Advanced Web Services

Athman Bouguettaya · Quan Z. Sheng
Florian Daniel
Editors

Advanced Web Services

Foreword by Michael P. Papazoglou

Editors
Athman Bouguettaya
School of Computer Science
and Information Technology
RMIT University
Melbourne, VIC
Australia

Florian Daniel
Dipartimento di Ingegneria e Scienza
dell'Informazione
Università di Trento
Povo, Trento
Italy

Quan Z. Sheng
School of Computer Science
University of Adelaide
Adelaide, SA
Australia

ISBN 978-1-4939-0071-8 ISBN 978-1-4614-7535-4 (eBook)
DOI 10.1007/978-1-4614-7535-4
Springer New York Heidelberg Dordrecht London

Printed on acid-free paper

Springer is part of Springer Science+Business Media (www.springer.com)

To my parents, Horia and Mahmoud,
and my wife Malika

Athman Bouguettaya

To my parents Shuilian and Jianwu,
my brothers Guanzheng and Xinzheng,
my wife Yaping and my daughters Fiona
and Phoebe

Quan Z. Sheng

To Cinzia, my family, my friends

Florian Daniel

Foreword

Service-Oriented Computing (SOC) is the computing paradigm that utilizes software services as fundamental elements for developing and deploying distributed software applications. Services are self-describing, platform-agnostic computational elements that support rapid, low-cost composition of distributed applications. They perform functions, which can be anything from simple requests to complicated business processes. Services allow organizations to expose their core competencies programmatically via a self-describing interface based on open standards over the Internet (or intra-net) using standard (XML-based) languages and protocols. Because services provide a uniform and ubiquitous information distributor for wide range of computing devices (such as handheld computers, PDAs, cellular telephones, or appliances) and software platforms (e.g., UNIX or Windows), they constitute a major transition in distributed computing.

A Web service is a specific kind of service that is identified by a URI that exposes its features programmatically over the Internet using standard Internet languages and protocols, and can be implemented via a self-describing interface based on open Internet standards (e.g., XML interfaces which are published in network-based repositories).

Understanding the conceptual underpinnings and mastering the technical intricacies of Web services is anything but trivial and is absolutely necessary to construct a well-functioning service-based system or application. Web service technology is undergoing continuous, rapid evolution, thanks to both standardization efforts pushed forward by the industry and the research efforts of the scientific community.

Web services standards are still evolving. However, they seem to converge today on a handful of standards: the Simple Object Access Protocol (SOAP) for service communication, Web Services Description Language (WSDL) for service description, Universal Description, Discovery, and Integration Infrastructure (UDDI) for registering and discovering services, and the Business Process Execution Language (BPEL) for service composition. A plethora of WS-* specifications also exists to describe the full spectrum of activities related to Web services in topics such as reliable messaging, security, privacy, policies, event processing, and coordination, to name but a few.

Leading international conferences, such as the International Conference on Service Oriented Computing (ICSOC), the International Conference on Web Services (ICWS), the International Conference on Service Computing (SCC), and others, have spearheaded groundbreaking research efforts. This has led to the emergence of novel topics such as semantic Web services, automated Web service composition, Web service recommendations, quality of service, trust, and a range of other interesting themes. Related conference series such as Web Engineering, Cloud Computing, Business Process Management, HCI, and Database-related conferences have all been strongly influenced by the emergence of Web services and consistently feature Web service-related topics in their calls for papers. These conferences contribute to the wealth of knowledge that is growing exponentially around Web services.

The content of this book and that of its companion book *Web Services Foundations* (Springer, 2013) reflect such activities. It is a testimonial of the leading role of its editors and their highly influential work in the area of Web services. Together, both books cover an enormous wealth of important topics and technologies that mirror the evolution of Web services. They provide an exhaustive overview of the challenges and solutions of all major achievements pertaining to Web services. Each chapter is an authoritative piece of work that synthesizes all the pertinent literature and highlights important accomplishments and advances in its subject matter.

To my knowledge, this is the first attempt of its kind, providing complete coverage of the key subjects in Web services. I am not aware of any other book that is as thorough, comprehensive and ambitious in explaining the current state of the art of scientific research and in synthesizing the perspectives and know-how of so many experts in the field. Both books are a must-read for everyone interested in the field. They cater for the needs of both novices to the field as well as seasoned researchers and practitioners. They are a major step in this field's maturation and will serve to unify, advance, and challenge the scientific community in many important ways.

It is a real pleasure to have been asked to provide the foreword for this book collection. I am happy to commend the editors and authors on their accomplishment, and to inform the readers that they are looking at a landmark in the development of the Web services field. Anybody serious about Web services ought to have handy a copy of *Web Services Foundations* and *Advanced Web Services* in their private library!

Tilburg, The Netherlands, December 2012 Michael P. Papazoglou

Preface

Web Service technology is undeniably the preferred delivery method for the Service-Oriented Computing (SOC) paradigm. It has evolved over the years to be a comprehensive, interdisciplinary approach to modern software development. Web services have gone beyond software componentization technology to embody and express the software manifestation of a general trend transforming our modern society from an industrial, production-centric economy into a digital, service-centric economy. Web services aim to provide the missing conceptual links that unify a variety of different disciplines, such as networking, distributed systems, cloud computing, autonomic computing, data and knowledge management, knowledge-based systems, and business process management. Web services are the technological proxies of services that power much of the developed and increasingly developing economies. In this respect, Web services play a central role in enabling and sustaining the growth of service-centric economies and help modernizing organizations, companies, and institutions also from an IT perspective.

Over the last decade, Web services have become a thriving area of research and academic endeavors. Yet, despite a substantial body of research and scientific publications, the Web services community has been hitherto missing a one stop-shop that would provide a consolidated understanding of the scientific and technical progress of this important subject. This book (the second of a two-book collection) is a serious attempt to fill this gap and serve as a primary point of reference reflecting the pervasive nature of Web services.

This book is the second installment of a two-book collection (we discuss the foundational topics in the first book, *Web Services Foundations*, Springer, 2013). Together, they comprise approximately 1,400 pages covering state-of-the-art theoretical and practical aspects as well as experience using and deploying Web services. The collection offers a comprehensive overview of the scientific and technical progress in Web services technologies, design, architectures, applications, and performance. The second book of the collection consists of three major parts:

I *Advanced Services Engineering and Management* (11 chapters)—It explores advanced engineering problems, such as Web service transactions and recovery, security and identity management, trust and contracts, and Web service evolution and management;

II *Web Service Applications and Case Studies* (5 chapters)—It covers concrete scenarios of the use of Web service technology and reports on empirical studies of real-world Web service ecosystems;

III *Novel Perspectives and Future Directions* (10 chapters)—It surveys approaches of the applications on how the Web service paradigm can be applied to novel contexts, such as human-centric computing, human work, and the Internet of Things, and discusses the value of Web services in the context of mobile and cloud computing.

The first book (*Web Services Foundations*, Springer, 2013) consists of two major parts:

I *Foundations of Web Services* (12 chapters)—It explores the most representative theoretical and practical approaches to Web services, with a special focus on the general state-of-the-art approaches to Web service composition;

II *Service Selection and Assisted Composition* (16 chapters)—It focuses on other aspects of Web service composition problem, specifically takes a deep look at non-functional aspects (e.g., quality of service), Web service recommendations, and how Web service composition is made easy for less expert developers.

The topics covered in the collection are reflective of their intent: they aim to become the primary source for all pertinent information regarding Web service technologies, research, deployment, and future directions. The purpose of the two books is to serve as a trusted and valuable reference point to researchers and educators who are working in the area of Web services, to students who wish to learn about this important research and development area, and to practitioners who are using Web services and the service paradigm daily in their software development projects.

This collection is the result of an enormous community effort, and their production involved more than 100 authors, consisting of the world's leading experts in this field. We would like to thank the authors for their high-quality contributions and the reviewers for their time and professional expertise. All contributions have undergone a rigorous review process, involving three independent experts in two rounds of review. We are also very grateful to Springer for their continuous help and assistance.

Melbourne, Australia, December 2012 Athman Bouguettaya
Adelaide, Australia Quan Z. Sheng
Trento, Italy Florian Daniel

Contents

Contributors

Marco Anisetti Dipartimento di Informatica, Università degli Studi di Milano, Bramante 65, Crema 26013, Italy, e-mail: marco.anisetti@unimi.it

Claudio A. Ardagna Dipartimento di Informatica, Università degli Studi di Milano, Bramante 65, Crema 26013, Italy, e-mail: claudio.ardagna@unimi.it

Youakim Badr INSA de Lyon, Villeurbanne 69621, France, e-mail: youakim.badr@insa-lyon.fr

Luciano Baresi Deep-SE Group, Dipartimento di Elettronica e Informazione, Politecnico di Milano, Piazza L. da Vinci 32, Milan I-20133, Italy, e-mail: luciano.baresi@polimi.it

Michele Bezzi SAP Research Sophia-Antipolis, 805, Av. du Docteur Maurice Donat, Mougins 06254 Mougins Cedex, France, e-mail: michele.bezzi@sap.com

Domenico Bianculli SnT Centre, University of Luxembourg, 4 rue Alphonse Weicker, Luxembourg, Luxembourg, e-mail: domenico.bianculli@uni.lu

Tobias Binz IAAS, University of Stuttgart, Universitätsstr. 38, 70569 Stuttgart, Germany, e-mail: binz@iaas.uni-stuttgart.de

Athman Bouguettaya School of Computer Science and Information Technology, RMIT, Melbourne, Australia, e-mail: athman.bouguettaya@rmit.edu.au

Uwe Breitenbücher IAAS, University of Stuttgart, Universitätsstr. 38, Stuttgart 70569, Germany, e-mail: breitenbuecher@iaas.uni-stuttgart.de

Muhammad Z. C. Candra Distributed Systems Group, Vienna University of Technology, Argentinierstrasse 8/184-1, Vienna 1040, Austria, e-mail: m.candra@dsg.tuwien.ac.at

Mauro Caporuscio Dipartimento di Elettronica e Informazione, Politecnico di Milano, Piazza L. da Vinci 32, 20133 Milan, Italy, e-mail: mauro.caporuscio@polimi.it

Rubén Casado Department of Computing, University of Oviedo, Asturias, Spain, e-mail: rcasado@lsi.uniovi.es

Yi-Min Chee IBM Thomas J. Watson Research Center, Hawthorne, NY, USA, e-mail: ymchee@us.ibm.com

Jun-Liang Chen State Key Laboratory of Networking and Switching Technology, Beijing University of Posts and Telecommunications, Beijing, China, e-mail: chjl@bupt.edu.cn

Dickson K. W. Chiu Dickson Computer Systems, 7 Victory Avenue, Kowloon, Hong Kong; Department of Computer Science and Engineering, Hong Kong University of Science and Technology, Hong Kong, China, e-mail: dicksonchiu@ieee.org

Marco Comerio University of Milano-Bicocca, Viale Sarca 336, 20126 Milan, Italy, e-mail: comerio@disco.unimib.it

Ernesto Damiani Dipartimento di Informatica, Universitaà degli Studi di Milano, Bramante 65, 26013 Crema, Italy, e-mail: ernesto.damiani@unimi.it

Flavio De Paoli University of Milano-Bicocca, Viale Sarca 336, 20126 Milan, Italy, e-mail: depaoli@disco.unimib.it

Peter Dolog Department of Computer Science, Aalborg University, Selma Lagerloefs Vej 300, 9220 Aalborg, Denmark, e-mail: dolog@cs.aau.dk

Marlon Dumas University of Tartu, Tartu, Estonia, e-mail: marlon.dumas@ut.ee

Schahram Dustdar Distributed Systems Group, Vienna University of Technology, Argentinierstrasse 8/184-1, 1040 Vienna, Austria, e-mail: dustdar@dsg.tuwien.ac.at

Noura Faci Claude Bernard Lyon 1 University, Lyon, France, e-mail: noura.faci@univ-lyon1.fr

Matthias Farwick Institute of Computer Science, University of Innsbruck, Innsbruck, Austria, e-mail: csae8781@uibk.ac.at

José Eduardo Fernandes Bragana Polytechnic Institute, Bragana, Portugal, e-mail: jef@ipb.pt

Nuno Ferreira I2S Informtica, Sistemas e Servios S.A., Porto, Portugal, e-mail: nuno.ferreira@i2s.pt

Marios Fokaefs Department of Computing Science, University of Alberta, Edmonton, AB, Canada, e-mail: fokaefs@ualberta.ca

Marco Funaro Dipartimento di Elettronica e Informazione, Politecnico di Milano, Piazza L. da Vinci 32, 20133 Milan, Italy, e-mail: funaro@elet.polimi.it

Dragan Gasević School of Computing and Information Systems, Athabasca University, Athabasca, Canada, e-mail: dgasevic@acm.org

Carlo Ghezzi Dipartimento di Elettronica e Informazione, Politecnico di Milano, Piazza L. da Vinci 32, 20133 Milan, Italy, e-mail: carlo.ghezzi@polimi.it

Sam Guinea Dipartimento di Elettronica e Informazione, Politecnico di Milano, Piazza L. da Vinci 32, 20133 Milan, Italy, e-mail: sam.guinea@polimi.it

Jing He Victoria University, Melbourne, Australia, e-mail: jing.he@vu.edu.au

Guangyan Huang Victoria University, Melbourne, Australia, e-mail: guangyan.huang@vu.edu.au

Patrick C. K. Hung Faculty of Business and Information Technology, University of Ontario Institute of Technology, Oshawa, Canada, e-mail: patrick.hung@uoit.ca

Valérie Issarny Domaine de Voluceau, INRIA Paris-Rocquencourt, Le Chesnay 78153, France, e-mail: valerie.issarny@inria.fr

Samuel Paul Kaluvuri SAP Research Sophia-Antipolis, 805, Av. du Docteur Maurice Donat, Mougins 06254 Mougins Cedex, France, e-mail: samuel.kaluvuri@sap.com

Oliver Kopp IAAS, University of Stuttgart, Universitätsstr. 38, Stuttgart 70569, Germany, e-mail: kopp@iaas.uni-stuttgart.de

Peep Küngas University of Tartu, Tartu, Estonia, e-mail: peep.kungas@ut.ee

Sau Chan Lai Department of Computer Science and Engineering, Hong Kong University of Science and Technology, Hong Kong, China, e-mail: chanlaze@ust.hk

Frank Leymann IAAS, University of Stuttgart, Universitätsstr. 38, Stuttgart 70569, Germany, e-mail: leymann@iaas.uni-stuttgart.de

Lei Li Department of Computing, Macquarie University, Sydney, NSW 2109, Australia, e-mail: lei.li@outlook.com

Guanfeng Liu Department of Computing, Macquarie University, North Ryde, NSW, Australia, e-mail: guanfeng.liu@mq.edu.au

Hua Liu Xerox Research Center at Webster, Webster, USA, e-mail: hua.liu@xerox.com

Xumin Liu Department of Computer Science, Rochester Institute of Technology, Rochester, USA, e-mail: xl@cs.rit.edu

Zakaria Maamar Zayed University, Dubai, U.A.E, e-mail: zakaria.maamar@zu.ac.ae

Ricardo J. Machado Centro ALGORITMI, Escola de Engenharia, Universidade do Minho, Guimares, Portugal, e-mail: rmac@dsi.uminho.pt

Mihhail Matskin Royal Institute of Technology, Stockholm, Sweden, e-mail: misha@kth.se

Shahab Mokarizadeh Royal Institute of Technology, Stockholm, Sweden, e-mail: shahabm@kth.se

Wolfgang Nejdl L3S Research Center, University of Hannover, Appelstr. 9a, Hannover 30167, Germany, e-mail: nejdl@l3s.de

Surya Nepal CSIRO ICT Centre, Sydney, Australia, e-mail: Surya.Nepal@csiro.au

Nick L. L. NG Department of Computer Science and Engineering, Hong Kong University of Science and Technology, Hong Kong, China, e-mail: nickng@ust.hk

Talal H. Noor School of Computer Science, The University of Adelaide, Adelaide, SA 5005, Australia, e-mail: talal@cs.adelaide.edu.au

Daniel V. Oppenheim IBM Thomas J. Watson Research Center, Hawthorne, NY, USA, e-mail: music@us.ibm.com

Matteo Palmonari University of Milano-Bicocca, Viale Sarca 336, 20126 Milan, Italy, e-mail: palmonari@disco.unimib.it

Luca Panziera University of Milano-Bicocca, Viale Sarca 336, 20126 Milan, Italy, e-mail: panziera@disco.unimib.it

Antonino Sabetta SAP Research Sophia-Antipolis, 805, Av. du Docteur Maurice Donat, Mougins 06254 Mougins Cedex, France, e-mail: antonio.sabetta@sap.com

Nuno Santos CCG-Centro de Computaao Gráfica, Campus de Azurm, Guimares, Portugal, e-mail: nuno.santos@ccg.pt

Michael Schäfer L3S Research Center, University of Hannover, Appelstr. 9a, 30167 Hannover, Germany, e-mail: Michael.K.Schaefer@gmx.de

Quan Z. Sheng School of Computer Science, The University of Adelaide, Adelaide, SA 5005, Australia, e-mail: qsheng@cs.adelaide.edu.au

Wanita Sherchan IBM Research, Melbourne, Australia, e-mail: wanitash@au.ibm.com

Satish Narayana Srirama Mobile Cloud Laboratory, Institute of Computer Science, University of Tartu, J Liivi 2, Tartu 50409, Estonia, e-mail: srirama@ut.ee

Eleni Stroulia Department of Computing Science, University of Alberta, Edmonton, AB, Canada, e-mail: stroulia@ualberta.ca

Hong-Linh Truong Distributed Systems Group, Vienna University of Technology, Argentinierstrasse 8/184-1, 1040 Vienna, Austria, e-mail: truong@dsg.tuwien.ac.at

Javier Tuya Department of Computing, University of Oviedo, Asturias, Spain, e-mail: tuya@uniovi.es

Lav R. Varshney IBM Thomas J. Watson Research Center, Hawthorne, NY, USA, e-mail: lrvarshn@us.ibm.com

Yan Wang Department of Computing, Macquarie University, Sydney, NSW 2109, Australia, e-mail: yan.wang@mq.edu.au

Muhammad Younas Department of Computing and Communication Technologies, Oxford Brookes University, Oxford, UK, e-mail: m.younas@brookes.ac.uk

Rostyslav Zabolotnyi Distributed Systems Group, Vienna University of Technology, Argentinierstrasse 8/184-1 1040 Vienna, Austria, e-mail: rstzab@dsg.tuwien.ac.at

Yanchun Zhang Victoria University, Melbourne, Australia, e-mail: yanchun.zhang@vu.edu.au

Yang Zhang State Key Laboratory of Networking and Switching Technology, Beijing University of Posts and Telecommunications, Beijing, China, e-mail: yangzhang@bupt.edu.cn

Yufeng Zhang National Laboratory for Parallel and Distributed Processing, School of Computer Science, The National University of Defense Technology, Changsha, China, e-mail: yufengzhang@nudt.edu.cn

George Zheng Science Applications International Corporation, McLean, VA, USA, e-mail: george.zheng@saic.com

Hong Zhu Department of Computing and Electronics, School of Technology, Oxford Brookes University, Oxford OX33 1HX, UK, e-mail: hzhu@brookes.ac.uk

Part I
Advanced Services Engineering and Management

Chapter 1
Design and Management of Web Service Transactions with Forward Recovery

Peter Dolog, Michael Schäfer and Wolfgang Nejdl

Abstract In this chapter we describe a design of compensations using forward recovery within Web service transactions. We introduce an approach to model compensation capabilities and requirements using feature models, which are the basis for defining compensation rules. These rules can be executed in a Web service environment that we extend with the concept of an abstract service, which is a management component for flexible compensation capabilities. We describe the design and also discuss advantages and disadvantages of such an approach.

1.1 Introduction

A Web service allows a *provider* to encapsulate functionality and to make it available for use via a network. A *client* can invoke such a Web service to use its functionality. By combining existing Web services from different service providers, a new and more complex *distributed application* can be created, which in turn can be offered as a new value-added *composite service*. Such a distributed application is usually created based on a *business process*, which consists of a logical sequence of actions that can include the invocation of a Web service. Accordingly, it is vitally important to control the processing of each single action and the overall process in order to be able to guarantee correct execution. This is done by using *transactions*.

P. Dolog (✉)
Department of Computer Science, Aalborg University, Selma Lagerlöefs Vej 300, 9220 Aalborg, Denmark
e-mail: dolog@cs.aau.dk

M. Schäfer · W. Nejdl
L3S Research Center, University of Hannover, Appelstr. 9a, 30167 Hannover, Germany
e-mail: Michael.K.Schaefer@gmx.de

W. Nejdl
e-mail: nejdl@l3s.de

A. Bouguettaya et al. (eds.), *Advanced Web Services*,
DOI: 10.1007/978-1-4614-7535-4_1,

A transaction consists of a set of *operations* ("units of work") that are executed within a system. Before and after the transaction, this system has to be in a consistent state [6]. The concept of transaction originates from database systems, which require an effective control of operations in order to guarantee data consistency. This is achieved by requiring that transactions fulfill the ACID properties [6, 7]: *Atomicity*, *Consistency*, *Isolation*, and *Durability*.

In the context of a distributed application, a *distributed transaction* [6] controls the execution of operations on multiple loosely-coupled Web services (*participants*) from different providers. Each operation is an invocation of one of the services and executes functionality provided by the particular service that is called. Any kind of service, independent of the actual functionality it implements (e.g. reserving a flight, performing a money transfer, transforming data), can in principle participate in such a transaction. A *coordinator* is responsible for the creation of the transaction, the registration of participants, and the evaluation of the participant's results.

Due to the fact that a distributed transaction has to include external sources via a network connection, it is usually not possible to fulfill all ACID properties, as each one imposes restrictions on the system which can be a disadvantage in such an environment. For example, in order to be able to handle long-running transactions, which take a long time until they complete, it is necessary to relax the isolation property. This means that locks on resources are removed even though the overall transaction is not yet complete, so that other transaction can access these resources and are not blocked. However, it can still happen that the transaction fails, and if this is the case it is necessary for the coordinator to initiate a *compensation*, which reverts all operations that were already performed in order to restore the state of the system before the transaction was started. The Web services that were already processed have to do a *rollback*, i.e. they have to execute a predefined set of actions that undo their original operation. This notion of rolling back the system to a previous state is known as *backward recovery* [16], as it reverses the operations that have been performed. Whether such rollback operations exist, and what steps they consist of, depends highly on the system and the Web services involved. A compensation protocol can only provide the orchestration of compensative activities, the developer of a rollback operation has to ensure that its result represents the consistent state before the transaction was started.

There are alternative approaches how to relax the isolation property within a Web service environment. Reference [9] describes the "Promises" pattern, which defines a "Promise Manager" that receives resource promise requests from a service. In comparison to the classic ACID isolation, this promise does not lock an individual resource but instead ensures that one from a pool of (anonymous) resources with the same properties will be available.

Web service coordination and transaction specifications [11–13] have been defined that provide the architecture and protocols required for transaction coordination of Web services. Several extensions have been proposed to enhance these protocols to add more flexibility [2, 20]. While these protocols provide the means for transactions in a distributed environment, it is still a challenge to guarantee its consistency.

[10] describes an approach to check already at application design time whether the distributed application will always terminate in a consistent state.

The specifications in their original form provide only limited compensation capabilities [8]. In most cases, the handling of a service failure is restricted to backward recovery. Subsequently, the aborted transaction will usually have to be restarted, because the failed distributed application still has to perform its tasks. Backward recovery therefore results in the loss of time and money, and additional resources are needed to restart the transaction. Moreover, the provider of the service that has encountered an error might have to pay contractual penalties because of a violated *Service Level Agreement* (*SLA*). The rollback of the complete transaction due to the failure of one service can also have widespread consequences: All *dependent transactions* on the participating Web services (i.e. transactions that have started operations on a service after the currently aborting transaction and therefore have a completion dependency [3]) have to abort and perform a rollback, which in turn can trigger the abort of other transactions and thus lead to cascading compensations. This is sometimes called the *domino effect* [16].

In addition to the problematic consequences of backward recovery, current approaches do not allow any changes in a running transaction. If for example erroneous data was used in a part of a transaction, then the only possible course of action is to cancel the transaction and to restart it with correct data.

An alternative to backward recovery is *forward recovery*. The goal of this approach is to proactively change the state and structure of a transaction after a service failure occurred, and thus to avoid having to perform a rollback and to enable the transaction to finish successfully.

To illustrate forward recovery in a Web service environment, consider as example a company's monthly payroll processing. In the first step, the company has to calculate the salary for each employee, which can depend on a multitude of factors like overtime hours or bonuses. In the next step, the payment of the salary is performed, which comprises several operations: Transfer of the salary from the company's to the employee's account, transfer of the employee's income tax to the account of the fiscal authorities, and printing and mailing of the payslip. The employee has only one task, which he has to perform each month: He transfers the monthly installment for his new car to the car dealer's account.

The company's and the employee's operations are each controlled by a business process and are implemented using services from multiple providers (Fig. 1.1). The two business processes use transactions in order to guarantee a consistent execution of all required operations. For simplicity, only the services of transaction T1 are shown, although of course also transaction T0 and T2 consist of several services.

While this scenario is quite simple, it has multiple dependencies within and between the two running transactions. Therefore, it is important that both transactions can complete successfully and do not have to be aborted and rolled back. Nevertheless, a situation in which such a need arises can become imminent quite easily:

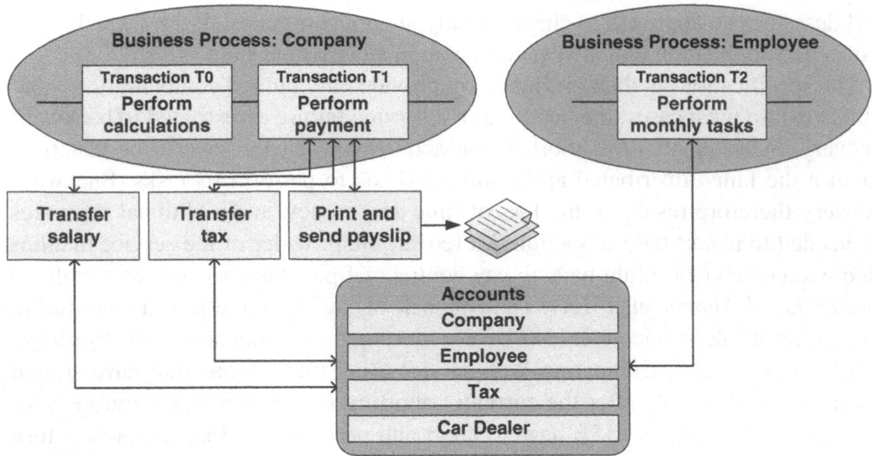

Fig. 1.1 The example scenario

- Situation 1: One of the Web services might encounter a problem during the execution of its operations. For example, it could be that the service that transfers the salary fails due to an internal error.
- Situation 2: A mistake might have been made regarding the input data of one of the operations. In this scenario, it could be that the calculation of the salary is flawed and too much has been transferred to the employee's account.

As explained above, using a backward recovery approach in such a scenario would be costly. However, using a forward recovery approach allows to handle both situations without a rollback:

- Situation 1: Although the Web service failed, it would still be possible to save the transaction by using a different service. Such a *replacement* of the original Web service is encouraged by the fact that usually multiple services from different providers exist that provide the same or similar capabilities.
- Situation 2: The operations with the erroneous input data have already been processed, and the transaction would have to be rolled back even if an administrator notices the failure before the transaction has been finished. However, the salary transfer could be easily corrected with another money transfer operation.

This scenario is only one example where a forward recovery of transactions would be beneficial. Similarly, such an approach could help in other situations such as overloaded services, timeouts, or other errors.

In this chapter we describe a design approach [17] and an environment which is able to handle forward recovery compensation of Web service transactions [19]. The approach is based on the idea that there is a possibility to replace a failed service in the transaction with another one with the same or similar capabilities and by doing so to avoid unnecessary rollbacks. In addition, the design includes an approach to model and match compensation capabilities and requirements. The contribution of this chapter is that it provides more detailed examples and explains the whole approach from design of the rules to their execution within the environment.

The main idea of the design is the introduction of a new component called an *abstract service*, which does not directly implement any functionality that is provided to the client, but instead functions as a management unit for flexible compensation capabilities [18]. As part of these capabilities, it specifies and manages potential replacements for participating Web services to be used. The compensations are performed according to predefined *rules*, and are subject to *contracts* [14]. An abstract service's functional and compensation capabilities can be specified using *feature models*, which allow a client to describe his requirements for a service, and a provider to specify a service's capabilities. These individual feature models can be used to automatically find matching services for a given set of requirements.

Such a solution has the following advantages:

- Compensation strategies can be defined on both, the service provider and the client side. They utilize local knowledge (e.g. the provider of a service knows best if and how his service can be replaced in case of failure) and preferences, which increases flexibility and efficiency.
- The environment can handle internally and externally triggered compensations.
- The client of a service is informed about complex compensation operations, which makes it possible to trigger additional compensations. Compensations can thus consist of multiple operations on different levels.
- By extending the already adopted Web service specification, it is not necessary to discontinue current practices if compensations are not required.
- The separation of the compensation logic from the coordination logic allows for a generic definition of compensation strategies, independent from the coordination specification currently in use. They are therefore more flexible and can easily be reused in a different context.

The rest of the chapter is structured as follows: Sect. 1.2 describes how we propose to represent compensation capabilities using feature models. Section 1.3 describes the specification of compensation rules and possible compensation activities. Section 1.4 describes the abstract service architecture where compensations can be executed according to compensation rules. Finally, Sect. 1.5 provides a discussion regarding advantages and shortcomings of the approach.

1.2 Compensations Design

We are introducing a compensation design approach which provides a set of models that describe both functional and compensation capabilities of a service:

- on the service provider side, *mandatory features* which are needed to provide at least the minimum functionality, as well *optional features* which extend the capabilities or level of service;
- on the service consumer side, features the client requires in order for the service to suit his needs.

We adopt a feature modeling approach and a methodology from [5, 17]. According to that methodology, first a *conceptual model* is defined which describes the main concepts and relationships between them. The configuration view on the concepts is described by means of *feature modeling* for both functionality and compensation capabilities.

Subsequently, the functionality and compensation models are merged to describe the offered capabilities by a service provider, or requested functionalities and restrictions posed on compensations by a service consumer. Different algorithms can then be employed to match feature models of a client and a service provider. In the following we will explain the introduced models in more detail.

1.2.1 Conceptual Model

In order to formalize different types of compensations, a conceptual model has been created that constitutes the basis for the feature models in the following sections. The result is the *compensation concept model* as seen in Fig. 1.2.

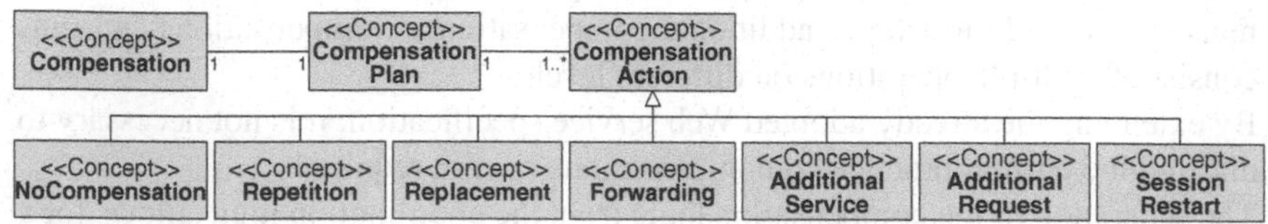

Fig. 1.2 The compensation concept model

Each *Compensation* contains a *CompensationPlan*, which in turn consists of one or more *CompensationActions*. Which CompensationActions exist and how they can be implemented depends on the actual environment. Accordingly, the ones listed are not necessarily complete and can be extended in the future.

Based on this definition of compensation concepts, it is now possible to create feature models in order to define what a service *can do*, *should be able to do*, and *is not allowed to do*.

1.2.2 Compensation Feature Model

The compensation concept model is the basis for the definition of the *compensation feature model*, which is depicted in Fig. 1.3. It describes the mandatory and optional features of the compensation concept, and will be used in the next step to define service-specific feature models, which can be part of a contract between a service provider and a service client.

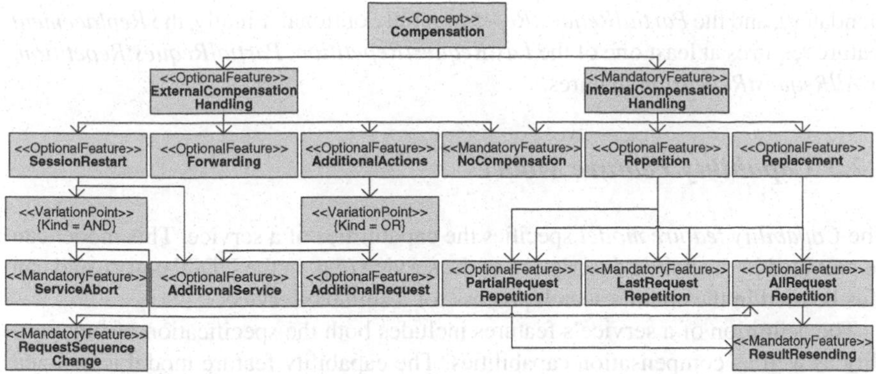

Fig. 1.3 The compensation feature model

The main two features of the model are the *InternalCompensationHandling* and the *ExternalCompensationHandling* features. An internal compensation is triggered by an internal service error, while an external compensation is triggered from outside of the transaction. An example for an externally triggered compensation could be the handling of the salary transfer mistake from the scenario described in Sect. 1.1 that is spotted by an administrator.

These main features structure the available compensation types as features according to their application: *Repetition* and *Replacement* are only available for internal compensation operations, and *SessionRestart*, *Forwarding* and *AdditionalActions* are only available for external compensation operations. The exception for this separation is *NoCompensation*, which is the only common compensation feature. Only two of these features are mandatory, the *InternalCompensationHandling* and the *NoCompensation* feature. This is due to the fact that the elementary feature of a compensation in our context is inactivity: If no rule or compensation capabilities exist, then the service has to fail without any other operations. Accordingly, the ability to perform external compensations is only optional.

The *SessionRestart* includes as an optional feature the invocation of an additional service (*AdditionalService*), and requires via a variation point (AND) the *ServiceAbort*, *RequestSequenceChange*, and *AllRequestRepetition* features. The capability to abort the service, change the request log, and resend all requests is needed to perform the session restart, and therefore these three features are mandatory. Likewise, the *AllRequestRepetition* feature cannot work without the *ResultResending* feature.

Within an externally triggered compensation, it is possible to invoke additional services and to create and send additional requests to the service. That is why the *AdditionalActions* feature includes the *AdditionalService* and *AdditionalRequest* features. They are connected via an OR variation point as the *AdditionalActions* feature needs at least one of these two features.

The basic operation mode of the *Repetition* compensation feature is the resending of the last request to the service. Therefore, the *LastRequestRepetition* feature is mandatory, and the *PartialRequestRepetition* only optional. Finally, the *Replacement* feature requires at least one of the *LastRequestRepetition*, *PartialRequestRepetition*, or *AllRequestRepetition* features.

1.2.3 Capability Feature Model

The *Capability feature model* specifies the capabilities of a service. This model can be provided in the public description of the service (e.g. in the UDDI entry), and can thus be used in the client's search process for a suitable service.

The definition of a service's features includes both the specification of functionality as well as compensation capabilities. The capability feature model is realized by merging the service's functionality feature model with its compensation feature model. The *functionality feature model* describes the features of the service that constitute the offered operations, e.g. the booking of a flight. The compensation feature model describes the service's compensation capabilities. It is created by using the compensation feature model described in the previous section as a basis, and then altering it by deleting features that are not offered (e.g. a service that does not provide external compensation capabilities will delete this part of the model completely), by changing the mandatory/optional properties, or by adding features at certain parts (e.g. by specifying the additional services that can be used in the compensation process).

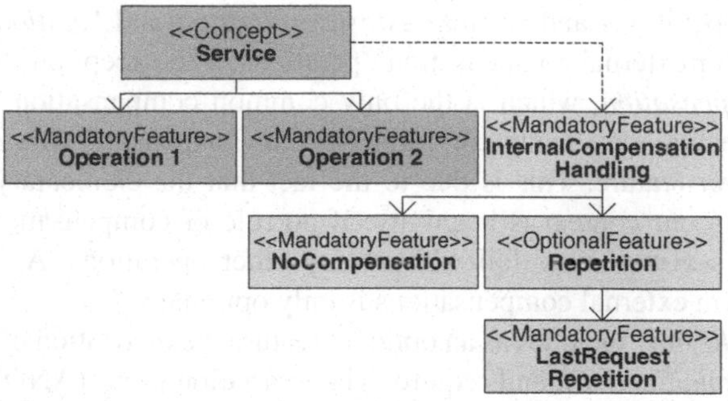

Fig. 1.4 Merging of the functionality and compensation models

This process of merging the two different models is depicted in Fig. 1.4. Here, a service offers two basic operations, "Operation 1" and "Operation 2", which form the functionality feature model (dark grey). The service is able to handle internal compensations by either doing nothing (the mandatory default action), or by repeating the last request. This forms the compensation model (light grey). The two models are merged (symbolized by the dashed arrow), and thus form the service's capability feature model. The mandatory/optional properties are interpreted in this context as "will be used by the service" and "can be used by the service", respectively. The interpretation is different in the requirement feature model.

1.2.4 Requirement Feature Model

The client creates a requirement description in order to be able to initiate a search for a suitable service. The specification is being done very much like the definition of the capability feature model described in the previous section: A common model is being created that includes the required functionality and compensation features. This model is called the *requirement feature model*.

However, although the basic process of creating the requirement feature model is the same, the interpretation of the mandatory/optional properties differs. A mandatory feature *has* to be provided by the service and is thus critical for the comparison process, while an optional feature *can* be provided by the service, and is seen as a bonus in the evaluation of the available services.

In the search process, each service's capability feature model will be compared to the client's requirement feature model, and the client can thus decide which service is suitable for its needs.

1.2.5 Restriction Feature Model

After the client has found the necessary services that offer the required functional and compensation features, the contract negotiation with each service will be performed. A vital part of this contract is the specification of compensation features that the service is allowed to use. While it is of course possible to do this restriction by simply searching for services that only perform the allowed compensation actions, such an approach significantly reduces the available services. Moreover, it is quite possible that a client wants to use the same service in multiple applications, where each has its own rules regarding the compensation actions that are permitted. Therefore, it is beneficial to use a *restriction feature model* that can be part of the contract, and to which the service dynamically adapts its compensation actions.

The restriction feature model can be defined by using the compensation feature model described in Sect. 1.2.2. By removing features from this model, the client can state that these are not allowed to be used in the compensation process. Only those features that are still in the model are permitted. Therefore, it is not necessary to distinct between mandatory and optional features.

When the service wants to invoke a specific compensation action, it will first consult the contract's restriction feature model. If the compensation action is part of the model, then the service is allowed to use it. This way, the service can dynamically adapt to the requirements of each single client.

1.2.6 Model Comparison Algorithm

We define a comparison algorithm to match the requirement model of a client and the capability model of a service. These two models are the input for the algorithm, which iteratively compares them and calculates a numerical *compatibility score*:

- Using the requirement feature model as a basis, the features are compared stepwise. In this process, it is required that the same features are found in the same places, because the same feature structure is expected.
- Each mandatory feature in the requirement model has to be found in the capability feature model. If this is not the case, the comparison has failed and a negative compatibility score is returned to indicate this. However, if a mandatory feature is included in the capability model, this will not have any impact on the comparison score, as the mandatory features are the minimum this is expected.
- Each optional feature in the requirement model can exist in the capability model, but does not have to. Each one found counts as a bonus added to the compatibility score. This accounts for the fact that a service that provides more than the minimum is better, as it can more easily be used in different applications.
- Additional features in the service's capability model, like the specification of additional services used in the compensation process, are ignored as long as they are found in the appropriate place, e.g. as a subfeature to the "AdditionalService" feature. Any other additional features will lead to a failure of the comparison.

Once the comparison is completed, the compatibility score will be returned. At the moment, a very simple score is used that does not include advanced properties like feature priorities, which could be used in the future:

- If the comparison has failed, the compatibility score will be *−1*.
- Each mandatory feature that is found does not increase the score. A service which provides only the mandatory features (and is thus suitable) will therefore have a compatibility score of *0*.
- Each optional feature in the capability model increases the score by *1*.

As it can be seen, every compatibility score equal to or higher than 0 classifies a service as suitable for the client's needs. Moreover, the higher the score is, the more features a service provides. Using this simple score, it is easy to compare multiple services and their capabilities.

1.2.7 Example

The use of feature models will now be examined based on the "Transfer salary" service of the scenario described in Sect. 1.1. The services in this scenario can be used in different distributed applications, and it is therefore important that their compensation capabilities can be adapted.

Capability Feature Model (depicted in Fig. 1.5): The functional features of this service are the "Debit" and "Credit" operations, which are mandatory. The service is capable of performing all compensation actions, and accordingly the complete compensation feature model is merged with the functional model. Finally, the service

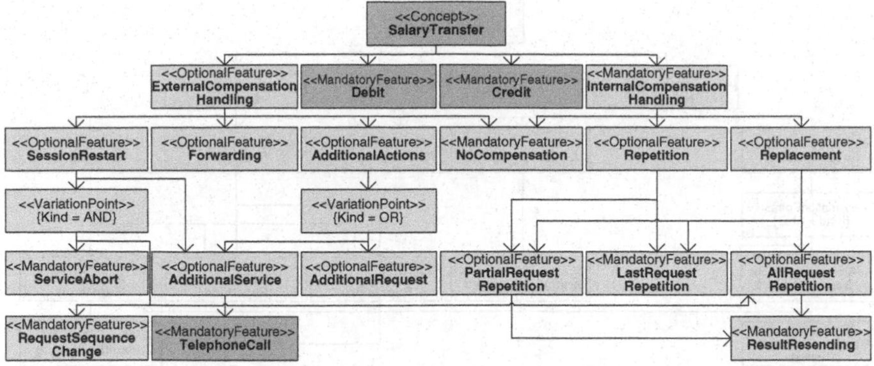

Fig. 1.5 The SalaryTransfer capability feature model

specifies that an additional service will be used in the compensation procedures: This is defined by adding the "TelephoneCall" feature to the "AdditionalService" feature. By providing this feature model, the service can state its capabilities and informs the client about a special operation it uses for this purpose.

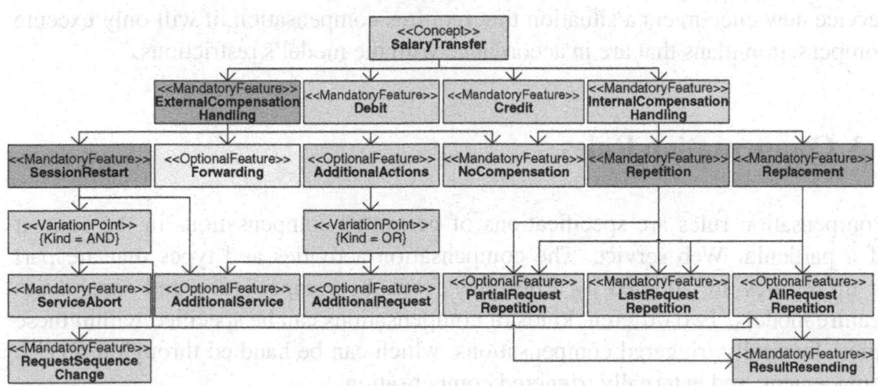

Fig. 1.6 The SalaryTransfer requirement feature model

Requirement Feature Model (Fig. 1.6): The client that creates the payment processing application specifies its requirements for the "Salary Transfer" service in a requirement feature model. The functional features are the "Debit" and "Credit" operations. Regarding the required compensation features, the client is looking for a service that is able to perform the "Repetition" and "Replacement" compensation actions for internal error handling, and the "SessionRestart" for external compensation handling. Accordingly, these features are marked as "mandatory".

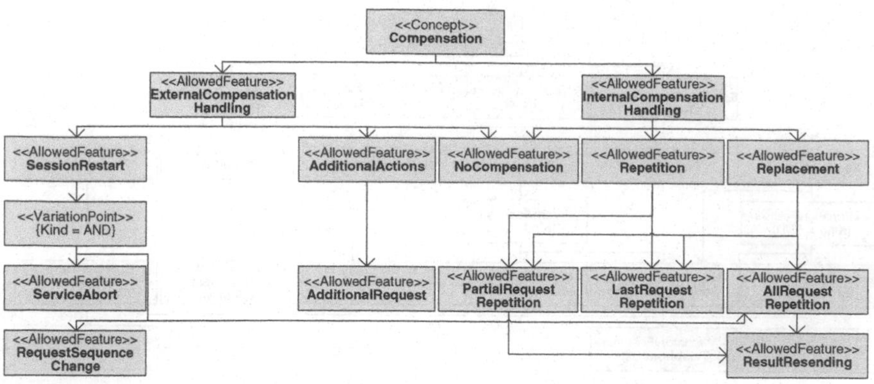

Fig. 1.7 The restriction feature model

Restriction Feature Model (Fig. 1.7): After the client has found a suitable service that offers the required capabilities, he defines the permitted compensation actions. In this example, the client does not want for the new application's service that it uses additional services in the event of a compensation. Therefore, the respective feature ("AdditionalService") is removed from the compensation feature model. This restriction model is part of the contract that the client has with the service. When the service now encounters a situation that requires compensation, it will only execute compensation plans that are in accordance with the model's restrictions.

1.3 Compensation Rules

Compensation rules are specifications of permitted compensations in the context of a particular Web service. The compensation activities and types that are part of these rules are adopted by a designer from the compensation and capabilities feature models. Two different kinds of compensations can be specified within these rules: Internally triggered compensations, which can be handled through a service replacement, and externally triggered compensations.

Each rule specifies the exact steps that have to be performed in the compensation process. For the purpose of defining the available compensation operations, we distinguish between basic *compensation activities*, which constitute the available single compensation operations, and complex *compensation types*, which are composed compensation processes consisting of multiple activities. This is shown in Fig. 1.8.

The compensation types specify which *combinations* of compensation activities can be defined in rules for handling internal and external compensations, as it is not desirable to allow every possible combination within the environment. When a service receives a request for a compensation, it will first of all check whether a rule for the current situation exists, and if this is the case, it will validate each rule before executing the given set of compensation activities in order to guarantee that they are consistent with the available compensation types.

Nr		Compensation Type	ServiceReplacement	LastRequestRepetition	PartialRequestRepetition	AllRequestRepetition	CompensationForwarding	AdditionalServiceInvocation	AdditionalRequestGeneration	ServiceAbortInitiation	RequestSequenceChange	ResultResending
01		NoCompensation										
02	Internal	Repetition		■								
03	Internal	Repetition			■							■
04	Internal	Replacement	■	■								
05	Internal	Replacement	■		■							■
06	Internal	Replacement	■			■						■
07	External	Forwarding	□	□	□	□	■	□	□	□	□	□
08	External	AdditionalService						■				
09	External	AdditionalRequest							■			
10	External	SessionRestart				■				■	■	■

■ Included compensation activity □ Possibly included compensation activity

Fig. 1.8 The compensation types and their included activities

Therefore, although the combination of different compensation activities allows the definition of flexible and complex rules, it is not permitted to define arbitrary compensation handling processes. Only the predefined compensation types can be used, and it is thus guaranteed that a service does not execute a process defined in a compensation rule that is not permitted or possible. At the same time, this approach allows the future extension of the environment with new compensation strategies: In order to test or include new compensation strategies, it is possible to simply define a new compensation type and extend the service to accept it.

1.3.1 Basic Compensation Activities

Compensation activities are the basic operations which can be used in a compensation process. *ServiceReplacement* replaces the currently used Web service with a different one, which offers the same capabilities. *LastRequestRepetition* resends the last request to the service. *PartialRequestRepetition* resends the last *n* requests from the request sequence of the current session (i.e. within the current transaction) to the service, while *AllRequestRepetition* resends all requests. *CompensationForwarding* forwards the external compensation request to a different component that will handle it. *AdditionalServiceInvocation* invokes an additional (external or internal) service, which performs a particular operation required for the compensation (e.g. the invocation of a logging service). *AdditionalRequestGeneration* creates and sends an additional request to the Web service. Such a request is not influenced by the client, and the result will not be forwarded to the client. *ServiceAbortInitiation* cancels the operations on the service, i.e. the service aborts and reverses all operations which have been performed so far. *RequestSequenceChange* performs changes in the sequence of requests that have already been sent to the Web service. *ResultResending* sends new results for old requests, which have already returned results.

1.3.2 Compensation Types

Compensation types aggregate multiple compensation activities, and thus form complex compensation operations (Fig. 1.8). These types are the compensation actions which can be used for internal and external compensations.

The most simple type is *NoCompensation*, which does not perform any operation.

The *Repetition* type is important for the internal error handling, as it repeats the last request or the last *n* requests. The last request can for example be resent to a service after a response was not received within a timeout period. A partial resend of *n* requests can for instance be necessary if the request which failed was part of a sequence. A partial repetition of requests will result in the resending of results for old requests to the client, which has to be able to process them.

The compensation type *Replacement* can be used if a service fails completely. It replaces the current service with a different one, and resends either all requests, a part of the requests, or only the last one. Resending only the last request is possible if a different instance of the service that has failed can be used as replacement, which works on the same local data and can therefore simply continue with the operations.

Forwarding is special in comparison with the other types as it only indirectly uses the available activities. It forwards the handling of the compensation to a different component, which can potentially use each one of the compensation activities (which are therefore marked as "possibly included") in the process.

In an externally triggered compensation, it is sometimes necessary to invoke additional services and send additional requests to the service. For this purpose, the compensation types *AdditionalService* and *AdditionalRequest* exist.

The final compensation type is *SessionRestart*. This operation is required if the external compensation request cannot be handled without a restart of the complete session, i.e. the service has to be aborted and subsequently the complete request sequence has to be resent. The requested change will be realised by a change in the request sequence prior to the resending.

1.3.3 Example of a Compensation Rule

Figure 1.9 shows an example of an external compensation rule specified in an XML document. This example rule handles the refund of excess salary that has been transferred to the employees account as described in the example in Sect. 1.1.

```
<cmp:ExternalCompensationRule identifier="refundSalaryDifference">
  <cmp:CompensationCondition>
    <cmp:RequestMethod identifier="transferSalaryMethod" />
    <cmp:ParticipantRequest identifier="getAccountBalanceMethod"
      parameterFactory="CheckEmployeeAccountParameterFactory">
      <cmp:Result resultEvaluator="AccountInCreditResultEvaluator" />
    </cmp:ParticipantRequest>
  </cmp:CompensationCondition>
  <cmp:CompensationPlan>
    <cmp:Compensation>
      <cmp:AdditionalRequest identifier="transferSalaryMethod"
        parameterFactory="RefundSalaryDifferenceParameterFactory" />
    </cmp:Compensation>
    <cmp:Compensation>
      <cmp:ServiceRequest
        serviceAddress="http://localhost:8080/axis/services/TelephoneCall"
        methodName="initializeTelephoneCall" />
    </cmp:Compensation>
  </cmp:CompensationPlan>
</cmp:ExternalCompensationRule>
```

Fig. 1.9 An example compensation rule

The compensation condition consists of two single condition elements:

1. *RequestMethod*—The rule applies to external compensation requests, which aim at changing requests that originally invoked the service's method "transferSalaryMethod", i.e. it applies to external compensations that try to change the details of an already completed salary transfer.
2. *ParticipantRequest*—The second condition element specifies a request that has to be sent to the current service. The goal of the request is to check whether the account of the employee will still be in credit after the excess amount has been refunded. The condition's request invokes the service's method "getAccountBalanceMethod". The request parameters are created by the parameter factory "CheckEmployeeAccountParameterFactory". After the request has returned the current balance, the predefined result evaluator "AccountInCreditResultEvaluator" is responsible for checking whether the salary refund can be performed, and thus whether the rule's condition is fulfilled or not.

The rule's compensation plan consists of two steps as well:

1. *AdditionalRequest*—An additional request is sent to perform the required changes, i.e. the money transfer back to the company's account. It invokes the service's method "transferSalaryMethod". The parameters for this request are created by the parameter factory "RefundSalaryDifferenceParameterFactory".
2. *ServiceRequest*—An additional external service is used as part of the compensation. The method "initializeTelephoneCall" has to be invoked. This external service performs a precautionary telephone call which informs the employee about the error in the salary calculation and the refund that has been performed.

This is of course only a simple example. External compensation rules can consist of a multitude of single conditions and/or compensation operations.

1.4 Web Service Environment with Transaction Coordination

The compensation rules from the previous section can be interpreted by an environment we have designed and implemented as a prototype. The environment builds upon adapted Web service coordination and transaction specifications [11–13]. They provide a conceptual model and architecture for environments where business activities performed by Web services are embedded in a transactional context.

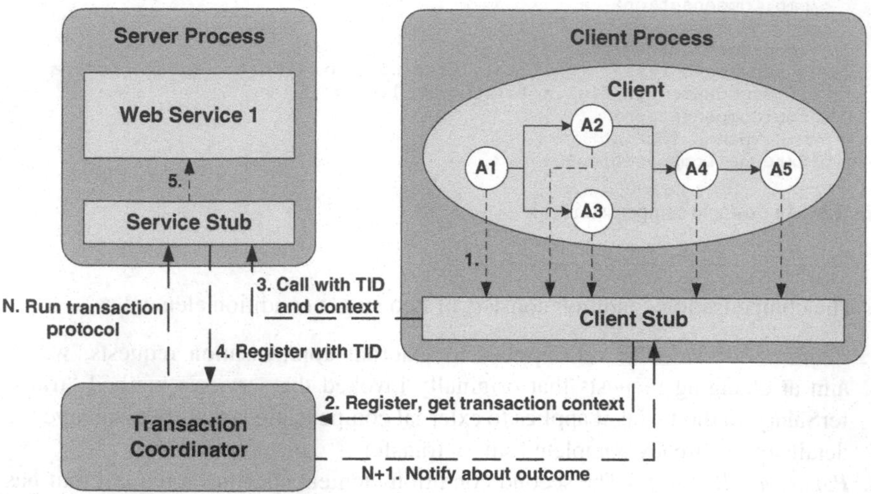

Fig. 1.10 Transactional environment for Web services adopted from [1]

Figure 1.10 depicts an excerpt of such an environment with the main components. The client runs business activities A1 to A5, which are part of a transactional context that is maintained by a transaction coordinator. Client and server stubs are responsible for getting and registering the activities and calls for Web services in the right context. The sequence of conversation messages is numbered. For clarity, we only show a conversation with a Web service provider that performs business activity A1. The coordinator is then responsible for running appropriate protocols, for example a distributed protocol for Web service environments such as [2].

We extend the architecture and the infrastructure based on the specifications [11–13] in order to enable it to handle both internally and externally triggered compensations as described in the previous sections.

Figure 1.11 depicts the extension to the transaction Web service environment, namely the *abstract service* and the *adapter* components. This extension does not change the way how client, coordinators and providers operate. Instead of invoking a normal Web service, a client invokes an abstract service, which looks like a standard Web service to the outside. However, the abstract service is a management component for forward recovery compensation handling, which wraps multiple *con-*

crete services that offer the same functionalities and can thus replace each other. The abstract service is therefore a *mediator* between a client and the concrete service that performs the required operations. At the same time, the adapter functions as a mediator between transaction coordinator, abstract service and concrete service to ensure proper transactional context and to provide the means to intercept failure notifications and create messages required in the compensation handling process.

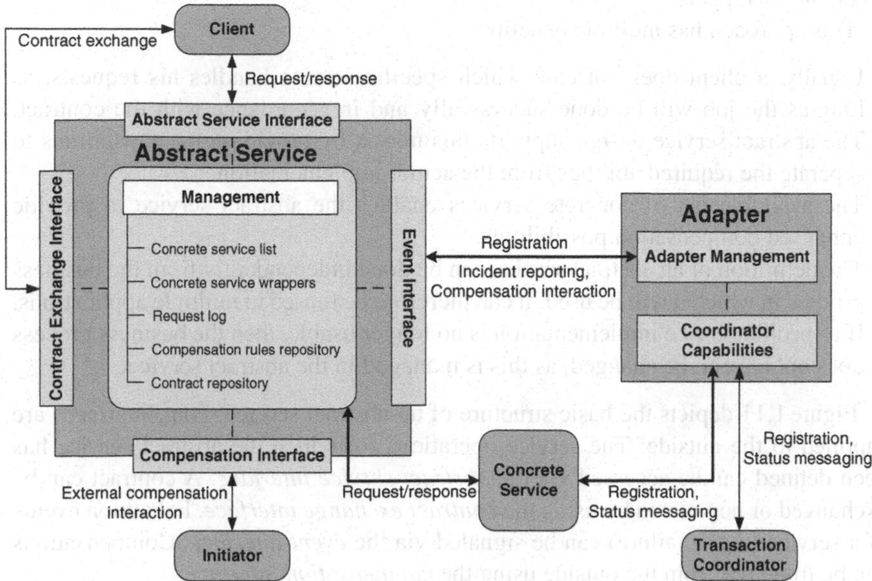

Fig. 1.11 The abstract service and adapter transaction environment

1.4.1 Abstract Service

The central element of the extension is the notion of the *abstract service*. The client stub communicates with the Web service provider stub through the abstract service. An abstract service does not directly implement any operations, but rather functions as a management unit, which allows to:

- define a list of Web services which implement the required capabilities,
- invoke a service from the list in order to process requests which are sent to the abstract service,
- replace a failed service with another one from the list without a failure of the transaction, and
- process externally triggered compensations on the running transaction.

To the outside, it provides an abstract interface and can be used like any other Web service, and uses the same mechanisms like SOAP [15] and WSDL [4]. On the inside, it manages a list of concrete services which provide the required capabilities. When the abstract service receives a request, it chooses one of these services and invokes it. Which concrete service is chosen depends on the abstract service's implementation. In the simplest case, the abstract service only selects the next concrete service on the list. However, it would be possible to give the abstract service the capability to dynamically assess each concrete service and to choose the one that optimizes the client's QoS requirements. Interface and data incompatibilities are solved by predefined wrappers.

This approach has multiple benefits:

- Usually, a client does not care which specific service handles his requests, as long as the job will be done successfully and in accordance with the contract. The abstract service design supports this notion by providing the capabilities to separate the required abilities from the actual implementation.
- The available list of concrete services enables the abstract service to provide enhanced compensation possibilities.
- The definition of an abstract service can be done independently from the business process in which it will be used. It can therefore be reused in multiple applications. If a specific service implementation is no longer usable, then the business process does not have to be changed, as this is managed in the abstract service.

Figure 1.11 depicts the basic structure of an abstract service. Four interfaces are supplied to the outside: The service operations for which the abstract service has been defined can be accessed via the *abstract service interface*. A contract can be exchanged or negotiated by using the *contract exchange interface*. Execution events of a service (e.g. a failure) can be signaled via the *event interface*. Compensations can be triggered from the outside using the *compensation interface*.

On the inside, the main component is the *management* unit, which receives and processes requests, selects and invokes concrete services, and handles compensations. In order to do so, it has several elements at its disposal:

- *Concrete service list*: Contains the details of all available concrete services.
- *Concrete service wrappers*: Define the mapping of the generic abstract service interface to the specific interface of each concrete service.
- *Request log*: Holds all requests of the current session.
- *Compensation rules repository*: Manages the rules that control the compensation handling process.
- *Contract repository*: Contains the existing contracts with the different clients.

1.4.2 Adapter

Abstract services could be used in conjunction with a wide variety of technologies. Therefore, it would be preferable if the definition of the abstract service itself could be generic. However, the participation in a transaction requires capabilities that are different for each transaction management specification.

That is why the transaction specific requirements are encapsulated in a so-called *adapter* (see Fig. 1.11). An abstract service registers with this adapter, which in turn registers with the transaction coordinator. To the coordinator it appears as if the abstract service itself has registered and sends the status messages. When the abstract service invokes a concrete service, it forwards the information about the adapter, which functions as a coordinator for the service. The service registers accordingly at the adapter as a participant in the transaction.

As can be seen, the adapter works as a mediator between the abstract service, the concrete service, and the transaction coordinator. The adapter receives all status messages from the concrete service and is thus able to process them before they reach the actual coordinator. Normal status messages can be forwarded directly to the coordinator, while failure messages can initiate the internal compensation handling through the abstract service. If the adapter receives such an error message, it informs the abstract service that can then assess the possibility of compensation, which includes checking both the existing compensation rules and the restriction feature model. The adapter will be informed about the decision, and can act accordingly. If for example the replacement of a failed concrete service is possible, then the adapter will deregister this service and wait for the replacement to register. In this case, the failure message will not be forwarded to the transaction coordinator. The compensation assessment could of course also show that a compensation is not possible (or permitted). In such a case, the adapter will simply forward the failure message to the coordinator, which will subsequently initiate the abort of the transaction.

1.4.3 Compensation Protocol

While the compensation rules specify when and how a compensation can be performed, the compensation protocol controls the external compensation process itself and its interaction with the different participants.

An externally triggered compensation always has the purpose of changing one particular request that has already been processed at the service. More specifically, the compensation request contains the original request with its data that has to be changed (`request1(data1)`), and the new request-data (`data2`) to which the original request has to be changed to (`request1(data2)`). The participants in the protocol are the *abstract service*, the *client* which uses the abstract service in its business process, the *initiator* which triggers the external compensation (either the client itself, or any other authorized source like an administrator), the *concrete service* which is currently being utilized by the abstract service, and the *transaction coordinator*. An externally triggered compensation can only be performed if the transaction in which the abstract service participates has not yet finished, as this usually has consequences for the client due to result resending.

The protocol consists of two stages. The first stage is the *compensation assessment*: As soon as the abstract service receives a request for a compensation, it checks whether it is feasible and what the costs would be. To that end, predefined compensation rules are being used, which consist of a *compensation condition* (defines when a compensation rule can be applied) and a *compensation plan* (defines the compensation actions that have to be performed). The second stage of the protocol is the *compensation execution*, which performs the actual compensation according to the plan. Whether this stage is actually reached depends on the initiator: After the assessment has been completed and has come to a positive conclusion, the initiator, based on this data, has to decide whether the compensation should be performed.

As the client and the initiator of an external compensation can differ, the protocol contains the means to inform the client about the compensation process. It also ensures that the current concrete service and the transaction coordinator are informed about the status of the external compensation, as it is possible that the concrete service's (and thus the abstract service's) state changes due to the external compensation. The concrete service has to enter a specific external compensation handling procedure state for this purpose. While the concrete service is in this state, it will wait for additional requests from the abstract service, and the coordinator is not allowed to complete the transaction. While assessing the possibilities for a compensation, and while performing it, the abstract service cannot process additional requests (and either has to store the requests in a queue, or has to reject them with an appropriate error message).

Because of the requirements of the compensation protocol, it is necessary to adapt the normal transaction protocol with additional state changes regarding the coordinator and participant (i.e. the concrete service). This has been done in our implementation for the `BusinessAgreementWithCoordinatorCompletion` protocol (refer to [11]), using an extended version introduced in [2] as a basis that uses transaction dependency graphs in order to solve cyclic dependencies. The result of the state diagram adaptation for the compensation protocol is depicted in Fig. 1.12.

Two new states have been introduced, `ExCompensation I` and `ExCompensation II`. While both represent the external compensation handling procedure state which the concrete service has to enter, it is necessary to distinct between them, because depending on the former state different consequential transitions exist.

If the concrete service as participant is currently either in the `Active` state or the `Completing` state when receiving an `ExCompensate` notification from the adapter, it will enter the `ExCompensation I` state. While the concrete service is in this state, it will wait for new requests from the abstract service, and the coordinator will not finish the transaction. If the external compensation procedure is canceled after the assessment has been performed, the concrete service will be instructed to re-enter its former state by receiving either an `Active` or a `Complete` instruction from the adapter. The transaction processing can then continue in the normal way. In contrast, if the external compensation is executed and performed successfully, the concrete service will receive an `ExCompensated` message, which instructs it to enter the `Active` state. This is necessary for two reasons: Firstly, because any additional requests as part of the external compensation handling require that the participant again performs the `Completing` operations. And secondly, because the abstract service's client will be informed about the external compensation that

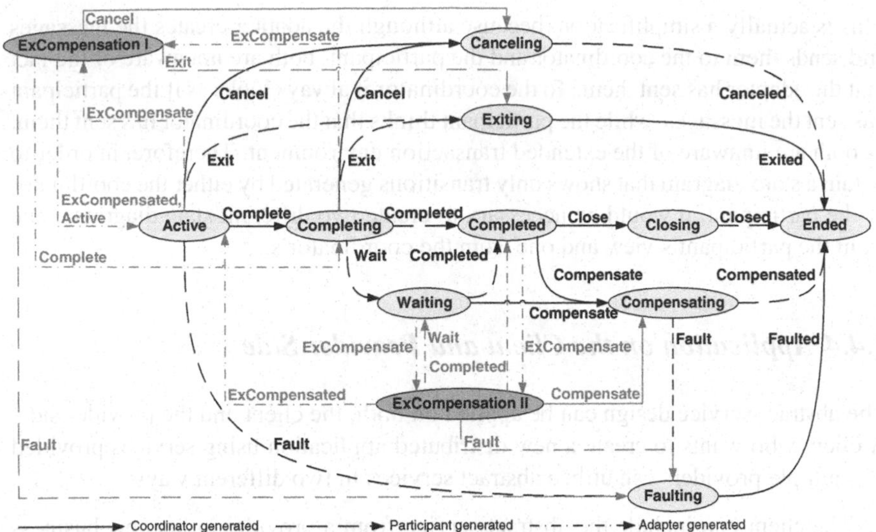

Fig. 1.12 The state diagram of the `BusinessAgreementWithCoordinatorCompletion` protocol with extensions for the external compensation handling

has been performed, and it is possible that additional operations are required by the client as a consequence of the compensation.

In addition to these options within the `ExCompensation I` state, the same transitions exist as in the `Active` and `Completing` states, i.e. the coordinator can `Cancel` the operations, and the participant can `Exit` or send a `Fault` notification.

If the concrete service is either in the `Waiting` or `Completed` state when receiving an `ExCompensate` message, it will enter the `ExCompensation II` state. In principle, the state has the same meaning as `ExCompensation I`: The concrete service will wait for new abstract service requests, and at the same time the coordinator is not allowed to finish the transaction. The concrete service will be notified to enter the `Active` state through an `ExCompensated` message after a successful external compensation execution. However, in contrast to `ExCompensation I`, different consequential transitions are available, and therefore it is necessary to separate these two states. In case of a compensation abort, the concrete service can be instructed to re-renter its former state through a `Wait` or `Completed` message. Moreover, a `Fault` message can be sent to signal an internal failure. Finally, the coordinator can send a `Compensate` instruction while the concrete service is in the `ExCompensation II` state. The concrete service can only be instructed to `Compensate` if it is either in the `Waiting` or the `Completed` state. Therefore, it is necessary to introduce `ExCompensation II`, as this option is not available for the `Active` and `Completing` states and thus may not be permitted within `ExCompensation I`.

The extended state diagram contains new transitions generated by the adapter in addition to the ones from the participant (i.e. the concrete service) and the coordinator.

This is actually a simplification, because although the adapter creates the messages and sends them to the coordinator and the participant, both are not aware of the fact that the adapter has sent them. To the coordinator it always looks as if the participant has sent the messages, while the participant thinks that the coordinator has sent them, as both are unaware of the extended transaction environment. Therefore, in order to obtain a state diagram that shows only transitions generated by either the coordinator or the participant, it would be necessary to create two different state diagrams, one from the participant's view and one from the coordinator's.

1.4.4 Application on the Client and Provider Side

The abstract service design can be applied on both, the client and the provider side. A client who wants to create a new distributed application using services provided by multiple providers can utilize abstract services in two different ways:

1. The client can include the abstract service from a provider in his new business process, and can use the added capabilities.
2. The client can define a new abstract service, which manages multiple concrete services that can perform the same task.

The main goal of a Web service provider is a successful and stable execution of the client's requests in accordance with the contracts. If the service of a provider fails too often, he might face contractual penalties, or the client might change the provider. He can use abstract services in order to enhance the reliability and capability of his services by creating an abstract service which encapsulates multiple instances or versions of the same service. These can be used in case of errors to compensate the failure without the need for a transaction abort.

1.4.5 Client Contracts

While the different compensation capabilities of an abstract service allow the handling of internal and external compensations, it may not always be desirable for a client that these functionalities are applied. The abstract service environment therefore allows the definition and evaluation of *contracts*.

A client will negotiate a contract with the abstract service before sending the first request. This contract not only contains legal information and the Service Level Agreement, but can also specify (using a restriction feature model as described in Sect. 1.2.5) which compensation operations the abstract service is permitted to apply. The abstract service adapts dynamically to this contract by checking the restrictions defined in it prior to performing a compensation: A compensation rule may only be applied if all necessary compensation operations are permitted via the contract. It can thus happen that although a compensation rule exists for handling a compensation, the abstract service will not apply it because the contract restricts the use of required compensation operations. Accordingly, an abstract service that is not allowed to use any compensation capabilities will act exactly like a standard Web service. A client therefore *can* make use of the forward recovery capabilities, but he does not *have* to, and thus always has the control over the environment's forward recovery compensation handling features.

Because of this ability to dynamically adapt to each client's contract, it is possible to use the same abstract service in a wide variety of distributed applications with differing requirements regarding compensation handling.

1.4.6 Transaction Environment Adaptation

The abstract service and adapter approach has been designed as an extension of the current transaction coordination structure so that it is easy to integrate it into existing environments and different transaction protocols. Therefore, it is not necessary to change either the client, coordinator or concrete service in order to use the internal compensation handling capability: An abstract service that manages different concrete services and that is able to replace failed concrete services can be used like a normal Web service and without any changes to the transaction protocol.

However, the introduced external compensation functionality for changing already processed requests requires some changes in the transaction environment:

1. It is necessary to extend the existing transaction specification protocols to provide the capability to perform external compensations. This has been shown for the `BusinessAgreementWithCoordinatorCompletion` protocol in Sect. 1.4.3. Accordingly, the coordinator and the participating concrete service have to be able to handle this adapted protocol.
2. The external compensation process requires that reports about a performed compensation or the resending of results can be sent to the client of a transaction. It is therefore necessary that the client provides the expected interfaces and that he is able to process these reports in accordance with his business process.

The extent of the changes thus depends on the compensation requirements.

1.4.7 Middleware Prototype

The described design approach has been implemented as a prototype in order to verify the design and the protocols. The implementation has been done using Apache Tomcat as Web container, and Apache Axis as SOAP engine. The WS-Transaction specification has been chosen for the transaction coordination, more specifically the adapted `BusinessAgreementWithCoordinatorCompletion` protocol that has been introduced in Sect. 1.4.3. The implementation has been published online at SourceForge.net as the *FROGS* (**f**orward **r**ecovery c**o**mpensation handlin**g** **s**ystem) project: http://sourceforge.net/projects/frogs/.

1.5 Discussion

The evaluation of the approach is discussed in detail in [19]. Here we provide a summary of the findings: The experiments showed that in our environment about twice as many transactions as in a standard environment finish successfully. Furthermore, a similar improvement can also be found if we look at how many transactions finish in one minute. The number of messages sent in the environment is of course higher, which is, however, compensated by the increased number of transactions that do not have to roll back. Also, the number of additional messages is justified well enough if the overall cost of forward recovery is lower than the cost of the rollback and cumulative cascading rollbacks.

The current approach still has some shortcomings. The transition from design to compensation rules needs to be studied in order to support it via semi-automatic tools. Also, the algorithms for matching capability and requirement models require further studies, as the proposed algorithm is limited to an exact match. Especially approximation and similarity methods can be beneficial in this context. In addition, the support for different types of configuration models seems quite useful to study. So far, we have concentrated our efforts on defining the architecture and the required protocol. It will be necessary to do a further analysis of the proposed protocol to ensure that it is complete and is not susceptible to race conditions, which can occur in a real-life environment where less than optimal conditions exist, messages can be delayed or lost, and many concurrent accesses can exist.

References

1. Alonso, G., Casati, F., Kuno, H., Machiraju, V.: Web Services - Concepts, Architectures and Applications. Springer (2003)
2. Alrifai, M., Dolog, P., Nejdl, W.: Transactions Concurrency Control in Web Service Environment. In: ECOWS '06: Proceedings of the European Conference on Web Services, pp. 109–118. IEEE, Washington, DC, USA (2006). DOI 10.1109/ECOWS.2006.37
3. Choi, S., Jang, H., Kim, H., Kim, J., Kim, S.M., Song, J., Lee, Y.J.: Maintaining Consistency Under Isolation Relaxation of Web Services Transactions. In: A.H.H. Ngu, M. Kitsuregawa, E.J. Neuhold, J.Y. Chung, Q.Z. Sheng (eds.) WISE, *Lecture Notes in Computer Science*, vol. 3806, pp. 245–257. Springer (2005)
4. Christensen, E., Curbera, F., Meredith, G., Weerawarana, S.: Web Services Description Language (WSDL) 1.1. W3C note, W3C (2001)
5. Dolog, P., Nejdl, W.: Using UML-Based Feature Models and UML Collaboration Diagrams to Information Modelling for Web-Based Applications. In: T. Baar, A. Strohmeier, A. Moreira, S.J. Mellor (eds.) Proc. of UML 2004 — The Unified Modeling Language. Model Languages and Applications. 7th International Conference, *LNCS*, vol. 3273, pp. 425–439. Springer (2004)
6. Dostal, W., Jeckle, M., Melzer, I., Zengler, B.: Service-orientierte Architekturen mit Web Services. Spektrum-Akademischer Verlag (2005)
7. Gray, J.: The Transaction Concept: Virtues and Limitations. In: VLDB 1981: Intl. Conference on Very Large Data Bases, pp. 144–154. Cannes, France (1981)

8. Greenfield, P., Fekete, A., Jang, J., Kuo, D.: Compensation is Not Enough. In: 7th International Enterprise Distributed Object Computing Conference (EDOC 2003), pp. 232–239. IEEE Computer Society, Brisbane, Australia (2003)
9. Greenfield, P., Fekete, A., Jang, J., Kuo, D., Nepal, S.: Isolation Support for Service-based Applications: A Position Paper. In: CIDR, pp. 314–323 (2007)
10. Greenfield, P., Kuo, D., Nepal, S., Fekete, A.: Consistency for Web Services Applications. In: Proceedings of the 31st international conference on Very large data bases, VLDB '05, pp. 1199–1203. VLDB Endowment (2005). URL http://dl.acm.org/citation.cfm?id=1083592.1083731
11. Ltd., A.T., Systems, B., Ltd., H., Corporation, I., Technologies, I., Corporation, M.: Web Services Business Activity Framework (2005). Published at ftp://www6.software.ibm.com/software/developer/library/WS-BusinessActivity.pdf
12. Ltd., A.T., Systems, B., Ltd., H., Corporation, I.B.M., Technologies, I., Corporation, M.: Web Services Coordination (2005). Published online at ftp://www6.software.ibm.com/software/developer/library/WS-Coordination.pdf
13. Ltd., A.T., Systems, B., Ltd., H., Corporation, I.B.M., Technologies, I., Inc., M.C.: Web Services Atomic Transaction (2005). Published at ftp://www6.software.ibm.com/software/developer/library/WS-AtomicTransaction.pdf
14. Meyer, B.: Applying "Design by Contract". IEEE Computer **25**(10), 40–51 (1992)
15. Nielsen, H.F., Mendelsohn, N., Moreau, J.J., Gudgin, M., Hadley, M.: SOAP Version 1.2 Part 1: Messaging Framework. W3C recommendation, W3C (2003)
16. Pullum, L.L.: Software Fault Tolerance — Techniques and Implementation. Artech House, Inc., Norwood, MA, USA (2001)
17. Schäfer, M., Dolog, P.: Feature-Based Engineering of Compensations in Web Service Environment. In: M. Gaedke, M. Grossniklaus, O. Díaz (eds.) Web Engineering, 9th International Conference, ICWE 2009, *Lecture Notes in Computer Science*, vol. 5648, pp. 197–204. Springer, San Sebastián, Spain (2009)
18. Schäfer, M., Dolog, P., Nejdl, W.: Engineering Compensations in Web Service Environment. In: P. Fraternali, L. Baresi, G.J. Houben (eds.) ICWE2007: International Conference on Web Engineering, *LNCS*, vol. 4607, pp. 32–46. Springer Verlag, Como, Italy (2007)
19. Schäfer, M., Dolog, P., Nejdl, W.: Environment for Flexible Advanced Compensations of Web Service Transactions. ACM Transactions on Web **2**(2) (2008)
20. Yang, Z., Liu, C.: Implementing a Flexible Compensation Mechanism for Business Processes in Web Service Environment. In: ICWS '06. Intl. Conference on Web Services, pp. 753–760. IEEE Press, Salt Lake City, Utah, USA (2006)

Chapter 2
A Generic Framework for Testing the Web Services Transactions

Rubén Casado, Muhammad Younas and Javier Tuya

Abstract This chapter focuses on web services transactions which support creating robust web services applications by guaranteeing that their execution is correct and the data sources are consistent. More specifically, it investigates into the *testing* of such transactions which has not received proper attention from the current research. It presents a generic framework for testing different models and standards of web services transactions. The framework is implemented as a prototype system using the case study of Jboss Transactions and is applied to test the predominant web services models and standards such as Web Services Business Activity (WS-BA). The results show that the framework automatically generates test cases and detects possible faults or failures during the processing of web services transactions running under different model and standards.

2.1 Introduction

Web services provide a new computing paradigm in which functional and non-functional requirements of specialised services are published over the Internet such that they can be dynamically discovered and composed in order to create composite services that provide integrated and enhanced functionality. Web services transactions (or WS transactions) are used to ensure reliable execution of services and to maintain the consistency of data. WS Transactions are defined as sequences of web services operations or processes that are executed under certain criteria in order to

---

R. Casado (✉) · J. Tuya
Department of Computing, University of Oviedo, Asturias, Spain
e-mail: rcasado@lsi.uniovi.es

J. Tuya
e-mail: tuya@uniovi.es

M. Younas
Department of Computing and Communication Technologies, Oxford Brookes University, Oxford, UK
e-mail: m.younas@brookes.ac.uk

A. Bouguettaya et al. (eds.), *Advanced Web Services*,
DOI: 10.1007/978-1-4614-7535-4_2,

achieve mutually agreed outcome regardless of system failures or concurrent access to data sources i.e., either all the web services operations succeed completely or fail without leaving any incorrect or inconsistent outcomes. The classical and most widely used criteria are the ACID (Atomicity, Consistency, Isolation, Durability) which require that a transaction be treated as a single atomic unit of work in order to maintain consistency and persistency of data. Consider, for example, an online service provider (e.g., Amazon) that develops web services based solutions to automate the order and delivery of online books as part of a WS transaction. Such transaction can only be considered as successful once the books (purchased) are delivered to a customer and the payment has received.

Numerous models and protocols have been developed for WS Transactions, including, the OASIS Business Transaction Protocol (BTP) [24], Web Services Business Activity (WS-BA) [29], Web Services Transaction Management (WS-TXM) [25] and other models and frameworks [1, 20]. These aim to improve the quality of WS transactions in terms of response time efficiency, failure recovery, flexibility and support for long running and complex business applications. For example, [1] present an optimistic concurrency control protocol in order to optimise the throughput and response time of WS transactions. The authors in [20] propose an algorithm for selecting QoS-aware transactional web services that meet user's requirements.

This chapter focuses on another quality dimension which is the testing of WS transactions. Though there exists research work on testing non-transactional web services [4, 5], the area of WS transactions testing has not been properly researched yet.

Generally, the software testing aims to systematically explore the behaviour of a system or a component in order to detect unexpected behaviours. In other words, testing identifies whether the intended and actual behaviours of a system differ, or (at gaining confidence) that they do not. In our case, the focus of testing is to detect possible faults or failures in WS transactions running under different models or standards (e.g., BTP, WS-BA). The objective is to identify the observable differences between the behaviours of implementation and what is expected on the basis of specification of WS transaction models and standards. Based on our previous work [8, 9], this chapter presents a generic framework for testing WS transactions. The framework is comprised of the following phases:

- To design a generic model that abstractly represents the commonly used WS transaction models and standards (e.g., BTP, WS-BA).
- To automatically generate test cases and map them to different WS transactions models and standard.
- To perform testing and evaluation using the standard case study of Night Out, which is provided by Jboss [19] in their implementation of the WS-BA standard.
- To automatically compare the expected and actual outcomes in order to identify possible faults or failures in WS transactions.

The chapter is organized as follows. Section 2.2 gives an analysis of WS transaction models and standards. Section 2.3 presents the proposed framework. It also presents the generic transaction model and illustrates the process of representing some of the WS Transactions standards using the proposed transaction model. Section 2.4

presents the evaluation and results. Section 2.5 gives a critical analysis of the proposed framework. Conclusions are presented in Sect. 2.6.

2.2 WS Transactions

WS transactions are defined as sequences of web services operations or processes that are executed under certain criteria in order to achieve mutually agreed outcome regardless of system failures or concurrent access to data sources. But WS transactions have distinct characteristics than the classical database transactions. They are based on various models ranging from classical ACID criteria to advanced or extended transaction models. Two Phase Commit (2PC) protocol and its variants [12] have commonly been used for maintaining ACID properties. ACID properties are vital for WS transactions that need strict isolation and data consistency. However, they are not suitable for long running WS transactions as they result in resource locking/blocking problems. Advanced transaction models have been developed to address 2PC and ACID related issues. These includes, nested transaction model [23], SAGA model [15], open-nested [33], Split-join [31], Contracts [32], Flex [35], and WebTram [34]. The underlying strategy of these models is to relax the strict ACID criteria and to allow for compensation of partially completed transactions in order to maintain application correctness and data consistency.

The work in [11] proposes a theoretical approach in order to specify, analyze and synthesize advanced transaction models. Transactional patterns that combine workflow process adequacy and the transactional processing reliability are identified in [2]. In [16], the authors present a high level UML-based language to design transaction process with diverse transactional semantics. An XML representation is proposed in [18]. In our previous work [7], a risk-based approach is used to define general test scenarios for compensatable transactions. Further, in [6], we present test criteria for transactional web services composition. The approach is based on the dependencies which are defined between participants of a WS transaction. In [21], authors have developed a model of communicating hierarchical timed automata in order to describe long-running transactions. This approach verifies the properties of transactions using model checking. The work presented in [13] translates programs with compensations to tree automata in order to verify compensating transactions. The authors in [22] proposes a formal model to verify the requirement of relaxed atomicity with temporal constraints whilst [14] uses event calculus to validate the transactional behaviour of WS compositions.

In addition to the above, several standards have been developed for WS transactions. For instance, the OASIS Business Transaction Protocol (BTP) [24] coordinates loosely web services. BTP was designed and developed by several major vendors including BEA, Hewlett-Packard, Sun Microsystems, and Oracle. BTP adapts 2PC for short lived transactions and nested transaction model for long-lived transactions.

Web Services Composite Application Framework (WS-CAF) [25] is a set of WS specifications in order to support composite web services applications. Basically, WS-CAF uses WS-Transaction Management (WT-TXM) to manage transactions

Table 2.1 Test execution results

Standards	Coordination	Transaction model		Relationship
		Short	Long	
BTP	✓	ACID/2PC	Nested	✗
TXACID	✓	ACID/2PC	✗	WS-TXM
TXLRA	✓	✗	SAGA	WS-TXM
TXBP	✓	✗	Open-nested	WS-TXM
WS-AT	✓	ACID/2PC	✗	WS-COOR
WS-BA	✓	✗	SAGA	WS-COOR

in composite services. WT-TXM is built around three models: ACID Transaction (TXACID), Long Running Transaction (TXLRA) and Business Transaction Process (TXBP). These models are defined in order to meet the different requirements of web services. For example, if a web service is required to abide by strict isolation and consistency policy then it adapts the TXACID model.

Web Services Atomic Transactions (WS-AT) [28] and Web Services Business Activity (WS-BA) [29] are built on top of Web Services Coordination (WS-COOR) [27]. WS-AT and WS-BA thus follow the coordination mechanism of WS-COOR. WS-AT follows 2PC protocol while WS-BA uses the SAGA model.

The above standards and their underlying transaction models and protocols are summarized in Table 2.1. 'Coordination' represents whether a particular standard provides coordination facilities. 'Transaction Model' shows the underlying transaction models and protocols on which the WS transaction standard is based on. 'Short' and 'Long' respectively represent short-lived and long-lived WS transactions. 'Relationship' represents the relationship between the WS transaction standards.

From Table 2.1, we make some useful observations that motivate the need for a generic model for testing the WS transactions. Our first observation is that all the standards separate the coordination and the management of transactions and also distinguish between short-lived and long-lived transactions. Second, these standards have proprietary definitions of their underlying transaction models despite the fact that some of them are based on similar concepts. Third, the support for long-lived transactions is based on different advanced transaction models. For instance, TXLRA adapts SAGA while TXBP adapts open-nested transaction model. This reveals that WS transactions do not have a homogeneous transaction models or protocols. Instead they are characterized by a diversity of transaction models and protocols.

Given the diversity of WS transactions standards it is essential to develop a generic model that has the capability to represent and test WS transactions running under different standards. In the next section we define the proposed framework.

2.3 The Generic Framework

This section presents the proposed framework for testing the WS transactions. It first describes the transaction model and then illustrates the process of modelling the current WS transaction standards.

2.3.1 The Transaction Model

This section presents the first phase of the proposed framework i.e., to design a generic model that abstractly represents the commonly used WS transaction models and standards. It provides the basic definitions and relationships of WS transactions and also explains the different roles played by the participants (component systems) in the execution of WS transactions.

WS Transaction: A *WS Transaction, wT*, is defined as a set $S = s_1, \ldots, s_n$ of sub-transactions (or activities) which are executed in order to consistently and (semi) atomically acquire web services. Each wT is associated with one *Coordinator*, k, while each sub-transaction, s_i, is executed by an *Executor*, e_i. *Transaction context* is defined as a set of functional information and transaction configuration shared by the sub-transactions. Each s_i can be represented as a single level sub-transaction or as nested sub-transactions, which is denoted as wT_c. wT, s_i, and wT_c are related in a *parent:child* relationship. The outcome of wT is called atomic if all its sub-transactions complete their execution in an agreed manner. Alternatively, the outcome is called mixed if subtransactions can have different final states or outcomes, i.e., some completed and others not.

In the proposed model, subtransactions have different types [3, 20]. A subtransaction, s_i, is *lockable* if the resources (or data) that it uses can be locked until the completion of the parent transaction. A sub-transaction is *compensatable* if its effect can be semantically undone through a compensating transaction. If a sub-transaction is successfully completed and its effects cannot be semantically undone, then it is called *pivot*. A sub-transaction is *retriable* if it guarantees a successful termination after a finite number of invocations. A sub-transaction is *replaceable* if there is an alternative sub-transaction that can perform a similar task. Note that the different types of sub-transactions are defined as these are commonly used in WS transaction models and standards.

The execution of a wT involves different participants, each of which plays a certain role. We identify four different roles for the participants involved in processing the wT and its sub-transactions:

- *Executor*: represents a participant which is responsible for executing and terminating a sub-transaction.
- *Coordinator*: coordinates the overall execution of wT. For instance, it collects the results (votes) from participants in order to consistently process wT.
- *Initiator*: represents a participant which starts wT. That is, it submits wT to the coordinator and requests a transaction context.

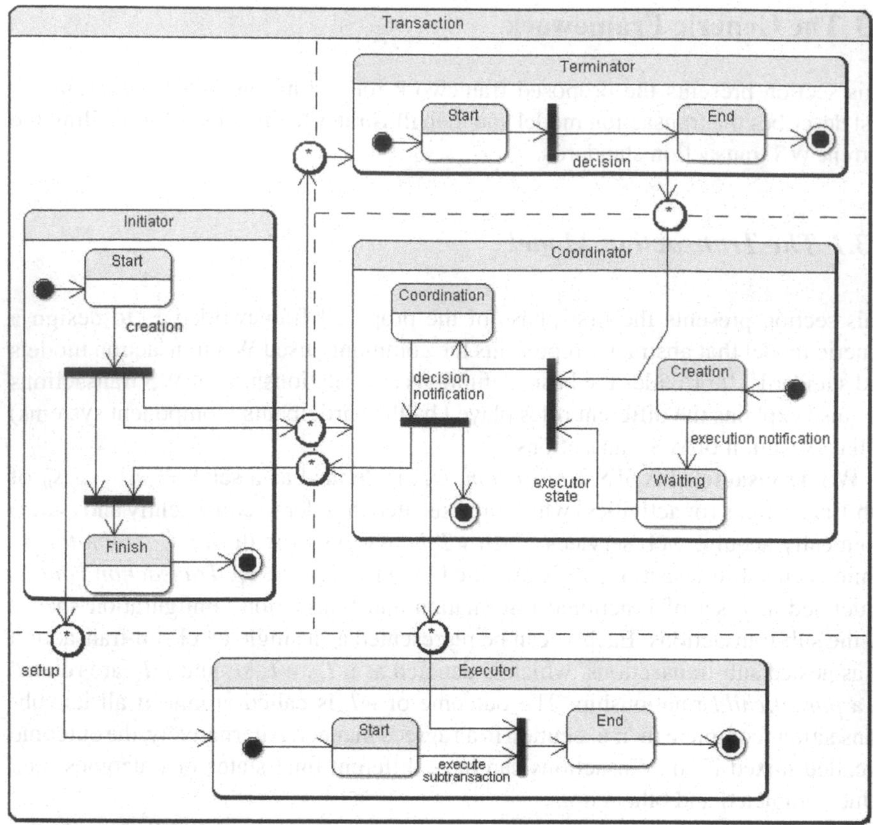

Fig. 2.1 Participant and roles in the proposed transaction model

- *Terminator*: represents a participant which decides when and how *wT* has to be terminated. It also participates in the coordination tasks. In some situations, it can play the role of a sub-coordinator.

The above roles are diagrammatically represented in Fig. 2.1 using UML state chart notation. The purpose of defining the above roles is to automatically and uniformly represent the different roles of participants in different WS transactions standards. As shown in Fig. 2.1, each participant plays a certain role and makes transition from one state to another during the processing of *wT*.

2.3.2 Representation of WS Transaction Models and Standards

This section describes the process of modelling WS transaction models and standards using the proposed framework. As proof of concept we model the BTP and WS-BA standards as these are the commonly accepted standards in WS transactions. The modelling process is composed of the following steps:

2.3.2.1 Role Identification and Modelling

This step identifies the roles of participants in a target WS transaction standard and models it using the roles defined in the proposed framework.

The BTP implements the nested transaction model [23] and defines two main roles; *Superior* and *Inferior*. In other words, it defines *Superior:Inferior* relationship between a parent transaction, *wT*, and its sub-transactions, s_i. Figure 2.2a shows the BTP representation of *wT* and its sub-transactions using the Superior:Inferior relationship, and Fig. 2.2b represents the same *wT* using the proposed framework. In BTP the superior makes the decision and the inferior abides such decision in order to complete the transaction. The superior of BTP is modelled as Initiator in the proposed framework. Also the superior can be modelled as Coordinator and Terminator as it decides on the outcome of the subtransactions. Inferior of BTP executes a subtransaction and is therefore modelled as Executor in the proposed framework.

The WS-BA defines two outcomes of wT: (i) *MixedOutcome* allows that sub-transactions may have distinct outcomes or final states, (ii) *AtomicOutcome* requires all the subtransactions to complete their execution in an agreed manner. The main roles are played by the: *Executor* and *Coordinator*. Figure 2.3 depicts the modelling of WS-BA using the proposed framework. Figure 2.3a shows the *AtomicOutcome*, whilst Fig. 2.3b shows the *MixedOutcome* scenario. In both scenarios the role of *Initiator* is taken by the first participant who interacts with a *Coordinator*. In *AtomicOutcome* the role of *Terminator* is taken by the *Coordinator*. This is due to the fact that *Coordinator* can be the participant that knows all Executors's output. It also knows the final outcome: close or terminate *wT* if all executors have successfully executed their sub-transactions, or compensated otherwise. In *MixedOutcome*,

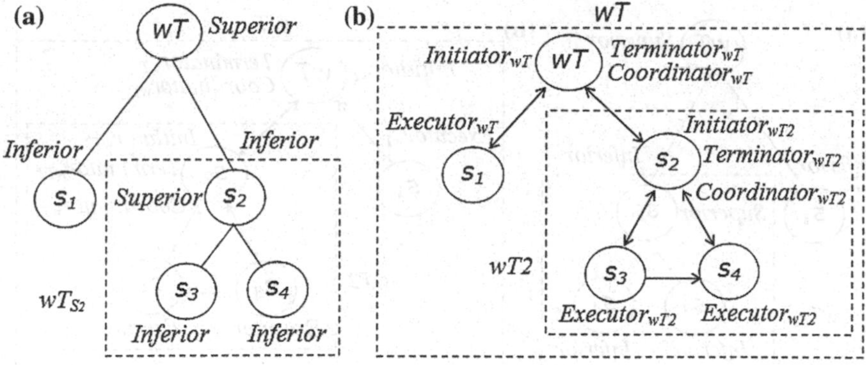

Fig. 2.2 Representation of BTP roles and relationships

the *Initiator* is the *Terminator* since each *Executor* may have its specific or distinct decision so the outcome depends on the business logic.

2.3.2.2 State Transitioning and Messages

This section describes the mapping of the state transitions and messages between a target WS transaction standard and the proposed framework.

Figures 2.4 and 2.5 give more details on the state transitions and message communication between Executor and Coordinator during the processing of *wT*. Note that here we only model these two participants as they play a major role in executing *wT*. The Inferior and Superior (in BTP) are respectively represented by Executor and Coordinator. Similarly Executor and Coordinator are used to represent WS-BA participants involved in *wT*.

BTP mapping: When a *wT* is started at the initiative of an Initiator a request is sent to the Coordinator for creation of a context for the new transaction. The Coordinator replies the Initiator and other Executors with the context information and then moves from INITIAL state to ACTIVE state. Each Executor receives a context, enrols with the Coordinator and then moves from READY to ACTIVE state. The Executor moves to COMPLETED state after processing its sub-transaction. Coordinator moves to PREPARE state awaiting decisions from Executors. The Executor sends its outcome to the Coordinator and moves to DECISION state. The Coordinator collects the outcomes from all Executors and takes the final decision by moving from PREPARE state to DECISION state. The final decision is sent to each Executor and the Coordinator then moves to CONFIRM state. Each Executor sends acknowledgement and changes its state to END state through the transition (either completed rollback or completed successfully). Once the Coordinator has received all confirmations, it moves to END state. Note that an Executor can leave the *wT* before confirming the completion of sub-transaction. So it can move from ACTIVE state to CANCEL state.

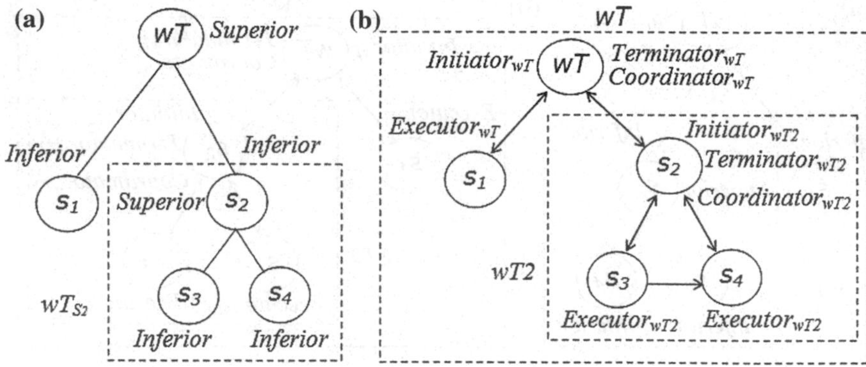

Fig. 2.3 WS-BA relationships modeling

Although BTP uses the 2PC protocol, Executors are not required to lock data on becoming prepared (i.e., in prepared state). This can produce a contradictory decision since the Coordinator could take a decision for all the Executors but some Executors may take their own decisions. When the Coordinator detects any contradiction it notifies the concerned Executor and moves to the END state. If the Coordinator wants to cancel, the Executor uses *completed pivot*. In some cases, it uses *completed rollback*. Further, BTP allows replaceable subtransactions. Thus if an Executor is not able to start or carry on with its sub-transaction, it moves to FAILED state. A new Executor is selected and the previous one moves to END state.

WS-BA mapping: The Initiator initiates *wT* and requests a context from Coordinator. The Coordinator responds with a context. After *wT* initiation, Executors join the current *wT* and move from READY to ACTIVE state, wherein they execute their sub-transactions. After processing sub-transaction, each Executor moves from ACTIVE to COMPLETED state. Coordinator moves from ACTIVE to PREPARE state after receiving decision from all the Executors. In WS-BA, when the transaction is of *MixedOutcome*, the decision for each sub-transaction is taken independently by each Executor. In this case, the Coordinator moves from PREPARE to DECISION state whenever it receives an Executor's notification. The Coordinator decides about its outcome and moves from DECISION to CONFIRM state. In the case of *AtomicOutcome* type, the Coordinator moves from PREPARE to DECISION state after receiving decisions from each Executor. The Coordinator then sends the global decision to all Executors and moves from DECISION to CONFRIM state. Finally it awaits the acknowledgements from Executors. Once these are received, the Coordinator then moves to END state. When an Executor is not able to start executing its sub-transaction it moves from READY to ABORTED state. If the sub-transaction was cancelled while it was still under execution, the Executor moves from ACTIVE to CANCELLED state. In case of failure it moves from ACTIVE to FAILED state.

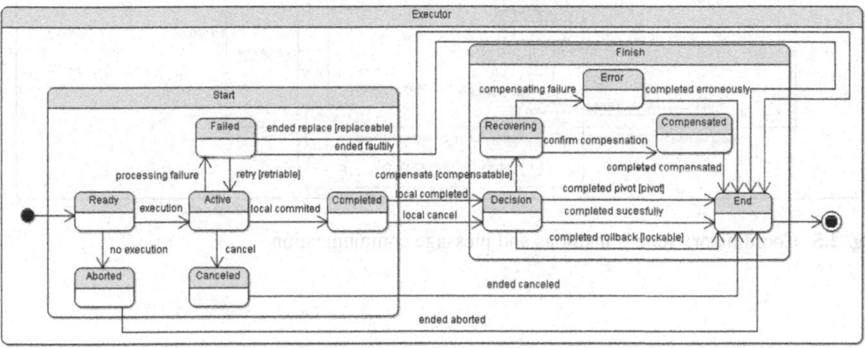

Fig. 2.4 Executor: State transitions and message communication

2.4 Implementation and Evaluation of the Proposed Framework

The process of testing aims at showing whether the intended and actual behaviours of a system differ, or at gaining confidence that they do not. The main goal of testing in our context is failure detection, i.e., the observable differences between the behaviours of implementation and what is expected on the basis of the specification of WS Transaction standards. We exploit a model-based testing approach that encodes the intended behaviour of a system and the behaviour of its environment. Model-based testing is capable of generating suitable test cases and it has also been successfully used in others WS domains [10].

In order to validate and evaluate our framework we have designed a test process which comprises test design, test implementation, test execution and outcome evaluation. In the following, we first explain the testing process. We then illustrate the implementation of the proposed framework. Finally, we discuss the evaluation of the framework.

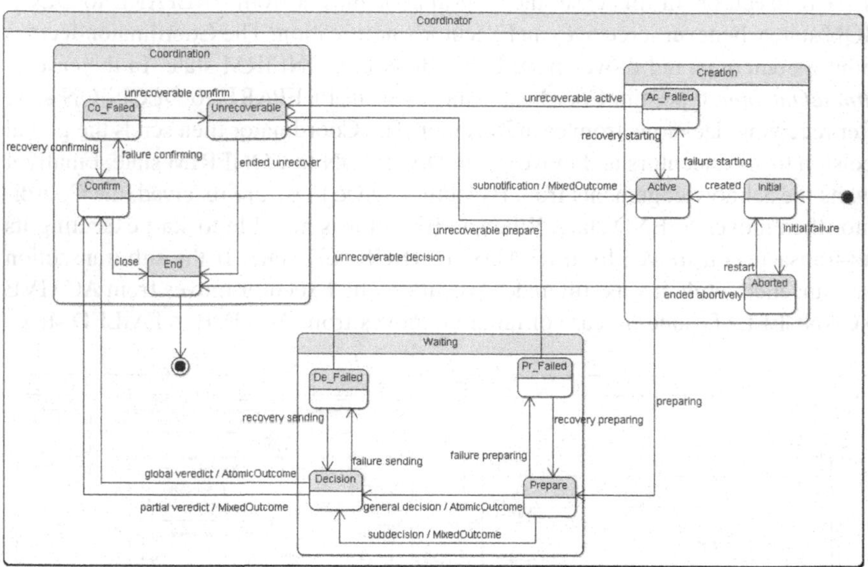

Fig. 2.5 Coordinator: State transitions and message communication

2.4.1 Testing Process

The testing process includes selecting a test criterion, test design, test implementation, test execution and outcome evaluation. This section presents how the proposed framework implements those phases using the generic transaction model.

The first step to design the tests is to select a test criterion. Since the model is based on states and transitions, we use the well known criterion of transition coverage [30]. By applying a test criterion over the generic transaction model, we obtain a set of abstract test cases. Each abstract test case is mapped to a concrete test case which is composed of the test scenario and the expected system outcome. The basic concepts used in the test process are defined as follows.

- *Test criterion*: This defines a rule that imposes constraints (or requirements) on a set of test cases.
- *Transition coverage criterion*: The set of test cases must include tests that cause every transition between states in a state-based model (e.g., as in Figs. 2.4 and 2.5)
- *Abstract Test case*: This represents a sequence of states and transitions of a participant using the generic transaction model. The notation $S_i \rightarrow S_i^{\prime}$ is used to denote that the participant p_i changes its current state S to $S^{\prime}$ executing the transition labelled, t. If the participant is the Coordinator, it is denoted by k. We use $S_i^a \rightarrow S_i^b \cdots S_i^c \rightarrow S_i^d$ to denote a sequence of state transitions.
- *Test scenario*: This represents a sequence of actions in a human-understandable way to provide guidance to the tester to execute a test case.
- *System outcome*: The internal state of the process defined by a sequence of exchanged messages between participants using a specific WS transaction standard. The notation $i[m_1]j$ is used to denote that the participant p_i sends message m_1 to participant p_j. We use $i[m_1]j - l[m_2]o - \cdots - v[m_n]z$ to denote a sequence of messages.

The test phases included in the proposed framework are depicted in Fig. 2.6 and are described as follow:

Test design: This phase defines the test requirements for an item and derives the logical (abstract) test cases. At this stage the test cases do not have concrete values for input and the expected results. The abstract test cases are automatically generated by applying transition coverage criterion over the abstract model. It is obtained from a set of different paths where each path defines an abstract test case. Thus the tests achieved using this criterion are a set of paths that cover all states and transitions of a model.

Test implementation: The sequence of states and transitions specified by the abstract test cases generated in the test design phase are mapped to a specific WS transaction standard, for example, BTP or WS-BA (see Sect. 2.3). As discussed above the proposed generic model has the ability to capture the behaviours of WS transaction standards as well as mapping the abstract cases to different WS transaction standards. These features provide the capability of automatically obtaining the test scenario and the expected system output.

Test execution and outcome evaluation: Once the test cases are implemented, they are executed over the system under test (e.g., BTP or WS-BA) and the actual outcome is obtained. Finally, for each test case, the expected outcome is compared to the actual outcome to find differences in behaviour and to detect failures. Two outcomes are considered: (i) *user outcome*: this refers to what the user perceives; for instance, to reserve theatre tickets and to see whether the number of booked tickets is correct. (ii) *system outcome*: this refers to the non-visible process that the system

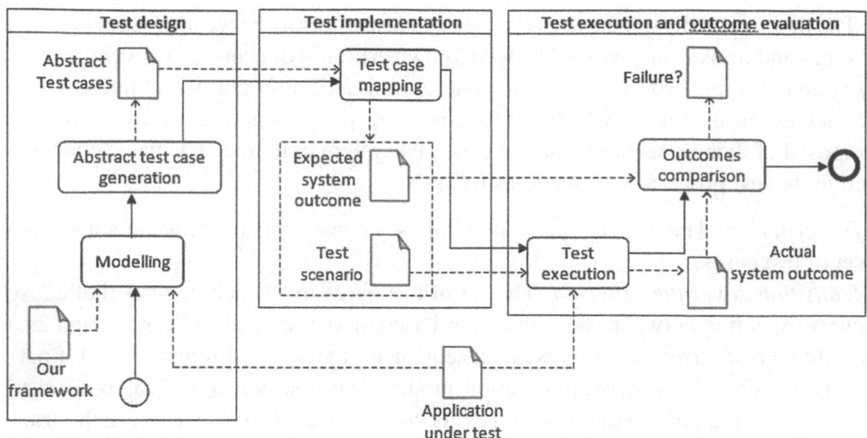

Fig. 2.6 Test process of the proposed framework

has carried out to achieve the requirements e.g., the correct exchange of messages between the participants according to the given transaction standard.

Both outcomes are necessary for detecting the differences in the behaviour of WS transactions. Consider a simple application that runs as a WS transaction in order to book theatre tickets. Assume that there is a fault in creating messages and the format of confirmation messages is incorrect. In a test scenario where the user confirms a reservation, the systems outcome would be to inform the user that the booking was successfully completed because the application has already sent the confirmation message to the theatre service. Since the message was incorrectly created, the theatre service would reject the reservation and, as a result, the tickets cannot be booked. Thus, the tester needs not only the user outcome, but also the internal state of the process to know whether a test case has detected a failure or not. In this work we focus on Excutors internal behaviours related to the WS transactions. Thus we only need to evaluate the system outcome.

2.4.2 Prototype System

We have developed a prototype system that implements the main phases of the proposed framework (Fig. 2.6).

- *Modelling*: The prototype system prompts the tester to provide information (e.g. services, roles, transaction standard, etc) and to create the WS transaction.
- *Abstract test case generation*: the abstract test cases for all the participants (Coordinator, Executor, etc) are automatically generated by the prototype system.
- *Test case mapping*: Abstract test cases are mapped to WS transaction standards (e.g., BTP or WS-BA). That is, the prototype system automatically generates the

concrete test cases (for each WS transaction standards) which are composed of the test scenario and the expected system outcome. A test scenario is defined as a sequence of actions in a human-readable way to provide guidance to the tester to execute a test case.

- *Outcomes comparison*: test cases are executed in order to produce the actual systems outcome. The prototype system automatically compares the actual systems outcome with the expected systems outcome in order to detect any fault or failure.

The prototype system is implemented in Java 1.5. It includes three components: *Model*, *Tests* and *Outcome*. The *Model* implements the generic transaction model. It also includes a graphic interface to allow the tester to enter all the necessary information such about the system under test such as roles, URL, WS transaction standard, etc. The *Model* component sends the information to the *Tests* component. The *Tests* component implements two activities: first, it applies the transition coverage criterion in order to generate the abstract test cases for all the participants. It then maps all the abstract test cases into concrete test cases. That is, the *Model* component generates the test scenario (text file) and the expected systems outcome (as an XML file). Finally, the *Outcome* component compares two XML files to identify any possible faults. This component has a graphic interface that allows the tester to add an XML file (the actual systems outcome obtained from the execution of test scenario) and to select the test case for comparison purpose. The result of both outcomes is shown to the tester.

2.4.3 Evaluation

In order to evaluate the proposed framework we utilise the *Night Out* case study which is adopted from the Jbosss implementation of the WS-BA standard [29]. This study concerns booking three independent services for night time leisure: *Restaurant* service allows customers to reserve a table for a specified number of dinner guests. *Theatre* service provides reservation of seats in a theatre and allows customers to book a specified number of tickets for different categories such as seats in circle, stalls, or balcony. *Taxi* service provides the facility to book a taxi. These services are implemented as transactional web services. The client side of the application is implemented as a servlet which allows users to select reservations and then book a night out by invoking each of the services within the scope of a WS transaction. For example, if seats are not available in a restaurant or a theatre, then taxi will not be required. Each service, exposed as Java API for XML Web Services (JAX-WS) [17] endpoint, has a GUI with state information and an event trace log.

In this chapter we described the process of modelling and testing the WS-BA standard using the prototype system. But the prototype system is capable of representing different WS transaction models and standards.

2.4.3.1 Modelling of WS-BA-Based Transactions

The transactional aspects of WS-BA included in the *Night Out* application has been modelled according to the aforementioned procedure. As shown in Fig. 2.7, *Night Out* (client side) takes the role of Initiator since it starts the transaction and asks the other web services to participate in the transaction. *Restaurant*, *Theatre* and *Taxi* services are modelled as Executors as they execute individual sub-transactions. Some sub-transactions (e.g. *Theatre*) are independent of others (e.g. *Restaurant*). That is, if one sub-transaction cannot complete its execution the others are allowed to commit. The *Taxi* activity is dependent on some of the services. For instance, if a table is not available in the restaurant, the customer still needs a taxi to go to the theatre. The role of Coordinator is taken by an external service, *WSCoor11*, provided by the server. It follows the WS-COOR [27] and WS-BA [29] standards to exchange required messages.

2.4.3.2 Abstract Test Case Generation and Mapping

This phase generates various abstract cases for each Executor, i.e., *Restaurant*, *Theatre* and *Taxi*. The abstract test cases are automatically generated and mapped to specific standard in this case, the WS-BA standard. As explained above, these tests cases define the test scenario and the expected system outcome. For example, in the following we explain the process of mapping the abstract test cases to a specific sequence of WS-BA messages. Consider the sequence shown in Fig. 2.8 of state transitioning and messages wherein an Executor moves from Ready to End state (see Fig. 2.4).

Applying the transition coverage criterion over the above, abstract test case is mapped to a specific sequence of WS-BA message (see Fig. 2.9). From this sequence of messages, our prototype system automatically generates the test scenario which is shown in Fig. 2.10.

Based on the above, the prototype system can generate and map various test cases for *Restaurant*, *Theatre* and *Taxi* services. Figure 2.11 contains eight test cases for the *Restaurant*, *Theatre* and *Taxi*. Res_1, Thr_1, and Tax_1 respectively represent test case 1 for *Restaurant*, *Theatre* and *Taxi* services. Res_2, Thr_2, and Tax_2 mean test case 2 and so on. Note that these eight are example test cases. But the prototype system is capable of generating other possible test cases.

2.4.3.3 Test Execution and Outcome Evaluation

The prototype system executes the generated test cases using the Night Out services. The results of test execution are summarised in Table 2.2. 'Pass' means that a test case is executed but has not detected any failure during the processing of a service (e.g., booking a restaurant, theatre or taxi). 'Fails' means that the actual outcome differs from the expected outcome (i.e. a fault has been detected). 'Blocked' means that a test case cannot be executed because the application does not have the interface to perform the required actions.

Pass: Test cases 3, 6, and 7 are executed but the prototype system has detected no failures. That is, Rest_3, 6, 7, Thr_3, 6, 7, and Tax_3, 6, 7 have passed the tests.

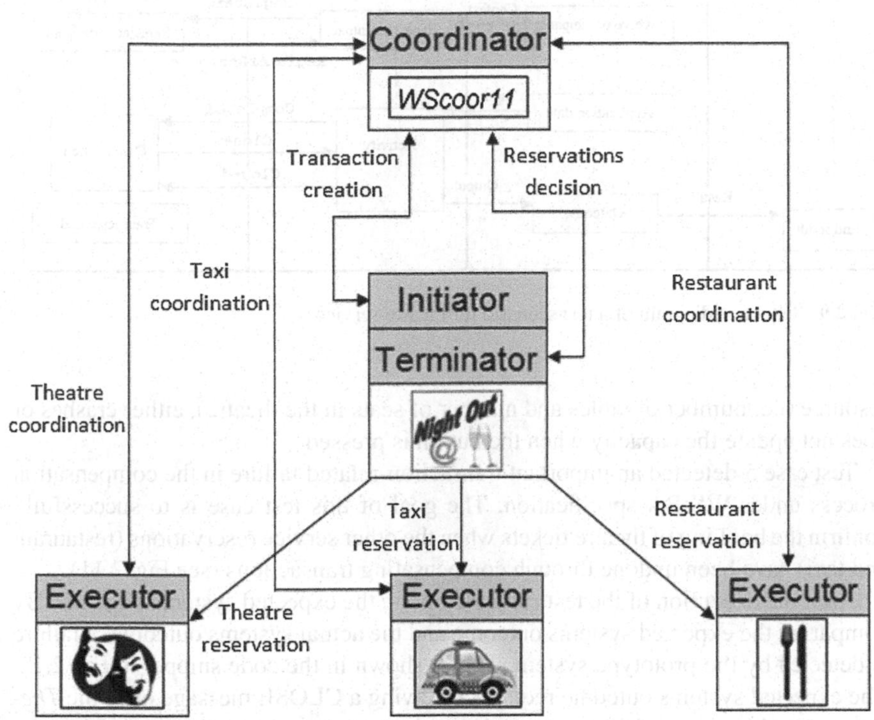

Fig. 2.7 Roles and representation of Night Out Services

$$\mathit{READY} \xrightarrow{\mathit{Execution}} \mathit{ACTIVE} \xrightarrow{\mathit{Local\_commited}} \mathit{COMPLETED} \xrightarrow{\mathit{Local\_completed}} \mathit{DECISION} \xrightarrow{\mathit{Completed\_sucesfully}} \mathit{END}$$

Fig. 2.8 Executor abstract sequence

Blocked: Two of the test cases were blocked due to the following reasons. Test case 1 requires cancelling the activity (*Cancel* message) once the Executor has started but has not finished yet. But WS-BA standard does not allow cancelling a concrete booking once the service has started executing its activity. Test case 8 defines a scenario where the Executor is not able to complete its activity (*CanNotComplete* message) but has retried executing its action. However, the WS-BA does not allow the services to retry its activity without starting a new transaction.

Fail: During the execution of test cases 3 and 4 interface-related failures were detected. The application, which allows changing manually the capacity of each

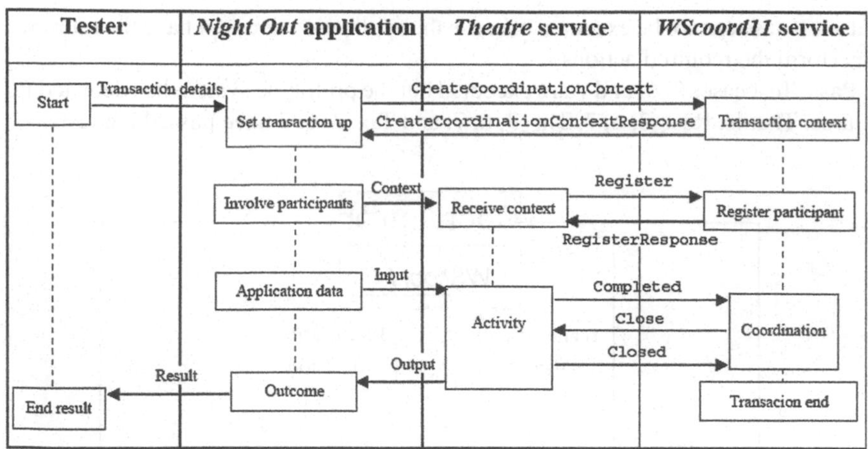

Fig. 2.9 Sequence diagram of a test scenario for theatre service

resource (i.e. number of tables and number of seats in the theatre), either crashes or does not update the capacity when the button is pressed.

Test case 5 detected an important transaction-related failure in the compensation process under WS-BA specification. The goal of this test case is to successfully confirm the booking of theatre tickets when the other service reservations (restaurant and taxi) have been undone through compensating transactions (see Fig. 2.11).

After the execution of the test case, we obtain the expected systems outcome. By comparing the expected systems outcome and the actual systems outcome, a failure is detected by the prototype system. This is shown in the code snippet in Fig. 2.12. The expected systems outcome requires receiving a CLOSE message once the *Theatre* service has successfully completed its activity (see sequence diagram in Fig. 2.9). However, the actual outcome has a COMPENSATED message since *Restaurant* service was not able to commit. As a result, the *Theatre* reservations were automatically undone. The fault which causes such failure is detected by the prototype system as there is a difference (or discrepancy) in the 'Register' message the way *Theatre* service is registered in the *Night Out* under the WS-BA specification. That is, it registers the Theatre service as an *AtomicOutcome* when a *MixedOutcome* was expected (Fig. 2.13). In other words, if *Taxi* or *Restaurant* services are not able to make their reservations, the *Theatre* service will automatically undo the reservation even if the customer would wish to keep the theatre tickets.

The results obtained from the test comparison are also useful for a debugging process. In the above tests, the faults mean that the transaction was not correctly configured or coded. This can help in identifying the faults in the code. For example, the above fault was found in *BasicClient.java* file, at line number 496 in the code shown in Fig. 2.14. The configuration of the transaction is made using the class *UserBusinessActivityImple*, through the factory pattern using *UserBusinessActivityFactory* class. By looking at the implementation of that class we found (in Fig. 2.15) that the transaction is defined as an *AtomicOutcome*.

STEP 1: *NightOut* starts the process. It sends a context request (`CreateCoordinationContext` message) to the coordinator *WScorr11*

STEP 2: WScorr11 sends the transaction context (`CreationCoordinationContextResponse` message) to *NightOut*

STEP 3: *Theatre* receives a transaction context from the initiator *NightOut*

STEP 4: *Theatre* accepts to participate in the process. It requests to be registered in the transaction, thus it sends `Register` message to *WScorr11*

STEP 5: *WScorr11* receives Register message from *Theatre* and registers *Theatre* in the transaction. It sends `RegisterResponse` message to *Theatre*

STEP 6: *NightOut* sends the application data to *Theatre*

STEP 7: *Theatre* successfully completes its activity. *Theatre* sends `Completed` message to notify its outcome to the Coordinator *WScorr11*

STEP 8: Theatre has successfully completed its activity. *Theatre* notifies the results and leaves the transaction. *Theatre* sends `Close` message to notify the Coordinator *WScorr11* which in turn replies with a `Closed` message

Fig. 2.10 Test scenario for theatre service

2.5 Discussion

This section gives a critical overview of the proposed framework and illustrates its merits and demerits. The prototype system implements the main phases of the testing process. But it still lacks full automation of the overall process. For instance, the tester has to model the given WS standard under test according to the roles defined by the framework such as Initiator, Coordinator, Executor and Terminator. Information on each service such as its URL or the transaction standard used has to be provided by the tester. With such information, the framework automatically generates the abstract test cases and maps them to WS transaction standards. Further, the tester has to manually execute the test scenario in order to get the actual systems outcome. The actual systems outcome is provided to the prototype system by the tester which then automatically compares both outcomes in order to detect faults. Despite the semi-automatic nature of the framework, it still helps the tester in two ways: (i) defining specific test cases for WS transactions and (ii) automating some of the most tedious and error-prone phases of testing. Our future work includes the full automation of the overall testing process.

The framework relies on the capability of the proposed generic transaction model in order to capture the behaviour of existing transaction standards. The generic model,

Test Case Ids			Description
Restaurant	Theatre	Taxi	
Rest_1	Thr_1	Tax_1	Cancel the in-progress booking (of restaurant, theatre, taxi). That is, a service is started but has not confirmed the reservation yet.
Rest_2	Thr_2	Tax_2	Service is executed but is unsuccessful as there is no taxi or seat available in restaurant or theatre
Rest_3	Thr_3	Tax_3	Cancel (undo) booking by executing the compensating action
Rest_4	Thr_4	Tax_4	Confirm successful booking after the commit of the transaction
Rest_5	Thr_5	Tax_5	Successfully confirm the theatre tickets booking when the other services reservations have been undone through compensating transactions
Rest_6	Thr_6	Tax_6	Abort service before it has started its execution
Rest_7	Thr_7	Tax_7	Failure occurs during the compensation process of completed booking
Rest_8	Thr_8	Tax_8	Use retry action if there is a failure during the booking process

Fig. 2.11 Test cases for the Night Out services

Table 2.2 Test execution results

Executor	Generated test cases	Pass	Fail	Blocked
Restaurant	8	3	3	2
Theatre	8	3	3	2
Taxi	8	3	3	2

presented in this chapter, has been designed after an in-depth study of the existing solutions of WS transactions. Currently BTP, WS-BA and WS-TXM transaction standards have been modelled using the generic transaction model. Our analysis revealed that though these standards are incompatible between each other, they are based on same theoretical concepts. Thus they can be modelled using the roles specified in the generic transaction model. In future, we intend to study the capability of the generic transaction model to model transaction-based applications running under non-transaction standards such as [26].

In terms of the test case generation, the proposed framework applies transition test criterion that ensures the coverage of all transitions and states specified in the generic transaction model. The framework however does not guarantee the code coverage. As a part of the future research work we plan to enhance the prototype system in order to monitor the execution of the code.

```
<soap:Envelope
xmlns:soap="http://schemas.xmlsoap.org/soap/envelope/">
<soap:Header>
<Action
xmlns="http://www.w3.org/2005/08/addressing">
http://docs.oasis-open.org/ws-tx/wsba/2006/06/Close
</Action>
```

(a) Expected outcome

```
<soap:Envelope
xmlns:soap="http://schemas.xmlsoap.org/soap/envelope/">
<soap:Header>
<Action
xmlns="http://www.w3.org/2005/08/addressing">
http://docs.oasis-open.org/ws-tx/wsba/2006/06/Compensate
</Action>>
```

(b) Actual outcome

Fig. 2.12 Fault in message exchange

```
<wscoord:CoordinationType>
http://docs.oasis-open.org/ws-tx/wsba/2006/06/MixedOutcome
</wscoord:CoordinationType>
```

(a) Expected outcome

```
<wscoord:CoordinationType>
http://docs.oasis-open.org/ws-tx/wsba/2006/06/AtomicOutcome
</wscoord:CoordinationType>
```

(b) Actual outcome

Fig. 2.13 Fault in registration process

```
private boolean testBusinessActivity(int restaurantSeats, int
theatreCircleSeats, int theatreStallsSeats, int
theatreBalconySeats, boolean bookTaxi) throws Except
{
System.out.println("CLIENT: obtaining
userBusinessActivity..."); UserBusinessActivity uba =
UserBusinessActivityFactory.userBusinessActivity();
```

Fig. 2.14 Fault identification: transaction setup

2.6 Conclusion

This chapter investigated into the issue of testing the WS Transactions. In it we designed, developed and evaluated the generic framework which is capable of dynamically modelling different WS transaction models and standards. The framework exploits model-based testing technique in order to automatically generate test cases for testing the WS transaction standards. The framework is implemented as a prototype system with which various test cases were automatically generated and mapped to different WS transaction standards. The evaluation was performed using the case study of *Night Out*, which is an open source application provided by Jboss [19].

```
public class UserBusinessActivityImple extends User
BusinessActivity {

   public void begin(int timeout) throws
WrongStateException,SystemException {
   try {
       if (_contextManager.currentTransaction() != null)
           throw new WrongStateException();
      CoordinationContextType ctx = _factory.create(
      BusinessActivityConstants.WSBA_PROTOCOL_ATOMIC_OUTCOME,
null, null);
```

Fig. 2.15 Fault identification: protocol implementation

The experiments show that our framework can effectively be used to define different test cases as well as test the different WS transactions models and standards.

References

1. Alrifai, M., Dolog, P., Balke, W.T., Nejdl, W.: Distributed management of concurrent web service transactions. Services Computing, IEEE Transactions on **2**(4), 289–302 (2009)
2. Bhiri, S., Godart, C., Perrin, O.: Transactional patterns for reliable web services compositions (2006)
3. Bhiri, S., Perrin, O., Godart, C.: Ensuring required failure atomicity of composite web services (2005)
4. Bozkurt, M., Harman, M., Hassoun, Y.: Testing web services: A survey. Tech. rep., Department of ComputerScience, King's College London (2010)
5. Canfora, G., Penta, M.: Service-Oriented Architectures Testing: A Survey, pp. 78–105. Springer-Verlag (2009)
6. Casado, R., Tuya, J., Godart, C.: Dependency-based criteria for testing web services transactional workflows. In: Next Generation on Web Services Practices, pp. 74–79. IEEE (2011)
7. Casado, R., Tuya, J., Younas, M.: Testing long-lived web services transactions using a risk-based approach. In: 10th International Conference on Quality Software, pp. 337–340. IEEE Computer Society, 1849260 (2010)
8. Casado, R., Tuya, J., Younas, M.: Evaluating the effectiveness of the abstract transaction model in testing web services transactions. Concurrency and Computation: Practice and Experience pp. n/a–n/a (2012)
9. Casado, R., Tuya, J., Younas, M.: Testing the reliability of web services transactions in cooperative applications (2012)
10. Cavalli, A., Cao, T.D., Mallouli, W., Martins, E., Sadovykh, A., Salva, S., Zadi, F.: Webmov: A dedicated framework for the modelling and testing of web services composition. In: IEEE International Conference on Web Services (2010)
11. Chrysanthis, P.K., Ramamritham, K.: Synthesis of extended transaction models using acta. ACM Trans. Database Syst. **19**(3), 450–491 (1994)
12. Elmagarmid, A.K.: Database transaction models for advanced applications. Morgan Kaufmann Publishers (1992)

13. Emmi, M., Majumdar, R.: Verifying compensating transactions. In: International Conference Verification, Model Checking, and Abstract, Interpretation, pp. 29–43 (2007)
14. Gaaloul, W., Rouached, M., Godart, C., Hauswirth, M.: Verifying composite service transactional behavior using event calculus (2007)
15. Garcia-Molina, H., Salem, K.: Sagas (1987)
16. Gioldasis, N., Christodoulakis, S.: Utml: Unified transaction modeling language. In: The Third International Conference on Web Information Systems Engineering (2002)
17. GlassFish: Jax-ws (2005)
18. Hrastnik, P., Winiwarter, W.: Using advanced transaction meta-models for creating transaction-aware web service environments. International Journal of Web Information Systems (2005)
19. Jboss: Jboss transactions (2006)
20. Joyce El, H.: Tqos: Transactional and qos-aware selection algorithm for automatic web service composition. IEEE Transactions on Services Computing **3**, 73–85 (2010)
21. Lanotte, R., Maggiolo-Schettini, A., Milazzo, P., Troina, A.: Design and verification of long-running transactions in a timed framework. Science of Computer Programming pp. 76–94 (2008)
22. Li, J., Zhu, H., He, J.: Specifying and verifying web transactions. In: International conference on Formal Techniques for Networked and Distributed Systems, pp. 149–168 (2008)
23. Moss, E.: Nested transactions: An approach to reliable distributed computing. Massachusetts Institute of Technology (1981)
24. OASIS: Business transaction protocol (2004)
25. OASIS: Web services composite application framework (2005)
26. OASIS: Web services business process execution language v2.0 (2007)
27. OASIS: Web services coordination, http://docs.oasis-open.org/ws-tx/wscoor/2006/06 (2007)
28. OASIS: Web services atomic transaction (2009)
29. OASIS: Web services business activity (2009)
30. Offutt, J., Liu, S., Abdurazik, A., Ammann, P.: Generating test data from state-based specifications. Journal of Software Testing, Verification and Reliability **13**(13), 25–53 (2003)
31. Pu, C., Kaiser, G.E., Hutchinson, N.C.: Split-transactions for open-ended activities (1988)
32. Reuter: Contracts: A means for extending control beyond transaction boundaries. Proceedings of the 3rd International Workshop on High Performance Transaction Systems (1989)
33. Weikum, G., Schek, H.J.: Concepts and applications of multilevel transactions and open nested transactions. Database transaction models for advanced applications. Morgan Kaufmann Publishers Inc. (1992)
34. Younas, M., Eaglestone, B., Holton, R.: A formal treatment of a sacred protocol for multidatabase web transactions. Database and Expert Systems Applications **1873**, 899–908 (2000)
35. Zhang, A., Nodine, M., Bhargava, B., Bukhres, O.: Ensuring relaxed atomicity for flexible transactions in multidatabase systems. ACM, SIGMOD Record (1994)

Chapter 3
Universal Identity Management Based on Delegation in SOA

Yang Zhang and Jun-Liang Chen

Abstract Relationship-focused and credential-focused identity management are both user-centric notions in Service-oriented architecture (SOA). For composite services, pure user-centric identity management is inefficient because each sub-service may authenticate and authorize users and users need to participate in every identity provisioning transaction. If the above two paradigms are unified into universal identity management, where identity information and privileges are delegatable, user-centricity will be more feasible in SOA. The credential-focused system is a good starting point for constructing a universal identity management system. However, how to implement a practical delegation scheme is still a challenge although some delegatable anonymous credential schemes have been theoretically constructed. This paper aims to propose a practical solution for universal identity management. For this, a pseudonym-based signature scheme is firstly designed, where pseudonyms are self-generated and unlinkable for realizing user privacy. Next, a proxy signature is presented with the pseudonyms as public keys where delegation can be achieved through certificate chains. Finally, the WS-Federation is extended to build a universal identity management solution.

Y. Zhang (✉) · J.-L. Chen
State Key Laboratory of Networking and Switching Technology,
Beijing University of Posts and Telecommunications, Beijing, China
e-mail: YangZhang@bupt.edu.cn

J.-L. Chen
e-mail: chjl@bupt.edu.cn

A. Bouguettaya et al. (eds.), *Advanced Web Services*,
DOI: 10.1007/978-1-4614-7535-4_3,

3.1 Introduction

3.1.1 Motivation

In Service-oriented architecture (SOA), individuals often use identity providers to provide their identity information and the identities are represented by a set of attributes [1, 2]. Based on the user-centricity philosophy, identity management systems [3, 4] are classified into relationship-focused and credential-focused systems [5]. In the relationship-focused system, identity providers play an important role and are involved in each transaction that conveys identity information to a service provider. The users only adopt identity providers to provide identity information and have control over their attributes. Therefore, the users participate in every identity provisioning transaction. On the contrary, in the credential-focused system, the users obtain long-term credentials from identity providers and store them locally. Then, these credentials are used to provide identity information without involving the identity provider. The users are still involved in every identity transaction as in the relationship-focused approach.

The above two paradigms provide user-centric privacy management in personal data dissemination. The apparent major advantage of user centricity is that users retain control through their involvement in each transaction. In fact, this is also the major drawback of user centricity because it cannot handle delegations. A universal identity management system incorporates the advantages of these user-centric systems and provides a delegation capability. The credential-focused system is suitable for constructing a universal identity management system. However, constructing a universal identity management system from credential-focused identity management systems is non-intuitive and complex, because the specific properties of anonymity, minimal data disclosure and various anonymity revocation capabilities involve multi-party transactions. These render delegation a formidable task to tackle.

In SOA, the users may access more than one service at any given time. When they use the same pseudonym to access different services, all their transactions are linkable. It would be ideal for the users to be able to self-generate different pseudonyms based on their credentials without interacting with identity providers. On the other hand, the users should use the same pseudonym to link different actions in one transaction and delegate their privilege to others in order to improve the runtime performance of composite services. Therefore, the features of self-generation of pseudonyms and delegation of identity information are essential in the universal identity management system. For instance, let it be assumed that a user called Liming visits a hospital called People-Health. Following the visit, he has to get certain clinical tests done in some examination centers several times, the results of which are required for proper comprehensive diagnosis. Owing to privacy restrictions, most of the test centers do not reveal this data to anyone but the user. Therefore, Liming himself has to retrieve the data every time it is needed by the People-Health. As this exercise is cumbersome, Liming is looking for a method that enables the People-Health to directly retrieve the desired data from the various centers and to generate the pseudonyms without online identity providers. Such a capability, besides being more efficient, is vital to handle cases of emergency.

When the delegation scheme is defined, the universal identity management system can be realized based on web service technologies. As a public specification, WS-Federation [4] defines a framework to allow different security domains to federate, such that authorized access to web services can be realized in distributed realms. That includes mechanisms for brokering of identity, attribute, authentication and authorization assertions between domains, and privacy of federated claims. Based on WS-Trust [40], WS-Federation supports delegation by using identity providers to issue appropriate security tokens for providers in different security domains. As a relation-focused framework, it also has the undesirable features of general relation-focused paradigms. Our solution extends this relation-focused framework with enhanced credentials to achieve universal identity management.

Users are a key component of the SOA environment. Therefore, how to realize easy-to-use identity management systems and provide consistent experiences and transparent security is very critical in our solution. The notion of Identity Metasystem [36, 37] has been introduced to put an abstract identity management layer on the Internet to allow existing identity systems based on various technologies to interoperate with each other. The identity metasystem introduces the important concept of an "information card" modeled after a business card, licence, etc. In general, an information card is a digital representation of user identity to realize easy-to-use and consistent experiences. However, the identity metasystems do not support delegation and composite services. In SOA, a service often consists of sub-services, and delegation mechanisms are critical for efficiency. We combine the identity metasystem which is the user perspective and WS-Federation framework which is the service federation perspective, and extend them to construct the universal identity management solution.

3.1.2 Related Work

There is no straightforward transformation of anonymous credential schemes without delegation into delegatable schemes. Classic anonymous credential systems were introduced by Chaum [6] in 1985, as a way of allowing the user to work effectively, but anonymously, with multiple organizations. The works of [7–10] developed the model and implementation of anonymous credential systems. Camenisch and Lysyanskaya [11–13] proposed anonymous credential systems, which are more efficient than the earlier ones, by constructing a signature scheme with efficient protocols. All the above systems use interactive zero-knowledge protocols to prove the possession of credentials without optimizing the rounds of interaction. Belenkiy [14] introduced non-interactive anonymous credentials in 2007 to solve this problem. However, the scheme could not be directly transformed into a delegatable anonymous credential scheme.

Delegatable anonymous credential schemes were proposed in [15, 16] where users can obtain credentials from identity providers and delegate their credentials to other users. If an identity provider issues user A a credential for his given pseudonym Nym_A, user A can prove to user B that Nym_A has a credential from the identity provider. Credentials received directly from the identity provider are level 1 credentials, those that have been delegated once are level 2 credentials, and so on. User A can also delegate his credential to user B, and user B can then prove that he has a level 2 credential from the identity provider where user B proves to others his possession of a credential without involving any identity information on A. However, the size of the possession proof increases with the increase in delegation level, and cannot be bounded to a constant number by aggregating proofs. Further-more, in these schemes, identity providers are involved in issuing credentials when a new pseudonym is generated, and these schemes are not efficient either as far as network resources are concerned.

Camenisch, Sommer, and Zimmermann proposed a general certification framework for SOA where identity information can be privacy-enhanced [17]. They claim that their framework can be integrated into today's Public Key Infrastructure (PKI) on the Internet. The framework includes cryptographic primitives for realizing the functionality, definition of protocol interfaces for the *CertificateIssuance* and *CertificateProof* protocols and a powerful specification language with well-defined semantics that allows defining the data to be released in a transaction. However, the framework and implementation do not specify how to realize delegation. The solution offered here not only utilizes the advantage of the general certification framework, but also provides a new way of implementing the *CertificateIssuance* and *CertificateProof* protocols to realize delegation.

In this paper, a pseudonym-based signature scheme is proposed to construct practical delegation solutions for universal identity management where users can self-generate pseudonyms based on their credentials. The self-generated pseudonyms are used as public keys. The privacy is ensured by the unlinkability between different pseudonyms. According to this idea, we get a natural solution to the delegation problem. A conventional signature scheme often immediately allows for (non-anonymous) delegatable credentials: A, who has a public signing key and a certification chain of length L, can sign B's public key, giving B a certification chain of length $L+1$. Therefore, the delegation solution consists of two signature schemes in which the pseudonyms are used as public keys: a pseudonym-based signature scheme and a conventional proxy signature scheme [18–21]. The pseudonym-based signature scheme provides anonymous proof of possession of credentials to protect the user's privacy where service providers verify the signature to decide whether the signer has the rights to access the services. In the conventional proxy signature scheme, the original signers delegate their signing capability to proxy signers without divulging their private keys. Then, the proxy signer creates a valid signature on behalf of the original signer. The receiver of the signature verifies the signature and the original signer's delegation together. Our proxy signature scheme has the delegation capability by warrant. A warrant explicitly states the signer's identity, delegation period and the qualification of the message on which the proxy signer can sign, etc.

Zero-knowledge proofs of credential possession in classic anonymous credential systems can be converted to signatures via the Fiat-Shamir heuristic [22]. Compared with pseudonym-based signature schemes, the converted signature schemes have four undesirable features: First, the pseudonyms in the converted signature schemes are not self-generated; second, an identity provider must provide an online issuing service; third, the ability to sign under the pseudonyms is lacking; fourth, the signature size is often too long. Compared with group signature schemes [23–27], the pseudonym-based signature scheme requires self-generated pseudonyms that can be used as public keys, while group signature schemes do not need any pseudonym, nor do they specify how to generate them. Therefore, besides the self-generation feature, the scheme proposed here has the desirable feature that the pseudonyms are used as temporal public keys for signatures. This feature can be compared to that of the ID-based signature schemes where signers have the ability to sign with their identities. Unlike the identity in ID-based signature schemes, pseudonyms are not directly bound to real identities or certificates because pseudonyms are self-generated. Thus, the security notion is a bit different from that of the ID-based signature schemes. To prove the unforgeability of pseudonym-based schemes, the challenger should distinguish between forged pseudonyms and valid randomized pseudonyms generated by adversaries who have obtained some valid credentials.

Our pseudonym-based scheme is similar to the DAA (Direct Anonymous Attestation) scheme [28, 29] which coordinates a TPM (Trust Platform Module) and a host together to generate pseudonyms and signatures. The scheme was adopted by the Trusted Computing Group as the method for remote authentication of a TPM, while preserving the privacy of the user of the platform that contains the module. Compared with DAA, this scheme does not require a TPM to work online, which improves the performance of the scheme. Although DAA adopts group signature schemes [23–27] to generate pseudonyms that link transactions, it is not clear how it can be used to build a delegation solution for universal identity management. While DAA uses pseudonyms to link transactions, ours uses pseudonyms to achieve privacy because one pseudonym is unlinkable to the other. Moreover, ours uses pseudonyms as public keys for signatures.

In a distributed federated identity environment, there exists some leading specification such as SAML (Security Assertion Markup Language) [42], Liberty ID-FF (Identity Federation Framework) [43] and WS-Federation [4]. These specifications support privacy-preservation and have capabilities to prevent identity tracking and collusion through issuance of an opaque handle for each user. The work of [44] extended the existing framework for federated identity management to support delegation. However, these specifications do not address the issue of anonymous delegation. In this relation-focused model, the identity provider is involved in almost every identity provision transaction, systems are difficult to use in a long-term credential setting, and the token is often issued with a limited audience set which in turn pre-determines the use of the token.

3.1.3 Contributions

The contribution of this paper is three-fold. Our first contribution is that a signature-based natural approach is adopted to define the delegation model for universal identity management in SOA. Our second contribution is that the novel concept of a pseudonym-based signature scheme is introduced where pseudonyms are self-generated and messages can be bound to the self-generated pseudonyms which are used as the public keys for signatures. Based on this, the novel pseudonym-based signature scheme is constructed. Our third contribution is the application of our scheme to universal identity management systems where the delegation of the privilege to access services is realized by adopting warrant proxy signature schemes [18–21] based on time-varying pseudonyms.

3.1.4 Organization of the Paper

The remainder of the paper is structured as follows. Section 3.2 gives a description of preliminaries. Section 3.3 contains our delegation model. Section 3.4 focuses on the construction of the universal identity management solution. Section 3.5 presents how to design the implementation of a delegation model. Section 3.6 gives our deployment. Finally, conclusions are drawn in Sect. 3.7.

3.2 Preliminaries

Suppose we have groups G_1 and G_2 of the same prime order p and security parameter κ. Assume the discrete logarithm problem is hard in both groups. Then we need a cryptographic bilinear map $e : G_1 \times G_1 \rightarrow G_2$ to satisfy the following properties [30, 31]:

1. Bilinearity: $\forall a, b \in Z_p^*, P, Q \in G_1, e(aP, bQ) = e(P, Q)^{ab}$.
2. Non-degeneracy: For any point $P \in G_1, e(P, P) \neq 1_{G_2}$.
3. Computability: there exists an efficient algorithm to compute $e(P, Q)$ for $\forall P, Q \in G_1$.

To give the security proof of our scheme, we introduce a problem which is slightly different from the one proposed by Mitsunari et al. [32] and is called (k,n)-CAA (Collusion Attack Algorithm with k Traitors and n Examples).

Definition 3.1 (k,n)-CAA. Collusion Attack Algorithm with k Traitors and n Examples

Let (G_1, G_2, e) *be as above, k,n be integers,* $P, P_1, \ldots, P_n \in G_1, x \in Z_p$. *Given* $P, P_j, a_i \in Z_p, xP, xP_j, 1/(x + a_i)p | 1 \leq i \leq k, 1 \leq j \leq n$, *to compute* $1/(x + a)P$ *for some* $aP_i \notin a_i P_j | 1 \leq i \leq k, 1 \leq j \leq n$.

The (k,n)-CAA is considered to be hard in the literature. That is, the probability of success of any probabilistic, polynomial-time, 0/1 valued algorithm in solving (k,n)-CAA problem is negligible. A function $F(y)$ is said to be negligible if it is less than $1/y^l$ for every fixed $l > 0$ and sufficiently large integer y.

3.3 Delegation Model for Universal Identity Management

Participants in a delegation model for universal identity management comprise identity providers (who grant credentials), user u (who obtains credentials), user v (who is delegated by u to access services, and can be a service provider) and service providers. Our model is different from the delegatable anonymous credential systems. In the latter, the user first registers a pseudonym with the identity provider, and then the identity provider grants to the user a credential associated with the registered pseudonym. Our model, on the other hand, allows the users to first get a credential from the identity provider, and then to generate multiple new pseudonyms as needed while the identity provider does not participate. Without interacting with the identity provider, the users can show service providers that they possess the right credentials. Compared with a relationship-based delegation scheme, in our model, the users can self-generate different pseudonyms and directly delegate privileges to others without the identity provider's participation.

The delegation model can be defined by the following six sub-protocols'

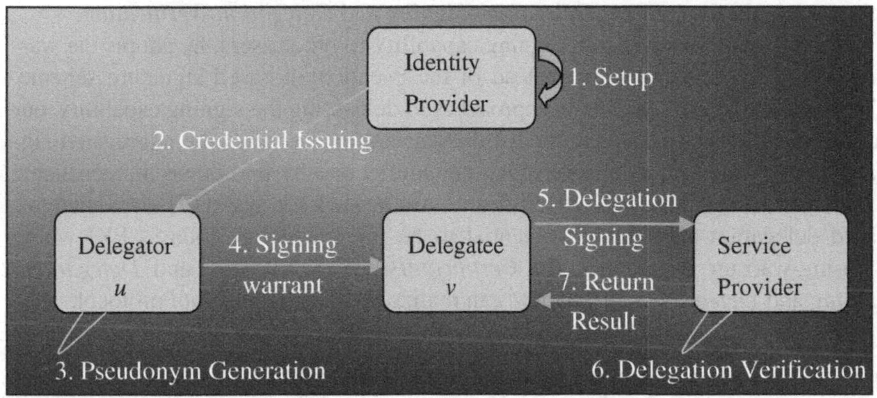

Fig. 3.1 Delegation model

Setup: The identity provider generates system parameter and system public/private key pairs.

Credential Issuing: The identity provider grants a secret credential to user u.

Pseudonym Generation: User u generates a new pseudonym in a current time slot according to its secret credential and timestamp. Two pseudonyms are unlinkable and only loose time synchronization is required.

Signing-warrant: User u signs a warrant that contains delegation period, delegated pseudonyms, and the services to be accessed, etc. User v obtains a proxy key according to his private key and the signature of the warrant.

Delegation-Signing: User v generates proxy signatures on behalf of user u.

Delegation-Verification: Service providers verify proxy signatures from v together with u's delegation.

The relationship among the six sub-protocols is illustrated in Fig. 3.1. If the service provider trusts the identity provider (IdP) and a secret credential is issued to the delegator u by the IdP, u can grant to the delegatee v the access privilege to the service when v does not have the privilege. u uses the pseudonym generation protocol to protect its privacy and the signing-warrant protocol to grant the privilege.

Our delegation model can be implemented by two signature schemes. The first one is the pseudonym-based signature scheme which provides anonymous proof of the possession of credentials to protect the user's privacy. Service providers verify the signature to decide whether the signer has the rights to access the services. The second one is a warrant proxy signature scheme, where the original signer u delegates his signing capability to the proxy signer v without leaking his private key, and then the proxy signer creates a valid signature on behalf of the original signer. The pseu-donym-based signature scheme mainly implements *Credential Issuing*, *Pseudonym Generation* and *Signing–warrant*, and the warrant proxy signature scheme mainly implements *Delegation–Signing* and *Delegation–Verification*.

When v again delegates his signing capability to other users, he adopts the warrant proxy signature scheme, instead of the pseudonym-based signature scheme. Compared with certificate chain approaches to delegating the signing capability, our solution can aggregate signatures for the warrant m_w, verifies the aggregated signature only once and avoids verifying signatures one by one down the certificate chain. According to the general certification framework for SOA [17], our signature-based delegation solution has potential to be integrated into today's PKI where Sign-ing-warrant can realize the *CertificateIssuance protocol*, and *Delegation–Signing* and *Delegation–Verification* can realize the *CertificateProof* protocol.

3.4 Universal Identity Management Solution

Our solution takes the credential-focused identity approach as a starting point, which may be trivially set to short-term credentials. With delegation enhanced, users can reissue security tokens based on long-term credentials stored in their personal identity metasystem. The underlying credential-focused approach can provide strong data minimization and anonymity.

In this solution, it is assumed that different security domains are federated, and there exists a personal identity metasystem to aid a user to manage his identities.

Figure 3.2 illustrates a framework focusing on a relationship among a requestor, a delegatee, a resource and a personal identity metasystem. The requestor (user) uses his personal identity metasystem to log in to his local security domain. The local security domain and delegatee (web service B) security domain trust each other such that the requestor can use a short-term credential to access the delegatee based on the trust relationship of identity providers in the two domains. When it wants to access the resource (web service C) in the resource domain, the delegatee (web service B) can be appointed to represent the requestor anonymously with certain attributes if the requestor has the privilege to access the resource and the delegatee hasn't.

The detailed runs in Fig. 3.2 are as follows.

Step 1: A secret credential is issued to the requestor by the IdP C in domain C if the requestor has not stored the credential to access resource C (web service C). That is to say, the *Credential Issuing* sub-protocol in the delegation model is executed between the IdP C and the requestor's selector.

Step 2: The secret credential is stored in the requestor's storage service which is a part of her personal identity metasystem.

Step 3: The requestor makes a compound resource request (involving web service B and web service C). Web service B is in security domain B and web service C is in security domain C.

Step 4: The client application uses its short-term credential obtained from IdP A in the requestor's security token to make the request. IdP A and IdP B trust each other. IdP B is in security domain B.

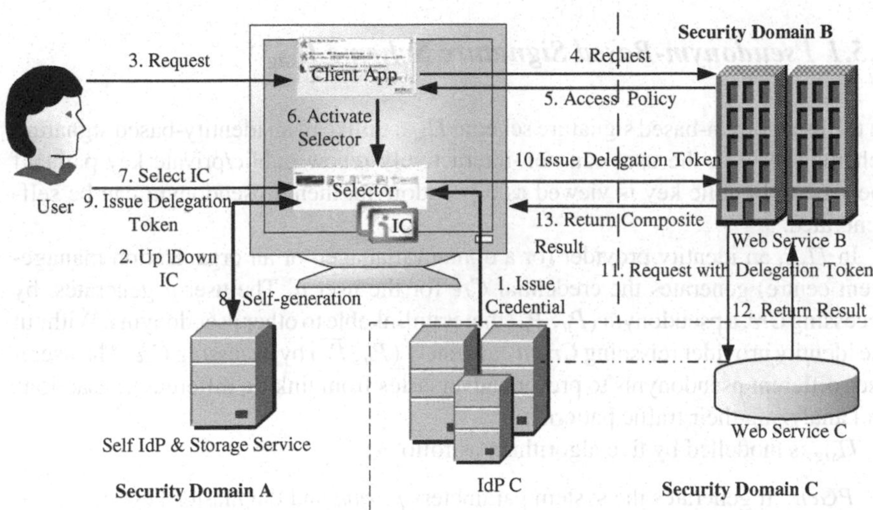

Fig. 3.2 Universal identity management solution

Step 5: Web service B finds that the request is compound, and involves web service C. It returns an access policy which specifies that the requestor should delegate it her privileges such that it can efficiently interact with web service C.
Step 6: The client application activates the Selector which is the visual window for the user to select one information card (IC).
Step 7: The requestor uses her Selector to select one appropriate IC according to the access policy.
Step 8: The requestor's self-IdP self-generates pseudonyms based on its stored credential using the *Pseudonym Generation* sub-protocol in the delegation model.
Step 9, 10: The requestor's metasystem uses the *Signing–warrant* sub-protocol in the delegation model to issue a delegation token with respect to the self-generated pseudonym.
Step 11: Web service B uses the *Delegation–Signing* sub-protocol in the delegation model to sign an access-token request to the IdP in the domain C. The IdP in domain C uses the *Delegation–Verification* sub-protocol in the delegation model to verify the request. If the verification is successful, it returns an access token to the requestor. Web service B makes a service request to the resource using the access token.
Step 12, 13: The resource returns the service response to the delegatee, and the delegatee returns a composite service response to the requestor.

3.5 Delegation Construction

3.5.1 Pseudonym-Based Signature Scheme Π_{sig}

In the pseudonym-based signature scheme Π_{sig}, unlike in an identity-based signature scheme [33, 34], the user can non-interactively renew public/private key pairs. If the renewed public key is viewed as a pseudonym, then a pseudonym can be self-generated.

In Π_{sig}, an identity provider (or a domain manager, or an organization management centre) generates the credential *Cre* for the user u. The user u generates, by accessing *Cre*, a pseudonym $(P_u, \overline{P_u})$ that is unlinkable to other pseudonyms. Without the identity provider reissuing *Cre*, u can renew $(P_u, \overline{P_u})$ by accessing *Cre*. The user u uses different pseudonyms to prevent adversaries from linking different transactions and analyzing their traffic patterns.

Π_{sig} is modelled by five algorithms as follows:

PGen: It generates the system parameters *param* and the master-key *ms*.
Gen: Executed by the identity provider, it generates the credential *Cre* for the user u.

$\Delta - Gen$: Executed by u, it generates the pseudonym $(P_u, \overline{P_u})$ and corresponding secret value $\mu^{'}$.

$Sign$: It takes as input the user's private key $(Cre, \mu^{'})$ and the message m to return the signature of m under $(Cre, \mu^{'})$.

$Verify$: It takes as input $u^{'}s$ pseudonym $(P_u, \overline{P_u})$, the organization public key (W, W_i), the message m, and the signature sig to return either 1 or 0.

In our construction, the identity provider periodically publishes a set of public restriction keys $W_i, \ldots, W_j$ which correspond to the time slots $slot_i, \ldots, slot_j$. A new public restriction key begins to work when a new time slot starts. The public restriction keys are used to enable the user to update his pseudonyms. The function $T(time)$ takes $time$ as input and outputs a time slot where only loose time synchronization is required.

Definition 3.2 Π_{sig} is made up of the following five algorithms:

$PGen(1^{\kappa})$: *Setup* G_1, G_2, e *and* $P \in G_1$,
pick cryptographic hash functions $H_1, H_2 : \{0,1\}^* \rightarrow G_1$,
compute $Q_i = H_1(T(time_i))$,
choose a master-key $s \in_R Z_p$,
compute organization's public keys $W = sP$, $W_i = sQ_i$,
return $ms = s' param = (G_1, G_2, e, P, W, W_i, H_1, H_2)$.

$Gen(ms, param, u)$: $\mu \in_R Z_p$,
$Cre = (\mu, S_u) = (\mu, 1/(s+\mu)P)$,
return Cre.
User u can verify the correctness by checking $e(\mu P + W, S_u) = e(P, P)$.

$\Delta - Gen(Cre, param, time_i)$: $Q_i = H_1(T(time_i)), \mu^{'} \in_R Z_p$,
$P_u = (\mu + \mu^{'})Q_i$, $\overline{P_u} = \mu^{'} S_u$,
return $((P_u, \overline{P_u}), \mu^{'})$.
The key pair $(P_u, \overline{P_u})/(\mu, \mu^{'}, S_u)$ *of the user u satisfy*
$e(P_u + W_i, S_u) = e(Q_i, P)e(Q_i, S_u)^{\mu^{'}} = e(Q_i, P)e(Q_i, \overline{P_u})$.

$Sign(m, (P_u, \overline{P_u}), (\mu, \mu^{'}, S_u), param, time_i)$: $r, r^{'} \in_R Z_p$,
$R_G = rQ_i$, $R = [e(Q_i, P)e(Q_i, \overline{P_u})]^{r^{'}}$,
$c = H_2(m||R_G||R||P_u||\overline{P_u}||T(time_i))$,
$z_1 = c(\mu + \mu^{'}) + r$, $z_2 = c\mu^{'} + r^{'}$,
return $sig = (c, z_1, z_2)$.

Verify$(m, sig, (P_u, \overline{P_u}), param, time_i)$: *Parse* $sig = (c, z_1, z_2)$,
$\underline{Q_i} = H_1(T(time_i))$,
$\overline{R_G} = z_1 Q_i - cP_u$,
$\overline{R} = [e(Q_i, P)e(Q_i, \overline{P_u})]^{z}/e(P_u + W_i, \overline{P_u})^c$,
$\overline{c} = H_2(m||\overline{R_G}||\overline{R}||P_u||\overline{P_u}||T(time_i))$,
if $c = \overline{c}$ *then return 1, otherwise return 0.*

This signature scheme is converted from a zero-knowledge proof via the Fiat-Shamir heuristic [22]. The prover and verifier undertake a proof of knowledge values satisfying the following equation:

$$e(P_u + W_i, \overline{P_u}) = e((\mu + \mu^{'})Q_i + sQ_i, \mu^{'}/(s + \mu)P)$$
$$P_u = (\mu + \mu^{'})Q_i.$$

The protocol for proving knowledge of the discrete logarithm is as follows:

Prover u: chooses $r, r^{'} \in_R Z_p$,
computes $R_G = rQ_i$, $R = [e(Q_i, P)e(Q_i, \overline{P_u})]^{r^{'}}$,
sends (R_G, R) to the verifier v.

Verifier v: receives (R_G, R),
chooses $c \in_R Z_p$,
sends c to the prover u.

Prover u: receives c,
computes $z_1 = c(\mu + \mu^{'}) + r$, $z_2 = c\mu^{'} + r^{'}$,
sends (z_1, z_2) to the verifier v.

Verifier v: receives (z_1, z_2),
verifies the correctness by checking
$z_1 Q_i = cP_u + R_G$ and
$e(P_u + W_i, \overline{P_u})^c R = [e(Q_i, P)e(Q_i, \overline{P_u})]^{z_2}$.

In our pseudonym-based signature scheme, the value c is non-interactively obtained by computing the hash value of $(m||R_G||R||P_u||\overline{P_u}||T(time_i))$ according to the Fiat-Shamir heuristic [22]. If u proves possession of the knowledge of the discrete logarithm $(\mu^{'}, \mu + \mu^{'})$ satisfying

$$e(P_u + W_i, \overline{P_u}) = [e(Q_i, P)e(Q_i, \overline{P_u})]^{\mu^{'}},$$
$$P_u = (\mu + \mu^{'})Q_i,$$

the verifier v will believe that the credential $Cre = (\mu, S_u) = (\mu, 1/(s + \mu)P)$ is issued to $(P_u, \overline{P_u})$ by the identity provider. When the user u signs a message under $(P_u, \overline{P_u})$, the identity provider can track the transcripts by iteratively computing

$$e(P_u + W_i, S_u) = e(Q_i, P)e(Q_i, \overline{P_u})$$

according to its stored private keys $\{S_1, S_2, \ldots\}$.

3.5.2 Proxy Signature Scheme Π_{psig}

Assume the user v has a public/private key pair $(PK_v = vQ_i, v)$ and the user u has some rights to access one service *serv* with a public/private key pair $(PK_u = (P_u, \overline{P_u}), (\mu, \mu', S_u))$. The user u can grant the user v to delegate himself to access the service *serv*. It does not matter whether the user v has the rights to access *serv*. The service provider of *serv* verifies the proxy signature from v and then knows whether v is indeed delegated by PK_u. If v is delegated by PK_u and has rights to access *serv*, v will be allowed to access *serv*. v creates the warrant which contains related information such as $\overline{P_u}$, a part of the pseudonym of u, the delegation period, etc. Also, u generates the signature α for m_w and conveys both the signature and m_w to v. v creates a proxy key from α and m_w. The following proxy signature scheme is from the work of [35], where the key generation algorithm of the original signer is slightly different.

Definition 3.3 Π_{psig} is made up of the following five algorithms:

$Setup(1^\kappa)$: *Generate* G_1, G_2, e *and* $Q_i \in G_1$,
pick cryptographic hash functions $H_1, H_2{:}\{0,1\}^* \rightarrow G_1$,
return $param = (G_1, G_2, e, P, W, W_i, H_1, H_2)$.

KGen$(param, u, v)$: *The key of the original signer u:*
$\tau = \mu + \mu', PKey_u = P_u = \tau Q_i, SK_u = \tau,$
The key of the proxy signer v:
$PKey_v = vQ_i, SK_v = v, v \in_R Z_p$.

$PKGen(param, \tau, v, PKey_u)$: *Generate a proxy key for v:*
Create the warrant m_w.
u signs m_w: $\alpha = \tau H_1(m_w)$,
v checks whether (m_w, α) *satisfies*
$e(\alpha, Q_i) = e(H_1(m_w), PKey_u)$.
If true, v gets a proxy key (α, v).

$PSign(m, param, m_w, (\alpha, v))$: *v generates proxy signatures:*
$\sigma = \alpha + vH_2(m\|m_w)$,
return $sig = (m, \sigma)$.

$PVerify(m, sig, param, PKey_u, PKey_v)$: *If*
$e(\sigma, Q_i) = e(H_1(m_w), PKey_u)e(H_2(m\|m_w), PKey_v)$,
then return 1.
Otherwise, return 0.

The security proof of this scheme can be found in [35]. When u delegates his signing capability to the user v, v will possess u's privilege to access the services. u adopts the pseudonym-based signature scheme Π_{sig} to generate time-varying pseudonyms for privacy and the proxy signature scheme Π_{psig} to realize delegation. Therefore, the delegation solution consists of Π_{sig} and Π_{psig}. When v again delegates the privilege to another user x, Π_{psig} is executed as follows:

$Setup(1^{\kappa})$: *Generate* G_1, G_2, e *and* $Q_i \in G_1$,
pick cryptographic hash functions $H_1, H_2 : \{0,1\}^* \rightarrow G_1$,
return $param = (G_1, G_2, e, P, W, W_i, H_1, H_2)$.

$KGen(param, u, v)$: *The key of the original signer* v:
$PKey_v^{'} = PKey_u + PKey_v, SK_v = v$,
The key of the proxy signer x:
$PKey_x = \chi Q_i, SK_x = \chi, \chi \in_R Z_p$.

$PKGen(param, v, \chi, PKey_v^{'})$: *Generate a proxy key for* x:
v signs m_w:
$\alpha^{'} = \alpha + vH_1(m_w)$,
where m_w *is created by* u *and* α *is the signature for* m_w *produced by* u. x *checks whether* $(m_w, \alpha^{'})$ *satisfies*
$e(\alpha^{'}, Q_i) = e(H_1(m_w), PKey_v^{'})$.
If true, x *gets a proxy key* $(\alpha^{'}, \chi)$.

$PSign(m, param, m_w, (\alpha^{'}, \chi))$: *v generates proxy signatures:*
$\sigma = \alpha^{'} + \chi H_2(m||m_w)$,
return $sig = (m, \sigma)$.

$PVerify(m, sig, param, PKey_x, PKey_v^{'})$: *If*
$e(\sigma, Q_i) = e(H_1(m_w), PKey_v^{'})e(H_2(m||m_w), PKey_x)$,
then return 1.
Otherwise, return 0.

Compared with certificate chain approaches to delegating the signing capability, our solution can aggregate signatures for the warrant m_w, verify the aggregated signature only once and thus avoids verifying signatures one by one down the certificate chain. That is to say, if $x_1 \rightarrow x_2 \rightarrow \cdots \rightarrow x_n$ is the user chain for delegation and $\alpha_1 \rightarrow \alpha_2 \rightarrow \cdots \rightarrow \alpha_n$ is the signature chain for the warrant m_w which are respectively produced by these users, then x_n obtains the aggregated signature $\alpha = \alpha_1 + \cdots + \alpha_n$ and the proxy key (α, SK_n). x_n generates the proxy signature for the message m as follows: $\sigma = \alpha + SK_n H_2(m||m_w)$. Service providers compute $PKey = PKey_{x_1} + PKey_{x_2} + \cdots + PKey_{x_n}$ and verify the signature under $PKey$. If the signature is valid and x_1 has proved the possession of the issued credentials, the service providers will allow x_n to access the services. The service providers verify only one signature and not the signatures produced by each delegation user in order to show that the last delegatee has the privilege for accessing the services. In addition, the conventional certificate chain can also be used in our solution.

Reverting to the health-care example cited in the introduction, Liming can adopt Π_{sig} to generate the new pseudonym, and signs the warrant that contains the pseudonym, time period, and the names of those health examination services. Then, Liming conveys the signature and the warrant to People-Health to enable them to obtain the proxy key. Therefore, People-Health can directly request the results of health examinations from the test centres by signing the request messages under the proxy key according to the algorithm *PSign* in Π_{psig}. The examination centres concerned have stored the test results of the user because Liming adopted the pseudonym as his identity and proved by using Π_{sig} that has the rights to consume the examination services and access the results, which protects the privacy of Liming by not disclosing his real identity, exact age and other identity information. When the request messages signed by People-Health are received, the examination centres verify the corresponding signature according to the algorithm *PVerify* in Π_{psig}. If the signature is valid, the stored results will be conveyed to People-Health.

In some settings, the identity provider of a service domain may want to control the generation of pseudonyms. For example, when users require adequate protection of their personal information, anonymous communication services are often used to deliver the consumer services [2]. If the users are just in an ad hoc network, they will be not only service consumers but also service providers. In this case, the pseudonym-generation approach is required to have the pseudonym-uniqueness property for a period of time. Otherwise, if adversaries have controlled one node, they can forge different pseudonyms according to different neighbours, that is, they can forge false topology. They can also use a different pseudonym for a different instance of anonymous communication services and infer their traffic patterns by distinguishing messages relating to different pseudonyms, which often expose the VIP's private information or their action characteristics. Therefore, the identity providers should have the means to manage how to self-generate pseudonyms besides delegation of identity information. We propose a variation of the pseudonym-based signature scheme to satisfy the requirement in the next section.

3.5.3 Pseudonym-Controlled Variation of Π_{sig}

In order to provide control over the self-generation properties of pseudonyms, the algorithm $\Delta - Gen$ of Π_{sig} is modified such that the new pseudonyms do not take effect until the start of a new time slot and publication of new restriction keys. Identity providers manage pseudonym-generation by adopting restriction keys and time slots.

The identity provider periodically publishes a set of public restriction keys $\{W_i, \ldots, W_j\}$ which correspond to time slots $\{slot_i, \ldots, slot_j\}$. A new public restriction key begins to work when a new time slot starts. The public restriction keys are used to ensure the uniqueness of the pseudonym of a user in a single time slot and make it possible for the user to generate his pseudonyms. The pseudonym-controlled variation Π_{vsig} of the pseudonym-based signature is as follows:

Definition 3.4 Π_{vsig} is made up of the following five algorithms:

$PGen(1^{\kappa})$: *Setup* G_1, G_2, e *and* $P \in G_1$,
pick cryptographic hash functions $H_1, H_2 : \{0, 1\}^* \rightarrow G_1$,
compute $Q_i = H_1(T(time_i))$,
choose a master-key $s \in_R Z_p$,

compute organization's public keys $W = sP$, $W_i = sQ_i$,
return $ms = s$*'* $param = (G_1, G_2, e, P, W, W_i, H_1, H_2)$.

$Gen(ms, param, u)$: $\mu \in_R Z_p$,
$Cre = (\mu, S_u) = (\mu, 1/(s+\mu)P)$,
return Cre.
User u can verify the correctness by checking $e(\mu P + W, S_u) = e(P, P)$.

$\Delta - Gen(Cre, param, time_i)$: $Q_i = H_1(T(time_i))$,
$P_u = \mu Q_i$
return P_u.
The key pair $P_u/(\mu, S_u)$ *of the user u satisfy*
$e(P_u + W_i, S_u) = e(Q_i, P)$.

$Sign(m, P_u, (\mu, S_u), param, time_i)$: $\alpha, r, r' \in_R Z_p$,
$T = \alpha S_u$, $R_{G_i} = rQ_i$, $R = e(Q_i, P)^{r'}$,
$c = H_2(m||T||R_{G_i}||R||P_u||T(time_i))$,
$z_1 = c\alpha + r'$, $z_2 = c\mu + r$,
return $sig = (T, c, z_1, z_2)$.

Verify$(m, sig, (P_u, \overline{P_u}), param, time_i)$: *Parse* $sig = (T, c, z_1, z_2)$,
$\underline{Q_i} = H_1(T(time_i))$,
$\overline{R_{G_i}} = z_2 Q_i - cP_u$,
$\overline{R} = e(Q_i, P)^{z_1}/e(P_u + W_i, T)^c$,
$\overline{c} = H_2(m||T||\overline{R_{G_i}}||\overline{R}||P_u||T(time_i))$,
if $c = \overline{c}$ *then return 1, otherwise return 0.*

When the identity provider in the domain publishes some pseudonyms $\{P_u^i, \ldots, P_u^j\}$ of user u in its certificate revocation list, the credential of u is revoked in time slots $\{slot_i, \ldots, slot_j\}$. This revocation solution is simple and attractive because the computation is efficient and the pseudonyms of u that are not in these timc slots are still unlinkablc. The signatures produced by u are also traceable since the identity provider can compute all the users' pseudonyms in all the time slots according to $\{\mu_1, \mu_2, \ldots\}$.

When Π_{vsig} is adopted to construct delegation solutions combined with Π_{psig}, the warrant m_w will contain related information such as the delegation period, service name, and so on. Unlike the Π_{sig}-based scheme, it does not include one part of the public key of u. The security proof of Π_{vsig} is similar to that of Π_{sig}.

3.6 Deployment Framework for Delegation Model

SOA is a very popular paradigm for system integration and interoperation. Web service is the current standard for SOA. Therefore, the industry is pursuing the deployment of identity management systems in distributed different security domains, called FIM (Federated Identity Management) [3, 4], to build one cornerstone of the web service security. Current user-centricity FIM systems are mostly relationship-focused, and can enhance the user's privacy by following the data minimization and transaction unlinkability principles. Multiple industry products [36, 37] embrace this paradigm. However, the bottle-neck effect will become more serious for identity providers if the delegation function is implemented only based on the relationship-focused model. Some credential-focused systems are also developed to achieve FIM. The example is idemix [38, 39], but it does not support self-generation and efficient delegation. This section describes how to deploy our solution in the relationship-focused paradigm by integrating the credential-focused paradigm to realize universal identity management.

We adopt the concept from WS-Federation [4] to describe how to deploy the delegation scheme for universal identity management. As a public specification, WS-Federation defines a framework to allow different security domains to federate, such that authorized access to web services can be realized in distributed realms. That includes mechanisms for brokering of identity, attribute, authentication and authorization assertions between domains, and privacy of federated claims. Based on WS-Trust [40], WS-Federation supports delegation by using identity providers to issue appropriate security tokens for entities in different security domains. As a relation-ship-focused framework, it also has the undesirable features of general relation-ship-focused paradigms. Our scheme can be deployed in this relationship-focused framework with enhanced credentials to achieve universal identity management. The basic entities mapping between the delegation solution and WS-Federation is provided as follows.

IdP: An Identity Provider is an entity that acts as an authentication service to end-requestors and as a data origin authentication service to service providers. IdPs are third parties trusted to maintain some of the requestor's identity information. The original IdP is enhanced to issue secret credentials by adding the Credential Issuing interface.

Requestor: An end user—an application or a machine—is typically represented by a digital identity and may have multiple valid digital identities. The original requestor is enhanced to self-generate pseudonyms and delegate privileges by adding the issued party interface of Credential Issuing and a Signing-warrant interface.

Resource: A web service, service provider, or any valuable thing. Sometimes, it can act as another requestor. The original resource is enhanced to sign messages and verify signatures by adding Delegation-Signing and Delegation-Verification interfaces. When it acts as a requestor, it delegates privileges to other resources by adding a Signing-warrant interface.

Before describing general deployment in typical scenarios, we revert to the healthcare example cited in the introduction. Assume the Citizen Identity Provider (CIP) issues Liming a digital identity credential which can be used to prove he is a citizen in that city. Figure 3.3 illustrates the application of the delegation model with privacy-preserving in this example, where People-Health can directly retrieve the desired data from the test centres. Such a capability, besides being more efficient, is vital to handle cases of emergency.

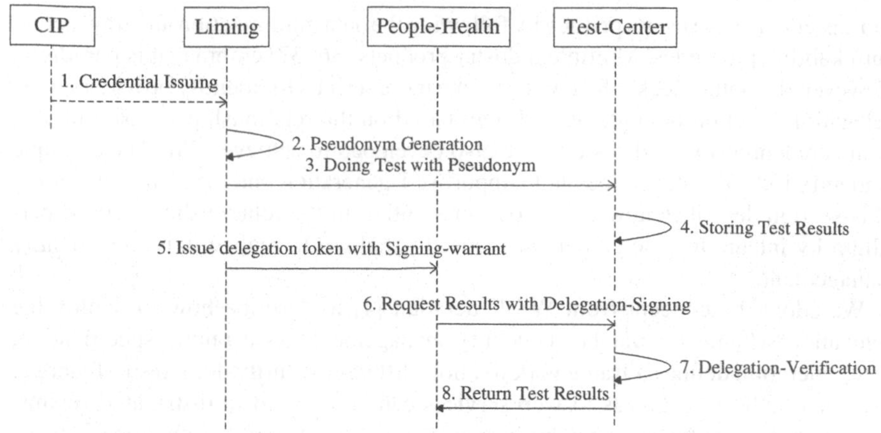

Fig. 3.3 Delegation procedure for health-care example

The example runs as follows:

Step 1: A secret credential is issued to Liming by the Citizen Identity Provider where the *Gen* of Π_{sig} is used. That is to say, the $CredentialIssuing$ sub-protocol in the solution is executed between the CIP and Liming.

Step 2: Liming adopts the $\Delta - Gen$ of Π_{sig} to generate the new pseudonym $(P_{Liming}, \overline{P}_{Liming})$. That is to say, the $PseudonymGeneration$ sub-protocol in the solution is executed by Liming.

Step 3: Liming uses the pseudonym $(P_{Liming}, \overline{P}_{Liming})$ as his identity to undergo health examination in the test centres, where he may prove his citizenship by using the $Sign$ of Π_{sig} (This is not illustrated in the figure).

Step 4: The test centre stores the test results under the user $(P_{Liming}, \overline{P}_{Liming})$ because Liming adopted the pseudonym as his identity.

Step 5: Using the $Sign$ of Π_{sig}, Liming signs the warrant m_w that contains $\overline{P}_{Liming}$, time period, and the names of those test centres. Then, Liming conveys the signature α and the warrant m_w to People-Health to enable them to obtain the proxy key (α, v). That is to say, the *Signing–warrant* sub-protocol in the solution is executed between People-Health and Liming.

Step 6: People-Health can directly request the results of health examinations from the test centres by signing the request messages under the proxy key (α, v) according to the algorithm *PSign* in Π_{psig}.

Step 7: When the request messages signed by People-Health are received, the test centre concerned verifies the corresponding signature according to the algorithm *PVerify* in Π_{psig}.

Step 8: If the signature is valid, the stored results will be conveyed to People-Health.

For general deployment, some typical scenarios are used to illustrate the delegation model. In Figs. 3.4 and 3.5, the requestor has stored some long-term credentials which

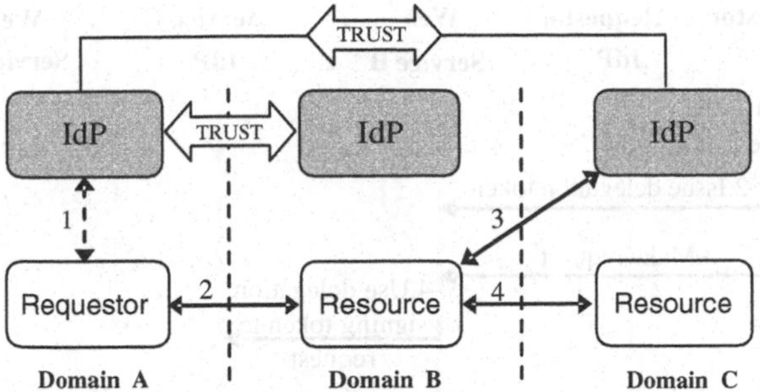

Fig. 3.4 The requestor IdP issues credentials

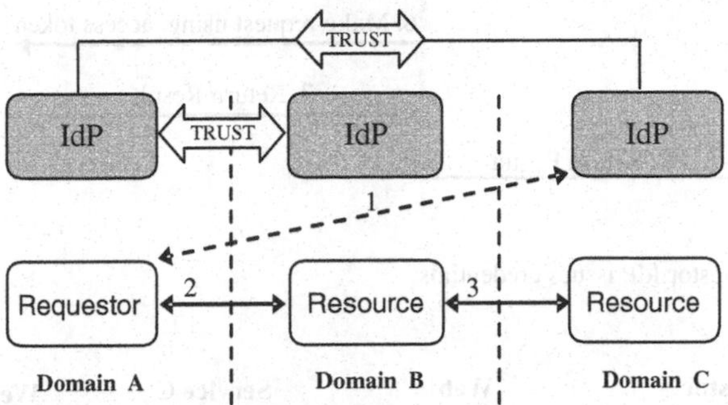

Fig. 3.5 The target service IdP issues credentials

may be from his IdP or C's IdP. Credentials from the IdP in other domains mean that if that IdP issues the requestor a long-term credential in one transaction, it can be used sub-sequently in other transactions for efficiency and convenience. Each arrow represents a possible communication path between the participants. Each dashed arrow represents that the possible communication can be executed offline or has been completed between the participants.

In Fig. 3.4, a secret credential is issued to the requestor by the IdP in the requestor's trust realm (domain A) (1). The requestor self-generates identity security tokens (pseudonyms) based on its credential, and sends a delegation token to the resource/service in domain B (2). The delegation signing tokens are then provided to the IdP in domain C and access security tokens are returned from C (3). Resource B uses the access token to access resource C. In Fig. 3.5, a secret credential to access resource C is issued to the requestor from the IdP in domain C (1). The requestor self-generates pseudonyms based on its credential, and sends a delegation token to the resource/service in domain B (2). Resource B uses the delegation signing token to access resource C. Unlike the classic delegation process in WS-Federation, no IdP is involved when new identity and delegation tokens are needed if the requestor has stored the credentials, and the privacy of the requestor is protected using unlinkable

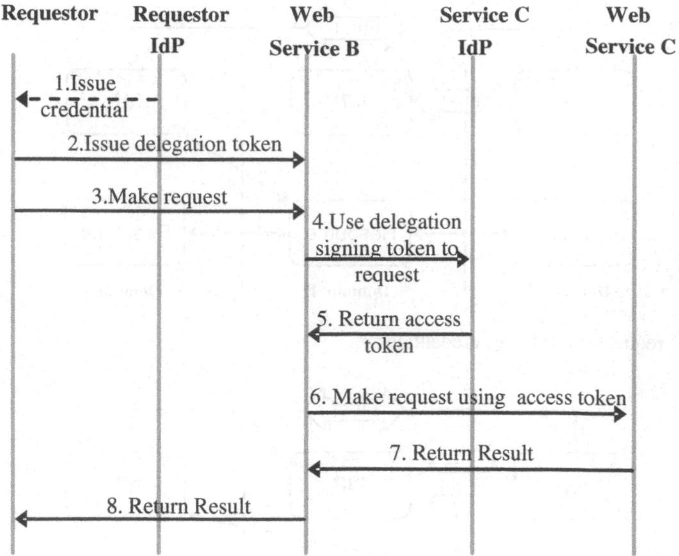

Fig. 3.6 The requestor IdP issues credentials

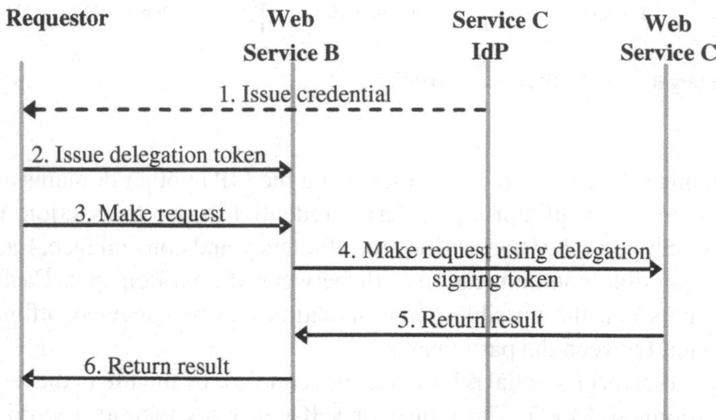

Fig. 3.7 The target service IdP issues credentials

pseudonyms. In both cases, it does not matter whether IdP B and IdP C trust each other.

Figures 3.6 and 3.7 illustrates the message sequence of the delegation procedure in these typical scenarios where a resource accesses data from another resource on behalf of the requestor. In Fig. 3.6, the delegation solution runs as follows.

Step 1: A secret credential is issued to the requestor by the IdP in domain A if the requestor has not stored the credential. That is to say, the *Credential Issuing* sub-protocol in the solution is executed between the IdP and the requestor.
Step 2: The requestor self-generates pseudonyms based on its stored credential using the *Pseudonym Generation* sub-protocol in the solution. Then, it uses the *Signing–warrant* sub-protocol to issue a delegation token with respect to the self-generated pseudonym.
Step 3: The requestor makes a composite service request to service B.
Step 4: Service B uses the *Delegation–Signing* sub-protocol to sign an access token request to the IdP in domain C.
Step 5: The IdP in domain C uses the *Delegation–Verification* sub-protocol to verify the request. If the verification is successful, it returns an access token to the service in domain B.
Step 6: Service B makes a service request to service C using the access token.
Step 7,8: Service C returns the service response to service B, and service B returns a composite service response to the requestor.

In Fig. 3.7, the delegation scheme runs on almost the same lines as those of Fig. 3.6, which corresponds to Fig. 3.5, and is as follows.

Step 1: A secret credential is issued to the requestor by the IdP in domain C if the requestor has not stored the credential to access resource C and is trusted. That is to say, the *CredentialIssuing* sub-protocol in the solution is executed between the IdP in domain C and the requestor.
Step 2: The requestor self-generates pseudonyms based on its stored credential using the *PseudonymGeneration* sub-protocol in the solution. Then, it uses the *Signing–warrant* sub-protocol to issue a delegation token with respect to the self-generated pseudonym.
Step 3: The requestor makes a composite service request to service B.
Step 4: Service B uses the *Delegation–Signing* sub-protocol to sign a service request to the resource in domain C. Because the credential is issued by the IdP in domain C, service C can directly verify the signature produced by service B, where IdP C may not involve the transactions and service C knows the public keys of its IdP.
Step 5: Service C uses the *Delegation–Verification* sub-protocol to verify the request. If the verification is successful, it returns a request result to service B.
Step 6: Service B forms composite results and returns them to the requestor.

For a delegation chain $x_1 \rightarrow x_2 \rightarrow \cdots \rightarrow x_n$ where the requestor is denoted by x_1, resource A is denoted by x_2, and so on, the delegation solution works as above by iterating delegation token issuance. Therefore, we describe in detail the delegation token in the chain as follows:

$$\{\alpha, KSet\}$$

where $\alpha = \alpha_1 + \cdots + \alpha_n$ is the signature and $\alpha_1 \to \alpha_2 \to \cdots \to \alpha_n$ is the signature chain for the warrant m_w which are respectively produced by $x_1 \to x_2 \to \cdots \to x_n$; $KSet$ is a list of pseudonyms, i.e., $\{PKey_{x_1}, PKey_{x_{n_1}}, PKey = PKey_{x_1} + PKey_{x_3} + PKey_{x_4} \cdots + PKey_{x_{n_1}}\}$, where middle pseudonyms can be hidden.

In the above deployment, we use the relationship-focused framework and trust model from WS-Federation. Requestors use stored credentials to reduce interaction rounds, and enhance the controllability of identity transactions with self-generating identities and self-issuing credentials.

3.7 Conclusions

In this paper, a practical delegation solution for universal identity management, as well as a novel notion of a pseudonym-based signature scheme, is introduced. In our proposal, the users prove the possession of valid credentials without interacting with identity providers. Beyond user-centricity, our delegation solution also allows for privilege delegation to improve the runtime performance of composite services. As the natural certificate chains, the solution consists of two signature schemes: a pseudonym-based signature scheme and a conventional warrant proxy signature scheme. The pseudonym-based signature scheme can be used to self-generate pseudonyms, to prove the possession of credentials, and to achieve privacy based on time-varying pseudonyms. The proxy signature scheme is used to delegate the signing capability where the proxy key includes the signature of warrants produced by the signing protocol in the pseudonym-based signature scheme. Therefore, the model and constructions will provide strong building blocks for the design and implementation of universal identity management systems [41, 45].

References

1. Cameron K (2005) Laws of identity http://www.identityblog.com. May 2005
2. PRIME Consortium. Privacy and Identity Management for Europe (PRIME). http://www.prime-project.eu
3. Identity-management. Liberty alliance project. http://www.projectliberty.org
4. Kaler C, Nadalin A (2003) Web services federation language.
5. Bhargav-Spantzel A, Camenisch J (2006) User Centricity: A Taxonomy and Open Issues. In: The Second ACM Workshop on Digital Identity Management - DIM, 493–527.
6. Chaum D (1985) Security without identification: transaction systems to make big brother obsolete. Communications of the ACM, 28(10): 1030–1044.
7. Chaum D, Evertse JH (1986) A secure and privacy-protecting protocol for transmitting personal information between organizations. Advances in Cryptology-CRYPTO'86, p 118–167.
8. Damgard IB (1988) Payment systems and credential mechanisms with provable security against abuse by individuals. Advances in Cryptology-CRYPTO'88, p 328–335
9. Chen LD (1995) Access with pseudonyms. Lecture Notes in Computer Science, 1029: 232–243
10. Lysyanskaya A, Rivest R, Sahai A (1999) Pseudonym systems. In: Selected Areas in Cryptography, 6th Annual International, Workshop, SAC'99, p 184–199

11. Camenisch J, Lysyanskaya A (2001) Efficient non-transferable anonymous multi-show credential system with optional anonymity revocation. In: Pfitzmann B (ed) EUROCRYPT 2001, vol 2045 of LNCS, Springer Verlag, p 93–118
12. Camenisch J, Lysyanskaya A (2002) A signature scheme with efficient protocols. In: SCN 2002, vol 2576 of LNCS, p 268–289
13. Camenisch J, Lysyanskaya A (2004) Signature schemes and anonymous credentials from bilinear maps. In: CRYPTO 2004, vol 3152 of LNCS, p 56–72
14. Belenkiy M, Chase M, Kohlweiss M (2008) Non-Interactive Anonymous Credentials. Theoretical Cryptography Conference (TCC) 2008. http:// eprint.iacr.org/2007/384.
15. Chase M, Lysyanskaya A (2006) On signatures of knowledge. In: Dwork C (ed) CRYPTO 2006, vol 4117 of LNCS, p 78C96
16. Belenkiy M, Camenisch J, Chase M, Kohlweiss M, Lysyanskaya A, Shacham H (2008) Delegatable Anonymous Credentials. http://eprint.iacr.org/2008/428.
17. Camenisch J, Sommer D, Zimmermann R (2006) A General Certification Framework with Applica-tions to Privacy-Enhancing Certificate Infrastructures. IFIP International Federation for Information Processing, p 25–37
18. Mambo M, Usuda K, Okamoto E (1996) Proxy signatures: Delegation of the power to sign mes-sages. IEICE Transaction on Fundamentals, vol. E79-A, no. 9, p 1338–1354.
19. Kim S, Park S, Won D (1997) Proxy signatures revisited. Proceedings of ICICS97, LNCS 1334, Springer-Verlag, p 223–232
20. Okamoto T, Tada M, Okamoto E (1999) Extended proxy signatures for smart card. Proceedings of Information Security Workshop99, LNCS 1729. Springer-Verlag, p 247–258
21. Herranz J, Saez G (2004) Revisiting fully distributed proxy signature schemes. Proceedings of Indocrypt04, LNCS 3348. Springer-Verlag, p 356–370
22. Fiat A, Shamir A (1986) How to prove yourself: Practical solutions to identification and signature problems. In: Odlyzko AM (ed) Proceedings of Crypto 1986, vol 263 of LNCS. Springer-Verlag, p 186–194
23. Chaum D, van Heyst E (1991) Group signatures. In: Davies DW (ed) Proceedings of Eurocrypt 1991, vol 547 of LNCS. Springer-Verlag, p 257–265
24. Bellare M, Micciancio D, Warinschi B (2003) Foundations of Group Signatures: Formal Definitions, Simplified Requirements, and a Construction Based on General Assumptions. Eurocrypt 03, LNCS 2656. Springer-Verlag, p 614–629
25. Boneh D, Boyen X (2004) Short Signatures without Random Oracles. Eurocrypt04, LNCS 3027. Springer-Verlag, p 56–73
26. Bellare M, Shi H, Zhang C (2005) Foundations of Group Signatures: The Case of Dynamic Groups. In: CT C RSA05, LNCS 3376. Springer-Verlag, p 136–153
27. Delerablee C, Pointcheval D (2006) Dynamic Fully Anonymous Short Group Signatures. Progress in Cryptology - VIETCRYPT 2006, Hanoi, Vietnam, p 193–210
28. Brickell E, Camenisch J, Chen LQ (2004) Direct anonymous attestation. Proceedings of the ACM Conference on Computer and Communications Security, Washington, DC, p 132–145
29. Camenisch J (2006) Protecting (anonymous) credentials with the trusted computing groups trusted platform modules, vo1.2. In: Proceedings of the 21st IFIP International Information Security Confer-ence (SEC 2006)
30. Boneh D, Franklin M (2001) Identity-based encryption from the Weil pairing. In Proc. of CRYPTO'01, vol 2139, p 213–229
31. Barreto P, Kim H, Bynn B, Scott M (2002) Efficient algorithms for pairing-based cryptosystems. In Proc. CRYPTO'02, p 354–368
32. Mitsunari S, Sakai R, Kasahara M (2002) A new traitor tracing. IEICE Trans. Vol. E85-A, No.2, p 481–484
33. Hess F (2002) Efficient identity based signature schemes based on pairings. SAC 2002, LNCS 2595, p 310–324
34. Zhang F, Kim K (2002) ID-based blind signature and ring signature from pairings. Advances in Cryptology-Asiacrypt 2002.

35. Huang X, Mu Y, Susilo W, Zhang F, Chen X (2005) A short proxy scheme: efficient authentication in the ubiquitous world. In: EUC Workshops 2005, LNCS 3823, Berlin. Springer-Verlag, p 480–489
36. MICROSOFT (2005) A technical reference for InfoCard v1.0 in Windows
37. Higgins Trust Framework, 2006. http://www.eclipse.org/higgins/.
38. Camenisch J, Herreweghen EV (2002) Design and implementation of the idemix anonymous cre-dential system. Proceedings of the 9th ACM Conference on Computer and Communications, Security, p 21–30
39. Camenisch J, Gross T, Sommer D (2006) Enhancing Privacy of Federated Identity Management Protocols. Proceedings of the 5th ACM workshop on Privacy in Electronic Society, p 67–72
40. IBM, Microsoft, Actional, BEA, Computer Associates, Layer 7, Oblix, Open Network, Ping Identity, Reactivity, and Verisign. Web Services Trust Language (WS-Trust). February 2005.
41. Segev A, Toch E (2009) Context-Based Matching and Ranking of Web Services for Composition. IEEE Transactions on Service Computing, vol 2(3): 210–222
42. OASIS (2005) Assertions and Protocol for the OASIS Security Assertion Markup Language (SAML) V2.0. OASIS Standard, March 2005.
43. Liberty Alliance Project (2003) Liberty ID-FF Protocols and Schema Specification. Version 1.2, November 2003. http://www.projectliberty.org/specs.
44. Gomi H, Hatakeyama M, Hosono S, Fujita S (2005) A Delegation Framework for Federated Identity Management. Proceedings of the 2005 Workshop on Digital Identity Management, p 94–103
45. Zhang Y, Chen JL (2011) A Delegation Solution for Universal Identity Management in SOA. IEEE Transactions on services computing, p 70–81

Chapter 4
The Roadmap of Trust and Trust Evaluation in Web Applications and Web Services

Lei Li and Yan Wang

Abstract In the 1980s and 1990s, the issue of trust in many aspects of life has drawn much attention in a significant number of studies in social science. Nowadays, with the development of Web applications, trust evaluation has become a significant and important issue, especially when a client has to select a trustworthy one from a pool of unknown service providers. An effective and efficient trust evaluation system is highly desirable and critical to clients for identifying potential risks, providing objective trust results and preventing huge monetary losses.This research roadmap presents an overview of the general structure of trust, the bases of trust and the concepts of trust in different disciplines. Then the typical trust evaluation methods in each area of Web applications, including e-commerce, P2P networks, multi-agent systems, recommendation systems, social networks and service-oriented computing, are briefly introduced from technology, state of the art and scientific challenges standpoints. This roadmap provides not only the necessary background for on-going research activities and projects, but also the solid foundations for deciding on potential future research on trust evaluation in broader contexts.

4.1 Introduction

In our daily life, there are many occasions when we have to trust others to behave as they promised or as we expect them to do. For example, we trust a bus driver can take us to our destination on time; we trust a doctor to conduct a physical examination and check whether we have an illness; we trust a motor mechanic to find out whether there is a problem in our car and then repair it; we trust a bank and deposit our money. Each time when we trust, we have to put something at risk: our lives, our

L. Li (✉) · Y. Wang
Department of Computing, Macquarie University, Sydney, NSW 2109, Australia
e-mail: lei.li@outlook.com

Y. Wang
e-mail: yan.wang@mq.edu.au

A. Bouguettaya et al. (eds.), *Advanced Web Services*,
DOI: 10.1007/978-1-4614-7535-4_4,

assets, our properties, and so on. On these occasions, we may use a variety of clues and past experiences to believe in these individuals' good intentions towards us and decide on the extent to which we can trust them. This is the general procedure of trust evaluation in daily occasions [36].

Nowadays, with the development of information communication technologies, from time to time it is necessary to have some interactions with others on the Web. For example, download some files from others, or purchase some products or services from online e-commerce or e-service websites. In Web applications, when a client intends to have an interaction selected from a large pool of service providers, in addition to functionality, the trustworthiness of a service provider is a key factor in service provider selection. This is due to the fact that any service client would like to have transactions with reputable service providers so as to reduce the possibility to be deceived. This makes trust evaluation a significant and important issue in Web applications, especially when the client has to select one from unknown service providers.

Conceptually, trust is the measure taken by one party of the willingness and ability of another party to act in the interest of the former party in a certain situation [31]. If the trust value is in the range of [0, 1], it can be taken as the subjective probability by which one party expects that another party can perform a given action [29].

The issue of trust has been actively studied in Peer-to-Peer (P2P) networks (e.g., [14, 30, 91]), which can be used for information-sharing systems (e.g., GNutella[1]). In a P2P system, it is quite natural for a client peer to doubt if a serving peer can provide the complete file prior to any download action, which may be quite time-consuming and network bandwidth-consuming. Unlike some trust management systems in e-commerce (EC) or service-oriented environments (SOC), in the P2P trust management system a requesting peer needs to inquire the trust data of a serving peer (target peer) from other peers who may have transacted with the serving peer [30, 57, 91]. The computation of the trust level of the serving peer from the collected trust ratings is then performed by the requesting peer rather than a central management server, because of the decentralized architecture of the P2P system.

Unlike P2P information-sharing networks or the eBay[2] reputation management system where a binary rating system is used [91], in SOC environments a trust rating is usually a value in the range of [0, 1] given by a service client [81, 85, 87], representing the subjective belief of the service client on their satisfaction with a service or a service provider. The trust value of a service or a service provider can be calculated by a trust management authority based on the collected trust ratings representing the reputation of the service or the service provider.

In general, in a trust management enabled system, service clients can provide feedback and trust ratings after completed transactions. Based on the ratings, the trust value of a service provider can be evaluated to reflect the quality of services in a certain time period. This trust evaluation approach in service-oriented environments is the focus of research works nowadays in service-oriented computing.

[1] http://www.gnutella.com/

[2] http://www.eBay.com/

Effective and efficient trust evaluation is highly desirable and critical to service clients for identifying potential risks, providing objective trust results and preventing huge monetary loss [83].

In this chapter, the literature review on trust is organized as follows:

- Section 4.2 presents a general structure of trust, which provides a general global picture of trust. With this structure, it is easy to start a preliminary theoretical analysis of trust.
- Section 4.3 identifies the bases of trust, with which trust can be established from a variety of diverse sources of trust-related information.
- Section 4.4 briefly introduces the concepts of trust defined in multiple disciplines, including sociology, history, psychology, economics and so on.
- Section 4.5 focuses on trust evaluation models used in different areas of Web applications, including e-commerce, P2P networks, multi-agent systems, recommendation systems and social networks.
- Section 4.6 focuses on the typical trust evaluation methods used in service-oriented computing.
- In Sect. 4.7, the above mentioned trust evaluation methods in Web applications are categorized into different taxonomies with respect to trust evaluation techniques, the structure of trust and the bases of trust respectively.
- Finally, Sect. 4.8 concludes our work in this chapter.

4.2 General Structure of Trust

The general structure of trust has been proposed in [55] and graphically represented in Fig. 4.1. This structure provides a general global picture of trust, with which professionals, scientists and even ordinary citizens can start a preliminary theoretical analysis of trust. With primary trust and reflective trust as the horizontal axis, and micro-social trust and macro-social trust as the vertical axis, this presentation creates four spaces which correspond to four orthogonally placed forms of trust.

- Vertically, passing from the bottom half of Fig. 4.1 toward the top, we move from micro-social trust (i.e., personal, private and interpersonal trust) toward macro-social trust (i.e., professional, group and organizational trust).
- Horizontally, the left-hand side of Fig. 4.1 is characterized by trust as feelings, either based on the interdependence between the self and other, or associated with security or social cohesion [1]. As we move toward the right-hand part of Fig. 4.1, trust becomes conceptualized and rationalized [1]. Trust in the right-hand part of Fig. 4.1 is contractual, and is based on obligations and morality.

  In other words, in the left-hand side we focus on primary trust (i.e., immediately apprehended [preconceptual] forms of trust), while in the right-hand side trust is established between the self and a stranger, an institutions or a kind of group (i.e., reflective trust [1]). However, once trust has been established, it transforms into common knowledge and becomes taken-for-granted and commonly understood.

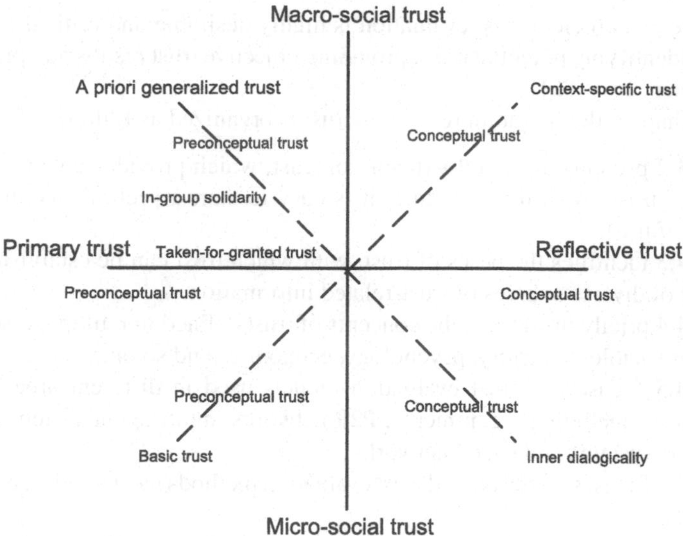

Fig. 4.1 General structure of trust

In contrast to the left-hand side of Fig. 4.1, this taken-for-grantedness arises from reflective thinking. There is also a case whereby, as a result of an individual's doubt trust is brought back into discourse explicitly. When trust is explicitly verbalized, it is no longer taken-for-granted and is partly or fully destroyed. It is necessary to establish trust from the very beginning again.

4.2.1 Basic Trust

Now let us focus on the bottom left quadrant of Fig. 4.1, in which there is what developmental psychologists describe as *basic trust* between a mother and her baby.

Basic trust is the first mark of an individual's mental life, even before feelings of autonomy and initiative develop [17]. Through the mutuality between a mother and her baby, basic trust evolves through mutual somatic experiences and "unmistakable communication" that creates security and continuity. With the presupposition that humans possess the capacity to make distinctions, the child, equipped with an innate capacity for intersubjectivity, learns through actions, experiences and communications to differentiate between the mental states of others, between feelings, and between trustworthy and untrustworthy relations [73].

4.2.2 A Priori Generalized Trust

Moving to the second quadrant in the top left part of Fig. 4.1, we can see that a *priori generalized trust* which is above all a fundamental psychosocial feeling, and is instantaneously apprehended, quite often without the awareness of those concerned [54]. Generally speaking, the top left quadrant contains trust which is characterized by the kinds of social relations in a society where individuals have certain kinds of social activities. Particularly, in a heterogeneous and complex society like ours, trust is person-specific and content-specific [73]. In our society, during daily life we have to deal with strangers all the time, but here we only deal with one aspect of a stranger and not with the whole person. For example, we trust a motor mechanic to find out whether there is a problem in our car and then repair it, but we don't trust him/her on anything else, such as conducting a physical examination and checking whether we have an illness.

In this quadrant, somewhere more towards the intersection, we can place *in-group solidarity* [11], which can be taken as a special form of trust. It includes the social binding and bounding of close in-groups, such as the social cohesion and social ties within family, friends, neighbors, coactivists, and other communities.

4.2.3 Context-Specific Trust

Now we focus on the third quadrant of Fig. 4.1, and this quadrant includes trust resulting from a variety of forms, ranging from cooperation to audits, strategies, calculations and so on. The typical form of trust located in this quadrant is *context-specific trust* [56], which can be derived from contextual information.

In the computer science discipline, it is firstly pointed out in [56] that trust is context sensitive: "Whilst I may trust my brother to drive me to the airport, I most certainly would not trust him to fly the plane!" Generally, context is any information characterizing the situation of an entity [76]. An entity, in turn, can be a person, a place, or an object that is considered relevant to the interaction between a user and an application, including the user and the application themselves [78].

A typical and simple context-specific trust evaluation process in SOC environments is as follows: in a trust management system, regarding a service client A who has never interacted with a service provider B in the past, before making the decision to have an interaction with B, A asks other clients what are their trust ratings for B under the target context required by A. Then the trust from A to B will be established only if the weighted average of the trust ratings from other entities is larger than a threshold, where the weights of trust ratings are determined based on the similarity of the context of a trust rating and the target context required by A [66].

4.2.4 Inner Dialogicality

Finally, we arrive at the bottom right quadrant of Fig. 4.1, and in this quadrant we can place *inner dialogicality* [2]. By inner dialogicality, we mean the capacity of humans to carry out internal dialogues (i.e., dialogues within the self). For example, it could include evaluations of one's own and others' past experiences and present conduct, which reflects personal issues and predicts the future conduct. Inner dialogues include not only self-confidence but also self-doubt [55]. With inner dialogues, individuals can develop an awareness of how, where, when and why they can trust or have confidence in specific others (or in themselves).

With the proposed general structure of trust, any form of trust should fall into one of these four quadrants. As the forms of trust in the same quadrant have the similar properties, when we start to analysis a new form of trust, it is possible to begin the research with analyzing the evaluation approaches for other forms of trust in the same quadrant and then determine the corresponding evaluation approaches for the new form of trust.

4.3 Bases of Trust

In the proposed general structure of trust, there are a lot of forms of trust. But, how to establish trust? Research on identifying the bases of trust attempts to establish the conditions which lead to the emergence of trust, including psychological, social, and organizational factors that influence individuals' expectations about others' trustworthiness and their willingness to behave trustworthily during an interaction [1, 32]. The bases of trust are significant to understand trust and measure trust in computer science.

4.3.1 Dispositional Trust Establishment

Individuals behave differently in their general predisposition to trust different people [32]. To explain the origins of such dispositional trust, Rotter [69] proposed that individuals tend to build up general trustworthiness about other people from their early trust-related experiences (e.g., the basic trust proposed in Sect. 4.2.1). In addition, we usually assume that an individual has a relatively stable personality characteristic [69] in a certain situation, i.e., a relatively stable dispositional trust in a certain situation. However, as the dispositional trust is related to individuals' personal characteristic, it is usually hard to estimate its value directly.

4.3.2 History-Based Trust Establishment

In the literature, it has been pointed out that individuals' willingness to engage in trusting others is largely a history dependent process [6]. Interactional histories provide decision makers with useful trust information on the estimation of others' dispositions, intentions and motivations. With the assumption of a relatively stable personality characteristic, this historical information also provides a basis for making predictions about others' future behaviors.

Interactional histories have a significant effect on two psychological facets of trust judgment.

- First, individuals' estimations about others' trustworthiness depend on their prior expectations about others' behaviors.
- Second, these expectations vary with subsequent experience, which either validates or discredits the expectations.

In this regard, history-based trust can be taken as an important basis for establishing knowledge-based or personalized trust [35].

For example, in [12], with personalized weights on different transaction attributes introduced by a service client, the trust value of a service provider can be calculated from a collection of his/her service invocation history records.

Personalized knowledge about interaction history can provide important information for trust estimation. However, from time to time such knowledge is hard to obtain. In most situations, it is impossible for decision makers to accumulate sufficient knowledge about the potential individuals with whom they would like to transact. As a consequence, a variety of substitutes for such direct personalized knowledge about interaction history have to be utilized [13] and many other bases of trust have to be introduced.

4.3.3 Third Parties as Conduits of Trust

Considering the importance of personalized knowledge about interaction history regarding others' trustworthiness and its difficulty to obtain, third parties can be introduced as conduits of trust because of their diffusion of trust-related information.

In our daily life, the most common examples of using third parties as conduits of trust are gossip and word-of-mouth. These ways can provide a valuable source of second-hand knowledge about others [8], but the effects of these ways on trust estimations are complex and do not always have positive effects on the estimation of others' trustworthiness. That is because third parties usually tend to disclose only partial information about others [8]. In particular, when an individual has a strong relation to a prospective trustee, third parties usually prefer to convey the information which they believe the individual wants to hear, i.e., the information which strengthens the tie between third parties and the individual [32]. This will increase the certainty about the trustee's trustworthiness. Thus, in this situation, third parties tend to amplify such trust.

Third parties also play an important role in the development and diffusion of trust in social networks [79]. When there is no sufficient knowledge or interaction history available, individuals can turn to third parties for transferring their well-established trust relationships. This provides a base of trust which will be validated or discredited with subsequent experience.

4.3.4 Category-Based Trust Establishment

Category-based trust refers to trust estimation based on the information regarding a trustee's membership in a social or an organizational category. For example, we can take gender, race or age as a social category to establish the category-based trust. This category information usually unknowingly influences others' estimations about the trustee's trustworthiness.

The theoretical foundation of category-based trust is established from the fact that due to the cognitive consequences of categorization and ingroup bias, individuals tend to attribute positive characteristics such as cooperativeness and trustworthiness to other ingroup members [7]. As a result, individuals can establish a kind of depersonalized trust (i.e., category-based trust) on other ingroup members only based on the awareness of their shared category membership.

As pointed out in [70], in SOC environments, a service provider inherits by default the reputation of a social category it belongs to, especially when direct information about personal interactions with the service provider is lacking. In fact, this category-based trust is evaluated based on the trustworthiness of other members in this social category, which has already been known to the service client.

4.3.5 Role-Based Trust Establishment

Role-based trust focuses on trust estimation based on the knowledge that a trustee occupies a particular role in an organization rather than that a truster has the specific knowledge about the trustee's dispositions, intentions and motivations. To some extent, it is believable that technically competent role performance is usually aligned with corresponding roles in organizations [3]. For example, in the case of vehicle maintenance, we usually trust a motor mechanic to find out whether there is a problem with the car. Therefore, individuals can establish a kind of trust based on the knowledge of role relations, even without personalized knowledge or interaction history.

Role-based trust is established from the fact that there are some prerequisites to occupy a role in an organization, such as the training and socialization processes that role occupants have undergone, and their intentions to ensure their technically competent role performance.

Role-based trust can also be quite vulnerable, especially during organizational crises or when novel situations occur which confuse organizational roles or break down role-based interactions.

4.3.6 Rule-Based Trust Establishment

Both formal and informal rules capture much of the knowledge about tacit understandings regarding transaction behaviors, interactional routines, and exchange practices [53]. Formal rules are determined by a trust management authority to establish trust between truster and trustee. For example, with the help of PayPal[3], a buyer can trust an unknown seller for a certain transaction. In contrast, informal rules are not explicitly determined by any trust management authority. Instead, they are formed by tradition, religion or routines. For example, in academic environments, early career researchers usually trust senior researchers to help them and guide their research path.

Rule-based trust is estimated not on a conscious calculation of consequences, but rather on shared understandings regarding rules of appropriate behaviors. Regarding the effects of rules on individuals' self-perceptions and expectations about other participants in a social network, rules can create and sustain high levels of trust within the social network [53].

4.4 Concept of Trust in Multiple Disciplines

Complex social phenomena like trust cannot be properly understood from the perspective of a single discipline or in separation from other social phenomena [55]. Although considerable attention to the problem of defining trust has been afforded [32], as it is understandable that a single researcher cannot master all the knowledge related to trust in all related disciplines, thus a concise and universally accepted definition of trust has remained elusive, and the concept of trust is usually based on analysis from the viewpoint of a single discipline, as discussed below.

From the perspective of sociology and history, according to Seligman [72], "trust enters into social interaction in the interstices of systems, when for one reason or another systematically defined role expectations are no longer viable". If people play their roles according to role expectations, we can safely conduct our own transaction accordingly. The problem of trust emerges only in cases where there is "role negotiability", i.e., there is "open space" between roles and role expectations [72].

Seligman [72] also points out that trust is a modern phenomenon. What might appear as trust in premodern societies was nothing but "confidence in well-regulated and heavily sanctioned role expectations". Modernity saw the rise of individualism and the proliferation of societal roles. There was thus a greater degree of negotiability of role expectations and a greater possibility for role conflicts, and this resulted in a greater potential for the development of trust in modern society.

From the perspective of sociology, Coleman [10] proposes a four-part definition of trust.

- Placement of trust allows actions that otherwise are not possible, i.e., trust allows actions to be conducted based on incomplete information on the case in hand.
- If the person in whom trust is placed (i.e., a trustee) is trustworthy, then the trustor will be better off than if s/he had not trusted. Conversely, if the trustee is untrustworthy, then the trustor will be worse off than if s/he had not trusted.

[3] http://www.paypal.com.au/

- Trust is an action that involves a voluntary transfer of resources (e.g., physical, financial, intellectual, or temporal) from the truster to the trustee with no real commitment from the trustee.
- A time lag exists between the extension of trust and the result of the trusting behavior.

This definition allows for the discussion of trust behaviors, which is useful in reasoning about human-computer trust and trust behaviors in social institutions.

From the perspective of psychology, trust is the belief in the person who you trust to do what you expect. Individuals in relationships characterized by high levels of social trust are more apt to exchange information and to act with benevolence toward others than those in relationships lacking trust. Misztal [64] points out three basic things that trust does in the lives of people: It makes social life predictable, creates a sense of community, and makes it easier for people to work together.

From the perspective of economics, trust is often conceptualized as reliability in transactions [55].

In all cases, trust involves many heuristic decision rules, requiring the trust management authority to handle a lot of complex information with great effort in rational reasoning [9].

4.5 Trust Evaluation in Web Applications

The issue of trust has been studied in some Web application fields.

4.5.1 Trust Evaluation in E-Commerce Environments

Trust is an important issue in e-commerce (EC) environments. At eBay (see Footnote 2), after each transaction, a buyer can give feedback with a rating of "positive", "neutral" or "negative" to the system according to the service quality of the seller. eBay calculates the feedback score $S = P - N$, where P is the number of positive ratings left by buyers and N is the number of negative ratings. The positive feedback rate $R = \frac{P}{P+N}$ (e.g., $R = 99.1\,\%$) is then calculated and displayed on web pages. This is a simple trust management system providing valuable trust information to buyers.

In [97], the Sporas system is introduced to evaluate trust for EC applications based on the ratings of transactions in a recent time period. In this method, the ratings of later transactions are given higher weights as they are more important in trust evaluation. The Histos system proposed in [97] is a more personalized reputation system compared to Sporas. Unlike Sporas, the reputation of a seller in Histos depends on who makes the query, and how that person rated other sellers in the online community. In [75], Song et al. apply fuzzy logic to trust evaluation. Their approach divides sellers into multiple classes of trust ranks (e.g., a 5-star seller, or a 4-star seller). In [86], Wang and Lin present some reputation-based trust evaluation mechanisms (such as transaction-specific trust, raters' credibility and the social relationship between a rater and ratee) to more objectively depict the trust level of sellers on forthcoming transactions and the relationship between interacting entities.

4.5.2 Trust Evaluation in P2P Information Sharing Networks

The issue of trust has been actively studied in Peer-to-Peer (P2P) information sharing networks as a client peer needs to know prior to download actions which serving peer can provide complete files. In [14], Damiani et al. propose an approach for evaluating the trust of peers through a distributed polling algorithm and the *XRep* protocol before initiating any download action. This approach adopts a binary rating system and is based on the Gnutella (see Footnote 1) query broadcasting method. EigenTrust [30] adopts a binary rating system as well, and aims to collect the local trust values of all peers to calculate the global trust value of a given peer. Some other P2P studies also adopted the binary rating system. In [91], Xiong and Liu propose a *PeerTrust* model which has two main features. First, they introduce three basic trust parameters (i.e., the feedback that a peer receives from other peers, the total number of transactions that a peer performs, the credibility of the feedback sources) and two adaptive factors in computing the trustworthiness of peers (i.e., transaction context factor and the community context factor). Second, they define some general trust metrics and formulas to aggregate these parameters into a final trust value. In [57], Marti and Garcia-Molina propose a voting reputation system that collects responses from other peers on a target peer. The final trust value is calculated by aggregating the values returned by responding peers and the requesting peer's experience with the target peer. In [100], Zhou and Hwang discover a power-law distribution in peer feedbacks, and develop a trust system with a dynamical selection on a small number of power nodes that are the most trustworthy in the system.

4.5.3 Trust Evaluation in Multi-Agent Systems

Trust has also drawn much attention in the field of multi-agent systems. In [77], Teacy et al. introduce the TRAVOS system (Trust and Reputation model for Agent-based Virtual OrganisationS) which calculates an agent's trust on an interaction partner using probability theory, taking into account the past interactions between agents. In [21], Griffiths proposes a multi-dimensional trust model which allows agents to model the trust value of others according to various criteria. In [70], Sabater and Sierra propose a model discussing trust development between groups. When calculating the trust from individual *A* to individual *B*, a few factors are considered, e.g., the interaction between *A* and *B*, the evaluation of *A*'s group to *B* and *B*'s group, and A's evaluation to B's group. In [15], a community-wide trust evaluation method is proposed where the final trust value is computed by aggregating the ratings (termed as votes in [15]) and other aspects (e.g., the rater's location and connection medium). In addition, this approach computes the trust level of an assertion (e.g., trustworthy or untrustworthy) as the aggregation of multiple fuzzy values representing the trust resulting from human interactions. In [26], during trust evaluation, the motivations of agents and the dependency relationships among them are also taken into account.

4.5.4 Trust-Aware Recommendation Systems

Conventional recommender systems mainly employ the information filtering techniques for making recommendations. In such systems, collaborative filtering approaches [25] or content-based filtering approaches [16, 65] are used for making recommendations, which collect ratings from the users with similar profiles or the items similar to the one a user liked in the past, respectively. However, these conventional approaches take users individually and do not address the trustworthiness of recommendations directly. In addition, as pointed out in [71], the sparsity of data in recommender systems has been an outstanding problem, which makes the filtering techniques less effective. Nevertheless, the ultimate goal of recommender systems is to provide high quality and trustworthy recommendations that can very likely be accepted by users. To this end, using the reviews/recommendations from social networks has drawn much attention in recent studies [49, 50].

Social influence occurs when one's emotions, opinions or behaviours are affected by others.[4] As indicated in Social Psychology [5, 18, 93], in the real society, a person prefers the recommendations from trusted friends. In addition, based on statistics, Sinha and Swearingen [74] and Bedi et al. [4] have demonstrated that given a choice between the recommendations from trusted friends and those from recommender systems, in terms of quality and usefulness, trusted friends' recommendations are more preferred.

Social networks are important to recommender systems due to the data sparsity problem [49, 71] and the scenarios in real life that people turn to friends and friends' friends for soliciting opinions [5, 93], raising the need of trust propagation/inference in social networks (i.e., evaluating the trust between two non-adjacent participants). Earlier studies have adopted the averaging strategies [19], multiplication strategies [42, 82], or probabilistic approaches [33, 34] based on the trust values between adjacent participants. However, they ignore contextual factors that influence trust relations and trust inference (e.g., a person's recommendation role [89] or the social intimacy between people [46]), and/or simply take the confidence to other people as a probabilistic value without discussing from where the confidence comes. Most of the existing studies usually model their approaches intuitively, without following the principles from Social Science or Social Psychology. In some recent work [46–48],

[4] http://qualities-of-a-leader.com/personal-mbti-type-analysis/

following the principles in Social Psychology [1, 62], both the recommendation role resulting from social positions (e.g., a professor) and expertise, and trust and social intimacy degree between adjacent participants in social networks have been taken into account.

4.5.5 Trust Evaluation in Social Networks

The studies of social network properties can be traced back to 1960s when the small-world characteristic in social networks was validated by Milgram [61] (i.e., the average path length between two Americans was found to be about 6.6 hops). In recent years, sociologists and computer scientists investigated the characteristics of popular online social networks (OSNs) [63] (e.g., Facebook,[5] MySpace[6] and Flickr[7]), and validated the small-world and power-law characteristics (i.e., the probability that a node has a degree k is proportional to $k^{-r}, r > 1$).

In recent years, the new generation of social network based web application systems has drawn the attention from both academia and industry. The study in [45] has pointed out that it is a trend to build up social network based web applications (e.g., e-commerce or online recruitment systems). In real applications, according to a survey on 2600 hiring managers in 2008 by CareerBuilder (careerbuilder.com, a popular job hunting website), 22 % of those managers used social networking sites to manually investigate potential employees. The ratio increased to 45 % in June 2009 and 72 % in January 2010. In Oct. 2011, eBay (see Footnote 2) announced their strategic plan to deepen the relationship with Facebook (see Footnote 5) for creating a new crop of e-commerce applications with social networking features, integrating both their e-commerce platform and social networking platform seamlessly.[8]

In the literature, the issue of trust becomes increasingly important in social networks. In [82], Walter et al. identify that network density, the similarity of preference between agents, and the sparseness of knowledge about the trustworthiness of recommendations are crucial factors for trust-oriented recommendations in social networks. However, the trust-oriented recommendation can be attacked in various ways, such as sybil attack, where the attacker creates a potentially unlimited number of identities to provide feedback and increase trust level. In [95], Yu et al. present SybilGuard, a protocol for limiting the corruptive influences of sybil attacks, which depends on the established trust relationship between users in social networks.

Trust propagation, during which the trust of a target agent can be estimated from the trust of other agents, is an important problem in social networks. In [20], Golbeck and Hendler present trust propagation algorithms based on binary ratings. In social

[5] http://www.facebook.com

[6] http://myspace.com

[7] http://flickr.com

[8] Refer to the Reuters news "eBay and Facebook unveil e-commerce partnership" at http://www.reuters.com/article/2011/10/12/ebay-facebook-idUSN1E79B22Y20111012.

networks, many more non-binary trust propagation approaches have been proposed. In [22], Guha et al. develop a framework dealing with not only trust propagation but also distrust propagation. In [24], Hang et al. propose an algebraic approach to propagating trust in social networks, including a concatenation operator for the trust aggregation of sequential invocation, an aggregation operator for the trust aggregation of parallel invocation, and a selection operator for trust-oriented multiple path selection. In [80], Victor et al. present a trust propagation model, which takes into account fuzzified trust, fuzzified distrust, unavailable trust information and contradictory trust information simultaneously.

4.6 Trust Evaluation in Service-Oriented Environments

In recent years, Service-Oriented Computing (SOC) has emerged to be an increasingly important research area attracting attention from both the research and industry communities [51, 67]. In SOC applications, various services are provided to clients by different providers in a loosely-coupled environment. In such context, a service can refer to a transaction, such as selling a product online (i.e., the traditional online services), or a functional component implemented by Web service technologies [42]. When a client looks for a service from a large set of services offered by different service providers, in addition to functionality, the reputation-based trust level of a service provider is a very important concern from the view point of the service client [29, 42, 44, 51]. It is also a critical task for the trust management authority to be responsible for maintaining the list of reputable and trustworthy services and service providers, and making these information available to service clients [67].

In general, in a trust management mechanism enabled system, service clients can provide feedback and trust ratings after transactions. Then, the trust management system can calculate the trust value based on collected ratings reflecting the quality of recent transactions, with more weights assigned to later transactions [37, 83]. The trust value can be provided to service clients by publishing it on web or responding to their requests [37, 43]. An effective and efficient trust management system is highly desirable and critical for service clients to identify potential risks, providing objective trust results and preventing huge financial loss [29].

In the literature, the issue of trust has received much attention in the field of SOC. In [81], Vu et al. present a model to evaluate service trust by comparing the advertised service quality and the delivered service quality. If the advertised service quality is as good as the delivered service quality, the service is reputable. In [87], Wang et al. propose some trust evaluation metrics and a formula for trust computation with which a final trust value is computed. In addition, they propose a fuzzy logic based approach for determining reputation ranks that particularly differentiate the service periods of new and old (long-existing) service providers. The aim is to provide incentives to new service providers and penalize those old service providers with poor service quality. In [52], Malik and Bouguettaya propose a set of decentralized techniques aiming at evaluating reputation-based trust with the ratings from clients to facilitate the trust-oriented selection and composition of Web services. In [12], Conner et al. present a trust model that allows service clients with different trust requirements to use different weight functions that place emphasis on different transaction attributes. This customized trust evaluation provides flexibility for service clients to have different trust values from the same feedback data.

Now let us introduce some important topics on trust evaluation in service-oriented environments.

4.6.1 Trust Vector and Its Evaluation

In the literature, in most existing trust evaluation models [14, 30, 44, 77, 81, 85, 87, 91, 97], a single final trust level (*FTL*) is computed to reflect the general or global trust level of a service provider accumulated in a certain time period (e.g., in the latest 6 months). This *FTL* may be presumably taken as a prediction of trustworthiness for forthcoming transactions. Single-trust-value approaches are easily adopted in trust-oriented service comparison and selection. However, a single trust value cannot preserve the trust features well, e.g., whether and how the trust trend changes. Certainly, a full set of trust ratings can serve for this purpose, but it is usually a large dataset as it should cover a long service period. A good option is to compute a small dataset to present a large set of trust ratings and well preserve its trust features.

In [37, 43], Li and Wang propose a trust vector with three values, including final trust level (*FTL*), service trust trend (*STT*) and service performance consistency level (*SPCL*), to depict a set of trust ratings. In addition to *FTL*, the service trust trend indicates whether the service trust ratings are becoming worse or better. *STT* is obtained from the slope of a regression line that best fits the set of ratings distributed over a time interval. The service performance consistency level indicates the extent to which the computed *STT* fits the given set of trust ratings. However, the computed trust vector can represent the set of ratings well only if these ratings imply consistent trust trend changes and are all very close to the obtained regression line.

In a more general case with trust ratings for a long service history, multiple time intervals (MTI) have to be determined, within each of which a trust vector can be obtained and can represent well all the corresponding ratings. In [41], Li and Wang propose three trust vector based MTI analysis approaches, which are better than the two existing boundary included MTI algorithms in [83]. The proposed bisection-based boundary excluded greedy MTI algorithm has a lower time complexity, and it is much faster than any of the other four MTI algorithms. The proposed boundary mixed optimal MTI analysis algorithm can guarantee the representation of a large set of trust ratings with a minimal set of values while highly preserving the trust features. Therefore, a small set of data can represent well a large set of trust ratings with well preserved trust features.

In the literature, there exist some other approaches using trust vectors, with different focuses. In [68], Ray and Chakraborty propose a trust vector that consists of the experience of a truster about a trustee, the knowledge of the truster regarding the trustee for a particular context, and the recommendation of other trustees. The focus of this model is how to address these three independent aspects of trust in evaluations. In [99], Zhao and Li propose a method using a trust vector to represent the directed link with a trust value between two peers. The trust vector includes a truster, a trustee and the trust value that the truster gives to the trustee. In [85], Wang and Lim propose an approach to evaluate situational transaction trust in e-commerce environments, which binds a new transaction with the trust ratings of previous transactions. Since the situational trust vector includes service specific trust, service category trust, transaction amount category specific trust and price trust [84], it can deliver more objective transaction specific trust information to buyers and prevent some typical attacks.

4.6.2 Trust Evaluation in Composite Services

To satisfy the specified functionality requirement, a service may have to invoke other services forming composite Web services with complex invocations and trust dependency among services and service providers [60]. Meanwhile, given a set of various services, different compositions may lead to different service structures. In [58, 59], Medjahed et al. present some frameworks and algorithms for automatically generating composite services from specifications and rules. Although these certainly enrich the service provision, they greatly increase the computation complexity and thus make trustworthy service selection and discovery a very challenging task.

In real applications, the criteria of searching services should take into account not only functionalities but also other properties, such as QoS (quality of service) and trust. In the literature, a number of QoS-aware Web service selection mechanisms have been developed, aiming at QoS improvement in composite services [23, 90, 98]. In [98], Zeng et al. present a general and extensible model to evaluate the QoS of composite services. Based on their model, a service selection approach has been introduced using linear programming techniques to compute optimal execution plans for composite services. The work in [23] addresses the selection and composition of Web services based on functional requirements, transactional properties and QoS characteristics. In this model, services are selected in a way that satisfies user preferences, expressed as weights over QoS and transactional requirements. In [90], Xiao and Boutaba present an autonomic service provision framework for establishing QoS-assured end-to-end communication paths across domains. Their algorithms can provide QoS guarantees over domains. The above works have their merits in different aspects. However, none of them has taken parallel invocation into account, which is fundamental and one of the most common existing invocations in composite services [60, 96].

Menascé [60] adopts an exhaustive search method to measure service execution time and cost involving probabilistic, parallel, sequential and fastest-predecessor-triggered invocations. However, the algorithm complexity is exponential. Yu et al. [96] study the service selection problem with multiple QoS constraints in composite services, and propose two optimal heuristic algorithms: the combinatorial algorithm and the graph-based algorithm. The former one models the service selection as a multidimension multichoice 0-1 knapsack problem. The latter one can be taken as a multiconstraint optimal path problem. Nevertheless, none of these works addresses any aspect of trust.

As pointed in [94], in richer service environments such as SOC or e-commerce, a rating in [0, 1] is more suitable. In [92], Xu et al. propose a reputation-enhanced QoS-based Web service discovery algorithm for service matching, ranking and selection based on existing Web service technologies. Malik and Bouguettaya [52] propose a set of decentralized techniques aiming at evaluating reputation-based trust with the ratings from peers to facilitate trust-based selection and composition of Web services.

4.6.3 Subjective Trust Evaluation

Conceptually, if the trust value is in the range of [0,1], it can be taken as the subjective probability by which, one party expects that another party can perform a given action [29].

In [28], Jøsang describes a framework for combining and assessing subjective ratings from different sources based on Dempster-Shafer belief theory, which is a generalization of the Bayesian theory of subjective probability. Wang and Singh [88] set up a bijection from subjective ratings to trust values with a mathematical understanding of trust in a variety of multiagent systems. However, their models use either a binary rating (positive or negative) system or a triple rating (positive, negative or uncertain) systems that are more suitable for security-oriented or P2P file-sharing trust management systems.

Considering service invocation structures in composite services, in [38] Li and Wang propose a global trust evaluation approach, in which each rating is in the range of [0, 1]. However, this approach has not taken the subjective probability property of trust into account. In [42], Li et al. propose a Bayesian inference based subjective trust evaluation approach which aggregates the subjective ratings from clients. Nevertheless, this approach still has some drawbacks. Firstly, it assumes that the trust ratings of each service component conform to a normal distribution, which is continuous. However, trust ratings adopted in most existing rating systems (see Footnote 2)[9,10] are discrete numbers. Thus, they cannot conform to a continuous distribution. Secondly, the proposed subjective probability approach (Bayesian inference) is to evaluate the trust values of service components, which is not used in the global trust evaluation of composite services. Therefore, although service invocation structures have been taken into account, the global trust evaluation of composite services does not keep the subjective probability property of trust. As in most existing rating systems (see Footnotes 2, 9 and 10) trust ratings are discrete numbers, the numbers of

---

[9] http://www.epinions.com/

[10] http://www.youtube.com/

the occurrences of all ratings of each service component conform to a multinomial distribution [39]. Hence, in [39] Li and Wang propose a subjective trust estimation approach for service components based on Bayesian inference, which can aggregate the non-binary discrete subjective ratings given by service clients and keep the subjective probability property of trust ratings and trust results. Although the joint subjective probability approach proposed in [39] considers the trust dependency between service components caused by direct invocations, it does not take into account the composition of trust dependency, which is caused by indirect invocations in composite services. To solve this problem, in [40], on the basis of trust dependency caused by direct invocations, Li and Wang propose a SubjectivE probabiLity basEd deduCTIVE (SELECTIVE) approach to evaluate the subjective global trustworthiness of a composite service. All these processes follow subjective probability theory and keep the subjective probability property of trust in evaluations.

4.7 Trust Evaluation Taxonomy

Trust evaluation is based on the trusters' knowledge of trust, which is only in the trusters' minds. This makes the analysis process highly human-dependent and therefore prone to errors. Knowledge of trust can be abstract/general, or domain/application specific, etc. From different viewpoints, the trust evaluation approaches in Web applications (e.g., the ones presented in Sect. 4.5) can be categorized into different taxonomies as follows.

4.7.1 Trust Evaluation Technique Based Taxonomy

Similar to the taxonomy in [15, 83], we can categorize the above mentioned trust evaluation approaches in Web applications as follows according to their computation techniques. Some approaches may correlate to more than one category. Please refer to Table 4.1 for details.

- *Category 1*: In this category, to evaluate the trust value it adopts the approach of calculating the summation or weighted average of ratings, like the models in [15, 21, 85, 87, 91, 97].
  In addition, based on this additive approach, a few studies address how to compute the final trust value by considering appropriate metrics. For example,
  - later transactions are more important [97], in which the ratings from later transactions are assigned larger weights;
  - the evaluation approach should provide incentive to consistently good quality services and punish malicious service providers [87, 91].

Table 4.1 Trust evaluation approaches under trust evaluation technique based taxonomy

	Category 1	Category 2	Category 3	Category 4	Category 5
[12]				√	
[15]	√				√
[20]				√	
[21]	√				
[22]				√	
[24]				√	
[28]		√			
[39]		√			
[52]					
[77]			√		
[80]				√	
[82]				√	
[85]	√				
[87]	√				√
[91]	√				
[95]				√	
[97]	√			√	
[100]				√	

- Some other studies also consider context factors, e.g., the new transaction amount and service category [85], the rater's profile and location [15], or the relationship between the rater's group and the ratee [21].

- *Category 2*: This category addresses the subjective property of trust for trust rating aggregation, e.g., the work in [28, 39], where subjective probability theory [27] is adopted in trust evaluation.
- *Category 3*: The approaches in this category (e.g., [77]) adopt Bayesian systems, which take binary ratings as input and compute reputation scores by statistically updating beta probability density functions (PDF).
- *Category 4*: This category uses flow models (or network structures), e.g., in [12, 20, 22, 24, 80, 82, 95, 97, 100], which compute the trust of a target through some intermediate participants and the trust dependency between them.
- *Category 5*: While each of the above categories calculates a crisp value, the last category adopts fuzzy models, e.g., in [15, 87], where membership functions are used to determine the trustworthiness of targets.

4.7.2 Trust Structure Based Taxonomy

According to the general structure of trust described in Sect. 4.2, the trust evaluation approaches in Web applications (e.g., the ones presented in Sect. 4.5) can be categorized into the *first quadrant* of Fig. 4.1. This is not a big surprise since each trust evaluation approach in Web applications focuses on trust in a specific environment (e.g., e-commerce, P2P networks, service-oriented computing, multi-agent systems or social networks), and reflective and macro-social trust belongs to the first quadrant.

In contrast, the second and third quadrants focus on primary (taken-for-granted) trust, and there is no necessity to have any trust evaluation approach in these quadrants. The fourth quadrant focuses on self trust evaluation.

4.7.3 Trust Bases Based Taxonomy

According to the bases of trust proposed in Sect. 4.3, the trust evaluation approaches presented in Sect. 4.5 can be analyzed as follows to find out which base of trust is adopted in each trust evaluation approach. Some approaches may be based on more than one bases of trust. Please refer to Table 4.2 for details.

Table 4.2 Trust evaluation approaches under trust bases base taxonomy

	Dispositional	History-based	Third Parties as Conduits	Category-based	Role-based	Rule-based
[12]		√				
[14]		√				
[15]					√	
[20]			√			
[21]						√
[22]			√			
[24]			√			
[26]		√	√		√	
[28]			√			√
[30]		√				
[52]		√				
[57]		√				
[70]		√	√	√		
[75]		√				
[77]	√		√			
[80]			√			
[81]		√				
[82]			√			
[85]		√				
[86]		√			√	
[87]		√				√
[91]		√				
[95]			√			
[97]		√				
[100]		√	√			

- *Dispositional Trust* focuses on the personality of a truster, with the assumption of a relatively stable personality characteristic, like the model in [77].
- *History-based Trust* is the most widely adopted trust base in trust evaluation. For example, it has been taken into account in [12, 14, 26, 30, 52, 57, 70, 75, 81, 85–87, 91, 97, 100].
- *Third Parties as Conduits of Trust* is another widely adopted trust base to evaluate trust. For example, it has been adopted by the models in [20, 22, 24, 26, 28, 70, 77, 80, 82, 95, 100].
- *Category-based Trust* addresses the information regarding a trustee's membership in a social or organizational category, e.g., in [70].
- *Role-based Trust* uses the knowledge that a trustee occupies a particular role in the organization, e.g., the work in [15, 26, 86].
- *Rule-based Trust* specifies formal or informal rules, which can determine trust, like the models in [21, 28, 87].

4.8 Conclusions

This chapter provides a general overview of the research studies on trust and trust evaluation. Conceptually, we present the general structure of trust, the bases of trust and the concepts of trust in different disciplines. The general structure of trust presents a general cross-disciplinary analysis of trust, and provides a general picture containing all kinds of trust. The bases of trust illustrate what leads to the emergence of trust. The concepts of trust present different aspects of trust from the different viewpoints of different disciplines.

In addition, the typical trust evaluation methods are introduced in a variety of Web application areas, including e-commerce, P2P networks, multi-agent systems, recommendation systems, social networks and service-oriented computing. Finally, these trust evaluation methods in Web applications can be categorized into different taxonomies. The trust evaluation methods presented in this chapter cover a wide range of applications and are based on many different types of mechanisms, and there is no single trust evaluation method that will be suitable in all contexts and applications. This roadmap provides not only the necessary background for on-going research activities and projects, but also the solid foundations for deciding on potential future research on trust evaluation in broader contexts.

References

1. P. S. Adler. Market, hierarchy, and trust: The knowledge economy and the future of capitalism. *Organization Science*, 12(2):215–234, 2001.
2. M. Bakhtin. *Speech Genres and Other Late Essays*. University of Texas Press, 1986.
3. B. Barber. *The logic and limits of trust*. Rutgers University Press, 1983.

4. P. Bedi, H. Kaur, and S. Marwaha. Trust based recommender system for semantic web. In *IJCAI 2007*, pages 2677–2682, 2007.
5. E. Berscheid and H. T. Reis. *Attraction and Close Relationships in The Handbook of Social Psychology*. Oxford University Press, 1998.
6. S. D. Boon and J. G. Holmes. The dynamics of interpersonal trust: Resolving uncertainty in the face of risk. In R. Hinde and J. Groebel, editors, *Cooperation and Prosocial Behavior*, pages 167–182. Cambridge Univ. Press, 1991.
7. M. B. Brewer. In-group favoritism: the subtle side of intergroup discrimination. In D. M. Messick and A. E. Tenbrunsel, editors, *Codes of Conduct: Behavioral Research and Business Ethics*, pages 160–171. Russell Sage Found, 1996.
8. R. S. Burt and M. Knez. Kinds of third-party effects on trust. *Rationality and Society*, 7:255–292, 1995.
9. C. Castelfranchi and R. Falcone. Trust is much more than subjective probability: Mental components and sources of trust. In *HICSS 2000*, 2000.
10. J. Coleman. *Foundations of Social Theory*. Belknap Press of Harvard University Press, 1998.
11. R. Collins. *Sociological Insight: an Introduction to Non-obvious Sociology*. Oxford University Press, 1992.
12. W. Conner, A. Iyengar, T. A. Mikalsen, I. Rouvellou, and K. Nahrstedt. A trust management framework for service-oriented environments. In *WWW 2009*, pages 891–900, 2009.
13. D. W. Creed and R. E. Miles. Trust in organizations: a conceptual framework linking organizational forms, managerial philosophies, and the opportunity costs of controls. In R. Kramer and T. Tyler, editors, *Trust in organizations: Frontiers of Theory and Research*, pages 16–38. Sage Publications, 1996.
14. E. Damiani, S. D. C. di Vimercati, S. Paraboschi, P. Samarati, and F. Violante. A reputation-based approach for choosing reliable resources in peer-to-peer networks. In *ACM Conference on Computer and Communications Security (CCS 2002)*, pages 207–216, 2002.
15. E. Damiani, S. D. C. di Vimercati, P. Samarati, and M. Viviani. A wowa-based aggregation technique on trust values connected to metadata. *Electr. Notes Theor. Comput. Sci.*, 157(3):131–142, 2006.
16. M. Deshpande and G. Karypis. Item-based top- n recommendation algorithms. *ACM Trans. Inf. Syst.*, 22(1):143–177, 2004.
17. E. Erikson. *Identity: Youth and Crisis*. W. W. Norton & Company, 1968.
18. S. Fiske. *Social Beings: Core Motives in Social Psychology*. John Wiley and Sons Press, 2009.
19. J. Golbeck. Generating predictive movie recommendations from trust in social networks. In *iTrust 2006*, pages 93–104, 2006.
20. J. Golbeck and J. A. Hendler. Inferring binary trust relationships in web-based social networks. *ACM Trans. Internet Techn.*, 6(4):497–529, 2006.
21. N. Griffiths. Task delegation using experience-based multi-dimensional trust. In *AAMAS 2005*, pages 489–496, 2005.
22. R. V. Guha, R. Kumar, P. Raghavan, and A. Tomkins. Propagation of trust and distrust. In *WWW 2004*, pages 403–412, 2004.
23. J. E. Haddad, M. Manouvrier, G. Ramirez, and M. Rukoz. QoS-driven selection of web services for transactional composition. In *ICWS 2008*, pages 653–660, 2008.
24. C.-W. Hang, Y. Wang, and M. P. Singh. Operators for propagating trust and their evaluation in social networks. In *AAMAS 2009*, pages 1025–1032, 2009.
25. J. L. Herlocker, J. A. Konstan, A. Borchers, and J. Riedl. An algorithmic framework for performing collaborative filtering. In *SIGIR 1999*, pages 230–237, 1999.
26. T. D. Huynh, N. R. Jennings, and N. R. Shadbolt. An integrated trust and reputation model for open multi-agent systems. *Autonomous Agents and Multi-Agent Systems*, 13(2):119–154, 2006.
27. R. Jeffrey. *Subjective Probability: The Real Thing*. Cambridge University Press, April 2004.
28. A. Jøsang. Subjective evidential reasoning. In *IPMU 2002*, 2002.
29. A. Jøsang, R. Ismail, and C. Boyd. A survey of trust and reputation systems for online service provision. *Decision Support Systems*, 43(2):618–644, 2007.

30. S. D. Kamvar, M. T. Schlosser, and H. Garcia-Molina. The eigentrust algorithm for reputation management in p2p networks. In *WWW 2003*, pages 640–651, 2003.
31. D. H. Knight and N. L. Chervany. The meaning of trust. Technical Report WP9604, University of Minnesota, Management Information Systems Research Center, 1996.
32. R. M. Kramer. Trust and distrust in organizations: Emerging perspectives, enduring questions. *Annual Review of Psychology*, 50:569–598, 1999.
33. U. Kuter and J. Golbeck. Sunny: A new algorithm for trust inference in social networks using probabilistic confidence models. In *AAAI 2007*, pages 1377–1382, 2007.
34. U. Kuter and J. Golbeck. Using probabilistic confidence models for trust inference in web-based social networks. *ACM Trans. Internet Techn.*, 10(2), 2010.
35. R. J. Lewicki and B. B. Bunker. Trust in relationships: a model of trust development and decline. In B. Bunker and J. Rubin, editors, *Conflict, Cooperation, and Justice*. Jossey-Bass, 1995.
36. L. Li. *Trust Evaluation in Service-Oriented Environments*. PhD thesis, Macquarie University, 2011.
37. L. Li and Y. Wang. A trust vector approach to service-oriented applications. In *ICWS 2008*, pages 270–277, 2008.
38. L. Li and Y. Wang. Trust evaluation in composite services selection and discovery. In *IEEE SCC 2009*, pages 482–485, 2009.
39. L. Li and Y. Wang. Subjective trust inference in composite services. In *AAAI 2010*, pages 1377–1384, 2010.
40. L. Li and Y. Wang. A subjective probability based deductive approach to global trust evaluation in composite services. In *ICWS 2011*, pages 604–611, 2011.
41. L. Li and Y. Wang. The study of trust vector based trust rating aggregation in service-oriented environments. *World Wide Web*, In press, 2012.
42. L. Li, Y. Wang, and E.-P. Lim. Trust-oriented composite service selection and discovery. In *ICSOC/ServiceWave 2009*, pages 50–67, 2009.
43. L. Li, Y. Wang, and V. Varadharajan. Fuzzy regression based trust prediction in service-oriented applications. In *ATC 2009*, pages 221–235, 2009.
44. M. Li, X. Sun, H. Wang, Y. Zhang, and J. Zhang. Privacy-aware access control with trust management in web service. *World Wide Web*, 14(4):407–430, 2011.
45. G. Liu, Y. Wang, and L. Li. Trust management in three generations of web-based social networks. In *CPSC 2009*, pages 446–451, 2009.
46. G. Liu, Y. Wang, and M. A. Orgun. Optimal social trust path selection in complex social networks. In *AAAI 2010*, pages 1391–1398, 2010.
47. G. Liu, Y. Wang, and M. A. Orgun. Quality of trust for social trust path selection in complex social networks. In *AAMAS 2010*, pages 1575–1576, 2010.
48. G. Liu, Y. Wang, M. A. Orgun, and E.-P. Lim. A heuristic algorithm for trust-oriented service provider selection in complex social networks. In *IEEE SCC 2010*, pages 130–137, 2010.
49. H. Ma, H. Yang, M. R. Lyu, and I. King. Sorec: social recommendation using probabilistic matrix factorization. In *CIKM 2008*, pages 931–940, 2008.
50. H. Ma, T. C. Zhou, M. R. Lyu, and I. King. Improving recommender systems by incorporating social contextual information. *ACM Trans. Inf. Syst.*, 29(2):9, 2011.
51. Z. Malik and A. Bouguettaya. Rater credibility assessment in web services interactions. *World Wide Web*, 12(1):3–25, 2009.
52. Z. Malik and A. Bouguettaya. RATEWeb: Reputation assessment for trust establishment among web services. *VLDB J.*, 18(4):885–911, 2009.
53. J. G. March. *Primer on Decision Making: How Decisions Happen*. Free Press, 1994.
54. I. Marková. *Trust and Democratic Transition in Post-Communist Europe*. Oxford University Press, 2004.
55. I. Marková, A. Gillespie, and J. Valsiner. Trust and Distrust: *Sociocultural Perspectives*. Information Age Publishing, 2008.
56. S. Marsh. *Formalising Trust as a Computational Concept*. University of Stirling, 1994.
57. S. Marti and H. Garcia-Molina. Limited reputation sharing in p2p systems. In *ACM EC 2004*, pages 91–101, 2004.

58. B. Medjahed and A. Bouguettaya. A multilevel composability model for semantic web services. *IEEE Trans. Knowl. Data Eng.*, 17(7):954–968, 2005.
59. B. Medjahed, A. Bouguettaya, and A. K. Elmagarmid. Composing web services on the semantic web. *VLDB J.*, 12(4):333–351, 2003.
60. D. A. Menascé. Composing web services: A QoS view. *IEEE Internet Computing*, 8(6):88–90, 2004.
61. S. Milgram. The small world problem. *Psychology Today*, 2(30), 1967.
62. R. Miller, D. Perlman, and S. Brehm. *Intimate Relationships*. McGraw-Hill College Press, 2007.
63. A. Mislove, M. Marcon, P. K. Gummadi, P. Druschel, and B. Bhattacharjee. Measurement and analysis of online social networks. In *Internet Measurement Conference 2007*, pages 29–42, 2007.
64. B. Misztal. *Trust in Modern Societies: The Search for the Bases of Social Order*. Polity Press, 1996.
65. R. J. Mooney and L. Roy. Content-based book recommending using learning for text categorization. In *ACM DL 2000*, pages 195–204, 2000.
66. L. Mui. *Computational Models of Trust and Reputation: Agents, Evolutionary Games, and Social Networks*. PhD thesis, Massachusetts Institute of Technology, Dec 2002.
67. M. P. Papazoglou, P. Traverso, S. Dustdar, and F. Leymann. Service-oriented computing: a research roadmap. *Int. J. Cooperative Inf. Syst.*, 17(2):223–255, 2008.
68. I. Ray and S. Chakraborty. A vector model of trust for developing trustworthy systems. In *9th European Symposium on Research Computer*, Security, pages 260–275, 2004.
69. J. B. Rotter. Interpersonal trust, trustworthiness, and gullibility. *American Psychologist*, 35(1):1–7, 1980.
70. J. Sabater and C. Sierra. REGRET: reputation in gregarious societies. In *Agents 2001*, pages 194–195, 2001.
71. B. M. Sarwar, G. Karypis, J. A. Konstan, and J. Riedl. Item-based collaborative filtering recommendation algorithms. In *WWW 2001*, pages 285–295, 2001.
72. A. B. Seligman. *The Problem of Trust*. Princeton University Press, 2000.
73. G. Simmel. *The Sociology of Georg Simmel*. The, Free Press, 1950.
74. R. R. Sinha and K. Swearingen. Comparing recommendations made by online systems and friends. In *DELOS Workshop 2001: Personalisation and Recommender Systems in Digital Libraries*, 2001.
75. S. Song, K. Hwang, R. Zhou, and Y.-K. Kwok. Trusted p2p transactions with fuzzy reputation aggregation. *IEEE Internet Computing*, 9(6):24–34, 2005.
76. T. Strang, C. Linnhoff-Popien, and K. Frank. Cool: A context ontology language to enable contextual interoperability. In *IFIP WG6.1 International Conference on Distributed Applications and Interoperable Systems 2003*, pages 236–247, 2003.
77. W. T. L. Teacy, J. Patel, N. R. Jennings, and M. Luck. Travos: Trust and reputation in the context of inaccurate information sources. *Autonomous Agents and Multi-Agent Systems*, 12(2):183–198, 2006.
78. S. Toivonen, G. Lenzini, and I. Uusitalo. Context-aware trust evaluation functions for dynamic reconfigurable systems. In *Proceedings of the WWW'06 Workshop on Models of Trust for the Web (MTW'06)*, 2006.
79. B. Uzzi. Social structure and competition in interfirm networks: The paradox of embeddedness. *Administrative Science Quarterly*, 42(1):35–67, 1997.
80. P. Victor, C. Cornelis, M. D. Cock, and P. P. da Silva. Gradual trust and distrust in recommender systems. *Fuzzy Sets and Systems*, 160(10):1367–1382, 2009.
81. L.-H. Vu, M. Hauswirth, and K. Aberer. QoS-based service selection and ranking with trust and reputation management. In *CoopIS 2005*, pages 466–483, 2005.
82. F. E. Walter, S. Battiston, and F. Schweitzer. A model of a trust-based recommendation system on a social network. *Autonomous Agents and Multi-Agent Systems*, 16(1):57–74, 2008.
83. Y. Wang and L. Li. Two-dimensional trust rating aggregations in service-oriented applications. *IEEE T. Services Computing*, 4(4):257–271, 2011.

84. Y. Wang, L. Li, and E.-P. Lim. Price trust evaluation in e-service oriented applications. In *CEC/EEE 2008*, pages 165–172, 2008.
85. Y. Wang and E.-P. Lim. The evaluation of situational transaction trust in e-service environments. In *ICEBE 2008*, pages 265–272, 2008.
86. Y. Wang and K.-J. Lin. Reputation-oriented trustworthy computing in e-commerce environments. *IEEE Internet Computing*, 12(4):55–59, 2008.
87. Y. Wang, K.-J. Lin, D. S. Wong, and V. Varadharajan. Trust management towards service-oriented applications. *Service Oriented Computing and Applications*, 3(2):129–146, 2009.
88. Y. Wang and M. P. Singh. Formal trust model for multiagent systems. In *International Joint Conference on Artificial Intelligence (IJCAI 2007)*, pages 1551–1556, 2007.
89. Y. Wang and V. Varadharajan. Role-based recommendation and trust evaluation. In *CEC/EEE 2007*, pages 278–288, 2007.
90. J. Xiao and R. Boutaba. QoS-aware service composition and adaptation in autonomic communication. *IEEE Journal on Selected Areas in Communications*, 23(12):2344–2360, 2005.
91. L. Xiong and L. Liu. Peer Trust: Supporting reputation-based trust for peer-to-peer electronic communities. *IEEE Trans. Knowl. Data Eng.*, 16(7):843–857, 2004.
92. Z. Xu, P. Martin, W. Powley, and F. Zulkernine. Reputation-enhanced QoS-based web services discovery. In *ICWS 2007*, pages 249–256, 2007.
93. I. Yaniv. Receiving other peoples' advice: Influence and benefit. *J. Artif. Intell. Res. (JAIR)*, 93(1).
94. B. Yu, M. P. Singh, and K. Sycara. Developing trust in large-scale peer-to-peer systems. *IEEE Symposium on Multi-Agent Security and Survivability*, pages 1–10, 2004.
95. H. Yu, M. Kaminsky, P. B. Gibbons, and A. D. Flaxman. Sybilguard: defending against sybil attacks via social networks. *IEEE/ACM Trans. Netw.*, 16(3):576–589, 2008.
96. T. Yu, Y. Zhang, and K.-J. Lin. Efficient algorithms for web services selection with end-to-end Qos constraints. *TWEB*, 1(1), 2007.
97. G. Zacharia and P. Maes. Trust management through reputation mechanisms. *Applied Artificial Intelligence*, 14(9):881–907, 2000.
98. L. Zeng, B. Benatallah, M. Dumas, J. Kalagnanam, and Q. Z. Sheng. Quality driven web services composition. In *WWW 2003*, pages 411–421, 2003.
99. H. Zhao and X. Li. Vectortrust: Trust vector aggregation scheme for trust management in peer-to-peer networks. In *18th International Conference on Computer Communications and Networks*, pages 1–6, 2009.
100. R. Zhou and K. Hwang. Powertrust: A robust and scalable reputation system for trusted peer-to-peer computing. *IEEE Trans. Parallel Distrib. Syst.*, 18(4):460–473, 2007.

Chapter 5
Web Service-Based Trust Management in Cloud Environments

Talal H. Noor and Quan Z. Sheng

Abstract Trust is one of the most concerned obstacles for the adoption and growth of cloud computing. Although several solutions have been proposed recently in managing trust feedbacks in cloud environments, how to determine the credibility of trust feedbacks is mostly neglected. In addition, guaranteeing the availability of the trust management service is a difficult problem due to the unpredictable number of cloud service consumers and the highly dynamic nature of cloud environments. In this chapter, we propose a framework that uses Web services to improve ways on trust management in cloud environments. In particular, we introduce an adaptive credibility model that distinguishes between credible and malicious feedbacks by considering the cloud service consumers' capability and majority consensus of their feedbacks. We also present a replication determination model that dynamically decides the optimal replica number of the trust management service so that the trust management service can be always maintained at a desired availability level. The approaches have been validated by a prototype system and experimental results.

5.1 Introduction

Over the past few years, cloud computing is gaining a considerable momentum as a new computing paradigm for providing flexible services, platforms, and infrastructures on demand [3, 6]. Government agencies, businesses and researchers can benefit from the adoption of cloud services. For instance, it only took 24 h, at the cost of

---

T. H. Noor (✉) · Q. Z. Sheng
School of Computer Science, The University of Adelaide, Adelaide, SA 5005, Australia
e-mail: talal@cs.adelaide.edu.au

Q. Z. Sheng
e-mail: qsheng@cs.adelaide.edu.au

A. Bouguettaya et al. (eds.), *Advanced Web Services*,
DOI: 10.1007/978-1-4614-7535-4_5,

merely $240, for the New York Times to archive its 11 million articles (1851–1980) using Amazon Web Services (AWS[1]).

Given the quick adoption of cloud computing in the industry, there is a significant challenge in managing trust among cloud service providers and cloud service consumers. Indeed, trust is one of the top obstacles for the adoption and growth of cloud computing [3, 6, 17]. Recently, a considerable amount of research works have recognized the significance of trust management and proposed several solutions to assess and manage trust based on trust feedbacks collected from participants [7, 10, 17, 35]. However, one particular problem has been mostly neglected: to what extent can these trust feedbacks be credible. On the one hand, it is not unusual that a trust management system will experience malicious behaviors from its users. On the other hand, the quality of the trust feedbacks differs from one person to another, depending on how experienced she is. This chapter focuses on improving ways on the trust management in cloud environments. In particular, we distinguish the following key issues of the trust management in cloud environments:

- **Results Accuracy.** Determining the credibility of trust feedbacks is a significant challenge due to the dynamic interactions between cloud service consumers and cloud service providers. It is difficult to know how experienced a cloud service consumer is and from whom malicious trust feedbacks are expected. Indeed, the trust management protection still requires extensive probabilistic computations [18, 37] and trust participants' collaboration by manually rating trust feedbacks [22].
- **Availability.** In a cloud environment, guaranteeing the availability of the trust management service is a difficult problem due to the unpredictable number of cloud service consumers and the highly dynamic nature of cloud environments. Consequently, approaches that requires understanding of the trust participants' interests and capabilities through similarity measurements [34] are inappropriate in the cloud environment. Trust management systems should be adaptive and highly scalable.
- **Assessment and Storage.** The trust assessment of a service in existing techniques is usually centralized, whereas the trust feedbacks come from distributed trust parties. Trust models that follow a centralized architecture are more prone to several problems including scalability, availability, and security (e.g., Denial of Service (Dos) attack) problems [16]. Given the open and distributed nature of cloud environments we believe that a centralized solution is not suitable for trust feedback assessment and storage.

In this chapter, we overview the design and implementation of the proposed framework. This framework helps distinguish between the credible trust feedbacks and the malicious trust feedbacks through a credibility model. It also guarantees high availability of the trust management service. In a nutshell, the salient features of the proposed framework are:

- **Feedback Credibility.** We develop a credibility model that not only distinguishes between trust feedbacks from experienced cloud service consumers and feedbacks

[1] http://open.blogs.nytimes.com/2007/11/01/self-service-prorated-super-computing-fun/

from amateur cloud service consumers, but also considers the *majority consensus* of feedbacks, i.e., how close a trust feedback is to the majority trust feedbacks.

- **Replication Determination.** High availability is an important requirement to the trust management service. We propose to spread replicas of the trust management service and develop a *replication determination model* that dynamically determines the optimal number of the trust management service replicas, which share the trust management workload, thereby always maintaining the trust management service at a desired availability level.
- **Distributed Assessment and Storage.** To avoid the drawbacks of centralized architectures, our trust management service allows trust feedback assessment and storage to be managed distributively. Each trust management service replica is responsible for trust feedbacks given to a set of cloud services.

The remainder of the chapter is organized as follows. In Sect. 5.2, we present some background of cloud services and their deployment models. The design of the framework is briefly presented in Sect. 5.3. Section 5.4 details the trust management service, including distributed trust feedback collection and assessment, as well as the replication determination model for high availability of the trust management service. Section 5.5 describes the credibility model. Section 5.6 reports the implementation and several experimental evaluations. Finally, Sect. 5.7 overviews the related work and Sect. 5.8 provides some concluding remarks.

5.2 Background

Cloud services are established based on five essential characteristics [26], namely, (i) *on-demand self-service* where cloud service consumers are able to automatically provision computing resources without the need for human interaction with each cloud service provider, (ii) *broad network access* where cloud service consumers can access available computing resources over the network, (iii) *resource pooling* where computing resources are pooled to serve multiple cloud service consumers based on a multi-tenant model where physical and virtual computing resources are dynamically reassigned on-demand, (iv) *rapid elasticity* where computing resources are elastically provisioned to scale rapidly based on the cloud service consumers need, and (v) *measured service* where computing resources usage is monitored, metered (i.e., using pay as you go mechanism), controlled and reported to provide transparency for both cloud service providers and consumers.

5.2.1 Cloud Service Models

Cloud services have three different models, including *Infrastructure as a Service* (IaaS), *Platform as a Service* (PaaS), and *Software as a Service* (SaaS) based on different Service Level Agreements (SLAs) between a cloud service provider and a

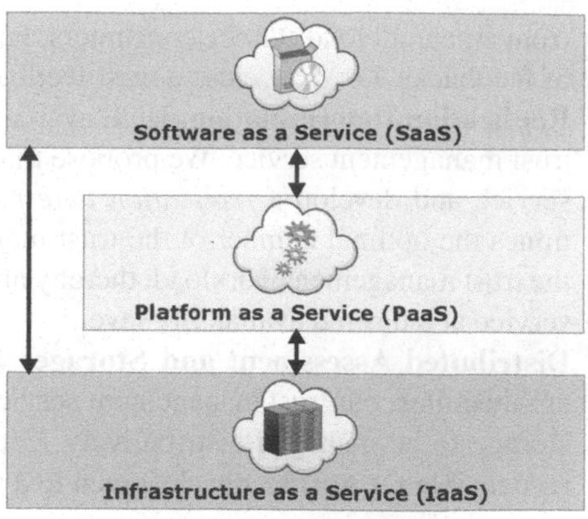

Fig. 5.1 Cloud service models

cloud service consumer [5, 9, 26]. Figure 5.1 depicts the structured layers of cloud services:

- *Infrastructure as a Service* (*IaaS*). This model represents the foundation part of the cloud environment where a cloud service consumer can rent the storage, the processing and the communication through virtual machines provided by a cloud service provider (e.g., Amazon's Elastic Compute Cloud (EC2) [1] and Simple Storage Service (S3) [2]). In this model, the cloud service provider controls and manages the underlying cloud environment, whereas the cloud service consumer has control over his/her virtual machine which includes the storage, the processing and can even select some network components for communication.
- *Platform as a Service* (*PaaS*). This model represents the integration part of the cloud environment and resides above the IaaS layer to support system integration and virtualization middleware. The PaaS allows a cloud service consumer to develop his/her own software where the cloud service provider provisions the software development tools and programming languages (e.g., Google App [13]). In this model, the cloud service consumer has no control over the underlying cloud infrastructure (e.g., storage network, operating systems, etc.) but has control over the deployed applications.
- *Software as a Service* (*SaaS*). This model represents the application part of the cloud environment and resides above the PaaS layer to support remote accessibility where cloud service consumers can remotely access their data which is stored in the underlying cloud infrastructure using applications provided by the cloud service provider (e.g., Google Docs [14], Windows Live Mesh [27]). Similarly, in this model, the cloud service consumer has no control over the underlying cloud infrastructure (e.g., storage network, operating systems, etc.) but has control over his/her data.

5.2.2 Cloud Service Deployment Models

Based on the Service Level Agreement (SLA), all cloud service models (i.e., IaaS, PaaS, SaaS) can be provisioned through four different cloud service deployment models, namely *Private*, *Community*, *Public*, and *Hybrid* [26, 36] depending on the cloud service consumer's needs. Figure 5.2 depicts how cloud services are arranged to support these four cloud services deployment models and shows different interactions between cloud service providers and consumers. The interactions include business-to-business (B2B) and business-to-client (B2C).

- *Private Cloud.* In this deployment model, computing resources are provisioned for a particular organization (e.g., a business organization as shown in Fig. 5.2a), which involves several consumers (e.g., several business units). Essentially, interactions in this deployment model are considered as B2B interactions where the computing

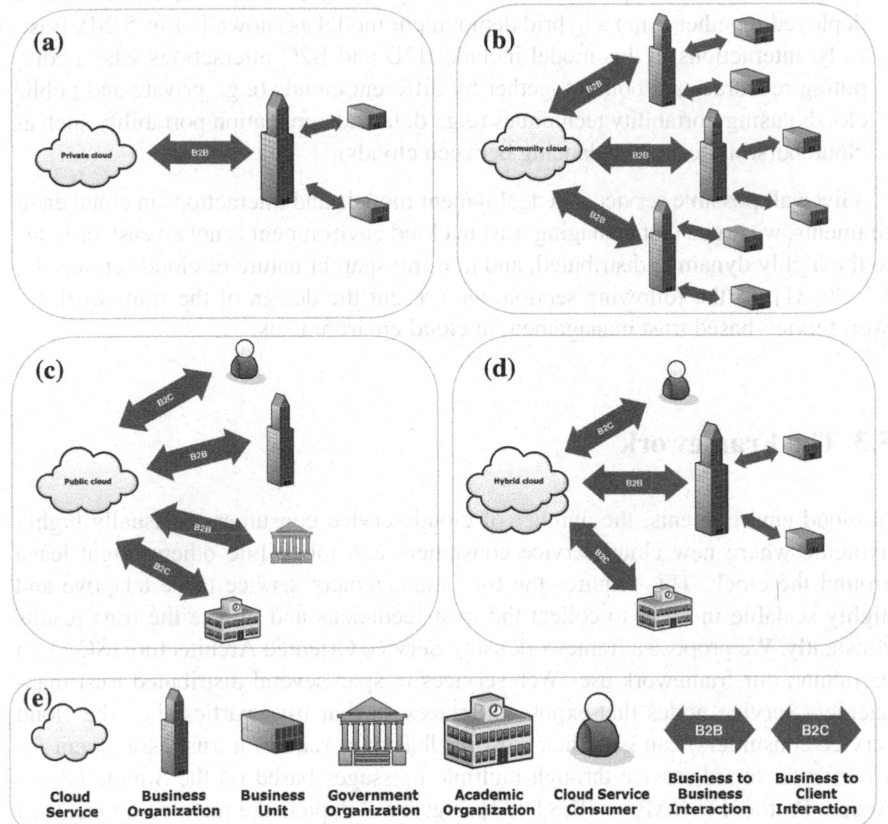

Fig. 5.2 Cloud service deployment models. **a** Private cloud, **b** community cloud, **c** public cloud, **d** hybrid cloud

resources can be owned, governed, and operated by the same organization, a third party, or both.

- *Community Cloud.* In this deployment model, computing resources are provisioned for a community of organizations, as shown in Fig. 5.2b, to achieve a certain goal (e.g., high performance, security requirements, or reduced costs). Basically, interactions in this model are considered as B2B interactions where the computing resources can be owned, governed, and operated by the community (i.e., one or several organizations in the community), a third party, or both.
- *Public Cloud.* In this deployment model, computing resources are provisioned for the public (e.g., an individual cloud service consumer, academic, government, business organizations or a combination of these cloud service consumer types as shown in Fig. 5.2c). Essentially, interactions in this model are considered as B2C where the computing resources can be owned, governed, and operated by an academic, government, business organization, or a combination of them.
- *Hybrid Cloud.* In this deployment model, computing resources are provisioned using two or more deployment models (e.g., private and public clouds can be deployed together using a hybrid deployment model as shown in Fig. 5.2d). Basically, interactions in this model include B2B and B2C interactions where computing resources are bound together by different clouds (e.g., private and public clouds) using portability techniques (e.g., data and application portability such as cloud bursting for load balancing between clouds).

Given all possible service and deployment models and interactions in cloud environments, we argue that managing trust in cloud environment is not an easy task due to the highly dynamic, distributed, and non-transparent nature of cloud services [3, 17, 29–31]. In the following section, we present the design of the framework for Web service-based trust management in cloud environments.

5.3 The Framework

In cloud environments, the number of cloud service consumers is usually highly dynamic where new cloud service consumers can join while others might leave around the clock. This requires the trust management service to be adaptive and highly scalable in order to collect the trust feedbacks and update the trust results constantly. We propose a framework using Service Oriented Architecture (SOA). In particular, our framework uses Web services to span several distributed trust management service nodes that expose interfaces so that trust parties (i.e., the cloud service consumers) can give their trust feedbacks or request a trust assessment for a particular cloud service through multiple messages based on the Simple Object Access Protocol (SOAP) or REST [33]. Figure 5.3 depicts the main components of the framework, which consists of three different layers, namely the *Provider Layer*, the *Trust Management Service Layer*, and the *Consumer Layer*.

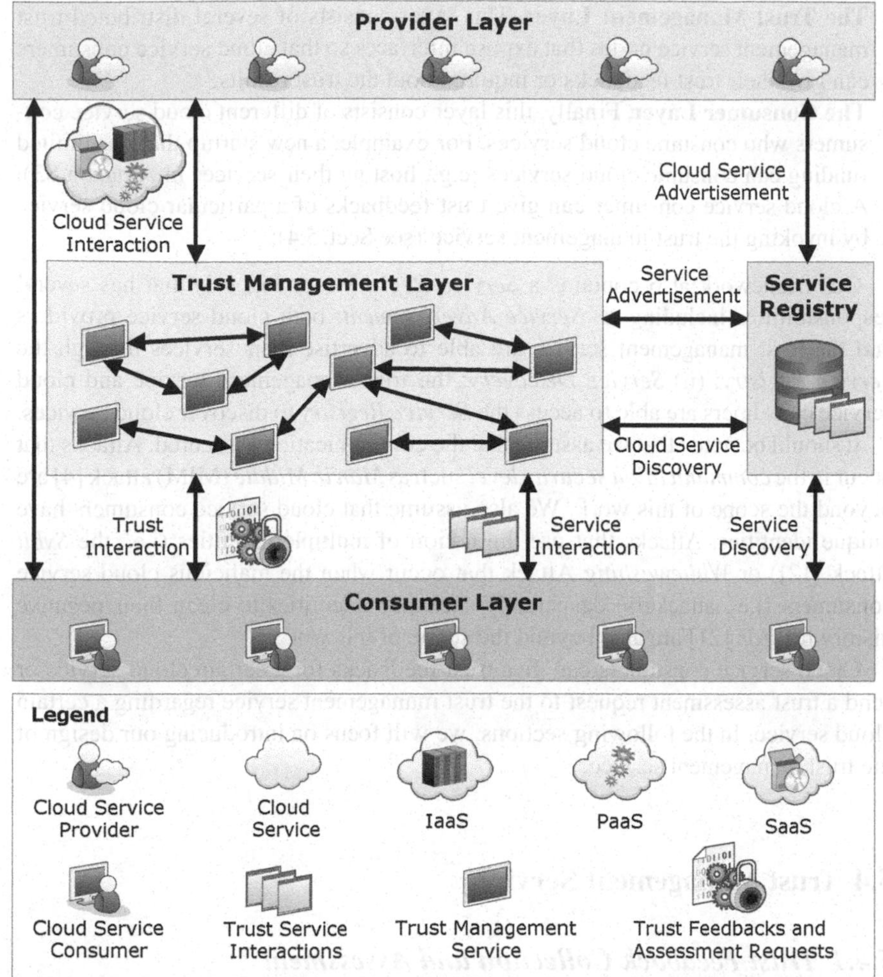

Fig. 5.3 Architecture of the WS-based trust management in cloud environments framework

- **The Providers Layer.** This layer consists of different cloud service providers who are providing cloud services. The minimum indicative feature that every cloud service provider should have is to provide the infrastructure as a service (i.e., the cloud service provider should have a data center that provides the storage, the process, and the communication). In other words, the cloud service providers can provide either IaaS (Infrastructure as a Service) only, IaaS and PaaS (Platform as a Service), IaaS and SaaS (Software as a Service), or all of the cloud services models.

- **The Trust Management Layer.** This layer consists of several distributed trust management service nodes that expose interfaces so that cloud service consumers can give their trust feedbacks or inquire about the trust results.
- **The Consumer Layer.** Finally, this layer consists of different cloud service consumers who consume cloud services. For example, a new startup that has limited funding can consume cloud services (e.g., hosting their services in Amazon S3). A cloud service consumer can give trust feedbacks of a particular cloud service by invoking the trust management service (see Sect. 5.4).

Our framework also contains a *Service Registry* (see Fig. 5.3) that has several responsibilities including (i) *Service Advertisement*: both cloud service providers and the trust management service are able to advertise their services through the *Service Registry*; (ii) *Service Discovery*: the trust management service and cloud service consumers are able to access the *Service Registry* to discover cloud services.

It should be noted that we assume that the communication is secured. Attacks that occur in the *communication security level* such as *Man in Middle* (MIM) attack [4] are beyond the scope of this work. We also assume that cloud service consumers have unique identities. Attacks that use the notion of multiple identities (i.e., the *Sybil* attack [12]) or *Whitewashing* Attack that occur when the malicious cloud service consumers (i.e., attackers) desperately seek new identities to clean their negative history records [21] are also beyond the scope of this work.

Cloud service consumers can give trust feedbacks for a certain cloud service or send a trust assessment request to the trust management service regarding a certain cloud service. In the following sections, we will focus on introducing our design of the trust management service.

5.4 Trust Management Service

5.4.1 Trust Feedback Collection and Assessment

In our framework, the cloud service trust behavior is represented by a collection of invocation history records denoted as H. Each cloud service consumer c hold her point of view regarding the trustworthiness of a specific cloud service s in the invocation history record which is managed by the assigned trust management service. Each invocation history record is represented in a tuple that consists of the cloud service consumer primary identity C, the cloud service identity S, a set of trust feedbacks F and the aggregated trust feedbacks weighted by the credibility F_c (i.e., $H = (C, S, F, F_c)$). Each feedback in F is represented in numerical form in which the range of the normalized feedback is [0, 1], where 0, +1, and 0.5 means negative feedback, positive feedback, and neutral respectively.

Whenever a cloud service consumer inquires the trust management service regarding the trustworthiness of a certain cloud service s, the trust result, denoted as $Tr(s)$, is calculated using:

$$Tr(s) = \frac{\sum_{l=1}^{|V(s)|} F_c(l, s)}{|V(s)|} \tag{5.1}$$

where $V(s)$ is all of the feedbacks given to the cloud service s and $|V(s)|$ represents the length of the $V(s)$ (i.e., the total number of feedbacks given to the cloud service s). $F_c(l, s)$ are the trust feedbacks from the lth cloud service consumer weighted by the credibility.

The trust management service distinguishes between credible trust feedbacks and malicious trust feedbacks through assigning the *cloud service consumer's Experience* aggregated weights $Exp(l)$ to the trust feedbacks $F(l, s)$ as shown in Eq. 5.2, where the result $F_c(l, s)$ is held in the invocation history record h and updated in the assigned trust management service. The details on how to calculate $Exp(l)$ is described in Sect. 5.5.

$$F_c(l, s) = F(l, s) * Exp(l) \tag{5.2}$$

5.4.2 Availability of Trust Management Service

Guaranteeing the availability of the trust management service is a significant challenge due to the unpredictable number of invocation requests the service has to handle at a time, as well as the dynamic nature of the cloud environments. An emerging trend for solving the high-availability issue is centered on replication. In our approach, we propose to spread trust management service replicas over various clouds and dynamically direct requests to appropriate clouds (e.g., with lower workload), so that its desired availability level can be always maintained.

However, there is clearly a trade-off between high availability and replication cost. On the one hand, more clouds hosting the trust management service means better availability. On the other hand, more replicas residing at various clouds means higher overhead (e.g., cost and resource consumption such as bandwidth and storage space). Thus, it is essential to develop a mechanism that helps determine the optimal number of the trust management service replicas in order to meet the trust management service's availability requirement.

We propose a replication determination model to allow the trust management service to know how many replicas are required to achieve a certain level of availability. Given the trust management service s_{tms} failure probability denoted p that ranges from 0 to 1, the total number of s_{tms} replicas denoted r, and the availability threshold denoted e_a that also ranges from 0 to 1. The desired goal of the replication is to ensure that at least one replica of the trust management service is available, represented in the following formula:

$$e_a(s_{tms}) < 1 - p^{r(s_{tms})} \tag{5.3}$$

where $p^{r(s_{tms})}$ represents the probability that all trust management service replicas are failed, and $1 - p^{r(s_{tms})}$ represents the opposite (i.e., the probability of at least

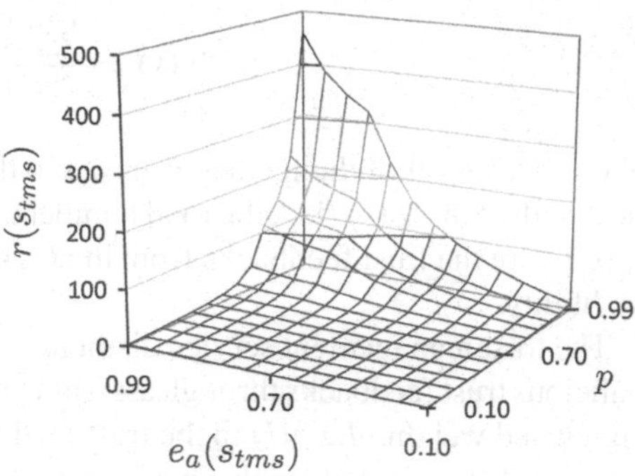

Fig. 5.4 Trust management service replication number determination

one trust management replica is available). As a result, the optimal number of trust management service replicas can be calculated as follows:

$$r(s_{tms}) > log_p(1 - e_a(s_{tms})) \tag{5.4}$$

For example, if the availability threshold $e_a(s_{tms}) = 0.99$ and the failure probability of trust management service $p = 0.2$ (low), $r(s_{tms}) > 2.86$, meaning that at least 3 trust management service replicas are needed. Similarly, if $e_a(s_{tms}) = 0.99$ and the failure probability of the trust management service $p = 0.8$ (high), $r(s_{tms}) > 20.64$ which means at least 21 replicas are required. Figure 5.4 depicts the relationship between the main components of the replication determination model. It can be clearly seen that the relationship between p and $r(s_{tms})$ is a direct or positive relationship (i.e., any change in p is associated with a change in $r(s_{tms})$ in the same direction). The relationship between $e_a(s_{tms})$ and $r(s_{tms})$ is also a direct or positive relation. However, it should be noted that p has a larger influence on $r(s_{tms})$ than $e_a(s_{tms})$.

Whenever a cloud service consumer needs to send the invocation history record or a trust assessment request of a certain cloud service, $h(c, s)$ can be sent to a particular trust management service decided by using a consistent hash function (e.g., sha-256). Unlike previous work such as in [10] where consistent hashing technique is used to map all of the invocation history records for a certain client to a particular trust

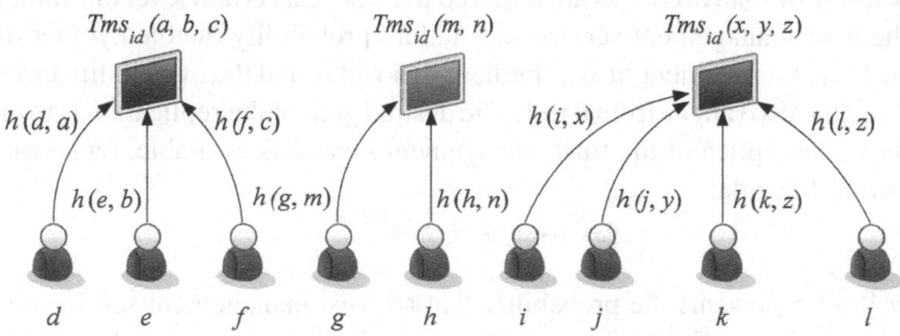

Fig. 5.5 Trust management service replicas identification example

management service instance (e.g., all trust feedback given to a certain cloud service in our case), in our framework each trust management service replica is responsible for trust feedbacks given to a set of cloud services where trust feedbacks are handled as follows:

$$Tms_{id}(s) = \left(\sum_{i=1}^{|hash(s)|} byte_i \left(hash(s)\right) \right) mod \ r(s_{tms}) \tag{5.5}$$

where the first part of the equation represents the sum of each byte of the hashed cloud service identity $hash(s)$. The second part of the equation represents the optimal number of the trust management service replicas $r(s_{tms})$. This insures that the chosen trust management service replica is within the optimal number range.

Figure 5.5 depicts an example of the trust management service nodes' identification where many cloud service consumers (d to l) have interacted with cloud services a, b, c, m, n, x, y and z. All aggregated invocation history records H for interactions with cloud services a, b, and c are sent to the first trust management service replica (i.e., the trust management service that holds the identifier $Tms_{id}(a, b, c)$). Similarly, all H for interactions with other cloud services (m to z) are sent to trust management service replicas that hold the identifier $Tms_{id}(m, n)$ and $Tms_{id}(x, y, z)$ respectively. We can see that each trust management service replica is holding all of the invocation history records H for interactions with a set of cloud services.

5.5 Credibility Model

Sine the trust behavior of a cloud service in our framework is represented by a collection of invocation history records that contain cloud service consumers trust feedbacks, there is a considerable possibility that the trust management service receives *inaccurate* or even *malicious* trust feedbacks from amateur cloud service consumers (e.g., who lack experience) or vicious cloud service consumers (e.g., who submit lots of negative feedbacks in a short period in order to disadvantage a particular cloud service). To overcome these issues, we propose a *credibility model*, which is centered on the *cloud service consumer's experience*.

In our model, a cloud service consumer with considerable experience of giving trust feedbacks can gain a credibility as an *expert*. To be able to differentiate between expert cloud service consumers and amateur cloud service consumers, we further consider several factors including the *cloud service consumer's Capability* and the *Majority Consensus*.

5.5.1 Cloud Service Consumer's Capability

It is a common sense that older people are likely to be more experienced in judging things than younger people [32]. However, this is only true if the elder people have experienced considerable number of judging practices. As a result, we believe that "elder" cloud service consumers who have many judging practices are likely to be more experienced and capable than "younger" cloud service consumers with little experience. A cloud service consumer's capability, denoted as B, is measured as follows:

$$B(c) = \begin{cases} 1 + \frac{|Vc(c)|}{Ag(c)} & if \ \ |Vc(c)| \leq Ag(c) \\ 2 & otherwise \end{cases} \tag{5.6}$$

where $Vc(c)$ represents all of the feedbacks given by the cloud service consumer c and $|Vc(c)|$ represents the length of $Vc(c)$ (i.e., the total number of feedbacks given by the cloud service consumer c). $Ag(c)$ denotes the virtual *Age* of a certain cloud service consumer, measured in days since the registration in the trust management service. The idea behind adding the number 1 to this ratio is to increase the value of a cloud service consumer experience based on the capability result. In other words, we use $B(c)$ as a *reward* factor. The higher the value of $B(c)$ is, the more experienced a cloud service consumer is. It should be noted that even if a malicious cloud service consumer attempts to manipulate the capability result by giving numerous trust feedbacks in a short period of time, the capability result will not exceed 2.

5.5.2 Majority Consensus

It is well-known that the majority of people usually agree with experts' judgments about what is good [8]. Similarly, we believe that the majority of cloud service consumers agree with *Expert cloud service consumers'* judgments. In other words, any cloud service consumer whose trust feedback is close to the majority trust feedbacks is considered an *Expert Cloud Consumer*, *Amateur cloud service consumers* otherwise. In order to measure how close the cloud service consumer's trust feedbacks to the majority trust feedbacks (i.e., the *Majority Consensus*, $J(c)$), we use the standard deviation (i.e., the root-mean-square) which is calculated as follows:

$$J(c) = 1 - \sqrt{\frac{\sum_{h \in Vc(c)} \left(\sum_{k=1}^{|Vc(c,k)|} \left(\frac{F(c,k)}{|Vc(c,k)|} - \left(\frac{\sum_{l \neq c, l=1}^{|Vc(l,k)|} F(l,k)}{|V(k)| - |Vc(c,k)|} \right) \right) \right)^2}{|Vc(c)|}} \tag{5.7}$$

where the first part of the numerator represents the mean of the cloud service consumer c's trust feedbacks $F(c,k)$ for the kth cloud service. The second part of the numerator represents the mean of the majority trust feedbacks given by other cloud service consumers denoted $F(l,k)$ (i.e., the lth cloud service consumer trust feedbacks, except the cloud service consumer c's trust feedbacks) to the kth cloud service. This procedure is done for all cloud services to which cloud service consumer c give trust feedbacks (i.e., $Vc(c)$).

Table 5.1 Notation and meanings

Notation	Meaning	Notation	Meaning
$J(c)$	The majority consensus	$F(c, k)$	The cloud service consumer c's trust feedback instance for the kth cloud service
$Vc(c, k)$	All trust feedbacks given by the cloud service consumer c for the kth cloud service	$F(l, k)$	The majority trust feedbacks given by other cloud service consumers for the kth cloud service
$V(k)$	All trust feedbacks given for the kth cloud service	$Vc(c, k)$	All trust feedbacks given by the cloud service consumer c for the kth cloud service
$B(c)$	The cloud service consumer's capability	$Vc(c)$	All cloud services to which cloud service consumer c give trust feedbacks to
$Ag(c)$	The virtual *Age* of a certain cloud service consumer	$Exp(c)$	Cloud service consumer's experience

Based on the specified cloud service consumer's experience factors (i.e., cloud service consumer's capability and majority consensus), the trust management service distinguishes between the *Expert cloud service consumers* and the *Amateur cloud service consumers* through assigning the *cloud service consumer's Experience* aggregated weights $Exp(c)$ to each of the cloud service consumers trust feedbacks as shown in Eq. 5.2. The *cloud service consumer's Experience* aggregated weights $Exp(c)$ is calculated as follows:

$$Exp(c) = \frac{\beta * B(c) + \mu * J(c)}{\lambda} \tag{5.8}$$

where β and $B(c)$ denote the *cloud service consumer's Capability* factor's normalized weight (i.e., parameter) and the factor's value respectively. The second part of the equation represents the *Majority Consensus* factor where μ denotes the factor's normalized weight and $J(c)$ denotes the factor's value. λ represents the number of factors used to calculate $Exp(c)$. For example, if we only consider cloud service consumer's capability, $\lambda = 1$; if we consider both cloud service consumer's capability and majority consensus, $\lambda = 2$ (Table 5.1).

We use the majority consensus as a *penalty* factor. The lower the value of $J(c)$ is, the lower the experience of the cloud service consumer c is. It should be worth mentioning that this is not the case for the cloud service consumer capability factor $B(c)$, which is used as a reward factor.

5.6 Implementation and Experimental Evaluation

In this section, we report the implementation and preliminary experimental results in validating the proposed approach. Our implementation and experiments were developed based on the NetLogo platform [28], which was used to simulate the cloud environments. We particularly focused on validating and studying the performance of the proposed credibility model (see Sect. 5.5).

Since it is hard to find some publicly available real-life trust data sets, in our experiments, we used Epinions[2] rating data set which was collected by Massa and Avesani [25]. The reason that we chose Epinions data set is due to its similar data structure (i.e., consumers opinions and reviews on specific products and services) with our cloud service consumer trust feedbacks. In particular, we considered `user_id` in Epinions as the cloud service consumer primary identity C, `item_id` as the cloud service identity S, and we normalized the `rating_value` as the cloud service consumers trust feedbacks F to scale of 0 to 1. The data set has 49,290 users, 139,738 items, and 664,824 trust feedbacks.

Figure 5.6 depicts the prototype system interface for a cloud service. We imported the Epinions data sets to create the cloud environment that we are intending to analyze. Figure 5.6[3] depicts the cloud environment network for a particular cloud service. The cloud shape represents the cloud service, the circles represent the cloud service consumers and the links represent the interactions between the cloud service consumers and the cloud service. The sizes of the circles indicate the credibility of cloud service consumers. For example, a smaller-sized cloud service consumer means that her feedbacks are less credible.

We evaluate our credibility model using both *analytical analysis* and *empirical analysis*. The analytical analysis focuses on measuring the trust result accuracy when using the credibility model and without using the credibility model. The analytical model calculates the trust results without weighting the trust results (i.e., we turn the $Exp(c)$ to 1 for all cloud service consumers). The empirical analysis focuses on measuring the trust result accuracy for each factor in our credibility model (i.e., the *Cloud Consumer's Capability* factor and the *Majority Consensus* factor). The parameters setup for each corresponding experiment factor are depicted in Table 5.2.

Figure 5.7 depicts the analytical analysis of the trust results for a particular cloud service. From the figure, it can be seen that the trust results are oscillating more significantly when calculating the trust without considering the credibility factors than when calculating the trust with all credibility factors. In other words, even if the trust management service receives inaccurate or malicious trust feedbacks from amateur or malicious cloud service consumers, it is difficult to manipulate the trust results by using our credibility model.

---

[2] http://www.trustlet.org/wiki/Downloaded_Epinions_dataset

[3] Please note that the lengths of the links do not represent anything because the cloud service consumers' positions were assigned randomly around the corresponding cloud service.

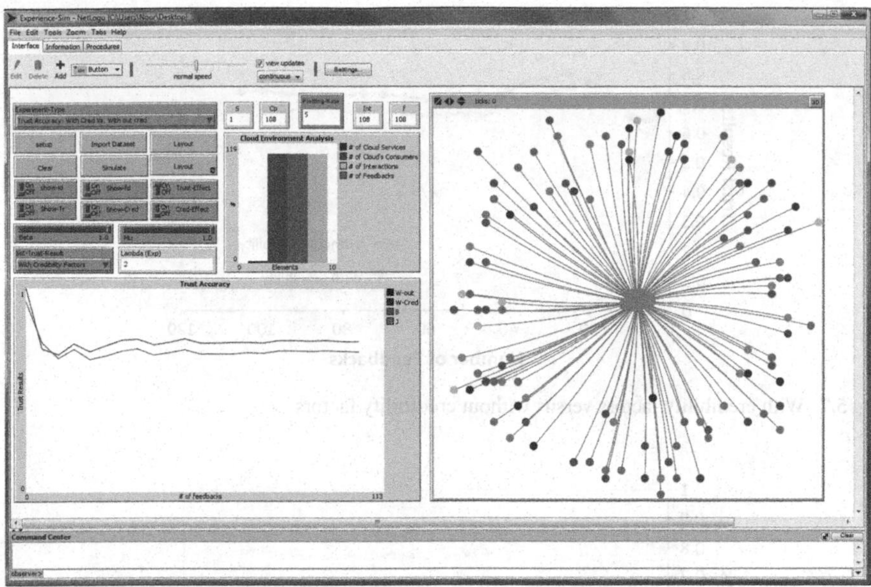

Fig. 5.6 Netlogo-based prototype system

Table 5.2 Experiment factors and parameters setup

Experiment design	β	μ	λ	$Exp(c)$
With credibility factors	1	1	2	
Without credibility factors				1
Cloud service consumer's capability factor	1	0	1	
Majority consensus factor	0	1	1	

Figure 5.8 shows the empirical analysis of the trust results for the same cloud service. It is clear that the trust results obtained by only considering the cloud service consumer's capability factor are higher than the trust results by only considering the majority consensus factor. This is true, because we use the cloud service consumer capability factor as a reward factor and the majority consensus factor as a penalty factor. This reflects how adaptive our credibility model is where the credibility factors can easily be tweaked according to the trust management service's needs. For instance, for optimistic situations where only a few cloud service consumers have high values of capability, increasing the cloud service consumer's capability factor (i.e., β) will help the trust management service to distinguish between experienced cloud service consumers and inexperienced ones. On the other hand, for pessimistic situations where many cloud service consumers have high values of capability, the majority consensus factor (i.e., μ) needs to be increased.

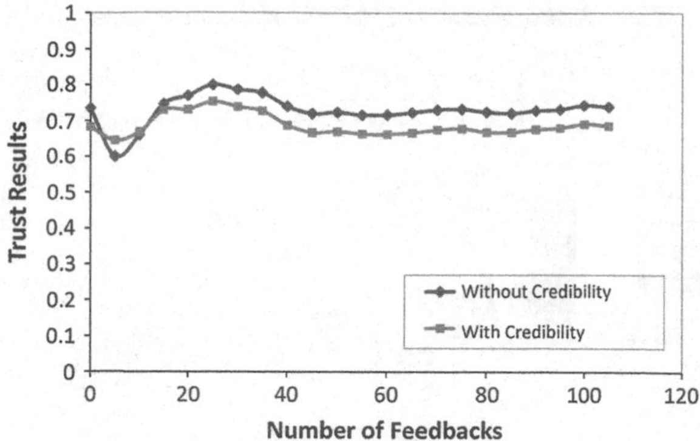

Fig. 5.7 With credibility factors versus without credibility factors

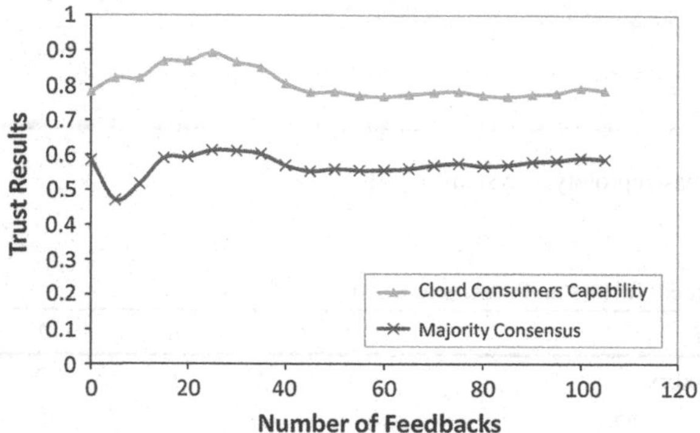

Fig. 5.8 Cloud service consumer's capability factor vs. majority consensus factor

5.7 Related Work

Trust management is considered as one of the critical issues in cloud computing and a very active research area [5, 17, 20, 24].

Ko et al. [19] proposed TrustCloud framework for accountability and trust in cloud computing. In particular, TrustCloud consists of five layers including workflow, data, system, policies and laws, and regulations layers to address accountability in the cloud environment from all aspects. All of these layers maintain the cloud accountability life cycle which consists of seven phases including policy planning, sense and trace, logging, safe-keeping of logs, reporting and replaying, auditing, and optimizing and rectifying. Brandic et al. [5] proposed a novel approach for compliance management in cloud environments to establish trust between different parties. The approach is developed using a centralized architecture and uses compliant management technique to establish trust between cloud service consumers and cloud service providers. Unlike previous works that use policy-based trust management techniques, we evaluate the trustworthiness of a cloud service using reputation-based trust management techniques. Reputation represents a high influence that cloud service consumers have over the trust management system [11] especially that the opinions of the various cloud service consumers can dramatically influence the reputation of a cloud service either positively or negatively.

Other research works also use reputation-based trust management techniques. For instance, Habib et al. [15] proposed a multi-faceted Trust Management (TM) system architecture for cloud computing to help the cloud service consumers to identify trustworthy cloud service providers. In particular, the architecture models uncertainty of trust information collected from multiple sources using a set of Quality of Service (QoS) attributes such as security, latency, availability, and customer support. The architecture combines two different trust management techniques including reputation and recommendation where operators (e.g., AND, OR, NOT , FUSION, CONSENSUS, and DISCOUNTING) are used. Hwang et al. [17] proposed a security aware cloud architecture that assesses the trust for both the cloud service provider and the cloud service consumers. To assess the trustworthiness of cloud service providers, Hwang et al. proposed the trust negotiation approach and the data coloring (integration) using fuzzy logic techniques. To assess the trustworthiness of cloud service consumers, they proposed the Distributed-Hash-Table (DHT)-based trust-overlay networks among several data centers to deploy a reputation-based trust management technique. Unlike previous works which did not consider the problem of unpredictable attacks against cloud services, we present an occasional attacks detection model that not only detects misleading trust feedbacks from collusion and Sybil attacks, but also has the ability to adaptively adjust and tweak the trust results for cloud services that have been affected by occasional and periodic malicious behaviors.

Conner et al. [10], proposed a trust management framework for service-oriented architecture (SOA) that focuses on service provider's perspective to protect resources from unauthorized access. This framework has a decentralized architecture that offers multiple trust evaluation metrics to allow trust parties to have customized evaluation to assess their clients (i.e., cloud service consumers). Malik and Bouguettaya [23] proposed reputation assessment techniques based on the existing quality of service (QoS) parameters that enable the cloud service consumers to personalize the criteria in assessing the reputation of Web services. The approach has a decentralized architecture where each cloud service consumer records their own perceptions of the reputation of a particular service provider. The proposed framework supports different assessment metrics such as rater credibility, majority rating, past rating history, personal experience for credibility evaluation, personal preferences, personal experience for reputation assessment, and temporal sensitivity.

Unlike previous works that require extensive computations or trust parties' collaboration by rating the trust feedbacks, we present a credibility model supporting the distinguishment between trustworthy feedbacks and malicious trust feedbacks. We were inspired by Xiong and Liu who differentiate between the credibility of a peer and the credibility of the feedback through distinguishing several parameters to measure the credibility of the trust participants feedbacks [38]. However, their approach is not applicable in cloud environments.

5.8 Conclusions and Future Work

Given the quick adoption of cloud computing in the last few years, there is a significant challenge in managing trust among cloud service providers and cloud service consumers. In this chapter, we have presented a framework that uses Web services to improve ways to manage trust in cloud environments. We introduced an adaptive credibility model that assesses cloud services' trustworthiness by distinguishing between credible trust feedbacks and amateur or malicious trust feedbacks. We particularly introduced two trust parameters including the *cloud service consumer's capability* factor and the *majority consensus* factor in calculating the trust value of a cloud service. In addition, our trust management service allows trust feedback assessment and storage to be managed in a distributed way. In the future, we plan to deal with more challenging problems such as the *Sybil* attack and the *Whitewashing* attack. Performance optimization of the trust management service is another focus of our future research work.

Acknowledgments Talal H. Noor's work has been supported by King Abdullah's Postgraduate Scholarship, the Ministry of Higher Education: Kingdom of Saudi Arabia.

References

1. Amazon-EC2: Elastic Compute Cloud (Amazon EC2) (2011), accessed 01/04/2011, Available at: http://aws.amazon.com/ec2
2. Amazon-S3: Amazon Simple Storage Service (Amazon - S3) (2011), accessed 29/03/2011, Available at: http://aws.amazon.com/s3
3. Armbrust, M., Fox, A., Griffith, R., Joseph, A., Katz, R., Konwinski, A., Lee, G., Patterson, D., Rabkin, A., Stoica, I., Zaharia, M.: A View of Cloud Computing. Communications of the ACM 53(4), 50–58 (2010)
4. Aziz, B., Hamilton, G.: Detecting Man-in-the-Middle Attacks by Precise Timing. In: Proc. of the 3rd Int. Conf. on Emerging Security Information, Systems and Technologies (SECURWARE'09). Athens/Glyfada, Greece (Jun 2009)
5. Brandic, I., Dustdar, S., Anstett, T., Schumm, D., Leymann, F., Konrad, R.: Compliant Cloud Computing (C3): Architecture and Language Support for User-Driven Compliance Management in Clouds. In: Proc. of IEEE 3rd Int. Conf. on Cloud Computing (CLOUD'10). Miami, Florida, USA (Jul 2010)
6. Buyya, R., Yeo, C., Venugopal, S.: Market-oriented Cloud Computing: Vision, Hype, and Reality for Delivering it Services as Computing Utilities. In: Proc. of IEEE 10th Int. Conf. on High Performance Computing and Communications (HPCC'08). Dalian, China (Sep 2008)
7. Chen, K., Hwang, K., Chen, G.: Heuristic Discovery of Role-Based Trust Chains in Peer-to-Peer Networks. IEEE Transactions on Parallel and Distributed Systems 20(1), 83–96 (2008)
8. Child, I.: The Psychological Meaning of Aesthetic Judgments. Visual Arts Research 9(2 (18)), 51–59 (1983)

9. Clark, K., Warnier, M., Brazier, F., Quillinan, T.: Secure Monitoring of Service Level Agreements. In: Proc. of the 5th Int. Conf. on Availability, Reliability, and Security (ARES'10). Krakow, Poland (Feb 2010)
10. Conner, W., Iyengar, A., Mikalsen, T., Rouvellou, I., Nahrstedt, K.: A Trust Management Framework for Service-Oriented Environments. In: Proc. of the 18th Int. Conf. on World Wide Web (WWW'09). Madrid, Spain (Apr 2009)
11. Dellarocas, C.: The Digitization of Word of Mouth: Promise and Challenges of Online Feedback Mechanisms. Management Science 49(10), 1407–1424 (2003)
12. Friedman, E., Resnick, P., Sami, R.: Algorithmic Game Theory, chap. Manipulation-Resistant Reputation Systems, pp. 677–697. Cambridge University Press, New York, USA (2007)
13. Google-Apps: Google Apps (2011), accessed 03/04/2011, Available at:http://www.google.com/apps/intl/en-au/business/index.html#utm_campaign=en-au&utm_source=en-ha-apac-au-bk-google&utm_medium=ha&utm_term=google-20app
14. Google-Docs: Google Docs - Online documents, spreadsheets, presentations, surveys, file storage and more (2011), accessed 11/04/2011, Available at: https://docs.google.com/
15. Habib, S., Ries, S., Muhlhauser, M.: Towards a Trust Management System for Cloud Computing. In: IEEE 10th Int. Conf. on Trust, Security and Privacy in Computing and Communications (TrustCom'11). Changsha, China (Nov 2011)
16. Hoffman, K., Zage, D., Nita-Rotaru, C.: A Survey of Attack and Defense Techniques for Reputation Systems. ACM Computing Surveys (CSUR) 42(1), 1–31 (2009)
17. Hwang, K., Li, D.: Trusted Cloud Computing with Secure Resources and Data Coloring. IEEE Internet Computing 14(5), 14–22 (2010)
18. Jøsang, A., Quattrociocchi, W.: Advanced Features in Bayesian Reputation Systems. In: Proc. of the 6th Int. Conf. on Trust, Privacy and Security in Digital Business (TrustBus'09). Linz, Austria (Sep 2009)
19. Ko, R., Jagadpramana, P., Mowbray, M., Pearson, S., Kirchberg, M., Liang, Q., Lee, B.: TrustCloud: A Framework for Accountability and Trust in Cloud Computing. In: IEEE World Congress on Services (SERVICES'11). Washington, DC, USA (Jul 2011)
20. Krautheim, F., Phatak, D., Sherman, A.: Introducing the Trusted Virtual Environment Module: A New Mechanism for Rooting Trust in Cloud Computing. In: Proc. of the 3rd Int. Conf. on Trust and Trustworthy Computing (TRUST'10). Berlin, Germany (Jun 2010)
21. Lai, K., Feldman, M., Stoica, I., Chuang, J.: Incentives for Cooperation in Peer-to-Peer Networks. In: Proc. of the 1st Workshop on Economics of Peer-to-Peer Systems. Berkeley, CA, USA (Jun 2003)
22. Malik, Z., Bouguettaya, A.: Rater Credibility Assessment in Web Services Interactions. World Wide Web 12(1), 3–25 (2009)
23. Malik, Z., Bouguettaya, A.: RATEWeb: Reputation Assessment for Trust Establishment Among Web services. The VLDB Journal 18(4), 885–911 (2009)
24. Manuel, P., Thamarai Selvi, S., Barr, M.E.: Trust Management System for Grid and Cloud Resources. In: Proc. of the 1st Int. Conf. on Advanced Computing (ICAC'09). Chennai, India (Dec 2009)
25. Massa, P., Avesani, P.: Trust Metrics in Recommender Systems. In: Computing with Social Trust, pp. 259–285. Human-Computer Interaction Series, Springer London (2009)
26. Mell, P., Grance, T.: The NIST Definition of Cloud Computing (Sep2011), accessed: 05/06/2012, Available at: http://csrc.nist.gov/publications/drafts/800-145/Draft-SP-800-145/Draft/800_145_cloud-efinition.pdf
27. Microsoft: Windows Live Mesh 2011 (2011), accessed 09/05/2011, Available at:https://www.mesh.com/
28. NetLogo: Netlogo home page (2011), accessed 1/3/2011, Available at: http://ccl.northwestern.edu/netlogo/
29. Noor, T.H., Sheng, Q.Z.: Credibility-Based Trust Management for Services in Cloud Environments. In: Proc. of the 9th Int. Conf. on Service Oriented Computing (ICSOC'11). Paphos, Cyprus (Dec 2011)

30. Noor, T.H., Sheng, Q.Z.: Trust as a Service: A Framework for Trust Management in Cloud Environments. In: Proc. of the 12th Int. Conf. on Web and Information Systems (WISE'11). Sydney, Australia (Oct 2011)
31. Pearson, S., Benameur, A.: Privacy, Security and Trust Issues Arising From Cloud Computing. In: Proc. IEEE 2nd Int. Conf. on Cloud Computing Technology and Science (CloudCom'10). Indianapolis, Indiana, USA (Nov - Dec 2010)
32. Roosevelt, E.: Facing the problems of youth. The P.T.A. magazine: National Parent-Teacher Magazine 29(30), 1–6 (1935)
33. Sheth, A.P., Gomadam, K., Lathem, J.: SA-REST: Semantically Interoperable and Easier-to-Use Services and Mashups. IEEE Internet Computing 11(6), 84–87 (2007)
34. Skopik, F., Schall, D., Dustdar, S.: Start Trusting Strangers? Bootstrapping and Prediction of Trust. In: Proc. of the 10th Int. Conf. on Web Information Systems Engineering (WISE'09). Poznan, Poland (Oct 2009)
35. Skopik, F., Schall, D., Dustdar, S.: Trustworthy Interaction Balancing in Mixed Service-Oriented Systems. In: Proc. of ACM 25th Symp. on Applied Computing (SAC'10). Sierre, Switzerland (Mar 2010)
36. Sotomayor, B., Montero, R., Lorente, I., Foster, I.: Virtual Infrastructure Management in Private and Hybrid Clouds. IEEE Internet Computing 13(5), 14–22 (2009)
37. Weng, J., Miao, C., Goh, A.: Protecting Online Rating Systems from Unfair Ratings. In: Proc. of the 2nd Int. Conf. on Trust, Privacy, and Security in Digital Business (TrustBus'05). Copenhagen, Denmark (Aug 2005)
38. Xiong, L., Liu, L.: Peertrust: Supporting Reputation-based Trust for Peer-to-Peer Electronic Communities. IEEE Transactions on Knowledge and Data Engineering 16(7), 843–857 (2004)

Chapter 6
Web Service Contracts: Specification and Matchmaking

Marco Comerio, Flavio De Paoli, Matteo Palmonari and Luca Panziera

Abstract Web services promise universal interoperability through integration of services developed by independent providers. The coming of the Cloud Computing paradigm extends the need to share resources (e.g., platform, infrastructure, data) that are accessible as Web services. This means that a key factor to build complex and valuable business processes among cooperating organizations relies on the efficiency of automate the discovering of appropriate Web services. The increasing availability of Web services that offer similar functionalities requires mechanisms to go beyond the pure functional discovery. This chapter proposes the evaluation of *Web service contracts*, which define non-functional properties (NFPs) and applicability conditions associated with Web services, as a solution to automate process composition and enactment. Today, there is a lack of tools and algorithms that fully support this solution due to several open issues. First, existing languages don't provide the right constructs for the specification of Web service contracts. Second, the lack of standard languages determines heterogeneity in Web service contract specifications raising interoperability issues. Third, Web service contract evaluation is only partially supported by existing discovery engines and composition tools when combining different services from different providers. This chapter proposes some research efforts on addressing these open issues.

M. Comerio (✉) · F. De Paoli · M. Palmonari · L. Panziera
University of Milano-Bicocca, Viale Sarca 336, 20126 Milano, Italy
e-mail: comerio@disco.unimib.it

F. De Paoli
e-mail: depaoli@disco.unimib.it

M. Palmonari
e-mail: palmonari@disco.unimib.it

L. Panziera
e-mail: panziera@disco.unimib.it

A. Bouguettaya et al. (eds.), *Advanced Web Services*,
DOI: 10.1007/978-1-4614-7535-4_6,

6.1 Introduction

Web services aim at addressing interoperability and integration issues to deliver complex business processes by discovering and composing services distributed over the Internet and developed by independent providers. The building of such complex and valuable processes requires efficient discovery and composition techniques. Moreover, the emerging cloud computing paradigm that offers resources (software, platform, infrastructure, and data) as on-demand services accessible through Web services makes the development of enhanced discovery and composition processes urgent.

There is a growing consensus that pure functional discovery and composition of Web services are inadequate to develop valuable processes. This is due to the increasing availability of Web services, in the Internet and cloud computing environments, which offer similar functionalities but with different non-functional properties (e.g., price, availability and copyright). Therefore, a promising path towards the automatic definition of valuable business processes is the development of Web service discovery and composition tools and techniques to evaluate non-functional properties (NFPs).

Currently, NFPs that state the conditions to access and use services are expressed by means of policies, licenses, and service level agreements. Despite of differences, their common goal is to regulate a business transaction between the service provider and the service consumer and thereby, commonly considered under the umbrella term *Web Service Contract* (WS contract, for short). A WS contract includes one or more *contractual terms* described in forms of conditions established on NFPs, such as quality of service (e.g., response time and availability), legal aspects (e.g., fair use and copyrights), intellectual rights (e.g., allowing or denying composition), and business aspects (including financial terms such as payment and tax).

Despite enhancement of Web service discovery and composition with the evaluation of WS contracts is increasingly considered strategic, currently there is a lack of tools and algorithms that fully support it. This is mainly due to the lack of shared standard ways to express descriptions of contractual terms. Basically, service providers represent these terms as they wish, causing strong ambiguity and redundancies that make difficult, or even impossible without specific techniques, the automatic interpretation in multi-provider service-oriented contexts.

This chapter discusses some research efforts on addressing WS contract specification and matchmaking, which are at the core of the possible solutions. In particular, we present (i) a semantic meta-model that provides a sound and robust base to formally describe WS contracts, (ii) a set of techniques and rules to extract contractual terms from available WS contract descriptions and (iii) an effective approach to WS contract matchmaking, and a framework that implements it.

The chapter is organized as follows. Section 6.2 discusses motivations and state of the art of the research on WS contracts. Sections 6.3 presents the semantic meta-model and the set of rules and techniques to extract contractual terms. Section 6.4 describes the approach to WS contract matchmaking. Section 6.5 concludes the chapter.

6.2 Motivation and State of the Art

In the literature, the mutual understanding between providers and consumers is typically established by specifying policies, service level agreements and licenses.

A *policy* establishes a relationship between involved parties by specifying obligations and authorizations. A policy provides the means for specifying and modulating the behavior of a feature to align its capabilities and constraints with the requirements of its users [18].

A *Service Level Agreement (SLA)* is a bilateral statement signed between a service provider and a service consumer, that describes the minimum performance criteria a provider commits to meet while delivering a service and typically sets out the remedial actions and penalties that take effect when the actual performance falls below the promised standard. Thus, an SLA specifies the expected operational characteristics of a service in business oriented terms between a provider and a consumer in such a way that they can be measured, monitored, and managed [26].

A *license* includes all transactions between the licensor (e.g., service provider) and the licensee (e.g., service consumer) in which the licensor establishes the rights granted to the licensee when using some specific services for a specific tenure under predefined terms and conditions [13].

In general, policies, SLAs, and licenses serve as a common denominator to specify normative aspects of services and establish business relationships between providers and consumers. In the literature, terms like policies, SLAs, and licenses are often considered synonyms; therefore, we prefer to use the term *Web Service Contract* to include all possible contractual terms, including the ones addressed by policies, SLAs, and licenses.

Definition 6.1 Web Service Contract. Given a Service s offered by a Provider p to potential Customers C, a Web service contract WSC is a legal binding exchange of promises or agreements between p and C expressed through a set of contractual terms $CT = \{ct_1, \ldots, ct_n\}$ that regulate the provisioning of s.

Definition 6.2 Contractual Term. Given a Web service contract WSC associated with a Service s, a Contractual Term ct in WSC is a non-functional property referred to a concern of s.

Example 6.1 **Web Service Contract and Contractual Term**. The *Safe Logistic Operator* offers the *Freight Transportation* service with a Web service contract including a contractual term specifying that the transportation is covered by a *blanked insurance*.

Currently, the literature focuses on the definition of models for WS contract specification. In particular, recent contributions deal with the analysis of the different contractual terms. According to [8], contractual terms can be classified into: (i) *Quality of Service (QoS) terms* that represent technical issues of a service (e.g., security and performance); (ii) *Business terms* that describe financial terms and conditions (e.g., price, insurance and compensation agreements); (iii) *Service Context terms* that define technical aspects (e.g., compliancy to available devices and connections) as well as profile aspects (e.g., service coverage) of the context associated with a service and (iv) *License terms* that state responsibilities among involved parties and conditions on service usage (e.g., compliancy to legal statements and regulations).

This classification can be further detailed as defined in [24], where a customizable part of a service contract (namely, *individual contract)* has been introduced to include contractual terms on: (i) *Provider Obligation* (e.g., quality of service guarantees), (ii) *Use of Information* (e.g., data licenses), (iii) *Warranties and Liabilities* (e.g., warranty on the accuracy of the provided information), (iv) *Delivery Time* (e.g., time conditions on service delivery) and (v) *Price and Payment Terms* (e.g., business terms related to service usage).

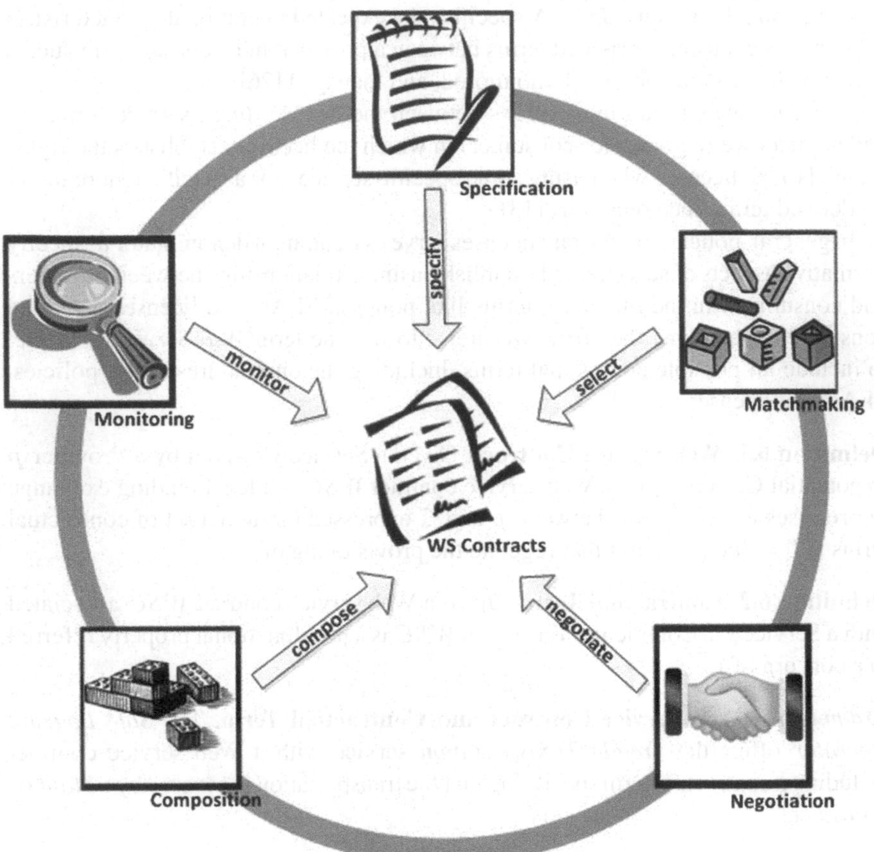

Fig. 6.1 WS Contracts in service lifecycle

WS contracts have a role in several activities in service lifecycle, as illustrated in Fig. 6.1:

- *Web Service Specification*: in order to support efficient discovery and composition of Web services, service specifications should also include offered non-functional properties. Such properties are described in WS contracts. Several approaches have been presented in the literature, among others, the most relevant are [1, 22, 24, 39, 48].
- *Web Service Matchmaking*: when more than one Web service satisfies the requested functional requirements, the evaluation of WS contracts allows for the identification of services that best match the requirements on non-functional properties. The most relevant approaches to contract-based Web service matchmaking are [6, 14, 23, 28, 41, 42, 45].
- *Web Service Negotiation*: in many real business situations, WS contracts cannot be considered static documents, instead they define reference terms to be negotiated between providers and consumers to reach a tailored agreement. The most relevant approaches to contract-based Web service negotiation are [9, 44].
- *Web Service Composition*: when two or more Web services are to be composed, WS contract should be evaluated to validate the composition from a non-functional-property point of view in order to avoid illegal or unauthorized compositions. The most relevant approaches to contract-based Web service composition are [37, 47].
- *Web Service Monitoring*: during the execution of a Web service, the contractual terms need to be checked against the actual state and behavior of the service. When a violation of the contract terms is detected, exception handling actions should be put in place. The most relevant approaches to contract-based Web service monitoring are [16, 48].

Due to space reasons, in the rest of the chapter we will focus on issues and research results related to Web service specification and matchmaking.

6.2.1 Issues on Web Service Contract Specification

The specification of contractual terms defining non-functional properties of a service is a complex task since the following aspects must be considered:

- *synonym and homonym*: similar properties may have different names (e.g., in different languages or domains) or the same name may refer to different properties (e.g., in different domains a property may have different implications).
- *quantitative and qualitative values*: contractual terms can be expressed with numeric values defined in different units (e.g., price in Euro or in USD), or they can be purely qualitative (e.g., usability is *good*, trust is *high*, software is *open source*).
- *technological and business interdependencies*: contractual terms present technological interdependencies (e.g., the WS has a higher price since it guarantees a certain bandwidth) and business interdependencies (e.g., some contractual terms are offered only to business users, others to private users).

Table 6.1 Shortcomings of current WS contract descriptions

	Semantic	XML-based	Template-based	Free-text
Machine interpretability	✔	✔	✘	✘
Interoperability	✔	Limited	Limited	Limited
Expressivity	✔	Limited	✔	✔
Reasoning	✔	✘	✘	✘

As mentioned in Sect. 6.1, there are many way to specify WS contracts that bring to heterogeneous descriptions that can be categorized as follows:

- *semantic descriptions*: defined by means of semantic Web languages and based on domain ontologies.
- *XML-based descriptions*: defined by $< attribute, value >$ clauses, where *attribute* identifies an offered NFP and *value* specifies the value of that NFP.
- *template-based descriptions*: defined according to a predefined template. The contractual terms are plain texts in natural language.
- *free-text descriptions*: defined by unstructured textual documents written in natural language.

The mentioned descriptions present different levels of machine interpretability, interoperability, expressivity and reasoning (see Table 6.1). Machine interpretability represents the possibility for a machine to conceive the significance of a WS contract. Interoperability defines the possibility to automatically interpret the WS contract meaningfully and accurately in different contexts and domains. Expressivity represents the capability to define articulated contractual terms supporting the specification of technological and business interdependencies. Reasoning is the capability of a machine to automatically form inferences from terms specified into a WS contract. In Table 6.1, the symbol "✔" means that the contract description type covers the capability; otherwise the symbol "✘" is used. In case in which the capability is partially covered, the label "*limited*" is used.

Semantic descriptions fully support machine interpretability, interoperability and reasoning due to the explicit definition of relations between property names and property values. Moreover, the specification of expressive contractual terms is also supported at the cost of describing technological and business interdependencies through the use of articulated axioms [2, 39].

XML-based descriptions present contractual terms defined by text labels; there is not a formal definition of NFP names and values, nor measurement methods and units. Therefore, semantic misunderstandings are likely to occur causing limited interoperability. Moreover, expressivity is also limited since the specification of articulated contractual terms is not allowed. Finally, reasoning cannot be supported since relations among names and values are not explicitly stated.

Template-based and free-text descriptions present an high-level of expressivity due to the use of natural language that can express specifications of articulated WS contracts. On the contrary, they are not machine-processable and cannot be exploited for reasoning. Interoperability is limited since different terminology can be used in different domains to express the same contractual terms (i.e., synonyms and homonyms are not explicitly stated).

According to the above criteria, semantic descriptions represent the best solution to define WS contracts. This conclusion is confirmed by the survey in [2], where languages based on Logic programming or Description logics appear to have enough expressivity for the description of articulated contractual terms regarding privacy and security concerns of a service. The languages analyzed in [2] are classified in two main groups: standard-oriented languages and research-oriented languages. The former provide a well-defined but restricted set of features (e.g., possibility to specify actions to be performed at runtime); the latter strive toward generality and extensibility and provide a number of more advanced features (e.g., support for negotiation).

Such languages cover only the specification of contractual terms on privacy and security concerns of a service. To the best of our knowledge, no languages have been proposed in the literature to cover all types of terms discussed above. As a matter of facts, the most popular research-oriented models for semantic Web service descriptions, namely OWL-S [30] and WSMO [43], and the associated languages, OWL and WSML respectively, only marginally cover the specification of contractual terms. OWL-S does not natively support the specification of contractual terms; an extension of the model is required for their specification. WSMO basically allows for attribute-value descriptions of contractual terms that are not included in the logical model and thus reasoning activities on them cannot be performed. Several papers [22, 39] try to overcome such limitations. As demonstrated in [11], these solutions support the definition of expressive service contracts with the disadvantage of strong effort required for their specifications.

The following research issue emerges: *there is a lack of semantic meta-models to provide sound and robust bases for describing WS contracts.* A proper meta-model should be:

- independent from the specific language used for actual semantic specifications, so it can be adopted in different contexts providing for interoperability;
- expressive enough to represent all the needed properties, but simple enough to require low effort for its usage;
- flexible enough to support the definition of automatic techniques and rules to extract contractual terms from available descriptions, whether they are semantic, XML-based, template-based or free-text.

This research issue has been addressed by the Policy Centered Meta-model (PCM) [11]. The PCM supports: (i) expressive descriptions addressing qualitative contractual terms by means of logical expressions and quantitative terms by means of expressions including ranges and inequalities and, (ii) structured descriptions that aggregate different term descriptions into a single entity with an applicability condition. Moreover, the PCM outperforms other models providing a good trade-off between provided expressiveness and effort required for its application. Finally, the PCM is independent from a single language: it has been expressed both in WSMO and OWL to overcome their limitations. Details about the semantic of the PCM and techniques and rules to perform the mapping from heterogeneous sources to the PCM are provided in Sect. 6.3.

6.2.2 Issues on Web Service Contract Matchmaking

The WS contract matchmaking problem can be defined as follows: given a set of WS contracts $WSC = \{wsc_1, \ldots, wsc_n\}$, and a specification R of requested contractual terms, define a sorting relation on WSC based on R. In this chapter, we assume that each $wsc_i \in WSC$ consists of an *eligible contract* associated with a Web service identified by a discovery engine (e.g., GLUE2 [5] or OWLS-MX [21]) according to its functional properties.

Historically, the first approaches proposed for WS contract matchmaking focused only on QoS terms, which were expressed by numeric values. Syntactic matching of contractual terms were performed and matching scores were computed by mathematical functions [28, 41, 45]. These approaches are very efficient, but not very precise due to the syntactic approach, which may cause semantic misunderstandings when dealing with qualitative contractual terms.

Tools and approaches based on the evaluation of semantic descriptions have been proposed to improve the effectiveness of QoS-based matchmaking [6, 42]. In particular, the coming of WSMO and its extensions to support the specification of all types of contractual terms, promoted the development of more precise WS contract semantic matchmakers [12, 14, 15, 20, 31, 36]. Semantic approaches take advantage of reasoning techniques to mediate between different terminologies and data models by means of logical axioms and rules. Therefore, reasoning techniques are very suitable to handle qualitative values of contractual terms. However, reasoning tools are not very practical to deal with numeric expressions and formulae, since they show very low efficiency.

Therefore, pure semantic and non-semantic approaches appear to be inadequate to solve the WS contract matchmaking problem. In particular, they show the following limitations: (i) *expressivity*: service contracts that include logical expressions on ontology values and numeric expressions including ranges and inequalities are not supported; (ii) *generality*: semantic mediation between contractual term descriptions based on different domain ontologies is not supported; (iii) *extensibility*: parametric matching evaluation by means of customized evaluation functions cannot be defined; (iv) *flexibility*: evaluation of incomplete specifications (i.e., unspecified contractual terms in requests or offers) is not supported.

The following research issue emerges: *there is a lack of an effective approach to WS contract matchmaking that combines high level of expressivity, generality, extensibility and flexibility.*

In [23, 46] this issue is partially addressed by extending WSMO or OWL-S with the integration of mathematical techniques. However, both are not able to evaluate multi-value qualitative and quantitative expressions defined by ranges. The research issue is completely addressed by the Policy Matchmaker and Ranker (PoliMaR) framework,[1] which implements an hybrid approach to exploit logic-based techniques for qualitative evaluations, and algorithmic techniques for numeric expressions. Details on the hybrid approach and PoliMaR are provided in Sect. 6.4.

6.3 Towards Web Service Contract Specification

Here we discuss the experience in defining the Policy Centered Meta-model (PCM) [11] that has been developed to address representation and evaluation of non-functional properties collected into requested and offered WS contracts. PCM has been designed to be independent of any specific language. Currently, PCM has been formalized in WSML and OWL.[2] The usage of PCM as an extension of the WSMO logical model has been accepted by the WSMO working group [38].

PCM provides a step towards the development of an expressive, flexible and technology-independent framework for specifying Web Service contracts. The main advantages of PCM in relation to other proposed models have been discussed in several works (e.g., [11]) and can be summarized as follows:

- Expressivity: PCM provides a good trade-off between expressiveness and complexity of the model. Besides PCM provides a simplified structure for organizing contract descriptions (e.g. arbitrary logical axioms for specifying NFPs are not allowed, while these are allowed in [38]), it has been showed that PCM supports the representation of the most significant types of contract (policies, SLAs, license), and mappings to existing languages, such as WSOL [40], WSLA [19] and ODRL-S [13] have been defined [8].
- Flexibility: the model has been easily extended along time to represent NFPs extracted from heterogeneous data formats (semantic, XML-based, template-based and textual descriptions) [8, 32, 33]; as a result, a large number of semantic PCM-based descriptions of real services extracted from existing (non semantic) sources have been made available to semantic matchmaking tools.
- WS technology independence: PCM has been applied to describe contracts for SOAP-based services [7] and RESTful services [32, 33]; PCM descriptions can be associated with service descriptions represented in any model, provided that the description has a unique identifier.

6.3.1 The Policy Centered Meta-Model

Informally, PCM is centered around the concept of *policy* as aggregation of single *non-functional properties* (NFPs) to form a bundle of offers or requests, that is, a *WS contract* according to the terminology defined in Sect. 6.2. A policy offered by a service, Service Policy in the following, is associated with a *Condition* that defines

[1] Available at: http://sourceforge.net/projects/polimar/.

[2] PCM formalizations are available at: http://www.siti.disco.unimib.it/research/ontologies/.

the requirements a consumer or the execution context should fulfill to select that policy. For example, a service provider in the logistic domain may offers a shipment service associated with a service policy (namely, Premium Policy) with a condition (namely, Premium Condition) stating that the consumer must be subscribed to at least 10 shipments. Each NFP in a policy is defined by a *Constraint Expression* (Expression for short) that can involve either quantitative or qualitative criteria. For example, the mentioned Premium Policy may offer a base price equal to 100 Euros and a blanket insurance. On the other side, a policy defining user requirements, Requested Policy in the following, consists of *Requests*, which are NFPs associated with a weight named *Relevance*. For example, a requested policy may state, among others, a mandatory constraint on the service price (i.e., price less than or equal to 120 Euros) and a preference on the service insurance (i.e., fire insurance or any insurance type that includes it).

Formally, the meta-model can be defined as follows.

Definition 6.3 Non-Functional Property. Let L be a set of property labels, C a set of constraint operators, $\Delta = \{D_1, \ldots, D_n\}$ a set of disjoint domains, U a set of units of measure; an *Expression* is a triple $exp =< c, V, u >$, where $c \in C$, $V \subseteq D$, for some $D \in \Delta$, and $u \in U$. A *NFP specification* (NFP for short) is a couple $p =< l, exp >$, where $l \in L$ and exp is an Expression. With l^p, c^p, V^p, and u^p we denote the property label, the constraint operator, the set of values and the unit of measure of the NFP p, respectively.

PCM makes a distinction between qualitative and quantitative Expressions and qualitative and quantitative NFPs. A *Qualitative Expression* $< c, V, u >$ refers to objects taken from a given domain, that is, the domain D such that $V \subseteq D$ is a set of arbitrary objects; since different measurement systems need not to be considered, whereas objects are denoted by identifiers, u takes "id" (identifier) as default value in qualitative expressions. A *Quantitative Expression* $< c, V, u >$ refers to numerical values, that is, the domain D such that $V \subseteq D$ is a numerical domain, e.g. $\mathcal{N}$, $\Re$ and so on. The Unity of measure for *Qualitative NFPs* are NFPs whose Expressions are qualitative expressions; *Quantitative NFPs* are NFPs whose Expressions are quantitative expressions.

Example 6.2 **Quantitative NFP**. The quadruple $< off.BasePrice1, =100, Euros >$ represents the base price specification of the Premium Policy.

Example 6.3 **Qualitative NFP**. The quadruple *<off.Insurance1, all, blanketInsurance, id>* represents the insurance specification of the Premium Policy.

Definition 6.4 Service Policy. Given a set of Services S, and a set of applicability conditions identifiers PC, a Service Policy is a tuple $sp = \{P, pc, S\}$, with P denoting a set of NFPs $P = \{p_1, \ldots, p_k\}$ such that $\bigcap_{i=1}^{k} l^k = \emptyset$ (non shared labels), $pc \in PC$, and S is a set of services associated with the policy.

Given a service s, we denote with SP^s the set of all the policies sp such that $sp = \{P, pc, s\}$ for some P and some pc.

Example 6.4 **Service Policy**. The triple *<P1, Premium Condition, Freight Transport>* represents the premium policy associated with the Freight Transport service where P1 includes the NFPs in Examples 6.2 and 6.3.

Definition 6.5 Request and Requested Policy. A Request r is a couple $< p, rel >$, where p is a NFP and $rel \in [0..1]$. A Requested Policy is defined by a set of requests $rp = \{r_1, \ldots, r_n\}$.

Example 6.5 **Request and Requested Policy**. A Requested Policy includes the following requests *<req. BasePrice, lessEqual, 120, Euros, 0.8>* and *<req. Insurance, include, fire insurance, id, 0.6>*.

6.3.2 Semantic Representation of the PCM

The PCM conceptual syntax has been designed to be independent of any specific language. The concrete syntax in OWL and WSML has been defined to provide for: (i) the definition of constraint expressions and operators by introducing specific classes (e.g. the class of set operators and set expressions); (ii) the exploitation of ontology axioms to formally define the mutual relationship among constraints (e.g., set expressions can have only ontology instances as values); (iii) the representation of qualitative expression values as instances of ontologies, formally defining constraints on the value domain (i.e., ontology concepts and their mutual relationships) and (iv) the exploitation of logical inferences and semantic technologies for matching and evaluating properties.

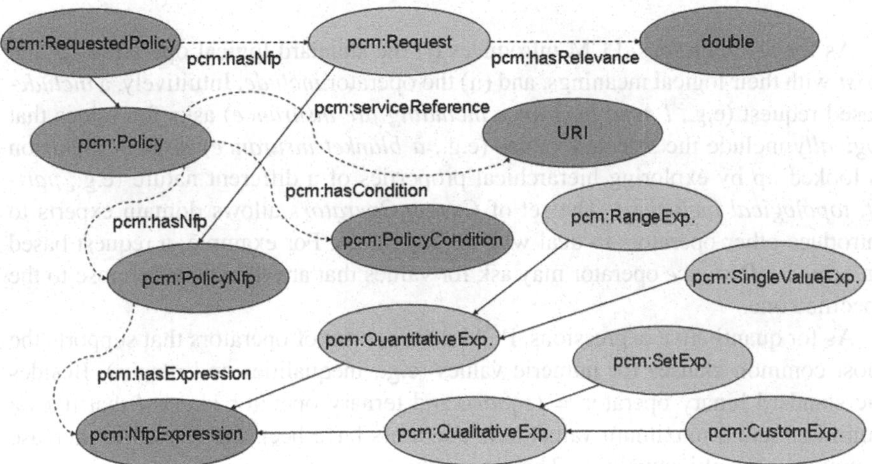

Fig. 6.2 PCM main classes. *Dashed arcs* represent domain/range restrictions over the properties and *continuous arcs* represent subclass relationships

The main classes of the PCM are represented in Fig. 6.2 (refer to [11] for details). Policies are represented by the class *Policy*, and NFPs are represented by the class *PolicyNfp* (labels identifying NFPs are URIs); the class *Request* is a subclass of *PolicyNfp* with the specification of a relevance value; the class *RequestedPolicy* is a subclass of *Policy* with NFPs of class *Request*; the class *NfpExpression* is the superclass of different types of expressions: qualitative and quantitative. Figure 6.3 shows the properties that characterize each class of Expressions, the respective ranges, and a set of built-in constraint operators.

	Expression Class	Attribute	Range
Qualitative	Set Expression	pcm:hasOperator	pcm:SetOperator // {**all**, **exist**, **include**}
		pcm:hasParameters	URI *(instance)*
	Custom Expression	pcm:hasOperator	pcm:CustomOperator // e.g. **semanticDistance**
		pcm:hasParameters	-
Quantitative	Single Value Expression	pcm:hasOperator	pcm:BinaryOperator // {≥↑, ≥↓, ≤↑, ≤↓}
		pcm:hasParameter	Lit *(numerical value)*
		pcm:hasUnit	pcm:Unit
	Range Expression	pcm:hasOperator	pcm:TernaryOperator // {**interval**}
		pcm:hasMinParameter	Lit *(numerical value)*
		pcm:hasMaxParameter	Lit *(numerical value)*
		pcm:hasUnit	pcm:Unit

Fig. 6.3 Expression classes

As for *SetOperators*, PCM introduces (i) the standard logical operators *all* and *exist* with their logical meanings, and (ii) the operator *include*. Intuitively, a *include*-based request (e.g., *I need insurance including fire insurance*) asks for values that *logically* include the selected values (e.g., *a blanket insurance*); logical inclusion is looked up by exploring hierarchical properties of a different nature (e.g., *part-of, topological inclusion*). The set of *CustomOperators* allows domain experts to introduce other operators to deal with object values. For example, a request based on *semanticDistance* operator may ask for values that are semantically close to the specified one.

As for quantitative expressions, PCM defines a set of operators that supports the most common clauses for numeric values (e.g., inequalities and ranges). Besides the standard binary operator = (*equal*), and ternary operator *interval* that fixes a minimum and a maximum value, new operators have been introduced to increase expressiveness of inequalities. These operators are:

(i) $\geq\uparrow$ (*greaterEqual*) to specify a lower bound, so that the highest possible value is better;

(ii) ≥↓ (*atLeast*) to specify a lower bound, so that the lowest possible value is better;

(iii) ≤↓ (*lessEqual*) to specify an upper bound, so that the lowest possible value is better;

(iv) ≤↑ (*atMost*) to specify an upper bound, so that the highest possible value is better.

6.3.3 Web Service Contract Extraction from Heterogeneous Sources

As discussed in Sect. 6.2, heterogeneity prevents from automatic evaluation of contracts; therefore, techniques to deliver comparable descriptions is needed. Currently, no comprehensive solutions to solve this problem have been presented in the literature. Recent proposals, such as the VieSLAF framework [3] and the Integrated Service Engineering (ISE) workbench [35], are innovative but partial solutions since only the management of service level agreement (SLA) mappings is supported.

The definition of techniques and rules to extract contractual terms from available semantic, XML-based, template-based and free-text descriptions and to map them to a reference meta-model is still a open research issue.

6.3.3.1 Semantic Descriptions

A possible solution to extract contractual terms from heterogeneous semantic descriptions of WS contracts is to develop wrappers that use ontology matching systems (e.g., AgreementMaker [10]) to create mappings to a reference meta-model, such as PCM [8]. Since WS contracts can be described according to different semantic models (e.g., OWL-S, WSMO, MicroWSMO, WSOL) and by means of multiple ontologies, a wrapper for each semantic model must be defined. The ontology matching systems can find pairs of related concepts and evaluate semantic affinity between concepts to create correct mappings.

Let us consider the mapping between a WSOL specification [40] and a PCM-based WS contract. The concept of *service offering* in WSOL is mapped to a pcm:Policy; *QoS constraints* and *access rights* are represented as pcm:PolicyNfp and pcm:PolicyCondition, respectively. The mapping required a preliminary step in which an ontology matching system is used to identify semantic matching between concepts in the user ontology and concepts in the reference ontology. In the example shown in Fig. 6.4, the concept ont:MaxRequestNumber specified in the user ontology matches with the concept ref:RequestLimit in the reference ontology. After this preliminary step, pre-defined rules are used to complete the mapping. For example, for each identified *QoS constraints* in the WSOL specification (e.g., *reqNumber* in Fig. 6.4), a new instance (*requestLimit1*) of the correspondent pcm:PolicyNfp is created. The instance is defined by means of an expression having operator, parameter

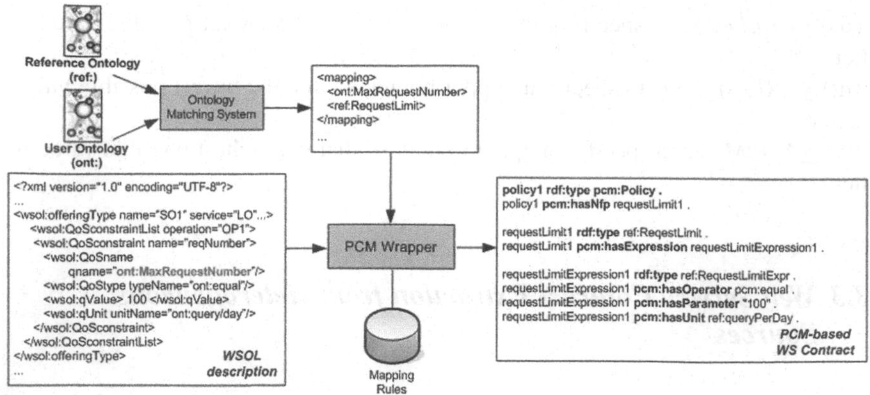

Fig. 6.4 An example of semantic WS contract mapping

and unit equals to *wsol:QoStype.typeName*, *wsol:qValue* and *wsol:qUnit.unitName* of the QoSConstraint. In the example, the resulting sematic descrition is expressed in OWL, according to *N-Triples* format.[3]

6.3.3.2 XML-Based Descriptions

A possible approach to extract semantic WS contracts from XML-based documents, and represents them according to a reference meta-model (e.g., PCM) is described in [33]. The approach is based on the usage of two main data structures and knowledge elements: *source-to-policy templates* and *semantic mappings*.

A *Source-to-Policy Template* is an XML document defined by the following main elements (the datatypes and the allowed values for each element are specified within round brackets):

- **WSName** (XPath): represents the path defined by an XPath expression to extract the name of the Web service;
- **WSProperty***[propertyValue(XPath), propertyType(String), propertyDescription (String)]: represents a property that describes a characteristic of a WS. Each WSProperty is described by a XPath expression to extract the value of the property, the type (qualitative or quantitative) of the PCM property to which the property is mapped, and the label associated with the property in the extracted contracts.

The XPath query expression is exploited by a wrapper to formulate the query over semi-structured documents to extract the desired data. An example of Source-to-Policy Template is represented in Listing 6.1. The elements tagged by "WSName" and "WSProperty" are the ones used to build PCM-based WS contracts.

[3] Specification available at: http://www.w3.org/TR/rdf-testcases/#ntriples.

Listing 6.1 An example of Source-to-Policy Template.

```
encoding="UTF-8"?> <tns:template
 xmlns:tns="http://pcm. itis. disco. unimib. it/s2ptemplate"
 xmlns:xsi="http://www. w3. org/2001/ XML Schema-instance">
 < tns:WS Name >
   /feed /entry /content /name
 </tns:WS Name >
 <tns:WS Property >
   <tns:property Value >
     /feed /entry /content /dataFormats
   </tns:property Value >
   <tns:property Type >qualitative</tns:property Type >
   <tns:property Descpription>
     Data formats
   </tns:property Description>
 </tns:WS Property>
</tns:template>
```

A set of *semantic mappings* are defined between properties in the Source-to-Policy Template at design time. Mappings are defined by equivalence relations between properties $< p, q >$ and the transitive closure of the mappings is computed. Mappings are established between properties of the same type (i.e., qualitative/quantitative properties are mapped only to qualitative/quantitative properties). Intuitively, a mapping between properties states that those properties address the same characteristic with no particular regards to possible different units of measure. For example, two different properties that adopt different scales for user-rating values (e.g. user ratings expressed in range [1..5] versus user ratings expressed in range [1..10]) are considered equivalent. Therefore, each mapping is associated with functions to convert the values expressed in a unit into values expressed in the other, and vice versa.

6.3.3.3 Template-Based and Free-Text Descriptions

As a matter of facts, template-based and free-text are the most common kind of WS contracts available. In both cases, service characteristics are described by text in natural language, which makes difficult the identification of contractual terms. A possible approach is to apply simple Information Retrieval (IR) techniques, such as keyword extraction (words and terms are identified and extracted from the service contract textual description), and stop words removal (terms that are non-significant or don't provide any meaning are removed) to index such descriptions.[4] The result is a set of keywords that are potential terms to be included in a WS contract. An IR-based approach to extract contractual terms from textual descriptions and to include them into a PCM-based WS contract has been defined in [4]. Basically, the approach consists in (i) using the IR techniques to extract a vector of keywords representing potential contractual terms and (ii) adding the vector into an existing PCM-based description to be used for matchmaking.

---

[4] For simplicity, the description of IR techniques is omitted, interested readers can to refer to [29].

A more sophisticated approach exploits natural language processing (NLP) techniques [17] such as Word splitting (for parsing concatenated text), Stemming (for reducing inflected words to their stem, base, or root form), Part Of Speech (POS) tagging (for marking up the words in a text as corresponding to a particular part of speech), Word Sense Disambiguation (WSD) (for identifying which sense of a word is used in a sentence, when the word has multiple meanings). An example of usage of such such techniques is proposed in [25].

6.4 Towards Web Service Contract Matchmaking

Here we discuss some research efforts on addressing issues on WS contract matchmaking. In particular, we present an hybrid approach to WS contract matchmaking that combines logic-based and algorithmic techniques. Logic-based techniques are used for mediation and qualitative NFP evaluation instead more practical algorithmic techniques are used for quantitative NFP evaluation. The aim of the proposal is to overcome the limitations of purely semantic or non-semantic approaches (see Sect. 6.2.2) using logical reasoning techniques on semantic WS contract descriptions only when they are strictly needed to improve the precision of the matchmaking. The hybrid approach has been implemented in the Policy Matchmaker and Ranker (PoliMaR) framework, which evolved along time in order to consider the issues discussed in Sect. 6.2.2.

The proposed hybrid approach to service matchmaking provides a step towards the development of effective, flexible, and Web-scale matchmaking systems handling different types of contracts. The main advantages over others approaches, discussed in details in [7, 32, 33], can be summarized as follows:

- Effectiveness: PoliMaR performs effective semantic-based non-boolean matchmaking dealing with, possibly under specified, qualitative and quantitative contract terms [7]; these semantic matchmaking techniques have been applied to descriptions of contracts of different kinds [8], including user-generated descriptions of contracts available in existing Web sources [32, 33].
- Extensibility: the decomposition of the matching process and architectural modularity supports different matching strategies and customized processes to fulfill application domain needs; this feature have been tested by adopting different matching functions, and different configuration of matching components without changes to the core matching strategy [4, 7, 27, 32, 33];
- Web-compliant Scalability and Performance: recent results showed that the adoption of caching and lightweight service-based distributed architectures can overcome scalability and performance limitations, which often affect semantic-based tools. By balancing loads for tasks that require significant computational resources and using different computing nodes, the proposed approach can perform matching over thousands of contract specifications extracted from the Web at run-time [32, 33].

6.4.1 An Hybrid Approach to Web Service Contract Matchmaking and Ranking

In [7], a four-phase process for WS contracts Matchmaking and Ranking has been proposed and formalized. As shown in Fig. 6.5, given a PCM-based requested contract and a set of PCM-based offered contracts the process is composed as follows: the **term matching** phase identifies the terms in the offered contracts that match with each requested term in the requested contract. The result is a set of matching term couples; the **local evaluation** phase evaluates, for each identified matching couple, how the offered term satisfies the requested one. Results are in range [0, 1]; the **global evaluation** phase evaluates, for each offered contract, the results of the previous phase to compute a global matching score. Results are values in range [0, n]; finally, the **contract ranking** phase sorts the offered contracts according to their global matching scores.

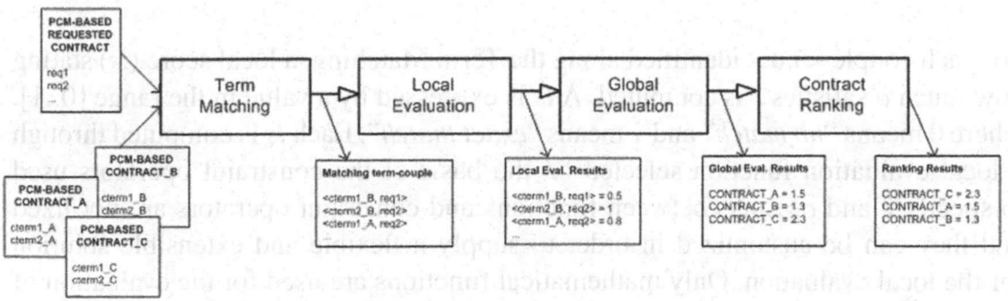

Fig. 6.5 The four-phase process for WS contract matchmaking and ranking

6.4.1.1 Term Matching

In order to identify matching term couples, the proposed mediator-centric hybrid approach exploits domain ontologies, rule-based mediators and an inference engine to solve semantic mismatches. In particular, mediators are defined as logic programming rules and stored in a rule domain ontology; rules have the following form:

$$(\tilde{s}, \tilde{p}, \tilde{o},) \leftarrow (s_1, p_1, o_1), (s_2, p_2, o_2), \ldots, (s_n, p_n, o_n)$$

Rules are composed by a head and a body. The body represents a condition through a conjunction of statements defined by the RDF triples (s_i, p_i, o_i) with $1 \leq i \leq n$. Each triple specifies a relation, through a *predicate* p, between two concepts, defined by a subject s and an object o. If the condition is verified, the relation defined by the triple $(\tilde{s}, \tilde{p}, \tilde{o})$ exists.

An example of *term matching rules* is defined in Listing 6.2. The three rules specify that every instance o of *BasePrice* and *ServicePrice* classes matches with

Listing 6.2 An Example of Term Matching Rules

```
(?r,pr:pricingMatches,?o) <- (?r,rdf:type,nfpr:BasePriceRequest),(?o,rdf:type,nfpo1:BasePrice)
(?r,pr:pricingMatches,?o) <- (?r,rdf:type,nfpr:BasePriceRequest),(?o,rdf:type,nfpo2:ServicePrice)
(?r,pcm:matches,?o) <- (?r,pr:pricingMatches,?o)
```

every instance *r* of the class *BasePriceRequest*. Moreover, the matching is defined as a *pricing* relation type (*pricingMatches*). Prefixes (e.g., *nfpo1:*) define namespaces of the ontologies in which the related concepts are specified. These prefixes permit the mediation across several ontologies.

Term matching rules can be modelled through standard rule languages, such as *SWRL*,[5] *Jena Rules*,[6] for OWL descriptions.

6.4.1.2 Local Evaluation

For each couple <*r,o*> identified along the Term Matching, a local score (*ls*) stating how much *o* satisfies *r* is computed. A *ls* is expressed by a value in the range [0..1], where 0 means "*no match*" and 1 means "*exact match*". Each *ls* is computed through a local evaluation function selected on the basis of the constraint operators used to specify *r* and *o*. Links between functions and constraint operators are not fixed and they can be customized in order to supply a flexible and extensible solution for the local evaluation. Only mathematical functions are used for the evaluation of quantitative terms; while for the evaluation of qualitative properties, mathematical functions are used in combination with logic programming rules that exploit semantic dependencies among terms based on the domain ontologies [7]. For example, let us consider an ontology for the insurance domain, where the *fireInsurance* is defined as *partOf* the *blanketInsurance*. Therefore, a WS contract offering *blanketInsurance* satisfies a requested contract specified through an *include* operator and asking for a *fireInsurance*.

6.4.1.3 Global Evaluation and Contract Ranking

Different Multi-Criteria Decision Making (MCDM) approaches can be used to perform the global score *gs* evaluation of a WS contract. An example is the Simple Additive Weighting (SAW) technique that consists in multiplying the value of each *ls* for the relevance (*rel*) that the consumer associates with the requested term. The formula is defined as follows:

[5] Specification available at: http://www.w3.org/Submission/SWRL/.

[6] Specification available at: http://jena.apache.org/documentation/inference/.

$$gs^{WScontract} = \sum_{i=1}^{n} ld^{<r,o>_i} * rel^r$$

Different techniques can be used to perform the WS contract ranking according to their *gs*. The simplest technique consists of using a traditional sorting algorithm.

6.4.2 The PoliMaR Framework

The Policy Matchmaker and Ranker (PoliMaR) framework implements the hybrid approach to WS contract matchmaking and ranking proposed in the previous section. During its development lifecycle, three different versions have been released.

After the implementation of the first core version [7], testing activities denoted a high system response time when performing reasoning activities. This issue made the first PoliMaR version inadequate to be used as a Web application. Therefore, two other versions have been developed: a cache-based and a distributed version.

6.4.2.1 The Core Architecture

The process of enabling WS contract matchmaking can be divided in two phases:

- *setup-time*: a number of offered contracts are stored into the *ontology repository* together with all the ontologies necessary for their evaluation. Moreover, a *configuration file* defining configuration parameters to be used along the matchmaking process is specified.
- *run-time*: a requested contract is submitted to the engine and the term matching, local evaluation, global evaluation and contract ranking activities are performed. The result is a list of offered contracts ordered respect to their compliance with the requested one.

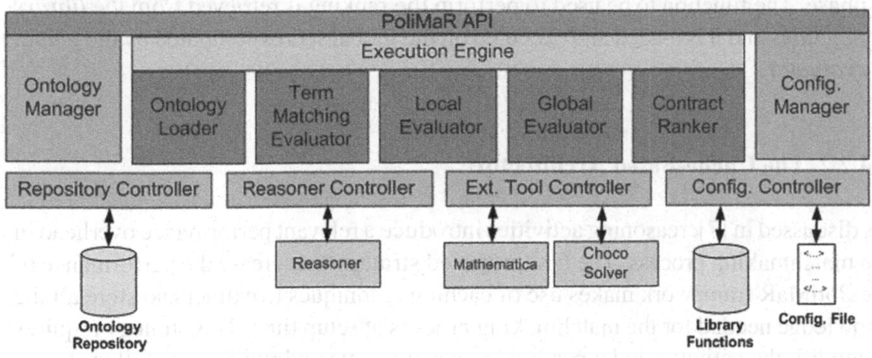

Fig. 6.6 The core PoliMaR architecture

The PoliMaR tool supports setup-time and run-time activities, from the storages of contracts by the service providers and the submission of requested contract by the service consumers, to the definition of the ranked list of contracts.

The architecture of the core version of the PoliMaR tool, illustrated in Fig. 6.6, is composed of independent modules that supply services through an API that gives access to: (i) an *ontology manager*, which is in charge of receiving contract descriptions and storing them into an appropriate repository; (ii) an *execution engine*, which receives the requested contract and implements the execution strategies to fulfill the matchmaking process; (iii) a *configuration manager*, which allows the client to specified configuration parameters to be used to perform the matchmaking.

The *execution engine* relies on a set of components providing for specific features that can be extended by new components without disrupting the architecture. Since the adopted interaction model prevents components to communicate each other, they act as servers that provide their services to the *execution engine* and make it the orchestrator of the matchmaking process, which can enact different workflows to implement different logics.

The PoliMaR core components are the following:

- *Ontology loader*: is in charge of loading into the *reasoner* through the *reasoner controller* all the knowledge necessary to realize the term matching and the local evaluation of qualitative terms.
- *Term matching evaluator*: implements the process necessary to perform the term matching phase. Through the *reasoner controller*, this component submits the matching rules to the *reasoner* and receives a set of matching couples as results.
- *Local evaluator*: implements the process necessary to perform the local evaluation phase. For each matching couple produced by the *term matching evaluator*, the local score evaluation is performed exploiting a specific function retrieved from the *library functions*.
- *Global evaluator*: implements the process necessary to perform the global evaluation phase. This component retrieves from the *library functions* the function to be used for the global score evaluations. The function is loaded and executed on the local scores computed by the *local evaluator*.
- *Contract ranker*: implements the process necessary to perform the contract ranking phase. The function to be used to perform the ranking is retrieved from the *library functions* and it is loaded and executed on the global scores computed by the *global evaluator*.

6.4.2.2 The Cache-Based Architecture

As discussed in [7], reasoning activities introduce a relevant performance overhead in the matchmaking process. The first proposed strategy to increase the performance of the PoliMaR framework makes use of caching techniques to extract and store all the knowledge needed for the matchmaking process at setup time. This strategy requires to modify the activities to be performed at setup-time and run-time as follows:

- *setup-time*: different types of caches must be created in order to make available in practical data structures all the knowledge needed for the run-time evaluation. The caches are created through the *reasoner* that extracts relevant information from the *ontology repository*.
- *run-time*: a requested contract is submitted to the engine and the cache-based matchmaking process is performed. The use of a *reasoner* is no longer needed.

In order to support both term matching and local evaluation, two different types of caches are created: (i) *matching cache* that includes, for each possible requested term, all the instances of concepts defined in the *ontology repository* that satisfy predefined matching rules; (ii) *relation cache* that includes, relations (e.g., inclusion, equality) between instances of concepts defined in the *ontology repository*.

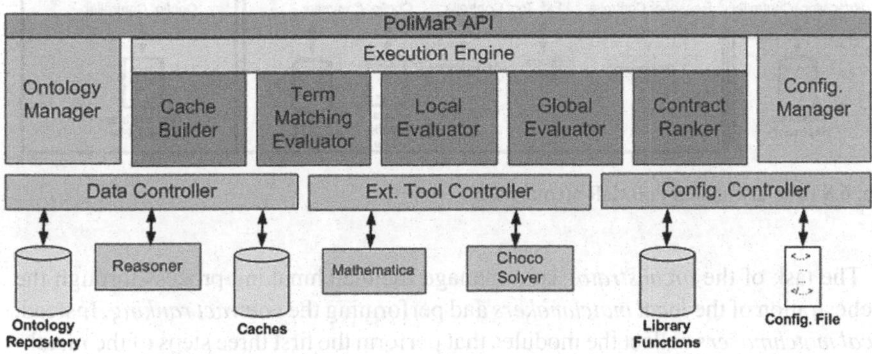

Fig. 6.7 The cache-based PoliMaR architecture

The cache-based PoliMaR architecture (shown in Fig. 6.7) introduces two new components:

- *Cache builder*: replaces the *ontology loader* and implements the functionalities required for cache management. It is in charge of creating the caches at setup-time and updating them at run-time when new ontologies are stored in the *ontology repository*.
- *Data controller*: replaces the original *repository controller* and *reasoner controller* and aims at making the upper components independent of the actual underlying *reasoner* and of the technology used to manage the *ontology repository* and the *caches*.

6.4.2.3 The Distributed Architecture

The cache-based architecture dramatically reduces the response time of the PoliMaR framework, but at the cost of another limitation: the management of dynamic properties (e.g., QoS) requires continuous cache refreshing in order to preserve data consistency, but the *cache building* performance is low since reasoning is required. To increase the response time, a distributed version of PoliMaR has been defined.

The architecture of the distributed PoliMaR is shown in Fig. 6.8. The high modularity of the core architecture allows us to create two distributed components, the *orchestrator* and the *local matchmaker*, that collects existing modules.

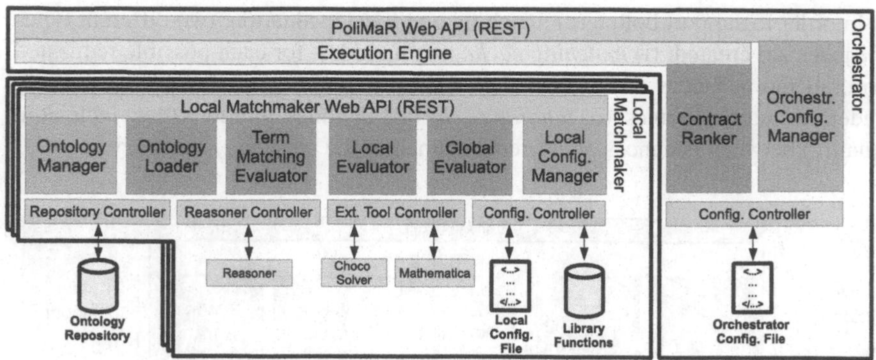

Fig. 6.8 The distributed PoliMaR architecture

The task of the *orchestrator* is to manage the matchmaking process through the orchestration of the *local matchmakers* and performing the *contract ranking*. Instead, *local matchmakers* collect the modules that perform the first three steps of the matchmaking process: term matching, local evaluation and global evaluation. The communication overhead is kept low thanks to the adoption of REST style interfaces to deliver a lightweight and flexible service-oriented architecture [34].

As discussed in details in [33], this distributed architecture ensures a relevant performance improvement. This improvement is enabled by a partial parallelization of the matchmaking process performed by the *local matchmaker*. Moreover, each *local matchmaker* performs a more efficient reasoning exploiting a smaller and less complex knowledge base.

6.5 Concluding Remarks

Web service contracts are legally binding exchange of promises and agreements between service providers and potential service consumers expressed through sets of contractual terms on non-functional properties covering QoS, legal, intellectual right, and business characteristics of services and their data.

The enhancement of Web service discovery and composition with the evaluation of WS contracts is promising, but currently not supported by Web service discovery and composition engines. This is due to the fact that service providers represent WS contracts using heterogeneous formalisms, causing strong ambiguity and redundancies and preventing their right interpretation in multi-provider service-oriented environments.

From the analysis of the literature two main issues emerge: (i) the definition of a semantic meta-model that provides a sound and robust base to formally describe WS contracts and (ii) the definition of an effective approach to WS contract matchmaking with high levels of expressivity, generality, extensibility and flexibility.

The chapter reports research experiences that addressed the mentioned issues. The Policy Centered Meta-model (PCM) [11] is a semantic meta-model that supports the definition of expressive and structured WS contract descriptions aggregating qualitative and quantitative contractual terms into a single entity with an applicability condition. Different techniques can be used to extract contractual terms from available WS contract descriptions and to map them into PCM-based WS contracts. Examples are in [4, 8, 33] where (i) wrapping techniques appear to be a valid solution for the extraction of terms from semantic descriptions, (ii) template-based and semantic mappings are proposed to manage XML-based descriptions and, (iii) IR and NLP are proposed to extract terms from free-text descriptions.

The hybrid approach implemented into the Policy Matchmaker and Ranker (PoliMaR) framework [7] that combines logic-based and algorithmic techniques represents an effective solution to WS contract matchmaking with high levels of expressivity, generality, extensibility and flexibility.

References

1. Bochicchio, M.A., Longo, A.: Modelling contract management for cloud services. In: IEEE International Conference on Cloud Computing (CLOUD 2011), pp. 332–339. Washington, DC, USA (2011)
2. Bonatti, P.A., Coi, J.L.D., Olmedilla, D., Sauro, L.: Rule-based policy representations and reasoning. In: In Semantic Techniques for the Web, The REWERSE Perspective, *Lecture Notes in Computer Science*, vol. 5500, pp. 201–232. Springer (2009)
3. Brandic, I., Music, D., Leitner, P., Dustdar, S.: Vieslaf framework: Enabling adaptive and versatile sla-management. In: In proc. of International Workshop on Grid Economics and Business Models 2009 (GECON 09), pp. 60–73. Delft, The Netherlands (2009)
4. Calegari, S., Comerio, M., Maurino, A., Panzeri, E., Pasi, G.: A semantic and information retrieval based approach to service contract selection. In: Proc. 9th International Conference on Service-Oriented Computing (ICSOC 2011), pp. 389–403. Paphos, Cyprus (2011)
5. Carenini, A., Cerizza, D., Comerio, M., Della Valle, E., De Paoli, F., Maurino, A., Palmonari, M., Turati, A.: Glue2: a web service discovery engine with non-functional properties. In: Proc. of the Fifth European Conference on Web Services (ECOWS '07). Dublin, Ireland (2008)
6. Chaari, S., Badr, Y., Biennier, F.: Enhancing web service selection by qos-based ontology and ws-policy. In: Proceedings of the 2008 SAC ACM, SAC '08, pp. 2426–2431. ACM (2008)
7. Comerio, M., De Paoli, F., Palmonari, M.: Effective and flexible nfp-based ranking of web services. In: Proc. of Inter. Conf. on Service Oriented Computing (ICSOC), pp. 546–560. Stockholm, Sweden (2009)
8. Comerio, M., Truong, H.L., De Paoli, F., Dustdar, S.: Evaluating contract compatibility for service composition in the seco2 framework. In: Proc. of Inter. Conf. on Service Oriented Computing (ICSOC), pp. 221–236. Stockholm, Sweden (2009)

9. Comuzzi, M., Pernici, B.: Negotiation support for web service selection. Technologies for E-Services pp. 29–38 (2005)
10. Cruz, I.F., Antonelli, F.P., Stroe, C.: Agreementmaker: Efficient matching for large real-world schemas and ontologies. PVLDB **2**(2), 1586–1589 (2009)
11. De Paoli, F., Palmonari, M., Comerio, M., Maurino, A.: A Meta-Model for Non-Functional Property Descriptions of Web Services. In: Proc. of the IEEE International Conference on Web Services (ICWS), pp. 393–400. Beijing, China (2008)
12. Domingue, J., Cabral, L., Galizia, S., Tanasescu, V., Gugliotta, A., Norton, B., Pedrinaci, C.: IRS-III: A broker-based approach to semantic Web services. Web Semantics: Science, Services and Agents on the World Wide Web **6**(2), 109–132 (2008)
13. Gangadharan, G.R., D'Andrea, V., Iannella, R., Weiss, M.: Odrl service licensing profile (odrl-s). In: 5th International Workshop for Technical, Economic, and Legal Aspects of Business Models for Virtual Goods (2007)
14. Garcia, J.M., Toma, I., Ruiz, D., Ruiz-Cortes, A.: A service ranker based on logic rules evaluation and constraint programming. In: Proc. of 2nd Non Functional Properties and Service Level Agreements in SOC Workshop (NFPSLASOC). Dublin, Ireland (2008)
15. Haller, A., Cimpian, E., Mocan, A., Oren, E., Bussler, C.: Wsmx-a semantic service-oriented architecture. In: Proc. of IEEE International Conference on Web Services (ICWS 2005), pp. 321–328. IEEE (2005)
16. Jarma, Y., Boloor, K., Dias de Amorim, M., Viniotis, Y., Callaway, R.: Dynamic service contract enforcement in service-oriented networks. Services Computing, IEEE Transactions on **PP**(99), 1 (2011). doi:10.1109/TSC.2011.45
17. Jurafsky, D., Martin, J.H.: Speech and Language Processing: An Introduction to Natural Language Processing, Computational Linguistics and Speech Recognition, second edn. Prentice Hall (2008). http://www.worldcat.org/isbn/013122798X
18. Kamoda, H., Yamaoka, M., Matsuda, S., Broda, K., Sloman, M.: "Policy Conflict Analysis Using Free Variable Tableaux for Access Control in Web Services Environments". In: "Proceedings of the 14th International World Wide Web Conference (WWW)" (2005)
19. Keller, A., Ludwig, H.: The WSLA framework: Specifying and monitoring service level agreements for web services. Journal of Network and Systems Management **11**(1), 57–81 (2003)
20. Keller, U., Lara, R., Lausen, H., Polleres, A., Fensel, D.: Automatic location of services. In: The Semantic Web: Research and Applications, *Lecture Notes in Computer Science*, vol. 3532, pp. 1–16. Springer Berlin / Heidelberg (2005)
21. Klusch, M., Fries, B., Sycara, K.: Owls-mx: A hybrid semantic web service matchmaker for owl-s services. Web Semant. **7**(2), 121–133 (2009). http://dx.doi.org/10.1016/j.websem.2008.10.001
22. Kritikos, K., Plexousakis, D.: Semantic qos metric matching. In: Proc. of the European Conference on Web Services (ECOWS), pp. 265–274. IEEE Computer Society, Washington, DC, USA (2006)
23. Lamparter, S., Ankolekar, A., Studer, R., Grimm, S.: Preference-based selection of highly configurable web services. In: Proc. of the 16th international conference on World Wide Web (WWW '07), pp. 1013–1022. ACM, New York, NY, USA (2007). http://doi.acm.org/10.1145/1242572.1242709
24. Lamparter, S., Luckner, S., Mutschler, S.: Semi-automated management of web service contracts. International Journal of Services Sciences **1**(3/4) (2008)
25. Lee, K.H., Lim, J.: Constructing composite web services from natural language requests. Web Semantics: Science, Services and Agents on the World Wide Web **8**(1) (2011)
26. Lewis, L., Ray, P.: Service level management definition, architecture, and research challenges. In: Global Telecommunications Conference, 1999. GLOBECOM '99, vol. 3, pp. 1974–1978 vol. 3 (1999). doi:10.1109/GLOCOM.1999.832515
27. Li, P., Comerio, M., Maurino, A., De Paoli, F.: Advanced non-functional property evaluation of web services. In: Proceeding of Seventh IEEE European Conference on Web Services (ECOWS'09), pp. 27–36. IEEE (2009)

28. Liu, Y., Ngu, A., Zeng, L.: Qos computation and policing in dynamic web service selection. In: Proc. of the 13th international World Wide Web conference on Alternate track papers and posters (WWW Alt. '04), pp. 66–73 (2004)
29. Manning, C.D., Raghavan, P., Schütze, H.: Introduction to Information Retrieval. Cambridge University Press (2008)
30. Martin, D.: Semantic Markup for Web Services. Formalization available at: http://www.w3.org/Submission/OWL-S/ (2004)
31. Mokhtar, S., Preuveneers, D., Georgantas, N., Issarny, V., Berbers, Y.: Easy: Efficient semantic service discovery in pervasive computing environments with qos and context support. Journal of Systems and Software **81**(5), 785–808 (2008)
32. Panziera, L., Comerio, M., Palmonari M. De Paoli, F., Batini, C.: Quality-driven Extraction, Fusion and Matchmaking of Semantic Web API Descriptions. Journal of Web Engineering **11**(3), 247–268 (2012)
33. Panziera, L., Comerio, M., Palmonari, M., De Paoli, F.: Distributed matchmaking and ranking of web apis exploiting descriptions from web sources. In: Proceedings of the IEEE International Conference on Service-Oriented Computing and Applications (SOCA 2011). Irvine, USA (2011)
34. Pautasso, C., Zimmermann, O., Leymann, F.: Restful web services vs. "big" web services: making the right architectural decision. In: Proceedings of the 17th International Conference on World Wide Web (WWW) 2008, pp. 805–814 (2008)
35. Spillner, J., Winkler, M., Reichert, S., Cardoso, J., Schill, A.: Distributed contracting and monitoring in the internet of services. In: Proc. of the 9th International Conference on Distributed Applications and Interoperable Systems (DAIS), pp. 129–142. Lisbon, Portugal (2009)
36. Stollberg, M., Keller, U., Lausen, H., Heymans, S.: Two-phase web service discovery based on rich functional descriptions. In: E. Franconi, M. Kifer, W. May (eds.) The Semantic Web: Research and Applications, *Lecture Notes in Computer Science*, vol. 4519, pp. 99–113. Springer Berlin / Heidelberg (2007)
37. Surya, N., John, Z.: Issues on the compatibility of web service contracts. In: L. Jie-Zhang (ed.) Innovations, Standards and Practices of Web Services: Emerging Research Topics, pp. 154–188. IGI Global (2012)
38. Toma, I., Foxvog, D., Paoli, F.D., Comerio, M., Palmonari, M., Maurino, A.: Non-functional properties in web services. wsmo d28.4 v0.2. Tech. rep., http://www.wsmo.org/TR/d28/d28.4/v0.2/20080416 (2008)
39. Toma, I., Roman, D., Fensel, D.: On describing and ranking services based on non-functional properties. In: Third International Conference on Next Generation Web Services Practices (NWESP '07), pp. 61–66. IEEE Computer Society, Washington, DC, USA (2007)
40. Tosic, V., Patel, K., Pagurek, B.: Wsol - web service offerings language. In: CAiSE '02/ WES '02: Revised Papers from the International Workshop on Web Services, E-Business, and the Semantic Web, pp. 57–67. Springer-Verlag, London, UK (2002)
41. Vu, L., Hauswirth, M., Porto, F., Aberer, K.: A search engine for QoS-enabled discovery of semantic web services. International Journal of Business Process Integration and Management **1**(4), 244–255 (2006)
42. Wang, X., Vitvar, T., Kerrigan, M., Toma, I.: A qos-aware selection model for semantic web services. In: Proc. of the 4th Intl Conference on Service-Oriented Computing (ICSOC'06), pp. 390–401. Chicago, IL, USA (2006)
43. WSMO: The Web Service Modeling Ontology (WSMO). Final Draft. Available at: http://www.wsmo.org/TR/d2/v1.2/20050413/ (2005)
44. Yan, J., Kowalczyk, R., Lin, J., Chhetri, M., Goh, S., Zhang, J.: Autonomous service level agreement negotiation for service composition provision. Future Generation Computer Systems **23**(6), 748–759 (2007)
45. Yu, H.Q., Reiff-Marganiec, S.: A method for automated web service selection. In: proc. of the Congress on Services (SERVICES), pp. 513–520 (2008)
46. Zaremba, M., Migdal, J., Hauswirth, M.: Discovery of optimized web service configurations using a hybrid semantic and statistical approach. In: Web Services, 2009. ICWS 2009. IEEE International Conference on, pp. 149–156. IEEE (2009)

47. Zeng, L., Benatallah, B., Ngu, A., Dumas, M., Kalagnanam, J., Chang, H.: Qos-aware middleware for web services composition. IEEE Trans. Softw. Eng. 30(5), 311–327 (2004). http://dx.doi.org/10.1109/TSE.2004.11
48. Zou, J., Wang, Y., Lin, K.J.: A formal service contract model for accountable saas and cloud services. In: Proc. of IEEE International Conference on Services Computing (SCC 2010), pp. 73–80. Miami, Florida, USA (2010)

Chapter 7
A Certification-Aware Service-Oriented Architecture

Marco Anisetti, Claudio A. Ardagna, Michele Bezzi, Ernesto Damiani, Samuel Paul Kaluvuri and Antonino Sabetta

Abstract The widespread development of Service-Oriented Architecture (SOA) and web services is changing the traditional view of information technology. Today, software applications are increasingly distributed and consumed as a service, and business processes are implemented by selecting and composing services provided by different suppliers at run-time and with a minimal human intervention. In this scenario, where services are usually selected on the basis of clients' functional preferences, the risk of providing powerful but insecure applications raises, and the problem of guaranteeing and preserving the security of services and business processes becomes stringent. To this aim, we put forward the idea that security certification techniques can be adopted to provide the evidence that a service system has some security properties and behaves as expected. However, existing security certification techniques are not well-suited to the service scenario, since they are designed for static and monolithic software and then cannot support the intrinsic SOA dynamics. In this chapter, we discuss recent developments in the area of extending security

M. Anisetti (✉) · C. A. Ardagna · E. Damiani
Dipartimento di Informatica, Università degli Studi di Milano,
Via Bramante 65, 26013 Crema, Italy
e-mail: marco.anisetti@unimi.it

C. A. Ardagna
e-mail: claudio.ardagna@unimi.it

E. Damiani
e-mail: ernesto.damiani@unimi.it

M. Bezzi · S. P. Kaluvuri · A. Sabetta
SAP Research Sophia-Antipolis, 805, Av. du Docteur Maurice Donat,
06254 Mougins Cedex, France
e-mail: michele.bezzi@sap.com

S. P. Kaluvuri
e-mail: samuel.kaluvuri@sap.com

A. Sabetta
e-mail: antonino.sabetta@sap.com

A. Bouguettaya et al. (eds.), *Advanced Web Services*,
DOI: 10.1007/978-1-4614-7535-4_7,

certifications to web services. In particular, we first review current certification approaches, and highlight requirements and challenges for applying them to the service ecosystem. We then present an advanced methodology for security certification based on testing, as a crucial part of a novel approach for security certification developed in the context of the FP7 EU project *Advanced Security Service cERTificate for SOA* (ASSERT4SOA).

7.1 Introduction

Recent enhancements of Internet technologies and the growing success of SOA and web services are moving current vision of ICT towards the Internet of Services [40]. Today, in fact, many software applications are released as service-based products, and business processes are implemented by composing loosely-coupled services provided by different suppliers. SOA and Web service standards provide a powerful framework to specify distributed applications by defining their *messaging* (e.g., using the Web Service Description Language (WSDL) [24]), *conversation* (e.g., using the Web Service Conversation Language (WSCL) [2]), and/or *coordination* (e.g., using the Business Process Execution Language (BPEL) [1]).

The price we pay for such a convenient way of specifying distributed applications and developing business processes is an increasing difficulty in the evaluation of their non-functional properties. This is especially true for security properties, since runtime selection and composition of services provided by unknown parties can increase the risk of security issues. As a consequence, the users are much more concerned about the risk of developing powerful but insecure services. There is therefore the need of providing new assurance techniques that fit the SOA environment and allow users to evaluate a service not only using its functional properties but also verifying non-functional ones. The availability of service-oriented assurance techniques aims to increase the confidence of the users that a given service is secure and behaves as expected.

The research community is trying to address the above issues by adapting current development, verification, and certification techniques to the SOA environment (e.g., [7, 9, 14, 19, 20, 22, 30, 45]). These techniques have to manage the intrinsic dynamics of SOA applications and environments, and must be integrated within the selection, discovery, and composition processes which are at the basis of the SOA success. Among the different assurance techniques that can be used to address the above problems, *security certification* is increasingly adopted. Originally, security certification schemes have been defined for traditional static and monolithic software systems, to the aim of proving some properties that are then used at deployment and installation time [18]. These solutions cannot be adopted in a SOA scenario as they are, but they need to be enhanced to meet SOA requirements.

In this chapter, the challenges and issues of security certification schemes for services are analyzed from two different perspectives: (i) we analyze how a test-based security certification scheme can be defined and integrated within SOA to provide a certification-aware selection process; (ii) we analyze how a suitable framework for managing the full life-cycle of services with certified security properties can be provided, including certificate issuing and management, certification-aware service discovery, certificate validation, and service consumption. The remaining of this chapter is organized as follows. First, we analyze requirements on certification schemes for services (Sect. 7.2) also discussing how they are changing the trust model underlying the SOA infrastructure (Sect. 7.3). Then, we present a possible specification of a test-based security certification scheme for SOA (Sect. 7.4). Moreover, we illustrate the framework provided by ASSERT4SOA to support a certification-aware SOA (Sect. 7.5), giving an overview of the high-level components of the framework and a certification-aware development environment. Finally, we discuss the next steps in the certification of evolving and composed services (Sect. 7.6).

7.2 Requirements on Security Certification of Services

Currently available certification schemes aim to provide trustworthy evidence that a particular software system has some features, conforms to specified requirements, and behaves as expected [18]. Some of these schemes have focused on security properties and requirements. The Trusted Computer System Evaluation Criteria (TCSEC) (commonly referred as *Orange Book*) [46], provided by the U.S Department of Defense (DoD) in 1985, has been the first security certification solution. TCSEC aimed to propose a standard for security certification of software that (i) provides guidelines to develop products satisfying security requirements, (ii) defines a means to measure the level of trust provided by the system, and (iii) allows software purchasers to state their requirements on the software. Following the TCSEC effort, many other solutions have been provided world-wide, as for instance, Information Technology Security Evaluation Criteria (ITSEC) [26] in 1991, Canadian Trusted Computer Product Evaluation Criteria (CTCPEC) [18] in 1993. A major drawback of these solutions is that they implement national certifications that are totally independent from each other. As a consequence, the cost of certifying a software system at an international level has been very high for a long time. The Common Criteria (ISO 15408) certification scheme [24] has been defined to address this limitation and provides an international standard for affordable software security certification, including a general framework to specify, design, and evaluate security properties of IT products. Common Criteria therefore reduces the costs of certifying a system, while it maintains high complexity. Recently, some lightweight software certification processes have been specified with the goal of reassuring the users without the complexities of existing processes. As an example, Certificat de Sécurité de Premier Niveau (CSPN) [3] has been designed as an alternative to Common Criteria and provides a lightweight security certification infrastructure. If, on one side, CSPN provides a lower level of security assurance than Common Criteria, on the other side, it is less complex and allows to achieve security certification in less time.

Although the many advantages of the above certification schemes, they are not suitable for a service ecosystem. In fact, they usually consider static and monolithic software, provide certificates including human-readable statements signed by a trusted third party, and consider system-wide certificates to be used at deployment and installation time. A promising direction to increase the level of assurance of existing SOA applications and web services must (i) extend existing schemes to fit the SOA dynamics and (ii) support the selection and composition of services on the basis of the evidence that proves a set of security properties for each single service. We therefore identify the following requirements that are fundamental for the definition of a service-oriented certification scheme.

- *Machine-readable certificates*. A service provider should be able to retrieve a machine-readable certificate for its services by interacting with a trusted certification authority. The certificate proves a set of properties and can be consumed at run-time by clients searching for a service that provides a set of functionalities with a given level of assurance. Also, clients should be able to access and analyze (if needed) the evidence supporting the properties. There exist two classes of evidence that can be included in the certificate to support the claim that a service holds a property [18]: (i) *test-based evidence* providing test-based proofs that a test carried out on the service has given a certain result, which in turn shows that a given property holds for that service; or (ii) *model-based evidence* providing formal proofs that a service holds some properties and meets formal specifications in terms of security requirements. The generation, management, and availability of accurate evidence are fundamental aspects to integrate the security certification process and outcomes within the SOA infrastructure. Some approaches for software systems (e.g., Common Criteria [24]) integrate both test-based and model-based evidence to provide different levels of assurance on software properties. In this chapter, as explained in Sect. 7.4, we focus on *test-based evidence* as the means to provide a first level of security assurance for services.
- *Support for certification-aware service selection and composition*. The certification scheme should be designed to enhance the run-time service selection and composition processes, which are at the basis of the SOA paradigm. First, the SOA infrastructure should be extended to allow clients to select only those services that address their security preferences. This requirement introduces the need of a solution that matches clients' preferences with assurance information (i.e., evidence) in the certificates. Second, the SOA infrastructure should provide a composition process that aims to implement a composed service with some security properties. This process is driven by the properties to be certified on the composition and selects only those services that have a security certificate compatible with the target properties.
- *Certificate life-cycle management*. A service provider should be able to maintain the freshness of certificates awarded to its services, also upon a new delivery of the service code. Given the high dynamics of services, a low-cost solution for incremental certification of evolving services is required to limit the need of re-certification from scratch. A proper solution should then re-use as much as

possible the evidence and information in certificates awarded to older versions of the service, to release a certificate for the new version.

- *Service-based framework*. The certification scheme should be enriched by a service-based framework that is responsible for all certification activities, including certificate release/revocation, certificate life-cycle management, and certificate-based selection and composition of services. The framework should include a certification-aware service registry and all components needed to manage certified services.

7.3 A Trust Model for Service Certification

The adoption of security certification techniques for services has a double impact on the SOA infrastructure. On one side, it changes the traditional trust model underlying SOA [6, 16], while on the other side, as discussed in Sect. 7.2, it would enhance the selection and composition processes with requirements on non-functional properties of services.

In general, when no certification techniques are used, the process of service purchase involves two parties: (i) a *service provider* implementing and deploying a service, and (ii) a *client* (either a human being or another service provider) selecting and composing services implemented by different service providers to build complex applications. Each service provider makes claims in the form of human-readable statements on their services' functionalities, as well as on their non-functional properties. These claims can be of two types: (i) assertions on functionalities of a service (e.g., "*the service supports functionalities for storing, retrieving, updating, and deleting files*"), and assertions linking functionalities and some abstract properties (e.g., "*a mechanism to encrypt-decrypt messages in transit is implemented and implies confidentiality of the communications*"). In this case, the assertions are usually self-certified by the service provider and added to the service specifications. The service provider can optionally provide a set of evidence supporting its assertions, as for instance, testing results, bug fixing reports, and the like. The client trust in an assertion k made by a service provider s can be denoted with a variable $T_{k,s}$, taking a value on an ordinal scale or in the interval [0, 1]. This value can be influenced by many factors, as for instance, the market standing and reputation of the service provider, the evidence type, the way in which the evidence supporting the assertion has been generated.

The integration of a security certification scheme within the SOA infrastructure modifies the trust relationship between a client and a service provider. In this new scenario, a trusted external entity (i.e., a certification authority—CA) is responsible to collect, validate, and publish security assertions (and related evidence) on services. The client trust in an (set of) assertion k made by a certification authority CA can be denoted with a variable $T_{k,CA}$, and implicitly represents the level of trust the client has on a service certifying a set of properties. In particular, assertions produced by the security certification process are used as follows.

- *Security property definition.* Certified assertions are used to define the security properties supported by a given service. These properties belong to the well-known confidentiality, integrity, or availability classification [7, 21, 25]. The client trust in a service will then depend on it having all functionalities required to achieve some security properties.
- *Certification authority.* Certified assertions are used to identify who has validated the security functionalities of the service. The client trust in a service will depend on the entity (i.e., certification authority) signing the assertions, how the entity has been accredited, and the adopted collection and validation processes. Usually, a certification scheme also provides a set of criteria for entities, called *security evaluation facilities*, to ensure that these entities are capable and competent of performing security evaluations under a clearly defined quality system.
- *Security functionality validation.* Certified assertions are used to specify the nature of the evidence supporting the validation of a security functionality. The client trust in a service will depend on the nature of the available evidence. A security functionality can be verified using a test-based approach; alternatively, its properties can be proven based on a formal model. The focus of the validation can be on security functionality alone, or the development process may also have been taken into account. Certification schemes clearly define how evidence has been collected and stored, and how the product has been validated.

A trust model for service certification involves three main parties: a *client* that searches for a certified service, a *service provider* that communicates with a certification authority to certify its services, and a *certification authority* that produces assertions on service functionalities, provides evidence supporting the assertions, and specifies properties implied by evidence and assertions for the service under certification. Upon a request for service certification by a service provider, the certification authority collects the needed information by the service provider and starts the evaluation activities. These activities result in the certification of a set of security properties for the service. The client trust $T_{k,CA}$, where k is the set of assertions supporting a set of properties for the service, depends on the assertions themselves, the produced evidence, the mechanisms used by the CA to produce the evidence, and the reputation of the CA. As said, there are cases in which the service provider itself may provide the set k of assertions on its services, on which the client has a given level of trust $T_{k,s}$. It is important to stress that certifications are often used as a selling argument, compared to a competitor's product with no certificate or self-signed certificate. In general, the service provider assumes that $T_{k,CA} \geq T_{k,s}$, and the increase in revenue due to increased trust will be greater than the cost of certification. This is indeed the case because the credibility and reputation of a service provider rarely outperform the trust in a certificate signed by a certification authority which is internationally recognized.

7.4 Machine-Readable Certification of Services

Current certification schemes lack of a machine-readable, semantics-aware format for expressing security properties, and cannot be used to support and automate run-time security assessment in a highly-dynamic SOA environment. As a consequence, existing certification schemes do not support, from a client perspective, a reliable way to assess the trustworthiness of a web service (composed or not) in the context where (and at the time when) it will be actually executed. In this section, we present a service-oriented approach that aims to fill this gap by expressing, assessing, and certifying security properties of complex service-oriented applications. The proposed solution, which consists of a test-based security certification scheme, permits to specify machine-readable certificates (e.g., using an XML-based language) proving that a service has a security property. Clearly, also the evidence in the certificate supporting the property is in a machine-readable form, in such a way that it can be used to query and compare different certificates. In the following of this section, we present the test-based certification scheme and how it fits the SOA environment.

7.4.1 Test-Based Certification of Services

According to Damiani et al. [18], "*test-based certificates are evidence-based proofs that a test carried out on the software has given a certain result, which in turn shows (perhaps with a certain level of uncertainty) that a given property holds for that software. In particular, test-based certification of security-related properties is a complex process, identifying a set of high-level security properties and linking them to a suitable set of white- and black-box software tests*". Starting from this definition, a machine-readable certificate should link a set of security properties with the evidence supporting them. More in detail, a service-oriented certification scheme needs to define (i) the set of security properties that can be certified on the services, (ii) the categories of tests that can be used to provide the evidence supporting a property, (iii) a model of the services under test that is used to generate the test cases of a given category, and in turn the test evidence supporting a given property.

Hierarchy of security properties. A security property is defined as a pair $p = (\hat{p}, A)$ where $\hat{p}$ is an abstract property (e.g., confidentiality, integrity) and A is the set of class attributes that refer to a set of threats the service proves to counteract, to a security function implemented by the service, or to specific characteristics of the implemented security function [7]. The domain of each attribute $a \in A$ is characterized by a (partial/total) order relationship $\preceq_a$ and the value of a is denoted as $v(a)$. Security properties can be formally organized in a hierarchy defined as a pair $(\mathscr{P}, \preceq_P)$, where $\mathscr{P}$ is the set of all security properties, and $\preceq_P$ is a partial order relationship over $\mathscr{P}$. Given two properties p_i and p_j in $\mathscr{P}$, we write that $pi \preceq_P p_j$ (i.e., p_i is an abstraction of p_j), if $p_i.\hat{p} = p_j.\hat{p}$ and $\forall k = 1, \ldots, |A|$, either $v_i(a_k)$ is not specified

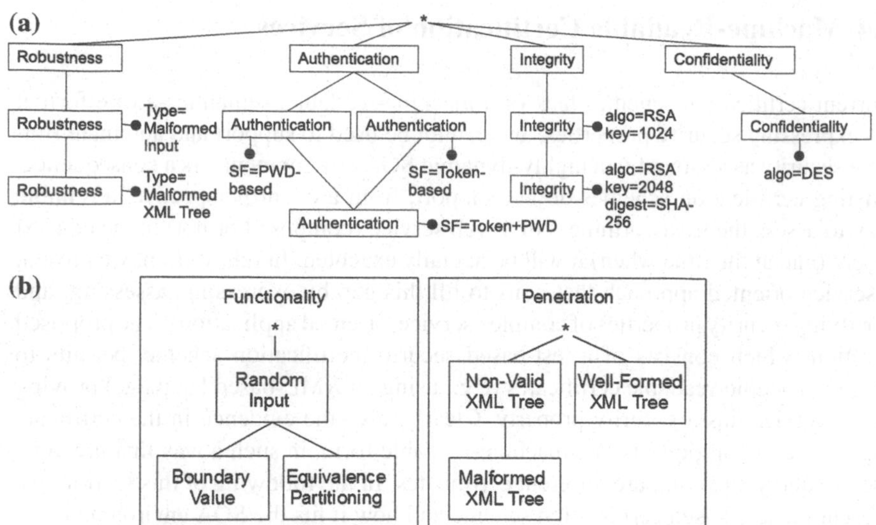

Fig. 7.1 An example of a hierarchy of security properties (**a**) and categories of tests (**b**) [7]

or $v_i(a_k) \preceq_{ak} v_j(ak)$. In general, a service proving property p_j always proves p_i. Figure 7.1a shows an example of a hierarchy of security properties.

Categories of tests. Each category T (e.g., functionality) specifies a set of test types (e.g., random input), which represent the test design technique used to generate the test cases and the certification evidence. Test types are organized in a hierarchy $(\mathscr{T},\preceq_T)$, one for each test category T, where $\mathscr{T}$ is the set of all test types for the category T, and $\preceq_T$ is a partial order relationship over $\mathscr{T}$. Given two test types t_i and t_j in $\mathscr{T}$, $t_i \preceq_T t_j$ if t_i is an abstraction of t_j. Figure 7.1b shows a first example of categories of tests, which can be extended to embrace additional testing categories and types in [47]. We note that each test category has a set *TA* of test attributes. Each test attribute $ta \in TA$ is characterized by a total order relationship $\preceq_{ta}$.

Service model. In the literature, different approaches model services as state automata and transition systems (e.g., [22, 30]). These approaches are mainly aimed to improve testing performance and test generation, and to evaluate the correctness of the service under test. Starting from the work in [22], we model a service as a Symbolic Transition System (STS) [23]; STS, in fact, is a suitable solution to represent and certify complex Web services involving communications over the Net. A symbolic transition system is a tuple $\langle \mathscr{S}, s_0, \mathscr{V}, \mathscr{I}, \mathscr{A}, \rightarrow \rangle$, where $\mathscr{S}$ is a set of states, $s_0 \in \mathscr{S}$ is the initial state, $\mathscr{V}$ is the set of internal variables, $\mathscr{I}$ is the set of interaction variables, $\mathscr{A}$ is the set of actions (web service operations), and $\rightarrow$ is the transition relation. Each transition relation consists of a set of edges connecting two states and labeled with an action, a guard (conditions on transition), and an update mapping (new assignments to variables). Service models can be specified at different levels including information coming from different sources as: (i) information

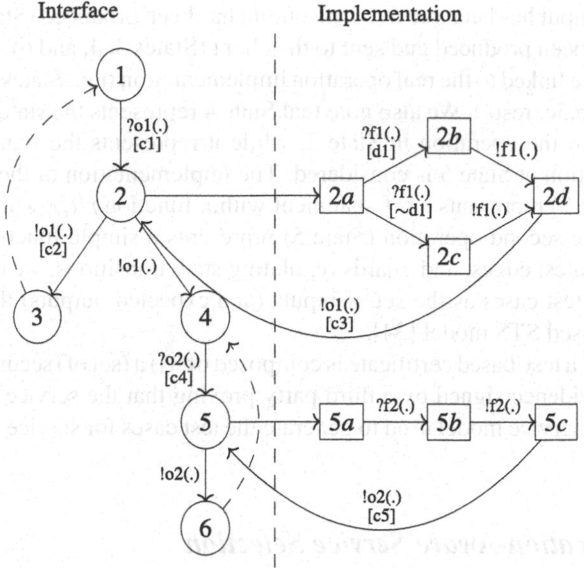

Fig. 7.2 An example of STS-based model

in the WSDL interface only (WSDL-based model), which defines the interface of a service in terms of operations and messages; (ii) information in the WSDL interface extended with information about the conversation (communication flow between clients and services) in the WSCL document (WSCL-based model). WSCL defines the service interactions as the messages to be exchanged and the expected transitions based on the results of these interactions; (iii) information in the WSDL interface and WSCL document extended with details on the implementation of the WSDL operations (implementation-based model). We note that in case (i) we have an STS-based model for each WSDL operation, while in cases (ii) and (iii), we have a single STS-based model involving conversations and operation implementations, respectively. The service model is used to automatically generate those test cases that will be used to certify a service and produce the supporting evidence. We note that the generation of test cases is pretty simple in case we consider basic data types (e.g., integers, strings), while it is more difficult for complex data types (e.g., XML fragments). In the latter scenario, the test cases can be manually constructed and then automatically selected according to the test category. Figure 7.2 shows an example of STS-based model that presents the flow of communication of a service both at the interface level (operations in WSDL and conversations in WSCL) and at the implementation level (operation implementation). Operations in the WSDL interface and functions in the implementation are denoted as $o_i(.)$ and $f_j(.)$, respectively. Each transition edge can be labeled with an input action *?o(.)/?f(.)*, the corresponding output *!o(.)/!f(.)*, and conditions (i.e., guards) on transitions presented in square brackets. Each WSDL operation consists of three states as follows: (i) no input has been received (States 1 and 4), (ii) the input has been received, no output has been produced (States 2 and 5), (iii) output has been produced and sent to the client (States 3, 4, and 6). We note that States 2 and 5 are linked to the real operation implementation (i.e., States 2a,2b,2c,2d, and States 5a,5b,5c, resp.). We also note that State 4 represents the state at point (iii) when it refers to the operation in State 2, while it represents the state at point (i) when the operation at State 5 is considered. The implementation of the first WSDL operation (State 2) represents an *if* statement within function *f1(.)*, while the implementation of the second operation (State 5) represents a simple function call *f2(.)*. Based on the states, edges, and guards regulating state transitions, we can automatically generate test cases as the set of inputs (and expected outputs) that permit to cover the proposed STS model [34].

To conclude, a test-based certificate is composed of: (i) a (set of) security property; (ii) a (set of) evidence signed by a third party proving that the service supports the property; (iii) a service model used to generate the test cases for service certification.

7.4.2 Certification-Aware Service Selection

The traditional SOA infrastructure permits dynamic and run-time selection and composition of services based on the clients' preferences. Current service selection and discovery approaches (e.g., UDDI business registries and service search engine) mostly rely on functional matching between services and clients' preferences [27, 35, 41] or support non-functional matching based on QoS properties [37, 48]. It is important to note that only few of the selection approaches supporting non-functional matching consider the mechanisms implemented by the service to achieve a non-functional property (e.g., [44]), while none of them considers the assurance level and the certification metadata in the matching process. Furthermore, the selection of the best service, which is achieved by comparing and ordering (usually in a ranked list) services satisfying clients' preferences, is mainly based on the property strength without considering how the property has been proven.

The certification scheme proposed in this chapter can be integrated within the existing SOA infrastructure, to enhance service selection and composition processes with a mechanism where clients define their security preferences in terms of properties, models, and evidence, and match them against the certificates awarded to the services. The best service is then retrieved by evaluating information in the certificates including the mechanisms behind the property, the evidence supporting the property, and the assurance level. In the following, we define (i) a *matching process*, which permits clients to evaluate if the assurance level provided by a service certificate is compatible with their own preferences; (ii) a *comparison process*, which permits clients to identify the best service among the ones identified at point (i).

Matching process. We introduce a triple-matching strategy which involves a check on security properties (property-match) [31], service model (model-match), and evidence (evidence-match) in the certificate [7]. Let $C(p, m, e)$ be a certificate awarded to a service, where $p = (\hat{p}, A)$ is a security property, m is a model level (e.g., WSDL-, WSCL-, or implementation-based model), and $e = (t, TA)$ is the evidence including the test type t and related attributes TA. Also let $R(p',m',e')$ be a user request over security property p', model m', and evidence e'. The matching process compares p and p' (property-match), m and m' (model-match), e and e' (evidence-match). The matching process is successful if both property-match, model-match, and evidence-match succeed, and provides an output as follows:

1. *match*, if and only if: (i) $p' \preceq_{P} p$ (property-match), (ii) m' is less detailed than m (model-match), and (iii) $t' \preceq_{T} t$ and $\forall k = 1 \ldots |TA|$, either $v'(ta_k)$ is not specified or $v'(ta_k) \preceq_{ta_k} v(ta_k)$ (evidence-match).
2. *no match*, otherwise.

In the following we discuss the match/no match scenarios by means of two examples based on the hierarchies in Fig. 7.1.

Example 7.1 (*Match*) Let us consider a service s that has a certificate C proving the security property $p = (\hat{p}, A) = (\textit{Robustness}, \{\texttt{Type} = \textit{Malformed XML Tree}\})$ with service model m = *WSCL-based* and evidence $e = (t, TA) =$ (*Penetration test using Malformed XML Tree*,$\{\texttt{card} = k\}$). Suppose now that a client submits a request R to a registry searching for a service that has a certificate proving a generic security property $p' = (\hat{p}', A') = (\textit{Robustness}, \{\texttt{Type} = \textit{Malformed Input}\})$ with service model m' = *WSDL-based* and evidence $e' = (t', TA') =$ (*Penetration test using Non-Valid XML Tree*,$\{\texttt{card} = m\}$), with $TA.\texttt{card} > TA'.\texttt{card}$, where $TA.\texttt{card}$ and $TA'\texttt{card}$ are the cardinalities of the test sets. The registry searches among its services and selects those that expose a certificate $C(p,m,e)$ that satisfies $R(p',m',e')$. Service s is selected since $p' \preceq_{P} p$ based on the hierarchy in Fig. 7.1a, m' is less detailed than m, and $t' \preceq_{T} t$ and $TA'.\texttt{card} < TA.\texttt{card}$ based on the hierarchies in Fig. 7.1b.

Example 7.2 (*No Match*) Let us consider the same service s in Example 7.1. Suppose now, that a user is submitting a request R that differs from the one in Example 7.1 because it requires a model m' = *implementation-based*. As in Example 7.1, the matching between C and R provides a successful property- and evidence-match. However, in this example, there is no model-match because m is less detailed than m'.

The output of a matching process is a set of services which satisfy the client's preferences. The client's preferences can vary from being very specific (e.g., expressing concrete properties, test-based evidence, and model) to more general (e.g., expressing just an abstract property). Although the proposed matching approach allows to produce a very specific query, we claim that the prototypical client of a SOA platform will not specify a fine-grained request, but a more general one leaving some details unspecified. The fact that a client will not specify every possible parameter in the request, leaves some degree of freedom that the matching process must manage. In general, the more these degrees of freedom, the bigger the set of services selected as the output of the matching process. To be the selection process more effective, there is the need of an approach that provides an ordering of the services that match the preferences of the client, thus giving to the client a more useful comparative evaluation of the services. This process is called comparison process and is discussed in the following of this section.

Comparison process. The comparison process receives as input the set of services that satisfy the client's preferences (matching process) and returns as output a ranked list of these services, that is, a partial order calculated on the basis of information contained in the service certificates. Several approaches are possible to generate the ranked list, which can be grouped into two broad categories as follows.

- A cumulative metric computed using quality indexes on the information in the certificate (i.e., property, model, evidence). This is the simplest approach and introduces compensation effects between indexes (e.g., using weighted average). Every information in the certificate is used in the definition of the ranked list and its importance depends on the weight used for aggregation.
- Rule-based aggregation of metrics, in which the ranked list is computed following some pre-defined rules. For instance, a simple rule can impose a specific evaluation order, where properties are evaluated first; if two services cannot be ordered using their properties, models and evidence are compared.

In both categories, the ranked list is generated comparing services that match the client's preferences on the basis of some specific metrics ordering properties, models, and evidence in their certificates. Based on the certification scheme in this section, properties in the certificates of two different services can be compared using the security property hierarchy in Fig. 7.1. Then, models can be compared by evaluating their level of detail (i.e., WSDL, WSCL, implementation). We note that a set of indexes (e.g., number of nodes, edges, linearly independent paths) can be defined to evaluate the quality of the service model, and used to rank and compare services. Finally, the evidence can be compared using the hierarchies of test types and the specified test attributes. Also in this case, a set of metrics (e.g., evaluating the test case coverage on the service model) can be defined to evaluate the certification quality and used to rank and compare services.

To conclude, we note that different approaches can produce different ranked lists of services that match the clients' preferences. Clients' profiles can then be defined to make the ranked list closer to their expectations. As an example, if a client expresses a profile with trust on property definition only, a rule-based aggregation considering the property first should be used.

7.5 ASSERT4SOA Framework

In this section, we describe the ASSERT4SOA framework, which implements a certification-aware service-oriented architecture based on the test-based certification scheme described in Sect. 7.4. The framework provides a set of features through which the full life-cycle of services with certified security properties can be managed, including certificate issuing and management, certification-aware discovery and matchmaking,[1] certificate verification, and service consumption [11].

7.5.1 Functionalities

To address the requirements described in Sect. 7.2, the ASSERT4SOA implementation provides the following set of functionalities.

- *Certificate model and language.* A model (see Sect. 7.4) and an XML-based language have been developed to enable the representation of service certificates (*Assert* in the following). The model and language allow the specification of the security properties of a service and the evidence that under-pins them (i.e., test cases used in the certification process).
- *Service discovery.* A client can query the framework and retrieve a list of services with certificates that match its functional and security preferences (i.e., matching process in Sect. 7.4.2). As an example, a business process modeler or a developer for a banking application specifies the functional preferences, that is, a service which provides credit worthiness of a customer, as well as the security preferences, that is, proper access control restrictions on the service provider side, in the query that is sent to the discovery framework. Service discovery matches certificates and the certified properties in the services with the specified preferences to retrieve a set of compatible services. This is done dynamically without any human intervention as the framework can receive queries from service-based applications at runtime.
- *Certificate comparison.* A core function of the framework is to rank services based on their certificates (see comparison process in Sect. 7.4.2). This is a complex process that involves ontological reasoning to the aim of comparing functionally-equivalent services with different certificates. For example, we may need to compare two services with the same security property that has been certified using different categories and types of tests. This problem becomes even more complex when two services have been certified using different classes of evidence, such as for instance, model-based evidence and test-based evidence. In addition, the reasoning algorithms have to take into account that there exists relations among security properties specified in ontologies.
- *Certificate issuing and management.* The framework includes tools and user interfaces that allow assert issuers and managers to create certificates and to manage their life-cycle (i.e., their issuing, update, and revocation).

[1] We note that in the ASSERT4SOA terminology the certification-aware matchmaking process refers to the matching and comparison processes in Sect. 7.4.2.

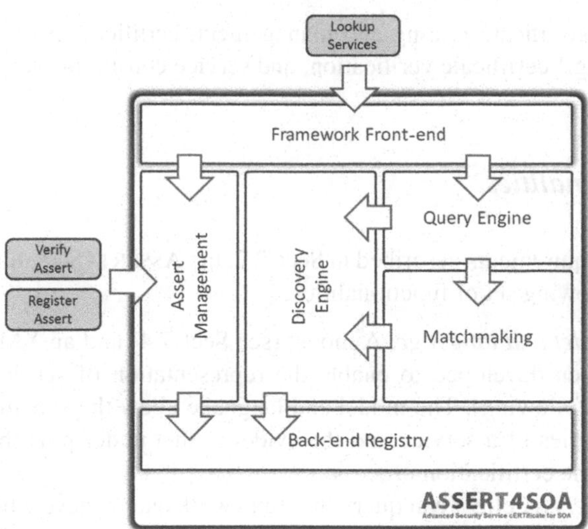

Fig. 7.3 Component overview

7.5.2 High-Level Component Overview

Figure 7.3 presents a high-level overview of the ASSERT4SOA framework [12]. Here, we mainly focus on the subsystems that are responsible for the core ASSERT4SOA functionalities; other components that are related to somewhat "standard" functions (e.g., system management, access control, logging) are left out of this description for the sake of conciseness.

Front-end. This is the common entry-point providing an uniform API through which clients can consume the functionalities provided by the ASSERT4SOA framework. The Front-end protects the framework providing access control functionalities; also, it represents an important source of security-relevant events, which are captured in a secure Audit Trail. Clients may want to access the front-end to: (i) use the discovery and matchmaking capabilities of the framework, and find a list of candidate services that correspond to the criteria specified in the query (see Sect. 7.4.2), and (ii) manage the lifecycle of certified services and of the related asserts, including registering, updating, and verifying them.

Query Engine. This component is connected to the Front-end, the Discovery Engine, and the Matchmaking. It is in charge of parsing the query coming from the client and passing it on to the Discovery Engine. Queries contain both a specification of the functionalities that candidate services must offer as well as a set of conditions on their non-functional properties. This component decouples the query language used by the client from the language that is used internally by the ASSERT4SOA framework. The queries coming from the client may specify a subscription option; in this case, the query is periodically evaluated and the client can receive continuous updates as new matches are found that satisfy the query.

Discovery Engine and Matchmaking. Based on the information in the client queries, the Discovery Engine coordinates several different subsystems. First, it accesses the Back-end Registry to retrieve an initial set of candidate services, based on their functional description. Then, it instantiates a matchmaking strategy. Such a strategy is basically a description of how various *types* of matchmaking modules should be coordinated and how their results should be aggregated to determine the final list of candidate services, ranked according to their degree of fit, to be returned to the client. The strategy and the initial list of services obtained from the Registry Abstraction Layer is given as input to the Matchmaking Subsystem (not depicted in Fig. 7.3).

The Matchmaking Subsystem is controlled by the Discovery Manager which activates it by passing as input (i) an initial set of (functionally matching) candidates, and (ii) a matchmaking strategy (produced based on the content of the query). As a result of the matchmaking process, the candidate services are filtered (discarding those that do not match the non-functional preferences) and ranked according to their degree of fit. Internally, the Matchmaking Subsystem is organized as a hierarchical, dynamically configurable architecture. It is *hierarchical* since a Master Matchmaker controls a set of Slave Matchmakers and aggregates the results coming from each slave in a single measure; it is *dynamically configurable* since the organization of the slaves is determined and realized at run-time, based on the matchmaking strategy, which in turn is determined based on the query.

This design allows each slave to be realized as a very targeted, domain-specific evaluator of a particular property or dimension, whereas the master matchmaker is only concerned with the coordination of slaves. In this way, additional (or alternative) slave matchmakers can be plugged into the system, thus supporting the evaluation of an extensible range of properties. While the focus of ASSERT4SOA is on security-related properties, the architecture accommodates a sophisticated coordination of different pluggable matchmaking components, in such a way that the decision as to which candidate has to be chosen can be taken on a more comprehensive basis (e.g., capturing constraints related to performance, reliability, cost, and so on). Slave matchmakers may be provided by external third-party services, giving an additional level of dynamism and diversity and possibly enhancing availability and fault-tolerance (although raising, at the same time, additional security and trust concerns).

Assert Management. This module includes a tool used by assert issuers to express the results of their assessment in a certificate. The tool provides a graphical user interface that guides the issuer (typically a certification authority) in the process, and produces as output an assert that conforms to the assert XML-schema and that is digitally signed by the issuer. Furthermore, an assert validation component is used to check the assert validity. This component is used both server-side, before the results of matchmaking are pushed to the client, and client-side, where clients may want to check the asserts on their own, before consuming a service. The validation involves several steps. First, the signature on the assert is checked to ensure it is authentic. Then, the well-formedness of the assert is verified. Finally, the credentials of the assert issuer are checked, based on the preferences of the client. The Assert Management module includes the functionality to publish certified services in the Back-end Registry, available through the registry abstraction module, for managing their life-cycle.

Back-end Registry. While service descriptions may be stored in several (possibly heterogeneous) back-end repositories, this component provides a uniform access to such repositories, regardless of the differences in their interfaces and protocols. The request coming from the Query Engine is split by the Discovery Engine into two parts that are treated separately: (i) the characterization of security properties required by the client, and (ii) the description of the interface, functionality, and other non-security QoS conditions that are expressed as part of service discovery queries. Based on the latter, the Discovery Engine queries the Back-end Registry to retrieve a set of candidate services that satisfy the required interface, functional, and non-security characteristics.

7.5.3 Certification-Aware Development Environment

A typical usage scenario would see a developer of a service-based application (SBA) who uses the ASSERT4SOA framework to identify and consume component services. In addition to the functional requirements for the SBA, the developer has also to take into account the security requirements for the application. These requirements are analyzed and translated by the developer into security requirements for the individual services that have to be composed in the application.

To access the functionalities provided by the ASSERT4SOA framework through its API, the developer may use a web-based front-end whereby she can browse and filter the services available in an ASSERT4SOA-enabled repository. Alternatively, using a dedicated extension to her IDE, the developer can access the same functionalities directly inside the development environment (e.g., through an ASSERT4SOA plugin) as depicted in Figs. 7.4 and 7.5. The interactions in the two cases are analogous; here we concentrate on the latter.

Enhanced Service Browser. The developer uses the service browser to lookup certified services by functionality, with services organized in categories. The security properties of the matching services are used as an additional dimension based on which services can be grouped, ranked, and filtered.

Service Security Properties Inspector. A dedicated view in the IDE is used to display the certified security properties of a service, as showed in Fig. 7.5. The basic information on the assert (such as, issuer information, time of issuing, and so on) is displayed together with a detailed view of the content of the certificate, including the certified properties, the service model, and the evidence on which the certification is based.

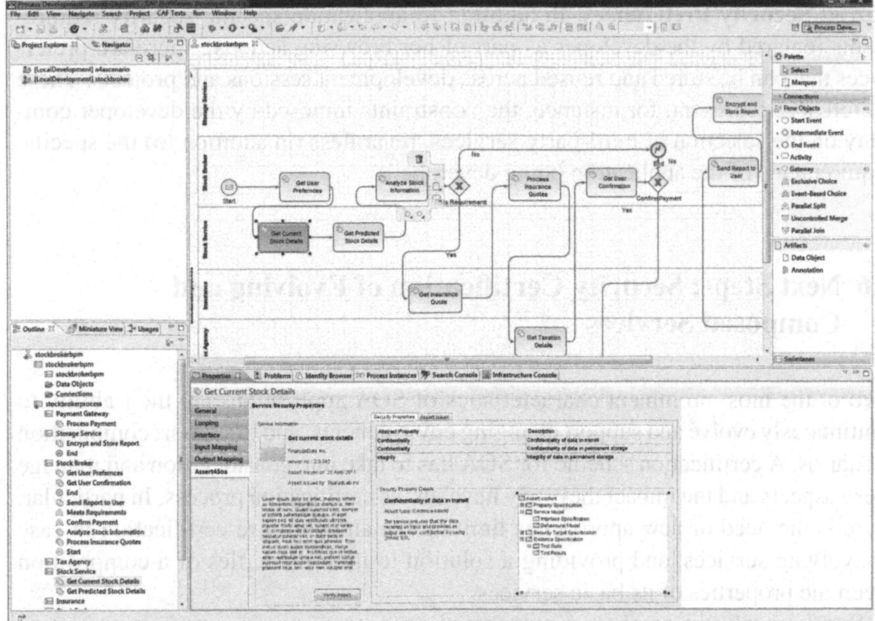

Fig. 7.4 Proof-of-concept of an Assert-enabled modeling environment

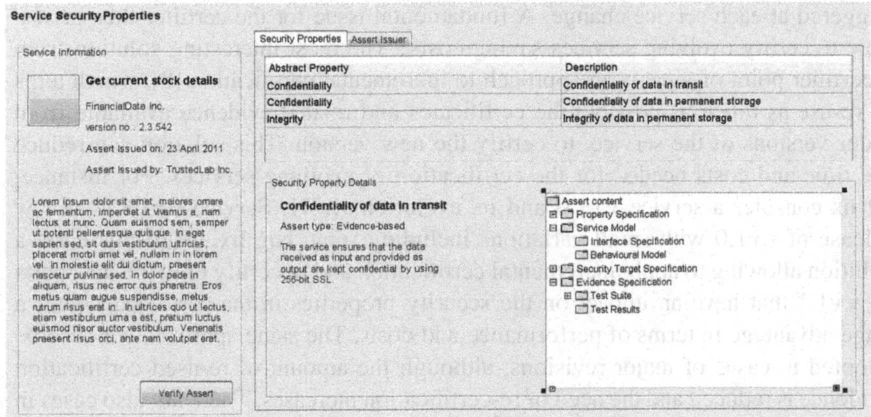

Fig. 7.5 Security property inspector

Assert Validation. The plugin allows the developer to trigger the assert validation at any time. The validation is automatic when the developer selects a service from a result set obtained in response to a query or browsing action. The developer may also choose to (re-)validate services that have already been included in the application (business process in Fig. 7.4).

Stored Security Preferences. In addition to application-specific security requirements (entered by the developer as part of her browsing actions), there are preferences that can be stored and reused across development sessions and projects. These preferences represent, for instance, the constraints imposed by the developer company on the selection of third-party services, regardless (in addition to) the specific requirements of the application being developed.

7.6 Next Steps: Security Certification of Evolving and Composed Services

Two of the most prominent characteristics of SOA applications are their ability to continuously evolve and support changing environments, and to support composition scenarios. A certification scheme for SOA has to take into consideration and manage these aspects and the impact they may have on the certification process. In particular, there is the need of new approaches limiting the amount of re-certification in case of evolving services, and providing a solution to infer properties of a composition given the properties of its basic services.

Service evolution can have a substantial impact on security certifications, since the release of a new version of a service may invalidate the certificates awarded to the old version. This scenario is costly and can reduce the increase in revenue given by the certified service, since a re-certification process from scratch can be triggered at each service change. A fundamental issue for the certifier then arises: how to certify evolving services saving costs? The most interesting solution from a certifier point of view is an approach to incremental certification [8], which aims to re-use as much as possible the certificates and related evidence available from older versions of the service, to certify the new version. This solution can reduce the time and costs needed for the certification of evolving services. For instance, let us consider a service $s.v1.0$ and its evolution $s.v1.1$. Service $s.v1.1$ is a new release of $s.v1.0$ with small variations including some bug fixing. In this case, a solution allowing to apply incremental certification and to certify only the new parts of $s.v1.1$ that have an impact on the security properties in the certificate, gives a huge advantage in terms of performance and costs. The same approach can also be adopted in cases of major revisions, although the amount of re-used certification evidence is reduced and the need of re-certification increases. There are also cases in which incremental certification is not applicable. For instance, if the change affects an horizontal functionality (e.g., a mechanism for message signature) that is used by all service operations, a re-certification from scratch is required.

Our solution, and in particular the test-based certification approach, provides some interesting functionalities that can be used by the CA to manage the certification of evolving services. As an example, the service model, that we use in the certification process to produce the test cases and related evidence, can help to identify which parts of the service and which subset of test cases are affected by changes among two different versions. Since the security property is directly associated with its model, changes in the model require incremental certification. Using this simple analysis, the CA can evaluate whether service changes have an impact on service certificates, and in this case can identify which of the existing test cases and evidence are not valid and need to be substituted/re-executed. If changes have no impact on the model and certificate, no activities are required. If changes have an impact on the whole service implementation, a re-certification from scratch is needed.

Let us again consider the two services $s.v1.0$ and $s.v1.1$, and suppose that the differences between them are captured by a service model m. Based on m, it is possible to produce the additional test evidence required to incrementally certify $s.v1.1$. We note that, in some cases, the CA can just adapt the previous certificate re-using the same evidence (or a subset of it) and signing the (reduced) certificate for the new service version. This activity can result in a decreasing quality of the certification process, thus affecting the ranking of the service in the comparison process.[2] In other cases, the CA applies incremental certification, by adding new test cases or by re-executing existing ones, to test m and generate new evidence for it.

Focusing on composition scenarios, composed services can be implemented by dynamically using orchestration or choreography approaches. Indeed, the certification of service compositions can be realized according to two approaches: (i) certify the composition as a single service (static composition with static binding), (ii) certify the composition by using certificates of basic services (dynamic or static composition with dynamic binding). The first approach recalls the certification of a single service. In particular, the CA certifies the composition using the complete model (that includes the model of every basic service and the BPEL of the composition) and the evidence produced for the entire composition. This approach is possible only for static compositions with static binding, and considers the composition as a single service in which basic services are statically integrated. Clearly this approach is not optimal, although it works correctly for static compositions. The second approach is based on the idea of re-using certificates of basic services to produce the certificate of the composed one. This approach assumes the knowledge of the service composition (i.e., BPEL composition), the property to be certified for the composition, and aims to reduce the effort required to the CA. A service composition defines how the basic services interact and exchange requests and responses. Furthermore, a set of composition patterns define simple rules that permit to derive the security properties of the composed service starting from the security properties of the basic services and by looking at their interactions.[3]

The process of certifying a composition of services based on testing has two fundamental steps: (i) select basic services to be composed on the basis of the property to be certified for the composition, the certified security patterns, the BPEL compo-

[2] This could sound contradictory from the software engineering point of view since service $s.v1.1$ is an updated version of $s.v1.0$ and thus it should be "better" than the previous version. From the certification point of view, however, if we do not have the evidence that $s.v1.1$ is "better" than $s.v1.0$, we should not claim it in the certificate.

[3] We note that the patterns can be certified themselves increasing the trust in the composition.

sition, and the security properties of the basic services, (ii) derive the evidence that supports the certified composition, since no real testing is done on the composition. The first step is simply obtained by selecting services having certificates that permit to infer the expected property for the composition, based on certified composition pattern. Although in some cases this can be considered enough from a CA point of view, the service provider retrieves a certificate for the composed service with no evidence that a property holds. In this scenario, the service ranking is usually low and the service is put at the end of the ranked list. The second step instead aims to derive a "virtual" set of evidence for the composition using the evidence of each basic service. The term "virtual" means that the evidence of the composition is not generated using real testing. This "virtual" evidence is generally a subset of the evidence of the basic services, and is obtained by using composition patterns. At the end of this process, the composed service has its own certificate supported by a "virtual" evidence, which can be used to achieve a better ranking in the selection process.

To conclude, the certification scheme proposed in this chapter provides the basis to support the important characteristics of a SOA environment, and can be extended to address most of the issues involving incremental certification of evolving services and most of the challenging tasks in the certification of service compositions.

7.7 Related Work

Traditional approaches for the development, verification, validation, and certification of systems have mainly focused on monolithic software, which is evaluated at design-time before each system is really installed and used by a client. In this area, the research community has mostly considered software testing to assess and verify the correct functioning of services [4, 36]. However, some works have also focused on non-functional verification of software, as for instance, in [49], where the authors define a model based approach to automatic testing of attack scenarios, and in [29], where a systematic specification-based testing of security-critical systems is proposed based on UMLsec models. Moreover, as discussed in Sect. 7.2, several approaches have been defined for certifying software systems ranging from national specifications (e.g., [26, 46]) to international ones (e.g., [24]). Also, given the high overheads and costs of software certification, lightweight and domain-specific certification schemes have been recently defined (e.g., [3, 15]).

Today, solutions for service testing have been inspired by existing approaches for software systems and share a common ground with them. However, even if they come from the same scientific ground, service testing differs from standard software testing practices, because the loosely coupled nature of web services severely limits the way testers can interact with the services during the testing process. Similarly to the case of software testing, the research literature has initially focused on addressing the problem of testing functional properties of web services, and to automatically generate test cases for service verification [9, 13, 14]. Tsai et al. [45] first propose the idea of using and extending WSDL standard to cope with web service testing. They enrich the WSDL interface with input-output dependency, invocation sequence, hierarchical functional description, and concurrent sequence specification. Salva and Rabhi [39] provide a solution to evaluate the robustness of services, which automatically generates test cases from the WSDL. Mao [33] proposes a hierarchical testing framework, which evaluates services at both unit and system levels. The unit level considers information in the WSDL interface and applies combinatorial testing, while the system level uses a state model of the information in the BPEL process specification to generate test cases. Jokhio et al. [28] apply specification-based software techniques to semantic web services, and define a solution to test case generation starting from their goal specification. Test cases are used to test the correctness of the real implementation.

Other works have proposed model-based solutions for testing web services [10, 20, 22, 30]. These solutions provide a modeling of web services for automatic generation of test cases, verification of the functional correctness of services, and identification of faults. Frantzen et al. [22] use symbolic transition systems to model and test web service coordination. The transition systems are used as a starting point to automatically generate test cases which fit service composition. Keum et al. [30] propose a solution using extended finite state machine to automatically generate test cases. The authors enrich the WSDL interface with information about the dynamic behaviour of services to improve the testing coverage. Bentakouk et al. [10] propose a solution based on STS-based testing and STM solver to verify that a service composition conforms to its specifications and/or user requirements. Endo and Simao [20] present a solution based on finite state machines and a Java prototype, which aim to automatically generate test cases for functional verification of services.

A recent and active field of research is focusing on verification and certification of service non-functional properties. The US-based Software Engineering Institute (SEI) [42] has published a requirements document on the service certification and accreditation process for the US Army CIO/G-6. The document describes a process for certifying services to assure that they are not malicious to the service-oriented infrastructure they are deployed in or interacting with. Anisetti et al. [7] presents a test-based certification scheme for services. The proposed solution models services as symbolic transition systems using information in the WSDL interface and in the WSCL document, and details about their implementation. Test cases are generated using the service models. Kourtesis et al. [32] present an approach to conformance testing managed by the SOA registry to improve the reliability of SOA environments. In general, if the service is functionally equivalent to its specifications, a certificate is awarded to it. Serhani et al. [43] focus on Quality of Service (QoS) certification and propose an architecture relying on a QoS broker for efficient web service selection, on the basis of clients' functional and QoS requirements.

To conclude, some works are currently facing the problem of managing service evolution and their impact on clients and services. These solutions (e.g., [5, 12]) are mainly aimed to provide an approach that limits the impact that dynamic changes and variations on services may have on the involved parties, run-time active conversations, and existing business processes.

7.8 Conclusions

In this chapter we discussed how the advent and success of SOA and web services are changing traditional ICT systems and, in particular, we focused on the problem of providing powerful and secure services that prove support for security requirements using certification techniques. To this aim, we described challenges and issues to be considered in developing certification schemes for services and we also discussed how service security certification changes the trust model underlying SOA. We then presented a certification scheme for services, which relies on testing to provide the evidence that a security property is supported. In this context, we illustrated an approach to service certification, including a description of the FP7 EU Project ASSERT4SOA framework that integrates the service certification process within the SOA infrastructure. Although security certification schemes have been provided since long, there is the need to adapt them to SOA and its intrinsic processes, as for instance, the run-time selection and composition of services and the management of evolving applications.

Acknowledgments This work was partly supported by the EU-funded project ASSERT4SOA (grant no. 257351).

References

1. A. Alves et al.: Web Services Business Process Execution Language Version 2.0. OASIS (2007). http://docs.oasis-open.org/wsbpel/2.0/OS/wsbpel-v2.0-OS.html, Accessed in date September 2012
2. A. Banerji et al.: Web Services Conversation Language (WSCL) version 1.0. World Wide Web Consortium (W3C) (2002). http://www.w3.org/TR/wscl10/, Accessed in date September 2012
3. Agence Nationale de la Sécurité des Systèmes d'Information (ANSSI): Certificat de Sécurité de Premier Niveau. http://www.ssi.gouv.fr/fr/certification-qualification/cspn/, Accessed in date September 2012
4. Ammann, P., Offutt, J.: Introduction to Software Testing. Cambridge University Press, New York, NY, USA (2008)
5. Andrikopoulos, V., S., Benbernou, Papazoglou, M.: On the evolution of services. IEEE Transactions on Software Engineering **PP**(99) (2011)
6. Anisetti, M., Ardagna, C., Damiani, E.: Certifying security and privacy properties in the internet of services. In: L. Salgarelli, G. Bianchi, N. Blefari-Melazzi (eds.) Trustworthy Internet. Springer (2011)
7. Anisetti, M., Ardagna, C., Damiani, E.: Fine-grained modeling of web services for test-based security certification. In: Proc. of the 8th International Conference on Service Computing (SCC 2011). Washington, DC, USA (2011)
8. Anisetti, M., Ardagna, C., Damiani, E.: A low-cost security certification scheme for evolving services. In: Proc. of the 19th IEEE International Conference on Web Services (ICWS 2012). Honolulu, HI, USA (2012)
9. Baresi, L., Di Nitto, E.: Test and Analysis of Web Services. Springer, New York, USA (2007)
10. Bentakouk, L., Poizat, P., Zaïdi, F.: Checking the behavioral conformance of web services with symbolic testing and an SMT solver. In: Proc. of the 5th International Conference on Tests & Proofs (TAP 2011). Zürich, Switzerland (2011)

11. Bezzi, M., Kaluvuri, S., Sabetta, A.: Ensuring trust in service consumption through security certification. In: Proc. of the International Workshop on Quality Assurance for Service-Based Applications (QASBA 2011). Lugano, Switzerland (2011)
12. Bezzi, M., Sabetta, A., Spanoudakis, G.: An architecture for certification-aware service discovery. In: Proc. of the 1st IEEE International Workshop on Securing Services on the Cloud (IWSSC 2011). Milan, Italy (2011)
13. Bozkurt, M., Harman, M., Hassoun, Y.: Testing web services: A survey. In: Technical Report TR-10-01. Department of Computer Science, King's College London (2010)
14. Canfora, G., di Penta, M.: Service-oriented architectures testing: A survey. Software Engineering: International Summer Schools, ISSSE 2006–2008 **1**, 78–105 (2009)
15. CCHIT: Certification Commission for Healthcare Information Technology. http://www.cchit.org/, Accessed in date September 2012
16. Chang, E., Hussain, F., Dillon, T.: Trust and Reputation for Service-Oriented Environments: Technologies For Building Business Intelligence And Consumer Confidence. John Wiley & Sons, Ltd (2006)
17. Chinnici, R., Moreau, J., Ryman, A., Weerawarana, S.: Web Services Description Language (WSDL) version 2.0. World Wide Web Consortium (W3C) (2007). http://www.w3.org/TR/wsdl20/, Accessed in date September 2012
18. Damiani, E., Ardagna, C., El Ioini, N.: Open source systems security certification. Springer, New York, NY, USA (2009)
19. Damiani, E., De Capitani di Vimercati, S., Paraboschi, S., Samarati, P.: Securing SOAP e-services. International Journal of Information Security (IJIS) 1(2), 100–115 (2002)
20. Endo, A., Simao, A.: Model-based testing of service-oriented applications via state models. In: Proc. of the 8th IEEE International Conference of Service Computing (SCC 2011). Washington, DC, USA (2011)
21. Focardi, R., Gorrieri, R., Martinelli, F.: Classification of security properties (Part II: Network security). In: R. Focardi, R. Gorrieri (eds.) Foundations of Security Analysis and Design II - Tutorial Lectures. Springer Berlin / Heidelberg (2004)
22. Frantzen, L., Tretmans, J., de Vries, R.: Towards model-based testing of web services. In: Proc. of the International Workshop on Web Services - Modeling and Testing (WS-MaTe 2006). Palermo, Italy (2006)
23. Frantzen, L., Tretmans, J., Willemse, T.: Test generation based on symbolic specifications. In: Proc. of the 4th International Workshop on Formal Approaches to Software Testing (FATES 2004). Linz, Austria (2004)
24. Herrmann, D.: Using the Common Criteria for IT security evaluation. Auerbach Publications (2002)
25. Irvine, C., Levin, T.: Toward a taxonomy and costing method for security services. In: Proc. of the 15th Annual Conference on Computer Security Applications (ACSAC 1999). Phoenix, AZ, USA (1999)
26. Jahl, C.: The information technology security evaluation criteria. In: Proc. of the 13th International Conference on Software Engineering (ICSE 1991). Austin, TX, USA (1991)
27. Jeong, B., Cho, H., Lee, C.: On the functional quality of service (FQoS) to discover and compose interoperable web services. Expert Systems with Applications **36**(3, Part 1), 5411–5418 (2009)
28. Jokhio, M., Dobbie, G., Sun, J.: Towards specification based testing for semantic web services. In: Proc. of the 20th Australian Software Engineering Conference (ASWEC 2009). Gold Coast, Australia (2009)
29. Jürjens, J.: Model-based security testing using UMLsec: A case study. Electronic Notes in Theoretical Computer Science **220**(1), 93–104 (2008)
30. Keum, C., Kang, S., Ko, I.Y., Baik, J., Choi, Y.I.: Generating test cases for web services using extended finite state machine. In: Proc. of the 18th IFIP International Conference on Testing Communicating Systems (TestCom 2006). New York, NY, USA (2006)
31. Kim, A., Luo, J., Kang, M.: Security ontology for annotating resources. In: Proc. of the 4th International Conference on Ontologies, Databases, and Applications of Semantics (ODBASE 2005). Agia Napa, Cyprus (2005)

32. Kourtesis, D., Ramollari, E., Dranidis, D., Paraskakis, I.: Increased reliability in SOA environments through registry-based conformance testing of web services. Production Planning & Control 21(2), 130–144 (2010)
33. Mao, C.: Towards a hierarchical testing and evaluation strategy for web services system. In: Proc. of the 7th ACIS International Conference on Software Engineering Research, Management and Applications (SERA 2009). Haikou, China (2009)
34. Myers, G.: The Art of Software Testing, Second Edition. John Wiley & Sons, Inc., Hoboken, NJ, USA (2004)
35. Paliwal, A., Shafiq, B., Vaidya, J., Xiong, H., Adam, N.: Semantics-based automated service discovery. IEEE Transactions on Services Computing **5**(2), 260–275 (2012)
36. Pezzè, M., Young, M.: Software Testing and Analysis: Process, Principles, and Techniques. John Wiley & Sons, New York, NY, USA (2008)
37. Rajendran, T., Balasubramanie, P.: An optimal broker-based architecture for web service discovery with QoS characteristics. International Journal of Web Services Practices **5**(1), 32–40 (2010)
38. Ryu, S., Casati, F., Skogsrud, H., Betanallah, B., Saint-Paul, R.: Supporting the dynamic evolution of web service protocols in service-oriented architectures. ACM Transactions on the Web **2**(2), 13:1–13:46 (2008)
39. Salva, S., Rabhi, I.: Automatic web service robustness testing from WSDL descriptions. In: Proc. of the 12th European Workshop on Dependable Computing (EWDC 2009). Toulouse, France (2009)
40. Schroth, C., Janner, T.: Web 2.0 and SOA: Converging concepts enabling the internet of services. IT Professional **9**(3), 36–41 (2007)
41. seekda! http://webservices.seekda.com/browse, Accessed in date September 2012
42. Securing Web services for army SOA. http://www.sei.cmu.edu/solutions/softwaredev/securing-web-services.cfm, Accessed in date September 2012
43. Serhani, M., Dssouli, R., Hafid, A., Sahraoui, H.: A QoS broker based architecture for efficient web services selection. In: Proc. of the IEEE International Conference on Web Services (ICWS 2005). Orlando, FL, USA (2005)
44. Thakar, U., Dagdee, N., Agrawal, A.: A methodology to compose web services using compatible components based on QoS and security requirements of the users. International Journal of Computer Applications **46**(10), 30–37 (2012)
45. Tsai, W., Paul, R., Yamin, W., Chun, F., Dong, W.: Extending WSDL to facilitate web services testing. In: Proc. of the 7th IEEE International Symposium on High Assurance Systems Engineering (HASE 2002). Tokyo, Japan (2002)
46. USA Department of Defence: Department Of Defense Trusted Computer System Evaluation Criteria (1985)
47. van Veenendaal, E.: Standard glossary of terms used in Software Testing. International Software Testing Qualifications Board (ISTQB) (2010). http://www.astqb.org/documents/ISTQB_Glossary_of_Testing_Terms_2.1.pdf, Accessed in date September 2012
48. Yu, H., Reiff-Marganiec, S.: Non-functional property based service selection: A survey and classification of approaches. In: Proc. of Non Functional Properties and Service Level Agreements in Service Oriented Computing Workshop (NFPSLAM-SOC) 2008. Dublin, Ireland (2008)
49. Zulkernine, M., Raihan, M.F., Uddin, M.G.: Towards model-based automatic testing of attack scenarios. In: Proc. of the 28th International Conference on Computer Safety, Reliability and Security (SAFECOMP 2009). Hamburg, Germany (2009)

Chapter 8
A Test Automation Framework for Collaborative Testing of Web Service Dynamic Compositions

Hong Zhu and Yufeng Zhang

Abstract The dynamic composition of services owned by different vendors demands a high degree of test automation, which must be able to cope with the diversity of service implementation techniques and to meet a wide range of test requirements on-the-fly. These goals are hard to achieve because of the lack of software artefacts of the composed services and the lack of the means of control over test executions and the means of observations on the internal behaviours of composed services. Yet, such integration testing on-the-fly must be non-intrusive and non-disruptive while the composed services are in operation. This chapter presents a test automation framework for such on-the-fly testing of service compositions to facilitate the collaboration between test services through utilisation of Semantic Web Services techniques. In this framework, an ontology of software testing called STOWS are used for the registration, discovery and invocation of test services. The composition of test services is realized by using test brokers, which are also test services but specialized in the coordination of other test services. The ontology can be extended and updated through an ontology management service so that it can support a wide open range of test activities, methods, techniques and types of software artefacts. We also demonstrate the uses of the framework by two running examples.

H. Zhu (✉)
Department of Computing and Communication Technologies,
Oxford Brookes University, Oxford OX33 1HX, UK
e-mail: hzhu@brookes.ac.uk

Y. Zhang
National Laboratory for Parallel and distributed Processing School of Computer Science,
The National University of Defense Technology, Changsha, China
e-mail: yufengzhang@nudt.edu.cn

A. Bouguettaya et al. (eds.), *Advanced Web Services*,
DOI: 10.1007/978-1-4614-7535-4_8,

8.1 Introduction

The past few years have seen a rapid growth in the research on testing Web Services (WS) [15, 18], which mostly falls into the following categories.

- **Generation of test cases**. Techniques have been developed to generate test cases from syntax definitions of WS in WSDL [1, 2, 10, 12, 13, 21, 23, 34, 35, 37, 41, 45, 49], business process and behavioural models in BPEL [4, 5, 22, 31, 33, 36, 39, 40, 53], ontology based descriptions of semantics in OWL-S [3, 28, 48], and other formal models of WS such as finite state machines and labelled transition systems [6, 14, 38], grammar graphs [24, 25], and first order logic [46], etc.
- **Generation of testbed**. A service often relies on other services to perform its function. However, in service unit testing and also in progressive service integration testing, the service under test needs to be separated from other services that it depends on. Techniques have been developed to generate service stubs [8] or mock services [27] to replace the other services for testing.
- **Checking the correctness of test outputs**. Research work has been reported in the literature to check the correctness of service output against formal specifications, such as using metamorphic relations [19], or a voting mechanism to compare the output from multiple candidate services [44, 47], etc.

These techniques have addressed various WS specific issues, such as the *robustness* in dealing with invalid inputs and errors in invocation sequences, *fault tolerance* to the failures of other services that it depends on and broken communication connections, and *security* in the environment that is vulnerable to malicious attacks, and so on. A number of prototypes and commercial tools have also been developed to support various activities in testing WS, such as Coyote [45], WS-FIT [37], TAXI [11], PLASTIC [9], LTSA-WS [38]; just to mention a few.

However, despite the advances made in the past few years, great challenges remain. In particular, it is still an open question how to cope with the following difficult issues in WS integration testing [17, 18, 54].

- **The lack of software artefacts**. A service-oriented application commonly consists of services owned by many different stakeholders. Thus, typically, developers of a service have no access to the design document, source code, even the executable code of the other services. These software artefacts are crucial to perform test activities efficiently and effectively.
- **The lack of control over test executions**. A service-oriented application is intrinsically distributed, and typically contains components and services running on hardware owned by other stakeholders. Thus, a tester usually cannot control the test executions of the other owners' services.
- **The lack of a means of observation of internal behaviour**. Another consequence of distributed ownership of services is that testers often cannot observe the internal behaviours of the services owned by other vendors.

Moreover, it is widely recognized that an integration testing technology for WS dynamic composition must meet the following requirements.

- **Capability of dealing with diversity**. The distributed and shared ownership of services also implies that the parts of a service-oriented application may operate on a variety of hardware and software platforms with different deployment configurations and delivering services of differing quality. Testing has to be performed in a heterogeneous environment. On the other hand, different service requesters may well have different test requirements to meet their own business purposes. Testing must deal with all such varieties and their combinations.
- **Capability of testing on-the-fly**. A typical scenario of service-oriented computing is that a service requester searches for a required function in a registry, and then dynamically links to the service and invokes it. It is widely believed that testing before the invocation is necessary especially in mission critical applications. Such testing, called *testing on-the-fly*, differs from traditional integration testing due to the fact that the time of testing is just before the invocation while all parts to be integrated are already in operation. A consequence of testing on-the-fly is that it eliminates the possibility of manual testing. Thus, all test activities must be performed automatically.
- **Capability of testing non-intrusively and non-disruptively**. Another consequence of testing on-the-fly is that, from a service provider's point of view, the test invocations of a service must be distinguished from the real ones so that the normal operation of the service is not interrupted by test activities. On the other hand, from a client's point of view, test invocations should also be distinguished from real ones so that they do not actually receive the real services and do not pay for such test invocations as real services.

It has been recognized that to address all these issues, testing WS dynamic compositions should be a collaborative effort contributed to by all stakeholders [11, 44, 54]. In this chapter, we present a test automation framework for collaborative testing of web services. The framework presented here has its inception in 2006 [54] based on the author's previous work on agent-based approach to testing web-based systems [55, 56]. A preliminary implementation and case study of the framework was reported in [51]. In [57], the details of test brokers and ontology management were presented and further experiments with the prototype implementation were reported. In [52], the test broker were extended to a general service composition mechanism so that not only test services can be dynamically composed and integrated through service brokers.

The remainder of the chapter is organised as follows. In Sect. 8.2, the framework and its prototype implementation are presented. Section 8.3 illustrates its uses with two running examples in typical scenarios of WS dynamic composition. Section 8.4 discusses its main features and reports the main results of the experiments with the prototype. Finally, Sect. 8.5 concludes the chapter with a discussion of future work.

8.2 The Test Automation Framework

This section elaborates the framework and briefly outlines the prototype implementation. More details can be found in [57].

8.2.1 The Architecture of the Framework

As shown in Fig. 8.1, the architecture of the test automation framework consists of

- an ontology of software testing for web services called *STOWS*,
- an ontology manager, which is a web service for the extension and revision of the ontology STOWS, and
- a number of test services.

These components are based on the Semantics Web Service technology and interact with the UDDI and Matchmaker facility.

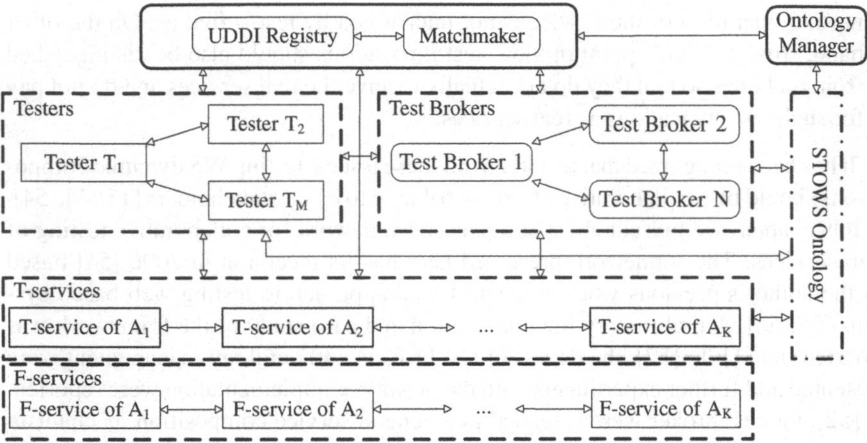

Fig. 8.1 Reference architecture of the framework

The following subsections will present these components of the architecture.

8.2.2 Test Services

The key notion of the framework is *test services* (*T-service* in short), which are services designated to perform various test tasks [54].

A T-service can be provided by the same organization of the normal service in order to perform the testing of a normal web service. For the sake of clarity, we use *functional service* (or *F-service* in short) to denote the normal services in the sequel.

A Test service can also be provided by a third party that is independent of the normal service provider, and specialized in performing certain testing tasks. A special type of such T-services is test brokers, which coordinate and compose test services in order to perform complicated test tasks.

8.2.2.1 Service Specific T-services

Ideally, each F-service should be accompanied by a special T-service to support the testing of the F-service. Such a T-service should provide the following three types of functions related to testing.

1. *Invoking test execution*. The T-service accompanying an F-service should enable test executions of the F-service to be invoked. Thus, the normal operation of the original F-service is not disturbed by test requests and the cost of testing is not charged as real invocations of the F-service. The F-service provider can distinguish real requests from the test requests so that no real world effect is caused by test requests. A T-service that only provides this test execution function can be regarded as a *mock service* [27]. However, T-service can be much more powerful by providing the following two functions.
2. *Providing required documents*. A T-service accompanying an F-service should also provide further support to other test activities. For example, the formal specification of the semantics of the F-service, the internal design of the F-service such as UML diagrams, the configuration of the hardware and software platform, the service policy, even the source code, etc., are of particular importance to testers. These kinds of information can be released to trusted T-services subject to preserve the intellectual property rights and privacy, but withheld from the general public.
3. *Observing internal behaviour*. Many test activities rely on the information of system's internal behaviours, such as the measurement of code coverage, the checking of the internal states of the program during test executions, etc. These can also be provided by the accompanying T-services.

To ensure that the testing carried out on a T-service faithfully represents the functional services, the following two principles should be maintained in the design and implementation of T-services.

- (a) A T-service should act in the same way as its functional service as much as possible so that the F-service is correct on an input if the T-service passes a test on the input.
- (b) A T-service should have a 'firewall' so that effects on the environment are stopped and the normal operation of the F-service is not disrupted.

An implication of principle (a) is that the business logic that a service implements may be duplicated by its corresponding T-service in order to test it adequately. On the other hand, an exact copy of the F-service may not achieve the goal of T-service according to principle (b). It is worth noting that in certain special cases the T-service can be absent and all testing are performed on the F-services. For example, if a service contains no internal state and has no effect on its environment, the T-service can be a simple duplicate of the F-service, even be the F-service itself. When the development and maintenance of a T-service is too expensive, or testing the service on-the-fly is unnecessary, the role of T-service can be performed by the F-service, or an identical copy of the F-service.

For example, the American's Insurance Industry Committee on Motor Vehicle Administration (IICMVA) requires that each insurance company provides a WS for online verification of car insurances and maintains two identical environments: one for test and one for production [29].

8.2.2.2 General Purpose Testers

Besides the service specific T-service that accompanies an F-service, a test service can also be a general purpose test tool that performs various test activities, such as test planning, test case generation, and test result checking, etc. A general purpose T-service can be specialized in certain testing techniques or methods such as the generation of test cases from WSDL or BPEL using certain WS testing techniques mentioned in Sect. 8.1. For the sake of convenience, such general purpose T-services are also called *testers* in the sequel to distinguish them from service specific T-services.

It is worth noting that the framework provides a facility for the integration of testing services rather than any specific testing techniques or tools. Most existing works on WS testing are complementary to the framework in the sense that their methods, techniques and tools can be implcmented as T-services. The framework facilitates their integration by providing the interfaces and collaboration mechanisms and enables test services to provide the software artefacts that testing processes require. The loosely coupled framework lays a foundation for composing various T-services by the utilization of Semantic WS technology.

8.2.2.3 Test Brokers

One particular type of general purpose T-services that will greatly improve the collaboration between the parties involved in WS testing is test broker. As discussed in Sect. 8.1, test tasks are usually too complicated to be performed directly by one T-service. A solution to this problem is to introduce test brokers, which compose and coordinate other T-services to carry out test tasks. Typically, there are multiple test brokers; for example, each specializes in one type of testing processes.

As a coordinator, a test broker receives test requests, decomposes the task into subtasks and generates test plans, searches for capable testers for each subtask, invokes testers and returns test results to users. It controls the process of testing. A test broker not only bridges the gap between the users and testers, but can also monitor the dynamic behaviours of T-services and keep a repository of tests performed on each service for future choices of T-services and optimization of test efforts.

We have developed a prototype test broker. Figure 8.2 shows the architecture of our prototype test broker. It receives test tasks from service requesters, decomposes a test task into a sequence of subtasks, sets a test plan, searches for other T-services capable of performing the subtasks, and then invokes the T-services according to the plan to carry out the subtasks and passes information between them. Finally, it assembles the results from the services and reports to the service requester. The broker is composed of the following four modules.

Communication Module provides an interface to the users. It receives test requests in the form of test tasks and sends out test results in SOAP format. It transfers test tasks to Task Analyzer and gets test results from the Task Execution Module. Failures to fulfil test requests are also reported to the requesters through this module.

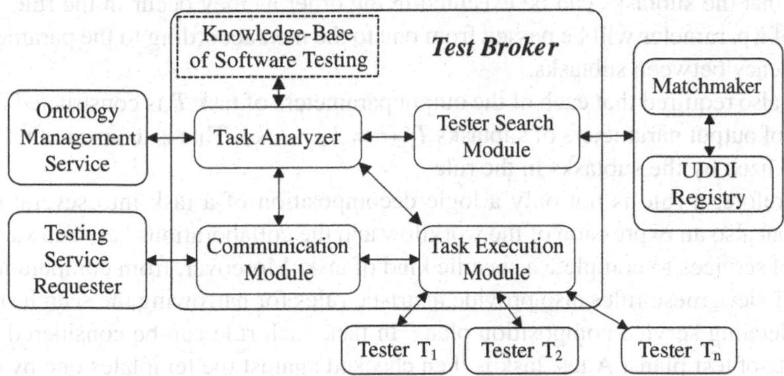

Fig. 8.2 The structure of a test broker

Task Analyzer decomposes a test task into several subtasks and produces test plans according to codified knowledge of software testing processes. It also keeps the track of test plan executions for each task so that backtracking can be made when a subtask fails.

Tester Search Module searches for testers for each subtask in the test plan generated by the Task Analyzer. A failure to find a suitable tester for a subtask is reported to the Task Analyzer and an alternative test plan may be generated if any, or the whole testing process fails.

Task Execution Module executes the test plan by invoking the testers and passing information between them. A failure to carry out a subtask is reported to the Task

Analyzer and an alternative tester will be employed if any, or an alternative test plan is generated if possible. Otherwise, the whole testing process fails.

The *knowledge-base of software testing processes* plays a central role in the test plan generation. It contains codified knowledge on how a task can be fulfilled by a number of subtasks. Each type of tasks is defined by a set of parameters. There are two kinds of parameters: *descriptive parameters* and *functional parameters*. The former describes the functionality of the task, such as the activity of the task, the execution environment of the task, and so on. The latter gives the data to be transformed by the task, including input and output data. The values of these parameters are concepts defined in the ontology.

The knowledge is represented in the form of rules:

$$T(p_1, \ldots, p_n) \Rightarrow T_1'(p_{1,1}, \ldots, p_{1,n_1}); \ldots; T_k'(p_{k,1}, \ldots, p_{k,n_k})$$

where T is a task and $p_1, \ldots, p_n$ are its parameters. It means that the task T can be decomposed into k subtasks $T_1' \cdots T_n'$, where $p_{i,1}$, ..., $p_{i,n_i} (1 \leq i \leq k)$ are parameters.

It is required that a parameter $p_{i,j}$ of subtask T_i' is constructed from $p_1, \ldots, p_n$ and the output parameters of its previous subtasks, i.e. $\{p_{x,y} | x < i, y \leq n_x\}$. This means that the subtasks can be executed in the order as they occur in the rule. The value of a parameter will be passed from one to the next according to the parameters dependency between subtasks.

It is also required that each of the output parameters of task T is constructed from the set of output parameters of subtasks T_i' $(i = 1, \ldots, k)$. This is to ensure that task T is realized by the subtasks in the rule.

Therefore, a rule is not only a logic decomposition of a task into several subtasks, but also an expression of the workflow and the collaborations between various kinds of services to complete a specific kind of task. Moreover, from computational point of view, these rules also provide heuristic rules for narrowing the search space for generating service composition plans. In fact, each rule can be considered as a template of test plans. A test task is then checked against the templates one by one. When a match is found, a test plan is produced by instantiating the template. Each rule can also be regarded as a collaboration pattern of T-services with heuristics about how to compose and coordinate T-services. This significantly reduces the size and complexity of the space in which T-services are searched for and combined. Thus, the complexity of T-service composition and collaboration can be reduced.

Our implementation of test brokers enables the user to write their own rules and instantiate the knowledge-base so that a number of test brokers can be registered and employed in testing. Figure 8.3 shows the process that the test broker interacts with Matchmaker and other T-services.

8.2.3 Registry and Matchmaker

As discussed above, in our framework, T-services interoperate with each other via SOAP messages. They need to advertise their service descriptions in a service registry to be discovered and invoked at runtime to achieve testing on-the-fly with a high degree of automation. Because of the complexity of the semantics of the service descriptions, we use Semantic WS registry to register T-services, which is composed of an UDDI registry and a Matchmaker [30].

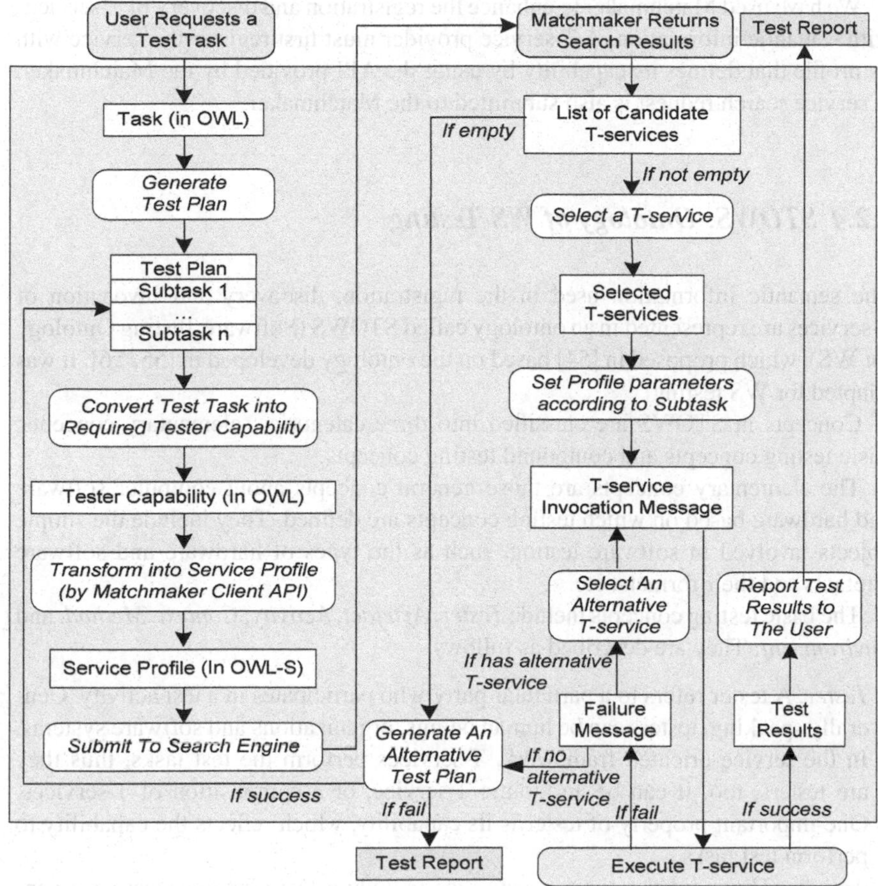

Fig. 8.3 Process model of test broker

The OWL-S/UDDI Matchmaker (Matchmaker for short) extends UDDI registry with a capability based service matching engine [30, 43]. It provides three levels of matching between capability and search request.

1. *Exact matching*: the capabilities in the registry and in the request match exactly.

2. *Plug-in matching*: the service provided is more general than the requested.
3. *Relaxed matching*: the service provided is similar to the requested.

The Matchmaker also provides filters for users to construct more accurate service discovery: which are namespace filter, domain filter, text filter, I/O type filter and constraint filter [32]. With these filters, users can construct necessary compound filters to control the precision of matching. The matching engine returns a numeric score for each candidate so that the higher the score, the more similar between the candidate and the request. Therefore, selection from the candidates can be based on the scores that tagged by the Matchmaker on the candidate services.

We have used Matchmaker to enhance the registration and discovery of T-services with semantic information. A T-service provider must first register the service with its profile that defines its capability by using the API provided by the Matchmaker. A service search request is also submitted to the Matchmaker.

8.2.4 STOWS: Ontology of WS Testing

The semantic information used in the registration, discovery and invocation of T-services are represented in an ontology called STOWS (Software Testing Ontology for WS), which proposed in [54] based on the ontology developed in [55, 56]. It was adapted for WS testing.

Concepts in STOWS are classified into three categories: elementary concepts, basic testing concepts and compound testing concepts.

The elementary concepts are those general concepts about computer software and hardware based on which testing concepts are defined. They include the simple objects involved in software testing, such as the types of hardware and software artefacts and their formats, etc.

The basic testing concepts include *Tester*, *Artefact*, *Activity*, *Context*, *Method*, and *Environment*. They are described as follows.

- *Tester*. A tester refers to a particular party who participates in a test activity. Generally speaking, testers can be human beings, organizations and software systems. In the service-oriented framework, T-services perform the test tasks, thus they are testers, too. It can be an atomic T-service, or a composition of T-services. One important property of tester is its capability, which reflects the capability to perform test tasks.
- *Activity*. There are various test activities including test planning, test case generation, test execution, result validation, adequacy measurement and test report generation, etc.
- *Artefact*. Various kinds of artefacts may be involved in test activities as input/output, such as test plan, test case, test result, program, specification and so forth. The most important property of class Artefact is Location, whose value is an URL referring to the location of the Artefact. Each type of artefacts is a subclass of Artefact, and

inherits the properties from Artefact. The subclasses of Artefact can be added into the ontology using the ontology management services.

- *Context*. Test activities may occur in different software development stages and have various test purposes. The concept context defines the contexts of test activities in testing processes and test methodologies. Typically, the contexts include unit testing, integration testing, system testing, regression testing, etc.
- *Method*. For each test activity, there may be multiple applicable test methods. Method is a part of the capability and also an optional part of test task. Test methods can be classified in a number of different ways. For example, test methods can be classified into program-based, specification-based, usage-based, etc. They can also be classified into structural testing, fault-based testing, error-based testing, etc. Structural testing methods can be further classified into control-flow testing, data-flow testing, etc. Therefore, test methods are represented as a hierarchy in the ontology.
- *Environment*. It is the hardware and software configuration in which a test activity is performed.

These basic concepts are combined together to express compound testing concepts, which include *Task* and *Capability*.

- *Capability*. The capability of a T-service represents its capability of performing test tasks. The class Capability in the ontology defines the aspects that affect the capability of a service to perform tasks, including the activities that the service can do, the test methods that the service uses, the artefacts that the service consumes and produces, the context in which the service performs test activities, and the environment in which test activities are carried out, etc. Therefore, it is composed of several basic test concepts. The structure of Capability is shown in the UML class diagram given in Fig. 8.4.
- *Task*. Task describes the test task to be carried out. It is used in service invocation. A test task also has six aspects: the activity to be performed, the context of the activity, the required test method and test environment, and the input and output artefacts. The compositions are in the same structure as capability as shown in Fig. 8.4, but have different semantics.

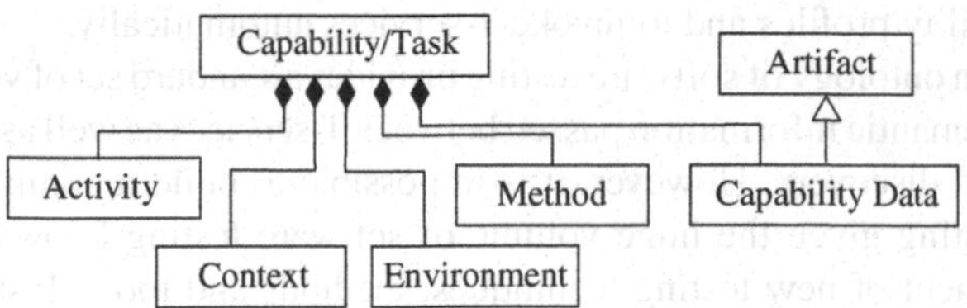

Fig. 8.4 The structure of capability and task

In OWL-S,[1] semantic descriptions are represented in the form of service profiles and used in service registration and discovery. The vocabulary of a subject domain is defined in a data model as classes with subclass relations.

To implement the ontology STOWS, we represent the concepts, including elementary, basic and compound concepts, as classes in OWL data model. To use the ontology for the registration, discovery and invocation of T-services, the compound concepts capability and task are transformed into service profiles. In OWL-S, a service profile contains the IOPR (Inputs, Outputs, Preconditions and Results) and a classification of the service. Figure 8.5 shows how the concept of capability is represented in service profile.

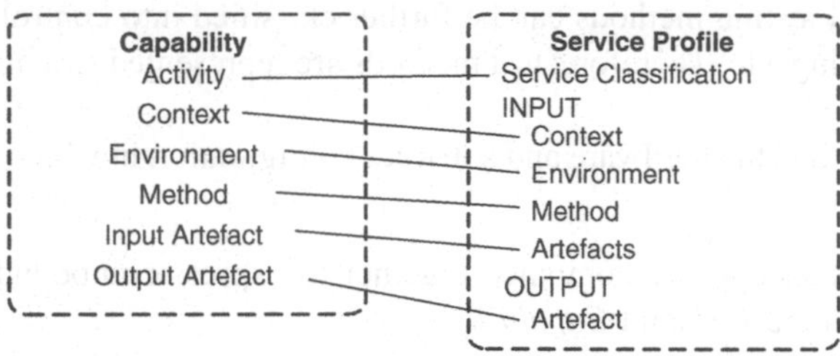

Fig. 8.5 Mapping between capability and service profile

In the service profile of T-service, the test context, the environment and the method aspects are represented as input parameters Context, Environment and Method. For example, Fig. 8.6 shows a part of a service profile, whose serviceClassification is TestCaseGeneration. The hasInput and hasOutput properties indicate that the service takes a Program as input and produces TestCase as output. By representing capability and task concepts in profiles, OWL-S/UDDI Matchmaker can be employed to perform semantic-based search of T-services.

It is worth noting that test tasks and capabilities have the similar structure and the corresponding semantics so that test requests (i.e. test tasks) can be easily transformed into search requests (i.e. testers' capabilities). Similarly, testers' capabilities can be transformed into test subtasks according to the test plan and submitted to the testers. In the implementation of the prototype, we used the Mindswap OWL-S API[2] to parse task and capability profiles and to invoke T-services automatically.

The use of an ontology of software testing provides a standard set of vocabulary for encoding the semantic information passed between T-services as well as for T-service registration and discovery. However, it is impossible to build a complete ontology of software testing given the huge volume of software testing knowledge and the rapid development of new testing techniques, methods and tools. Instead, we take the so-called *crowd-sourcing* approach to the construction of the ontology. It is the same approach that Wikipedia is developed. We achieve this by regarding STOWS

[1] http://www.w3.org/Submission/OWL-S/

[2] http://www.mindswap.org/2004/owl-s/api/

```
<profile:Profile rdf:about="#testcase_generation">
    <profile:serviceClassification rdf:datatype=
        "http://www.w3.org/2001/XMLSchema#anyURI">
        http://... /testingontology.owl#TestCaseGeneraton
    </profile:serviceClassification>
    <profile:hasInput>
        <process:Input rdf:ID="input_program">
            <process:parameterType rdf:datatype=
                "http://www.w3.org/2001/XMLSchema#anyURI">
                    http://.../testingontology.owl#Program
            </process:parameterType>
        </process:Input> </profile:hasInput>
    <profile:hasOutput>
        <process:Output rdf:ID="output_testcase">
            <process:parameterType rdf:datatype=
                "http://www.w3.org/2001/XMLSchema#anyURI">
                    http://.../testingontology.owl#TestCase
            </process:parameterType> </process:Output>
    </profile:hasOutput>
</profile:Profile>
```

Fig. 8.6 An example of service profile

as an ontology framework in which new vocabulary can be added and updated, and make it open to the public for population. This is supported by a facility for dynamic management of the ontology detailed in the next section.

8.2.5 Ontology Manager

The crowd-sourcing approach to ontology construction is achieved by dynamic management of the ontology through another special service, i.e. the ontology management service (OMS). It provides a mechanism to populate and update the ontology. It is delivered as a WS to facilitate the public access to the mechanism.

The ontology management service is implemented using the Protege-OWL API[3], which is an open source Java library for OWL and RDF. Using the API, OWL data model stored in OWL files or databases can be loaded, changed and saved, queries be made, and reasoning performed using a description logic inference engine. Therefore, the manipulation of the ontology can be implemented as operations on OWL files. Figure 8.7 shows the structure of OMS.

OMS provides a WS interface to read and update the ontology data model, which is open to the public. The kernel of OMS is the Manager module. It provides three services to users: AddClass, DeleteClass and UpdateClass to add new concept, delete concept and revise concept of the ontology.

[3] http://protege.stanford.edu/plugins/owl/api/guide.html

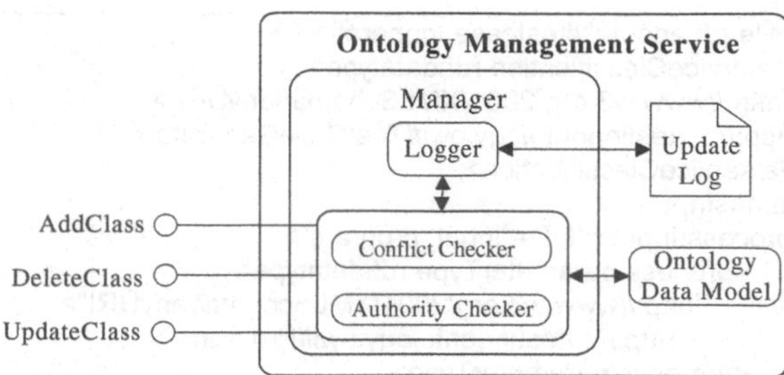

Fig. 8.7 The structure of OMS

For example, suppose that a T-service is developed to generate test cases using a new method not included in the ontology, say data mutation. Then, a new test method name DataMutation can be added to the ontology as a subclass of TestMethod. If a new T-service is to be registered that generates test cases from a new formal specification language called FSL, then a new type of software artefacts called FSL can be added to the ontology as a subclass of SoftwareArtefact. The relationship between classes in Ontology is represented as properties of classes. Adding or removing a relation can be done by applying operations on the ontology file via OMS. For example, if a subsumes relation from branch testing to statement testing is to be added, a Subsumes property can be added to class BranchTesting with the value that refers to the class StatementTesting.

However, to prevent misuses of the ontology management service, restrictions on the manipulation of the data model are imposed through two technical solutions.

First, we classify the classes in the ontology into two types: elementary classes and extended classes. Elementary classes are those that form the framework of the ontology STOWS. None of them could be pruned down from the ontology hierarchy to avoid structural damage to the ontology. The extended classes are those classes attached to the framework to populate the ontology with concrete concepts and instances of the concepts. They can be added by the users and deleted from the hierarchy. We have implemented an Authority Checker, which checks delete operations to ensure that the class to be deleted is an extended class.

Second, we have also implemented a Conflict Checker, which checks the operations on the ontology to ensure that the new class to be added does not exist in the ontology and that the class to be deleted has no subclasses in the hierarchy.

Due to the openness of ontology management, there is a risk of errors caused by update during task executions. If the update is only to add a new concept to the ontology, there should be no effect on existing tasks and services, thus no risk of such errors. However, if the update changes or deletes an existing concept or relation, a task running at the time of update may be affected if it uses the changed concept or relation and rely on the ontology to understand the messages. In such cases, errors may occur due to the updates during execution. How to prevent such errors and reduce the risk of such errors remains an open question that deserves further research.

8.3 Running Examples

We now illustrate how the framework works in WS integration testing using two running examples of typical scenarios in the dynamic composition of WS.

8.3.1 Example 1: Testing On-The-Fly for WS Dynamic Composition

Our first example is the integration testing in the dynamic composition of the services of a car insurance broker with the web services of an insurance company.

8.3.1.1 The Scenario

Suppose that a fictitious car insurance broker CIB operates a web-based system that provides online services of car insurance. In particular, they provide the following services to their end users.

The end users submit car insurance requirements to CIB and get quotes from various insurers that CIB is connected to, and then select one to insure the car. To do so, CIB takes information of the car, including its usage, and the payment. It uses the WS of its bank B to check the validity of user's payment information, passes the payment to the selected insurer and takes commissions from the insurer and/or the user. The car insurance broker's software system has a user interface to enable interactive uses, and a WS interface to enable other programs to connect as service requesters. Its binding to the bank's WS is static. However, since insurance is an active business domain, new insurance providers may emerge and existing ones may leave the market from time to time, the broker's software binds dynamically to multiple insurance providers to ensure that the business is competitive on the market. The structure of the system is shown in Fig. 8.8.

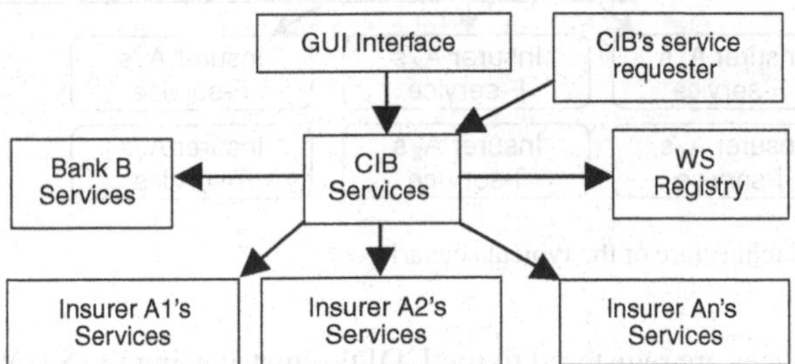

Fig. 8.8 Structure of car insurance broker services

The developer of CIB's service must test not only its own code, but also its integration with other WS, i.e. the WS of the insurers and the bank. Here, we focus on the integration with dynamic binding. Thus, suppose that CIB will dynamically compose with the WS of the PingAn Insurance Ltd. in China that provides car insurance to the customers through a web-based application.[4] It is a real-world example.

8.3.1.2 Architecture of Test Services

By applying the framework to the scenario, each of the functional WS of the bank B, CIB and insurer A_i has an accompanying T-service. Thus, we have the following architecture shown in Fig. 8.9. In particular, the following services are involved in the testing of the dynamic composition of CIB and the WS of PingAn Insurance.

- CIQS: the WS of the PingAn Insurance. It is the web service to be tested.
- TCE: a service specific T-service that executes the test cases for CIQS.
- TCG: a special purpose WS testing tool that generates test cases.
- CIB: the WS of the car insurance broker CIB. It acts as the testing requester, and generates and submits test tasks to the test broker to test CIQS.

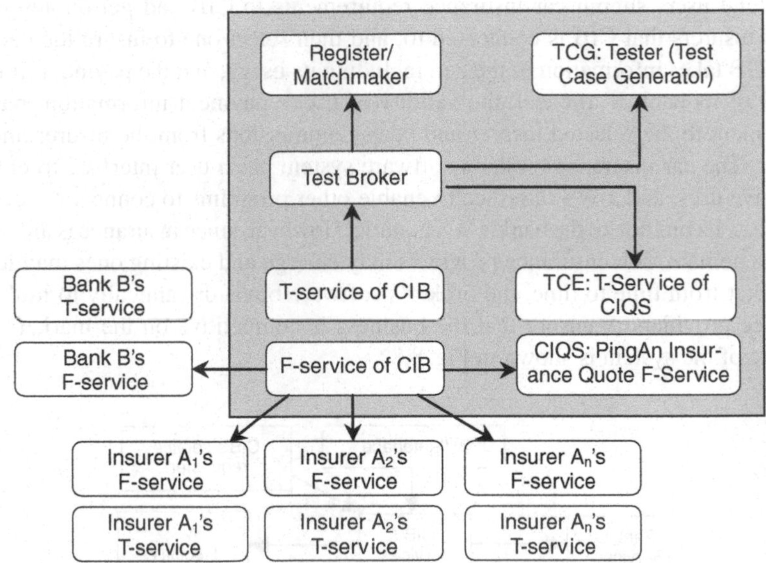

Fig. 8.9 System architecture of the typical scenario

These T-services are registered to the UDDI registry using the STOWS ontology. For example, TCG is a WS that takes the WSDL file of a service to be tested as input

[4] http://www.pingan.com/campaign/channels/pingan/car-quote/index.jsp

and generates random test cases as output. These artefacts are stored in files and referred to through URLs of the file locations. To describe this service, the following classes were added into the ontology.

- WSDL: a subclass of ServiceDescription, which is in turn the subclass of Artefact. It stands for the WSDL document of a service.
- ServiceTesting: a subclass of Context that stands for service testing.
- RandomTestingMethod: a subclass of Method that stands for the random testing method in test case generation.
- CarInsuranceQuoteServiceTestCase: a subclass of TestCase that stands for the test case file for testing car insurance quote service.

In the service profile that describes the capability of TCG, the serviceClassification is TestCaseGeneration. The Input artefact is WSDL. The context of TCG is ServiceTesting. Its environment is of type Environment, which is the ancestor of all the classes and stands for test environments. This means it imposes no specific requirement on the environment. Its method is RandomTestingMethod. The output artefact is of type CarInsuranceQuoteServiceTestCase.

8.3.1.3 Collaboration Process

Consider the situation that the CIB intends to establish a dynamic composition with insurer PingAn and to test the service on-the-fly. It delegates the task to a test broker TB. Figure 8.10 shows a typical example of collaboration processes managed by TB.

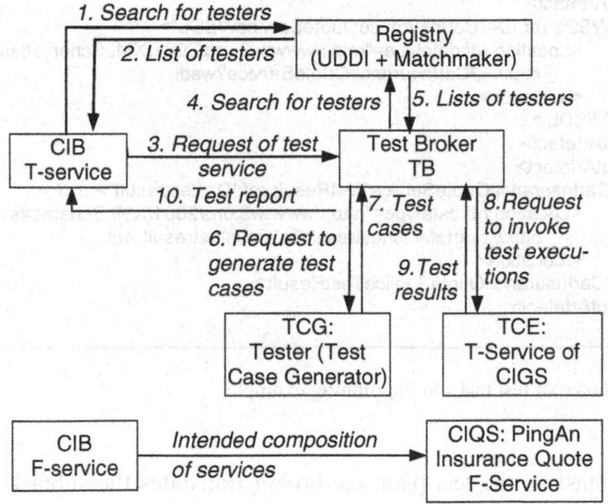

Fig. 8.10 The collaboration process in a typical scenario

The process starts with the generation of a test task by CIB's WS and submission of a search request for finding a proper tester to the service registry. The search request message contains a test task, which is matched against the capabilities of the registered testers. The search result is a list of testers who are capable of performing the task. From this list, the test broker TB is selected. A test request as shown in Fig. 8.11 is then sent to TB requesting to test CIQS.

Once the test broker receives the test task, it generates a test plan that consists of two subtasks:

- *Subtask 1*: Generating test cases according to a car insurance industry standard. The input artefact of the task is of type WSDL. The output of this subtask is of type CarInsuranceQuoteServiceTestCase.
- *Subtask 2*: Executing test cases and reporting test results. Its input is of type CarInsuranceQuoteServiceTestCase and its output type is CarInsuranceQuoteServiceTestResult.

```
<Task rdf:ID="insuranceQuoteServiceTestingTask">
    <needContext>
        <ServiceTesting rdf:ID="serviceTesting"/>
    </needContext>
    <needMethod>
       <RandomTestingMethod rdf:ID="randomTestingMethod"/>
    </needMethod>
    <needEnvironment>
        <Environment rdf:ID="environment"/>
    </needEnvironment>
    <needServiceClassification>
        <ServiceClassification rdf:ID="serviceClassification"/>
    </needServiceClassification >
    <inputArtefact>
        <WSDL rdf:ID="CarInsuranceQuoteServiceWSDL">
            <Location rdf:datatype="http://www.w3.org/2001/XMLSchema#string ">
                http://.../CarInsuranceQuoteService?wsdl
            </Location>
        </WSDL >
    </inputArtefact>
    <outputArtefact>
        <CarInsuranceQuoteServiceTestResult rdf:ID="testresult">
            <Location rdf:datatype="http://www.w3.org/2001/XMLSchema#string">
                http://.../artefacts/testresult/fictitioustestresult.xml
            </Location>
        </CarInsuranceQuoteServiceTestResult >
    </outputArtefact>
</Task>
```

Fig. 8.11 An instance of test tasks in the running example

For each subtask in the test plan, the broker translates the subtask into the corresponding capability description and constructs a service profile. The test broker then submits the service profile to the Matchmaker to search for appropriate testers. In this case, testers TCG and TCE are selected for the subtasks, respectively. The test planning finished with each subtask associated with a tester, and the test plan is passed to the execution module of the test broker for executing the subtasks.

The task execution module of the test broker calls the testers associated to each subtask according to the order given in the test plan. Data are passed from one subtask to another through invocation messages. In particular, the output artefact of the first subtask is passed to the second subtask. The output of the second subtask is the final result of the test, which is an OWL object. It is then returned to the client.

8.3.2 Example 2: Wrapping A Testing Tool into a Test Service

In this running example we demonstrate how to wrap an automated testing tool into a test service and how the tester can be composed together with other T-services to accomplish complex testing tasks.

8.3.2.1 Wrapping a Testing Tool

The testing tool in this running example is a general purpose testing tool called CASCAT [50], which generates test cases from algebraic specifications. It is wrapped into a web service by providing it with a WS interface. The web service version of the tool is referred to as TCG in the sequel. The following gives some technical details of the registration, search and invocation of the tester.

In the registration of TCG, the service takes a CASOCC specification file as input and generates test cases as output. These artefacts are stored in files and referred to through URLs of the file locations. To describe this service, the following new classes are added into the ontology.

- *CasoccSpecification*: a subclass of Specification that stands for algebraic specification in CASOCC.
- *ComponentTest*: a subclass of Context that stands for component testing.
- *CASOCCmethod*: a subclass of Method that stands for the method of test case generation from CASOCC.

In its service profile, the serviceClassification is set as TestCaseGeneration. The Input artefact is specified as the class CasoccSpecification. As described in the previous section, the service profile has three parameters that represent the aspects of the service capability. The context of TCG is ComponentTest. Its environment is Environment and represents no requirement on the test environment. Its method is CASOCCmethod. The output artefact is TestCase.

8.3.2.2 Collaboration Process

Similar to the first running example, suppose that a client wants to test a WS called NCS, which is a web service that provides numeric calculations of complex numbers. The client constructs a test task and submits it to the registry to search for a tester. As a result, a test broker is found to perform the testing.

Figure 8.12 shows the test task that client submitted to the test broker requesting test NCS against an algebraic specification written in CASOCC. The input artefact of the task is of type CasoccSpecification, and the output artefact type is TestResult.

Once the test broker receives the test task, it decomposes it into subtasks and generated a test plan that consisted of the following three subtasks:

- *Subtask 1*: Generating test cases from the specification. The input artefact of the task is of type CasoccSpecification. The output of this subtask is of type CasoccTestCase.
- *Subtask 2*: Transforming the test cases into the format that are executable by the T-service of NCS. Its input is of type CasoccTestcase and output is of type CalculatorTestCase.
- *Subtask 3*: Executing test cases and report test results. Its input is of type CalculatorTestCase and its output artefact type is TestResult.

```
<Task rdf:ID="thirdTask">
  <hasContext>
    <ServiceTest rdf:ID="serviceTest"/> </hasContext>
  <hasMethod rdf:resource="# CASOCCBasedMethod "/>
  <hasEnvironment rdf:resource="#notLimited"/>
  <hasActivity rdf:resource="#multiactivites"/>
  <inputArtefact>
    <CasoccSpecification rdf:ID="casoccSpecification">
      <Location rdf:datatype= "http://www.w3.org/2001/XMLSchema#anyURI">
        http://.../specification/Calculator.asoc
      </Location> </CasoccSpecification> </inputArtefact>
  <outputArtefact>
    <TestResult rdf:ID="testresult">
      <Location rdf:datatype= "http://www.w3.org/2001/XMLSchema#anyURI">
        http://.../artefacts/testresult/fictitioustestresult.txt
      </Location> </TestResult> </outputArtefact>
  <testObject>
    <TestObject rdf:ID="calculateService">
      <operationName rdf:datatype="http://www.w3.org/2001/XMLSchema#string">
        Add </operationName>
      <endpoint rdf:datatype="http://www.w3.org/2001/XMLSchema#string">
        http://.../axis/services/CalculatorImpl
      </endpoint> </TestObject> </testObject>
</Task>
```

Fig. 8.12 The task to test NCS based on algebraic specification

For each subtask in the test plan, the broker translates it into the corresponding capability description and constructs a service profile. The test broker then submits the service profile to the Matchmaker to search for appropriate testers. In this case, testers TCG, TFT and T-NCS are discovered for the subtasks, respectively. The test planning finishes with each subtask associated with a tester. The test plan is then passed to the execution module for executing the subtasks.

The task execution module calls the testers associated to each subtask according to the order given in the test plan. Data are passed from one subtask to another by the construction of invocation message to the testers. In particular, the output artefact of a subtask is passed to the next subtask. The output of the third subtask is the final result of the test, which is again an OWL object. It is returned to the client by the broker. Figure 8.13 summarises the collaboration process described above.

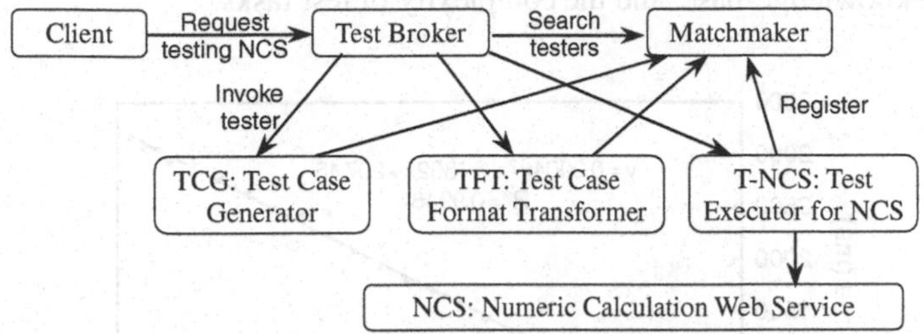

Fig. 8.13 The collaboration between the web services in running Example 2

8.4 Discussion: Main Feature of the Framework

The framework implements collaborative testing of WS within the service-oriented architecture using ontology and also the concept of T-services. In this framework, various testing functions are provided by T-services, such as generating test plan and test cases, invoking test executions, collecting test results, checking output correctness, measuring test adequacy and coverage, and so forth. It does not only applicable to functional testing as demonstrated in the running examples, but also applicable to non-functional tests, for example, through collaboration with a non-functional test service. The collaborations between test services are autonomous rather than enforced. That is, what to test and how to test is the choice of the service requester, but how to fulfil a client's test request is the choice of test service provider. A T-service requester need to search for T-services, negotiate the cost of test, select a T-service provider and invoke the T-service at runtime. The test activities are then performed by a T-service provider. Test brokers are also T-services but specialised in the composition of T-services. Complicated testing processes and interactions between T-services can be handled by such professionally developed T-services to simplify the uses of T-services. The approach has the following advantages.

A. Scalability

The framework is scalable since T-services are distributed and there is no extra-burden on UDDI servers. Experiments reported in [52, 57] shows that the average test service search time increases with the number of testers in the registry, but in almost a linear manner, as shown in Fig. 8.14. With the size of knowledge base increases, the time spent by a test broker to generate test service composition plans also increases, but again in an almost linear rate as shown in Fig. 8.15. With the increase of the complexity of testing tasks, which is measured by the number of different types of subtasks to fulfil the task, the time overhead increases in a quadratic polynomial function as shown in Fig. 8.16. Therefore, the test broker is capable of dealing with test problems of practical sizes with respect to the number of testers registered, the size of the knowledge-base, and the complexity of test tasks.

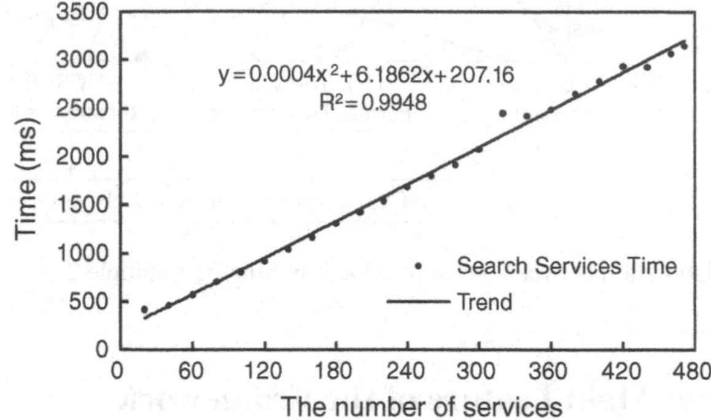

Fig. 8.14 Execution time dependence on the number of testers registered in UDDI

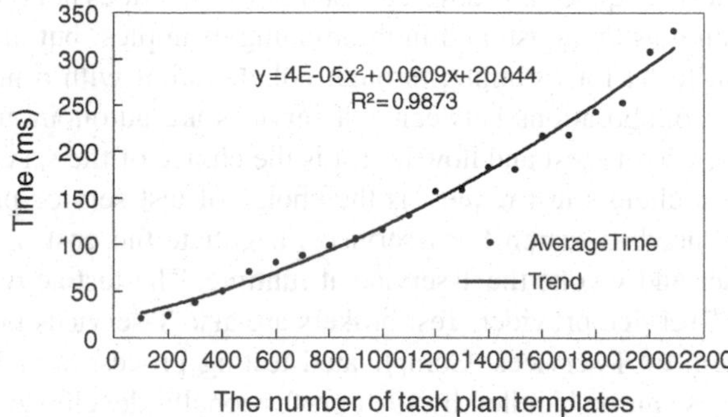

Fig. 8.15 Execution time dependence on the number of plan templates in knowledge-base

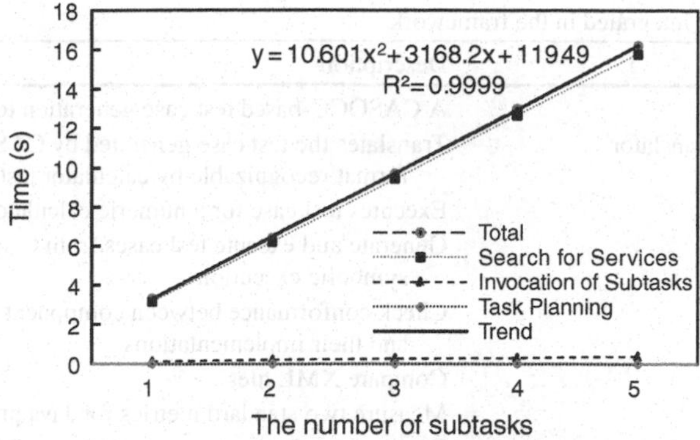

Fig. 8.16 Execution time dependence on the number of subtasks

B. Feasibility

The framework is implemented without any change to the existing standards of Semantic WS [7]. A case study reported in [57] demonstrated that a wide range of different types of test services can be supported and integrated into the framework. Table 8.1 summarises the services used in the case study.[5]

C. Capability of dealing with diversity

The need of dealing with variety is achieved through collaborations among many T-services and the employment of ontology of software testing to integrate multiple testing tools. An experiment applying data mutation testing techniques [42] shows clearly that the framework is capable of dealing with services of subtle differences so that the best match can be automatically selected to perform testing tasks [57].

D. Fully automated for testing on-the-fly

The automation of test processes for testing on-the-fly, especially the dynamic composition of T-services, can be also achieved by employing ontology of software testing and test brokers. Moreover, test executions can be performed by running a separate T-service, thus they do not interfere with the normal operations of the services under test.

E. Extendibility

This framework employs an ontology management facility to enhance its extendibility. With this, the software testing ontology can be extended and maintained through public services.

---

[5] Java NCSS can be found at URL: http://javancss.codehaus.org/, and PMD can be found at URL: http://pmd.sourceforge.net/

Table 8.1 Testers integrated in the framework

Name	Description
CASCAT [50]	A CASOCC-based test case generation tool
Test case format translator	Translates the test case generated by CASCAT into the format recognizable by calculator test case executor
Test case executor	Executes test case for a numeric calculator web service
Klee [16]	Generate and execute test cases from C source code by symbolic execution
Magic [20]	Check conformance between component specifications and their implementations
XML comparator	Compare XML files
Java NCSS	Measure two standard metrics for Java program
Findbugs [26]	Find bugs in Java program by static analysis
PMD	A static analysis tool for finding potential bugs and other problems in Java source code
WSDL-based test generator [2]	A WSDL based test case generation tool
Web service test case executor [2]	Execute the test case generated by WSDL based test case generator

8.5 Conclusion and Future work

In this chapter, we presented a service-oriented architecture for testing WS. In this architecture, various T-services collaborate with each other to complete test tasks. We employ the ontology of software testing STOWS to describe the capabilities of T-services and test tasks for the registration, discovery and invocation of T-services. The knowledge intensive composition of T-services is realized by the development and employment of test brokers, which are also T-services. We implemented the architecture in Semantic WS technology. Case studies have demonstrated the feasibility of the architecture and illustrated how to wrap up general purpose testing tools and turn them into T-services and how to develop service specific T-services to support the testing of a WS. Experimental evaluation also shows its scalability.

The test broker in the framework plays an important role in automation of testing processes. Further research on the design and implementation of powerful test brokers will have a significant impact on the usability of the T-services. In particular, using knowledge of software testing processes to generate test plans seems a promising topic for further work. Currently, such knowledge of software testing process is represented in the form of task decomposition rules. A question is whether such knowledge can be encoded in a process definition language such as BPEL. If yes, a careful analysis of the benefit and comparison of the two are necessary. Another direction to enhance the functionality of test brokers is to associate monitoring functions to brokers as Tsai et al. suggested so that the previous performance of T-services can be taken into consideration in the selection of testers.

An issue that has not been addressed adequately in the prototype is the testing of long running processes. A simple solution could be to allow testers to distinguish long running processes from short running tasks either in the test request message (i.e. in the test task description) or in the service description (i.e. in WSDL). An upper limit to the waiting time for test results should then be set accordingly to avoid infinite waiting. The broker could also set different running modes for short and long running tasks.

Moreover, as discussed in Sect. 8.1, a particular difficulty in testing WS is due to the lack of software artefacts to support test activities. The framework presented in this chapter offers the opportunity to incorporate a trust mechanism so that design documents, source code and many other types of internal information of services can be delivered to trustable T-services. Further research on how such a trust mechanism to interoperate with the T-services needs to be worked out in detail.

Another hard problem to be solved is associated to the management of ontology. Consistency problem may occur when the ontology is updated during the execution of a task. How to prevent such errors and to reduce the risk is still an open question.

Testing is one of the quality assurance activities for the development of services. It is worth investigating into how to extend and/or adapt the framework for a wider range of quality assurance activities such as static analysis and verification and dynamic monitoring of services, etc. This may need to extend the network model of WS to incorporate the internal structure of services.

Acknowledgments The work reported in this chapter is partly funded by the National Basic Research Program of China (973) under Grant No. 2011CB302603 and the National Natural Science Foundation of China under Grant No. 60725206.

References

1. de Almeida, L.F., Vergilio, S.R.: Exploring perturbation based testing for web services. In: Proc. of ICWS'06, pp. 717–726. IEEE CS (2006)
2. Bai, X., Dong, W., Tsai, W., Chen, Y.: Wsdl-based automatic test case generation for web services testing. In: Proc. of SOSE'05, pp. 215–220. IEEE CS (2005)
3. Bai, X., Lee, S., Tsai, W.T., Chen, Y.: Ontology-based test modeling and partition testing of web services. In: Proc. of ICWS'08, pp. 465–472. IEEE CS (2008)
4. Bartolini, C., Bertolino, A., Marchetti, E.: Introducing service-oriented coverage testing. In: Proc. of ASE'08, pp. 57–64. IEEE CS (2008)
5. Bartolini, C., Bertolino, A., Marchetti, E., Parissis, I.: Data flow-based validation of web services compositions: Perspectives and examples. In: R.e.a. Lemos V (ed.) Architecting Dependable Systems, LNCS, vol. 5135, pp. 298–325. Springer-Verlag (2008)
6. Belli, F., Linschulte, M.: Event-driven modeling and testing of web services. In: Proc. of COMPSAC'08, pp. 1168–1173. IEEE CS (2008)
7. Berners-Lee, T., Hendler, J., Lassila, O.: The semantic web. Scientific American **284**(5), 34–43 (2001).
8. Bertolino, A., Angelis, G.D., Frantzen, L., Polini, A.: Model-based generation of testbeds for web services. In: Proc. of TestCom/FATES'08, pp. 266–282 (2008)
9. Bertolino, A., Angelis, G.D., Frantzen, L., Polini, A.: The plastic framework and tools for testing service-oriented applications. In: Software Engineering: Int'l Summer Schools, (ISSSE'08), pp. 106–139 (2008)

10. Bertolino, A., Gao, J., Marchetti, E.: Xml every-flavor testing. In: Proc. of WEBIST'06, pp. 268–273. INSTICC Press (2006)
11. Bertolino, A., Gao, J., Marchetti, E., A.Polini: Taxi-a tool for xml-based testing. In: Proc. of ICSE'07 (Companion), pp. 53–54. IEEE CS (2007)
12. Bertolino, A., Gao, J., Marchetti, E., Polini, A.: Automatic test data generation for xml schema-based partition testing. In: Proc. of AST'07, p. 4. IEEE CS (2007)
13. Bertolino, A., Gao, J., Marchetti, E., Polini, A.: Systematic generation of xml instances to test complex software applications. In: N.e.a. Guelfi (ed.) Rapid Integration of Software Engineering Techniques, *LNCS*, vol. 4401, pp. 114–129. Springer (2007)
14. Bertolino, A., Polini, A.: The audition framework for testing web services interoperability. In: Proc. of EUROMICRO'05, pp. 134–142 (2005)
15. Bozkurt, M., Harman, M., Hassoun, Y.: Testing & verification in service-oriented architecture: A survey. Software Testing, Verification and Reliability (STVR) (To Appear).
16. Cadar, C., Dunbar, D., Engler, D.: Klee: Unassisted and Automatic Generation of High-Coverage Tests for Complex Systems Programs. OSDI (2008)
17. Canfora, G., Penta, M.: Testing services and service-centric systems: Challenges and opportunities. IT Professional **8**(2), 10–17 (2006)
18. Canfora, G., Penta, M.: Service-oriented architectures testing: A survey. In: A. Lucia, F. Ferrucci (eds.) Software Engineering: Int'l Summer Schools (ISSSE 2006–2008), Revised Tutorial Lectures, *LNCS*, vol. 5413, pp. 78–105. Springer-Verlag (2009)
19. Chan, W.K., Cheung, S.C., Leung, K.R.P.H.: A metamorphic testing approach for online testing of service-oriented software applications. Int'l Journal of Web Services Research **4**(2), 61–81 (2007)
20. Edmund, S.C., Clarke, E., Groce, A., Jha, S., Vienna, T.: Modular verification of software components in c. IEEE Trans. Softw. Eng. **30**, 388–402 (2004)
21. Emer, M.P., Vergilio, S.R., Jino, M.: A testing approach for xml schemas. In: Proc. of COMPSAC'05, pp. 57–62. IEEE CS (2005)
22. Garcia-Fanjul, J., Tuya, J., de la Riva, C.: Generating test cases specifications for bpel compositions of web services using spin. In: Proc. of WS-MaTe (2006)
23. Hanna, S., Munro, M.: An approach for wsdl-based automated robustness testing of web services. In: C.e.a. Barry (ed.) Information Systems Development: Challenges in Practice, Theory, and Education, vol. 2, pp. 493–504. Springer (2009)
24. Heckel, R., Lohmann, M.: Towards contract-based testing of web services. Electronic Notes in Theoretical Computer Science **82**(6) (2004)
25. Heckel, R., Mariani, L.: Automatic conformance testing of web services. In: Proc. of FASE'05, pp. 34–48. Springer (2005)
26. Hovemeyer, D., Pugh, W.: Finding more null pointer bugs, but not too many. In: Proc. of PASTE'07, pp. 9–14 (2007)
27. Huang, H., Liu, H., Li, Z., Zhu, J.: Surrogate: A simulation apparatus for continuous integration testing in service oriented architecture. In: Proc. of SCC'08, vol. 2, pp. 223–230. IEEE CS (2008)
28. Huang, H., Tsai, W., Paul, R., Chen, Y.: Automated model checking and testing for composite web services. In: Proc. of ISORC'05, pp. 300–307. IEEE CS (2005)
29. IICMVA: Model user guide for implementing online insurance verification, version 4, Insurance Industry Committee on Motor Vehicle Administration, USA. http://www.iicmva.com/IICMVAPublications.html (2010). (Accessed on 20 Oct. 2010).
30. K. Sycara M. Paolucci, A., Srinivasan, N.: Automated discovery, interaction and composition of semantic web services. J. Web Semantics **1**(1), 27–46 (2003)
31. Kaschner, K., Lohmann, N.: Automatic test case generation for services. In: Proc. of Fourth Int'l Workshop on Engineering Service-Oriented Applications: Analysis and Design (WESOA 2008), LNCS. Springer-Verlag (2008)
32. Kawamura, T., Blasio, J.A.D., Hasegawa, T., Paolucci, M., Sycara, K.: A preliminary report of a public experiment of a semantic service matchmaker combined with a uddi business registry. In: Proc. of ICSOC'03, pp. 208–224. IEEE CS (2003)

33. Lallali, M., Zaidi, F., Cavalli, A., Hwang, I.: Automatic timed test case generation for web services composition. In: Proc. of ECOWS'08, pp. 53–62 (2008)
34. Lee, S.C., Offutt, J.: Generating test cases for xml-based web component interactions using mutation analysis. In: Proc. of ISSRE'01, pp. 200–209. IEEE CS (2001)
35. Li, J.B., Miller, J.: Testing the semantics of w3c xml schema. In: Proc. of COMPSAC'05, pp. 443–448. IEEE CS (2005)
36. Li, Z., Sun, W., Jiang, Z.B., Zhang, X.: Bpel4ws unit testing: Framework and implementation. In: Proc. of ICWS'05, pp. 103–110. IEEE CS (2005)
37. Looker, N., Munro, M., Xu, J.: Ws-fit: A tool for dependability analysis of web services. In: Proc. of COMPSAC'04, pp. 120–123. IEEE CS (2004)
38. Magee, J., Kramer, J., Uchitel, S., Foster, H.: Ltsa-ws: a tool for model-based verification of web service compositions and choreography. In: Proc. of ICSE'06, pp. 771–774. IEEE CS (2006)
39. Mayer, P.: Design and implementation of a framework for testing bpel compositions. Master's thesis, Leibnitz Univ., Germany (2006)
40. Mei, L., Chan, W.K., Tse, T.H.: Data flow testing of service-oriented workflow applications. In: Proc. of ICSE'08, pp. 371–380. IEEE CS (2008)
41. Offutt, J., Xu, W.: Generating test cases for web services using data perturbation. SIGSOFT Softw. Eng. Notes **29**(5), 1–10 (2004)
42. Shan, L., Zhu, H.: Generating structurally complex test cases by data mutation. The Computer Journal **52**, 571–588 (2009)
43. Srinivasan, N., Paolucci, M., Sycara, K.: Adding owl-s to uddi, implementation and throughput. In: Proc. of The 1st Int'l Workshop on Semantic Web Services and Web Process Composition, pp. 169–182 (2004)
44. Tsai, W., Chen, Y., Paul, R., Liao, N., Huang, H.: Cooperative and group testing in verification of dynamic composite web services. In: Proc. of COMPSAC'04, vol. 2: Workshops and Fast Abstracts, pp. 170–173. IEEE CS (2004)
45. Tsai, W., Paul, R., Song, W., Cao, Z.: Coyote: An xml-based framework for web services testing. In: Proc. of HASE'02, pp. 173–174. IEEE CS (2002)
46. Tsai, W., Wei, X., Chen, Y., Paul, R., Bai, X.: Swiss cheese test case generation for web services testing. IEICE - Trans. Inf. Syst. **88**(12), 2691–2698 (2005)
47. Tsai, W., Zhou, X., Chen, Y., Bai, X.: On testing and evaluating service-oriented software. Computer **41**(8), 40–46 (2008)
48. Wang, Y., Bai, X., Li, J., Huang, R.: Ontology-based test case generation for testing web services. In: Proc. of ISADS'07, pp. 43–50. IEEE CS (2007)
49. Xu, W., Offutt, J., Luo, J.: Testing web services by xml perturbation. In: Proc. of ISSRE'05, pp. 257–266. IEEE CS (2005)
50. Yu, B., Kong, L., Zhang, Y., Zhu, H.: Testing java components based on algebraic specifications. In: Proc. of ICST'08, pp. 190–199. IEEE CS (2008)
51. Zhang, Y., Zhu, H.: Ontology for service oriented testing of web services. In: Proc. of SOSE'08. IEEE CS (2008)
52. Zhang, Y., Zhu, H.: An intelligent broker approach to semantics-based service composition. In: Proc. of COMPSAC 2011, pp. 20–25. IEEE CS, Munich, Germany (2011)
53. Zheng, Y., Zhou, J., Krause, P.: An automatic test case generation framework for web services. Journal of Software **2**(3), 64–77 (2007)
54. Zhu, H.: A framework for service-oriented testing of web services. In: Proc. of COMPSAC'06, pp. 679–691. IEEE CS (2006)
55. Zhu, H., Huo, Q.: Developing a software testing ontology in uml for a software growth environment of web-based applications. In: e. H. Yang (ed.) Software Evolution with UML and XML, pp. 263–295. IDEA Group Inc. (2005)
56. Zhu, H., Huo, Q., Greenwood, S.: A multi-agent software environment for testing web-based applications. In: Proc. of COMPSAC'03, pp. 210–215. IEEE CS (2003)
57. Zhu, H., Zhang, Y.: Collaborative testing of web services. IEEE Transactions on Services Computing **5**(1), 116–130 (2012)

Chapter 9
WSDARWIN: Studying the Evolution of Web Service Systems

Marios Fokaefs and Eleni Stroulia

Abstract The service-oriented architecture paradigm prescribes the development of systems through the composition of services, i.e., network-accessible components, specified by (and invoked through) their interface descriptions. Systems thus developed need to be aware of changes in, and evolve with, their constituent services. Therefore, the accurate recognition of changes in the specification of a service is an essential functionality in supporting the software lifecycle of service-oriented systems. In this chapter, we extend our previous empirical study on the evolution of web-service interfaces and we classify the identified changes according to their impact on client applications. To better understand the evolution of web services, and, more importantly, to facilitate the systematic and automatic maintenance of web-service systems, we introduce WSDARWIN, a specialized differencing method for web services. Finally, we discuss the application of such a comparison method on operation- (WSDL) and resource-centric (REST) web services.

9.1 Introduction

Service-system evolution and maintenance is an interesting variant of the general software-evolution problem. The problem is complex and challenging due to the fundamentally distributed nature of service-oriented systems, whose constituent parts may reside on different servers, across organizations and beyond the domain of any individual entity's control. At the same time, since the design of a service-oriented system is expressed in terms of the interface specifications of the underlying services, the overall system needs and can be aware only of the changes that impact

M. Fokaefs (✉) · E. Stroulia
Department of Computing Science,
University of Alberta, Edmonton, AB, Canada
e-mail: fokaefs@ualberta.ca

E. Stroulia
e-mail: stroulia@ualberta.ca

A. Bouguettaya et al. (eds.), *Advanced Web Services*,
DOI: 10.1007/978-1-4614-7535-4_9,

these interface specifications; any changes to the service implementations that do not impact their interfaces are completely transparent to the overall system. In effect, the specifications of the system's constituent services serve as a boundary layer, which precludes service-implementation changes from impacting the overall system.

The directly affected party in the evolution of service systems is the client, i.e., the consuming party. Figure 9.1 shows a typical evolution scenario from the client's perspective. Initially, the client invokes the service and a fault may be detected. It is not usual for the client to have a priori knowledge about any changes on the service, unless there is frequent and effective communication between the provider and the client. Once the fault is detected, the client has to compare the old service interface with the new one from the provider to identify the nature of the changes and possibly their effect on the application. The next step is to adapt the client application to the new version of the service. This requires as much information as possible in order to make the adaptation process systematic and, if possible, fully automatic. Finally, the client has to test the application to make sure the adaptation worked, since not all changes are automatically adaptable.

Fig. 9.1 The evolution process from the client's perspective

This is why recognizing the changes to the specification of a service interface and their impact on client applications is highly desirable and a necessary prerequisite for actually adapting the applications to the new version of the service. Further, assuming that a precise method for service-specification changes existed, it would be extremely useful if one could (a) characterize the changes in terms of their complexity, and (b) semi-automatically develop adapters for migrating clients from older interface versions to newer ones.

In this work, we introduce WSDARWIN, a domain-specific differencing method to compare (a variety of) web-service interfaces. Most frequently, services are developed following two approaches: operation-centric, whose interfaces are specified as Web Service Description Language (WSDL)[1] files, and data-centric (REST), which are specified as Web Application Description Language (WADL)[2] files. Although the two approaches are quite different in the syntax they use to specify web services and their associated technologies, they share a palette of building elements, namely functions and data. WSDARWIN takes advantage of this fundamental commonality to produce accurate comparison results in an efficient and scalable manner for service interfaces regardless of their specification syntax. In this work, we compare WSDARWIN with our old comparison approach VTRACKER [6] and discuss their differences with respect to performance and scalability. Finally, we apply

[1] http://www.w3.org/TR/wsdl

[2] http://www.w3.org/Submission/wadl/

WSDARWIN on Unicorn,[3] W3C's unified validator and Amazon Elastic Cloud Computing (EC2) web service and we present some special cases to demonstrate how the comparison method is used and how its results are presented.

In addition to comparing pairs of specifications to recognize their differences, we are also interested in analyzing the long-term evolution of real world services. We have already presented an empirical study [6], where we analyzed a set of commercial WSDL web services including the Amazon Elastic Cloud Computing (Amazon EC2),[4] the FedEx Package Movement Information and Rate Services,[5] the PayPal SOAP API[6] and the Bing search service,[7] using VTRACKER, as a comparison method. In that work, we studied the evolution of the aforementioned services and reported our findings on evolution patterns, we identified particular change scenarios and discussed them with respect to their impact on potential client applications and, finally, we correlated these changes with business decisions concerning the services in an effort to reason about the evolution of each service. In this chapter, we extend the findings of this empirical study by providing additional statistics about the changes that the examined services underwent and, more importantly, we provide a classification of the service change scenarios according to their impact on client applications.

The rest of the chapter is organized as follows. In Sect. 9.2 we present the extended results of our empirical study on the evolution of WSDL services and we present the classification of service changes. In Sect. 9.3, we introduce WSDARWIN as a comparison method for service interfaces and demonstrate its usage on a WSDL and a WADL service. Section 9.4 provides an overview of the literature related to our work. Finally, Sect. 9.5 concludes this chapter and discusses some of our future plans.

9.2 Study of Web Service Evolution

Before developing methods and tools to support the evolution process of web services, it is important to first study and understand how service interfaces change. This way, we can identify what is important to pay attention to and what can be simplified in order to build improved automated processes. In our work, we have studied five real-world web services offered by companies in the industry of web applications, whose evolution spans across different time periods and exhibits interesting evolution patterns.

- **Amazon EC2**. The Amazon Elastic Compute Cloud is a web service that provides resizable compute capacity in the cloud. We studied the history of the web service across 18 versions of its WSDL specification, dating from 6/26/2006 to 8/31/2010.

[3] http://code.w3.org/unicorn/

[4] http://aws.amazon.com/ec2/

[5] http://www.fedex.com/us/developer

[6] https://www.paypalobjects.com/en_US/ebook/PP_APIReference/architecture.html

[7] http://www.bing.com/developers

- The **FedEx Rate Service** operations provide a shipping rate quote for a specific service combination depending on the origin and destination information supplied in the request. We studied 9 versions of this service.
- The **FedEx Package Movement Information Service** operations can be used to check service availability, route and postal codes between an origin and destination. We studied 3 versions of this service.
- The **PayPal SOAP API** Service can be used to make payments, search transactions, refund payments, view transaction information, and other business functions. We studied 4 versions of this service.
- The **Bing Search** service provide programmatic access to Bing content Source-Types such as Image, InstantAnswer, MobileWeb, News, Phonebook, Related-Search, Spell, Translation, Video, and Web. We studied 5 versions of this service.

9.2.1 Analyzing the Evolution of the Services

Table 9.1 shows the evolution profile of all the examined services in terms of data types and operations. Each row corresponds to a service version. Columns 3–8 report the percentage of types and operations in this version that underwent edits (**C**hanges, **D**eletions, **A**dditions) from the previous version. The change columns include two types of changes: renaming or other changes in the "signature" of the object (type or operation), i.e., the attributes of the particular XML element and changes that were propagated from children nodes. For example, if the input or output of an operation or the contained elements of a type are changed, then these changes are propagated to the parent element.

Amazon EC2, as it can be seen from the tables, followed a very distinct pattern of evolution. The developers chose to augment a single service with new operations as they were being developed. For this reason, we observe many additions and changes and a complete lack of deletions. Although this policy eventually produced a rather long WSDL file, it was also prudent in the sense that deleting an operation creates a non-recoverable situation. In such a case a client application should be changed and recompiled. Furthermore, we can observe a correlation between adding new operations and adding new types. This is because in the Amazon services there is a 2-to-1 relationship between types and operations (one input type and one output type for each operation). The changes in the types are usually because of enhancements in previous functionality or to accommodate new functionality. In version 6, we can observe a special case: there are small changes and deletions in types and no other activity. Upon closer examination, it becomes clear that this change represents, in fact, a refactoring.

The FedEx services (Rate and Package Movement) do not follow the same evolution pattern. These services have a very small number of operations (1 and 2 respectively), which rarely change. On the other hand, the data types evolve vigorously with changes, deletions and additions of new types especially in the Rate service. An interesting change in the Rate service occurred between versions 3 and 4.

Table 9.1 The evolution profile of types and operations in the studied services

Service	Ver	Types			Operations		
		C(%)	D(%)	A(%)	C(%)	D(%)	A(%)
Amazon EC2	2	5.00	0.00	25.00	0.00	0.00	21.43
Amazon EC2	3	1.33	0.00	8.00	0.00	0.00	11.76
Amazon EC2	4	2.47	0.00	0.00	0.00	0.00	0.00
Amazon EC2	5	7.41	0.00	7.41	0.00	0.00	5.26
Amazon EC2	6	2.30	2.30	0.00	0.00	0.00	0.00
Amazon EC2	7	4.71	0.00	30.59	0.00	0.00	30.00
Amazon EC2	8	0.00	0.00	23.42	0.00	0.00	30.77
Amazon EC2	9	26.28	0.00	10.22	2.94	0.00	8.82
Amazon EC2	10	0.66	0.00	3.97	2.70	0.00	2.70
Amazon EC2	11	0.00	0.00	8.92	0.00	0.00	7.89
Amazon EC2	12	1.17	0.00	4.68	0.00	0.00	4.88
Amazon EC2	13	1.68	0.00	44.69	0.00	0.00	51.16
Amazon EC2	14	1.54	0.00	5.02	0.00	0.00	4.62
Amazon EC2	15	5.88	0.00	8.82	0.00	0.00	8.82
Amazon EC2	16	0.34	0.00	10.14	0.00	0.00	9.46
Amazon EC2	17	1.53	0.00	7.36	0.00	0.00	7.41
Amazon EC2	18	12.00	0.00	4.57	0.00	0.00	4.60
FedEx Rate	2	26.32	1.32	11.84	0.00	0.00	0.00
FedEx Rate	3	14.29	0.00	9.52	0.00	0.00	0.00
FedEx Rate	4	25.00	8.70	47.83	0.00	0.00	100.00
FedEx Rate	5	9.38	0.78	4.69	50.00	50.00	0.00
FedEx Rate	6	10.53	3.01	39.85	0.00	0.00	0.00
FedEx Rate	7	15.38	2.75	15.93	0.00	0.00	0.00
FedEx Rate	8	8.25	0.97	11.17	0.00	0.00	0.00
FedEx Rate	9	18.06	0.44	0.44	0.00	0.00	0.00
Bing	2.1	11.29	0.00	14.81	0.00	0.00	0.00
Bing	2.2	7.35	1.61	11.29	0.00	0.00	0.00
Bing	2.3	2.94	0.00	0.00	0.00	0.00	0.00
Bing	2.4	1.43	0.00	2.94	0.00	0.00	0.00
PayPal	53.0	12.35	0.00	107.69	0.00	0.00	110.53
PayPal	62.0	7.07	0.00	22.22	0.00	0.00	20.00
PayPal	65.1	1.82	0.00	11.11	0.00	0.00	10.42
FedEx Pack.	3	10.00	0.00	0.00	0.00	0.00	0.00
FedEx Pack.	4	5.00	0.00	0.00	0.00	0.00	0.00

Until version 3 the service offered a single operation named `getRate`. In version 3, a second operation, named `rateAvailableServices`, was introduced. In version 4, however, the new operation was promptly deleted, `getRate` was renamed to `getRates`, and based on the reorganization of the types, it appears that the responsibilities of the deleted operation were merged into the original one.

Bing and PayPal have both had a relatively short lifecycle but still exhibit interesting differences between them. Bing's history has been relatively stable, with few modifications given also the small number of elements in its WSDL specification

(1 operation and between 54 and 70 types). PayPal, on the other hand, follows an expansion pattern similar to the one Amazon follows; it is consistently enhanced with new operations. The great increase observed in Fig. 9.2a in the number of operations between the first two examined versions of PayPal is because there are a lot of intermediate versions for which we have no data.

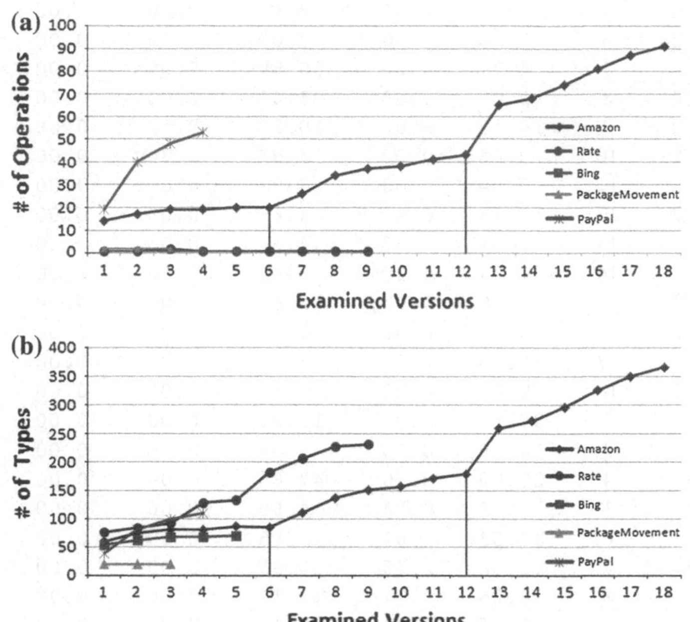

Fig. 9.2 The evolution of the examined services. **a** Evolution of number of operations. **b** Evolution of number of types

Figures 9.2a, b show the evolution of the operations and types of the examined services. An interesting observation from these figures concerns the Amazon service, where we can see that the particular service seems to have three distinct phases: the first is from version 1 to version 6, the second is from 7 to 12 and the third from 13 to 18. These phases are the result of the business decisions that have been described in [6].

9.2.2 Classification of Service Changes

Based on the discussion about specific changes that happened in the web services we examined in [6], we propose a classification of these changes based on their impact on client applications. Because of the distributed nature of service systems, clients usually have very little information to understand the changes in web services and contemplate their impact on their applications. Therefore, accurately recognizing and characterizing service changes will facilitate clients reason about these changes and systematically build adapters for their applications. We distinguish three types of changes with respect to their impact on clients.

1. *No-effect* changes do not impact the client at all. The client functionality is not disrupted and neither is the interface, which practically means that the client can still operate using the old stub. Changes in this category include adding new types (as long as these types are not used by existing operations) and adding new operations (assuming that the semantics of the service are preserved and there are no interdependencies between the new and the old operations).
2. *Adaptable* changes affect the interface of the client, but the functionality of the service remains the same. These changes, from the point of view of the provider, usually correspond to refactorings on the source code of the service. In other words, they are changes meant to improve the design of the service and leave the functionality unaffected. They can be easily addressed by generating a new stub and changing the old stub, still used by the client application, to invoke the new one and thus the evolved service [7]. This way we avoid changing the client code by modifying only autogenerated code. Changes in this category include refactorings, renaming and changing input or output for an operation (assuming that the new input or output are existing types and not new ones).
3. *Non-recoverable* changes imply that the functionality of the service is affected, in a way that the client breaks and we cannot address the issue without changing and recompiling the client code. In some cases, the change is so subtle as not to affect the interface of the client. In other words, the client still works but the results produced are not the desired ones. The problem in this case can be identified by means of unit and regression testing. Removing elements from the service interface (without replacing them) is a non-recoverable change.

Even after the identification of detailed changes between versions of the service interface and the classification of these changes, the adaptation of client applications may still not be plausible. Even in the first two categories, functionality may be affected and this impact may seem invisible or easily addressable by examining just the service interface. For this reason, testing of the adapted client application may still be needed and additional (manual) effort may be required.

9.2.3 Implications of the Empirical Study

Apart from drawing conclusions for the evolution of web service interfaces, including evolution patterns, lifecycles, good and bad practices, through the empirical studies we identified types of simple or more complex, but definitely recurring, changes. These examples, along with ones drawn from our experience in designing and developing software systems, have been used to design the comparison component of

WSDARWIN. The study has shown us what kind of changes to expect and the instances of these changes in commercial web services have helped us to understand how we can automatically identify such changes.

On the other hand, the classification of service changes primarily contributes to the adaptation and generally the evolution of client applications. In a recent work [7], we propose an adaptation algorithm that automatically adapts client applications to adaptable changes of the service interface. The knowledge of what category the change belongs to, can help us identify whether automatic adaptation can be applied. The classification can also improve the comparison method. For instance, in case of refactorings, these types of changes have very specific mechanics (see the work by Fowler [8]), which can be translated to comparison rules in WSDARWIN, thus expanding the system's capabilities to identify a greater variety of changes.

9.3 WSDARWIN

In order to be able to systematically adapt client applications to the changes of the web services on which they rely, we, first, should be able to accurately recognize the changes a web service undergoes. In developing a web-service differencing algorithm, one should consider two quality properties: (a) the efficiency and scalability of the algorithmic process, and (b) the understandability of the output it produces. The process has to be efficient and scalable because service-interface descriptions can be quite lengthy and complex, as they may contain many and complex types and numerous operations. On the other hand, as the differencing process is usually preformed in service of another task, such as adaptation for example, its output has to be understandable by the developers and it also has to be designed to be easily consumed by any downstream automated process.

In the WSDARWIN comparison method, we ensure efficiency by using a concise, domain-specific model to represent the relevant information of a service interface. The model captures the most important information of a service's elements such as *names*, *types*, their *structure* and the *relationships* with each other, thus, providing a simpler, more lightweight syntactic representation of the service representation than either WSDL or WADL. In addition, the algorithm employs certain heuristics on name comparisons to further improve the efficiency. The rationale underlying these heuristics is that within the same service (even between versions) names are unique and can therefore be treated as IDs. The use of the same name for different elements is not likely (and in many cases it is not allowed). For this reason, it only makes sense to compare strings using exact matching and not partial matching techniques such string-edit distance. Furthermore, instead of comparing named XML nodes like VTRACKER, WSDARWIN compares model entities based on their specific type (e.g. operations with operations, complexTypes with complexTypes etc.). This way it is not necessary to compare all elements against each other, thus avoiding false results due to fuzzy mapping and gaining further efficiency improvement over VTRACKER.

WSDARWIN's output follows the model shown in Fig. 9.3.[8] Figure 9.3a shows the model used to represent WSDL service interfaces. The operations, which are the invocation points between the provided service and the client application, have input and output types. The type hierarchy is in accordance with the XML Schema specification[9]: `PrimitiveTypes` include strings, integers, boolean etc.; `SimpleTypes` are based on certain restrictions on their values (e.g. enumerations); `ComplexTypes` are composed of other types. The model omits elements that add no further structural information for the clients, such as `messages` and high level `elements` from the schema, which only serve as references. Therefore, only the elements to which these references point were eventually included in the model.

Figure 9.3b corresponds to the WADL interface model. The element `resources` contains a set of `resource` elements, which in turn contain `methods` and these have `requests` and `responses`. Requests consist of a set of `parameters` and the responses, which are usually returned as a file of structured data such as XML or JSON, refer to elements in an XML schema file. The IType hierarchy is the same as in the WSDL model.

In both these models, the containment relationships (denoted by the black diamonds) indicate parent-child relationships between element types. For example, an operation in WSDL has two children: an input type and an output type. The children elements together represent the *structure* of a WS element. Structural information can be used to uniquely identify elements. If two elements across two web-service specifications have the same children, then there is high confidence that they are one and the same element.

Figures 9.4a, b[10] show examples of the instantiation of the WSDL and WADL models for the Amazon EC2 and the Unicorn validator, respectively. The figures clearly demonstrate the structure of elements, implemented by the parent-children relationship between WS elements as defined in the interface models.

Figure 9.3c models the changes. We can have different types of deltas including *changes*, *additions*, *deletions*, *moves* and *moves and changes*. The two hierarchies are connected through the Bridge design pattern [9] and their relationship is that each delta has a source WS element and a target WS element.

The interface models define the structure and the vocabulary of the diff scripts produced by WSDARWIN; the Delta model defines the annotations for each mapping reported in these scripts. Designing WSDARWIN in this manner, we have striven for a balance of specificity to the syntax of the compared specification (WSDL vs. WADL) and generality in the definition of the changes the interfaces go through. This design, we believe, makes the output clear to web-service system developers and enables them to understand and better reason about the changes in the services. Furthermore, the output is designed with consideration to a downstream automated adaptation process, since it provides a full mapping between the elements and the type of every change so that the process can assess its impact on the client application.

[8] The diagrams were designed using the Eclipse EMF toolkit.

[9] http://www.w3.org/XML/Schema

[10] The figures were generated by the Eclipse EMF toolkit.

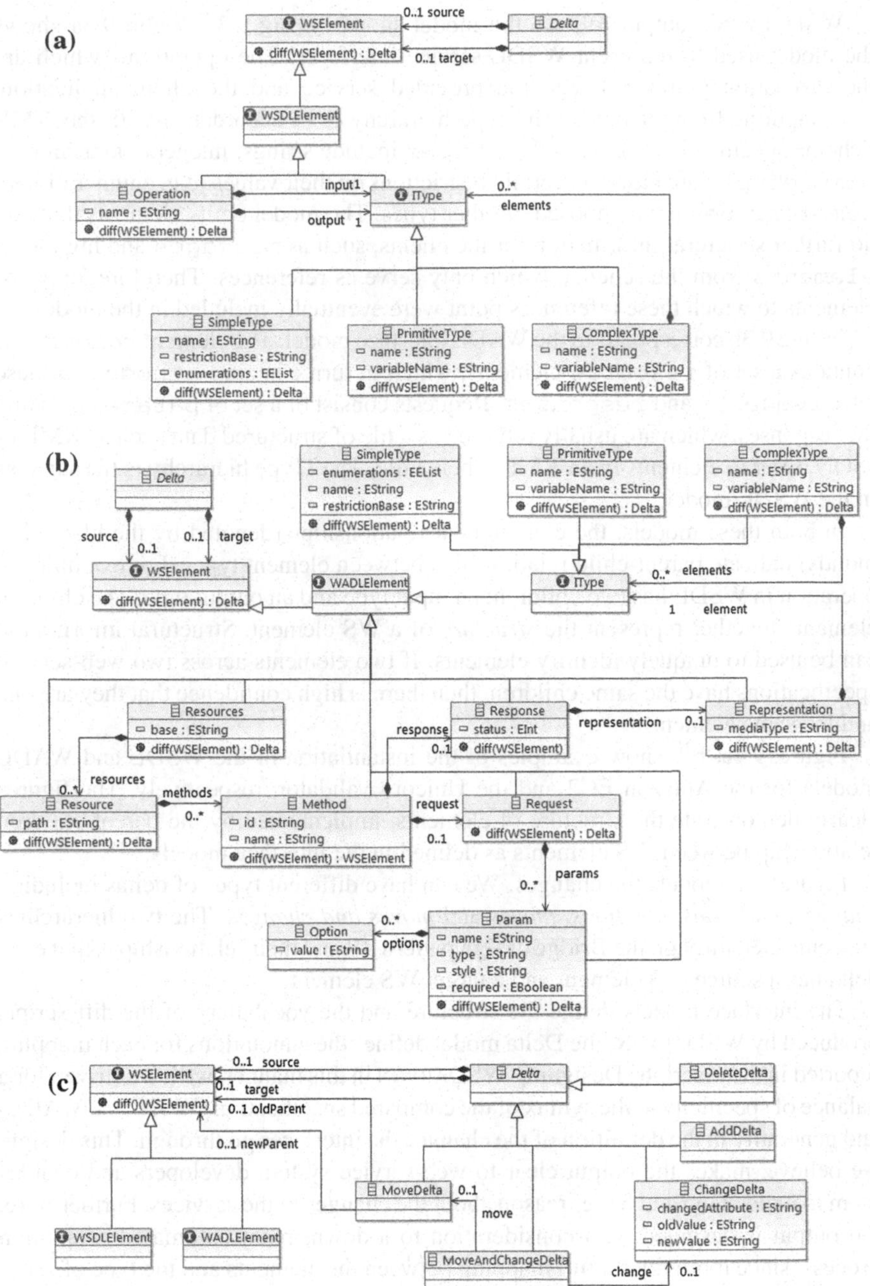

Fig. 9.3 The WSDARWIN comparison framework. **a** The WSDL service interface model. **b** The WADL service interface model. **c** The WSDARWIN delta model

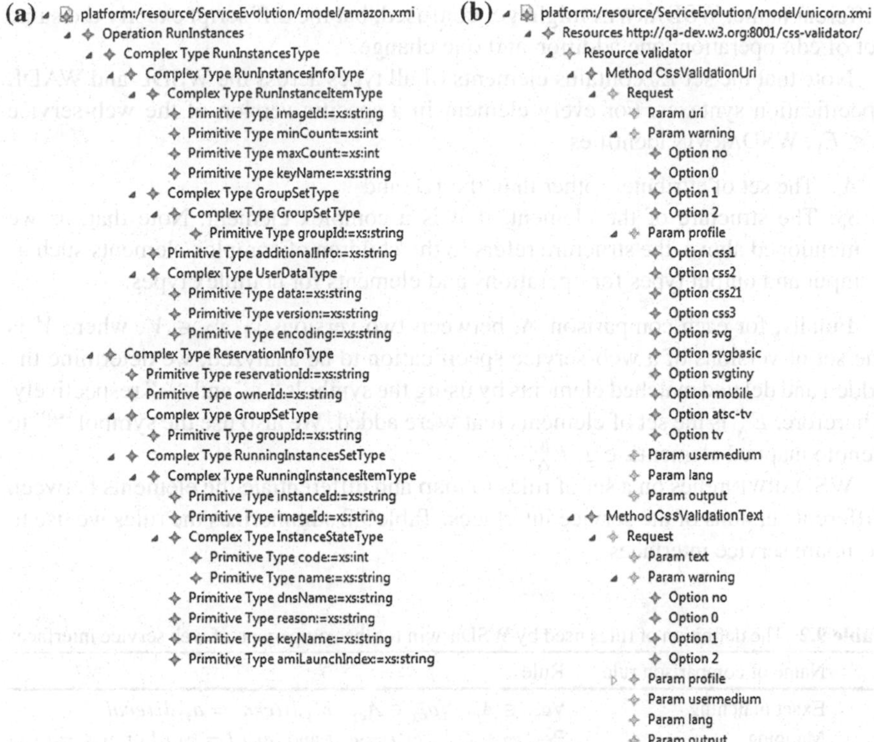

Fig. 9.4 Snippets of WSDL and WADL instances of the WSDARWINinterface models. **a** Amazon EC2. **b** W3C Unicorn CSS validator

Let us now review WSDARWIN in some detail. For each version v to be examined, WSDARWIN extracts E_v, the set of elements in the specification of the v version of the service. This set contains tuples (id, t, a, s) where id is the identifying attribute of the element (usually the name), t is the type of the element, a is the set of its attributes and s is the structure of the element.

In the context of the WSDARWIN comparison, the ID or the structure can uniquely identify an element. Therefore, if two elements, belonging in two different versions, share at least one of these two properties (ID and structure), then WSDARWIN considers them to be two versions of the same element. Since web service interfaces are artifacts generated by source code, they also follow the programming conventions of the underlying programming language. In principle, two entities in the same file cannot have the same name, or a compilation error occurs. Therefore, we can safely assume that the name of an entity is its unique identifier. On the other hand, we also consider structure to be a unique identifier so as to be able to identify cases of renaming. In the rare case, where the new version contains two elements, one with the same name as the old entity and the other with the old entity's structure but different name, WSDARWIN might get confused, but the diff script exactly the same set of edit operation: one addition and one change.

Note that the set E_v contains elements of all types across the WSDL and WADL specification syntaxes. For every element in a specific version of the web-service $e \in E_v$, WSDARWIN identifies

- A_e: The set of attributes, other than the ID, and
- S_e: The structure of the element, if it is a complex element. Note that, as we mentioned above, the structure refers to the children of complex elements such as input and output types for operations and elements for complex types.

Finally, for each comparison Δ, between two versions $v_1, v_2 \in V$, where V is the set of versions of a web-service specification to be analyzed, we determine the added and deleted matched elements by using the symbols "+" and "−" respectively. Therefore, E_Δ^+ is the set of elements that were added. We also use the symbol "#" to denote mapped elements, e.g. $E_\Delta^\#$.

WSDARWINrelies on a set of rules to map and differentiate the elements between different versions of the service interfaces. Table 9.2 summarizes the rules we use to compare service interfaces.

Table 9.2 The definition of rules used by WSDarwin for the comparison of web service interfaces

	Name of comparison rule	Rule
1	Exact matching	$\forall a_{e_1} \in A_{e_1}, \forall a_{e_2} \in A_{e_2} : a_{e_1}.literal = a_{e_2}.literal$
2	Mapping	$\exists e_1, e_2 \in E_\Delta^\# : e_1.t = e_2.t$ and $(e_1.id = e_2.id$ or $e_1.s = e_2.s)$
3	Changed	$\exists(id_i, t_i, a_i, s_i) \in E_\Delta^\#$ and $\exists(id_j, t_j, a'_j, s_j) \in E_\Delta^\#$
4	Propagated change	$\exists(id_i, t_i, a_i, s_i) \in E_\Delta^\#$ and $\exists(id_j, t_j, a_j, s'_j) \in E_\Delta^\#$
5	Matched	$\exists(id_i, t_i, a_i, s_i) \in E_\Delta^\#$ and $\exists(id_j, t_j, a_j, s_j) \in E_\Delta^\#$
6	Added	$\exists e_{v_2} \notin E_\Delta^\#$
7	Deleted	$\exists e_{v_1} \notin E_\Delta^\#$
8	Changed (Renamed)	$\exists(id_i, t_i, a_i, s_i) \in E_\Delta^-$ and $\exists(id'_j, t_j, a_j, s_j) \in E_\Delta^+$
9	Moved	$\exists(id_i, t_i, a_i, s_i) \in E_\Delta^-$ and $\exists(id_j, t_j, a_j, s_j) \in E_\Delta^+$
10	Moved and Changed	$\exists(id_i, t_i, a_i, s_i) \in E_\Delta^-$ and $\exists(id'_j, t_j, a'_j, s'_j) \in E_\Delta^+$

1. The first rule is the exact matching rule. In case of simple attributes (such as the element's ID and attributes belonging in the A_e set of the element), two attribute values are the same if and only if they have the same literal. In case of structure (i.e., the set of children of an element), two elements are considered structurally equal if and only if all their children are equal. Children equality is determined in an iterative manner.
2. The second rule states that two elements are "mapped" to each other, i.e., they are considered the same element across the two interface versions, if their type and at least one of their identifying properties, i.e., ID and structure, match. It is important to note that two mapped elements are not necessarily matched. There can still exist differences in which case a Change Delta is reported. On the other hand, matched elements are always mapped.

3. An element is considered "changed" if its ID was found in both versions but some of the values of its other attributes differ across the two versions.
4. If there is a change in the structure of the element (i.e., its children have changed), the element itself is considered "changed" even if none of the attributes of the parent element have changed. This is because the adaptation process starts from the root element of a service request which is considered to be the operation. Therefore, if some part of its input or its output is affected the operation is still considered affected.
5. If two elements are mapped and no differences are identified, they are labeled as "matched". The need to retain matched elements in the final comparison script is because an automated adaptation process needs a full mapping between the two versions.
6. An "addition" is identified if an element's name (its ID) that did not exist in the old version, but it was not found in the new version.
7. Correspondingly, a "deletion" is identified if an element's name existed in the old version, but it was not found in the new version.
8. In a second phase, the additions and deletions are reexamined to recognize potential changes in the element IDs or moves. If an element is identified as deleted from the old version and another element as added in the new version and the two elements have identical structure but differ with respect to their IDs then these elements are labeled as "changed (renamed)".
9. In a similar scenario, where elements are mapped between the deleted and added sets, these elements are marked as "moved". The reason they couldn't be identified in the first run of the comparison is because the process follows the structure of the service interface and elements are compared only in the context of their parents. Legitimate moves in a WSDL interface include primitive types being moved between complex types. Another also legal, but less probable, move can occur when two operations exchange their input or output types. In WADL, where the structure is more complicated, we can have `resource` elements being moved between `resources` elements and methods being moved between `resource` elements. Moves involving data types are also possible in this syntax.
10. If the moved elements also differ in their structures or their IDs, they are labeled as "moved and changed". If they differ with respect to both structure and ID, then they are considered different elements and are report as an addition and a deletion.

Based on the model and using the rules, in the first phase, the differencing method performs pairwise comparisons between the elements of the service interfaces starting from the more complex ones, such as the WSDL or WADL files themselves, and going down the hierarchy of the service elements as shown by Algorithm 1. First, the algorithm reports any changes in the attributes of the element (using the 3rd rule) or in the ID of the element (using the 8th rule) *(steps 1–4)*. Second, the children of the compared elements are mapped according to the 2nd rule *(step 7)*. Those that were not mapped are considered added, according to the 6th rule, or deleted, according to the 7th rule *(step 8)*. If a complex element is added or deleted all of its children are

Algorithm 1 diff(e_1, e_2) WSDARWIN service interface comparator

```
1: Compare the attributes of the two elements.
2: if Changes are detected then
3:   Set ElementDelta to ChangeDelta(e1, e2)
4: end if
5: for all c1 ∈ Children(e1) do
6:   for all c2 ∈ Children(e2) do
7:     if ¬Mapped(c1, c2) then
8:       Add DeleteDelta(c1) OR AddDelta(c2) to ElementDelta
9:       for all cc1 ∈ Children(c1) do
10:        Add DeleteDelta(cc1) to DeleteDelta(c1)
11:      end for
12:      for all cc2 ∈ Children(c2) do
13:        Add AddDelta(cc2) to AddDelta(c2)
14:      end for
15:    else
16:      Call diff(c1, c2)
17:      Add result to ElementDelta
18:      if The result contains only MatchDeltas AND ElementDelta != null then
19:        Set ElementDelta to MatchDelta(e1, e2)
20:      else
21:        //Change propagated.
22:        Augment ElementDelta with ChangeDelta(e1, e2)
23:      end if
24:    end if
25:  end for
26: end for
```

Algorithm 2 findMoveDeltas($Delta$)

```
for all AddDelta(e2) AND DeleteDelta(e1) ∈ Delta do
  if Mapped(e1, e2) then
    if Changed(e1, e2) then
      Create MoveAndChangeDelta(e1, e2)
      Replace DeleteDelta(e1) with MoveAndChangeDelta(e1, e2)
    else
      Create MoveDelta(e1, e2)
      Replace DeleteDelta(e1) with MoveDelta(e1, e2)
    end if
  end if
end for
```

also added or deleted to acquire a full mapping between the two versions *(steps 9–14)*. The elements that were mapped are then compared *(step 16)*. The comparisons continue this way until they reach simple elements, such as XSD elements or WADL `param` elements, which are only compared based on their attributes since they have no children and the comparison result is returned to the parent. In the final step, the algorithm checks if the children of the compared elements and the children of their children are matched according to the 5th rule, then the compared elements are matched as well *(step 19)*. Otherwise, a change is propagated to the parent according to the 4th rule *(step 22)*. In a second phase shown by Algorithm 2, WSDARWIN tries to identify moved elements among the added and the deleted ones. In the first phase, additions and deletions are identified within the scope of an element. In the second phase, the hierarchy is collapsed and additions and deletions are reexamined to detect moves based on the 9th and the 10th rule.

9.3.1 WSDARWIN *Versus* VTRACKER

VTRACKER, the first method we used for web-service differencing, is a generic domain-agnostic differencing algorithm that can be used to compare heterogeneous interfaces, i.e., interfaces described in different schemas. In other words, VTRACKER can be used to compare any pair of XML documents. For this reason, this method uses fuzzy mapping and partial matching. For the former option, since we don't always know a mapping between the elements of the two interfaces, the algorithm compares all elements with each other (regardless of their type) and establishes a mapping based on their structural similarity. As far as the partial matching is concerned, the algorithm uses the notion of distance to compare elements with each other. Then, using a stable marriage algorithm it matches the elements with the lowest edit distance. VTRACKER can be configured to include information about the specific XML syntax used by the files to be compared. In our previous study [6], we configured VTRACKER to work with WSDL interfaces. In the end, the output produced by the algorithm is a text-like document containing the appropriate XML edit operations to go from the first file to the second.

WSDARWIN, on the other hand, is a comparison method tailored to the web-service domain and it is developed from the beginning with knowledge about the structure of the interfaces, thus improving on quality properties such scalability and understandability. Fuzzy mapping can cause problems in the case of elements of different types named in a similar manner if they correspond to the same concept. In the case of web services, the convention is to name operations and their input and output types similarly to denote their relationship. Fuzzy mapping and partial matching also contribute to decreased efficiency and accuracy: when the algorithm considers a variety of increasingly relaxed methods for establishing correspondence between two elements, then it has to perform more computations (resulting to inefficiency) and it risks establishing correspondence on more "risky" grounds (resulting to inaccuracy). WSDARWIN takes advantage of the fact that web services share a common palette of elements, regardless of their syntax, namely data and functionality. In other words, this method is domain-specific, but technology-agnostic. Furthermore, having a priori knowledge, it compares elements according to their types and taking advantage of naming conventions, it uses exact matching to compare literals. Finally, the output of WSDARWIN is based on the Deltas and follows the structure of the service interface, which makes it not only understandable but also easily consumable by automated adaptation techniques. Table 9.3 summarizes the comparison between VTRACKER and WSDARWIN.

Figure 9.5 shows the execution time of VTRACKER and WSDARWIN with respect to the size of the compared service interfaces. Time measurements were performed in a machine with an Inter Core 2 Duo 1.87 GHz CPU, 3 GB RAM and 64-bit operating system. This figure clearly demonstrates the scalability of WSDARWIN even in the presence of large services. VTRACKER approximates an exponential execution time while WSDARWIN's is linear. Apart from the fuzzy mapping and partial matching, another factor that contributes to VTRACKER's large execution time is the fact that

Table 9.3 Comparison between VTRACKER and WSDARWIN

VTRACKER	WSDARWIN
Domain-agnostic	Domain-specific
Technology-specific	Technology-agnostic
Heterogeneous comparisons	Homogeneous comparisons
– Can be applied on any XML-like file	– Can be applied only on the WS domain
Less efficient	More efficient
– Fuzzy mapping	– Mapping according to type, structure and identifier
– Partial matching	– Exact matching (same literal)
Free text output	Structured output
– XML edit operations	– Deltas
	– Directly consumable by CASE tools

when comparing the structure of an element, the method has to resolve and compare references and this resolution takes place for each reference. WSDARWIN, on the other hand, resolves references only once during the parsing of the service interface and replaces the references with containment relationship, so the method avoids the time to seek for the element corresponding to a reference every time it encounters one.

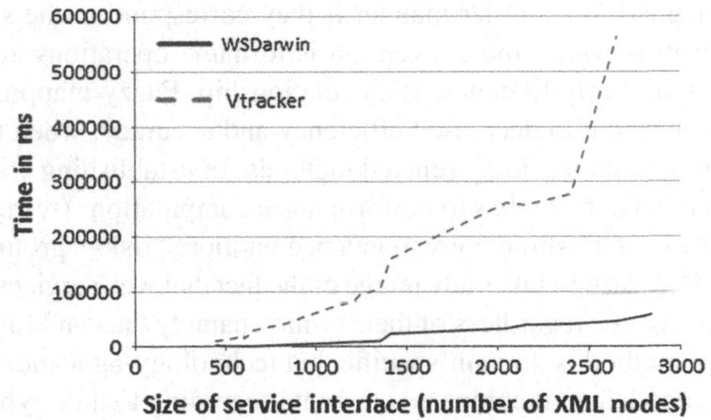

Fig. 9.5 Comparison between WSDARWIN and VTRACKER in terms of their execution time

9.3.2 *Applying* WSDARWIN *on the Comparison of Service Interfaces*

In this section, we demonstrate with examples how the WSDARWIN differencing method can be used to compare different versions of service interfaces. We applied the method on Amazon EC2, which has a WSDL-based interface, and Unicorn, which has a WADL-based interface. We chose these examples to show that given

(a)

```
1. ChangeOperation  RunInstances -> RunInstances
2.    Change ComplexType:RunInstancesType -> :RunInstancesType
3.        Add PrimitiveType       -> instanceType:string
4.        Add PrimitiveType       -> imageId:string
5.        Add PrimitiveType       -> keyName:string
6.        Add PrimitiveType       -> minCount:int
7.        Add PrimitiveType       -> maxCount:int
8.        Delete ComplexTypeinstancesSet:RunInstancesInfoType ->
9.            Delete PrimitiveType  keyName:string ->
10.           Delete PrimitiveType  imageId:string ->
11.           Delete PrimitiveType  minCount:int ->
12.           Delete PrimitiveType  maxCount:int ->
13.       Match  PrimitiveType addressingType:string -> addressingType:string
14.       Match  ComplexTypegroupSet:GroupSetType -> groupSet:GroupSetType
15.           Match  ComplexTypeitem:GroupItemType -> item:GroupItemType
16.               Match  PrimitiveType groupId:string -> groupId:string
17.       Match  ComplexTypeuserData:UserDataType -> userData:UserDataType
18.           Match  PrimitiveType  data:string -> data:string
19.       Match  PrimitiveType  additionalInfo:string -> additionalInfo:string
```

(b)

```
1. Change Operation   RunInstances -> RunInstances
2.    Change  ComplexType :RunInstancesType -> :RunInstancesType
3.        Add PrimitiveType           -> instanceType:string
4.        Add PrimitiveType           -> imageId:string
5.        Add PrimitiveType           -> keyName:string
6.        Add PrimitiveType           -> minCount:int
7.        Add PrimitiveType           -> maxCount:int
8.        Delete  ComplexType instancesSet:RunInstancesInfoType ->
9.            Move     PrimitiveType    keyName:string
                       instancesSet:RunInstancesInfoType ->:RunInstancesType
10.           Move     PrimitiveType    imageId:string
                       instancesSet:RunInstancesInfoType ->:RunInstancesType
11.           Move     PrimitiveType    minCount:int
                       instancesSet:RunInstancesInfoType ->:RunInstancesType
12.           Move     PrimitiveType    maxCount:int
                       instancesSet:RunInstancesInfoType ->:RunInstancesType
13.       Match   PrimitiveType   addressingType:string -> addressingType:string
14.       Match   ComplexType groupSet:GroupSetType -> groupSet:GroupSetType
15.           Match   ComplexType item:GroupItemType -> item:GroupItemType
16.               Match   PrimitiveType   groupId:string -> groupId:string
17.       Match   ComplexType userData:UserDataType -> userData:UserDataType
18.           Match   PrimitiveType    data:string -> data:string
19.       Match   PrimitiveType   additionalInfo:string -> additionalInfo:string
```

Fig. 9.6 Snippet of the diff script between two versions of the Amazon EC2 service. **a** Diff script without the detection of move operations. **b** Diff script with the detection of move operations

the proper model to represent the service interface, the comparison method, which is based on the delta model, can be applied to compare the interfaces regardless of their underlying specification technology.

Figure 9.6 shows a snippet of the output of WSDARWIN for the Amazon EC2 service. The diff script follows the hierarchy of the WSDL interface starting with the operations and then their input and output types. Each line is prefixed with the type of the edit operation performed for each element. The detection of move operations is activated for the script in Fig. 9.6a, and deactivated for the script reported in Fig. 9.6b. Comparing the two figures, we observe that the move operations are first perceived as additions and deletions, in the first phase of the comparison algorithm. In the second phase, the deletions are replaced by move operations but the additions are kept in the diff script.

In this example, we have a case of an "Inline Type" refactoring as described in our previous work [6]. As it can be seen from the figure, such a refactoring occurs when a type (`RunInstancesInfoType`), which is nested into another complex type (`RunInstancesType`, is deleted from the service and its constituent elements are *all* added in the parent type. By identifying the edit operations as moves and not as actual deletions, we can characterize this change as *adaptable* according to our classification. This is because the data exists in both versions but is "packaged" differently.

Also, edit operations of children elements are propagated as changes to the parent element. This is so that the adaptation process knows as early as possible which are the operations that are affected, since these are the contact elements between the service interface and client applications. For example, as it can be seen in the figure, because of the changes (additions and deletions) in the input of the `RunInstances` operation, these changes affect the operation which is marked as changed, despite not being directly changed.

```
1. Change  WADLFile files/unicorn/css-validator/css-validatorV1.wadl
2.                    -> files/unicorn/css-validator/css-validatorV8.wadl
3.     Change   Resources      http://jigsaw.w3.org/css-validator/
                          -> http://qa-dev.w3.org:8001/css-validator/
                          @base  http://jigsaw.w3.org/css-validator/
                             -> http://qa-dev.w3.org:8001/css-validator/
4.         Change   Resource validator -> validator
5.             Match    Method   CssValidationUri (GET) -> CssValidationUri (GET)
6.                 Match    Request  Request -> Request
7.                     Match    Param    usermedium -> usermedium
8.                     Match    Param    output -> output
9.                     Match    Param    uri -> uri
10.                    Match    Param    lang -> lang
11.                    Match    Param    warning -> warning
12.                    Match    Param    profile -> profile
13.            Change   Method   CssValidationText (POST) -> CssValidationText (GET)
                                 @name     POST -> GET
14.                Match    Request  Request -> Request
15.                    Match    Param    text -> text
16.                    Match    Param    usermedium -> usermedium
17.                    Match    Param    output -> output
18.                    Match    Param    lang -> lang
19.                    Match    Param    warning -> warning
20.                    Match    Param    profile -> profile
21.            Match    Method   CssValidationFile (POST) -> CssValidationFile (POST)
22.                Match    Request  Request -> Request
23.                    Match    Param    file -> file
24.                    Match    Param    usermedium -> usermedium
25.                    Match    Param    output -> output
26.                    Match    Param    lang -> lang
```

Fig. 9.7 The diff script between two versions of the WADL-based CSS validator of Unicorn

Figure 9.7 shows the output of WSDARWIN for the CSS validator service of Unicorn. The only major difference between the Unicorn and the Amazon diff scripts is that the former follows the WADL hierarchy. The edit operations are reported in exactly the same manner based on the delta model. In this case, we also have an instance of an attribute change (line 13). These changes are reported by identifying which attribute was changed (in this case attribute "name" of method "CssValidationText") prefixed by the symbol "@" for attribute, along with its old value and its new value. An attribute change subsumes a propagated change, since both edit operations mark the element as affected. For this reason, we do not need an additional type delta for either edit operation.

As we have already mentioned, while the structure and the vocabulary of the diff script are dictated by the underlying syntax model, the Deltas are used as annotations. This demonstrates and emphasizes the fact that WSDARWIN is technology-agnostic; regardless of the syntax model, the Delta language can be applied to provide the comparison context of the diff script.

9.4 Related Work

Our work relates to differencing, WSDARWIN's contribution, and service evolution, the substance of our empirical study.

9.4.1 Model- and Tree-Differencing Techniques

Fluri et al. [5] proposed a tree-differencing algorithm for fine-grained source code change extraction. Their algorithm takes as input two abstract syntax trees and extracts the changes by finding a match between the nodes of the compared trees. Moreover, it produces a minimum edit script that can transform one tree into the other given the computed matching. The proposed algorithm uses the bi-gram string similarity to match source code statements (such as method invocations, condition statements, and so forth) and the sub-tree similarity of Chawathe et al. [3] to match source code structures (such as if statements or loops). The method also uses names and types as IDs to map elements and can identify primarily changes, additions, deletions and moves for different types of elements.

Kelter et al. [10] proposed a generic algorithm for computing differences between UML models encoded as XMI files. The algorithm first tries to detect matches in a bottom-up phase by initially comparing the leaf elements and subsequently their parents in a recursive manner until a match is detected at some level. When detecting such a match, the algorithm switches into a top-down phase that propagates the last match to all child elements of the matched elements in order to deduce their differences. The algorithm reports four different types of differences, namely structural (denoting the insertion or deletion of elements), attribute (denoting elements that differ in their attributes' values), reference (denoting elements whose references are different in the two models) and move (denoting the move of an element to another parent element). Although the method does not use IDs to map elements, they are necessary to identify moves. For this reason, custom ones are constructed using the name of the element and its path along the XMI tree.

Xing and Stroulia [15] proposed the *UMLDiff* algorithm for automatically detecting structural changes between the designs of subsequent versions of object-oriented software. The algorithm produces as output a tree of structural changes that reports the differences between the two design versions in terms of additions, removals, moves, renamings of packages, classes, interfaces, fields and methods, changes to their attributes, and changes of the dependencies among these entities. UMLDiff employs two heuristics (i.e., name-similarity and structure-similarity) for recognizing the conceptually same entities in the two compared system versions. These two heuristics enable UMLDiff to recognize that two entities are the same even after they have been renamed and/or moved. The UMLDiff algorithm has been employed for detecting refactorings performed during the evolution of object-oriented software systems, based on UMLDiff change-facts queries [16].

Recently, Xing [14] proposed a general framework for model comparison, named *GenericDiff*. While it is domain independent, it is aware of domain-specific model properties and syntax by separating the specification of domain-specific inputs from the generic graph matching process and by making use of two data structures (i.e., typed attributed graph and pair-up graph) to encode the domain-specific properties and syntax so that they can be uniformly exploited in the generic matching process. Unlike the aforementioned approaches that examine only immediate common neighbors, GenericDiff employs a random walk on the pair-up graph to spread the correspondence value (i.e., a measurement of the quality of the match it represents) in the graph.

In our previous work [6], we adopted VTRACKER to recognize the differences between two versions of a web-service interface. VTRACKER is designed to compare and recognize thc similarities and differences between XML documents, based on the Zhang-Shasha tree-edit distance [17] algorithm.

WSDARWIN is tailored around a very specific domain, that of web services. Therefore, a lot of domain-specific information and characteristics are imbued in the comparison method. However, we do borrow some fundamental differencing techniques from the works described in this section. For example, many methods employ the concept of a model to describe the compared artifacts. In fact, the underlying model is the one that will determine the accuracy and the efficiency of the comparison method. Second, the use of identifiers for mapping compared elements is a widely used technique, also present in the VTRACKER algorithm. Finally, the propagation of changes as described in WSDARWIN, is a similar technique as the top-down/bottom-up approach used by Kelter et al.

Table 9.4 positions WSDARWIN among the aforementioned works with respect to whether they are generic or domain-specific, what kind of edit operations they can identify (**C**hange, **A**ddition, **D**eletion, **M**ove, comple**X** changes), if they employ IDs

Table 9.4 Comparison between differencing techniques

Method	Type	Edit Operations	IDs	Exact Matching	Model
Kelter	generic	CAD(M)	No(Yes)	No	UML/XMI
Fluri	domain-specific	CADM	Yes	No	AST
UMLDiff	domain-specific	CADMX	Yes	No	Custom/UML
GenericDiff	generic	CADM	Yes	No	UML
VTRACKER	generic	CADM	Yes	No	XML
WSDARWIN	domain-specific	CADM	Yes	Yes	Custom/WS

for the mapping of elements, whether they use exact matching in the comparison and finally what is the underlying model.

9.4.2 Service-Evolution Analysis

In addition to web-service (and web-service version) comparison, substantial efforts have been dedicated to the task of web-service evolution analysis. Wang and Capretz [13] proposed an impact-analysis model as a means to analyze the evolution of dependencies among services. By constructing the intra-service relation matrix for each service (capturing the relations among the elements of a single service) and the inter-service relation matrix for each pair of services (capturing the relations among the elements of two different services) it is possible to calculate the impact effect caused by a change in a given service element. A relation exists from element x to element y if the output elements of x are the input elements of y, or if there is a semantic mapping or correspondence built between elements of x and y. Finally, the intra- and inter-service relation matrices can be employed to support service change operations, such as the addition, deletion, modification, merging and splitting of elements.

Aversano et al. [2] proposed an approach, based on Formal Concept Analysis, to understand how relationships between sets of services change across service evolution. To this end, their approach builds a lattice upon a context obtained from service description or operation parameters, which helps to understand similarities between services, inheritance relationships, and to identify common features. As the service evolves (and thus relationships between services change) its position in the lattice will change, thus highlighting which are the new service features, and how the relationships with other services have been changed. This approach is useful to study the evolution of similar interchangeable services.

Ryu et al. [12] proposed a methodology for addressing the dynamic protocol evolution problem, which is related with the migration of ongoing instances (conversations) of a service from an older business protocol to a new one. To this end, they developed a method that performs change impact analysis on ongoing instances, based on protocol models, and classifies the active instances as migratable or non-migratable. This automatic classification plays an important role in supporting flexibility in service-oriented architectures, where there are large numbers of interacting services, and it is required to dynamically adapt to the new requirements and opportunities proposed over time.

In a similar vein, the WRABBIT project [4] proposed a middleware for wrapping web services with agents capable of communication and reflective process execution. Through their reflective process execution, these agents recognize run-time "conversation" errors, i.e., errors that occur due to changes in the rules of how the partner process should be composed and resolve such conversation failures.

Pasquale et al. [11] propose a configuration management method to control dependencies between and changes of service artifacts including web services, application servers, file systems and data repositories across different domains. Along with the service artifacts, Smart Configuration Items (SCIs), which are in XML format, are also published. The SCIs have special properties for each artifact such as host name, id etc. Interested parties (like other application servers) can register to the SCIs and receive notifications for changes to the respective artifact by means of ATOM feeds and REST calls. Using a discovery mechanism the method is able to identify new, removed or modified SCIs. If a SCI is identified as modified, then the discovery mechanism tracks the differences between the two items and adds them as entries in the new SCI. The changes that can be identified are delete, add, modify a property or delete, add, modify a dependency.

Andrikopoulos et al. [1] propose a service evolution management framework. The framework generally aims to support service providers evolve their services. It contains an abstract technology-agnostic model to describe a service system in its entirety, specifying all artifacts such as service interfaces, policies, compositions etc. and divide the artifacts in public and private. This division implies that the management framework has knowledge about the service's back-end functionality, which in turn means that it can be used only by the provider. The authors also propose a classification for the changes based on the basic operations (additions, deletions etc.) and guidelines on how to evolve, validate and conform service specifications to older versions. Although such a management framework may lead to a smooth evolution process, inconsistencies may still occur between services and their clients. Therefore, support to clients is equally important.

Table 9.5 summarizes the comparison between WSDARWIN and these other projects along 3 dimensions:

- what kind of dependencies the method examines:
  - inter-dependencies, requiring knowledge about different parts of the service system;
  - intra-dependencies, focusing on a particular part;
- whether the method provides any support to consumers of the service.
- what is the architectural level the method uses to study the service systems:
  - business protocol level, where the method needs information about various services in the system;

Table 9.5 Comparison between service evolution works

Method	Dependencies	Client Support	Level
Wang	Inter	Yes	Protocol
Aversano	Inter	No	Interface
WRABBIT	Inter	Yes	Protocol
Pasquale	Intra	Yes	Interface
Ryu	Inter	No	Protocol
Andrikopoulos	Intra	No	Source Code
WSDARWIN	Intra	Yes	Interface

- interface, where the method only examines boundary artifacts, such as service interfaces;
- source code, where the method needs back-end information.

9.5 Conclusion and Future Work

In this chapter, we introduced WSDARWIN as a comparison algorithm to support of web-service evolution tasks. Using a set of models to represent the service interfaces (whether this is WSDL or WADL) and to capture their differences, WSDARWIN perform efficient, scalable and accurate comparisons. Furthermore, the results of these comparisons are in a structured format that can potentially be used by other tools such as automatic client adaptation processes. The comparison method is precisely defined by a set of rules based on the representation and delta models. The usage of WSDARWIN was demonstrated on a WSDL and a WADL web service.

Using WSDARWIN we extended our previous empirical study on the evolution of several families of quite widely used commercial web services: Amazon EC2, FedEx Rate, Bing, PayPal and FedEx Package Movement Information. We examined what types of changes occur in the interfaces of actual, commercial web services and how these changes affect their client applications. Our main observation was that for the most part, as expected, web services were expanded rather than being changed or having their elements removed. This is because the addition of new features does not impact the behavior of clients that already use the service. Furthermore, changes, if made in a conservative manner, do not negatively impact clients much. On the other hand, deletion of elements should be avoided, as it will likely break a client application.

The most important result of the study was to identify a set of frequently applied changes and classify them in three categories according to how they can be handled by the client: *no*-effect, where changes don't affect the client at all, *non-recoverable*, where changes affect the functionality but cannot be addressed automatically and *adaptable*, where changes affect the interface of the service and the client can be automatically adapted to these changes.

In the future, we plan to extend our comparison method in two directions. The first direction involves identifying more complicated edit operation that consist of the simple ones, change, add, delete and move. This will help us characterize the changes from version to version according to our classification and easily assess their impact on client applications. Second, having defined separate models to represent WSDL and WADL service interfaces, we plan to merge the two into a single web service meta-model to describe service interfaces regardless of their specification. Since the rules and the comparison process are independent of the model, a unified model will allow us to compare any kind of service interface, even heterogeneous once.

Acknowledgments The authors would like to acknowledge the generous support of NSERC, iCORE, and IBM.

References

1. Andrikopoulos, V., Benbernou, S., Papazoglou, M.P.: Managing the evolution of service specifications. In: CAiSE '08, pp. 359–374. Springer-Verlag, Berlin, Heidelberg (2008)
2. Aversano, L., Bruno, M., Penta, M.D., Falanga, A., Scognamiglio, R.: Visualizing the Evolution of Web Services using Formal Concept Analysis. 8th International Workshop on Principles of Software, Evolution pp. 57–60 (2005)
3. Chawathe, S.S., Rajaraman, A., Garcia-Molina, H., Widom, J.: Change Detection in Hierarchically Structured Information. ACM Sigmod Internation Conference on Management of Data pp. 493–504 (1996)
4. Elio, R., Stroulia, E., Blanchet, W.: Using interaction models to detect and resolve inconsistencies in evolving service compositions. Web Intelli. and Agent Sys. **7**(2), 139–160 (2009)
5. Fluri, B., Würsch, M., Pinzger, M., Gall, H.C.: Change Distilling: Tree Differencing for Fine-Grained Source Code Change Extraction. IEEE Transactions on Software Engineering **33**(11), 725–743 (2007)
6. Fokaefs, M., Mikhaiel, R., Tsantalis, N., Stroulia, E., Lau, A.: An empirical study on web service evolution. In: ICWS 2011, pp. 49–56 (2011)
7. Fokaefs, M., Stroulia, E.: Wsdarwin: Automatic web service client adaptation. In: CASCON '12 (2012)
8. Fowler, M., Beck, K., Brant, J., Opdyke, W., Roberts, D.: Refactoring Improving the Design of Existing Code. Addison Wesley, Boston, MA (1999)
9. Gamma, E., Helm, R., Johnson, R., Vlissides, J.: Design Patterns: Elements of Reusable Object-Oriented Software, 1 edn. Addison-Wesley Professional (1994)
10. Kelter, U., Wehren, J., Niere, J.: A Generic Difference Algorithm for UML Models. Software Engineering 2005, Fachtagung des GI-Fachbereichs Softwaretechnik pp. 105–116 (2005)
11. Pasquale, L., Laredo, J., Ludwig, H., Bhattacharya, K., Wassermann, B.: Distributed cross-domain configuration management. In: Proceedings of the 7th International Joint Conference on Service-Oriented Computing, ICSOC-ServiceWave '09, pp. 622–636 (2009)
12. Ryu, S.H., Casati, F., Skogsrud, H., Benatallah, B., Saint-Paul, R.: Supporting the Dynamic Evolution of Web Service Protocols in Service-Oriented Architectures. ACM Transactions on the Web **2**(2), 1–46 (2008)
13. Wang, S., Capretz, M.A.M.: A Dependency Impact Analysis Model for Web Services Evolution. IEEE International Conference on Web Services pp. 359–365 (2009)

14. Xing, Z.: Model Comparison with GenericDiff. 25th IEEE/ACM International Conference on, Automated Software Engineering pp. 135–138 (2010)
15. Xing, Z., Stroulia, E.: Analyzing the Evolutionary History of the Logical Design of Object-Oriented Software. IEEE Transactions on Software Engineering **31**(10), 850–868 (2005)
16. Xing, Z., Stroulia, E.: Refactoring Detection based on UMLDiff Change-Facts Queries. 13th Working Conference on Reverse Engineering pp. 263–274 (2006)
17. Zhang, K., Shasha, D.: Simple fast algorithms for the editing distance between trees and related problems. SIAM Journal on Computing **18**, 1245–1262 (1989)

Chapter 10
SCML: A Change Management Language for Adaptive Long Term Composed Services

Xumin Liu and Athman Bouguettaya

Abstract We propose a Web Service Change Management Language (SCML) to manage top-down changes in Long term Composed Services (LCSs). A LCS is a collaboration between autonomous Web services that collectively provide a value-added service. Due to the dynamic environment, managing changes is a fundamental challenge for the successful deployment of a LCS. We first propose a change taxonomy that classifies changes into different categories. Based on the taxonomy, we define a set of change operators that specify different types of changes in a precise and formal way. The change operators can be mapped to a set of SCML statements, which are declarative and easy-to-use. We describe a systematic procedure to process SCML statements. We then propose our prototype implementation for the proposed SCML.

10.1 Introduction

Web services are gaining momentum as a new computing paradigm for delivering business functionalities on the Web. They are increasingly regarded as the most promising backbone technology that enables the modeling and deployment of the Service-Oriented Architecture (SOA) [11]. Web services are distinguished from other traditional applications by two major features: global availabilities and standardization. First, Web services take advantages of the powerful communication paradigm of the Web to provide global availabilities [15]. Second, Web services have enjoyed intensive standardization support. They are built upon XML-based standards as a vehicle for exchanging messages across heterogeneous Web applications [4, 7, 12, 17–22]. Typical Web service standards include WSDL for

X. Liu (✉)
Department of Computer Science, Rochester Institute of Technology, Rochester, USA
e-mail: xl@cs.rit.edu

A. Bouguettaya
School of Computer Science and Information Technology, RMIT, Melbourne, Australia

A. Bouguettaya et al. (eds.), *Advanced Web Services*,
DOI: 10.1007/978-1-4614-7535-4_10,

service description [22], UDDI for service discovery [19], and SOAP for service invocation [18]. Driven by the advantages offered by SOA, many service providers expose to move their business functionalities on the Web using Web services. This, in turn, has opened the opportunities for composing autonomous services on demand [3]. Thus, SOA has also opened the opportunities for building up cross-organization collaborations in a distributed, heterogeneous, and dynamic environment. A *composed Web service* is therefore an on-demand and dynamic collaboration between autonomous Web services that collectively provide a value added service. Each autonomous service specializes in a core competency, which reduces cost with increased quality and efficiency for the business entity and its consumers. A composed Web service can be *short term* or *long term*. Comparing with *short time* composed services, where the collaboration of services has a very limited time and will be resolved thereafter, a long term composed service (referred to as a LCS) has an open-ended lifetime. It usually has a long-run business goal and business commitment to its customers. The partnership among its component services is relatively stable unless the occurrence of some exceptional event [26]. LCSs have attracted a lot of attentions since they empower a *virtual enterprise*, which is a cross-organization collaboration to offer value-added and customized services [13].

A LCS consists of several outsourced Web services, but acts as a *virtually* coherent entity. Each service specializes in a core competency, which promotes cost reductions and increased quality for the LCS and its consumers. Business entities, in the form of Web services, are often geographically distributed and organizationally independent. LCSs will introduce new business opportunities through dynamic alliances. First, the provisioning of software services dramatically reduces the capital required to start a business. A LCS can built upon the legacy systems, which are wrapped as Web services. The services are readily available for integration and orchestration. It is superior to build up a complex software application from scratch. Second, as the number of business increases on the Web, it will be possible to select the "best" services from a pool of "similar" services [10]. The consumer or end user of the LCS will benefit from the open competition between businesses. Third, partners of a LCS can be selected dynamically. Each Web service is described in a standard format, which allows automatic and dynamic discovery and integration. Thus, business organizations will be able to form project-driven alliances. Current application domains of LCSs include the travel industry, computer industry, scientific community, automobile industry, etc.

One of the most challenging research issues in realizing LCSs is to deal with changes during the lifetime of a LCS. Because of the dynamic nature of Web service infrastructure, changes should be considered as the *rule* and managed in a structured and systematic way [6, 13, 24]. Changes are usually introduced by the occurrence of new market interests, business regulation, new technologies, etc. Such changes are always associated with a requirement on the modification of a LCS with respect to the functionality it provides, the way it performs, the partners it is composed of, and the performance it delivers. Once a change occurs, a LCS needs to quickly adjust itself to fulfill the requirement introduced by the change. The adjustment also needs to be performed in an automatic manner considering the frequent occurrence of changes.

By doing this, a LCS can maximize the market interests it attracts, optimize the way it outsources its functionality, and thus maintain its competitiveness among its peers. Changes in LCSs can be classified into two categories: *top-down changes* and *bottom-up changes* [25]. In this chapter, we focus on top-down changes. More specifically, top-down changes refer to the changes initiated by a LCS owner. An example of such changes is the addition of a local attraction service to a travel agency LCS.

Change management in the context of composed services poses a set of research issues.Changes need to be first captured and modeled in a formal way so that they can be understood and processed. The change reaction process then should be designed and implemented. Finally, the change reaction process needs to be evaluated for verification and correctness purpose. In this chapter, we address the issue of change specification. Changes may be specified in a literal way at first place, which is *informal* and sometimes *vague*. Examples of such change specifications include "*increase a LCS's profit*" and "*stop outsourcing the service that has a low reliability*". This type of specification obviously lacks sufficient formalization and semantics to support change management in a systematic way. Changes need to be machine comprehensible so that they can be automatically and correctly enacted. Therefore, a change specification should be *unambiguous*, *formal*, and *disciplined*, which are described as follows.

- *Unambiguous*: A change is always associated with a specific goal on a LCS. During the process of change management, the LCS will be modified and the goal will be reached ultimately. Therefore, a change specification should be unambiguous so that the goal can be deterministic.
- *Formal*: To improve the automation of change management, it is important that the software agents understand what change is intended to make to a LCS. Therefore, a change specification should contain machine-understandable semantics, such as pre-defined keywords and logic-base expressions.
- *Disciplined*: To ensure that a change is feasible, it is important that a change specification contains all the necessary information. For example, if a change requires to remove a service that has a low reliability, it needs to specify at what degree a service's reliability is considered as low. Therefore, a change specification should be disciplined. For different types of changes, different types of information are required to be contained in a change specification.

In this chapter, we present a Web Service Change Management Language (SCML) for the propose of modeling changes. SCML allows change specifications which achieve the above characteristics. Besides, it is also *complete* and *declarative*. By complete, it means that all meaningful top-down changes can be specified using SCML. By declarative, it means that SCML is non-operational. Using SCML, a LCS's owner only needs to specify *what* a change is, instead of specifying *how* to change. In another word, the ower does not need to concern the details of implementing a change when specifying it.

The reminder of this chapter is organized as follows. In Sect. 10.2, we describe a travel agency LCS, which will be used as a running example in this chapter.

In Sect. 10.3, we propose a supporting infrastructure that enables a LCS. In Sect. 10.4, we propose a change taxonomy that classify changes into different categories. Based on the schema and the taxonomy, we propose a set of change operators in Sect. 10.4. In Sect. 10.5, we propose a change language that provides comprehensive specification support for change management. In Sect. 10.6, we propose a procedure that processes the SCML change specifications. In Sect. 10.7, we describe a prototype that processes the proposed language. In Sect. 10.8, we discuss several representative related work and differentiate our work with them. In Sect. 10.9, we conclude our work.

10.2 Case Study

In this section, we describe a scenario from travel industry to motivate our work. It will also be used as a running example to illustrate the key idea of this chapter.

Consider a travel agency LCS that aims to provide a comprehensive travel package that outsources the functionalities from different service providers, including flight, hotel, taxi, weather, and online payment. Users can thus book airlines, reserve hotels, reserve taxis, or check weather information by directly accessing this LCS. Suppose that a recent market survey shows that car rental services have attracted more interests than taxi services serving as the ground transportation. In this case, the LCS's owner may want to replace the taxi service by a car rental service. Moreover, users that choose car rental service probably also take interest in the local traffic information, such as the router from the airport to the hotel. In addition, users may tend to include local activities to their travel packages nowadays. For example, when a user plans a trip to Orlando, he or she may also want to visit the local activities, such as the Universal Orlando and the SeaWorld Orlando. In this case, he or she may want to reserve the tickets for the activities via the travel agency. If the travel agency LCS does not incorporate the service into the enterprise, it risks becoming obsolete and loosing business.

10.3 An Infrastructure of Service-Oriented Enterprises

In this section, we present a supporting infrastructure of a LCS. We first give an overview of a LCS's architecture, as depicted in Fig. 10.1. It mainly consists of two key components: *LCS schema* and *LCS instance*. It also contains two supporting components: *ontology providers* and *Web service providers*. A LCS schema is the kernel of a LCS since it defines its high-level business logic. It guides the composition of outsourced Web services to perform the functionality of the LCS.The change language is built upon a LCS's schema.

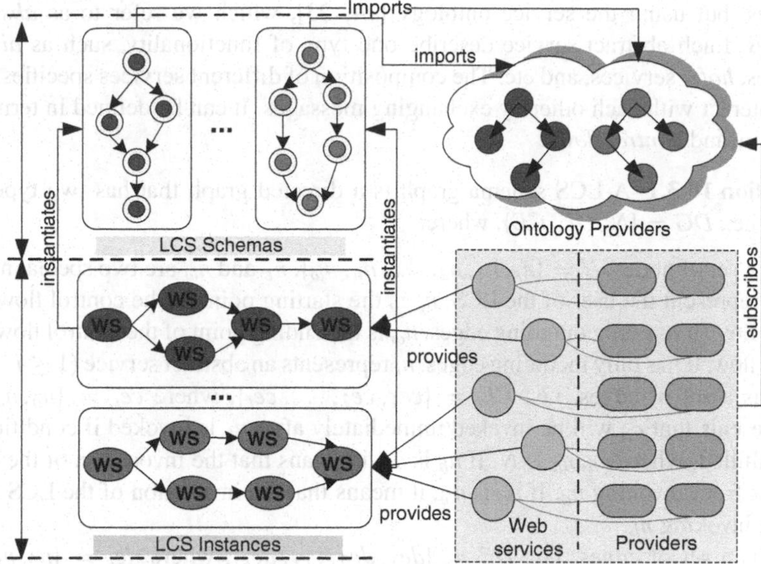

Fig. 10.1 The architecture of a LCS

10.3.1 LCS Architecture

A LCS schema consists of a set of abstract services and the relationships among these services. An abstract service specifies one type of functionality provided by the Web services. They are not bounded to any concrete services. They are defined in terms of service concepts in a Web service ontology. A LCS instance is a composition of a set of concrete services, which instantiates a LCS schema. It actually delivers the functionality and performance of a LCS.The ontology provider manages and maintains a set of ontologies that describe the semantics of Web services. A LCS outsources semantics from an ontology provider to build up its schema. Ontology providers also provide semantics for automating the process of change management [25]. The Web service providers offer a set of Web services, which can be outsourced to form LCS instances.

10.3.2 LCS Schema

The different between a LCS and the traditional enterprise is that a LCS outsources its functionality from individual and autonomous services. Therefore, a LCS's functionality can be specified as the combination of the functionalities of the services it outsources and their composition. We use a directed graph to specify a LCS's functionality. A LCS's functionality is typically not defined using the concrete Web services, but using the service ontology [14, 23], which we refer to as *abstract services*. Each abstract service describe one type of functionality, such as *airline* services, *hotel* services, and etc. The composition of different services specifies how they interact with each other by exchanging messages. It can be defined in terms of *data flow* and *control flows*.

Definition 10.3.1 A LCS schema graph is a directed graph that has two types of edges, i.e., $DG = \{N, DE, CE\}$, where:

- N is a set of nodes, $N = \{n_\varepsilon, n_1, n_2, \ldots, n_n, n_\omega\}$. n_ε and n_ω are two special nodes that represent the user of the LCS. n_ε is the starting point of the control flow and data flow. It has only outgoing edges. n_ω is the ending point of the control flow and data flow. It has only incoming edges. n_i represents an abstract service $(1 \leq i \leq n)$.
- CE is a set of edges, i.e., $CE = \{ce_1, ce_2, \ldots, ce_t\}$, where $ce_i = \{n_b, n_a, c_i\}$ represents that n_a will be invoked immediately after n_b is invoked if condition c_i is fulfilled, where $n_b, n_a \in N$. If n_b is n_ε, it means that the invocation of the LCS starts from invoking n_a. If n_a is n_ω, it means that the invocation of the LCS ends with invoking n_b.
- DE is a set of edges, i.e., $DE = \{de_1, de_2, \ldots, de_s\}$, where $de_i = \{n_f, n_t, d_i\}$ represents that n_f sends a message containing data d_i to n_t. Here, d_i is a subset of n_f's output and a subset of n_t's input. $n_f, n_t \in N$. If n_f is n_ε, it means the data d_i is part of the input of an LCS obtained from the users. If n_t is n_ω, it means the data d_i is part of the output of a LCS returning to the users.

Figure 10.2 shows the schema of the travel agency LCS in our running example.

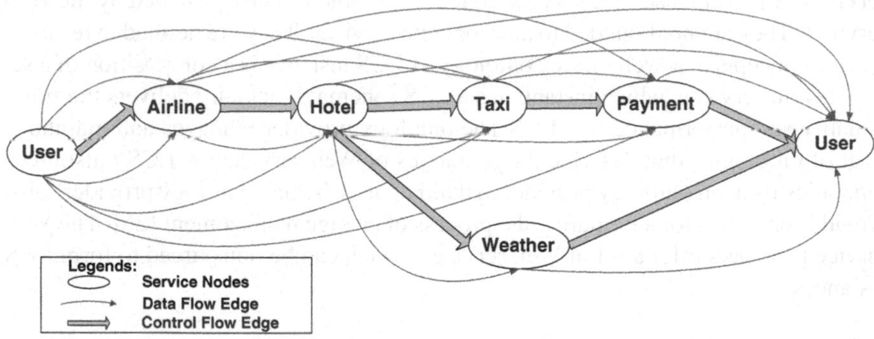

Fig. 10.2 The travel agency LCS schema

10.3.3 LCS Quality

The quality of a LCS consists of a set of quality parameters, such as *reliability*, *fee*, *invocation duration*, *reliability*, etc. These parameters constitute a quality model that is used to evaluate *how well* a LCS performs. The quality model is *domain-specific*.

A LCS outsources its functionality from multiple services. Meanwhile, it also outsources quality models from these services. Therefore, we define a LCS's quality model as follows.

Definition 10.3.2 *A LCS's quality model is a set* $Q = \{q_1, q_2, \ldots, q_n\}$, *where* q_i *is a quality parameter. Meanwhile* $Q \in (\bigcup_{n_i \in N} n_i.Q)$.

Since a LCS's quality is actually delivered by the Web services it outsources, the quality thus can be determined by these services. Since a LCS instance contains multiple services, the QoWS values of these services will be aggregated as the overall QoS of the LCS [27].

10.3.4 LCS Context

The context of a LCS consists of a set of context types, such as *location*, *time*, *user*, *travel type*, etc. The context carries important information for describing the interaction between a LCS and its users. Since a LCS outsources its functionality from multiple services, its context structure can be determined by these services. Therefore, we define a LCS's context model as follows.

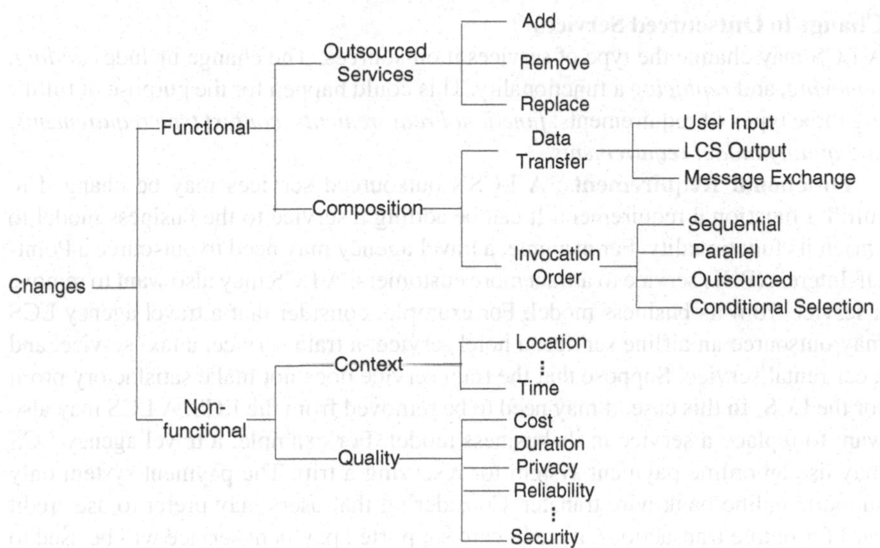

Fig. 10.3 A taxonomy of top-down changes in a LCS

Definition 10.3.3 *A LCS's context model is a set* $C = \{c_1, c_2, \ldots, c_n\}$, *where* c_i *is a context type. Meanwhile* $C \in (\bigcup_{n_i \in N} n_i.C)$.

10.4 Change Taxonomy

The first step of specifying a change of a LCS is to identify a clear classification of these changes. Thus, different types of changes will be specified in different ways. As depicted in Fig. 10.3, we use change requirements, which reflects the purpose of introducing a change, as a dimension, changes can be classified based on the key features of a LCS. This conforms to the classical change taxonomy approaches from the fields of software engineering and workflow systems [9, 16]. The features of a LCS can be classified into *functional* and *non-functional*. The functional feature refers to the *functionality* of a LCS. The non-functional features include *context* and *quality*. Top-down changes are expected to modify one or more of the features of a LCS. Therefore, we classify changes based on these features. We elaborate on each type of changes and define the corresponding change operators in this section.

10.4.1 Functional Changes

Functional changes are those that require to modify the functionality of a LCS. A LCS's functionality is specified by two types of information: the *abstract services* it outsources and their *composition*.

Change to Outsourced Services
A LCS may change the type of services it outsources. The change includes *adding*, *removing*, and *replacing* a functionality. This could happen for the purpose of fulfilling three types of requirements: *functional requirements*, *context type requirements*, and *quality model requirements*.

Functional Requirements: A LCS's outsourced services may be changed to fulfill a functional requirement. It can be adding a service to the business model to enrich its functionality. For example, a travel agency may need to outsource a Point-Of-Interest (POI) service to attract more customers. A LCS may also want to remove a service from its business model. For example, consider that a travel agency LCS may outsource an airline service, a hotel service, a train service, a taxi service, and a car rental service. Suppose that the train service does not make satisfactory profit for the LCS. In this case, it may need to be removed from the LCS. A LCS may also want to replace a service in its business model. For example, a travel agency LCS may use an online payment system for reserving a trip. The payment system only supports online bank wire transfer. Considering that users may prefer to use credit card for online transactions, a credit card supported payment service will be used to replace the original one.

As defined in a Web service ontology, the functionality of a Web service has two facets: *operations* and *data* [14, 23]. For the first facet, the intended service should provide the specified operations. An example of such a change is "adding a service that provides flight status checking operation". For the second facet, the intended service should provide the ability of transducing data. Put differently, it should be able to generate the specified output by using the given input. An example of such a change is "adding a service that can generate the weather information given a zip code". More specifically, a functional requirement (f) is a triplet (OP, D_I, D_O), where OP is a set of operations that a service should provide, D_I and D_O are two sets of data items stating that a service should be able to generate D_O by using D_I.

Context Type Requirements: A LCS's outsourced services may be changed due to a new context type requirement. Each abstract service is associated with a set of context types, which constitute the environment structure of the service. Suppose that a LCS is required to support a new context, such as historical data. It then needs to ensure that each outsourced service is able to embed the historical data information in the SOAP message during the interactions. This may trigger the change of "removing the service that does not support a context type of history data".

Quality Model Requirements: A LCS's outsourced services may be changed due to a new quality requirement. Each abstract service is associated with a quality model, which includes the parameters for service evaluation. For example, a top-down change may require a new quality parameter to evaluate the outsourced services, such as privacy. This may trigger the change of "removing the service that does not include privacy in its quality model".

We define the change operators for selecting abstract services based on the above requirements as follows.

- $\Pi^F_{op}(op, O)$: It will traverse the service ontology O to find the abstract services that provide the specified operation *op*. This operator takes *op* and O as input and returns an abstract service.
- $\Pi^F_d(D_I, D_O, O)$: It will traverse the service ontology O to find the abstract services that can generate the required output of D_O by using the given input D_I. This operator takes two sets of data, D_I, D_O as well as a service ontology O as input and returns an abstract service.
- $\Pi^C(c, O)$: It will traverse the service ontology O to find the abstract services that support a context type c. This operator takes c and O as input and returns a list of abstract services.
- $\Pi^Q(q, O)$: It will traverse the service ontology O to find the abstract services that include a quality parameter q in its quality model. This operator takes s and q as input and returns a list of abstract services.

For the selected service node, we define two change operators as below.

- Δ^S (s, M, op): It performs the operation *op*, by either *adding* an abstract service to or *removing* it from a LCS schema M. This operator takes s, M, and *op* as input and returns a new LCS schema as its output.
- $\Delta^{S\leftrightarrow}$ (s_{old}, s_{new}, M): It replaces an abstract service s_{old} with another abstract service s_{new} in a LCS schema M. This operator takes s_{old}, s_{new}, and M as input and returns a new LCS schema as its output.

Change to Composition

A LCS's composition defines *how* it performs its functionality. It specifies the collaboaration of the outsourced services in a LCS. A LCS's composition may change under two situations. First, when a new service is added to a LCS or a service is deleted from a LCS, a composition change will be introduced. For example, when adding a payment service to a travel agency LCS, the payment service needs to be combined with other services. Second, a LCS's owner may want to change the way that the component services are combined together for some purpose, such as optimization. For example, suppose that a hotel service and a car rental service are invoked sequentially. There is no invocation dependency between them since they do not exchange messages with each other. In this case, the LCS's owner may want to parallelize their invocation to decrease the overall duration time. The change to a LCS's composition can occur to both *data transfer* and *invocation order*.

Data transfer: Change to data transfer among services includes the modification of *user input*, *LCS output*, adding or deleting a message between two services. (1) *User input*: The user input is obtained from the user of a LCS. It contains the information that is necessary to invoke the services outsourced by the LCS. Once there is a change on the outsourced services, a change of the user input may be introduced. For example, when adding a car rental service, some information is required from the user to invoke the service, such as the car type (i.e., full size, compact, midsize, economy, etc.). A change of the user input may also be introduced by a LCS's owner. For example, a travel agency LCS provides the airline+hotel package. In this package, the information about location and check in/out time is typically determined by the result of invoking the airline service. The owner may now want to change it by letting users provide these information. In this way, users can have more options when they choose their hotels. (2) *LCS output*: The LCS output is generated by a LCS and returned to its users. It is contributed directly or indirectly by the services that the LCS outsources from. Once there is a change of the outsourced services, a change of the LCS output may be introduced. For example, when adding a car rental service, the LCS will generate more information, such as the pick up/drop off location, time, date, and charges. A change of LCS output may also be introduced by a LCS's owner. For example, a travel agency LCS is used to generate the weather information. The owner may want to stop providing such information in the future. (3) *Message exchange*: The message exchange is performed between outsourced services in a LCS. A Web service is interacted by its users or partners completely by exchanging message. It is invoked by an input message and reacts to the message with an output message. More specifically, a message (m) is a tuple $\{s^f, s^t, D\}$, where s^f is the service that the data comes from, s^t is the service that the data goes to, and D is a set of data items delivered. Once there is a change of the outsourced services, a change of the message exchange between services may be introduced. For example, when adding a traffic service to a travel package, the LCS owner may want to add the message exchanges from the airline service and the hotel service to the traffic service so that it can generate the corresponding driving direction between the airport to the hotel.We define the change operators for change of data flow as below.

- Δ^I (M, D, op): It performs the operation *op*, by either *adding* the data items in D to or *removing* them from a LCS's input. This operator takes M, D, and *op* as its input and returns a new schema as its output.

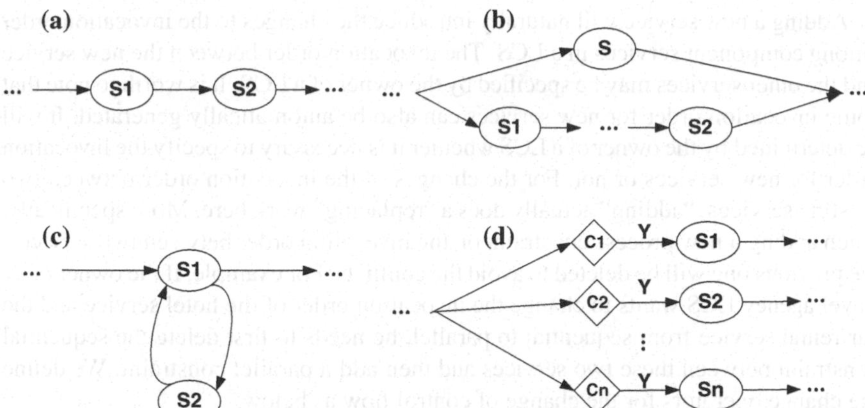

Fig. 10.4 Four types of process constraints. **a** Sequential constraint, **b** Parallel constraint, **c** Outsourcing constraint, and **d** Conditional selection constraint

- $\Delta^O(M, D, op)$: It performs the operation *op*, by either *adding* the data items in D to or *removing* them from a LCS's output. This operator takes M, D, and *op* as its input and returns a new schema as its output.
- $\Delta^{MX}(m, M, op)$: It performs the operation *op*, by either *adding* a data transfer m to or *removing* it from a LCS schema M.

Invocation order: The control flow of a LCS specifies the invocation order among component services. Meanwhile, it also specifies certain *process constraint* between two services, as depicted in Fig. 10.4. We define four types of process constraints below.

- *Sequential Constraint*: $P^{>>}(s_1, s_2)$ means that s_1 is invoked before the invocation of s_2. It usually exists between the services where one service requires the result of another service's invocation.
- *Parallel Constraint*: $P^{||}(s, s_1, s_2)$ means that s's invocation is in parallel with the invocation block from s_1 to s_2. It usually exists between two services where there is no direct or indirect data exchanges between them.
- *Outsourcing Constraint*: $P^{\dashv}(s_1, s_2)$ means that s_1 outsources functionality from s_2. It usually exists between two services where a service's (i.e., s_2's) invocation is totally embedded in another service's (i.e., s_1's) invocation. For the sake of simplicity and without the loss of generality, we assume that s_2 does not have any interaction with other services in a LCS than s_1.
- *Conditional Selection Constraint*: $P^?(s, (c_1, s_1), \ldots, (c_n, s_n))$ means that after the invocation of s, if c_i is fulfilled, s_i will be then invoked, where $1 \leq i \leq n$. It always exists among different services which provide the similar functionality in a coarse granularity. For example, taxi services and car rental services both provide the ground transportation.

Adding a new service will naturally introduce the changes to the invocation order among component services in a LCS. The invocation order between the new service and the other services may be specified by the owner of a LCS. It is worth to note that some invocation order for new services can also be automatically generated. It will be determined by the owner of a LCS whether it is necessary to specify the invocation order for new services or not. For the changes of the invocation order between two existing services, "adding" actually does a "replacing" work here. More specifically, when adding a new process constraint on the invocation order between two services, the previous one will be deleted to avoid the conflicts. For example, if the owner of an travel agency LCS wants to change the invocation order of the hotel service and the car rental service from sequential to parallel, he needs to first delete the sequential constraint between these two services and then add a parallel constraint. We define the change operators for the change of control flow as below.

- $\triangle_P^{>>}$ (s_1, s_2, M): It adds a sequential constraint on the order of invoking s_1 and s_2 defined in M. The operator takes s_1, s_2, M, as its input and returns a new schema as its output.
- $\triangle_P^{||}$ (s, s_1, s_2, M): It adds a parallel constraint on the order of invoking s_1 and s_2 defined in M. The operator takes s, s_1, s_2, M as its input and returns a new schema as its output.
- $\triangle_P^{\dashv}$ (s_1, s_2, M): It adds an outsourcing constraint on the order of invoking s and the block from s_1 to s_2 defined in M. The operator takes s_1, s_2, and M as its input and returns a new schema as its output.
- $\triangle_P^{?}$ (s, C, S, M): It will add a conditional selection constraint on the order of invoking services in S defined in M. The operator takes C, S, M, *op* as its input and returns a new schema as its output.

10.4.2 Non-Functional Changes

Non-functional changes are those that require to change the non-functional features of a LCS, including *context* and *quality* changes.

The context of a LCS specifies its environmental information. It can be any metadata that is related to the interactions between the LCS and its users, such as location, time, and payment methods. A top-down change may require to change the context of its component services. For example, in a travel agency LCS, the taxi service is located in the US. Suppose users tend to use the taxi service when they travel in Europe. The LCS owner may want to change the location of the taxi service it outsources to Europe to better serve user needs. The result of this change may be a replacement of the concrete taxi service in the LCS. For another example, in the LCS, the hotel service only accepts credit card payment. Suppose users tend to use other payment methods, such as paypal. The LCS owner may want to change the payment method of the hotel service it outsources accordingly. The result of this change may be that the LCS owner will find another hotel service which satisfies the new context requirement to replace the previous one.

The context change operator, $\triangle^{CM}$ (λ, M), will enforce a context constraint λ on a LCS with the schema M. λ is a triplet $\{S, v, e\}$, where *the services in* $\lambda.S$ *should have the value of* $\lambda.v$ *for the context* $\lambda.e$. This operator takes λ and M as its input and returns a new LCS instance as its output. For example, $\triangle^{CM}$ ({{*taxi*}, '*Europe*', *location*}, *travel_LCS*) means that the change requires the location of the taxi service in the travel agency LCS is in Europe.

The quality of a LCS refers to its non-functional features, such as its reliability, fee, invocation duration, and reputation. It evaluates the quality delivered by a LCS. A top-down change may require to modify the quality that a LCS delivers. For example, a LCS owner may want to guarantee that the providers of its component services should have a decent reputation. We define a quality change as follows.

The quality change operator, $\triangle^{QM}$ (δ, M), will enforce a quality constraint δ on a LCS with the schema M. δ is a triplet $\{S, r, i\}$, where the services in $\delta.S$ should have the value of $\delta.r$ for the quality parameter $\delta.i$. This operator takes δ and M as its input and returns a new LCS instance as its output. For example, $\triangle^{QM}$ ({{*car_rental*, *hotel*}, '*high*', *reputation*}, *travel_LCS*) means that the change requires that the car rental service and the hotel service in the travel agency LCS should have a high reputation.

10.5 SCML Language

Based on the proposed change model, we present a *Web Service Change Management Language* (SCML) in this section. Change operators can be used to describe a change. However, it is not a friendly way for LCS's owners due to the esoteric and uncommon notations. SCML paves the way for end users to input a change specification in a convenient fashion. SCML is an SQL-like language. It defines five types of commands: (1) *create command* for defining a LCS schema; (2) *select command* for querying both abstract services and concrete Web services; (3) *alter command* for specifying functional changes; (4) *update command* for specifying non-functional changes; (5) *drop command* for deleting a LCS schema. The commands are defined and elaborated on in this section.

10.5.1 Create Command

The create command is used to specify a new LCS schema. A LCS schema is given a name using two keywords: **CREATE** and **LCS**. For example, by writing

CREATE LCS travel-agency...

A LCS named as travel-agency is created. A LCS is associated with a Web service ontology from where it outsources semantics. Therefore, the Web service ontology is specified first. We use a keyword **ONTOLOGY** to specify the ontology provider that offers the ontology. For example, by writing

ONTOLOGY o http://wsms-dev.csiro.au:8080/.../OntologyAccessWithConfig

A LCS is associated with an ontology service which provides ontological semantics for the LCS.

After that, the abstract services in a LCS is specified. Each abstract service corresponds to a service concept in the Web service ontology. It is then described using the name of the service concept. We use the keyword, **SERVICES**, to specify one or more abstract services. For example, by writing

SERVICES s_a airline, s_t taxi, s_h hotel

SERVICES s_p payment

we specify four abstract services for the LCS.

We use a keyword, **CONTROL FLOWS**, to specify one or more control flow edges in a LCS schema graph. Each edge is given a name and a description. The description includes the information about the service node that the edge comes from, the service node the edge goes to, and the condition the edge delivers. For example, by writing

CONTROL FLOWS c1 (s_a, s_h, true), c2 (s_h, s_t, true)

we specify a control flow edge from the airline service to the hotel service.

We use a keyword, **DATA FLOWS**, to specify one or more data flow edges in a LCS schema graph. Each edge is given a name and a description. The description includes the information about the service node that the edge comes from, the service node that the edge goes to, and the data item the edge delivers. For example, by writing

DATA FLOWS d1 (s_a, s_p, ticket_price),

we specify a data flow edge from the airline service to the payment service with the information of a ticket's price.

Recall that there are two special service nodes: n_ω and n_ε, which refer to the user of a LCS. We use a keyword, **USER**, to specify these two service nodes when defining edges in a LCS schema graph. For example, by writing

DATA FLOWS d2 (**USER**, s1, user_Id), d3 (s1, **USER**, flight_schedule)

we specify two data flow edges. In d1, the information is obtained from a LCS's users and sent to the airline service. In d2, the data is generated by the airline service and returned to users.

After specifying a LCS schema graph, we use a keyword, **QUALITIES** to specify one or more quality parameters that are used to evaluate a LCS. A quality parameter is given a name and a description. For example, by writing

QUALITIES q1 availability, q2 cost

we specify two quality parameters.

We use a keyword, **CONTEXTS**, to specify one or more contexts of a LCS. A context is given a name and a description. For example, by writing

CONTEXTS c1 location, c2 time, c3 currency

we specify three contexts for the LCS.

Therefore, we can define a LCS schema as follows.

CREATE LCS travel-agency (
ONTOLOGY o http://wsms-dev.csiro.au:8080/.../OntologyAccessWithConfig
SERVICES s_a airline, s_t taxi, s_h hotel, s_p payment, s_w weather...
...
CONTROL FLOWS c1 (s_a, s_h, true), c2 (s_h, s_t, true)...
...
DATA FLOWS d1 (s_a, s_p, ticket_price),
...
QUALITIES q1 availability, q2 cost
...
CONTEXTS c1 location, c2 time, c3 currency
...
)

10.5.2 Select Command

The select command is used to specify a query on a Web service ontology. The corresponding change operators include: $\Pi^F_{op}(op, O)$, $\Pi^F_d(D_I, D_O, O)$, $\Pi^F_C(c, O)$, and $\Pi^F_Q(q, O)$. A query can be performed based on the features of a LCS: functional and non-functional. Similar to a select statement in SQL, a SCML select command is formed of the three clauses, which start with three keywords: **SELECT**, **FROM**, and **WHERE**, respectively.

SELECT <abstract service list>
FROM <ontology>
WHERE <condition>

where <abstract service list> is a list of abstract services that are intended to be retrieved by the query; <ontology> is the Web service ontology that the query is performed upon; and <condition> is a conditional expression (Boolean) that identifies the services to be retrieved by the query. In SCML, a conditional expression has the following format:

```
<abstract service> <operator> <values>
```

The operators include **hasOperation**, **hasInput**, **hasOutput**, **hasQuality**, and **hasContext**. They are defined for the four change operators that require a query on a Web service ontology. For each of these change operators, we give an example of a SCML query statement.

- $\Pi^F_{op}(op, O)$: **SELECT** s **FROM** o **WHERE** s **hasOperation** (airline_reservation)
- $\Pi^F_d(D_I, D_O, O)$: **SELECT** s **FROM** o **WHERE** s **hasInput** (location, date) **and** s **hasOutput** (weather_information)
- $\Pi^F_Q(q, O)$: **SELECT** s **FROM** o **WHERE** s **hasQuality** (privacy)
- $\Pi^F_C(c, O)$: **SELECT** s **FROM** o **WHERE** s **hasContext** (history_data)

10.5.3 Alter Command

The alter command is used to specify functional changes in a LCS. The possible *alter LCS schema actions* include (1) adding or deleting user input or LCS output, (2) adding, deleting, or replacing abstract services and/or data flow edges), and (3) adding a process constraint.

For (1) and (2), the alter command is formed as:

ALTER LCS <LCS name> <action> <element type> <value>

where an action can be **ADD, DELETE**, or **REPLACE**. An element type can be **INPUT, OUTPUT, SERVICES**, and **DATA FLOWS**. When the action is **REPLACE**, the element type has to be **SERVICES**. The value type for **REPLACE** action is a pair. For other actions, the value contains a service name and the name of its corresponding service concept in the service ontology. The alter command corresponds to the five functional change operators. We give an example of a SCML alter command for each of them.

- Δ^S (s, O, M, op): **ALTER LCS** travel-agency **ADD SERVICES**(s_f traffic, s_l local_activity, s_z address_to_zip);
- $\Delta^{S\leftrightarrow}$ (s_{old}, s_{new}, O, M): **ALTER LCS** travel agency **REPLACE SERVICES** (s_t, s_c car_rental);
- Δ^I (M, D, op): **ALTER LCS** travel-agency **ADD INPUT** (car_type)
- Δ^O (M, D, op): **ALTER LCS** travel-agency **DELETE OUTPUT** (taxi_charge, taxi_schedule)
- Δ^{MX} (m, M, op): **ALTER LCS** travel-agency **ADD DATA FLOWS** (<**USER**, s_c, car_type>)

When adding a process constraint, the alter command is formed as:

ALTER LCS <LCS name> **ADD PROCESS CONSTRAINT** <constraint type> <value>

where <constraint type> can be **SEQUENTIAL, PARALLEL, OUTSOURCING**, and **CONDITIONAL SELECTION**. The four constraint types correspond to the four change operators. We give an example of a SCML alter command for each of them.

- $\Delta_P^{>>}$ (s_1, s_2, M): **ALTER LCS** travel-agency **ADD PROCESS CONSTRAINT SEQUENTIAL** (s_a, s_c);
- $\Delta_P^{||}$ (s, s_1, s_2, M): **ALTER LCS** travel-agency **ADD PROCESS CONSTRAINT PARALLEL** (s_h, s_c, s_c);
- $\Delta_P^{\dashv}$ (s_1, s_2, M): **ALTER LCS** travel-agency **ADD PROCESS CONSTRAINT OUT SOURCING** (s_w, s_z);
- $\Delta_P^{?}$ (s, C, S, M): **ALTER LCS** travel-agency **ADD PROCESS CONSTRAINT CONDITIONAL SELECTION** (s_h, <travel_type="international", s_t >, <travel_type="domestic", s_c >);

10.5.4 Update Command

The update command is used to specify non-functional changes. The possible *update LCS actions* include: (1) changing a LCS quality, and (2) changing a LCS context. When changing a LCS quality, a update command is formed as:

UPDATE LCS <LCS name> **SET** <service list> <quality parameter>23 <operator> <value>

When changing a LCS context, a update command is formed as:

UPDATE LCS <LCS name> **SET** <service list> <context type> <operator> <value>

The operators can be "=", "<", "<=", ">", ">=", and "<>".

The command corresponds to the two non-functional change operators. We give an example of a SCML update command for each of them.

- Δ^{QM} (δ, M): **UPDATE LCS travel-agency SET** (s_a, s_h) **q1="high"**
- Δ^{CM} (λ, M): **UPDATE LCS travel-agency SET** (s_t) **c1="European"**

10.5.5 Drop Command

The drop command is used to drop a named LCS schema. We use two keywords: **DROP** and **LCS** to specify a drop command. For example, by writing

DROP LCS travel-agency

we delete the travel agency LCS schema.

10.5.6 Analysis on SCML

SCML needs to achieve the five characteristics to be qualified as a way to model changes in LCSs, including unambiguous, formal, disciplined, complete, and declarative. We give the analysis on SCML with respect to these five characteristics as follows.

SCML is built upon the proposed change taxonomy and change operators. Different types of change operators can be mapped to ALTER and UPDATE commands in SCML. For these commands, different keywords are used to specify the types of the changes and the related parameters. Therefore, a legal SCML statement contains the sufficient information to specify a change, which ensures the change specification to be unambiguous and disciplined.

Predefined keywords are used to constitute an SCML statement. The semantic of these keywords are understandable for machines, such as ALTER, LCS, SELECT, ADD, etc. The semantic of an SCML statement is understandable and processable for machines. Therefore, an SCML change specification is formal.

Each top-down change will fall into one or more categories defined in the change taxonomy. Each change category is mapped to a change operator. Therefore, for a simple change that falls into one change category, it can be specified in term of the corresponding change operator and then be mapped to an SCML statement. For a complex change which falls into more than one change categories, multiple change operators can be used to specify the change. It then can be specified by multiple SCML statement. Therefore, SCML can be used to specify all top-down changes. It is complete.

SCML is SQL-like language. Therefore, it is declarative. For example, if a LCS's owner wants to add a POI service to the LCS, he does not need to provide the operational information, i.e., how to integrate the POI service with other participated services.

10.6 SCML Processing

In this section, we propose a systematic procedure to process SCML statements. As showed in Fig. 10.5, there are several components that involve in the procedure, including an *SCML parser*, *Ontology manager*, *Change analyzer*, *LCS schema manager*, *schema-level processor*, and *Instance-level processor*. We describe these components as follows.

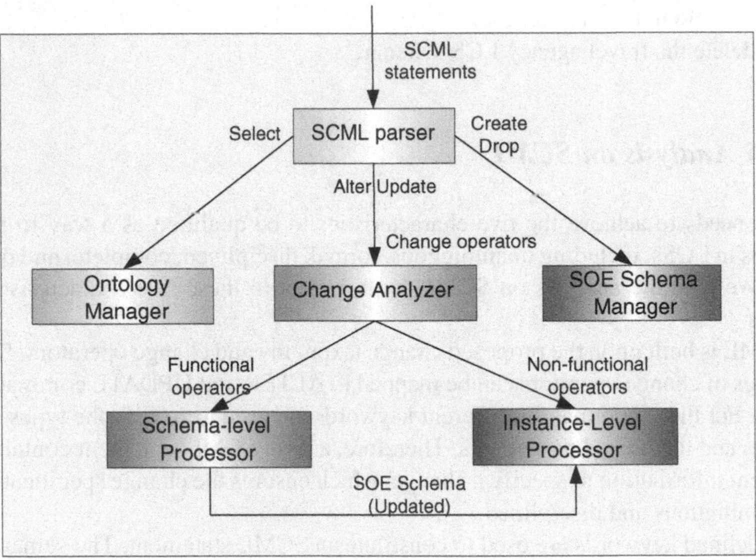

Fig. 10.5 SCML processing framework

10.6.1 SCML Parser

The SCML parser takes the first step of processing an SCML statement, which is initially expressed in term of strings. During this step, the parser first checks the syntax of the SCML statement. Besides syntax errors, semantic errors will also be detected. For example, the parser will check whether the service name appearing in the statement are names of the services in the ontology, whether the context of a service is included in the context type defined in the ontology, and so on. For create and drop SCML statements, the parser forwards them to the LCS schema manager for the further process. For other types of SCML statements, the parser translates them in format of change operators and forwards them to different SCML processing components.

10.6.2 Schema Manager and Ontology Manager

The LCS schema manager maintains two types of information: a set of LCS schema definitions and a set of Web service ontology definition. It processes two types of SCML commands: create and drop commands. When processing an SCML create statement, the LCS schema manager extracts the definition of the schema from the statement and add it to the schema definition set. It also extracts the ontology information from the statement. The ontology information is expressed as the URL of the service which provides the ontology information. The LCS schema manager stores the URL and connect it with the related LCS schema.

The ontology manager processes SCML SELECT commands. It retrieves the required semantics from the ontology service specify in the query. The ontology manager leverages the ontology query infrastructure offered by ontology providers [25].

10.6.3 Change Analyzer

The change analyzer takes a set of change operators translated from ALTER and UPDATE SCML commands as input. It first determines the feasibility of implementing the change. It then forwards the change operator to the two other components: schema-level processor and instance-level processor. A change is feasible if there will be an executable plan for implementing the change. The feasibility of a change will be checked in different stages: *initial* stage by the change analyzer, *schema-level* by the schema-level processor, and *instance-level* stage by the instance-level processor. In the initial stage, the change whose specification shows obvious unfeasibility will be identified. Such obvious unfeasibility includes (1): the service that is required to be added has already included in a LCS; (2): the service that is required to be removed does not participate in the LCS. Moreover, if a change specification consists of a set of change operators, the change analyzer goes through all the change operators and checks the conflict among the change operators. For example, adding and removing an airline service from a travel agency LCS are conflict with each other. For another example, adding a parallel and sequence order between two services at the same time are conflict with each other. The unfeasible changes will not be further processed. The second step of change analysis is to group the change operators and send them to different components based on their types. The functional change operators will be sent to the schema-level processor. The non-functional operators will be sent to the instance-level processor.

10.6.4 Schema-Level Processor

The schema-level processor takes a set of functional change operators as input. It then updates the schema based on the change operators. It first directly translates a change operators as the operations on the schema graph. The process is referred to as *change reaction*. For example, for a change that requires to add a new service to a LCS, a new node will be added to the schema graph. For a change that requires to delete a service from a LCS, the corresponding service node will be removed from the schema graph. The process is performed fulfill the functional requirement of a change. However, it may lead the schema graph in inconsistent state, i.e., services cannot collaborate properly. For example, if a new service is added, it may be an isolated node in the schema graph. It then cannot be invoked. For another example, a POI service depends on a hotel service to provide the input information, such as the location and activity time. If the hotel service is deleted, the POI service cannot be invoked since it does not have the enough information for the invocation.

The schema-level processor then further modifies the schema graph to maintain the correctness of the state. The process of referred to as *change verification* [26]. The schema-level processor first checks whether a service can be invoked based on the data flow. It checks each service can get enough input to be invoked. If not, it will make matching between the required input with the output of other services to create new data flows among them. The process is guided by the *dependency* between different services within a domain. A service S_A is depend on another service S_B if S_A relies on S_B to provide its input when they are combined together. An example of such a dependency is the one between a hotel service and an airline service. A user can book a airline or a hotel service individually via a travel agency. But when he wants a flight+hotel package, the information needed by the hotel service, such as check-in, check-out date, depends on the output of the airline service, i.e., the flight information. The dependency between different services is defined by domain experts and included in the Web service ontology definition [25]. The feasibility of a change will be checked at this step. A change is not feasible if it causes a cycle in data transfer. An example of a data transfer cycle is: service *A* waits for service *B*'s to provide its input; B waits for service C to provide its input; meanwhile, C waits for A to provide its input. The unfeasible change will be detected and it will not be further processed. The second step of change verification is to check whether a service can be invoked based on the control flow. For each data flow in the schema graph, there should be a corresponding execution path ensure the data transfer. The useless nodes will be detected and removed: *isolated* nodes and *unreachable* nodes. A node is isolate if it does not have incoming and outgoing edges. It is useless since there are no interaction between these nodes and other nodes in the schema graph. A node is unreachable if there is no path from the starting node to it. It is useless since it can not be invoked within the LCS. Any cycle in the control flow will also be detected and broken.

The output of the schema-level processor is an updated schema graph. The new graph ensures the functional requirement of the change. It is also in a correct configuration that ensures the proper composition of services.

10.6.5 Instance-Level Processor

The instance-level processor take a set of non-functional operators and the schema graph as input. If the schema graph has been changed by the schema-level processor, the instance-level processor will use the updated schema graph as input. the instance-level processor will perform two steps to generate the new LCS's instance: *service selection* and *service integration*.

For each newly added service node in the schema graph, the instance-level processor select the corresponding concrete Web services. The selection is based on the two criteria: functional and non-functional. Each service node the in the graph refers to a type of functionality of Web services. The concrete service that provides the functionality will be picked up. If there are non-functional requirements associated on the new service, the service that fulfills the requirement will be selected. An example of such a change is that the owner of a travel agency LCS wants to add a new POI service with a high reputation to the LCS. If there are new non-functional requirements associated on the existing services, the current service will be replaced by other service that fulfills the requirement. An example of such a change is that the owner of a travel agency LCS wants to replace the current hotel service with the one that has the availability higher than 99 %. If there are new non-functional requirements on the entire LCS, all the available orchestrations of services will be generated and the one that fulfills the requirement will be picked. An example of such a change is that the owner of a travel agency LCS wants to decrease the overall duration of the LCS to 5 s. The change feasibility is checked during this process. If there is no available services that can fulfill both the functional and the non-functional requirement of a change, the change is not feasible.

After selecting the services, the instance-level processor integrates these services together. It generates a BPEL process based on the schema graph [2]. The execution order among services is defined by the control flow. For the data flows between two services, a SOAP message is generated to delivered the information exchange between the services.

10.7 Implementation

In this section, we describe a prototype that implements the proposed SCML language. The prototype provides a graphic user interface for users to input an SCML specification and generates the result of language enactment. In this prototype, we focus on the two key SCML clauses: create command and alter command. We use a travel agency LCS in our running example as the scenario. For the sake of space, we only introduce some representative steps of using the system.

Users need to submit a create command to define a LCS schema graph. As depicted in Fig. 10.6, the information includes the nodes of the graph and the two sets of edges (i.e., data flow edges and the control flow edges). Each node represents an abstract Web service and is assigned to an id. An example of such a node id is Airline. Each node corresponds a concept in a Web Service Modeling Language (WSML) file, which contains the semantic definition of the abstract service. A data flow edge is represented as a triplet: the node that the edge comes from, the node that the edge goes to, and a data set pair delivered by the edge. An example of such a triplet is {Airline, Hotel, {arrival_date, check_in_date}}, which means that an airline service sends a message to a hotel service containing the information of the arrival_date, which can be used as the check_in_date for the hotel service. A control flow edge is represented as a triplet: the node invoked first, the node invoked afterwards, and the condition on the invocation of the second node. An example of such a triplet is {Airline, Hotel, "true"}, which means that a hotel service will be invoked after an airline service is invoked. After submitting the create command, users can click the execute button to create the LCS schema graph, which is depicted in Fig. 10.7.

Users need to submit an alter command to specify a change. As depicted in Fig. 10.8, an alter command contains the information of changes, such as the change operator (i.e., adding or removing), the type of change objectives (i.e., service, data flow, or control flow), and the change objectives. After editing the alter command, users can click the execution button to implement the change, which is depicted in Fig. 10.9. In the graph, there are three new services added (i.e., carRental, Traffic, and LocalActivity). The invocation orders and message exchanges among these services and other services in the LCS are automatically generated.

10.8 Related Work

Change management is an active research topic in database management, knowledge engineering, and software evolution. Research efforts are also underway to provide change management in a Web service community and adaptive workflow systems [1, 5]. There are some change models have been proposed to specify different types of changes. In this section, we will elaborate some representative works and differentiate them with our work.

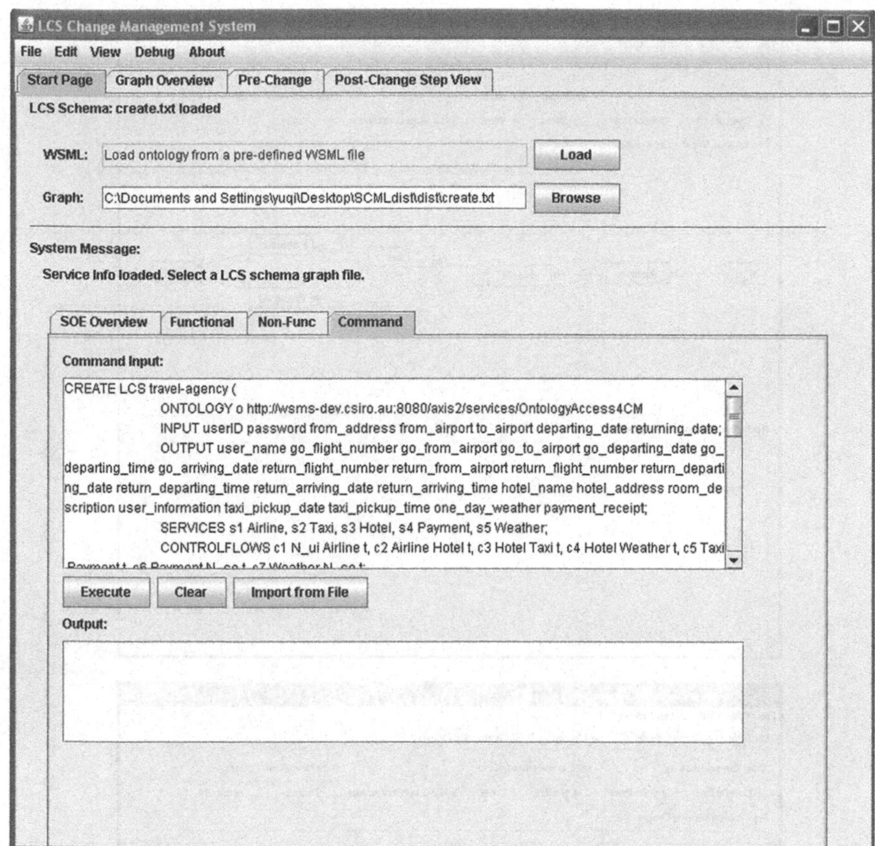

Fig. 10.6 The input of a create command

In [1], a petri-net based change model is proposed. The change model is used to specify bottom-up changes in LCSs, which are initiated at the service level and then propagated to the business level. built upon the differentiation the changes between two levels: service level and business level. The changes initiated at the service level is called as *triggering* changes. The changes initiated at the business level is called as *reactive* changes. A set of mapping rules are defined between triggering changes and reactive changes. These rules are used for propagating changes. The reactive changes are modeled as Petri-nets. In [1], the work mainly focus on devising handling mechanisms for exceptional changes. An example of such mechanisms is that the system will switch to use an alternative service if a sudden failure occurs to a service. Petri-nets are chosen to provide formal semantics for bottom-up changes. In this chapter, we focus on modeling the top down changes, which are initiated by a LCS's owner in case of the occurrence of new business requirements or new business regulations.

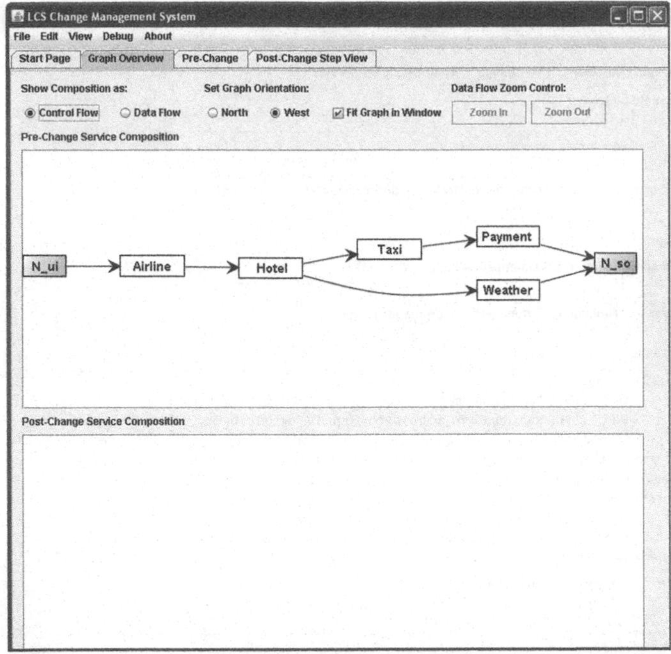

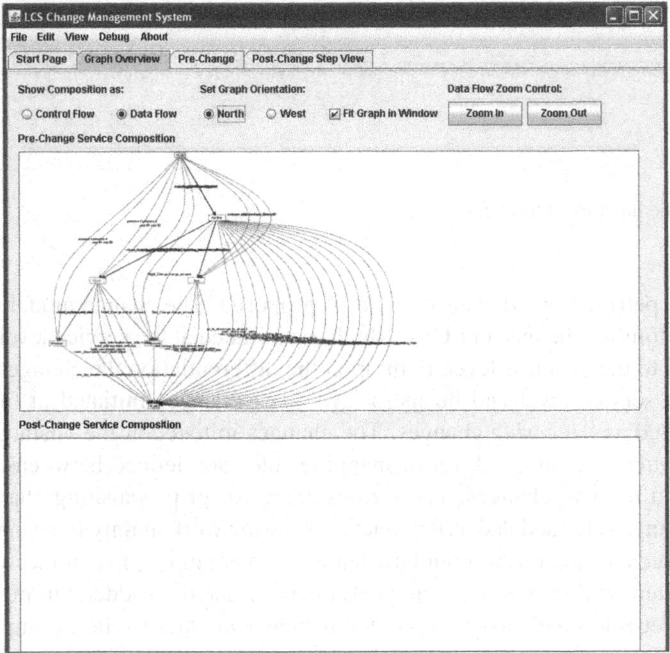

Fig. 10.7 The control flow and data flow of a LCS

In [5], the work focuses on modeling dynamic changes within workflow systems. It introduces a Modeling Language to support Dynamic Evolution within Workflow System (ML-DEWS). A change is modeled as a process class, which contains the information of *roll-out time*, *expiration time*, *change filter*, and *migration process*. The roll-out time indicates when the change begins. The expiration time indicates when the change ends. The change filter specifies the old cases that are allowed to migrate to the new procedure. The migration process specifies how the filtered-in old cases migrate to the new process. In [5], the language is defined for human consumption, not for machines. The change specification is not formal enough for completely understandable and processable by machines. The change management process based on ML-DEWS is not automated. SCML, in the other hand, is formal. It can be understandable and processable by machines. Based on the SCML change specification, the new LCS schema can be automatically generated.

In [8], a framework is presented to detecting and reacting to the exceptional changes that can be raised inside workflow-driven Web application is proposed. It

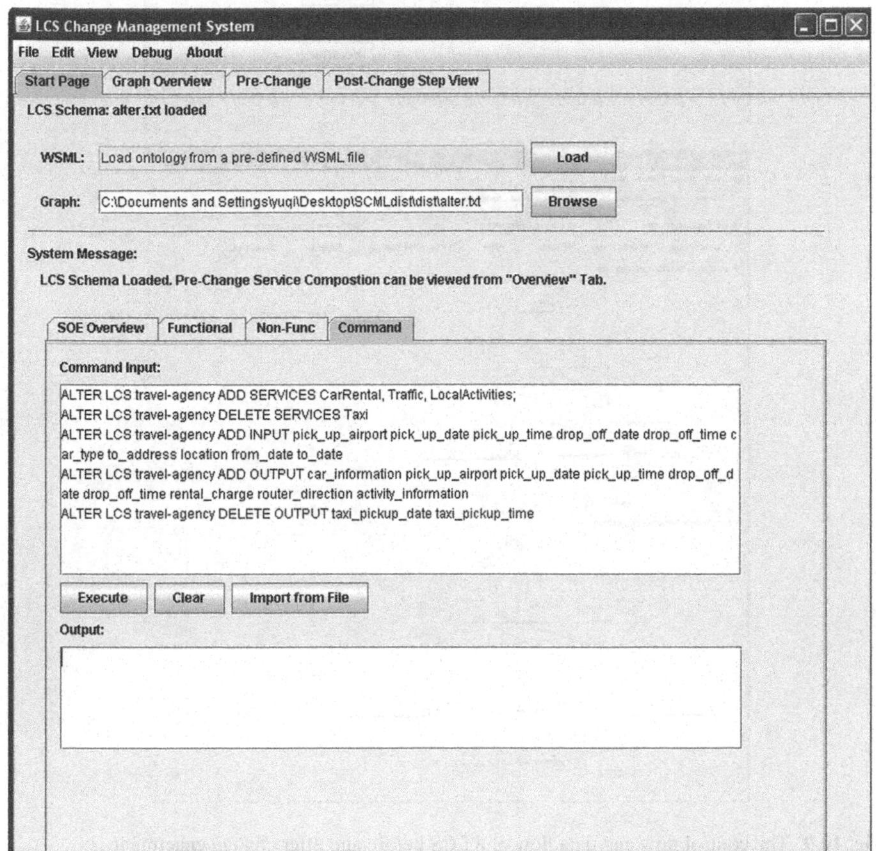

Fig. 10.8 The input of a set of alter commands

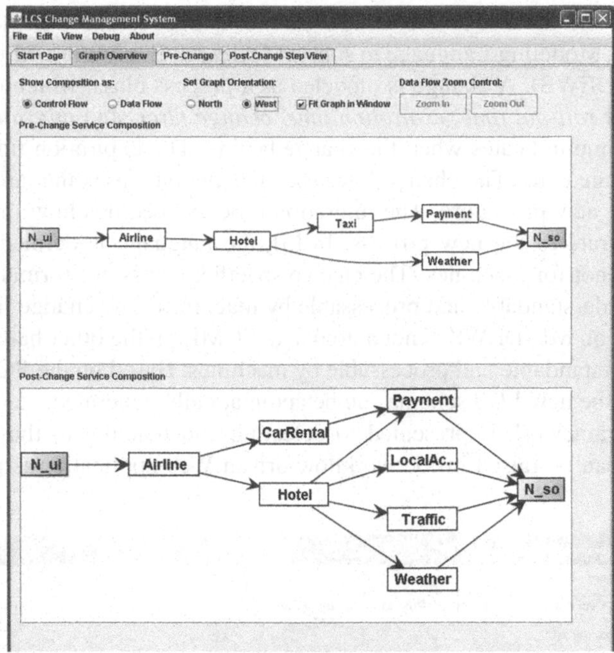

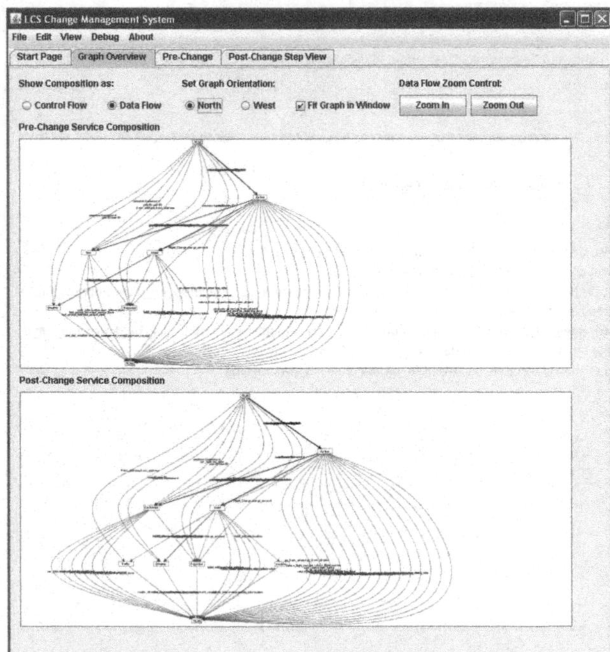

Fig. 10.9 The control flow and data flow of a LCS before and after change enactment

first classifies these changes into *behavioral (or user-generated), semantic (or application)*, and *system* exceptions. The behavior exceptions are driven by improper execution order of process activities. For example, the free user navigation through Web pages may result in the wrong invocation of the expired link, or double-click the link when only one click is respected. The semantic exceptions are driven by unsuccessful logical outcome of activities execution. For example, a user does not keep paying his periodic installments. The system exceptions are driven by the malfunctioning of the workflow-based Web application, such as network failures and system breakdowns. It then proposes a modeling framework that describes the structure of activities inside hypertexts of a Web application. The hypertext belonging to an activity is broken down into pages, where are univocally identified within an activity. framework to handle these changes. The framework consists of three major components: *capturing model*, *notifying model*, and *handling model*. The capturing model capture events and store the exceptions data in the workflow model. The notifying model propagate the occurred exceptions to the users. The handling model defines a set of recovery policy to resolve the exception. For different types of exceptions, different recovery policies will be used. In this chapter, we focus on different type of changes. Changes are treated as the "rule", not the "exception".

10.9 Conclusion

We propose SCML, a formal language, to specify top-down changes. The SCML is built upon a LCS schema, which is represented as a directed graph. The SCML focuses on a proposed change taxonomy, which classifies changes into two categories: functional and non-functional changes. It is centered around four types of clauses: definitive, query, change, and drop. The definitive clauses are used to define a LCS schema. The query clauses are used to specify a query on a Web service ontology. The change clauses are used to specify top-down changes. A procedure of processing SCML statements is presented. We also describe a prototype implemented to show the practicality of the proposed approach.

References

1. M. S. Akram, B. Medjahed, and A. Bouguettaya. Supporting Dynamic Changes in Web Service Environments. In *International Conferences on Service Oriented Computing (ICSOC)*, Trento, Italy, 2003.
2. T. Andrews, F. Curbera, H. Dholakia, Y. Goland, J. Klein, F. Leymann, K. Liu, D. Roller, D. Smith, S. Thatte, I. Trickovic, S. Weerawarana. Business Process Execution Language for Web Services Version 1.1. Technical report, BEA Systems and IBM Corporation and Microsoft Corporation and SAP AG and Siebel Systems, http://www.ibm.com/developerworks/library/ws-bpel/, May 2003.

3. Y. Baghdadi. A Web services-based business interactions manager to support electronic commerce applications. In *ICEC '05*, 2005.
4. BPMI. Business Process Modeling Language (BPML. http://www.bpmi.org/bpml.esp, 2003.
5. Clarence A. Ellis and Karim Keddara. A workflow change is a workflow. In *Business Process Management, Models, Techniques, and Empirical Studies*, pages 201–217, London, UK, 2000. Springer-Verlag.
6. Elisabetta Di Nitto, Carlo Ghezzi, Andreas Metzger, Mike Papazoglou, and Klaus Pohl. A journey to highly dynamic, self-adaptive service-based applications. *Automated Software Engineering*.
7. R. Khalaf and W. A. Nagy. Business Process with BPEL4WS: Learning BPEL4WS, Part 6. Technical report, IBM, http://www-106.ibm.com/developerworks/webservices/library/ws-bpelcol6/, 2003.
8. Marco Brambilla, Stefano Ceri, Sara Comai, and Christina Tziviskou. Exception handling in workflow-driven web applications. In *WWW '05: Proceedings of the 14th international conference on World Wide Web*, pages 170–179, New York, NY, USA, 2005. ACM Press.
9. Nazim H. Madhavji. The prism model of changes. *IEEE Trans. Softw. Eng.*, 18(5), 1992.
10. Qi Yu and Athman Bouguettaya. Framework for web service query algebra and optimization. *ACM Trans. Web*, 2(1):1–35, 2008.
11. Qi Yu, Xumin Liu, Athman Bouguettaya, and Brahim Medjahed. Deploying and managing web services: issues, solutions, and directions. *VLDB Journal*, 17(3):537–572, 2008.
12. Satish Thatte. XLANG Web Services for Business Process Design. http://www.gotdotnet.com/team/xml_wsspecs/xlang-c/default.htm, 2001.
13. Setrag Khoshafian. Service oriented enterprises. Auerbach Publications, Boston, MA, USA, 2006.
14. The OWL Services Coalition. Owl-s: Semantic markup for web services. Technical report, http://www.daml.org/services/owl-s/1.1B/owl-s/owl-s.html, July 2004.
15. A. Tsalgatidou and T. Pilioura. An Overview of Standards and Related Technology in Web Services. *Distributed and Parallel Databases*, 12(2):135–162, 2002.
16. W. M. P. van der Aalst and T. Basten. Inheritance of workflows: an approach to tackling problems related to change. *Theoretical Computer Science*, 270(1–2):125–203, 2002.
17. W3C. Extensible Markup Language (XML). http://www.w3.org/XML, 2003.
18. W3C. Simple Object Access Protocol (SOAP). http://www.w3.org/TR/SOAP/, 2003.
19. W3C. Universal Description, Discovery, and Integration (UDDI). http://www.uddi.org, 2003.
20. W3C. Web Service Choreography Interface (WSCI). http://www.w3.org/TR/wsci/, 2003.
21. W3C. Web Services Architecture. http://www.w3.org/TR/ws-arch/, 2003.
22. W3C. Web Services Description Language (WSDL). http://www.w3.org/TR/wsdl, 2003.
23. WSMO Working Group. Web Service Modeling Ontology (WSMO). http://www.wsmo.org/, 2004.
24. Xumin Liu and Athman Bouguettaya. Managing top-down changes in service oriented enterprises. In *IEEE International Conference on Web Services (ICWS)*, Salt Lake City, Utah, July 2007.
25. Xumin Liu and Athman Bouguettaya. Ontology support for managing top-down changes in composite services. In *CollaborateCom 2008*, Orlando, FL, Nov. 2008.
26. Xumin Liu, Athman Bouguettaya, Xiaobing Wu, and Li Zhou. Ev-lcs: A system for the evolution of long-term composed services. *IEEE Transactions on Services Computing*, 99(PrePrints), 2012.
27. Xumin Liu, Athman Bouguettaya, Qi Yu, and Zaki Malik. Efficient change management in long-term composed services. *Service Oriented Computing and Applications*, 5(2):87–103, 2011.

Chapter 11
A Semantic-Based Approach to Generate Abstract Services for Service Organization

Xumin Liu and Hua Liu

Abstract Service organization has been considered as the key enabler for efficient web service management. It gives a high-level and structured view of the important features of web services, including their functionality and inter-service relationships, which can be leveraged to allow a top-down declarative way of querying and composing web services. Abstract services that conceptualize the functionality provided by web services, has been widely adopted as the kernel component of web service organization. However, how to generate abstract services is non-trivial. Current approaches either assume the existence of abstract services or adopt a manual process that demands intensive human intervention. We propose a novel approach to fully automate the generation of abstract services. We first explain the process of generating homogeneous service spaces, i.e., service communities, which consist of a set of functionally similar services. We then present a process of generating abstract services within a service community. We leverage semantics to address the issues raised by syntactical-level service descriptions. An comprehensive experimental study on real world web service data is conducted to demonstrate the effectiveness and efficiency of the proposed approach.

11.1 Introduction

Efficient web service management has been an essential and long-lasting challenge since the introduction of Service-Oriented Computing (SOC). It becomes more critical when the emergence of Cloud Computing further impels the growth of SOC, which results in the dramatic increase in the number of web services on the web. This introduces significant difficulties of accessing to the services in an automatic

X. Liu (✉)
Department of Computer Science, Rochester Institute of Technology, Rochester, USA
e-mail: xl@cs.rit.edu

H. Liu
Xerox Research at Webster, Webster, USA

A. Bouguettaya et al. (eds.), *Advanced Web Services*,
DOI: 10.1007/978-1-4614-7535-4_11,

way, such as locating a desirable services and leveraging existing services to construct business processes. The natural solution to deal with the large number of web services and allow efficient web service management is to build up a *service organization*, where related services are grouped together and their relationships are clearly specified. Such a service organization gives a high-level and structured view of the important features of web services, including their functionality and inter-service relationships. It can be leveraged to allow a top-down and declarative way of querying and composing Web services [5].

The concept of *abstract services* has been introduced and widely adopted as the kernel component of web service organization [10]. The idea is to conceptualize the functionality provided by Web services in a service space as abstract services and use them as the basis of efficient service management [15]. Examples of such functionalities include *get_route*, *get_map*, *weather_inquiry* and so on. An abstract service is associated with the group of web services providing the defined functionality. The relationship between an abstract service and its associated actual services is anomalous to the one between a class and it objects. Based on the description of abstract services and their associations with actual services, service management tasks, including service description, service discovery, service composition, and change management, can be designed and performed in a top-down fashion. That is, they can be carried out first on the "*schema-level*", where only abstract services are involved, and then on "*instance-level*", where only the associated web services are dealt with. More specifically, service discovery can start at identifying the abstract services that match a query requirement and then search in the web services instantiating the abstract services. Hence, both the efficiency and accuracy of service discovery are expected to be greatly improved through narrowing down the searching space. Similar to service discovery, service composition can start at designing the composition schema by identifying suitable abstract services and building up a schema-level workflow. The schema will then be instantiated by finding actual services for the abstract services and orchestrate them [6, 8]. Following the same rationale, abstract services also facilitate the process of dealing with the frequent changes in service oriented enterprises [2, 13, 14].

While the usage of abstract services holds tremendous promise, how to generate abstract services poses a set of key challenges. Existing approaches usually adopt a manual process to create abstract services and generate the mapping to the concrete services. The process starts by designing an abstract service based on the designer's view of the service space and user query requirements. To have a complete and comprehensive view of the service space, the designer needs to manually go through all service descriptions. Moreover, the designer will also need to manually specify the mapping between an abstract service and the corresponding concrete services. This is simply infeasible considering that there are a large number of web services and the number still keeps increasing. An alternative way is to ask service providers to link their services to predefined abstract services when publishing their services. This is, however, impractical considering the autonomous and independent nature of service providers. An efficient approach for generating abstract services is needed, where human efforts should be minimized.

Some recent research efforts have been conducted for bootstrapping homogenous web service spaces, i.e., web service communities, where related services are grouped together [9, 11, 12, 20–22, 24]. The majority of these approaches leverages information retrieval techniques (e.g. TF/IDF) when computing the similarity between web service descriptions, where each web service is modeled as a vector of terms. WSDL documents are dominantly targeted since WSDL is the *de facto* way that service providers take to describe their services. It is thus practical to assume that a service's WSDL description is accessible. The approaches then apply various data clustering algorithms to generate service communities from the service similarity matrix. They differ mostly in the constructions of the term vectors, calculations of the similarity metrics, and clustering algorithms (e.g., QT, k-means, SVD, and SS-BVD). Inspired by these existing approaches, abstract service generation can be accomplished by following two steps. First, applying service community learning approaches to group web services providing similar functionalities together, i.e., forming service communities. This process can be fully automated by leveraging the existing web service community learning approaches. With the adoption of information retrieval technique, the process is proved to yield relatively high accuracy. This is due to the observation that some common naming are usually followed for web service development, especially for the WSDL documents which are automatically generated from programming source codes. Second, extracting common features of services within a service community to define abstract services.

The existing service community learning approaches only generate the mapping between a service community and its member services. The outcome lacks sufficient summative description of functionality of the member services, i.e., abstract services. Simply using cluster centroids or representative terms to label a service community is far away from being sufficient. First, such labels cannot precisely capture the functionality of all member services. Users still need to go through a service's description to determine whether the service provides the desired functionality. Second, it is not guaranteed that the labels have high coverage of member services' functionality. To address these issues, we propose an automatic abstract service generation process to extract functional features of a service community's member services. We define an abstract service in terms of its input and output. All possible definitions of abstract services can be generated by enumerating the possible combination of input and output data items. We choose those abstracts services that can be instantiated by sufficient number of actual services, i.e., having a supporting ratio no less than a predefined threshold, to ensure the representativeness of the abstract services. To improve the efficiency of the process, we leverage association rule mining techniques to generate and prune the candidate abstract services. We start with finding possible output of an abstract service by checking whether there are enough number of services generating the output. For each output as such, we enumerate all possible input and check whether there are enough number services from the result of the first step that consume the given input. The mapping between an abstract service and the member services are generated during the process. We apply a set of heuristics to improve the efficiency and scalability of the process.

The abstract service generation process could be suffered from the lack of semantical description contained in WSDL descriptions. This is due to the observation that web services in a service community are usually provided by independent and autonomous service providers. Various naming conventions and "dialects" are used to describe services. More specifically, different web service providers might use the same term to specify different meanings. For example, the term "courses" can be used to represent classes and also degrees. It is also the case that different web services use different terms to specify the same meaning. For example, some web service providers use the term of "geocode" and others use "coordinates". It is essential to reconcile the diversities among web service descriptions when generating abstract services. Furthermore, the ontological relationships between different terms, such as "graduate students" and "person" should also be considered to precisely define and compute the supporting ratio of an abstract service . In this chapter, we incorporate semantics to the process of abstract services generation to improve the accuracy of the produced outcome.

The remainder of this chapter is organized as follows. In Sect. 11.2, we describe a process of bootstrapping homogenous web service spaces. In Sect. 11.3, we formally define an abstract service and its support ratio. We then define the abstract service generation problem that we address. In Sect. 11.4, we propose a process of generating abstract services from a service community. Possible abstract services are enumerated in a heuristic way. We use a bitmap to efficiently check each abstract service's support ratio. We further improve this process by incorporating semantics to the process, which is presented in Sect. 11.4. In Sect. 11.5, we present a comprehensive experimental study to demonstrate the effectiveness and performance of the proposed algorithms. In Sect. 11.6, we discuss some representative related works. In Sect. 11.7, we conclude our chapter and discuss future work.

11.2 Web Service Community Generation

Abstract services are generated from a service community, where each community groups services that provide a certain type of functionality. As the process of service community generation is not the focus of this chapter, we present the general idea of this process. The detailed description of an advanced service community generation process can be found in [17]. The process takes WSDL documents as input since WSDL is *de facto* standard way of describing services. As depicted in Fig. 11.1, the process consists of several key steps, including *extract terms*, *model services*, *compute service similarity*, and *cluster services*. We elaborate on these steps as follows.

The first step is to use *web service crawlers* to retrieve WSDL documents by crawling the Web and store them in a service repository. Besides traditional web search engines, e.g., google and bing, existing web service search engines, e.g., seekda [1] and programmableWeb,[2] can be used as the sources of the service repository.

[1] http://webservices.seekda.com/

[2] http://www.programmableweb.com

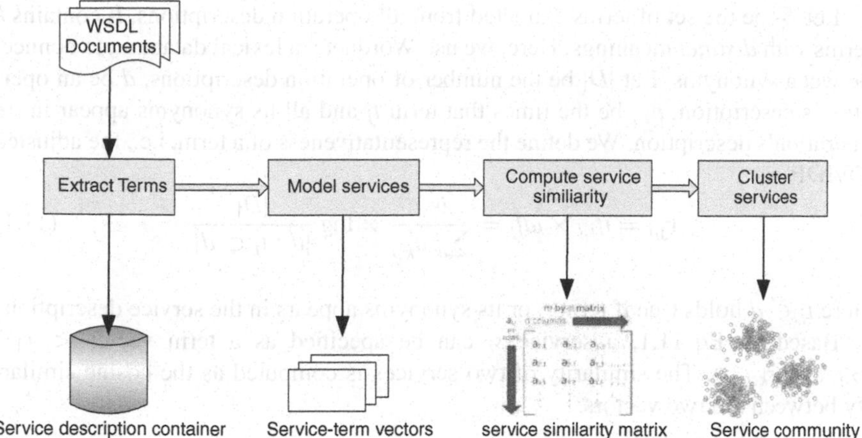

Fig. 11.1 The service community learning process

We then parse WSDL documents and store all the detailed description for each operation, including the operation name and detailed description of input and output messages. The message description includes the message name and the description of each part, which consists of the part name and its data type.

We adopt the current information retrieval approaches when comparing two services. Generally speaking, two services in the same community should have a higher similarity than the ones in different domains (e.g., travel, medical, and finance). For example, `flight_reservation` and `find_hotel` are expected to have a higher similarity than `flight_reservation` and `get_Medicine_name`. Although WSDL mainly describes a service at the syntactic level, information retrieval techniques can be adopted to extract semantics from WSDL descriptions. This is due to the observation that some common naming conventions are usually followed for Web service development, especially for the WSDL documents which are automatically generated from programming source codes. For example, an operation usually has the name of the original function, such as `TemperatureConversion`. Based on this observation, we can analyze the functional features of a service from the terms in its description. Following these lines, we extract *terms* from a service description to compute the service similarity.

It is very common that an element in a WSDL document appears in a composite format. For example, an operation may have a name like `get_Map`, `send PurchaseRequest`, or `order1`. Thus, tokenization is performed on an operation's description to extract simple terms. The tokenization process decomposes a given expression into simple terms. It consists of *case change*, *suffix numbers elimination*, *word stemming*, and *underscore separator* [19]. The output of the tokenization process is a set of terms that are used to model a service. The terms are stored in a *service description container*.

Let $\mathscr{T}$ be the set of terms extracted from all operation descriptions. It contains k terms with *distinct* meanings. Here, we use Wordnet,[3] a lexical database, to connect between synonyms. Let $|D|$ be the number of operation descriptions, d be an operation's description. $n'_{j,i}$ be the times that term t_j and all its synonyms appear in ith operation's description. We define the representativeness of a term, i.e., the adjusted TF/IDF, as:

$$\mathbf{r_{j,i}} = tf_{j,i} \times idf_j = \frac{n'_{j,i}}{\sum_k n'_{k,i}} \times \log \frac{|D|}{|d : t_j \in' d|} \tag{11.1}$$

Here $t_j \in' d$ holds true if term t_j or its synonyms appears in the service description.

Based on Eq. 11.1, a service s_i can be specified as a term vector $< r_{1,i}, r_{2,i}, \ldots, r_{k,i} >$. The similarity of two services is computed as the cosine similarity between the two vectors.

$$Sim(s_i, s_j) = \cos(v_i, v_j) = v_i^T v_j / (||v_i|| ||v_j||) \tag{11.2}$$

From Eq. 11.2, we can generate a service similarity relevance matrix $\mathscr{M}^S$, where $m^S_{s,t} = \text{Sim}(op_s, op_t)$. We then apply data clustering techniques to group related operations together. The objective here is to classify services into several groups (each group corresponds to a service community), so that the services assigned to each group are more similar to each other than the service assigned to different groups.

K-Means is a widely used centroid-based data clustering algorithm. The basic idea of applying K-Means is firstly randomly choose k operations as initial centroid. k is a predefined number that represents the number of resulting clusters. The algorithm then iteratively clusters operations, computes new centroids (c_i), re-clusters operations based on the new centroids, till centroids do not change. The process of clustering is guided to maximize the cohesion of a cluster, which is defined in Eq. 11.3. K-Means is efficient with time complexity of $\mathscr{O}(KIM)$, where K is the number of clusters, I is the number of iterations, and M is the size of the matrix.

$$cohesion = \sum_{i=1}^{k} \sum_{d \in C_i} \cos(d, c_i) \tag{11.3}$$

11.3 Problem Statement of Abstract Service Generation

In this section, we first formally define an abstract service and its support ratio. We then present the formal definition of abstract service generation problem.

[3] http://wordnet.princeton.edu/

11.3.1 Abstract Service and Support Ratio

An abstract service should be describe in terms of the functional capacity of member services of a service community. A query requirement specified in terms of abstract services will be mapped to concrete services if there is a match. A query requirement is usually formatted as *looking for a service that takes a given input and generates a given output*. An example would be: find a service that takes an address as input and returns weather information. Along with this line, we define an abstract service as:

Definition 11.3.1 An *abstract service* is a binary $l = \{l.I, l.O\}$, where $l.I = \{i_1, i_2, \ldots, i_m\}$ is its input, and $l.O = \{o_1, o_2, \ldots, o_n\}$ is its output.

Through an abstract service l of a service community c, users can understand what type of queries can be satisfied by c's member services. That is, being provided with the data items in $l.I$, the instances of l can generate all the data items in $l.O$. To measure the portion of services in c that can satisfy the query, we first define the *support* of a concrete service as follows.

Definition 11.3.2 A concrete service s is said to *support* an input $\mathscr{I}$, denoted as $\hat{s}.I(\mathscr{I})$, if $s.I \subseteq \mathscr{I}$; s is said to *support* an output $\mathscr{O}$, denoted as $\hat{s}.O(\mathscr{O})$, if $s.O \supseteq \mathscr{O}$; s is said to *support* an abstract service l, denoted as $\hat{s}(l)$, if $\hat{s}.I(l.I)$ **and** $\hat{s}.O(l.O)$.

Based on Definition 11.3.2, we compute the support ratio of an abstract service as follows. Let $S = \{s_1, s_2, \ldots, s_t\}$ be the set of all member services in a service community. The support ratio $\sigma(l)$ is calculated as follows:

$$\sigma(l) = \frac{|\{s_i | s_i \in S \wedge \hat{s}(l)\}|}{|S|} \tag{11.4}$$

Example 11.3.1 Suppose the `weather` community contains five services, whose input and output are listed in Table 11.1. Given an abstract service $l_1 = \{$`{zipcode}`, `{weather}`$\}$, the services that support l include: s_2, s_5. Therefore, l's support ratio is 0.4. Another abstract service $l_2 = \{$`{zipcode}`, `{weather,map_url}`$\}$ has a zero support ratio since there is no service supports it.

11.3.2 Abstract Service Generation Problem

A support ratio of an abstract service reflects the portion of the member services in a service community that have the functional capacity defined by the abstract

Table 11.1 Member services in weather community

ID	Input	Output
s_1	`city, state, country`	`weather, gas_price`
s_2	`zipcode`	`weather, gas_price`
s_3	`city, state, country`	`weather, map_url`
s_4	`geocode`	`map_url, gas_station`
s_5	`zipcode`	`weather`

service. A higher support ratio that an abstract service has, the more representative the abstract service is. We use a threshold τ, $0 < \tau \leq 1$, as the minimum support ratio of a *representative* abstract service.

Definition 11.3.3 An abstract service l is *representative* for a community c if its support ratio is no less than the threshold, i.e., $\sigma(L) \geq \tau$.

Moreover, based on Definition 11.3.2, if a concrete service s supports an input I, it supports all I's superset. If a service s supports an output O, it supports all O's subset. Therefore, for two abstract services, l, l', if the input of l' is a superset of the input of l and the output of l' is a subset of l's output, any service that supports l also supports l'. In this case, l is *dominated* by l' with respect to support ratio, denoted as $l' \succ l$. That is, if $l' \succ l$, $\sigma(l') \geq \sigma(l)$. If l is representative, l is more preferred than l' since it has fewer input and more output, meaning that users are required to provide fewer input but will gain more output from invoking l's instances than l''s instances. In another word, l defines stronger functional capability. To optimize the labeling result, we define an *optimal* abstract service as follows:

Definition 11.3.4 An abstract service l is *optimal* if it is *representative* **and** it does not *dominate* any other representative abstract services.

Therefore, the problem of abstract service generation is modeled as: *given $\mathcal{S}$, the set of a service community's member services, and a support ratio threshold τ, find a set of abstract services $\mathcal{L}$, where each abstract service $l \in \mathcal{L}$ is optimal.*

11.4 Candidate Abstract Service Generation and Pruning

To produce all candidate abstract services, a brute-force approach is to enumerate all possible inputs, denoted as $\mathcal{I}^{\mathcal{C}}$, enumerate all possible outputs, enumerate all combinations between $\mathcal{I}^{\mathcal{C}}$ and $\mathcal{O}^{\mathcal{C}}$, denoted as $\mathcal{C}$, and prune those that do not have enough support ratio. Let S be the set of the service community's member services. Let $\mathcal{D}_{\mathcal{I}}$ be the input data set, i.e., $\mathcal{D}_{\mathcal{I}} = \cup_{i=1}^{t} s_i.\mathcal{I}$, and $\mathcal{D}_{\mathcal{O}}$ be the output data set, i.e., $\mathcal{D}_{\mathcal{O}} = \cup_{i=1}^{t} s_i.\mathcal{O}$. We have:

$$|\mathcal{I}^{\mathcal{C}}| = \sum_{i=1}^{|\mathcal{D}_{\mathcal{I}}|} \binom{|\mathcal{D}_{\mathcal{I}}|}{i} = 2^{|\mathcal{D}_{\mathcal{I}}|-1}$$

$$|\mathcal{O}^{\mathcal{C}}| = \sum_{i=1}^{|\mathcal{D}_{\mathcal{O}}|} \binom{|\mathcal{D}_{\mathcal{O}}|}{i} = 2^{|\mathcal{D}_{\mathcal{O}}|-1}$$

$$|\mathcal{C}| = |\mathcal{I}^{\mathcal{C}}| \times |\mathcal{O}^{\mathcal{C}}| \approx 2^{|\mathcal{D}_{\mathcal{O}}|+|\mathcal{D}_{\mathcal{O}}|}$$

The brute-force approach has serious performance issue due to the exponentially increased computational complexity. To address this issue, we employ the idea of *Apriori* principle of frequent itemsets generation to heuristically generate candidate abstract services. We start with identifying all the possible outputs of an optimal abstract service. For each output as such, we then find the matching inputs. The mapping between the abstract service and the concrete services is also automatically generated during this process.

11.4.1 Candidate Output Generation

The overall idea of heuristic candidate output generation output is that we use the relationships between different outputs to filter out those outputs that are impossible to have a sufficient support ratio. By this, we narrow down the searching space. When compute the support ratio of an output, we only go through the concrete services that have the potential of supporting the output. By this, we decrease the number of comparisons between a candidate output and concrete outputs. We further optimize this process by using a *bitmap* structure to achieve $O(1)$ computational complexity. The whole process is guided by the following theorem.

Theorem 11.4.1 If an output's support ratio is less than the threshold, i.e., it is not associated with a representative abstract service, then all its superset must also not be associated with a representative abstract service. Moreover, if a concrete service does not support an output, it must also not support all the output's superset.

The proof of Theorem 11.4.1 directly follows Definition 11.3.2.

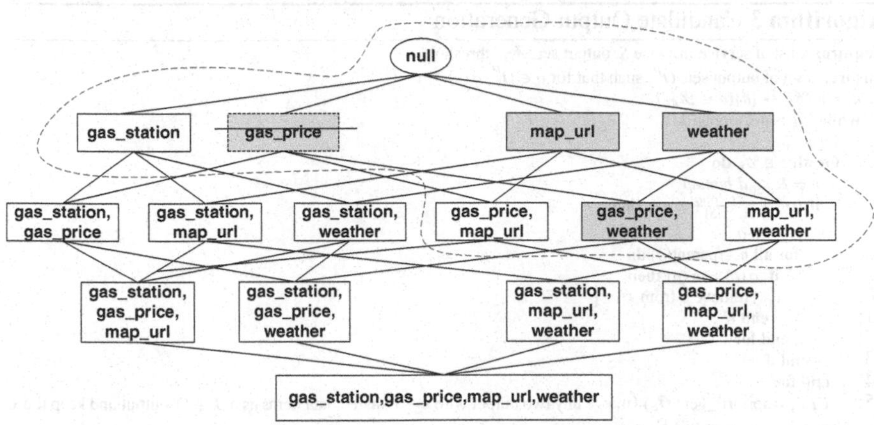

Fig. 11.2 A pruned output lattice using *Apriori* principle ($\tau = 0.3$)

We build a candidate output lattice where a node is a subset of all its child nodes, as shown in Fig. 11.2. The nodes in the lattice will be generated and evaluated in a breadth-first way. We use k-output to represent an output consisting of k data items. As described in Algorithm 3, the process starts with generating and evaluating candidate 1-output set from $\mathscr{D}_{\mathscr{O}}$ and filtering out those whose support ratios are less than the threshold (Line 1). When evaluating the support ratio of a node, we only go through the services that support the current node's parent nodes. We further optimize this process by using a *bitmap* structure to achieve $O(1)$ computational complexity.

An output data item d's occurrence in service outputs is bit encoded. The support ratio of an output can be computed by performing an *bitwise and* operation between the bit codes of all its data items (Line 5–6). In Example 11.3.1, weather is encoded as [11101] and map_url is encoded as [00110]. The bit code of the output, {weather, map_url}, is computed as [00100]. Therefore, the output's support ratio is 0.2. If an output node o has a sufficient support ratio, o will be included in the k-output set (Line 6–7). All the parent nodes of o will then checked whether they have the same support ratio as o. If there is such a parent, p, it can not be associated with an optimal abstract service since p and o share the same group of supporting services and p is a subset of o. All such p will be removed (Line 8–12).

After evaluating all the nodes in $\mathscr{C}_k$, k-output set, $\mathscr{O}_k$ is generated and be used to generate the next candidate output set, $\mathscr{C}_{k+1}$ (Line 15). This step follows the idea of apriori-gen method proposed in [1], i.e., merging two k-output nodes if they have $(k-1)$ shared items. For example, {a, b, c} will be merged with {a, b, d}, but not {a, d, e}. We then filter out those nodes that are impossible to be representative, i.e., one of its parents is not in $\mathscr{O}_k$. If all its parents are in $\mathscr{O}_k$, a $(k+1)$-output node will be generated $\binom{k+1}{2}$ times. We then only keep such nodes (Line 15). After removing the duplicates from $\mathscr{C}_{k+1}$, the algorithm goes to the next iteration if $\mathscr{C}_{k+1}$ is not empty. Let $|O_{max}|$ is the maximum length of data items in a service's output, the algorithm always stops before or on $k = |O_{max}|$. The result will be the union of all $\mathscr{O}_k$ (Line 18).

Algorithm 3 Candidate Output Generation

Require: a list of service instance S, output set $\mathscr{D}_{\mathscr{O}}$, threshold τ
Ensure: a set of output sets O^P, such that for $o \in O^P$, $\sigma(o) \geq \tau$
1: $k = 1$; $\mathscr{C}_k \leftarrow \{d\}(d \in \mathscr{D}_{\mathscr{O}})$
2: **while** $\mathscr{C}_k$ is not empty **do**
3: $\quad \mathscr{O}_k = \phi$
4: $\quad$ **for all** $o \in \mathscr{C}_k$ **do**
5: $\quad\quad r = \&_{d \in o} d.bitmap$
6: $\quad\quad$ **if** $(\sigma(o) = \frac{r.count}{|S|}) > \tau$ **then**
7: $\quad\quad\quad \mathscr{O}_k \leftarrow o$
8: $\quad\quad\quad$ **for all** $p \in$(parent(o)) **do**
9: $\quad\quad\quad\quad$ **if** $\sigma(o) = \sigma(p)$ **then**
10: $\quad\quad\quad\quad\quad$ remove p from $\mathscr{O}_{k-1}$
11: $\quad\quad\quad\quad$ **end if**
12: $\quad\quad\quad$ **end for**
13: $\quad\quad$ **end if**
14: $\quad$ **end for**
15: $\quad C_{k+1}$ = apriori'_gen($\mathscr{O}_k$) {merge any two output with $k-1$ shared data items as a $(k+1)$-output and keep those who are generated $\binom{k+1}{2}$ times}
16: $\quad k = k + 1$
17: **end while**
18: result=$\cup \mathscr{O}_k$

By applying Theorem 11.4.1, the searching space of candidate output set is significantly pruned. As shown in Fig. 11.2, the process has visited only seven out of fifteen nodes in the lattice. Four nodes out of them have a sufficient support ratio, including {gas_price}, {map_url}, {weather}, and {gas_price, weather}. Since `{gas_price}` has the same support ratio as its child node, `{weather, gas_price}`, it is not optimal. The other three nodes are returned.

11.4.2 Matching Input Generation

Once the candidate outputs are returned, the next step is to find each candidate output the *matching* inputs to construct candidate abstract services. Moreover, if an input i matches an output o, all its supersets matches o as well. Therefore an input should *minimally* match a candidate output so that the constructed abstract service is optimal. We define an *minimal matching input* as follows.

Definition 11.4.1 An input i is said to *match* an output o if the abstract service constructed from i and o has a support ratio no less than the threshold. i is *minimum* if it cannot still match o after removing a data item from it.

To find a matching input for an output o, a brute-force approach is to enumerate and evaluate all subsets of $\mathcal{D}_{\mathcal{I}}$. To improve the performance, we use the relationships between different input to filter out the ones that are impossible to match o. By this, we narrow down the searching space. When evaluating an input, we only go through the concrete services that support o and have the potential of supporting the input. By this, we decrease the number of comparison between a candidate input and concrete inputs. The whole process is guided by the following theorem.

Theorem 11.4.2 If an input i does not match an output o, then all of i's subsets must also not match o. Moreover, if a concrete service does not support an input, it must also not support all the input's subsets.

The proof of Theorem 11.4.2 directly follows Definition 11.3.2.

Algorithm 4 Candidate Input Sets Generation

Require: a list of service instance S, an output o, threshold τ
Ensure: a set of input sets $\mathcal{I}$, such that for $i \in \mathcal{I}$, $\sigma(l(i, o)) \geq \tau$

$\mathcal{D}'_{\mathcal{I}} = \cup s.I(s \in o.\hat{S})$
$k = |\mathcal{D}'_{\mathcal{I}}|$;
$\mathcal{C}_k \leftarrow$ node($\mathcal{D}'_{\mathcal{I}}$)
while $\mathcal{C}_k$ is not empty **and** $k > 1$ **do**
  $\mathcal{I}_k = \phi$
  for all $i \in \mathcal{C}_k$ **do**
    $i.count = 0$; $i.\hat{S} = \phi$
    for all $s \in \cap parent(i).\hat{S}$ **do**
      if $i \supseteq s.I$ **then**
        i.count++; $i.\hat{S} \leftarrow s$
      end if
    end for
    if $\frac{i.count}{|S|} > \tau$ **then**
      $\mathcal{I}_k \leftarrow i$
      remove all i's parents from $\mathcal{I}_{k+1}$
    end if
  end for
  $\mathcal{C}_{k-1}$=gen_next_level_input($\mathcal{I}_k$) {Intersect any two inputs with $k-1$ shared data items as a $(k-1)$-output and keep those who are generated $\binom{n-k+1}{2}$ times}
  k=k-1
end while
result=$\cup \mathcal{I}_k$

For each candidate output, we build an input lattice so that a node is a superset of all its child nodes, as shown in Figs. 11.3 and 11.4. The lattice will be traversed in a breadth-first way. We use k-input to represent an input consisting of k data items. As described in Algorithm 4, the process first merges the inputs of all the services that support o and uses the result, $\mathscr{D}'_{\mathscr{I}}$, as the root note of the lattice (Line 1–3). This will greatly decrease the size of the generated lattice without missing a potential matching input, as shown in Figs. 11.3 and 11.4. The searching process starts with generating k-input nodes, where $k = |\mathscr{D}'_{\mathscr{I}}|$. During each iteration, all the nodes in the candidate list, $\mathscr{C}_k$, will be examined by counting the number of o's supporting services that support the input. Based on Theorem 11.4.2, we only check those services that support all the parents of the current node (Line 8–12). For the root node, this step can be skipped since it is supported by all o's supporting services. If the current node matches o, the node will be added to k-input set (Line 13–14). All its parent nodes will be removed from $(k+1)$-input set since they are not minimum (Line 15). For example, in Fig. 11.4, all $\{d\}$'s ancestors are removed.

After evaluating all the nodes in $\mathscr{C}_k$, k-input set, $\mathscr{I}_k$ is generated and will be used to generate the next level input set, $\mathscr{C}_{k-1}$ (Line 18). This step uses the similar idea of apriori'-gen method in Algorithm 3, i.e., only generating the $(k-1)$-inputs that have the potential of matching o. The algorithm then goes to next iteration $k = k - 1$ if $\mathscr{C}_{k-1}$ is not empty. Let $|I_{min}|$ is the minimum length of a service's input, the algorithm always stops before or on $k = |I_{min}|$. The result will be the union of all $\mathscr{I}_k$ (Line 21).

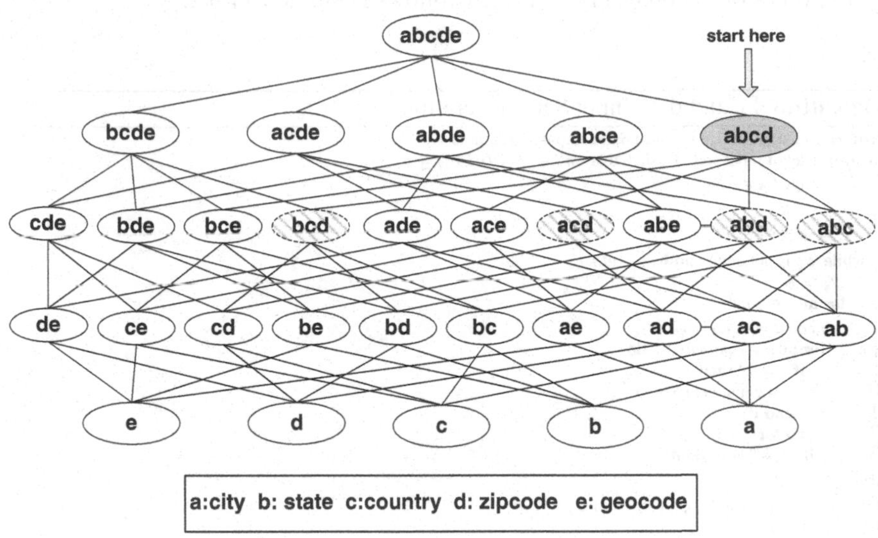

Fig. 11.3 A pruned input lattice using *Apriori* principle ($\tau = 0.3, O = \{weather, gas\_price\}$), the minimum matching input is {a, b, c, d}

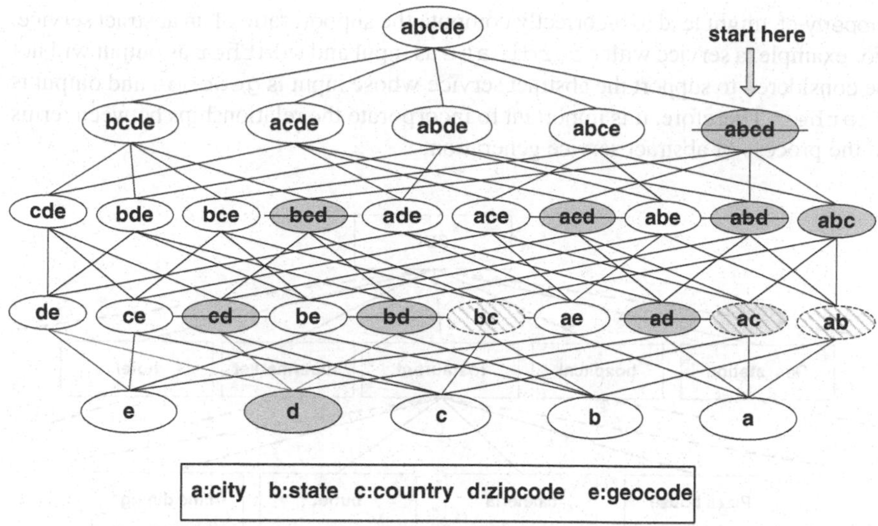

Fig. 11.4 A pruned input lattice using *Apriori* principle ($\tau = 0.3$, $O = \{\text{weather}\}$), the minimum matching inputs are {a, b, c} and {d}

Table 11.2 Optimal abstract services ($\tau = 0.4$)

ID	Input	Output	Support services
l_1	`zipcode, city, state, country`	`weather, gas_price`	s_1, s_2
l_2	`zipcode`	`weather`	s_2, s_5
l_3	`city,state,country`	`weather`	s_1, s_3
l_4	`city, state, country, geocode`	`map_url`	s_3, s_4

Table 11.2 shows the optimal abstract services generated from Example 11.3.1 with the support ratio threshold $\tau = 0.3$.

11.4.3 Semantic-Based Abstract Service Generation

Till now, we present a complete process of generating abstract services from a service community. The process is grounded with WSDL descriptions of web services. It could be suffered from the lack of semantics delivered in the syntactic-level service descriptions. More specifically, WSDL does not capture the relationships between terms so it only supports "keyword-based" scheme. This would lead to the two major accuracy issues of generating abstract services. First, failing to identify and handle synonyms, duplicate abstract services may be generated. For example, {*postalcode*} → {*weather*} and {*zipcode*} → {*weather*} will be considered and evaluated as two different abstract services. Second, failing to identify and handle relationships between two concepts, such as equivalent, subclass-of, and property-of, might lead to incorrectly compute the support ratio of an abstract service. For example, a service with `coordinate` as input and `weather` as output will not be considered to support the abstract service whose input is `geocode` and output is `weather`. Therefore, it is important to incorporate the relationships between terms to the process of abstract service generation.

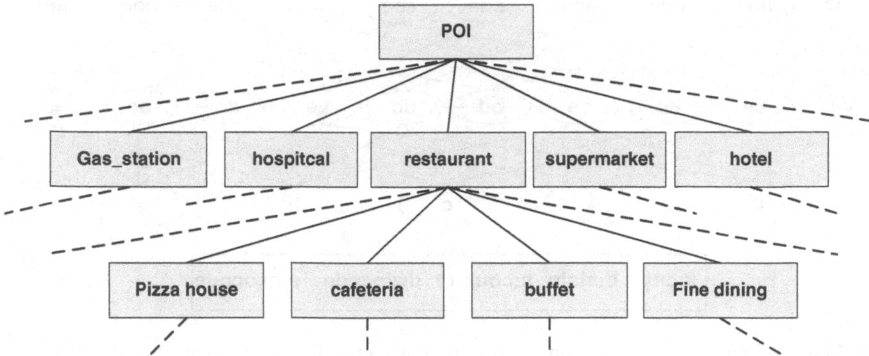

Fig. 11.5 An ontology of concepts in POI domain

Current web technologies, such as OWL, use *ontology* to describe terms and their relationships. Figure 11.5 depicts the snippet of a Point of Interests (referred to as POI) ontology structure. Three types of relationships are defined, including *equivalent*, *subclass of*, and *property of*, whose semantics are in line with the ones in RDF and OWL, including owl:sameAs, rdfs:subClassOf, and rdf:Property relations [3, 7]. A concept c_1 is *equivalent* to another concept c_2 iff $c_1 \sqsubseteq c_2$ and $c_1 \sqsupseteq c_2$. We identify synonyms if they are linked to the same or equivalent concepts. A concept c_1 is a *subclass* of another concept c_2 iff $c_1 \sqsubseteq c_2$, such as `buffet` is a subclass of *restaurant*. A concept c_1 is a *property* of another concept c_2 if c_1 is in c_2's property list. Description Logic (DL) [4] is used for reasoning concept relationships. The relationships between terms can be derived from the relationships between the concepts that they are linked to.

Once mapping the terms in WSDL descriptions to the nodes in an ontology tree, the following steps will be incorporated to the proposed abstract service generation process.

11.4.3.1 Replace Synonyms by a Unified Term

This step is to rewrite the web service WSDL descriptions to reconcile the syntactic difference among synonyms. For each group of synonyms, a unified term will be chosen and replace all other terms in the group. $\mathscr{D}_{\mathscr{I}}$ and $\mathscr{D}_{\mathscr{O}}$ will be regenerated with a smaller size. We use $\mathscr{D}'_{\mathscr{I}}$ and $\mathscr{D}'_{\mathscr{O}}$ to denote the new input data set and output data set.

11.4.3.2 Semantic-Based Support Ratio Calculation

We redefine '∈' for '⊆' and '⊇' in Definition 11.3.2 to take into account of relationships between concepts when computing the supporting ratio, as follows.

Definition 11.4.2 A data d is said to semantically be included in a data set D, i.e., d ∈' D, if either $d \in D$, or there is a data $d' \in D$ that d' is a descendent of d or d is a property f d'.

For example, a concrete service with the output {pizza house, address} can be counted as supporting the candidate output {restaurant, address}, which improve the accuracy of computing support ratio. Furthermore, by adding semantics, we can explore new representative abstract services. To help understand the idea, we revise our running example as follows by adding one service, which is depicted in Table 11.3.

Without incorporating semantics, adding s_6 to the list will not change the list of representative abstract services. When considering term relationships, we find that `gas-station` and `hotel` share a common ascendant, i.e., `POI`. Therefore, a new abstract service with the input {`geocode`} and output {POI} is found to be representative. It is supported by s_4 and s_6 so its support ratio is 0.33, which exceeds τ. Therefore, we change the process of enumerating candidate abstract services based on the following observation:

if a term t_1 is an ascendant of another term t_2, its support ratio is always higher then t_2's.

Therefore, we add these common ascendants to the data sets, $\mathscr{D}'_{\mathscr{O}}$, to fully explore potential candidate output. Two terms may have multiple ascendants. For example, `pizza house` and `buffet` have two ascendants, `restaurant` and POI in Fig. 11.5, we only consider *minimal common ascendant* (MCA), i.e., *restaurant*, to avoid redundancy. That is, for every pair $\{d_1, d_2\}$, where $d_1, d_2 \in \mathscr{D}'_{\mathscr{O}}$, add d to $\mathscr{D}'_{\mathscr{O}}$ if d is their MCA. Following the same line, we identify the *largest common descendants* (LCD) between two terms and add them to $\mathscr{D}'_{\mathscr{I}}$ when evaluating matching input items.

Definition 11.4.3 is also followed when using bitmap structure to encode a candidate output. In the example, after adding {POI} to $\mathscr{D}'_{\mathscr{O}}$, `POI` is encoded as [000101] since it is supported by s_4 and s_6.

Table 11.3 Revised list of member services in weather community

ID	Input	Output
s_1	`city, state, country`	`weather, gas_price`
s_2	`zipcode`	`weather, gas_price`
s_3	`city, state, country`	`weather, map_url`
s_4	`geocode`	`map_url, gas_station`
s_5	`zipcode`	`weather`
s_6	`geocode`	`map_url, hotel`

Table 11.4 Service communities

Community	Number of services
Communication	20
Food	17
Medical	16
Travel	16
Education	32

11.5 Experimental Study

To assess the effectiveness of the proposed abstract service generation algorithms, we performed a set of experiments on a real-world Web service dataset, whose WSDL descriptions are obtained from OWLS-TC, a service retrieval test collection [18]. All experiments were carried out on a Mac Pro with 2.66 GHz Quad-Core processor and 6GB DDR3 memory under Mac OS X operating system. To clearly illuminate the results, we randomly chose a subset of service descriptions from five different domains from the service collection. The randomly selected services are from five different application domains, including medical, communication, food, travel, and education.

We applied the service community construction algorithm we proposed in [16] to generate five different service communities. The community construction algorithm groups together services that provide similar functionalities by calculating the relevance of the operations provided by these services. Table 11.4 shows the service communities and their corresponding number of services. We applied out abstract service generation algorithm to these communities to produce the input/output labels for these services. In what follows, we present the result of output and input label generation. Limited by space, we choose the Medical service community to explain the result. Table 11.5 gives the details of all the services, including their inputs and outputs, in the Medical service community.

11.5.1 Output Label Generation

We applied Algorithm 3 to the Medical service community to generate the output labels. We set τ, the threshold for the support ratio, as 0.1. Table 11.6 reports the output labels for the medical services. The support ratio as well as the supporting services are listed together with each output label. Two labels are generated that include one output and three labels are generated with two outputs. Since the maximum number of outputs of all medical services is two, it is impossible to generate labels with more than two outputs.

The pruning strategy presented in Sect. 11.4 plays a key role to ensure the efficiency of the algorithm. As shown in Table 11.5, all the medical services generated 13 different outputs. Even for a relatively small community as such, a brute-force

Table 11.5 Services in the medical service community

SID	Service	Input	Output
0	get_DIAGNOSTICPROCESS	[_HOSPITAL]	[_DIAGNOSTICPROCESS] , [_TIMEDURATION]
1	get_DIAGNOSTICPROCESS _TIMEDURATION	[_HOSPITAL]	[_DIAGNOSTICPROCESS]
2	get_DIAGNOSTICPROCESS _TIMEINTERVAL	[_HOSPITAL]	[_DIAGNOSTICPROCESS] , [_TIMEINTERVAL]
3	get_DIAGNOSTICPROCESS _TIMEMEASURE	[_HOSPITAL]	[_DIAGNOSTICPROCESS] , [_TIMEMEASURE]
4	get_INTENTIONALPSYCHO-LOGICALPROCESS_ SUMMARY	[_HOSPITAL]	[_SUMMARY], [_INTENTIONALPSYCHOLOGICALPROCESS]
5	get_INVESTIGATING	[_HOSPITAL]	[_INVESTIGATING]
6	get_POSTAL-ADDRESS_INVESTIGATING	[_HOSPITAL]	[_POSTAL-ADDRESS] [_INVESTIGATING]
7	get_PREDICTING	[_HOSPITAL]	[_PREDICTING]
8	get_UPDATEPORTENTME-DICALRECORDS_ACKNOW-LEDGEMENTGETPATIENT-MEDICALRECORDS_AUTH-ORIZEDMEDICALRECORDS	[PATIENTTRANSPORT_PATIENTGPSPOSITION] [UPDATEPATIENTMEDICA-LRECORDS_TREATMENT] [GETPATIENTMEDICALRE-CORDS_PATIENTHEALTH-INSURANCENUMBER] [GETPATIENTMEDICALRECORDS_ AUTHORIZATIONENDTIME] [GETPATIENTMEDICAL-RECORDS_PHYSICIANPASSWORD] [GETPATIENTMEDICALRE-CORDS_PHYSICIANID]	[GETPATIENTMEDICALRE-CORDS_AUTHORIZEDMEDICALRECORDS] [UDPATEPATIENTMEDICAL-RECORDS_ACKNOWLEDGEMENT]

(continued)

Table 11.5 (continued)

SID	Service	Input	Output
9	getINFORMHOSPITAL_ACK-NOWLEDGEMENTRESPONSE	[INFORMHOSPITAL_DIAG-NOSEDSYMPTOMS] [INFORMHOSPITAL_SELEC-TEDHOSPITAL] [INFORMHOSPITAL_PATIE-NTARRIVALDATETIME]	[INFORMHOSPITAL_AKNO-WLEDGEMENTRESPONSE]
10	get_BIOPSY	[_MEDICALCLINIC]	[_BIOPSY]
11	get_DIAGNOSTICPROCESS	[_MEDICALCLINIC]	[_DIAGNOSTICPROCESS]
12	get_DIAGNOSTICPROCESS_TIMEDURATION	[_MEDICALCLINIC]	[_DIAGNOSTICPROCESS] [_TIMEDURATION]
13	get_DIAGNOSTICPROCESS_TIMEINTERVAL	[_MEDICALCLINIC]	[_DIAGNOSTICPROCESS] [_TIMEINTERVAL]
14	get_DIAGNOSTICPROCESS_TIMEMEASURE	[_MEDICALCLINIC]	[_DIAGNOSTICPROCESS] [_TIMEMEASURE]
15	get_INVESTIGATING	[_MEDICALCLINIC]	[_INVESTIGATING]

Table 11.6 Output labels for the medical service community

Output	Support	SID
One-output Labels		
[_DIAGNOSTICPROCESS]	0.5	0, 1, 2, 3, 11, 12, 13, 14
[_INVESTIGATING]	**0.1875**	**5, 6, 15**
Two-output Labels		
[_DIAGNOSTICPROCESS] [_TIMEINTERVAL]	0.125	2, 13
[_DIAGNOSTICPROCESS] [_TIMEMEASURE]	0.125	3, 14
]_DIAGNOSTICPROCESS] [_TIMEDURATION]	0.125	1, 12

approach requires to generate $2^{13} = 8192$ output labels. Algorithm 3 enumerated much less number of labels due to the proposed pruning strategy. Specifically, it first generates 13 output labels for the first level of the output lattice. Among these 13 labels, 8 are pruned as their support ratios are less than $\tau = 0.1$. The remaining outputs include [_DIAGNOSTICPROCESS], [_TIMEINTERVAL], [_INVESTIGATING], [_TIMEMEASURE], and [_TIMEDURATION]. Then, only these outputs will be used to generated labels with two outputs. Hence, $\binom{5}{2} = 10$ labels are generated, among which only the three as shown in Table 11.6 having a support ratio no less than τ are kept. Since no medical service has more than two outputs, the algorithm terminates. Therefore, the algorithm enumerates $10 + 13 = 23$ labels, which is 600 less times than a brute-force approach. This makes Algorithm 3 more efficient and scalable to very large sized service communities.

It is also worth to note that the three two-output labels have the same support ratio as their parent output labels [_TIMEINTERVAL], [_TIMEMEASURE], and [_TIMEDURATION], respectively. Hence, the three parent labels are removed as being dominated by their child output labels.

11.5.2 Input Label Generation

We applied Algorithm 4 to the generated output labels to identify their inputs. The result is a set of representative labels (i.e., input and output) for the service community. Table 11.7 shows the final representative labels for the medical services. We have some interesting observations. First, the final result has six labels whereas the size of the output labels is five. The reason is that the output label [_DIAGNOSTICPROCESS] is separated into two labels in the final result with different inputs. The supporting services for final abstract service [**output**([_DIAGNOSTICPROCESS]), **input**([_HOSPITAL])] consist of services, 0, 1, 2, and 3. Similarly, the supporting services for final abstract service [**output**([_DIAGNOSTICPROCESS]), **input**([_MEDICALCLINIC])] consist of services, 11, 12, 13, and 14.

Table 11.7 Optimal abstract services for the medical service community

Output	Input	Support	SID
One-output Labels			
[_DIAGNOSTICPROCESS]	[_HOSPITAL]	0.25	0, 1, 2, 3
	[_MEDICALCLINIC]	0.25	11, 12, 13, 14
[_INVESTIGATING]	[_HOSPITAL]	**0.125**	**5, 6**
Two-output Labels			
[_DIAGNOSTICPROCESS] [_TIMEINTERVAL]	[_HOSPITAL] [_MEDICALCLINIC]	0.125	2, 13
[_DIAGNOSTICPROCESS] [_TIMEMEASURE]	[_HOSPITAL] [_MEDICALCLINIC]	0.125	3, 14
]_DIAGNOSTICPROCESS] [_TIMEDURATION]	[_HOSPITAL] [_MEDICALCLINIC]	0.125	1, 12

Another interesting observation is that the support ratio of the final abstract service[**output** ([_INVESTIGATING]), **input**([_HOSPITAL])] is 0.125, which is lower than the support ratio of the corresponding output label [_INVESTIGATING]. This is because two inputs can generate [_INVESTIGATING], which includes [_HOSPITAL] and [_MEDICALCLINIC]. However, only one service (i.e., service 15) support final abstract service [**output**([_INVESTIGATING]), **input**([_MEDICALCLINIC])], which makes its support ratio fall below τ. Hence, this abstract service is removed. On the other hand, two services (i.e., 5 and 6) support final abstract service. [**output**([_INVESTIGATING]), **input**([_HOSPITAL])], which achieves a support ratio at $0.125 > \tau$. Therefore, only this abstract service is kept in the final result.

The proposed pruning strategy also ensures the efficiency and scalability of the input label generation algorithm. The analysis is similar to the one in the above section.

11.6 Related Work

This work is closely related to web service functionality-based labeling and web service community learning. In this Section, we discuss some representative related works and differentiate this work from them.

11.6.1 Service Functionality-Based Labeling

In [23], a system, "DeepMiner" is proposed to automatically derive domain ontologies for semantically marking up Web services. It takes a set of web sites that potentially provide Web services in a domain as input and uses machine learning approaches to incrementally learn domain ontologies. DeepMiner observes the query interfaces and data pages of the web sites. A base ontology is first generated from the query interfaces. DeepMiner then grows the ontology by investigating more information from the data pages. SLINK algorithm is used to discover distinctive concepts over multiple interfaces. The work mainly focuses on semantically annotate a web service's input and output. Our work mainly focuses on extract common functional features from a set of web services, forming an abstract service to represent the concrete services.

In [9], a self-organizing based clustering, "taxonomic clustering", is proposed to automatically generate an ontological organization of web services for each of the four dimensions: input, output, precondition, and effect. A set of web services is randomly selected as the sample space. Taxonomic web service clusters are generated over the sample space for each dimension independently. Such a cluster has a hierarchical structure where the relationships of services include ancestor/predecessor, sibling, or mutually disjoint. A sample web service is positioned by finding for the *most specific parents* (MSP) and *least specific children* (LSC). A service query can be answered by finding the MSP in the input cluster space and LSC in the output cluster space. This work clusters web services based on their input, output separately, which lacks an integrated view. Moreover, this work include all services in the hierarchy using exact match. Therefore, it is sensitive to outliers, which introduces difficulties in dealing with the service space with large volume and great diversity. In our work, we label a service community integrating both input and output of member services. We only keep the labels that are supported by a sufficient number of services to ignore outliers.

11.6.2 Web Service Community Learning

In [24], a co-clustering approach is proposed to generate web service communities based on WSDL descriptions. The approach improves the precision and recall of community generation by clustering web services and operations together. It builds up a service matrix and an operation matrix based on their term TF/IDFs. The similarity between a web service and an operation is computed as a dot product of the service vector and the operation vector. A co-occurrence matrix of services and operations is modeled as an undirected bipartite graph which consists a set of service nodes, a set of operation nodes, and the edges between them. Each edge is weighted as the similarity between the corresponding service and operation. Based on the bipartite graph model, the Singular Vector Decomposition (SVD) approach is used to group related web services and operations into the same communities.

The work proposed in [11] applies a clustering algorithm, Quality Threshold (QT), to cluster web services into functionally similar service groups. It measures the similarity between two services by comparing the elements in WSDL documents, including service names, complex data types, messages, portTypes, as well as terms.

In [19], URBE (Uddi Registry By Example) is proposed to intelligently retrieve Web services based on similarity between Web service interfaces. The similarity between two WSDL documents is computed based on the elements and the terms included in the documents. It defines a maximization function to calculate the similarity between the elements in two sets, based on a bipartite graph model. It then uses the maximization function to compute the similarity between names, operations, names, and parts. The work also utilizes Wordnet to solve the syntactic conflicts between synonyms. URBE is then extended to compute similarity between semantically annotated Web service descriptions, i.e., SAWSDL documents.

These approaches proposed in [11, 19, 24] mainly focus on bootstrapping web service communities. None of them takes a further step on labeling a service community by defining abstract services from it. This work is built upon these approaches and propose a heuristic process of generating abstract services in an automatic way.

11.7 Conclusion

We present an automatic approach to generate abstract services for constructing a functionality-based service organizaiton. The process starts with bootstrapping service communities, where similar services are grouped together. Within a service community, abstract services are generated in an automatic way. We model the problem as finding the abstract services whose supporting ratios are no less than a predefined threshold. The process enumerates all possible candidate abstract services and prune them using the threshold. The result is further optimized by filtering out those that can be represented by (i.e., dominate) other candidates. The mapping between an abstract service and the member services are also generated during the process. We apply a set of heuristics to improve the efficiency and scalability of the process. We further improve the accuracy of the generated outcome by incorporating semantics to the process. In the future work, we plan to apply our approach to large scale data sets to extensively evaluate the efficiency.

Acknowledgments This work is supported by a Xerox research grant.

References

1. R. Agrawal and R. Srikant. Fast algorithms for mining association rules in large databases. In *Proceedings of the 20th International Conference on Very Large Data Bases*, VLDB '94, pages 487–499, San Francisco, CA, USA, 1994. Morgan Kaufmann Publishers Inc.
2. S. Akram, A. Bouguettaya, X. Liu, A. Haller, and F. Rosenberg. A change management framework for service oriented enterprises. *IJNGC*, 1(1), 2010.
3. Grigoris Antoniou, Grigoris Antoniou, Grigoris Antoniou, Frank Van Harmelen, and Frank Van Harmelen. Web ontology language: Owl. In *Handbook on Ontologies in Information Systems*, pages 67–92. Springer, 2003.

4. Franz Baader, Diego Calvanese, Deborah L. McGuinness, Daniele Nardi, and Peter F. Patel-Schneider, Eds.. The description logic handbook: theory, implementation, and applications. Cambridge University Press, New York, NY, USA, 2003.
5. A. Bouguettaya, S. Nepal, W. Sherchan, X. Zhou, J. Wu, S. Chen, D. Liu, L. Li, H. Wang, and X. Liu. End-to-end service support for mashups. *IEEE T. Services Computing*, 3(3):250–263, 2010.
6. A. Bouguettaya, S. Nepal, W. Sherchan, X. Zhou, J. Wu, S. Chen, D. Liu, L. Li, H. Wang, and X. Liu. End-to-end service support for mashups. *IEEE Transactions on Services Computing*, 3:250–263, 2010.
7. Dan Brickley and R. V. Guha. Resource description framework (RDF) schema specification 1.0, March 2000.
8. G. Canfora, M.o Di Penta, R. Esposito, and M. Villani. An approach for qos-aware service composition based on genetic algorithms. In *Proceedings of the 2005 conference on Genetic and evolutionary computation*, GECCO '05, pages 1069–1075, 2005.
9. S. Dasgupta, S. Bhat, and Y. Lee. Taxonomic clustering and query matching for efficient service discovery. In *ICWS*, pages 363–370, 2011.
10. S. Dustdar and W. Schreiner. A survey on web services composition. *International Journal of Web and Grid Services*, 1:1–30, August 2005.
11. K. Elgazzar, A. E. Hassan, and P. Martin. Clustering wsdl documents to bootstrap the discovery of web services. In *ICWS 2010*, pages 147–154, 2010.
12. W. Liu and W. Wong. Discovering homogenous service communities through web service clustering. In *Proceedings of the 2008 AAMAS international conference on Service-oriented computing: agents, semantics, and engineering*, SOCASE'08, pages 69–82, Berlin, Heidelberg, 2008. Springer-Verlag.
13. X. Liu and A. Bouguettaya. Managing top-down changes in service oriented enterprises. In *IEEE International Conference on Web Services (ICWS)*, Salt Lake City, Utah, July 2007.
14. X. Liu, A. Bouguettaya, X. Wu, and L. Zhou. Ev-lcs: A system for the evolution of long-term composed services. *IEEE Transactions on Services Computing*, 99(PrePrints), 2012.
15. X. Liu, C. Liu, M. Rege, and A. Bouguettaya. Semantic support for adaptive long term composed services. In *ICWS*, pages 267–274, 2010.
16. X. Liu and H. Liu. Constructing operation-level ontologies for web services. In *ICWS* 2011 (Work-In-Progress), Washington DC, July 2011.
17. X. Liu and H. Liu. An integrated framework for web service ontology development. *International Journal of Next Generation Computing (IJNGC)*, to appear, 2012.
18. OWLS-TC. OWL-S service retrieval test collection. http://projects.semwebcentral.org/projects/owls-tc, 2005
19. P. Plebani and B. Pernici. URBE: Web service retrieval based on similarity evaluation. *IEEE Transactions on Knowledge and Data Engineering*, 21:1629–1642, 2009.
20. A. Salunke, M. Nguyen, X. Liu, and M. Rege. Web service discovery using semi-supervised block value decomposition. In *Proceedings of the IEEE International Conference on Information Reuse and Integration (IRI 2011)*, pages 36–41, 2011.
21. Amit Salunke, Minh Nguyen, Xumin Liu, and Manjeet Rege. Web service discovery using semi-supervised block value decomposition. In *IRI*, pages 36–41. IEEE Systems, Man, and Cybernetics Society, 2011.
22. A. Segev and Q. Z. Sheng. Bootstrapping ontologies for web services. *IEEE Transactions on Services Computing*, 5(1):33–44, 2012.
23. W. Wu, A. Doan, C. Yu, and W. Meng. Bootstrapping domain ontology for semantic web services from source web sites. In *In Proceedings of the VLDB-05 Workshop on Technologies for E-Services*, pages 11–22, 2005.
24. Q. Yu and M. Rege. On service community learning: A co-clustering approach. In *ICWS 2010*, pages 283–290, 2010.

Part II
Web Service Applications and Case Studies

Chapter 12
Exploring Service Networks of Biological Processes on the Web

George Zheng and Athman Bouguettaya

Abstract We propose a service-oriented framework for exploring networks of processes modeled as Web services. In particular, we apply this approach to biological processes that builds upon and extends existing biological representation methodologies. We present our prototype service exploration tool, named PathExplorer, to discover potentially interesting biological pathways linking service models of biological processes. We describe an innovative approach used by PathExplorer to identify useful pathways and its service-based simulation strategy to support predictive analysis.

12.1 Introduction

Worldwide research projects in genomics, epigenomics and proteomics have contributed to the recent explosion of the amount of data describing biological entities and processes at various levels. These processes are often manifested through entities' interactions with one another and the surrounding environment. The interactions themselves are the foundations for many of the pathways that are essential to the well being of our body. A biological pathway is a series of actions among molecules in a cell that leads to a certain product or a change in a cell [3]. Biological pathways have traditionally been discovered manually [37] based on experimental data such as gene expression data from microarrays, protein-protein interaction data from large-scale screening, and pathway data from previous discoveries. As a whole, biological

G. Zheng (✉)
Science Applications International Corporation, McLean, VA, USA
e-mail: george.zheng@saic.com

A. Bouguettaya
School of Computer Science and Information Technology, RMIT University, Melbourne, Australia
e-mail: athman.bouguettaya@rmit.edu.au

A. Bouguettaya et al. (eds.), *Advanced Web Services*,
DOI: 10.1007/978-1-4614-7535-4_12,

pathways form the bridges that link much of the diverse range of biological data into a logical picture of why and how human genes and cells function the way they do. Disturbances and alterations in many of these pathways are expected to be linked to various diseases. Although research projects have begun answering many questions regarding how the human biological machinery works, much of the gold mine of biological information generated from these projects is still unexplored to a large extent: critical links hidden across various lab results are still waiting to be identified; isolated segments of potentially more comprehensive pathways are yet to be linked together. While early exposure of these hidden pathway linkages is expected to deepen our understanding of how diseases come about and help expedite drug discovery for treating them, it is now obvious that the complexity and enormity of information involved in the exposure of such hidden linkages may be too overwhelming for an unaided human mind to comprehend. As a result, such exposure often requires the use of mining tools, which can be used to help identify pathways and conduct predictive pathway analysis, e.g., through simulation. Unfortunately, approaches taken today for representing biological data focus on either pathway identification or pathway simulation, but not both. This consequently makes it difficult to devise effective mining tools.

We propose a service-oriented framework to model and deploy biological entities and their processes as Web services to bridge the gap between the above two representation approaches. Using this strategy, biological processes are modeled as Web service operations and exposed via standard Web service interfaces. An operation may consume some input substance meeting a set of preconditions and then produce some output substance as a result of its invocation. Some of these input and output substances may themselves trigger processes that are known to us and thus can also be modeled and deployed as Web services. Domain ontologies containing definition of various entity types would be used by these Web services when referring to their operation inputs and outputs. This service oriented process modeling and deployment strategy opens up new interesting possibilities. First, like existing natural language processing approaches (e.g., [25, 34, 36, 38]), it allows us to use service mining tools to proactively and systematically sift through Web service description documents in the service registry for automatic discovery of previously hidden pathways. Second, it brings about unprecedented opportunity for validating such pathways right on the Web through direct invocation of involved services. This second capability also makes it possible to carry out simulation-based predictive analysis of interactions involving a large number of entities modeled by these services. When enough details are captured in the service process models, this in-place invocation capability allows for inexpensive and accessible simulations, which are expected to provide predictive results that can be validated *in vitro* and/or *in vivo* experiments. In the presence of a large amount of biological information already made available in many formats from various sources, the adoption of this approach will undoubtedly incur an initial cost. However, this cost is only one-time and will be relatively trivial compared to the on-going development cost of various coupling mechanisms required between applications hosting biological data and limited potential such coupling mechanisms can offer. To demonstrate the feasibility of our service-oriented modeling and mining approach, we have implemented our service mining tool in a prototype called PathExplorer, which can be used to discover potentially interesting biological pathways linking service models of biological processes. We have also implemented a service-oriented simulation strategy in PathExplorer for the purpose of predictive analysis.

We organize the remainder of the paper as follows. Section 12.2 first introduces the concept of service recognition, which forms the basis of much of our mining algorithms. Section 12.3 introduces our service-oriented framework. Section 12.4 describes our strategy for modeling biological processes as Web services. Section 12.5 presents the application of our framework to the service models and results obtained with respect to the discovery and analysis of biological pathways. Section 12.6 discusses related approaches that are currently used to represent biological entities. We conclude the paper in Sect. 12.7.

12.2 Web Service Recognition

Much like molecules in the natural world where they can recognize each other and form bonds in between [19], Web services and operations can also recognize each other through both syntax and semantics. Consequently, potentially interesting and useful service compositions may emerge from bottom up through such mechanism. In the following, we map behaviors/processes manifested by biological substances as operations. Operations from the same substance are grouped together and encapsulated in one service. We identify three relevant types of recognition between Web services and operations, as shown in Fig. 12.1.

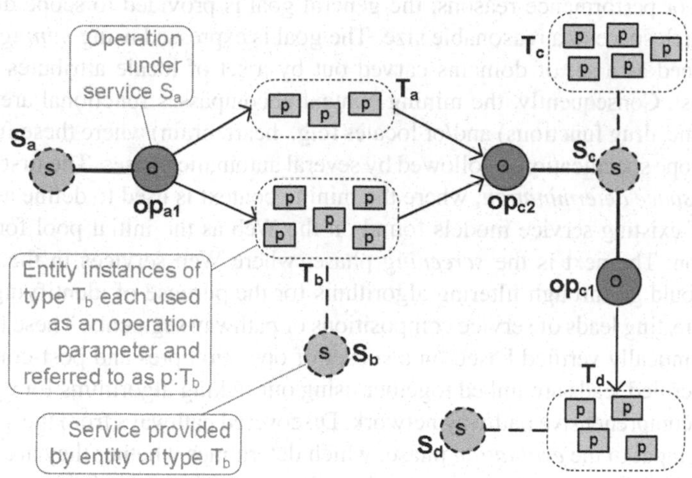

Fig. 12.1 Service/operation recognition mechanisms

Recognition. A *target* operation (e.g., op_{c2}) recognizes a *source* operation (e.g., op_{a1}), if the source operation generates some or all input parameters (e.g., $p : T_a$ and $p : T_b$) of the target operation.

In the following two patterns, we assume that the availability of a service is directly proportionate to the quantity of entity instances that provide the service. Thus, the increase in such quantity tends to promote the service and reduction in such quantity tends to inhibit the service.

Promotion. When an operation (e.g., op_{c1} of S_c) produces a substance (e.g., $p : T_d$ as output parameter of op_{c1}), which in turn manifests a set of behaviors/processes encapsulated in a service (e.g., S_d), we say that the operation promotes the service.

Inhibition. When an operation (e.g., op_{c2} of S_c) consumes a substance (e.g., $p : T_b$ as input parameter of op_{c2}), which in turn manifests a set of behaviors/processes encapsulated in a service (S_b), we say that the operation inhibits the service.

Note that in order for Web services and operations to recognize one another using these mechanisms, additional pre- and post-conditions may also need to be met.

12.3 Service Oriented Framework

Figure 12.2 shows our pathway exploration framework. It starts with *scope specification*, a manual phase involving a domain expert providing a general goal for the subsequent search. Different from traditional service composition approaches where specific search criteria are specified (e.g., compose a travel service that supports flight booking, car rental and hotel reservation), our search is driven by the desire to identify *any* interesting and useful service compositions that may come up in the search process. For performance reasons, the general goal is provided to scope down the initial search space to a reasonable size. The goal is expressed using *mining context* [44], defined as a set of domains carved out by a set of locale attributes of mining interest. Consequently, the mining context encompasses functional areas (e.g., cell enzyme, drug functions) and/or locales (e.g., heart, brain) where these functions reside. Scope specification is followed by several automatic phases. The first of these is *search space determination*, where the mining context is used to define a *focused library* of existing service models found on the Web as the initial pool for further exploration. The next is the *screening* phase, where Web services in the focused library would go through filtering algorithms for the purpose of identifying potentially interesting leads of service compositions or pathway segments. These leads are then semantically verified based on a subset of operation pre- and post-conditions. Finally, verified leads are linked together using our linking algorithms for establishing more comprehensive pathway network. Discovered pathways from the screening phase are input to the *evaluation* phase, which determines whether they are actually useful. In the following subsections, we describe each of these phases in more details.

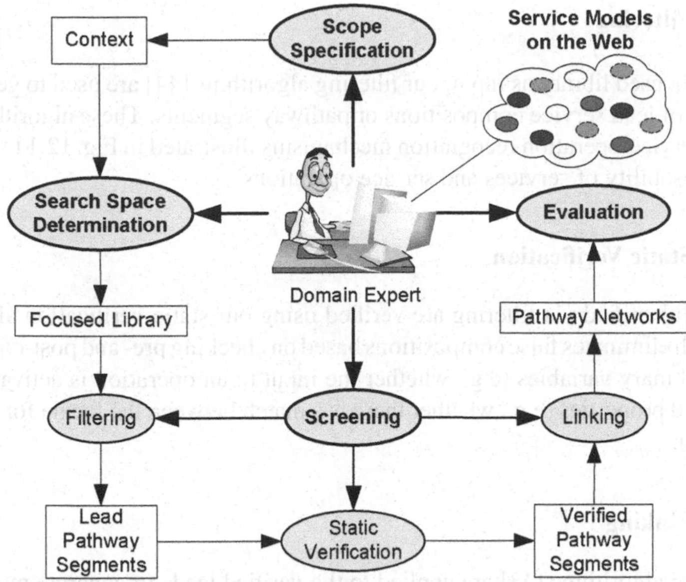

Fig. 12.2 Service-oriented pathway exploration framework

12.3.1 Scope Specification and Search Space Determination

The scope specification phase of our framework involves the specification of a *mining context* that determines a set of ontologies to use for the pathway discovery process [44]. These ontologies are referenced by Web services for defining the types of their operation input and output parameters. Consequently, the mining context defines the coverage of the search space when looking for composable component services for the purpose of pathway discovery. Usually the more specific a context is, the narrower a search space would be. Within the next search space determination phase, a *focused library* is determined based on the mining context [44]. The focused library consists of Web services from the service registry that are involved in the mining context. In other words, Web services contained in the focused library would reference some ontologies covered by the mining context.

12.3.2 Screening

The screening phase is used to identify composable biological service models and ultimately pathway networks. This phase contains three steps: *filtering*, *static verification*, and *linking*. We describe these in the following subsections.

12.3.2.1 Filtering

With the focused library as input, our filtering algorithms [44] are used to generate a collection of lead service compositions or pathway segments. These algorithms rely on three service/operation recognition mechanisms illustrated in Fig. 12.1 to identify the composability of services and service operations.

12.3.2.2 Static Verification

The leads identified via filtering are verified using our static verification algorithm [43], which eliminates false compositions based on checking pre- and post-conditions involving binary variables (e.g., whether the input to an operation is activated) and enumerated properties (e.g., whether there is a match between the locale for an input parameter).

12.3.2.3 Linking

Our linking algorithms [43] are applied to the verified leads to generate more comprehensive composition leads. In [43], we represented pathways discovered in the screening phase using the tree format due to its simplicity in implementation. However, this representation strategy has the inherent difficulty of merging potentially duplicate nodes in the pathways. In [45], we extended our rendering algorithms to represent pathways in GraphML [5], which can then be rendered and automatically arranged using yEd [16].

12.3.3 Evaluation

The goal of the evaluation is to identify interesting pathways out of those discovered from the screening phase. Evaluation is carried out in two steps: *objective evaluation* and *subjective evaluation*, as shown in Fig. 12.3.

12.3.3.1 Objective Evaluation

Objective evaluation aims at automatically highlighting interesting pathway subgraphs within a pathway network based on limited input from the user [46]. This is achieved in three substeps: automatic identification of interesting edges within a pathway network, user selecting interesting nodes for further pursuit based on such identification, and automatic establishment of a connected subgraph within the identified pathway network. The connected subgraph highlights interesting composition flows based on the heuristics that such flows would link user selected nodes with as many interesting edges as possible.

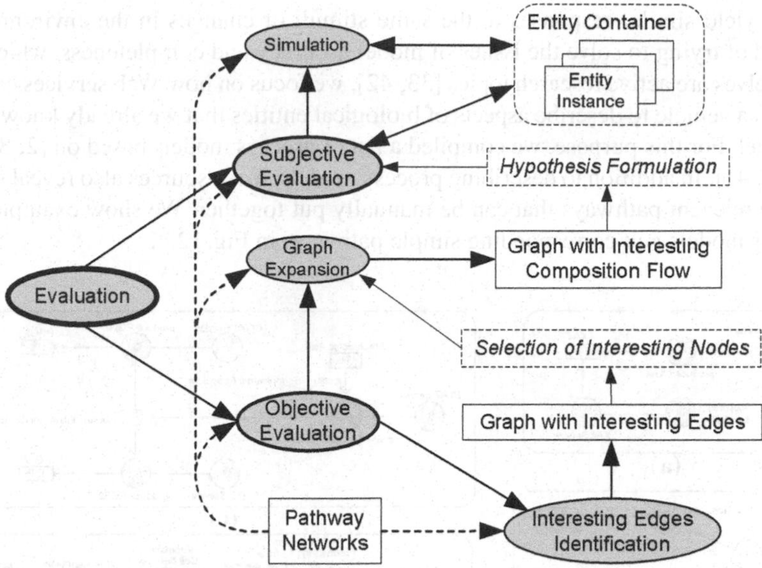

Fig. 12.3 Evaluation of pathway networks

12.3.3.2 Subjective Evaluation

Subjective evaluation aims at identifying useful pathways out of discovered pathway networks. Subjective evaluation contains two distinctive steps, namely *hypothesis formulation* and *simulation*. When presented with a pathway showing highlighted interesting composition flow, the user may attempt to formulate hypothesis based on the indirect relationships that are derived from the way the pathway network is laid out. Such hypothesis can then be tested out using simulation.

We will illustrate the above steps using real examples after we present how we model biological processes as Web services.

12.4 Service Model Development

Our service oriented framework for pathway discovery assumes that biological processes are modeled using Web services. We expect that these models will initially have minimal details about known attributes and processes based on lab discoveries. As our knowledge increases and the modeling techniques continue to mature, the fidelity and completeness of these models will also be increased accordingly. One of the most challenging issues in modeling biological entities is how to approximate the richness of their processes and contextual uncertainties (e.g., varying temperature and fluidity of the surrounding environment) in a way that the models themselves would yield similar responses to the same stimuli or changes in the environment. Instead of trying to solve the issues of model accuracy and completeness, which by themselves are active research topics [33, 42], we focus on how Web services can be used as a vehicle to describe aspects of biological entities that we already know how to model. For this purpose, we compiled a list of process models based on [2, 8, 18, 26, 32, 41]. In addition to describing process models, these sources also reveal some simple relevant pathways that can be manually put together. We show examples of process models and corresponding simple pathways in Fig. 12.4.

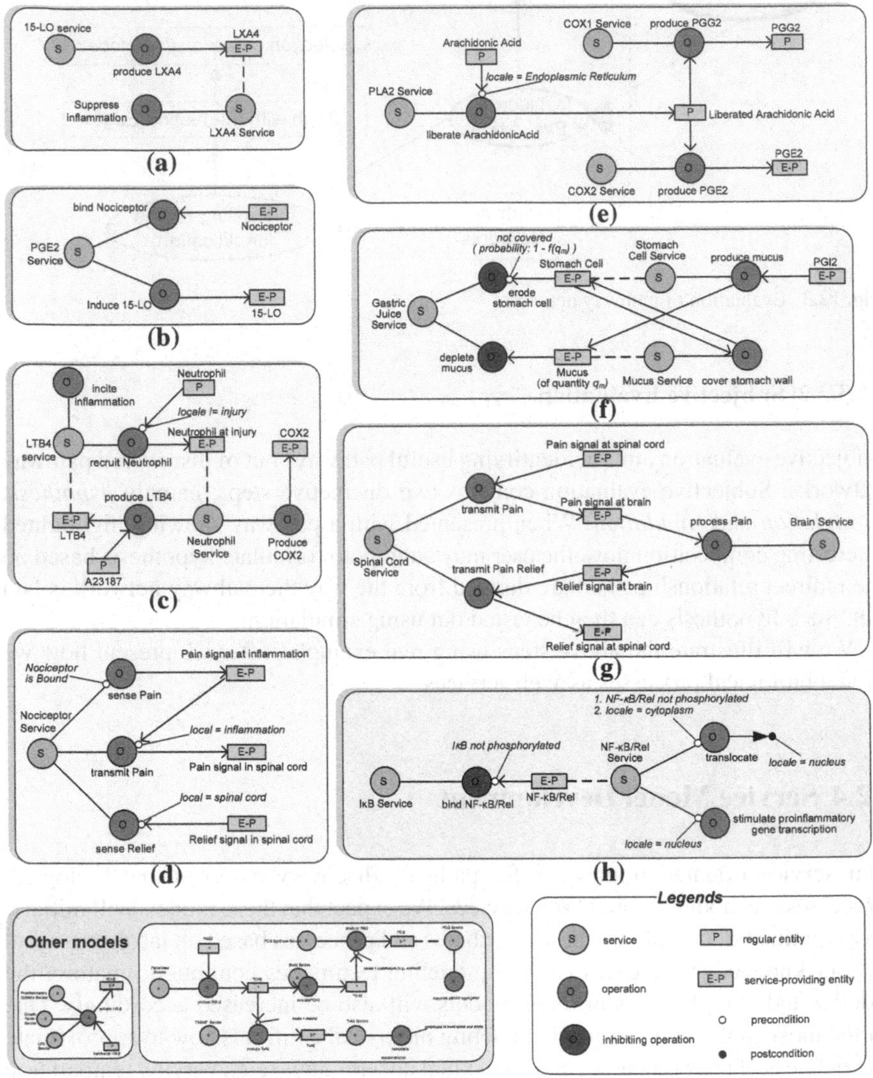

Fig. 12.4 Examples of conceptual process model and simple pathway

Multiple examples of *recognition*, *promotion* and *inhibition* can be found in these models. For example, Fig. 12.4a shows that an enzyme called 15 LO provides an operation called *produce LXA4*, which promotes the service of a lipoxin called LXA4. Figure 12.4c shows that upon injury, LTB4 recruits Neutrophil, promoting its service and hence its operation of producing COX2. Figure 12.4e shows that the service of an enzyme called PLA2 can liberate Arachidonic Acid, which can in turn be used as input to the *produce PGG2* operation of COX1's service or the *produce PGE2* operation of the COX2 service. Figure 12.4f shows that Gastric Juice's service can inhibit the services of both Stomach Cell and Mucus. Examples of pre- and post-conditions can be found in Fig. 12.4h, which shows that when not phosphorylated, a protein called NF-κB/Rel can translocate from cytoplasm to cell nucleus, where it can stimulate proinflammatory gene transcription. NF-κB/Rel's service, however, may be inhibited by the service of another protein called IκB through IκB's *bind NF-κB/Rel* operation. We use process models such as those in Fig. 12.4 as references when developing WSDL and WSML Web services in Sects. 12.4.1 and 12.4.2. We

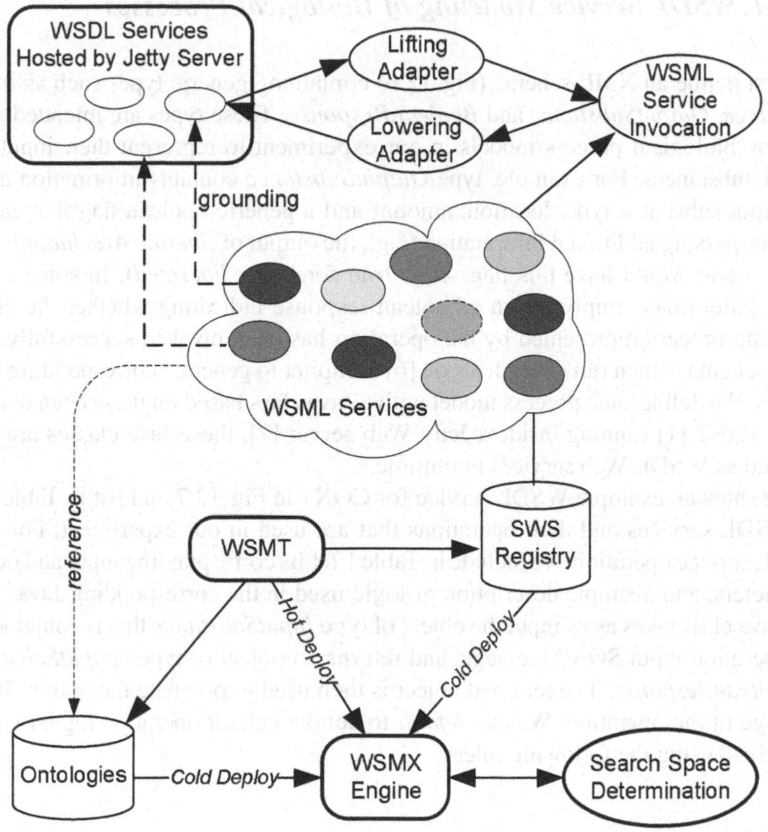

Fig. 12.5 Service model development

also use simple pathways manually constructed as references when we check the correctness of pathways automatically discovered using our mining algorithms.

To model biological processes as real Web services, we first capture the actual process details for each type of biological entity as a WSDL [13] service and deploy these services using a Jetty Web server [7], as shown in the upper left corner of Fig. 12.5. We then expose the semantic interface (i.e., ontological types of operation input and output, pre- and post-conditions) of each WSDL service using Web Service Modeling Language (WSML) [10] as a Semantic Web service. Web Service Modeling Toolkit (WSMT) [12] can be used to define both the ontologies and Semantic Web Services (SWS) in the registry. These can be either cold deployed to the Web Services Modeling eXecution environment (WSMX) [14] during WSMX startup or hot deployed by the WSMT at WSMX runtime. WSML service can be finally invoked during runtime with the help of lowering and lifting adapters. We discuss details involved in these steps in the following subsections.

12.4.1 WSDL Service Modeling of Biological Processes

We first define an XML schema (Fig. 12.6) containing generic types such as *InputSubstance*, *OutputSubstance* and *BooleanResponse*. These types are intended to be used by biological process models in our experiment to represent their input and output substances. For example, type *OutputSubstance* contains information about an output substance type, location, amount and a generic boolean flag that can be used for passing additional information (e.g., the output of *liberate ArachidonicAcid* in Fig. 12.4e would have this flag set to *true* for being *liberated*). In some cases, an operation may simply return a boolean response indicating whether the corresponding process represented by the operation has been invoked successfully. The XML schema is then run through an *xjc* [6] compiler to generate corresponding bean classes. We define each process model with a Java class based on these bean classes. Using Axis2 [1] running inside a Jetty Web server [7], these Java classes are then exposed as WSDL Web services at runtime.

We show an example WSDL service for COX1 in Fig. 12.7 and list in Table 12.1 all WSDL services and their operations that are used in our experiment. For each WSDL service operation, we include in Table 12.1 its corresponding input and output parameters, and a simple description of logic used in the corresponding Java class. The Java class takes as its input the object of type *InputSubstance* that is contained in the operation input SOAP message, and returns an object of type *OutputSubstance* or *BooleanResponse*. The returned object is then used to populate the output SOAP message of the operation. We use *default* to denote default operation logic that can be derived using the following rules:

- If the returned object is of type *OutputSubstance*, then the default logic is to set the *location* and *amount* attributes to be equal to those used in the input object.
- If the return object is of type *BooleanResponse*, then the default logic is to check whether the *type* attribute of the input object is the same as expected. If so, set the *result* attribute of *BooleanResponse* to *true*. Otherwise, set it to *false*.

We list for each operation in the third column of Table 12.1 the expected value for the *type* attribute.

```
<?xml version="1.0"?>
<xsd:schema xmlns:xsd="http://www.w3.org/2001/XMLSchema"
  xmlns="http://servicemining.org/"
  targetNamespace="http://servicemining.org/">

  <xsd:element name="ArachidonicAcid" type="InputSubstance" />

  <xsd:complexType name="InputSubstance">
    <xsd:sequence>
      <xsd:element name="type" type="xsd:string" minOccurs="1"
maxOccurs="1" />
      <xsd:element name="location" type="xsd:string" minOccurs="1"
maxOccurs="1" />
      <xsd:element name="amount" type="xsd:float" minOccurs="1"
maxOccurs="1" />
      <xsd:element name="flag" type="xsd:boolean" minOccurs="1"
maxOccurs="1" />
    </xsd:sequence>
  </xsd:complexType>
  <xsd:complexType name="OutputSubstance">
    <xsd:sequence>
      <xsd:element name="type" type="xsd:string" minOccurs="1"
maxOccurs="1" />
      <xsd:element name="location" type="xsd:string" minOccurs="1"
maxOccurs="1" />
      <xsd:element name="amount" type="xsd:float" minOccurs="1"
maxOccurs="1" />
      <xsd:element name="flag" type="xsd:boolean" minOccurs="1"
maxOccurs="1" />
    </xsd:sequence>
  </xsd:complexType>

  <xsd:complexType name="BooleanResponse">
    <xsd:sequence>
      <xsd:element name="result" type="xsd:boolean" minOccurs="1"
maxOccurs="1" />
    </xsd:sequence>
  </xsd:complexType>

</xsd:schema>
```

Fig. 12.6 Schema for WSDL services

```
<?xml version="1.0" encoding="UTF-8"?><definitions xmlns="http://
schemas.xmlsoap.org/wsdl/" xmlns:tns="http://servicemining.org/"
xmlns:xsd="http://www.w3.org/2001/XMLSchema" xmlns:soap="http://
schemas.xmlsoap.org/wsdl/soap/" targetNamespace="http://
servicemining.org/" name="COX1Service">
  <types>
    <xsd:schema>
      <xsd:import schemaLocation="http://servicemining.org:8001/
COX1?xsd=1" namespace="http://servicemining.org/"></xsd:import>
    </xsd:schema>
  </types>
  <message name="producePGG2">
    <part element="tns:producePGG2" name="parameters"></part>
  </message>
  <message name="producePGG2Response">
    <part element="tns:producePGG2Response" name="parameters"></part>
  </message>
  <portType name="COX1">
    <operation name="producePGG2">
      <input message="tns:producePGG2"></input>
      <output message="tns:producePGG2Response"></output>
    </operation>
  </portType>
  <binding name="COX1PortBinding" type="tns:COX1">
    <soap:binding style="document" transport="http://
schemas.xmlsoap.org/soap/http"></soap:binding>
    <operation name="producePGG2">
      <soap:operation soapAction="producePGG2"></soap:operation>
      <input>
        <soap:body use="literal"></soap:body>
      </input>
      <output>
        <soap:body use="literal"></soap:body>
      </output>
    </operation>
  </binding>
  <service name="COX1Service">
    <port name="COX1Port" binding="tns:COX1PortBinding">
      <soap:address location="http://servicemining.org:8001/COX1"></
soap:address>
    </port>
  </service>
</definitions>
```

Fig. 12.7 WSDL description of COX1 service

12.4.2 WSML Service Wrapping of WSDL Service

Although the internal details of biological processes can be modeled as WSDL Web services, WSDL itself does not provide elaborate mechanism for expressing the pre- and post-conditions of service operations. WSDL also lacks the semantics needed to unambiguously describe data types used by operation input and output messages. We choose WSML [10] among others (e.g., OWL-S [17], WSDL-S [15]) to fill this gap due to the availability of WSMX, which supports the deployment of ontologies and Web services described in WSML. Based on the conceptual service models captured in Fig. 12.4, we categorize biological entities into several ontologies as shown in Fig. 12.8. These include *DrugOntology*, *ProteinOntology*, *NervousSystemOntology*, *FattyAcidOntology* and *CellOntology*. They would all refer to a *CommonOntology* containing generic entity types such as *Substance*, the root concept of all entity types. We use *UnknownSubstance* as a placeholder for process inputs that are not fully described in the literature. We also create a *MiscOntology* capturing definitions of

Table 12.1 Descriptions of WSDL services

Service	Operations	InputSubstance attribute *type*	OutputSubstance attribute *type* or BooleanResponse	Operation logic
_15_LO	*produceLAX4*	UnknownStuff	LXA4	Set output location to inflammation
Aspirin	*acetylateCOX1*	COX1	BooleanResponse	Default
	acetylateCOX2	COX2	BooleanResponse	Default
	bindIKK_beta	IKKBeta	BooleanResponse	Default
Blood	*circulatePGH2*	ProstaglandinH2	ProstaglandinH2	Set output location to endothelium
Brain	*processPain*	Pain	Relief	Set output location to brain
COX1	*producePGG2*	ArachidonicAcid	ProstaglandinG2	Set output location to platelet
COX2	*producePGE2*	ArachidonicAcid	ProstaglandinE2	Default
GastricJuice	*erodeStomachCell*	StomachCell	StomachCell	If input is covered by mucus, flag output as not covered. Otherwise, set the amount of output to 0
	depleteMucus	Mucus	BooleanResponse	Default
IkappaB	*bindNFkappaBRel*	NFkappaBRel	BooleanResponse	Default
IKK_beta	*phosphorylateIkappaB*	IkappaB	BooleanResponse	Default
LPS	*activateIKKBeta*	IKKBeta	IKKBeta	Set output as activated
LTB4	*recruitNeutrophil*	Neutrophil	Neutrophil	Flag locale of output as injured
	inciteInflammation	UnknownStuff	BooleanResponse	Default
LXA4	*suppressInflammation*	UnknownStuff	BooleanResponse	Default
Mucus	*coverStomachWall*	StomachCell	StomachCell	Flag output as covered
Neutrophil	*produceLTB4*	A23187	LTB4	Default
	produceCOX2	UnknownStuff	COX2	Flag output as not acetylated
NFkappaBRel	*translocate*	NFkappaBRel	NFkappaBRel	Set output location to nucleus
	stimulatePGTranscription	NFkappaBRel	BooleanResponse	Default
Nociceptor	*sensePain*	Nociceptor	Pain	Set output location to inflammation
	transmitPain	Pain	Pain	Set output location to spinal cord
	senseRelief	Relief	BooleanResponse	Default

(Continued)

Table 12.1 (Continued)

Service	Operations	InputSubstance attribute *type*	OutputSubstance attribute *type* or BooleanResponse	Operation logic
Peroxidase	*producePGH2*	ProstaglandinG2	ProstaglandinH2	Default
PGE2	*induce15LO*	UnknownStuff	_15_LO	set the amount of output to 10 % of that of input
	bindNociceptor	Nociceptor	Nociceptor	Flag output as bound
PGI2	*suppressPlateletAggregation*	UnknownStuff	BooleanResponse	Default
PGI2Synthase	*producePGI2*	ProstaglandinH2	ProstaglandinI2	Default
PLA2	*liberateArachidonicAcid*	AA	AA	Flag output as liberated
SpinalCord	*transmitPain*	Pain	Pain	Set output location to brain
	transmitPainRelief	Relief	Relief	Set output location to spinal cord
StomachCell	*produceMucus*	ProstaglandinI2	Mucus	Default
TBXAS1	*produceTxA2*	ProstaglandinH2	TxA2	Default
TxA2	*vasoconstriction*	UnknownStuff	BooleanResponse	Default

entity types found in the literature that don't seem to belong to any domain. Table 12.2 shows ontological concepts that have attributes not depicted in Fig. 12.8. Since many of the ontological concepts are *subConceptOf Substance* in *CommonOntology*, they all inherit the *locale* and *quantity* attributes from *Substance*.

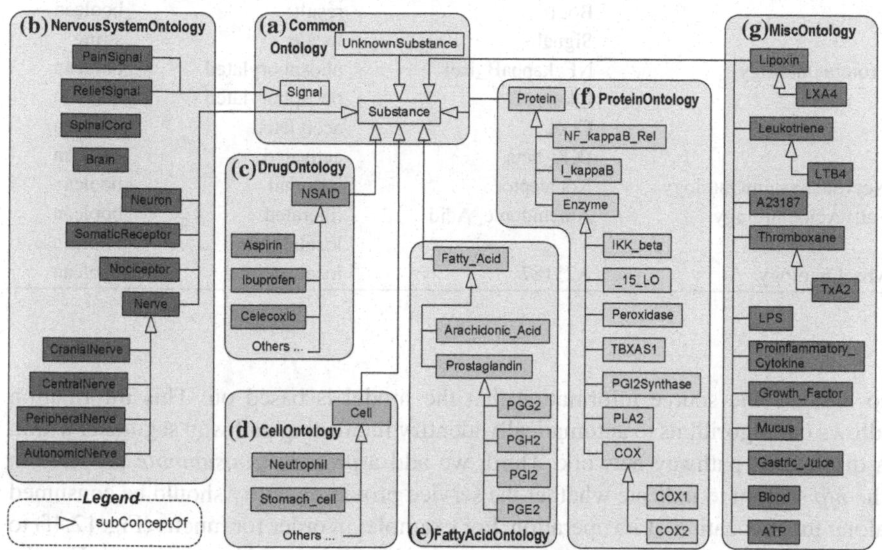

Fig. 12.8 Example ontologies

Using these ontologies, we then wrap the semantic interfaces of existing WSDL services as WSML services. Figure 12.9 gives an example of WSML service named *NF_kappaB_Rel_1_Service*. Note WSML uses the capability section to represent service operation. In addition, preconditions and postconditions are expressed in WSMO axiom logical expressions [11]. For the given example of operation *translocate*, the capability section states for the precondition that the input entity instance named *nfkbr* should be of type *NF_kappaB_Rel*, which is defined in *ProteinOntology*. In addition, *nfkbr*'s attribute *locale* should be equal to *cytoplasm* and its attribute *phosphorylated* should be equal to *false*. Similarly, the postcondition of the same operation states that the *locale* attribute has been changed to *nucleus*. The interface section states that input entity *NF_kappaB_Rel* has grounding with the input parameter of operation *translocate* of the corresponding WSDL service. The output from the WSDL service operation should be mapped to *NF_kappaB_Rel* as defined in the protein ontology.

In the non functional properties (nfp) section (towards the top of Fig. 12.9) of each WSML service, we add a *provider* property to indicate the corresponding ontological type of an entity that can provide the service. We use this information in our mining algorithms later to establish the relationship between a service providing entity and the service it provides. Second, we add a *modelSource* property in the *nfp* section

Table 12.2 Attributes of ontological concepts

Ontology	Concept	Attribute	Attribute type
CommonOntology	Substance	locale	_string
		quantity	_decimal
	UnknownSubstance	localeInjured	_boolean
	Bool	result	_boolean
	Signal	locale	_string
ProteinOntology	NF_kappaB_Rel	phosphorylated	_boolean
	I_kappaB	phosphorylated	_boolean
	COX	acetylated	_boolean
	IKK_beta	activated	_boolean
NervousSystemOntology	Nociceptor	isBound	_boolean
FattyAcidOntology	Arachidonic_Acid	liberated	_boolean
		localeInjured	_boolean
MiscOntology	A23187	localeInjured	_boolean

to indicate the source information that the model is based on. This information allows our algorithms to automatically identify interesting pathway segments within a discovered pathway network. Third, we add a *providerConsumable* property in the *nfp* section to indicate whether the service providing entity should be consumed along the invocation of its operation. For example, in order for mucus (Fig. 12.4f) to cover the wall of the stomach, the mucus itself will have to be consumed. Finally, one of the limitations of WSML is that it allows for the specification of pre- and post-conditions for only an entire service, but not its individual operations. Since different service operations in practice may have different pre- and post-conditions, we have to split services that each originally has multiple operations into several services (e.g., *NF_kappaB_Rel_1_Service* and *NF_kappaB_Rel_2_Service*) so that each new service would contain only one operation. This change allows us to specify different conditions individually for these operations. We use the name of these services to keep track of their relationship and use that information to merge these services towards the end of the screening phase.

Table 12.3 lists the preconditions and postconditions for some of the other WSML services that are used in our experiment. We use *default* listed for some of the pre- and post-conditions to indicate that the corresponding condition simply checks whether the parameter used during invocation is of the prescribed type.

12.4.3 WSML Service Invocation

The WSML service invocation module (top right of Fig. 12.5) is used in two cases. In the first case, after each pair of WSDL and WSML are developed and deployed, we need to verify that the services are themselves free of programming errors. In

```
wsmlVariant _"http://www.wsmo.org/wsml/wsml-syntax/wsml-rule"
namespace { _"http://servicemining.org/SWSs/NF_kappaB_Rel_1_Service#",
    po _"http://servicemining.org/Ontologies/ProteinOntology#",
    dc _"http://purl.org/dc/elements/1.1#",
    wsml _"http://www.wsmo.org/wsml/wsml-syntax#" }

webService NF_kappaB_Rel_1_Service
      nfp
              dc#contributor hasValue "George Zheng"
              _"http://owner" hasValue _"http://ServiceMining"
              _"http://modelSource" hasValue _"http://ServiceMining/h"
              _"http://provider" hasValue _"http://servicemining.org/
Ontologies/ProteinOntology#NF_kappaB_Rel"
              _"http://providerConsumable" hasValue _"http://
servicemining.org/true"
      endnfp

    importsOntology
    {
        po#ProteinOntology
    }

capability translocate

    precondition
        definedBy
            ?nfkbr memberOf NF_kappaB_Rel[
            locale hasValue ?l,
            phosphorylated hasValue ?p] and
            (?l = "cytoplasm") and
            (?p = false).

    postcondition
        definedBy
            ?nfkbr memberOf NF_kappaB_Rel[
            locale hasValue ?l] and
            (?l = "nucleus").

interface NF_kappaB_Rel_1_ServiceInterface

      choreography NF_kappaB_Rel_1_ServiceChoreography
    stateSignature NF_kappaB_Rel_1_ServiceStatesignature

    importsOntology
    {
        po#ProteinOntology
    }

        in
            concept po#NF_kappaB_Rel withGrounding _"http://
servicemining.org:8001/
NFkappaBRel?wsdl#wsdl.interfaceMessageReference(NFkappaBRel/translocate/in0)"

        out
            concept po#NF_kappaB_Rel

    transitionRules NF_kappaB_Rel_1_ServiceTransitionRules
```

For simplicity, we use the index in Fig. 12.4 as indication for modelSource

Fig. 12.9 Semantic interface description in WSML

the second case, we need to simulate the interactions among biological entities and their processes that are involved in a pathway network that has been discovered using our mining algorithms. The invocation of WSML services is realized with the help of both lowering and lifting adapters. For illustration purposes, we show both the input SOAP message packaged by a *lowering adapter* and output SOAP message consumed by a *lifting adapter* in Fig. 12.10 for operation *producePGG2*.

When a WSML service is to be invoked, the lowering adapter is used to parse out attribute values of the input entity and package them into an input SOAP message (Fig. 12.10a) to be used to invoke the corresponding WSDL service. Note in addition to the translation from ontological type *Arachidonic_Acid* to *ArachidonicAcid* for the *type* attribute, the following translations have also taken place in the lowering

Table 12.3 Preconditions and postconditions of WSML services

Service	Capability	Precondition	Postcondition
Aspirin_1_Service	*acetylateCOX1*	?cox1 memberOf COX1[acetylated hasValue ?a] and (?a = false)	Default
Aspirin_2_Service	*acetylateCOX2*	?cox2 memberOf COX2[acetylated hasValue ?a] and (?a = false)	Default
Aspirin_3_Service	*bindIKK_beta*	Default	Default
BrainService	*processPain*	?ps memberOf PainSignal[locale hasValue ?l] and (?l = "brain")	?rs memberOf ReliefSignal[locale hasValue ?l] and (?l = "brain")
COX1Service	*producePGG2*	?aa memberOf Arachidonic_Acid[liberated hasValue ?l] and (?l = true)	Default
COX2Service	*producePGE2*	?aa memberOf Arachidonicr_Acid[liberated hasValue ?l] and (?l = true)	Default
I_kappaBService	*bindNF_kappaB Rel*	?nfkb memberOf NF_kappaB_Rel[phosphorylated hasValue ?p] and (?p = false)	Default
IKK_betaService	*phosphorylateI_kappaB*	?ikb memberOf I_kappaB[phosphorylated hasValue ?p] and (?p = false)	Default
LPSService	*activateIKK_ Beta*	?ikkbeta memberOf IKK_beta[activated hasValue ?a] and (?a = false)	?ikkbeta memberOf IKK_beta [activated hasValue ?a] and (?a = true)
LTB4_1_Service	*recruitNeutrophil*	?neutrophil memberOf Neutrophil [localeInjured hasValue ?l] and (?l = false)	?neutrophil memberOf Neutrophil[locale Injured hasValue ?l] and (?l = true)
LTB4_2_Service	*incite_inflammation*	Default	Default
LXA4Service	*suppressInflammation*	?us memberOf UnknownSubstance[locale hasValue ?l] and (?l = "inflammation")	Default
MucusService	*coverStomachWall*	?sc memberOf Stomach_Cell[coveredByMucus hasValue ?c] and (?c = false)	?sc memberOf Stomach_Cell[coveredBy Mucus hasValue ?c] and (?c = true)
Neutrophil_1_Service	*produceLTB4*	?neutrophil memberOf Neutrophil[localeInjured hasValue ?l] and (?l = true)	Default

(Continued)

Table 12.3 (Continued)

Service	Capability	Precondition	Postcondition
Neutrophil_2_Service	*produceCOX2*	?uks memberOf UnknownSubstance[localeInjured hasValue ?l] and (?l = true)	Default
NF_kappaB_Rel_2_Service	*stimulateProinflammatory GeneTranscription*	?nfkbr memberOf NF_kappaB_Rel[locale hasValue ?l] and (?l = "nucleus")	Default
Nociceptor_1_Service	*sensePain*	?nccpt memberOf Nociceptor[isBound hasValue ?b] and (?b = true)	Default
Nociceptor_2_Service	*transmitPain*	?ps memberOf PainSignal[locale hasValue ?l] and (?l = "inflammation")	?ps memberOf PainSignal[locale hasValue ?l] and (?l = "spinal cord")
Nociceptor_3_Service	*senseRelief*	?ps memberOf ReliefSignal[locale hasValue ?l] and (?l = "spinal cord")	Default
PGE2_1_Service	*induce_15_LO*	Default	Default
PGE2_2_Service	*bindNociceptor*	?nccpt memberOf Nociceptor[isBound hasValue ?b] and (?b = false)	?nccpt memberOf Nociceptor[isBound hasValue ?b] and (?b = true)
PGI2SynthaseService	*producePGI2*	?pgh2 memberOf PGH2[locale hasValue ?l] and (?l = "endothelium")	Default
PLA2Service	*liberateArachidonicAcid*	?aa memberOf Arachidonic_Acid[liberated hasValue ?li, locale hasValue ?lo] and (?li = false) and (?lo = "endoplasmic_reticulum")	?aa memberOf Arachidonic_Acid [liberated hasValue ?l] and (?l = true)
SpinalCord_1_Service	*transmitPain*	?ps memberOf PainSignal[locale hasValue ?l] and (?l = "spinal cord")	?ps memberOf PainSignal[locale hasValue ?l] and (?l = "brain")
SpinalCord_2_ Service	*transmitPainRelief*	?rs memberOf ReliefSignal[locale hasValue ?l] and (?l = "brain")	?rs memberOf ReliefSignal[locale hasValue ?l] and (?l = "spinal cord")
TBXAS1Service	*produceTxA2*	?pgh2 memberOf PGH2[locale hasValue ?l] and (?l = "platelet")	Default

```
<?xml version="1.0" encoding="UTF-8"?>
<SOAP-ENV:Envelope xmlns:SOAP-ENV="http://
schemas.xmlsoap.org/soap/envelope/">
  <SOAP-ENV:Header/>
  <SOAP-ENV:Body>
    <q0:producePGG2 xmlns:q0="http://servicemining.org/">
      <q0:ArachidonicAcid>
        <type>ArachidonicAcid</type>
        <location>endoplasmic_reticulum</location>
        <amount>1.0</amount>
        <flag>true</flag>
      </q0:ArachidonicAcid>
    </q0:producePGG2>
  </SOAP-ENV:Body>
</SOAP-ENV:Envelope>
```


(a) Input


```
<?xml version="1.0" encoding="UTF-8"?>
<soapenv:Envelope xmlns:ns1="http://servicemining.org/"
  xmlns:soapenv="http://schemas.xmlsoap.org/soap/
envelope/" xmlns:xsd="http://www.w3.org/2001/XMLSchema">
  <soapenv:Body>
    <ns1:producePGG2Response>
      <ns1:ProstaglandinG2>
        <type>ProstaglandinG2</type>
        <location>platelet</location>
        <amount>1.0</amount>
        <flag>false</flag>
      </ns1:ProstaglandinG2>
    </ns1:producePGG2Response>
  </soapenv:Body>
</soapenv:Envelope>
```


(b) Output

Fig. 12.10 SOAP messages of COX1 WSDL service operation *producePGG2*: **a** input, **b** output

adapter: *locale* to *location*, *quantity* to *amount*, and *liberated* to *flag*. For simplicity, the lowering adapter expects only one extra attribute of *_boolean* type and converts it to a generic boolean *flag*.

After the WSDL service is invoked, the lifting adapter is used to parse out attribute values from the corresponding output SOAP message (Fig. 12.10b). These values are subsequently used to create an instance of an ontological entity type as specified in an adapter ontology (shown in Fig. 12.11) containing mappings for such conversion. According to this adapter ontology, *ProstaglandinG2* field in the output SOAP message is mapped to concept *PGG2* of *FattyAcidOntology*, *location* is mapped to *locale*, and *amount* is mapped to *quantity* (bottom of Fig. 12.11).

```
...
ontology AdapterOntology

concept xml2wsmlmapping
    instanceMappings impliesType (1 *) _string
    valueMappings impliesType  (1 *) _string
    conceptOutput impliesType  (1 1) _string
    inputMessage impliesType (1 1) _string

instance acetylateCOX2Response memberOf xml2wsmlmapping
    valueMappings hasValue { "//result=result"}
    conceptOutput hasValue "CommonOntology#Bool"
    inputMessage hasValue "//ns1:BOOL"

instance activateIKKBetaResponse memberOf xml2wsmlmapping
    valueMappings hasValue { "//location=locale(_string)",
"//amount=quantity", "//flag=activated"}
    conceptOutput hasValue "ProteinOntology#IKK_beta"
    inputMessage hasValue "//ns1:IKKBeta"

instance bindIKKBetaRelResponse memberOf xml2wsmlmapping
    valueMappings hasValue { "//result=result"}
    conceptOutput hasValue "CommonOntology#Bool"
    inputMessage hasValue "//ns1:BOOL"

instance bindNociceptorResponse memberOf xml2wsmlmapping
    valueMappings hasValue { "//location=locale(_string)",
"//amount=quantity", "//flag=isBound"}
    conceptOutput hasValue "NervousSystemOntology#Nociceptor"
    inputMessage hasValue "//ns1:Nociceptor"

instance bindNFkappaBRelResponse memberOf xml2wsmlmapping
    valueMappings hasValue { "//result=result"}
    conceptOutput hasValue "CommonOntology#Bool"
    inputMessage hasValue "//ns1:BOOL"

instance circulatePGH2Response memberOf xml2wsmlmapping
    valueMappings hasValue { "//location=locale(_string)",
"//amount=quantity"}
    conceptOutput hasValue "FattyAcidOntology#PGH2"
    inputMessage hasValue "//ns1:ProstaglandinH2"
instance coverStomachWallResponse memberOf xml2wsmlmapping
    valueMappings hasValue { "//location=locale(_string)",
"//amount=quantity", "//flag=coveredByMucus"}
    conceptOutput hasValue "CellOntology#Stomach_Cell"
    inputMessage hasValue "//ns1:StomachCell"
...
instance producePGG2Response memberOf xml2wsmlmapping
    valueMappings hasValue { "//location=locale(_string)",
"//amount=quantity"}
    conceptOutput hasValue "FattyAcidOntology#PGG2"
    inputMessage hasValue "//ns1:ProstaglandinG2"
...
```

Fig. 12.11 Adapter ontology for lifting adapter

12.5 Experiment

We have implemented our pathway exploration framework in PathExplorer, which is used in our experiment to discover pathways linking service models of biological processes. We included in the mining context all seven ontologies shown in Fig. 12.8. No locale (e.g., heart, brain) is explicitly specified. Thus, all locales are considered. During the search space determination phase (lower right of Fig. 12.5) in our experiment, PathExplorer is used to interrogate APIs of the WSMX runtime library to find WSML services that refer to each of the seven ontologies. These services are then collected as part of the focused library for later processing.

In Fig. 12.12a, we show pathways discovered using our screening algorithms and then represented in the graph format. For brevity, we display only shortened names for nodes in the graph. We keep the full name containing either the ontological path for entity nodes or the WSML service path for both service and operation nodes in a separate description field, which is not shown in Fig. 12.12a. In addition, for better diagram readability we omit pre- and post-condition details of operation linking edges such as the two forming a loop between operation *coverStomachWall* and entity *Stomach_Cell*.[1] However, we keep track of the pre- and post-conditions in *PathExplorer* as such information along with the ontological entity paths and WSML service paths are needed when we try to invoke these services during simulation. To ensure the correctness of our algorithms, we compared segments within the automatically discovered pathway network with those constructed manually in Fig. 12.4 and found them to be consistent in all cases. For example, if we follow the path starting with *COX2Service* at the bottom left of Fig. 12.12a, we see that *COX2 Service* has an operation called *produce PGE2*, which generates *PGE2*. This is consistent with Fig. 12.4e. Furthermore, *PGE2*'s corresponding service called *PGE2 Service* contains two operations: *bind Nociceptor* and *induce 15-LO*. This is consistent with Fig. 12.4b.

Identification of Interesting Edges—Interesting segments (or edges) of a lead composition network (highlighted in Fig. 12.12a) can be identified based on the outcome of comparing the source indicator of linkages in the pathway graph representing three types of service/operation recognitions as described in Sect. 12.3.2.1. These interesting edges highlight previously hidden linkages between individual services and operations. For example, Fig. 12.12a shows that connections from *produce PGE2* to *PGE2* and from *PGE2* to *PGE2 Service* are not only included as integral parts of the pathway network, but are highlighted as interesting edges as well. Such information is not obviously apparent if we examine a large number of simple pathways that are individually and independently put together in a manual fashion, such as those shown in Fig. 12.4.

Selection of Interesting Nodes—In this step, the user would use interesting edges highlighted in the previous step as visual clues to select nodes of interest to pursue further. For illustration purposes, we assume that the user has selected five such nodes

[1] The precondition along the upper edge states that Stomach_Cell is not covered by Mucus and the postcondition along the lower edge states that Stomach_Cell is covered by Mucus.

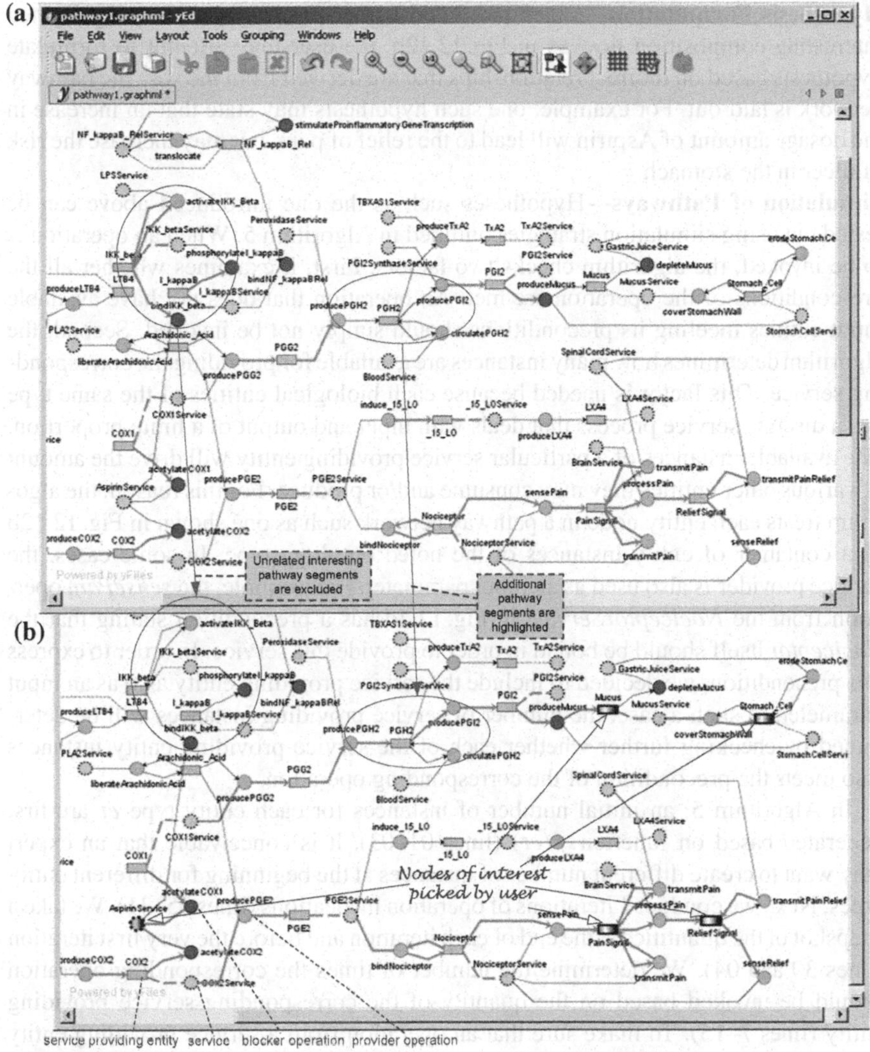

Fig. 12.12 Discovered pathways: **a** interesting pathway segments highlighted, **b** connected pathway subgraph highlighted

as shown in Fig. 12.12b. These are: service node *AspirinService*, parameter node *Mucus*, service providing entity node *Stomach_Cell*, parameter node *PainSignal*, and parameter node *ReliefSignal*.

Graph Expansion—Our graph expansion strategy [46] is applied next to link user identified interesting nodes with as many interesting edges as possible into a connected graph as highlighted in Fig. 12.12b. Using the same process, unrelated interesting pathway segments are excluded and no longer highlighted.

Hypothesis Formulation—When presented with a pathway showing highlighted interesting composition flow as in Fig. 12.12b, the user may attempt to formulate hypothesis based on indirect relationships that are derived from the way the pathway network is laid out. For example, one such hypothesis may state that an increase in the dosage amount of Aspirin will lead to the relief of pain, but may increase the risk of ulcer in the stomach.
Simulation of Pathways—Hypotheses such as the one introduced above can be tested out using simulation strategies outlined in Algorithm 5. When an operation is to be invoked, the algorithm checks two factors. First, it examines whether all the pre-conditions of the operation are met. An operation that does not have available input entities meeting its preconditions should simply not be invoked. Second, the algorithm determines how many instances are available for providing the corresponding service. This factor is needed because each biological entities of the same type has a discrete service process that deals with input and output of a finite proportion. The available instances of a particular service providing entity will drive the amount of various other entities they may consume and/or produce. For this reason, the algorithm treats each entity node in a pathway network such as one shown in Fig. 12.12b as a container of entity instances of the noted ontology type. In some cases, the service provider is also used as an input parameter. For example, the *sensePain* operation from the *NociceptorService* in Fig. 12.4d has a precondition stating that the *Nociceptor* itself should be bound in order to provide this service. In order to express this precondition, we decided to include the service providing entity also as an input parameter. In such a case, the number of service providing instances will be determined by checking further whether each of the service providing entity instances also meets the precondition of the corresponding operation.

In Algorithm 5, an initial number of instances for each entity type *et* are first generated based on function $f(et)$ (lines 01–03). It is conceivable that an expert may want to create different number of instances at the beginning for different entity types. Next, we conduct I iterations of operation invocations (lines 05–31). We take a snapshot of the quantitics at the end of each iteration and before the very first iteration (lines 30 and 04). We determine the number of times the corresponding operation should be invoked based on the quantity of the corresponding service providing entity (lines 7–15). To make sure that an operation from a service providing entity of a small quantity also gets the chance to be invoked, a random number generator is used (line 15). Upon invocation of the operation, we remove the corresponding entity instances consumed in the invocation (lines 19–24). Finally, we add the output parameter instance to the corresponding entity container (lines 25 and 26).

We start by simulating how the quantity of Aspirin affects the erosion of stomach and sensation of pain. The simulation results obtained from each run of *PathExplorer* are compiled into an Excel spreadsheet, which is then used to generate plots such as those in Figs. 12.13 and 12.14, where the horizontal axis represents the iterations of operation invocation and vertical axis represents the quantity of various substance involved. Figure 12.13a–c shows that given a fixed initial quantity of 60 for COX1, the increase in the dosage amount of Aspirin has a negative effect on the stomach, i.e., as the quantity of Aspirin continues to increase from (a) to (c), the severity of stomach

Algorithm 5 Simulation Algorithm

Input: Pathway Network PN, function $f()$ determining initial number of instances for an entity type, total number of iterations I, upper bound S for random number generator *random* with uniform distribution
Output: Statistics *Stats*
Variables: entity type et, entity instance container *Container(et)* of type et, operation op, input entity op_{in}, output entity op_{out} and precondition op_{pre}

```
for all et ∈ PN do
  Container(et) ← create f(et) instances;
end for
Stats ← Tally entity quantities in each container;
for i = 0 to I do
  for all op ∈ PN do
    s ← op.getProviderServce();
    et_parameter ← op.getInputParameter().getEntityType();
    et_provider ← s.getProviderEntityType();
    if et_parameter = et_provider then
      n ← number of entities of type et_provider that match op_pre
    else
      n ← number of entities of type et_parameter
    end if
    n ← n/S + ((random.nextInt(S) < (n modulo S))?1 : 0);
    for j = 0 to n do
      if ∃op_in ∈ Container(et_parameter) : op_in matches op_pre then
        op_out ← invoke(op) with op_in;
        if et_parameter ≠ et_provider ∧ provider is consumable then
          Container(et_provider).remove(0);
        end if
        if et_parameter ≠ et_provider ∨ provider is consumable then
          Container(et_parameter).remove(op_in);
        end if
        et_parameter ← op_out.getEntityType();
        Container(et_parameter).add(op_out);
      end if
    end for
  end for
  Stats ← Tally entity quantities in each container;
end for
```

erosion also increases. For example, when the quantity of Aspirin is 10, there is no sign of stomach erosion. When the quantity of Aspirin increases to 100, the quantity of stomach cell, after 150 iterations of operation invocation, drops to 20, which is one third of the initial quantity. This confirms the user hypothesis that Aspirin has a side effect on the stomach. In addition, we also noticed that given a fixed quantity of Aspirin, the reduction of the initial quantity of *COX1* also has a negative effect on the stomach (Fig. 12.13d–f). When the initial quantity of *COX1* is high, it takes longer for all the *COX1* to get acetylated by Aspirin. As a result, enough *PGG2* and consequently *PGH2* and *PGI2* will be built up to feed into the *produceMucus* operation of the *StomachCellService*. As the initial quantity of *COX1* becomes smaller and while the depletion rate of *Mucus* by *GastricJuiceService* remains the same, less *Mucus* is being produced by the *StomachCellService* as less *PGI2* becomes available.

While Fig. 12.13 clearly illustrates the relationships between Aspirin and *Stomach_Cell*, the relationship between the dosage amount of Aspirin and the sensation of pain is less obvious in the same figure. Except for Fig. 12.13a, which shows some accumulation of *PainSignal* when the quantity of Aspirin is 10, the rest of plots

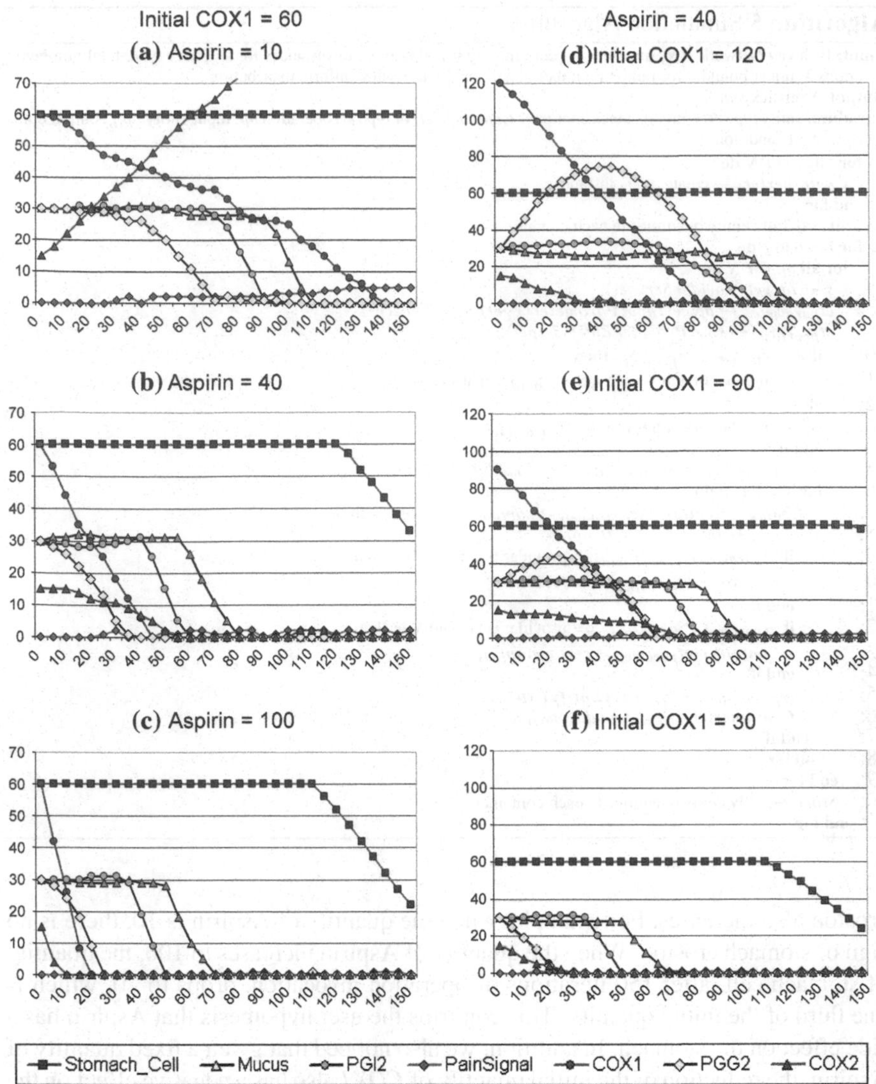

Fig. 12.13 Simulation results with original configurations

show no pattern of such accumulation or the variation thereof. A closer look at the highlighted pathway in Fig. 12.12b reveals that this is actually consistent with the way the simulation is set up. Since *PainSignal* is created and then converted by the *Brain* to *ReliefSignal*, which disappears after it is sensed by *Nociceptor*, this whole path at the bottom actually acts as a 'leaky bucket'. To examine exactly what is going on along that path, we decided to make two changes in the simulation setting. First, we reduced the maximum frequency of invoking the *Brain* service to half that

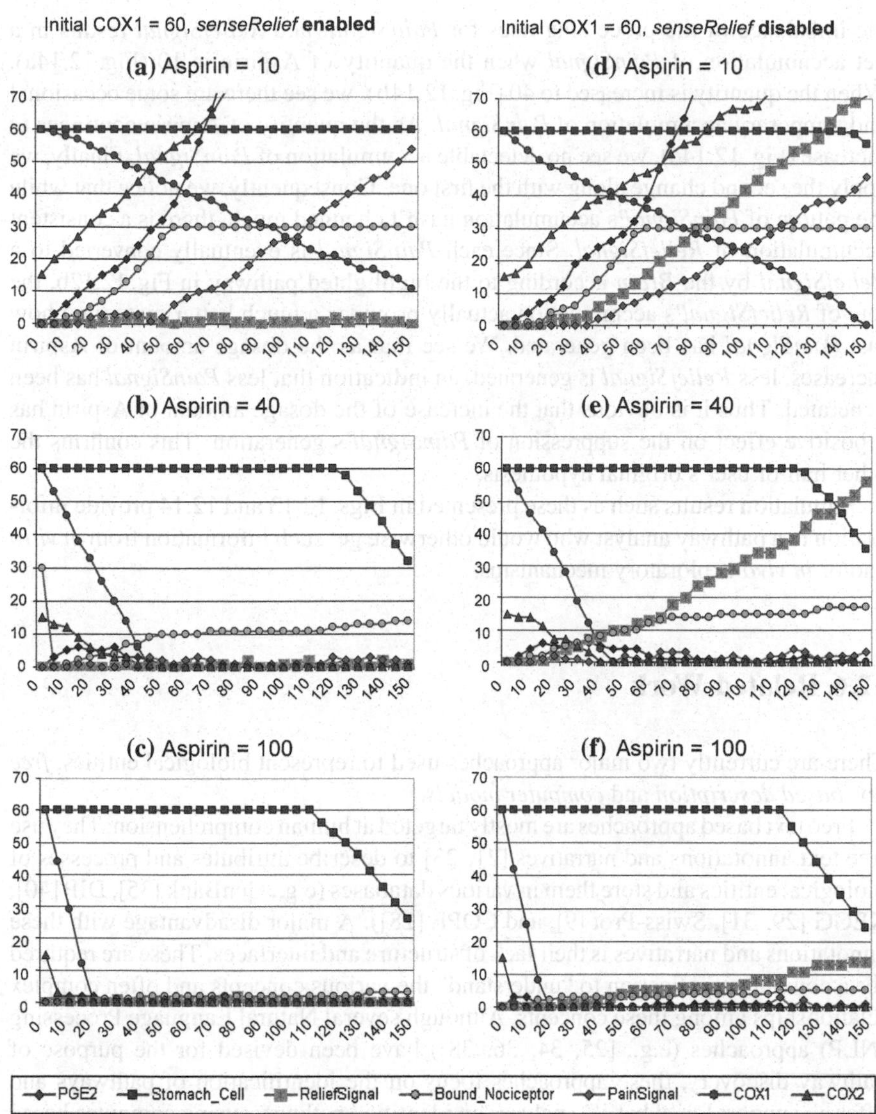

Fig. 12.14 Simulation results with modified configurations

of *Nociceptor*. This creates a potential imbalance between the production rate of *PainSignal* and *ReliefSignal* since the *processPain* operation from the *BrainService* will be consequently invoked less frequently than the *sensePain* operation from the *NociceptorService*. Second, we disabled the *senseRelief* operation of the *NociceptorService*. This essentially stops the leaking of the *ReliefSignal* that are generated as a result of the *PainSignal*. When we apply only the first change to the simulation, the imbalance of the processing rates for *PainSignal* and *ReliefSignal* results in a net accumulation of *PainSignal* when the quantity of Aspirin is 10 (Fig. 12.14a). When the quantity is increased to 40 (Fig. 12.14b), we see there are some occasional and temporary accumulation of *PainSignal*. As the quantity of Aspirin continues to increase (Fig. 12.14c), we see no detectable accumulation of *PainSignal*. Finally, we apply the second change along with the first one. Consequently, we notice that while the pattern of *PainSignal*'s accumulation hasn't changed much, there is a consistent accumulation of *ReliefSignal*. Since each *PainSignal* is eventually converted to a *ReliefSignal* by the *Brain* according to the highlighted pathway in Fig. 12.12b, the rate of *ReliefSignal*'s accumulation actually provides a much better picture on how fast *PainSignal* has been generated. We see that as the dosage amount of Aspirin increases, less *ReliefSignal* is generated, an indication that less *PainSignal* has been generated. Thus it is obvious that the increase of the dosage amount of Aspirin has a positive effect on the suppression of *PainSignal*'s generation. This confirms the other half of user's original hypothesis.

Simulation results such as these presented in Figs. 12.13 and 12.14 provide information to a pathway analyst who would otherwise get such information from *in vitro* and/or *in vivo* exploratory mechanisms.

12.6 Related Work

There are currently two major approaches used to represent biological entities: *free text based description* and *computer models*.

Free text based approaches are mostly targeted at human comprehension. They use free text annotations and narratives [21, 23] to describe attributes and processes of biological entities and store them in various databases (e.g., GenBank [35], DIP [40], KEGG [29, 31], Swiss-Prot [9], and COPE [28]). A major disadvantage with these annotations and narratives is their lack of structure and interfaces. These are required for a computer application to "understand" the various concepts and often complex relationships among these concepts. Although several Natural Language Processing (NLP) approaches (e.g., [25, 34, 36, 38]) have been devised for the purpose of pathway discovery, these approaches focus on the identification of pathways and offer no support for 'what-if' analyses on identified pathways using computer-based simulation.

A computer model of a biological entity can be created based on lab discoveries and hypotheses. Such models can be both expressive (for human comprehension) and structured (for computer consumption) and thus provide a better alternative to free-text annotations. They can be understood by a human through their visual representations and by a computer through their constituent constructs. A major advantage of computer models is their readiness for execution with their inherent processes. By executing processes of computer models in a simulation, we expect to verify the validity of previously identified pathways linking real biological entities as represented by these models. When their processes are expressed as a function of surrounding conditions (e.g., availability of nutrients and energy), computer models would also have the inherent capability of responding to perturbations in these conditions, making it possible to study the effects of the perturbations on the pathways to the extent allowed by these models. Computer models have been pursued in [4, 20, 22, 24, 27, 30, 39]. Unfortunately, these models are often constructed to simulate entities in an isolated local environment (as compared to the Web environment), limited to the study of known pathways (e.g., cell death, growth factor activated kinase in BPS [4]), and lack the ability to facilitate the discovery of new pathways linking models that are independently developed. The service-oriented modeling and exploration approach presented in this paper bridges the gap between the above two representation approaches. It not only allows for the automatic discovery of previously hidden pathways, but more importantly brings about unprecedented opportunity for validating such pathways right on the Web through direct invocation of involved services, making it possible to carry out simulation-based predictive analysis on the Web of interactions involving a large number of entities modeled by these services. Although we have chosen to model biological processes in this paper, we believe our approach is generic enough to be applicable to many other processes in life. These include, among others, knowledge production processes, which can be represented and mined in a similar fashion.

12.7 Conclusion

We described a service-oriented framework for modeling biological processes as Web services. We presented PathExplorer as a tool to discover pathways linking these process models. We also described the simulation-based approach used by PathExplorer to support predictive analysis of discovered pathways. Our framework allows for the interrelationships among various entities involved in pathway networks to be exposed in a more holistic fashion than traditional text-based pathway discovery mechanisms, which inherently lack the simulation capability. In addition, the framework allows such exposure to be achieved via the Web, consequently enabling better sharing of models and simulation results than traditional modeling and simulation approaches.

References

1. Apache axis2/java - next generation web services. http://ws.apache.org/axis2/.
2. Aspirin. http://www3.interscience.wiley.com:8100/legacy/college/boyer/0471661791/cutting_edge/aspirin/aspirin.htm
3. Biological pathways. http://www.genome.gov/27530687.
4. Bps: Biochemical pathway simulator. http://www.brc.dcs.gla.ac.uk/projects/bps/.
5. The graphml file format. http://graphml.graphdrawing.org/.

6. Java architecture for xml binding, binding compiler (xjc). http://java.sun.com/webservices/docs/1.6/jaxb/xjc.html.
7. Jetty. http://www.mortbay.org/.
8. Nf-kappab pathway. http://www.cellsignal.com/reference/pathway/NF_kappaB.html.
9. Uniprotkb/swiss-prot. http://www.ebi.ac.uk/swissprot/.
10. The web service modeling language wsml. http://www.wsmo.org/wsml/wsml-syntax.
11. Web service modeling ontology. http://www.wsmo.org/.
12. The web service modeling toolkit (wsmt). http://sourceforge.net/projects/wsmt.
13. Web services description language (wsdl) 1.1. http://www.w3.org/TR/wsdl.
14. Web services execution environment. http://sourceforge.net/projects/wsmx.
15. Web services semantics - wsdl-s. http://www.w3.org/Submission/WSDL-S/.
16. yed - java graph editor. http://www.yworks.com/en/index.html.
17. Owl-s: Semantic markup for web services. November 2004. http://www.w3.org/Submission/OWL-S/.
18. Sunny Y. Auyang. From experience to design - the science behind aspirin. http://www.creatingtechnology.org/biomed/aspirin.htm.
19. Philip Ball. *Designing the Molecular World - Chemistry at the Frontier*. Princeton University Press, Princeton, New Jersey, 1994.
20. Upinder S. Bhalla and Ravi Iyengar. Emergent properties of networks of biological signaling pathways. *Science*, 283:381 – 387, 1999.
21. Roger Brent and Jehoshua Bruck. Can computers help to explain biology? *Nature*, 440(23):416 – 417, March 2006.
22. Luca Cardelli. Abstract machines of, systems biology. pp. 145–168, 2005.
23. Jacques Cohen. Bioinformatics: An introduction for computer scientists. *ACM Computing Surveys*, 36(2):122 – 158, 2004.
24. H. de Jong and M. Page. Qualitative simulation of large and complex genetic regulatory systems. In *Proceedings of the 14th European Conference on Artificial Intelligence, ECAI*, pages 141–145, Amsterdam, 2000.
25. Daming Yao et al. Pathwayfinder: Paving the way toward automatic pathway extraction. 29:52 – 62, 2004.
26. Craig Freudenrich. How pain works. http://health.howstuffworks.com/pain.htm.
27. Stefan Hoops, Sven Sahle, Ralph Gauges, Christine Lee, Jrgen Pahle, Natalia Simus, Mudita Singhal, Liang Xu, Pedro Mendes, and Ursula Kummer. Copasi - a complex pathway simulator. *Bioinformatics*, 22:3067 – 3074, September 2006.
28. Horst Ibelgaufts. Cope - cytokines online pathfinder encyclopaedia. http://www.copewithcytokines.de/.
29. M. Kanehisa, S. Goto, M. Hattori, K. F. Aoki-Kinoshita, M. Itoh, S. Kawashima, T. Katayama, M. arki, and M. Hirakawa. From genomics to chemical genomics: new developments in kegg. *Nucleic Acids Research*, 34:354 – 357, January 2006.
30. Peter D. Karp, Suzanne Paley, and Pedro Romero. The pathway tools software. *Bioinformatics*, 18:S1 – S8, 2002.
31. Kanehisa Laboratories. Kegg: Kyoto encyclopedia of genes and genomes. http://www.genome.jp/kegg/.
32. Misia Landau. Inflammatory villain turns do-gooder. http://focus.hms.harvard.edu/2001/Aug10_2001/immunology.html.
33. Ben Lehner and Andrew G. Fraser. A first-draft human protein-interaction. Genome Biology, 5(9):R63, August 2004.
34. Daniel M. McDonald, Hsinchun Chen, Hua Su, and Byron B. Marshall. Extracting gene pathway relations using a hybrid grammar: the arizona relation parser. *Bioinformatics*, 20(18):3370 – 3378, July 2004.
35. NCBI. Genbank. http://www.ncbi.nlm.nih.gov/Genbank/.
36. See-Kiong Ng and Marie Wong. Toward routine automatic pathway discovery from on-line scientific text abstracts. volume 10, pages 104–112, 1999.

37. Reactome. Reactome - a curated knowledgebase of biological pathways. http://www.reactome.org/.
38. Carlos Santos, Daniela Eggle, and David J. States. Wnt pathway curation using automated natural language processing: combining statistical methods with partial and full parse for knowledge extraction. *Bioinformatics*, 21(8):1653 – 1658, November 2005.
39. Masaru Tomita, Kenta Hashimoto, Koichi Takahashi, Thomas Simon Shimizu, Yuri Matsuzaki, Fumihiko Miyoshi, K. Saito, S. Tanida, Katsuyuki Yugi, J. C. Venter, and C. A. Hutchison III. E-cell: software environment for whole-cell simulation. *Bioinformatics*, 15(1):72 – 84, 1999.
40. UCLA. Database of interacting proteins. http://dip.doe-mbi.ucla.edu/.
41. Min-Jean Yin, Yumi Yamamto, and Richard B. Gaynor. The anti-inflammatory agents aspirin and salicylate inhibit the activity of IκB kinase-β. *Nature*, 369:77 – 80, November 1998.
42. Jing Yu, V. Anne Smith, Paul P. Wang, Alexander J. Hartemink, and Erich D. Jarvis. Advances to bayesian network inference for generating causal networks from observational biological data. *Bioinformatics*, 20(18):3594 – 3603, 2004.
43. George Zheng and Athman Bouguettaya. Mining web services for pathway discovery. *2007 VLDB Workshop on Data Mining in, Bioinformatics*, September 2007.
44. George Zheng and Athman Bouguettaya. A web service mining framework. In *2007 IEEE International Conference on Web Services (ICWS)*, Salt Lake City, Utah, July 2007.
45. George Zheng and Athman Bouguettaya. Discovering pathways of service oriented biological processes. *The Ninth International Conference on Web information Systems Engineering (WISE 2008)*, September 2008.
46. George Zheng and Athman Bouguettaya. Service-based analysis of biological pathways. *BMC Bioinformatics*, October 2009.

Chapter 13
Automating Tendering Processes with Web Services: A Case Study on Building Construction Tendering in Hong Kong

Dickson K. W. Chiu, Nick L. L. NG, Sau Chan Lai, Matthias Farwick and Patrick C. K. Hung

Abstract With the recent advancements and adoption of Web Service technologies, improvements can be made for tendering processes to solve B2B interoperability and integration problems. In this paper, we detail our Tendering Process Meta-model (TPM) to improve inefficient manual or semi-automated tendering process. We further demonstrate our approach in a case study of the building and construction industries, where contracting authority invite tenderers to submit an estimate of prices, detailing the costs associated with completing a building. In this way, the contracting authority can base their decision on the tender submissions to select the most suitable contractor. Currently in Hong Kong, many of such tendering processes are still mainly manual and paper based. The tenderers need to collect the

---

An extended abstract of this paper was presented at the 2007 GDN meeting [9].

D. K. W. Chiu (✉)
Dickson Computer Systems, 117 Argyle Street, Kowloon, Hong Kong
e-mail: dicksonchiu@ieee.org

D. K. W. Chiu
Department of Computer Science and Engineering, Hong Kong University of Science and Technology, Kowloon, Hong Kong

N. L. L. NG · S. C. Lai
Computer Science and Engineering, Hong Kong University of Science and Technology, Kowloon, Hong Kong
e-mail: nickng@ust.hk

S. C. Lai
e-mail: chanlaze@ust.hk

M. Farwick
Institute of Computer Science, University of Innsbruck, Innsbruck, Austria
e-mail: csae8781@uibk.ac.at

P. C. K. Hung
Faculty of Business and Information Technology, University of Ontario Institute of Technology, Oshawa, Canada
e-mail: patrick.hung@uoit.ca

A. Bouguettaya et al. (eds.), *Advanced Web Services*,
DOI: 10.1007/978-1-4614-7535-4_13,

tender's booklet, price it, and bring it back to the contracting authority's office before the deadline. In this paper, we present a design and implementation of an e-tendering system (ETS) based on our TPM by using Web services for the automation of such tendering processes. We also show how e-tendering reduces the problems that occur in the manual process and helps decision making.

13.1 Introduction

Nowadays, technology plays an important role in many businesses, especially in roles such as automating many business processes and facilitating better decisions. Over the past several years, Web services have been expanded to become more and more popular for application development, mainly due to its competitiveness in applications integration [13]. Web services technology offers a unified platform for both *business-to-business* (B2B) and *business-to-customer* (B2C) communications. The goal of the Web service paradigm is to overcome some of the main drawbacks of traditional business-to-business applications that, in most cases, result in complex, custom, one-off solutions, that are not scalable, and costly and time consuming in the creation.

Unlike traditional client-server models, such as a Web server or webpage system, Web services do not provide the user with a Graphic User Interface (GUI) [4]. Instead, Web services share business logics, data, and processes through a standardized programmatic interface across a network. The applications interface with each other, but not with the users. Application developers can then add the Web service to a GUI (such as a Web page or an executable program) to offer specific functionalities to users. Besides, Web services realize a distributed computing model via application-to-application communication over the Internet. For example, a tendering application could reorder needed items via the Web service interface of a remote inventory application.

Tendering processes are complex. A typical one involves lots of business procedures such as tender specification preparation, tender advertisement, tender aggregation, tender evaluation, tender awarding, contract monitoring, etc. Besides, a tendering system often needs to communicate with other systems such as supply, order, purchase, procurement, and even account to complete its procedures. The total number of stakeholders involved can be numerous, and it is crucial for them to interoperate smoothly with one another through a programmatic interface written in a common language. Ideally, a well-suited tendering process model should be designed making use of this language to provide a framework for all stakeholders to follow strictly, so that application-to-application communication over the Internet in an organized manner becomes possible.

In particular, for the case that we study, the tendering process is a key business process in the construction industry. Many information exchanges occur between the contracting authorities and the contractors. Traditionally in Hong Kong, the tendering process is paper based and involves much manual work, this can cause many problems. Sometimes contractors even have to use handwritten submission, because some contract authorities still require them to fill in their own pre-printed tender booklets. Not only are such processes tedious however, handwriting is also extremely error-prone and sometimes difficult to read. In addition, traffic jams and accidents could cause submission deadlines to be missed.

Based on our earlier experience in developing e-Negotiation support with a meta-modeling approach with Web services [8], we apply and extend it for tendering processes. For the implementation, we are introducing an e-Tendering system (ETS). By using electronic forms as the means of tendering, companies are able to make split second decisions and last minute changes over the Internet. This is desirable because of the rapid changes in the material price (e.g., price of steel, see: http://hypertextbook.com/facts/2005/AlexGizersky.shtml) and labor cost (see: nominal Wage Index by Industry Sector, http://www.info.gov.hk/censtatd/eng/hkstat/fas/wages/w_nom_index.html). Further with the help of Web services, contractors can provide cost estimates automatically. The pricing of each item can automatically be calculated by using information from their corporate databases as well as immediate estimates from subcontractors. In addition, since all the information provided by the contractors is in a digital format, it is very easy for the contracting authority to generate tender evaluation reports in any format. Since different contractors have different systems and databases, a standard platform is required for the information exchange. Web services are therefore suitable because they use standardized XML, and are not tied to any particular operating system or programming language [4].

The rest of this paper is organized as follows. Section 13.2 introduces the background of tendering. Section 13.3 reviews related work. Section 13.4 describes the architecture and implementation for our ETS. Section 13.5 summarizes the paper with the advantage of our approach and our future work direction.

13.2 Tendering and Case Background

In general, no matter paper-based or computerized tendering process, both of them begin with a needs analysis, followed by supplier selection, tender invitation and ending with contract awarding and contract monitoring.

Need Analysis—Before a tender is issued, the responsible Contracting Authority (CA) ensures that it researches the needs of end-users to make sure that the tender specification meets these needs.

Supplier Selection—CA carries out their own supplier search for smaller contracts, or use pre-negotiated contracts of buying groups without tendering. Suppliers may even approach these buying groups separately to enquire about opportunities to supply.

Tender documents—usually called an Invitation to Tender (ITT), which contains the following sections:

a. Introduction—Background information of the tender
b. Tender Conditions—Legal parameters surrounding the tender

c. Specification—Description of the supplies, service or works to be provided
d. Instructions for Tender Submission—Instructions for the bidders
e. Qualitative Tender Response—Qualitative questions designed for bidder
f. Pricing and Delivery Schedule—Quantitative questions designed for bidder
g. Form of Tender—Declaration to be signed by the bidder
h. Certificate of Non-Collusion—Declaration that the bidder has not colluded with any other bidder on the tender
i. Draft of Proposed Contract—A draft of the contract that will be signed by the successful bidder

Tendering Procedures—Tenders are classified as 'Restricted', 'Open,' and 'Negotiated' tenders.

Restricted Tender follows a two-stage process. All suppliers that have expressed an interest are sent a pre-qualifying questionnaire (PQQ). The PQQ is split into a number of sections, such as General Company Details, Technical Resources, Financial Information, and References. Suppliers are short-listed based on the above information, and the ITT are sent to appropriate ones. Normally, suppliers have certain period of time to respond to PQQ and ITT.

Open Tender allows any supplier that expresses an interest in tendering to be sent the ITT documents. The supplier simply sends a letter referring to the contract, expressing an interest, and enclosing the relevant contact details. Normally, suppliers have a certain period of time to respond to the ITT.

Negotiated Tender is carried out only under special circumstances, such as when a project needs to be completed within a short period of time, or there is only one supplier or contractor who has the necessary supplies or expertise, where the technical and other parameters may not be capable of precise definition and where security projects of national importance are involved.

Award of Contract—Most contracts are awarded on a most economically advantageous tender basis. Therefore, the evaluation may not be restricted to just the cost. A contract is awarded after evaluating a range of criteria, which are usually weighted by importance [18]. Criteria other than cost may include quality, experience, proposed payment processes, and timetable for implementation.

Contract Award—The CA signs a contract with the selected supplier based on the "Draft of Proposed Contract" included in the tender documents once the contract has been awarded.

Contract Monitoring—The CA expects to meet with the selected supplier on a regular basis to review its performance and discuss any related issues.

In the Hong Kong construction industry, contracting authorities usually use tendering to find the most suitable contractors to construct buildings or perform building expiations and renovations [14]. A contract between a contracting authority and a contractor is formed when an express or implied offer is made by one party and is accepted without qualification or amendment by the other. The party making the offer is commonly referred to as the offerer and the party accepting is known as the offeree. The tender is an offer. The contracting authority invites tenderers (here, contractors) to submit the details of prices at which goods or services may be bought [3]. The contracting authority then selects one of the tenderers and makes a contract between them. A standard construction project tender should include at a minimum the following information:

- *Form of Tender* is used to ensure that all tenders are received on the same basis and should be simple to compare.
- *Condition of Contract* sets out the rights, responsibilities, and duties of the contractor in the form of numbered clauses.
- *Contract Drawings* are the graphic presentation, and details of works. It normally includes drawings showing the site location(s), the position of the building(s) on the site, floor plans, elevation and sections, as well as details of the components.
- *Specifications* are used to describe the nature, quality and class of materials and workmanship required, and any constraints to the methods of construction. So, the types of specifications used in the construction industry include design specifications, technical specifications, product specifications, and the performance specification.
- *Bill of Quantities* is a schedule of all the items of workers required to complete the project. It is in the form of a systematic and recognized list of items and represents the breakdown of all materials, together with laborers and plans required for the completion of the project. A bill of quantities is essential for contractors to price the work on the same basis in tendering for a construction project so that their total prices are directly comparable.

A tender also contains a *Form of Tender* to ensure that all tenders are received on the same basis and should be simple to compare. There are several types of tendering procedures commonly used in Hong Kong: open competitive tendering, selective competitive tendering, and negotiated tendering are all common forms [14].

- *Open competitive tendering* is a traditional approach in selecting a contractor. Competitive tendering is normally restricted to just price comparison. Any tenderer having interest in the project also can participate in the tendering process.
- *Selective competitive tendering* is almost the same as the open competitive tendering. The main difference between these two tendering methods is that selective tendering involves just a list of potential tenderers to be invited. They normally have good reputation, and the contracting authority has strong confidence in these choices.
- *Negotiated tendering* is different from open and selective competitive tendering. Negotiation is a process of conferring with the intent of finding terms of agreement.

In this paper, we use three typical types of the contracts typically used in Hong Kong construction projects to illustrate the applicability of our approach: Lump sum contracts are based on bill of quantities, Design and build without quantity, and Term contract based on the schedule of rates.

- *Lump sum contract* is a type of contract that is commonly used for building construction projects. The bill of quantities is provided to the tenderers. The tenderers only need to provide the cost data in the tender. With the quantities of the works

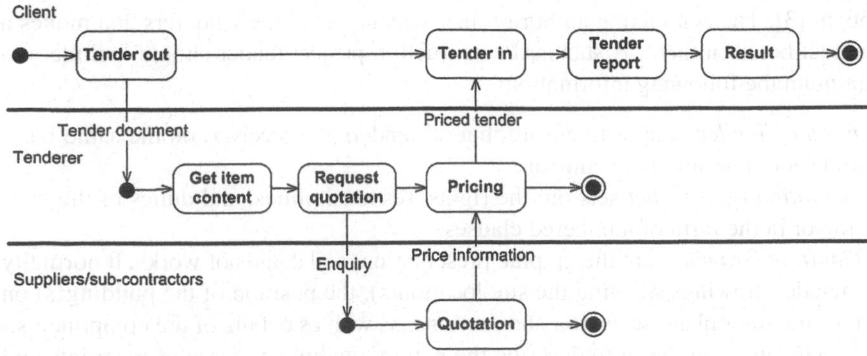

Fig. 13.1 Overview of a typical tendering process for building construction

and the cost data, a lump sum is produced and bound to the contract. The advantage of this type of contract is that the contracting authority can have easy control of the cost.

- *Design and build without quantity* is usually used for building services works or projects that need the contractor to design. The tenderers need to provide both the quantities and the price of the works with their design.
- *Term contract based on schedule of rates* is usually used in projects with an unclear scope, such as maintenance projects. For example, as we do not know how often and how many doors need repair, we need a schedule of rates for such costs. The tenderers also need to provide a trade discount for competition with others contenders.

In a construction project, there are several parties involved in the tendering process: contracting authority, professional teams (like architects, quantity surveyors), contractors, suppliers, sub-contractors. Architects are professional individuals who design the buildings. Quantity surveyors prepare the tender document. The contractors, suppliers, sub-contractors are the parties who actually construct the building. In this paper, the ETS automates some of the tendering process. So we introduce some details of these processes as depicted in Fig. 13.1.

- *Tender-out process*—In this process, based on the architect's design, the quantity surveyor prepares the tender document for the potential tenderers (traditionally the tender booklets and drawings).
- *Pricing process*—According to the information of the tender document (like bill of quantity), tenderers may make a request for further information or price them based on their own suppliers cost data or sub-contractor quotations in accordance with their profit. Tenderers usually have a database to store some frequently used materials cost data such as concrete and reinforcement.
- *Tender-in process*—After pricing a tender, the tenderer needs to submit it to the contracting authority, traditionally in a tender box at the contracting authority's location. Prior to the tender closing time, no one can gain access to the tender

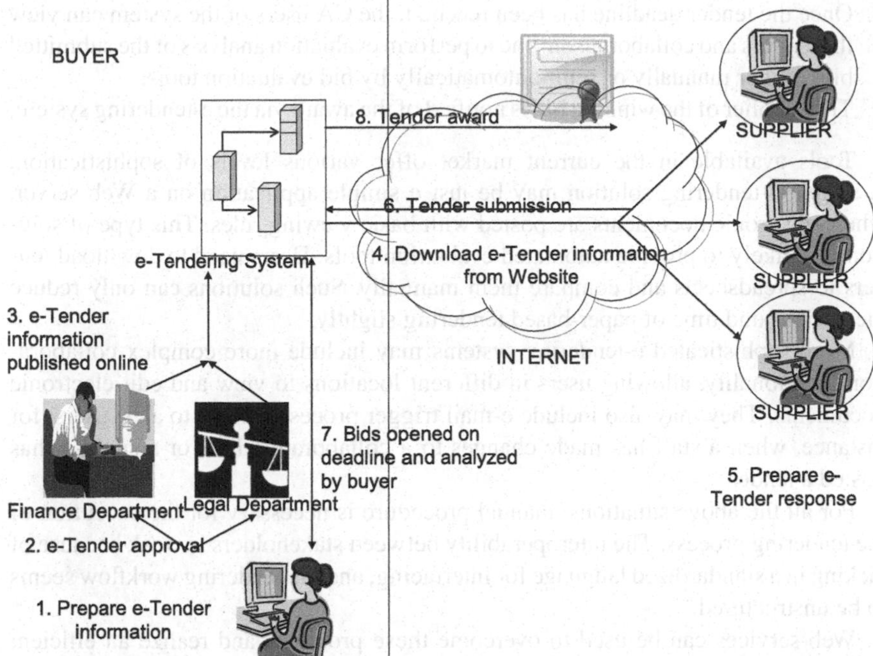

Fig. 13.2 Tradional e-tendering system

box to read the submitted tenders. After the tender closing time, the contracting authority's quantity surveyor will make the tender report of the submitted tenders.

Currently, This simple technical solution based on secure e-mail and electronic document management, involving uploading tender documents on to a secure Website with secure login, authentication, and viewing rules. So, the e-tendering approach is just an electronic paperless one, which is inadequate to solve the problem. Figure 13.2 describes a typical e-tendering System involving the following steps:

1. CA staff creates the electronic ITT document online.
2. ITT document is sent to all the parties involved in the approval process such as finance and legal departments.
3. ITT is published via the e-tendering system and is available online for interested suppliers to look into details.
4. Suppliers access the e-tendering system to view the ITT via the CA's website.
5. Suppliers plan and prepare their bids through their own systems and / or by manual calculations.
6. Suppliers respond to ITT by sending their bids using secure e-mail to the e-tendering system. Security features prohibit access to any of the tender responses until a specified deadline.

7. Once the tender deadline has been reached, the CA users of the system can view the tenders and collaborate on-line to perform evaluation analysis of the submitted bids, either manually or semi-automatically by bid evaluation tools.
8. The supplier of the winning bid is notified of the award via the e-tendering system.

Tools available in the current market offer various levels of sophistication. A simple e-tendering solution may be just a simple application on a Web server, where electronic documents are posted with basic viewing rules. This type of solution is unlikely to provide automated evaluation tools. Users need to download tenders to spreadsheets and compare them manually. Such solutions can only reduce the turn-around time of paper-based tendering slightly.

More sophisticated e-tendering systems may include more complex collaboration functionality, allowing users in different locations to view and edit electronic documents. They may also include e-mail trigger process control to alert users, for instance, when a staff has made changes to a collaborative ITT, or a supplier has posted a tender.

For all the above situations, manual procedure is necessary for the execution of the tendering process. The interoperability between stakeholders is weak because of lacking in a standardized language for interfacing, and the tendering workflow seems to be unstructured.

Web services can be used to overcome these problems and realize an efficient tendering process, reducing the time and cost significantly. Our approach automates most of the tendering process's procedures from preparing the tender specification, tender advertising, tender aggregation, to the evaluation and placing of the contract, under a structured model that has taken all business requirements into account after detailed analysis. Early adopters of Web services include several industries such as logistics businesses that may involve a set of diverse trading partners working closely together on Internet [13]. In summary, the properties of Web services can be summarized as follows:

- Loosely-coupled. Web services can run independently of each other on entirely different implementation platforms and run-time environments.
- Encapsulated. The only visible part of a Web service is the public interface.
- Standard Protocols and Data Formats. The interfaces are based on a set of XML standards.
- Invoked Over Intranet or Internet. Web services can be executed within or outside the firewall.
- Components. The composition of Web services can enable business-to-business transactions or connect the internal systems of separate companies, such as workflow.
- Ontology. Everyone must understand the functionality behind how data values are computed.
- Business Oriented. Web services are not end-user software.

As a result, a pool of Web services can provide an easier integration environment to achieve interoperability, reusability and robustness. Initial Web services-based applications are usually within businesses (behind the firewall or Intranet) in order to gain trust.

The overhead of streamlining the tendering process from start to finish requires more specific tender requirements for automatic evaluation of strict tender criteria and request responses from stakeholders to be in a particular format.

13.3 Related Work

Negotiation is a decision process in which two or more parties make individual decisions and interact with each other for mutual gain [27]. In the USA [24], the federal government spends about USD$200 billion annually buying goods and services from over 300,000 vendors. A typical supermarket chain requires negotiating of over 50,000 product items annually.

In tradition, negotiation is usually associated with contracts as an outcome [23]. A contract is a binding agreement between two or more parties, defining the set of obligations and rewards in a business process. This reduces uncertainty associated with the interactions between the parties. Therefore, contracts are important for attaining interoperability of business processes and enforcing their proper enactment. Negotiation of contracts also involves two or more parties multilaterally bargaining for mutual gain in order to achieve a mutual beneficial agreement, but each of them may have conflicting interests [5]. In many cases, the parties are searching for an integrative agreement. In particular, integrative agreements are likely to contribute to business effectiveness [21]. During negotiation, proposals are sent to the other parties, and a new proposal may be generated after receiving a counter proposal. The process continues until an agreement or a deadlock is reached, or even one or more party quits. During the process, each party needs to determine reactions of the other parties and obtain their responses, while estimating the outcomes that counter-parties would like to achieve. Whereas each party has its own utility function, they tend to be ignorant of the others' values and strategies, especially in a non-cooperative environment. As a result, negotiations may involve high transaction costs and therefore has to be streamlined, especially in high volume e-commerce environments.

The Internet has recently become a global communication platform and allows organizations as well as individuals to communicate among each other, to carry out various commercial activities, and to provide value-added services. Many business activities become automated as electronic transactions, causing both transaction costs and time to be greatly reduced. However, negotiation of contracts is often still performed manually unsupported by computer systems or just by email. The main problem of this is its slowness, which is further complicated by issues of culture, ego, and pride [27].

In general, negotiation processes can be classified into bidding and bargaining. An extended form of negotiation is to have a prelude phase of requirement and candidate identification in processes of request for proposals (RFP) [19]. Bidding is a multilateral distributive negotiation and it is a formal, competitive procurement procedure. Bidding offers to supply goods, works, or services, which are solicited, received, and evaluated. Bidding ends with a contract awarded to the bidder whose offer is the best in terms of price and other factors that should be taken into account in the evaluation of bids. A bargaining process involves two parties. Each party has a single but opposing objective such as paying less or being paid more. This is called divergence of interest between two parties. It means that the parties have incompatible preferences among a set of available options. Both parties have opposing preferences and the parties differ in their utility ordering for at least some of the options under consideration [22]. The difficulty of the bargaining process lies in learning the best value, which the opponent still would accept and in obtaining this value. In general, the degree of divergence of interest is a joint function of the parties' needs and the alternatives under consideration. However, it is usual for the parties to discover new alternatives that reduce or even eliminate a prior divergence of interest [21].

When the supplier has limited amount of goods, the supplier will sell to those to maximize the profit. Auction is an economic mechanism for determining the price of an item and hence the ownership of the item. Auction provides an effective, alternative means of price discovery, especially when sellers do not know the buyers' valuations [2]. This process is usually initiated by the supplier, and may be carried out through its own portal or an external e-Marketplace. Many (potential) buyers will bid at a time. Rothkopf and Park [25] provided an excellent review of different types of auctions (such as English and Dutch auctions) and related issues. On the other hand, tendering can be considered as a reversed situation, where the buyer wants to buy a limited number of items (or services) and the supplier with the lowest bid will win.

When buyers want to buy an item, they have some requirements about the item in mind. Given that, many issues in the requirements could still be left open. In this case, the item cannot be concretely identified. The buyer (usually big companies or government) may then advertise an RFP, aiming to attract suppliers to reply with the details of their solutions, i.e., providing concrete information and properties of the requested item. Upon receiving the proposals, the buyer evaluates them according to the criteria previously defined. The buyer may need to further interact with the candidates for clarifications and extra supporting information. The buyer may shortlist or rank candidates, or the buyer may also directly select a successful candidate. By this time, the buyer will have much more understanding on the details of product/service requirements, their issues, and thus also in the potential contract. Then, the buyer can negotiate further issues and criteria with the candidate(s), or initiate another tendering process. The tendering process is particularly suitable if the contract is complex, with many different issues [17].

Most studies on negotiation focus on interactive bargaining but not on B2B negotiation processes. In order to address this problem, we have conducted a preliminary study on the different requirements for different modes of negotiation [8]. We have been focused on more repeatable and structure negotiation processes in e-commerce (as opposed to political and governmental negotiations). In the paper, based on our experience on RFP, we extend our application to e-Tendering, which usually also involves more complex contracts than auctions [17].

However, manual tendering process is time-consuming and cumbersome, often taking months of turn-around time and numerous manual procedures, which is costly for the stakeholders involved. There are several approaches existing in the marketplace, most of which have been implemented for governmental tendering use. None of the found approaches offer a sophisticated infrastructure of public interfaces like in our approach.

E-NRTY is one of the most well-known approach [10]. It attempts to solve the problem by replacing paper-based tendering processes with electronically facilitated processes based on tendering practices to save turn-around time. However, this solution is incomplete, since the interoperability between stakeholders remains weak, i.e., the ability for two or more systems (or components) to exchange information and to use the information that has been exchanged is still lacking. For instance, the tendering process may not be efficient enough if buyers need to manage the tenders coming in by first storing them in one place, cut and paste data from the electronic tender documents for comparison in a spreadsheet, or make use of semi-automated evaluation tools to carry out the supplier selection process, and then reply selection result. The labor cost is further expensive if 7x24 operation is in need.

ETHICS [20] is a Danish e-tendering system, jointly developed by the Danish National Procurement Agency (SKI), International Business Machinery (IBM), and the software company [inno:vasion] (http://www.innovasion.dk/). The product is operational since 2003 and adheres to the European Union (EU) directives on digital certificates. Its initial development started in 1995. In contrast to our solution, ETHICS relies on the centralized IBM server product Domino/Lotus instead of an open Service-oriented Architecture (SOA). Although the implementers state that they are positioned for the use of SOA, considering the fact that the product was not built with SOA in mind, it means that a large amount of rebuilding would be required to decentralize it for SOA. Additionally the current product does not provide interfaces through which tenderers can use to integrate with their own computing environment.

Homann et al. [16] describe the technological and legal issues concerning security and trust in e-tendering systems. The technical report focuses on the EU public sector and especially on the qualified signatures prescribed by EU law for such transactions. This report gives an extensive comparison of existing e-tendering solutions in the public sector of which no system offers public interfaces like in our proposed solution. Specifically the article states: "If buyers and suppliers use or want to use e-Procurement solutions integrated within their (complete) work processes, e.g., at a hospital, it is clear that such a solution is very individual and depends on local circumstances. Therefore, the market of products for (public) e-Procurement solutions includes services for building up individual but completely new and needed e-Procurement solutions with integrated support for public e-Bidding as well as extending existing solutions for public e-Bidding support" [16]. This underlines the need for flexible SOA B2B implementations like our proposed architecture. The technical report expands on the German governmental e-tendering system eVergabe (see: http://www.evergabe-online.de/?selectedLanguage=en), which makes use of dedicated card readers to enable qualified signatures. Also due to legislation, the 4-eyes principle is enforced to open a tender process and to open the tender documents. In eVergabe the institution and the supplier are both clients to the Internet based bidding platform. Each role in the process runs different client software provided by eVergabe.

A similar study carried out by Betts et al. [1] outlines the security requirements of e-tendering systems. The authors also propose a distributed key and timestamp architecture, which allows suppliers and tenderers to receive keys and timestamps from trusted third parties. Although the article refers to the key and timestamp distribution mechanism as "services," the actual technology in favor has not been discussed, leaving it open whether a Web Service based SOA could be used.

As already mentioned, most implementations and publications focus on the public sector. One exception is the work of Singh and Thomson [26], who describe different e-Procurement models for business to business integration in the Australian context. These models are the buyer model which applies when there exist few buyers and many sellers, the marketplace model which applies when there are many buyers and many sellers, the long term relationship model which is relevant when there is a high degree of planning in the transaction involved, and the seller model that should be implemented when there are few sellers and many buyers. Again, all these approaches foresee a centralized platform to perform the integration without any public interfaces exposed for the integration with the internal information systems of each party.

13.4 Tendering Process Model

In this section, we introduce a model to cover different tendering procedures (open, restricted, negotiated), its architecture, model, and implementation with Web services. We illustrate our TPM with four typical kinds of tendering processes: Request To Participate (RTP), Invitation To Tender (ITT), Tender Submission, and Tender Award Notification. The tendering process can be classified into business procedures as shown in Fig. 13.3.

The tendering phase covers the preparation of an offer by a supplier in response to a call for competition, as well as its submission to and receipt by the CA. The awarding phase begins with the opening of tenders. After evaluating the tenders, a winning tender is selected and an award notice is published through the appropriate services. Suppliers are informed of the result of the selection. This model describes three of the award procedures: open, restricted, and competitive dialogue. The highlighted ones in the diagram are described with UML sequence diagrams afterwards.

Four typical tendering procedure meta-models are presented in the Unified Modeling Language (UML), which is a modeling language for visualizing, specifying, constructing, and documenting the artifacts of a software-intensive systems. UML offers a standard way to write a system's blueprints, including conceptual things such as business processes and system functions, as well as concrete things such as programming language statements, database schemas, and reusable software components. Note that UML standardizes only the notation, leaving software engineers the freedom to adopt their own software development process.

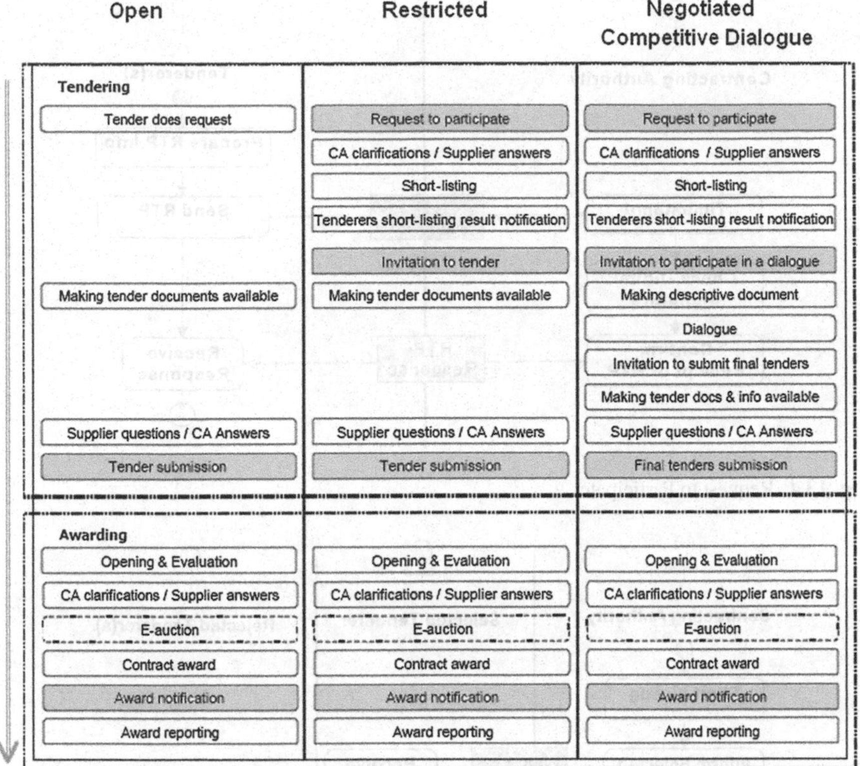

Fig. 13.3 Tendering business processes

13.4.1 Request To Participate

Figuer 13.4 presents a meta-model of RTP in UML. In response to the corresponding contract notice, suppliers (or bidders) may request to participate by sending the required information (legal, economic, financial, and technical information) to the CA. The request is duly signed and sent to the CA. The RTP is received by the tendering platform or directly by the CA, which time-stamps it, and checks the reception date against the deadline defined in the contract notice. The supplier is notified whether its RTP is accepted.

To illustrate the implementation, the following XML business documents (SOAP messages) are designed for the RTP Web service:

Message	Description
Request to participate	Sent by a supplier to the CA to request participation. Contains all required information
RTP response	Sent by the CA to a supplier in response to a previous request to participate to acknowledge receipt of RTP

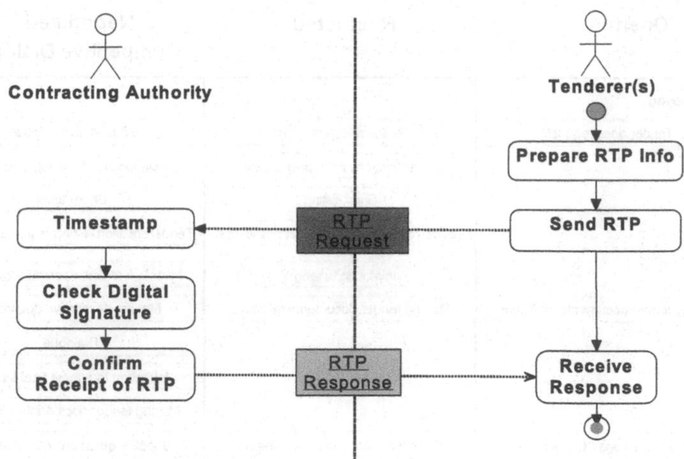

Fig. 13.4 Request to Participate

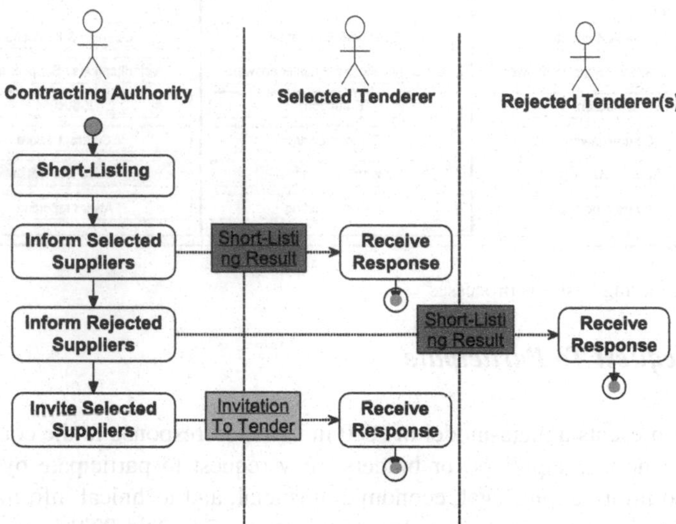

Fig. 13.5 Invitation to tender

13.4.2 Invitation To Tender

Figure 13.5 presents a meta-model of ITT in UML. The CA invites some or all pre-selected suppliers to tender. This applies also in the case of a reopening of competition between several suppliers. When using a tendering platform, the CA uploads the contract documents and makes them available to the suppliers it has invited to participate or tender. The following XML business documents (SOAP messages) are designed for the ITT Web service:

Message	Description
Short-listing result	Notification of rejected suppliers by the CA of the result of the short-listing process
Invitation to tender	Sent by the CA to a supplier in order to invite it to submit a tender, after a previous request to participate

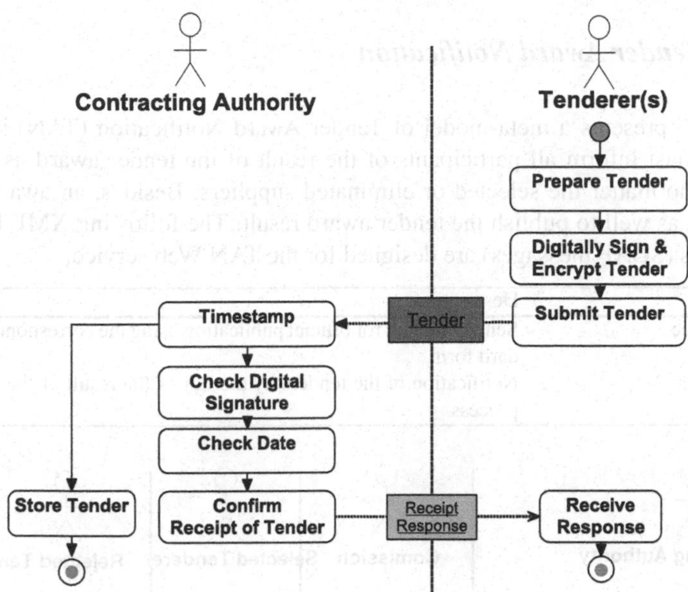

Fig. 13.6 Tender submission

13.4.3 Tender Submission

Figure 13.6 presents a meta-model of Tender Submission (TS) in UML. To submit the tender electronically, the supplier prepares its tender and then sends it to the tendering platform. The supplier may sign and encrypt it before uploading it. However, verification and evaluation of safety requirements (i.e., time stamping, signature features, etc.) constitute a separate process. Its sequencing depends on the type of security technology used (such as the Public Key Infrastructure). Moreover, time stamping and use of the digital signature may involve interactions with third parties. These are mainly exchanged at the software or hardware level and are not considered in our model and therefore, do not appear in the schema below. The submission date of the tender may be checked against the deadline defined in the contract notice. The tendering platform stores all submitted tenders in a secure vault. It issues a reception response to acknowledge receipt of the submitted tender. The following XML business documents (SOAP messages) are designed for the TS Web service:

Message	Description
Tender	Offer sent by the supplier to the CA. A tender may take the form of an electronic catalogue
Reception response	Sent by the CA to a supplier in response to a tender submitted. It acknowledges the receipt of the tender submitted

13.4.4 Tender Award Notification

Figure 13.7 presents a meta-model of Tender Award Notification (TAN) in UML. The CA must inform all participants of the result of the tender award as soon as possible, no matter the selected or eliminated suppliers. Besides, an award notice is sent out as well to publish the tender award result. The following XML business documents (SOAP messages) are designed for the TAN Web service:

Message	Description
Award notice	Sent by the CA for official publication using the corresponding standard form
Award result	Notification of the tenders by the CA of the result of the awarding process

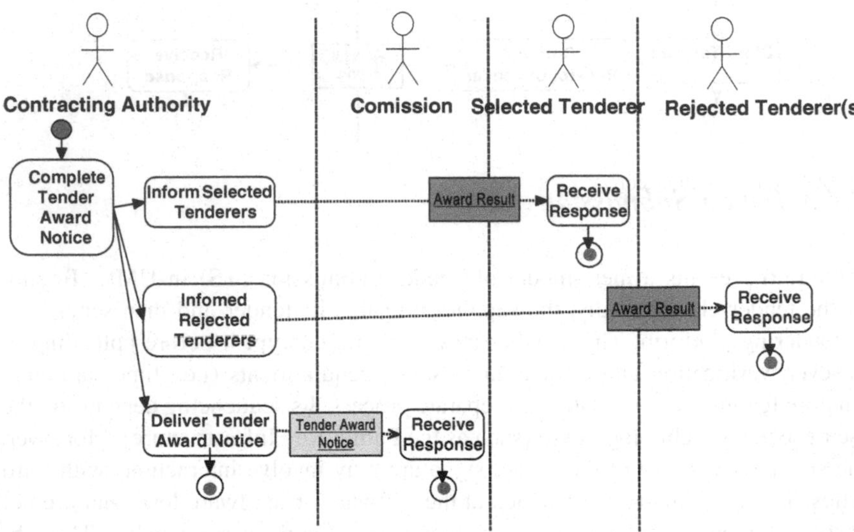

Fig. 13.7 Tender award notification

13.5 Implementation

In this section, we first introduce our overall architecture design for e-Tendering process integration. Then we detail some of the key Web service interfaces to illustrate how our approach works. We also highlight some technologies for tackling security issues.

13.5.1 Service-Oriented Architecture

The Web service SOAP messaging architecture described in Fig. 13.8 has been used to improve the integration and interoperability of the tendering process. The CA provides the tendering Web services for suppliers. The Web Services Description Language (WSDL) document has described the Web service technical details and Web service interface such as what operations it supports, what protocols are adopted, and how the data exchange should be organized [11, 15]. It is considered as a contract between the Web services requester and the provider.

First of all, the CA publishes the WSDL document to Universal Description, Discovery and Integration (UDDI) registries, which serve as "yellow pages" of WSDL documents that provide a standard means for describing organizations and their services thereby allowing online service discovery [11]. Then service requesters, such as suppliers, act as a requester entity that expects to make use of the tendering Web services for achieving its business requirements by using UDDI registries. UDDI provides the information for the matchmaking between the Web service provider

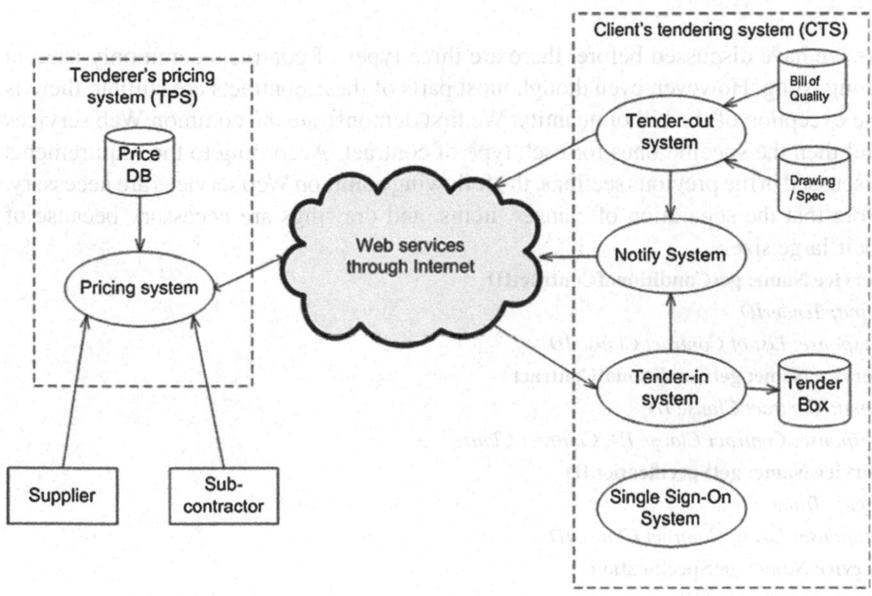

Fig. 13.8 Implementation architecture overview

and requester. UDDI works as a discovery agency, like a Web search engine such as Google.

Once suppliers find the tendering Web service at the UDDI registries, the suppliers gets the correspondent WSDL document and binds with the Web service via a SOAP message [11]. SOAP is an XML-based messaging protocol that is independent of the underlying transport protocol (e.g., HTTP, SMTP, and FTP). SOAP messages are used both by the suppliers to invoke tendering Web service, and by the tendering Web services to answer to their requests. Therefore, the tendering Web services provider (i.e., CA) receives the input SOAP message from and generates an output SOAP message to the suppliers. In the next subsection, we detail how Web services can facilitate the implementation of our TPM.

There are two main subsystems in the ETS: the Client tendering system (CTS) and the Tenderer Pricing System (TPS). In the CTS, there are two subsystems: the tender-out system and the tender-in system. In the TPS, the pricing elements are fundamental. These two main systems communicate by using Web services through the Internet for tender information exchange. We now detail some Web services implementations of each subsystem. We then show how tenderers can integrate those services into their environment and highlight some security issues and how the system handles some of the exceptions.

13.5.2 Web Services of the Tender-Out System

As we have discussed before, there are three types of contracts commonly used in Hong Kong. However, even though most parts of these contracts are similar, there is the exception of the bill of quantity. We first demonstrate the common Web services and then the specific ones for each type of contract. According to the requirements discussed in the previous sections, the following common Web services are necessary. Note that the separation of clauses, items, and drawings are necessary because of their large size.

Service Name: getConditionofContractID
Input: TenderID
Response: List of Contract Clause ID
Service Name: getConditionofContract
Input: Contract Clause ID
Response: Contract Clause ID, Contract Clause
Service Name: getSpecificationID
Input: Trade
Response: List of Contract Clause ID
Service Name: getSpecification
Input: Specification ID
Response: Specification ID, Trade, Specification Clause
Service Name: getDrawingID
Input: TenderID

Response: List of Drawing ID, List of Drawing Title
Service Name: getDrawing
Input: Drawing ID
Response: Drawing ID with the attachment of that drawing

Lump sum contract based on bill of quantities—In this type of contract, the contracting authority needs to provide all the data, and the tenderer only needs to return the price of the items. So the following Web services are provided.

Service Name: getItemID
Input: TenderID
Response: List of Item ID, Item trade, Item description
Service Name: getItemDetail
Input: Item ID
Response: Item ID, Item trade, Item description, Unit, Quantity

Design and build without quantity—In this type of contract, the tenderer should price the item and the quantity of the items. So, the parameters returned are slightly different.

Service Name: getItemID
Input: TenderID
Response: List of Item ID, Item trade, Item description
Service Name: getItemDetail
Input: Item ID
Response: Item ID, Item trade, Item description, Unit

Term contract base on the schedule of rates —In this type of contract, since the work details are still not specified, the price should be based on a schedule of rates. The tenderers also provide an overall trade discount. So, the following Web services are provided.

Service Name: getScheduleofRateID
Input: Trade
Response: List of Schedule of Rate ID, Item description

Service Name: getSchedulefRate
Input: Schedule of Rate ID
Response: Schedule of Rate ID, Trade, Item description, Rate

13.5.3 Web Services of the Tender-in System

Corresponding to the different types of contracts as discussed, the tender-in system provides the following Web services to support the reply from the TPS of tenderers. Note that not all the functions are used in a tender submission because of the different requirement in the submission (e.g., *lump sum contract base on bill of quantities* do not require the reply of quantities).

Service Name: priceItem
Input: Item ID, price
Response: Confirmation

Service Name: quantityItem
Input: Item ID, quantity
Response: Confirmation
Service Name: discountTrade
Input: Trade, Trade discount
Response: Confirmation
Service Name: commitTender
Input: Signed XML Format of Tender
Response: Confirmation

13.5.4 Web Services for Exception Handling

In a tendering process, some exceptions may occur. For example, a tenderer has not replied all the pricing information or the contracting authority wants to amend the tender. We demonstrate how some of these exceptions are supported with Web services.

Addendum—In the tendering period, sometimes although the tender has already been passed to the tenderer, the contracting authority may still want to amend some details. In this case, the system enters an addendum sub-process. Usually, there are three types of amendments: addition, modify, and deletion, as shown in Table 13.1. The CTS needs to notify the TPS about which statements or items are being amended. Once the TPS knows that an addendum will be issued. The TPS will request those amended items or clauses to be updated. So the tender-out system needs to provide the following Web service.
Service Name: getAddendumList
Input: Null
Response: List of amended clauses and items with the status of each item (addition, modify, deletion)

Consistency of the tender document—Since the whole tenderer document is downloaded by the TPS actively, we need to ensure that each tenderer has the identical tender document. So we need to know that the TPS gets all the clauses, items, and drawings from the CTS. The CTS has to monitor the download status of each tenderer. Once it finds that a tenderer has not downloaded all the details within a specific period, it will alert the TPS to immediately retrieve the needed details. Also, the tender-in system needs to monitor that all items have been priced. It will alert a TPS if it still has not committed the tender near to tender-in deadline. Once the CTS find that the

Table 13.1 Three types of action of the addendum

Action	Description
Addition	New clauses or items added
Modify	Clauses or items changed
Deletion	Clauses or items removed

tender is not completed after the deadline, the submission is disqualified; this is then marked in the tender report.

Bulk discount—In some cases, the tenderer may want to win the tender by offering a final bulk discount to the whole tender. Usually, this is in a discount rate format. For example, the final tender sum is $500,000,000.00 and the tenderer makes a bulk discount of 0.5 % off. So, the final tender sum becomes $487,500,000.00. In the CTS, it should be able to handle this kind of discount. So it will provide a service for the TPS to submit their discount.

Service Name: setBulkDiscount
Input: Input: Discount rate
Response: Confirmation

Additional information provided by tenderer—Sometimes the tenderer may submit additional information to the tender. For example, the tenderer may submit some detail designs or cost break downs of the works. This information sometimes facilitates it for the contracting authority to make better decisions. So, we need to provide a service for the TPS to submit any additional information. As the information may be in multimedia formats, the SOAP attachment format is used. After the CTS obtains the additional information, it makes notes on the tender report about this for the contracting authority's evaluation.

Service Name: submitAdditionInfo
Input: Tender ID, Information in attachment format
Response: Confirmation

Withdraw of tender—In some cases, the tenderer may want to withdraw the tender during the tendering process. Since this is a critical action, we need to have a further confirmation.

Service Name: withdrawTender
Input: Tender ID
Response: Confirmation Number

Service Name: confirmWithdrawal
Input: Tender ID, Confirmation Number
Response: Confirmation

13.5.5 Integration into the Tenderer's IT-Environment

The provision of the public web service interfaces by the tender-in and tender-out system allow suppliers for seamless integration of tendering processes into their e-business solutions. Since Web services do not provide graphical user interfaces, the tenderers can design their own, and integrate it into their existing environment. Also tenderers can make use of their own backend system to calculate the prices for their bid and to implement the TPS.

For instance, a construction company wants to take part in an e-tendering process for a large construction project, and also wants to integrate its system into the e-tendering infrastructure for the future. To accomplish this, the IT-department must create the necessary graphical (web-) interfaces to create the input for the tendering web services. Also, and very importantly, the IT department can make use of existing databases and services in the infrastructure of the enterprise to facilitate the price calculation and the compilation of the bid. These can, for example, be databases for the inventory, human resources and supply chain. Preexisting services that, i.e. calculate the parts of the cost can be reused.

Figure 13.9 shows such a scenario. A company has several existing databases and existing services access and process the data. The New Pricing Services are those services that need to be created if price calculation for bids has not been implemented. The New Bidding Services are those services that handle the communication with the remote Contracting Authority. Lastly the Integrated User Interface is the extended user interface that provides the bidding functionalities to the tenderer.

13.5.6 Security

Security is a very important issue in the ETS. Since all the data transfer between two parties involves trade secret, the data should be encrypted during transfer via the Internet. Since SOAP applications can run on top of HTTP, the message can passed via the Secure Sockets Layer (SSL) protocol, which is a proven technology and widely deployed. In addition, we can use the W3C XML Encryption Standard (see: http://www.w3.org/Encryption/2001/), which provides a framework for encrypting and decrypting XML documents.

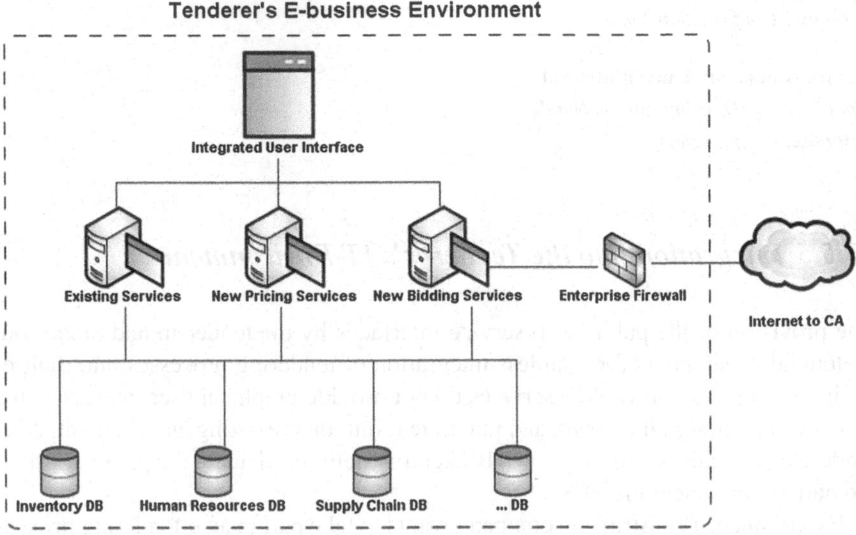

Fig. 13.9 The tenderer's e-business environment implementing the Tenderer Pricing System

Besides the confidentiality problem, we also need an authentication system to authenticate the tenderers. When a TPS first accesses the tender-out system, it will be directed to the single sign on system with the assignment of an identity key for subsequent log-on to the CPS. As discussed, there are several types of tendering processes, such as open competitive tendering and selective competitive tendering. For open competitive tendering, we have to allow all tenderers to access to the tender details. For selective competitive tendering, since only the selected tenderers can obtain the tender document, the TPS has to check the access against its shortlist of potential tenderers. For convenience, we can employ the technology of Single Sign-On (http://www.opengroup.org/security/sso/). Once a TPS logs on to the CTS, the CTS gives it a security token.

Also, we need to ensure that all the data transferred among the parties is indeed performed by the designated parties. The ETS (both the CPS and TPS) has to use digital signatures for identification. The SOAP technology provides a security extension SOAP-DSIG (http://www.w3.org/TR/SOAP-dsig/), which enables the validation of identities.

In cases where an extraordinary level of trust is needed, and where contract are digitally approved, the technique of qualified certificates can be employed to make the authentication procedure even more secure. This method involved smart cards that contain a private key of the signer, combined with card readers that can only retrieve the private key when a valid password is entered into the keypad of the card reader. This ensures that the private key (the smart card) has to be physically stolen from the owner, in order to impersonate the owner of the key. It also allows for the implementation of the four-eyes-principle that ensures the two persons with the correct authorization are physically present when a certain transaction is committed. This is especially important when contracts need to be digitally signed. The method of qualified signatures his currently required by law in all legal government transactions in the EU [12].

13.6 Facilitation of Decision Support with ETS

In this section, we provide an illustrative scenario how the contracting authority makes use of the TPM as discussed in the previous section to facilitate its decision making. It is a norm for the contracting authorities to look for the best tenderer's quotation meeting tender requirements. The degree of fitness may depend on their self-defined criteria such as cost, quality, experience, service level, past performance, scheduling, payment, etc. These criteria are considered as metrics for non-equally weighted average score calculation to find out the best tenderer [18], which should archive the *highest score* among all participated competitors. We highlight the implementation procedures as follows:

Initialization—During the invitation to tender (ITT) and tender submission procedures, stakeholders communicate with one another via an agreed schema to gather the relevant metrics-related information. The scale can be large, say, if the TPS needs to send out hundreds of RTP for each tender, and a significant proportion of bids are returned. All information for the *current* metrics is stored within their own database management systems (DBMS).

Metrics M_i	Score X_i	Weight W_i
M_1:Cost	$X = 0 :>= 3000K$ $X = 1 : 2000K <= M1 < 3000K$ $X = 2 : 1000K <= M1 < 2000K$ $X = 3 : 0 <= M1 < 1000K$	3
M_2:Location	X=0:Other Countries X=1: US-Based X=2:INDIA-Based X=3: CHINA-Based	1
M_3:Scale	X=0: Small-Scaled X=1: Middle-Scaled X=2:Large-Scaled X=3: Enterprise-Scaled	2

Tenderer	Metrics Status	Score	Weighted Average Score
S_i	M_i	X_i	$\bar{x} = \frac{\sum_{i=1}^{n} w_i x_i}{\sum_{i=1}^{n} w_i}$
S_1	M_1=2500K M_2=INDIA M_3=Enterprise	$X = 1$ $X = 2$ $X = 3$	$\{3(1) + 1(2) + 2(3)\}/6 = 1.83$
S_2	M_1=8500K M_2=US M_3=Enterprise	$X = 0$ $X = 1$ $X = 3$	$\{3(0) + 1(1) + 2(3)\}/6 = 1.17$
S_3	M_1=2100K M_2=CHINA M_3=Middle	$X = 1$ $X = 3$ $X = 1$	$\{3(1) + 1(3) + 2(1)\}/6 = 1.33$
S_4	M_1=1580K M_2=JAPAN M_3=Enterprise	$X = 2$ $X = 0$ $X = 3$	$\{3(2) + 1(0) + 2(3)\}/6 = 2$
S_5	M_1=2900K M_2=UK M_3=Large	$X = 1$ $X = 0$ $X = 2$	$\{3(1) + 1(0) + 2(2)\}/6 = 1.17$

Score ranking of the tenderers

RankR	Tenderer S_i	Weighted Average Score	Top-3 Decision
1st	S_4	2	Accept
2nd	S_1	1.83	Accept
3rd	S_3	1.33	Accept
4th	S_2, S_5	1.17	Reject

Fig. 13.10 Evaluation

Score Ranking—Non-equally weighted average score is calculated for all tenderers ($S_1, \ldots, S_N$) based on metrics criteria, and sorted with most ideal supplier S_{ideal} owns the greatest weighted average score ranked first on the list.

Ideal Tenderer(s) Identification—Normally, only one winner is chosen, while sometimes more than one tenderers can be awarded. Besides the normal procedure of awarding the tender to the highest scorer(s), the score ranking report provided by the TPS may be reviewed manually for the final decision, especially when the score difference is less than a certain threshold. In addition, sometimes when the overall score is too low, or when all the bids violate some constraints (especially price), the contract authority may award no tender at all.

Figure 13.10 shows an illustrative evaluation scenario. Suppose a contracting authority considers 3 different metrics M_i for tenderer selection S_{ideal} from its point of view, i.e., M_1: Cost, M_2: Location, and M_3: Scale. Besides, the metrics importance in supplier selection is $M_1 > M_3 > M_2$. With appropriate weighting assigned for different metrics, the following tables are obtained, which select S_2, S_1, S_4 accordingly.

13.7 Discussion and Conclusion

In this paper, we have presented a Tendering Process Meta-model based on UML for four typical business procedures: *Request To Participate* (RTP), *Invitation To Tender* (ITT), *Tender Submission* (TS), and *Tender Award Notification* (TAN). It is the responsibility for different types of enterprises to implement their own Tendering Process Model (TPM) that suits their own business requirements. They should also provide reliable tendering Web services so that interoperability and integration becomes possible for B2B application-to-application communication over the Internet, which is independent of platform, technology, and tools.

Based on this approach, we have presented our implementation of an e-Tendering system (ETS) based on a case study of the construction in Hong Kong with some details in the Web-service design specification. The ETS provides the tender document details for the tenderers, and the tenderers submit their tender price via Web services. In addition, we have also presented some of the exceptions that the system can handle, such as withdrawal of the tender, bulk discount, etc. Other elements discussed include some issues regarding security. We have two main stakeholders in the ETS, namely the contracting authority and the tenderers. We discuss our findings about their advantages as follows.

For the contracting authority, they have benefits in streamlining their work through the digitalization of the tender document. As previously mentioned, most of the information for the tender documents are currently prepared with a computer. They can easily be transferred to the CTS. So, the contracting authority can save the effort in printing them out and checking the tender booklet. Also, the electronically collected pricing information from the tenderers can be easily used for generating the tender report.

For the tenderers, the TPS can help them retrieve relevant rates from their cost database. So, the tendering pricing time can be shortened, and in this way the price is more up to date. The tenderer can make their final decisions right up until almost the last minute. There is also no need to worry about the delivery problems faced with physical tender documents.

The key advantage of applying Web services is to establish cross-organizational collaboration via existing Internet standards, supporting both human Web-based and application programmatic interactions. When both partners support Web services, a more efficient and preferred way for event passing with the publish-and-subscribe paradigm can be employed [7]. In addition, smaller business partners with varied degree of automation can still participate in these business processes manually or semi-automatically. Because of the process complexity, Web services based interactions also facilitate exception handling [6], which typically require human attention and decision.

Moreover, Web services enable external integration with e-marketplaces and brokers, expanding the opportunities of TSC and therefore businesses. Internally, Web services enable the integration of tendering processes with enterprise resource planning (ERP) and other enterprise information systems to facilitate decision support. These are on our future research agenda.

Lastly the Web service approach prescribes all participating parties precise rules on how to comply with the security policies that for example describe which kinds of certificates have to be used. Without complying with these Web service policies, a party cannot take part in the process. This is a major advantage over other business to business integration approaches, which often implement ad hoc security solutions.

For other continuing research, we are working on extending the ETS to subcontractors, who may further sub-contract their works. One problem for this in Hong Kong is the small sizes of many sub-contractors, who cannot be easily automated to such an extent. We are also working on other exception handling mechanisms. Another future work direction is to support e-negotiation on the price with the tenderers after the tendering process has finished. That is, we shall study the integration of the e-Tendering system with an e-Negotiation system [8] together for a more complete solution.

We are also looking into the integration with other logistics systems like delivery, order, purchase, and procurement. We can further customize the use of Web services as the communication channel between various logistics systems. Although the focus in this paper is on tendering processes, similar integration work can be done for other related processes involved in logistics to make scale-up feasible for proposed solution. The steps are similar, first of all, understand the business requirements to streamline the business procedures, design the message exchange specifications, and then set up the architecture for application-to-application communication over the Internet. The implementation approach for integration is similar to the one in this paper even though the business requirements are not exactly the same. We can foresee that the possible benefits for logistics industry are great. For this reason, we will also look into some ideas for developing such a methodology for Tendering Process Model (TPM).

References

1. Betts, M., Black, P., Christensen, S., et al. (2006). Towards secure and legal E-tendering. *Journal of Information Technology in Construction*, 11, 89–102.
2. Bichler, M. (2000). A Roadmap to Auction-based Negotiation Protocols for Electronic Commerce. *Proceedings of the 33th Hawaii International Conference on System Sciences*. Hawaii: IEEE Computer Society Press.
3. Brook, M. (2004). *Estimating and Tendering for Construction Work* (2nd ed.). Oxford: Elsevier.
4. Cerami, E. (2002). *Web Services Essentials*. Sebastopol, CA: O'Reilly.
5. Cheung, S. C., Hung, P. C. K., Chiu, D. K. W. (2003). On e-Negotiation of Unmatched Logrolling Views. *Proceedings of the 36th Hawaii International Conference on System Sciences*. Big Island, Hawaii: IEEE Computer Society Press.
6. Chiu, D. K. W., Cheung, S. C., Karlapalem, K., Li, Q., Till, S., Kafeza, E. (2004). Workflow View Driven Cross-Organizational Interoperability in a Web Service Environment. *Information Technology and Management*, 5(3/4), 221–250.
7. Chiu, D. K. W., Cheung, S. C., Till, S. (2003) An Architecture for E-Contract Enforcement in an E-service Environment. *Proceedings of the Hawaii International Conference on System Sciences 2003*. Big Island, Hawaii: IEEE Computer Society Press.
8. Chiu, D. K. W., Cheung, S. C., Hung, P. C. K., Chiu, S. Y. Y., Chung, A. K. K. (2005). Developing e-Negotiation support with a meta-modeling approach in a Web services environment. *Decision Support Systems*, 40(1), 51–69.
9. Chiu, D. K. W., Ng, N. L. L., Lai, S.C., Hung, P. C. K. (2007). Automating Tendering Processes with Web Services: A Case Study on Building Construction Tendering in Hong Kong. *Group Decision and Negotiation Meeting (GDN 2007)*, Mt. Tremblant (Montreal).
10. Coscia, E., Nicolodi, S., Doyle, R., Slade, A., Ginty, K., Shamsi, T.A. et al. (2000). The E-NTRY Web-based E-commerce Platform: an advanced infrastructure supporting Tendering. Bidding and Contract Negotiation. *Proceedings from E-Business and E-Work 2000 conference*. Madrid: IOS Press.
11. Erl, T. (2006). *Service-Oriented Architecture: Concepts, Technology, and Design*. Englewood Cliffs, NJ: Prentice-Hall.
12. EU Directive 1999/93/EC (1999). On a Community framework for electronic signatures.
13. Gortmaker, J., Janssen, M., Wagenaar, R. W. (2004). The Advantages of Web Service Orchestration in Perspective. *Proceedings from 6th international Conference on Electronic Commerce*, 506–515. Delft, Netherlands: ACM.
14. Hills, M. J. (1995). *Building Contract Procedures in Hong Kong*. Hong Kong: Longman.
15. Hull, R., Benedikt, M., Christophides, V., Su. J. (2003). E-services: a look behind the Curtain. *Proceedings of the Interna-tional Symposium on Principles of Database Systems (PODS)*. San Diego, CA: ACM.
16. Homann, F., Karabulut, Y., Voss, M., Fraikin, F. (2005). *Security and Trust in public eProcurement (Technical Report No. TUD-CS-2005-4)*, Darmstadt University of Technology / SAP Research Karlsruhe.
17. Lai, S. C., Chiu, D. K. W., Hung, P. C. K. (2007). e-Tendering with Web Services: A Case Study on the Tendering Process of Building Construction. *2007 IEEE International Conference on Services Computing (SCC 2007)*, Salt Lake City, Utah, 582–588.
18. Lau, G. K. T., Chiu, D. K. W., Hung, P. C. K. (2006). Web-service Based Information Integration for Decision Support: A Case Study on e-Mortgage Contract Matchmaking Service. *Proceedings of the Hawaii International Conference on System Science 2006*. Hilo, Hawaii: IEEE press.
19. Lomuscio, A. R., Wooldridge, M., Jennings, N. R. (2000). A Classification Scheme for Negotiation in Electronic Com-merce. *Agent-Mediated Electronic Commerce: A European Perspective*, Springer Verlag, 19–33.
20. Ostergaard, S., Mora-Jensen C. (2003). ETHICS - Best-of-Breed European e-Tendering Solution, *Global Purchasing & Supply Chain Strategies 2004*. London: Touch Briefings.

21. Pruitt, D. G. (1981). *Negotiation Behavior*. London: Academic Press.
22. Pruitt, D. G. and P. J. Carnevale. (1993). *Negotiation in Social Conflict*. Philadelphia: Open University Press.
23. Raiffa, H. (1982). *The Art and Science of Negotiation*. Cambridge, MA: Harvard University Press.
24. Robinson, W. N. (1997). Electronic Brokering for Assisted Contracting of Software Applets, *Proceedings of the 30th Hawaii International Conference on System Sciences*, 4,449–458.
25. Rothkopf, M. H. and S. Park. (2001). An Elementary Introduction to Auctions, *Interface*, 31(6), 83–97.
26. Singh, M., Thomson D. (2002). eProcurement Model for B2B Exchanges: An Australian Example. *15th Bled Electronic Commerce Conference eReality: Constructing the eEconomy*, 15, 293–307.
27. Thompson, L. (1998). *The Mind and Heart of the Negotiator*. Englewood Cliffs, NJ: Prentice-Hall.

Chapter 14
Service Trust Management for E-Government Applications

Surya Nepal, Wanita Sherchan and Athman Bouguettaya

Abstract Many services and service providers compete with each other to provide similar services in the service-oriented Web (also known as Service Web). Selection of the best services or service providers is an important and challenging problem. Trust plays an important role in identifying the best service provider for a customer, where trust information is computed from customer feedback ratings for the services. Such rating provides a measure of previous consumers' satisfaction with the services. The satisfaction value indicates the trustworthiness of a service provider in delivering the services as promised (also known as service trust). This situation exists in many E-Government applications where a large number of services are outsourced to the third party service providers and there is a need to select the best services for customers based on their current needs. In this chapter, we propose a community based approach of managing service trust for E-Government applications with the focus on a human services delivery system. We describe the architecture, implementation and a case study of the proposed service trust management framework in the context of delivering human services.

S. Nepal (✉)
CSIRO ICT Centre, Marsfield, Australia
e-mail: Surya.Nepal@csiro.au

W. Sherchan
IBM Research, Melbourne, Australia
e-mail: wanitash@au.ibm.com

A. Bouguettaya
RMIT University, Melbourne, Australia
e-mail: AthmanBouguettaya@rmit.edu.au

A. Bouguettaya et al. (eds.), *Advanced Web Services*,
DOI: 10.1007/978-1-4614-7535-4_14,

14.1 Introduction

Services computing is poised to transition computing to a new era where data is to take the back seat and services will take the driver seat—enabling, supporting and delivering tremendous benefits to new applications such as human services delivery. Central to service computing is the concept of Web services and Service Oriented Architectures (SOA). The fast increase in the number of deployed Web services is transforming the enterprises from a data-oriented system to a service-oriented system with a large repository of Web services. Therefore, there is a need to go beyond and above the basic building blocks of SOA to provide novel service management frameworks that deal with the whole life-cycle of services from inception to disbandment. Towards addressing this need, we have built a prototype end-to-end service management system called Web Service Management System (WSMS). This system has been used in applications ranging from bioinformatics [11] to human services [9]. This chapter describes the basic concepts behind WSMS and its application in human services delivery, with a focus on the service trust management framework, a significant component of WSMS.

The goal of every human services department is to design and deliver products and services efficiently and effectively to satisfy their stakeholders including individual citizens, residents, and other government agencies. The current human service delivery systems are typically under stress due to various reasons. These include unsustainable cost structures, requirement to deliver more services with limited resources and inability to deliver better-suited services because of changing demographics and an ageing population. It has been identified that new solutions are needed that require whole-of-government interoperability and strategic partnerships between government agencies and the private sector (e.g., enterprises and non-government agencies). To this end, we devise a novel Human Services Delivery System (HSDS) architecture that aims to address these major emerging challenges. Our architecture aims to assist human services departments in enhancing their capabilities of provisioning more services with lower cost (i.e., to "do more with less"). In addition, another important goal is to raise the quality of service delivered to achieve higher customer satisfaction. We have designed and developed a prototype human services delivery system using WSMS. The core components of HSDS include service query and composition, service selection and optimization, service organization, service change management and service trust management. In this book chapter, we present a case study of developing such a system with a particular focus on the service trust management component, we present a case study of developing such a system with a particular focus on the service trust management component.

The rest of the chapter is structured as follows. We next present the Human Services Delivery System architecture and describe each of the components in brief. We then describe the service trust management component of HSDS. This is followed by the implementation architecture and models for human services trust computation. Finally, we present a case study for service trust management framework within the human service delivery system.

14.2 Human Services Delivery System

Figure 14.1 shows the implementation architecture of the Human Services Delivery System (HSDS). This architecture aims to provide an end-to-end support for human services delivery. It leverages and manages the various required resources for delivering human services in an automated and coherent framework. When customers have new requirements or become eligible for new welfare services, their requests are described as a service query and forwarded to the service management framework. Then a series of activities such as service selection, service composition and service optimization create an integrated workflow that delivers the best set of services to meet the customers' requirements. When changes occur, either triggered by the customer or government legislation for example, the service change management module will automatically handle these changes in the form of a new workflow of services. The architecture is composed of seven modules that reflect the core components of the service management framework. In what follows, we provide a brief introduction of these modules.

Service & Process Repository (S &P Repository): The S &P Repository catalogues services, resources and business processes related to human services and relevant context information so that they can be uniquely identified and managed within their life-cycle. Whenever new services, resources and processes become available, they must be registered in the repository to be utilized in human service delivery. The repository utilizes a set of ontologies to enable fast retrieval of services and semantic interoperability for supporting automatic service composition.

Service Query & Composer: This component takes a user request and generates a composite service. The component provides support for the underlying query model and composition algorithms. The HSDS query model consists of a query interface, a query language, and a query engine. The interface allows users to specify what they want (goals) at semantic level and leave composite service generation to HSDS. The query interface is handled by the user interface component, which is discussed in

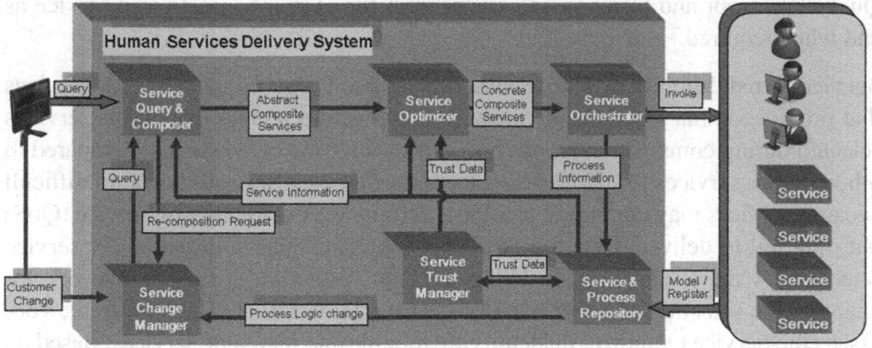

Fig. 14.1 Human services delivery system architecture

detail in [9]. The underlying query language is Service Query Language, an XML service query language we developed as an interface to HSDS query engine. Based on how services are composed to create composite services, HSDS allows three types of composition: horizontal, vertical, and hybrid [1]. Services in HSDS are organized using a semantic model in service organization. Upon receiving a user's query, HSDS will first identify relevant services and perform logical reasoning to generate a composite service at the semantic level. HSDS uses a matchmaking algorithm proposed in [4–10] and context-aware service weaving algorithm proposed in [2] to generate composite services.

Service Optimizer: The result of Service Query Processor and Composer may consist of several candidate services that fulfil the requirements of the customer. The Service Optimizer is responsible for evaluating the alternatives and generating the optimal integrated workflow expected to deliver the best possible user-centered quality of service to the customers. The service optimization aims to select the services that a user would prefer the most based on the available context information. The proposed techniques for service optimization are based on Quality of Service (QoS) parameters. These techniques aim to identify a service with the best quality based on context information. To conduct effective service optimization, HSDS adopts schemes aiming to handle both quantitative and qualitative properties of services. We propose some such techniques in [6].

Service Change Manager: The service change management is an important aspect of human services delivery as the services in a composition may need to be changed based on the contextual information. A service may go through frequent changes. The triggers for these changes could come from different sources. Changes in the services include changes in the functionality they provide, the way they work, the component services they are composed of and the quality of service they offer. The service change management component is designed to manage such changes all services. HSDS uses a number of approaches to deal with the changes in user and service contexts (refer to [7] for details). It provides a scheme for managing the life-cycle of a workflow to reflect and react to changes occurring within the human services department or its customers' life situation. The Service Change Manager will interact with the Service Query Processor and Composer to reconfigure the customer's delivered service as and when required.

Service Trust Manager: The service organization may contain several services that provide similar functionality. Service composition prefers that all the services selected during composition are the best services for the given context compared to other similar services [3]. However, selection of the best services becomes difficult because services may commit to provide a certain level of Quality of Service (QoS) but may fail to deliver. Therefore, trust acts as contextual information for service selection. A major challenge in HSDS includes providing a trust framework for enabling the selection of services based on trust information. The trust framework assists the Service Optimizer in identifying reliable and reputable services. Based on the statistics of service delivery and customers' feedback, the Service Trust Manager evaluates the trustworthiness of individual services and records the trust information in the S&P Repository. This the main focus of this chapter.

Service Orchestrator: The integrated optimal workflow created by the Service Optimizer is executed by the Service Orchestrator. The system guides the customer to consume the services step by step. It also helps coordinate the work of human services department staff delivering internal and external services to accomplish the tasks in the workflow. It is an important module of the implementation architecture that enables concrete delivery of human services.

14.3 Service Trust Management Framework

Human services departments, being the service delivery arm of the government, become the first point of contact and act as a coordinator to connect customers to the appropriate services which could be internal our outsourced. An important aspect of these outsourced services is that there may be more than one service provider providing similar types of services. Trust plays an important role in identifying the best service provider for a customer. Such trust information can be computed from customer feedback ratings for the services. Such *rating* provides a measure of previous consumers' satisfaction with the services. The satisfaction value indicates the trustworthiness of a service provider in delivering the services as promised (also known as *service trust*). We propose a community based approach of managing service trust in the human services delivery system. Our approach to the management of trust is based on the notion of community derived from social networks. Figure 14.2 depicts the basic elements of our framework and interactions among them. In the following, we explain them briefly using an example of Australian employment services model.

Community provider: A community provider is the entity that defines the service community. A community provider may be a government agency, a business council, an academic institution, etc. A provider may provide one or more communities, but each community has only one provider. Providers have publicly known identities. For example, Department of Employment Services is a community provider in the context of employment services. It defines the communities of employment service providers. In Australia, examples of employment service provider community include communities of Job Service Providers, Disability Employment Service Providers, and National Green Jobs Corps.

Service Community: A service community is a "container" that groups services related to a specific area (for example, employment service providers or social workers). We can use ontologies as templates for describing communities and their services. For example, in the context of Australian employment services model, Disability Employment Services are the members of the Employment Services Community and provide employment services to disabled job seekers.

Web Services: A Web service is a software application identified by a URI (Uniform Resource Identifier), whose interface and binding are defined, described and discovered by XML artefacts, and supports direct interaction with other software applications using XML messages via Internet-based protocols. Conceptually, a Web service may be viewed as a set of operations, where each operation is a "processing unit" that consumes input values (called its parameters) and generates output values called the result of that operation's invocation. In the context of human services, a Web service may include an operation service as defined above as well as human-assisted services. The human-assisted services are services that involve human beings. An example of a human service is a Job Capacity Assessment service provided by a job capacity assessor such as a medical doctor. We assume that there are corresponding Web services in the human services management framework to reflect the human activity.

Service provider: The service provider is the entity that provides the service and makes it available to consumers. A service provider may be a business, a government

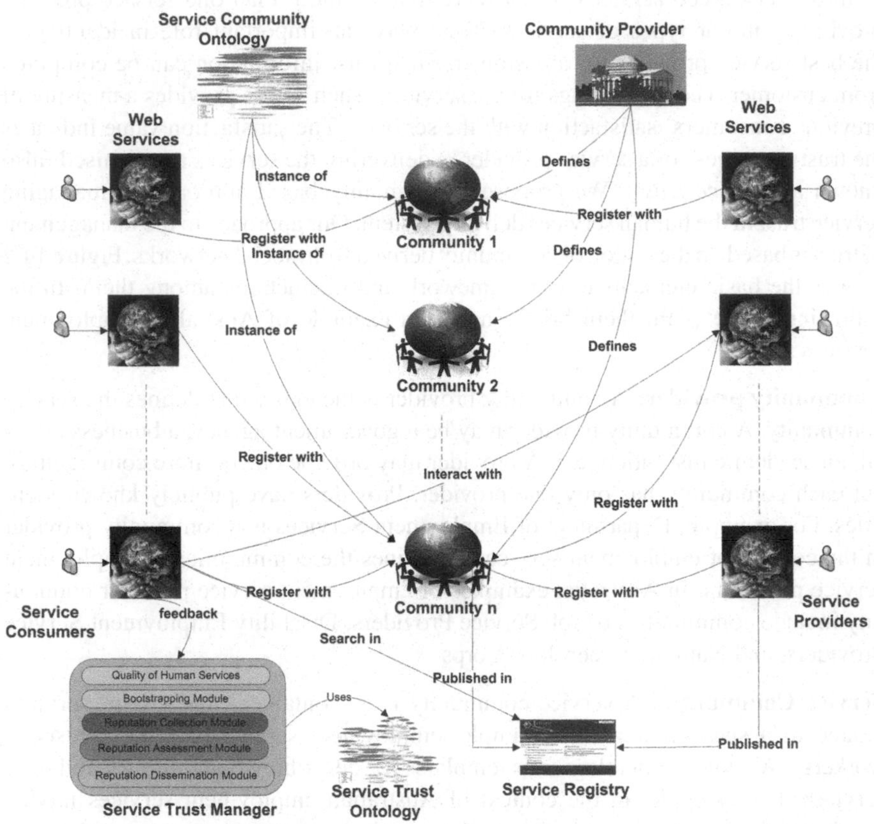

Fig. 14.2 A community based approach of managing trust

agency, or an academic institution. Providers have publicly known identities. A service provider registers with the community to offer one or more services. Each service is owned and offered by a single provider but may or may not be actually managed by the provider. For example, the provider of a service may outsource the task of actually operating the service to a third party. Service consumers may or may not be able to determine all the parties involved in delivering a given service. In our model, we do not make a distinction between the service provider and the provided service.

Service Community ontology: The service community ontology comprises of a hierarchical description of important concepts and their properties in a domain (for example, employment services domain). It also includes the ontological relationships between the concepts such as member of, subclass of or superclass of. In the context of employment services, we define an employment services community ontology. This ontology defines different types of employment service providers and their properties, the services they provide and the properties of these services and instances of the services and providers. For example, *DisabilityEmploymentService* is a subclass of concept *EmploymentService*. Similarly, *AuswideEnterprise* is an instance of *DisabilityEmploymentService*.

Service consumer: A service consumer is any entity that invokes a service, e.g., an intelligent agent, a Web application, or another Web service. A human user may also invoke a Web service, but we assume that each user is represented by a software component (defined proxy) in the system, similar to the human-assisted services represented by Web-based services. For example, a job seeker is a consumer of an employment service provided by employment service providers. Similarly, a Web service in the employment service provider' system is a consumer of Department of Employment Services' assessment service.

Service registry: A service registry is a searchable directory that contains a collection of descriptions of Web services and their communities. A service registry has two components: a repository of service descriptions and a registry engine that answers the requests sent to the registry by service providers and service consumers. A service registry may be private or public. Any provider may advertise its capabilities by publishing the Web service in a public registry. A private registry may be used only by a limited, known set of providers to publish services. In our framework, service registries are only used to locate prospective service providers, and the registries do not store any reputation related information.

Service trust ontology: The service trust ontology aims to improve knowledge reusability and semantic interoperability of trust services regardless of trust algorithms/mechanisms used by the services [8]. It provides a common framework to capture the relationships between various trust concepts and their relationships relevant to semantic service-oriented environments. In this ontology, we consider not only services trust but also trust as a service. Our service trust ontology captures the whole life cycle of services trust—from initialization of trust with trust bootstrapping to various phases specific to services trust, such as composition and propagation of trust in composite services. Each node of the ontology, representing a stage in trust life cycle, is mapped to the service providing this functionality. This enables easy representation of the whole life cycle of services trust. Separating trust algorithms from trust concepts enables us to model a large number of trust algorithms provided by different service providers.

Service trust manager: The trust manager is an entity that is responsible for computing trust values of the service providers. Some of the key tasks of the service trust manager include monitoring the quality of human services, providing mechanisms to collect and process customer feedback, and providing algorithms/protocols for collecting, evaluating and disseminating trust information. We describe them in detail in the following sections.

14.4 Service Trust Management Implementation

In this section, we first describe the architecture of the service trust management framework discussed earlier. This is followed by a discussion on Quality of Human Service (QoHS) parameters used to compute service trust. We then discuss the implementation of specific service ontology and trust ontology. This is followed by a discussion of various trust models for reputation information collection, bootstrapping, evaluation and dissemination.

14.4.1 Implementation Architecture

Figure 14.3 shows the service trust management implementation architecture along with key elements and interfaces. We describe them briefly below.

The service ontology manager includes an ontology base and an ontology query interface. The ontology base consists of two types of ontologies—a service community ontology and a service trust ontology. The service community ontology stores the ontology definitions of services within a specific domain. The service trust ontology stores the ontology definitions of services trust and trust services and models the relationships between different types of trust and the dependencies between different trust functionalities. A node in the service trust ontology defines a type of functionality offered by a service. Some examples of such nodes are *TrustBootstrapping*, *TrustPropagation* and *TrustEvaluation* (described in later subsections). Each node in the ontology is associated with a list of services that provide the defined functionality. This association enables functionality-based service discovery by first locating the corresponding node in the ontology, then locating the Web services that subscribe to the node.

The ontology query interface supports two types of queries in the ontology base: functionality query and Web service query. The functionality query is to locate a

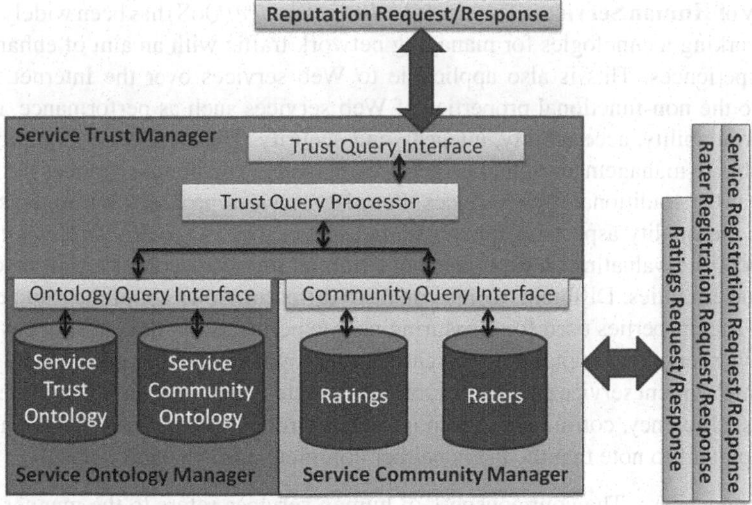

Fig. 14.3 A service trust management system architecture

node in the ontology and retrieve related information such as its relationship with other nodes. The Web service query is to find a list of Web services that provide a specific functionality, identified by a certain node in the ontology. The corresponding concrete Web services can be retrieved by checking whether they subscribe to a node. The community manager uses service community ontology to organise services into different types of communities. Services providing a similar type of service belong to the same community. The community manager also maintains *raters* and *ratings*. The raters are the consumers who are willing to share their experiences with others, and the ratings are the feedback given by the consumers against a service's quality parameters. We describe the quality parameters for human services, referred to as QoHS, in the following section. The community manager provides appropriate interfaces to communicate with other components of the Service Trust Management system.

The trust manager includes a trust query interface and a trust query processor. The trust query interface provides a query interface to the users of the trust management service. The current implementation supports two types of interfaces: Web service and Web portal. The Web service interface is used by other Web services to query trust of a service (or services). For example, a query optimizer in HSDS may invoke the trust service to inquire the trust value of a particular service using the Web service interface. The Web portal interface is designed to be used by an end user (or consumer). This enables the trust service to be used independently and directly by the consumer. The trust query processor interacts with the ontology manager to process a given trust query.

Quality of Human Services: The term *Quality of Service* (QoS) has been widely used in networking technologies for managing network traffic with an aim of enhancing user experiences. This is also applicable to Web services over the Internet. QoS refers to the non-functional properties of Web services such as performance, reliability, availability, accessibility, integrity and security. These aspects of quality are applicable to management of human services delivery. The human services not only represent the traditional Web services, but also services provided by humans. We refer to the quality aspects of human services in HSDS as *Quality of Human Service* (QoHS). Evaluating an experience of a human service is complex as it involves many uncertainties. Different people can have different views about the same experience. The properties used for measuring user experiences on human services may vary from scenario to scenario. In our case of employment services provided by third party employment service providers, QoHS parameters include courteousness, effectiveness, efficiency, convenience, responsiveness, reliability and breadth of choice. It is important to note that the list is neither complete nor exhaustive.

1. Courteousness: The courteousness of human services refers to the manner with which the provider provided the service to the consumers.
2. Effectiveness: Effectiveness refers to the degree to which stated objectives are achieved.
3. Efficiency: Efficiency refers to the ability to accomplish a job within minimum time.
4. Convenience: Convenience refers to the service providers being convenient to their consumers.
5. Responsiveness: Responsiveness refers to the service providers being quick to respond to their consumers' request.
6. Reliability: Reliability refers to degree of service providers being capable of maintaining the service and service quality.
7. Breadth of choice: Breadth of choice refers to the options provided by service providers to their consumers.

Service Community Ontology: As mentioned earlier, our approach to management of trust uses the concept of community. A variety of communities within the Department of Human Services come together to offer human services. For example, communities of employment service providers, financial advisors, job capacity assessors, and social workers. In order to manage these different communities, we introduce a concept of service community ontology. It typically comprises a hierarchical description of important concepts in a domain and describes their properties. The trust management framework provides trust service for each of these communities. We describe the main concepts below.

Community provider: This concept represents an entity that defines the communities. In our example, Department of Education is a community provider that defines the employment services communities. The WSML (Web Services Modelling Language) representation of the concept and its instance is shown below.

```
concept CommunityProvider
     hasName ofType _string
     hasCommunityProviderID ofType _string
     isCommunityProviderOf inverseOf(hasCommunityProvider)
                           ofType Community
instance Department_of_Education memberOf CommunityProvider
```

Community: This concept represents a group of providers providing similar services. In our example, job providers are the members of the Job community that belongs to the employment services community. The concept and its instance are shown below.

```
concept Community
     hasName ofType _string
     hasCommunityID ofType  _string
     hasCommunityProvider ofType CommunityProvider
     isCommunityOf inverseOf(hasCommunity) ofType
                              ServiceProvider
concept EmploymentServiceCommunity subConceptOf Community
instance JobCommunity memberOf EmploymentServiceCommunity
     hasCommunityID hasValue "JobCommunity"
     hasCommunityProvider hasValue DEEWR
```

Service provider: The service provider is the entity that provides the service and makes it available to consumers. A service provider may be a business, a government agency, an academic institution, etc. A service provider registers with the community. For example, *AuswideEnterprises* is an employment service provider that is registered with the *Job community*.

```
concept ServiceProvider
     hasName ofType _string
     hasProviderID ofType  _string
     hasCommunity ofType Community
concept EmploymentServiceProvider subConceptOf ServiceProvider
     hasService ofType ThirdPartyEmploymentService
     hasQoHSParameter ofType SetOfQoHSParameters
     hasCommunity ofType EmploymentServiceCommunity
     hasTrustValue ofType _string
concept JobProvider subConceptOf EmploymentServiceProvider
instance AuswideEnterprises memberOf JobProvider
     hasName hasValue "AuswideEnterprises"
     hasProviderID hasValue "AuswideEnterprises"
     hasCommmunity hasValue JobCommunity
     hasService hasValue AuswideEmploymentService
     hasQoHSParameter hasValue JobProviderQoHSParameters
     hasTrustValue hasValue "5.0"
```

QoHS: The QoHS parameters are used to record the past experience of service consumers on a particular service. For example, courteousness, effectiveness, efficiency, convenience, responsiveness, reliability and breadth of choice are QoHS parameters for Job providers. The QoS parameters for Web Services are also defined in the similar way.

```
concept SetOfQoHSParameters
     hasQoHSParameter ofType QoHSParameter
concept QoHSParameter
     hasQoHSValue ofType _integer
instance Courteousness memberOf QoHSParameter
instance Effectiveness memberOf QoHSParameter
instance Efficiency memberOf QoHSParameter
instance Convenience memberOf QoHSParameter
instance Responsiveness memberOf QoHSParameter
instance Reliability memberOf QoHSParameter
instance BreadthOfChoice memberOf QoHSParameter
```

Service consumer: A service consumer is any entity that consumes a service provided by service providers. Consumers are called raters if they are willing to share their experience with others. For example, a job seeker is a consumer of services provided by Job providers.

```
concept Consumer subConceptOf CSO#Customer
concept Rater subConceptOf Consumer
instance AliceSmithCCN20453 memberOf Rater
```

Service Trust Ontology: The service trust ontology defines trust concepts and their relationships specific to human services delivery system. In this ontology, we consider not only services trust but also trust as a service. Our service trust ontology captures the whole life cycle of services trust—from initialization of trust with trust bootstrapping to various phases specific to services trust, such as composition and propagation of trust in composite services. This is a major departure from the current approaches that focus on trust evaluation and trust decision making. We describe the main concepts below (see Fig. 14.4). The concept of *Trust* is defined as:

```
concept Trust
     hasTrustee ofType Trustee
     hasTimeStamp ofType _dateTime
     hasTrustValue ofType _string
     hasEvaluationCriteria ofType ESPO#SetOfQoHSParameters
     hasConfidence  ofType _string
     isBasedOnEvaluationPeriod ofType _duration
     isBasedOnNumOfInteractions ofType _string
```

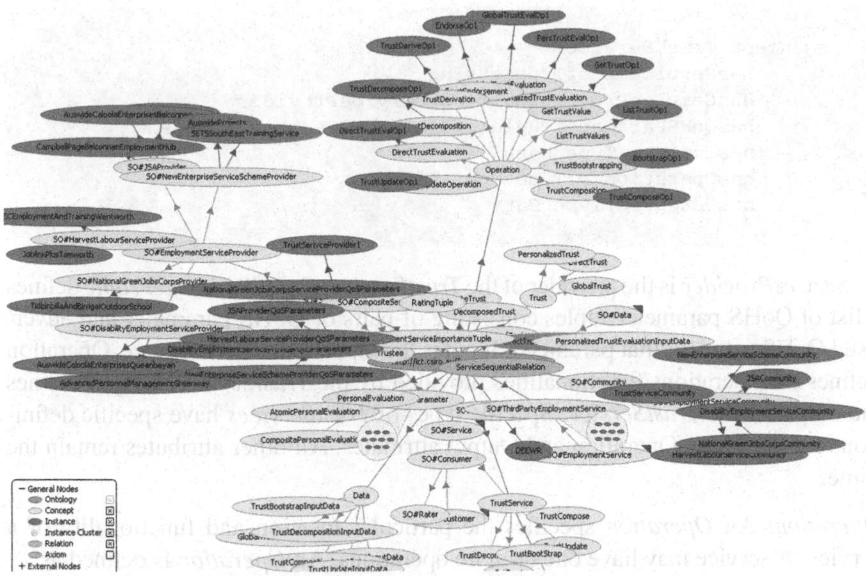

Fig. 14.4 Service trust ontology for employment service providers

where Trustee is a service/provider to which the Trust refers. *Trustor* is the entity whose level of trust on the trustee is captured by the Trust. *TimeStamp* is the time when the trust value was generated. *TrustValue* is the actual trust value such as "7" (numerical) or "very trustworthy" (fuzzy). *EvaluationCriteria* is the criteria based on which trust is evaluated (i.e., the QoHS parameters for trust evaluation). Confidence is the level of confidence on the trust evaluation. *EvaluationPeriod* is the duration of history considered in the trust evaluation. *NumOfInteractions* specifies the size of history (i.e., the number of past interactions) considered in the trust evaluation. Inclusion of information such as *TimeStamp*, *EvaluationCriteria*, *NumOfInteractions*, and *EvaluationPeriod* provides context to Trust such that two Trust instances for the same service/provider may be compared directly based on these properties. For example, two instances of Trust referring to the same service *AuswideCaloolaEnterprisesBelconnen* may have different *TimeStamp* values. This implies that one of the instances is more recent than the other and therefore more indicative of the current trustworthiness of that service.

Trust Service: A *TrustService* is a Web service that provides various trust functionalities such as trust bootstrapping, trust evaluation and trust propagation. *TrustService* can be of several types based on the type of functionality provided by the service. Each of these is defined as a *subconcept of TrustService*. At the abstract level, a *TrustService* is defined as:

```
concept TrustService
     hasServiceID ofType string
     hasServiceProvider ofType ServiceProvider
     hasQoHSParameterTuple ofType QoHSParameterTuple
     hasInput ofType Data
     hasOperation ofType Operation
     hasOutput ofType Data
```

ServiceProvider is the provider of the *TrustService*. *QoHSParameterTuple* defines a list of QoHS parameter tuples consisting of pairs of QoHS parameter and advertised QoHS value for that parameter. Input is the input to the *TrustService*. Operation defines the operations/functionalities provided by the *TrustService*. Output defines the output of the *TrustService*. Specific types of *TrustServices* have specific definitions for the Input, Operation and Output attributes. All other attributes remain the same.

Operation: An *Operation* specifies the particular location and functionality of a service. A service may have one or more operations. An *Operation* is defined as:

```
concept Operation
     hasOperationName ofType _string
     hasSoapLocation ofType _string
     hasSoapAction ofType _string
     isOperationOf inverseOf(hasOperation) ofType SO#Service
```

We have identified several types of services trust based on the purpose of trust evaluation (see Sect. 14.5). All of these trust types are sub-concepts of *Trust*.

BootstrappedTrust: A new service/provider in a community needs to be assigned a nominal trust value to ensure that newcomers are not unfairly disadvantaged. We define such initial trust as *BootstrappedTrust*. For example, a new employment service *CampbellPageEmploymentService* is registered in the JSA community. Since this service is new, its trust cannot be calculated from interaction history. Therefore, this service will be assigned a nominal *BootstrappedTrust*. As

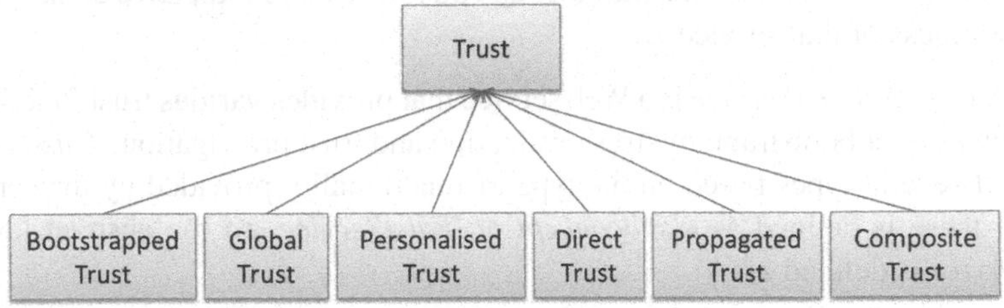

Fig. 14.5 Types of service trust

CampbellPageEmploymentService gets used and evaluated by job seekers, its *BootstrappedTrust* will be updated to reflect its trustworthiness. *BootstrappedTrust* is defined as:

```
concept TrustBootStrap subConceptOf TrustService
     hasInputData ofType TrustBootstrapInputData
     hasOperation ofType {TrustBootstrapping, TrustEndorsement}
     hasOutputData ofType BootstrappedTrust
```

Global Trust: In our community based environment, when trust evaluation is based on the collective perception of the whole community, such trust is termed as *GlobalTrust*. Everyone in the community has the same level of trust for a particular trustee (service/provider). The concept of community based trust (i.e., GlobalTrust) is defined as:

```
concept GlobalTrust subConceptOf Trust
     hasTrustor ofType ESPO#Community
     isBasedOnNumOfInteractions ofType _integer
```

Trustor is the community within which *GlobalTrust* is evaluated. In the employment service scenario, as *CampbellPageEmploymentService* gets invoked and evaluated by its consumers, its *BootstrappedTrust* will be updated and becomes its *GlobalTrust*. All feedback received by CampbellPageEmploymentService will be incorporated to obtain its GlobalTrust.

Personalised Trust: When trust evaluation incorporates the trustor's preferences with respect to various quality parameters, such trust is termed as *PersonalisedTrust*. When trust is personalised, the trust evaluation for the same trustee may be different depending on who the trustor is. Furthermore, trustor identification may be used to weigh the personalised trust values supplied by the trustor. *PersonalisedTrust* is defined as follows:

```
concept PersonalisedTrust subConceptOf Trust
     hasTrustor ofType ESPO#Consumer
     isBasedOnNumOfInteractions ofType _integer
     isBasedOnQoHSPreferences ofType  QoHSPrefTuple
```

Trustor is the consumer whose preferences have been considered in the personalised trust evaluation. *QoHSPreferences* defines the preferences of the trustor with value pairs of *QoHSParameter* and corresponding importance of that parameter to the user specified by Weight. In our example, for employment services, Alice considers the courteousness more important than effectiveness whereas John prefers efficiency over courteousness. Given these differences, for the same employment service

CampbellPageEmploymentService, Alice's *PersonalisedTrust* would be different from John's.
Direct Trust: The concept of trust based on direct past interactions between the trustor and trustee is defined as *DirectTrust*. Direct trust is a type of *PersonalisedTrust*. The concept of *DirectTrust* is defined as follows:

```
concept DirectTrust subConceptOf PersonalisedTrust
     hasTrustor ofType ESPO#Consumer
     isBasedOnNumOfDirectInteractions ofType _integer
```

For *DirectTrust*, trustor preferences for various QoHS parameters do not need to be specified. Trust evaluation is based on direct past evaluations, and therefore, trustor preferences are implicit in the evaluations. In our employment services example, Alice's *DirectTrust* on *CampbellPageEmploymentService* is computed based only on her past evaluations of *CampbellPageEmploymentService*.

Composite Trust: The concept of trust for a composite service, i.e., *CompositeTrust*, is based on the trust for the component services. This also includes the *BootstrapTrust* for composite services. Various algorithms may be used to determine the composite trust value from the atomic trust values of the component services. The concept of composite trust is defined as follows:

```
concept CompositeTrust
     hasTrustee ofType CSO#CompositeService
     hasTimeStamp ofType TimeStamp
     hasCompositeTrustValue ofType _string
```

CompositeTrust is typically used to facilitate selection among different service compositions providing the same functionality. Therefore, typically, *CompositeTrust* would be single use, i.e., used for comparisons and then discarded. For composite services that are likely to be used/invoked by many consumers, *CompositeTrust* is stored and will be regarded as the *GlobalTrust* for the composite service. In this respect, *CompositeTrust* can be considered as *BootstrappedTrust* for composite services. In our scenario, consider a new composite employment service combining different activities within EPP. When Alice is considering EPP activity options, the system will compute the *CompositeTrust* for EPP based on the trust for services providing different activities. If the EPP with same composition is needed for many job seekers, its *CompositeTrust* will be considered to be its *BootstrappedTrust* and stored. From this point onwards, JSA providers may evaluate the composite service just like an atomic service for different activities. Ratings provided for EPP will be used to update its *GlobalTrust*.
Propagated Trust: The concept of trust for the component services propagated from the trust score assigned to the composite service is termed as PropagatedTrust. The concept of *PropagatedTrust* is defined as follows:

```
concept PropagatedTrust
     hasTrustee ofType CSO#CompositeService
     hasTimeStamp ofType TimeStamp
     hasCompositeTrustValue ofType _string
```

TypeOfPropagation specifies whether the propagation is vertical, horizontal or hybrid, consistent with the type of service composition. In the above example, ratings assigned to the composite service EPP are propagated to the component activity services to obtain their *PropagatedTrust*. The *PropagatedTrust* for each component service is then used to update the corresponding *GlobalTrust*.

14.4.2 Trust Models

Reputation Information Collection Model: One of the important steps in the reputation-based trust management systems is to collect information that is necessary to evaluate the reputation of services. In our proposed trust management framework for human services, in particular employment services, we have proposed a community-based reputation information collection model. Figure 14.6 shows the interactions among different entities in our proposed model. We explain these interactions further below.

1. The first step is to register all service providers in the service registries. This step is a prerequisite for the community-based reputation information collection model. All service providers must be registered in the service registries so that they can be searched. For example, all JSA providers must be registered in an employment services registry.
2. The next step is registering service consumers to the community. The community provides a platform for a consumer to act as a *rater* and share its past experience with service providers. For example, a job seeker registers with the JSA community as a *rater*.
3. In this step, consumers search for providers in the service registries. It is important to note that other agents/services may request and search for the required services on behalf of consumers. For example, a human service related to a business process "looking for work" may search for all job providers meeting the job seeker's requirements.
4. The consumer selects a service and interacts with it. In our example, a job seeker selects one of the job providers and interacts with it. The interaction involves activities like creating employment plan, attending training, applying for jobs, preparing curriculum vitae, etc.
5. The next step is assessing the reputation of the service. The reputation assessment process involves getting feedback from the consumer on Quality of Human

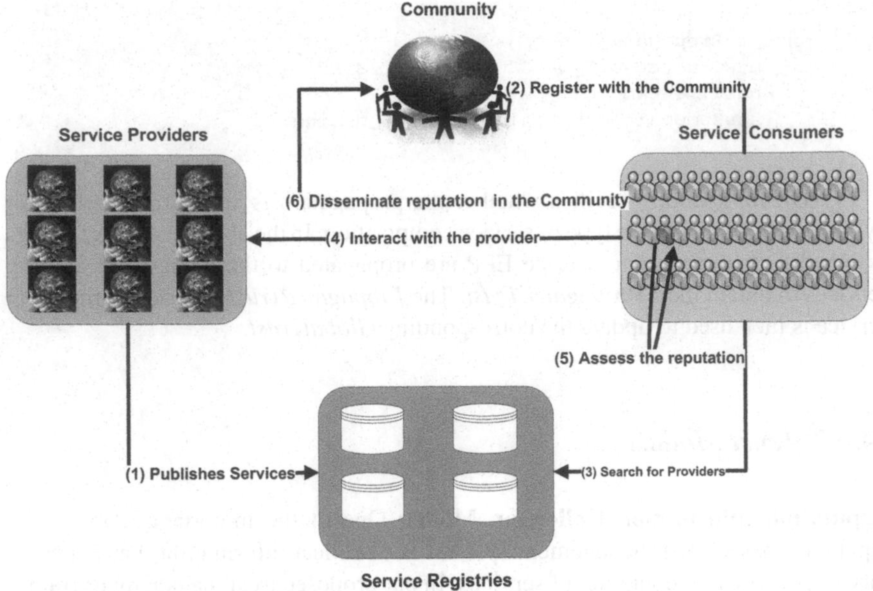

Fig. 14.6 Community based reputation information collection model

Service (QoHS) parameters and evaluating a reputation value (following the algorithm described in later).

6. The last step is to disseminate the evaluated reputation value to the community. The dissemination may include the final evaluated trust value or feedback values on each QoHS parameters or both. It depends on the underlying trust management service. In our implementation, a job seeker's feedback values on QoHS parameters are disseminated to the job provider community.

Reputation Evaluation Model: Once the trust related information is collected as described above, the trust management system must support a mechanism of evaluating trust value for each service provider. What do we understand by trust? We define trust as the belief that a service consumer has about the intention and the ability of a service provider to act as expected. How do we measure/establish a belief? The reputation is one of the mechanisms of establishing the belief about the provider's ability to deliver the service as expected by consumers. This is established through consumers' past behavior. Consumers past behavior is established through a collective perception of the consumers that have interacted with the service provider in the past. In this section, we first define the reputation based trust, and then propose a method of evaluating reputation considering a number of factors. We use the trust model based on the concept of community, where the reputation represents a collective perception of the users in the community regarding a service provider. The reputation of a given service is a collective perception of the consumers that have interacted with or used it in the past. The perception of each consumer about services they have invoked is called Personal Evaluation (PerEval). The personal evaluation could be a single value representing an overall perception or a vector representing a value for each Quality of Human Services (QoHS) attributes such as convenience, reliability and availability. For each service s_j that it has invoked, a service consumer c_i provides a *k-element* vector $PerEval^{ij}$ representing c_i's perception of s_j's behaviour. Then, the reputation of s_j, as perceived by a consumer c_i is defined as:

$$Reputation(s_j, c_i) = \bigwedge_{k \in K} (PerEval_k^{ij}) \tag{14.1}$$

where $\bigwedge$ represents the aggregation function. Equation 14.1 provides a first approximation of how the assessed reputation may be calculated for a service s_j. The service s_j could be a simple service or a composite service. In the case of a simple service, the reputation value calculated by the Eq. 14.1 is directly assigned to the service s_j. However, this gets complicated if the service s_j is a composite service. The reputation value received by s_j from the consumer c_i needs to be propagated to s_j's component services. We describe a method of propagating reputation value to component services later. Equation 14.1 shows a simple method of evaluating reputation value of a service provider based on a single consumer's feedback on QoHS parameters. Let us assume there are N number of consumers in a community who have interacted with the service s_j in the past. The reputation of the service in the community is calculated as:

$$Reputation(s_j) = \bigwedge_{k \in K, x \in N} (PerEval_k^{xij}) \tag{14.2}$$

There are a number of additional factors that influence the overall reputation value of a service such as credibility of the raters, preference of the consumer requesting the reputation value, and temporal sensitiveness of the feedback values. In our current model, we consider the consumer preference and temporal sensitivity in our calculation as follows.

Service consumers may have different preferences on QoHS parameters. This may result in different reputation values. For example, a job seeker may give higher preference to convenience over effectiveness, whereas another job seeker may give higher preference on courteousness than responsiveness. We allow the service consumers to calculate the reputation value of the service providers according to their own personal preference. Each service consumer defines a personal preference through a weight vector (w). Since service consumers can change their preferences from one request to another, the W is submitted with each reputation request submission. In this manner, the consumers have the ability to weigh the different QoHS parameters according to their own preferences. Let *w(k)* denote the preference assigned to QoHS parameter k by the service consumer c_i. The reputation value in Eq. 14.2 is then represented as:

$$Reputation(s_j) = \bigwedge_{k \in K, x \in N} w(k) \times (PerEval_k^{xij}) \tag{14.3}$$

Service consumers expect service providers to behave in a fair and consistent manner. Reputation values are directly affected by the consistency of offered services. However, there are situations where all the past data is of little or no importance. For instance, a service's performance may degrade over time. It may be the case that considering all historical data may provide an incorrect reputation value. In order to counter such discrepancies, we incorporate temporal sensitivity in our evaluation model. The rating submissions are time-stamped to assign more weight to recent observations and less to older ones for calculating the reputation value. This is termed as reputation fading where older perceptions gradually fade and fresh ones take their place. We adjust the value of the reputation as:

$$Reputation(s_j) = \bigwedge_{k \in K, x \in N} w(k) \times (PerEval_k^{xij}) \times f_d \qquad (14.4)$$

where f_d is the reputation fader. In our model, the most recent perception has the fader value 1 while older observations are decremented at equal intervals for each time instance passed. When $f_d = 0$, the perception is not included as it is considered to be outdated.

Reputation Bootstrapping Model: The reputation-based trust models rely on the feedback received from past interactions. How to deal with the newcomers with no past interactions? This means sometimes the reputation of a service has to be started on the basis of (a) no past experience of direct interactions, (b) a lack of experience in any meaningful role, (c) no witness reports, and (d) no evidence-based third party references. We refer to this issue as *bootstrapping* problem.

Bootstrapping is a major issue in human services because historical information may not be available regarding new services. For example, a new JSA provider is licensed to operate in a regional area to meet a growing demand in the region. When a new service is introduced, it is necessary to bootstrap its trust by assigning an initial reputation value. If the new service is assigned the lowest default reputation value, it may be overlooked over other existing services and treated unfairly in terms of competitive advantages. If the newcomer is assigned a high initial reputation value, then existing services are penalised. This may give a motivation to discard their identities and start fresh if their trust level falls below a certain threshold. Therefore, the trust bootstrapping mechanism should not only promote new services, but also encourage existing services to keep their reputation profiles. Here, the concept of trust bootstrapping refers to the process initialization of trust for a new service.

We have proposed a community-based reputation bootstrapping approach for human services. Figure 14.7 shows the interactions among different entities in the community-based reputation bootstrapping model. We describe these interactions in brief below.

1. The service consumer asks the reputation of a new service provider by submitting a query to the service trust manager. For example, a Centrelink service, on behalf of a job seeker, asks the reputation of a JSA provider by submitting a query to the service trust manager.

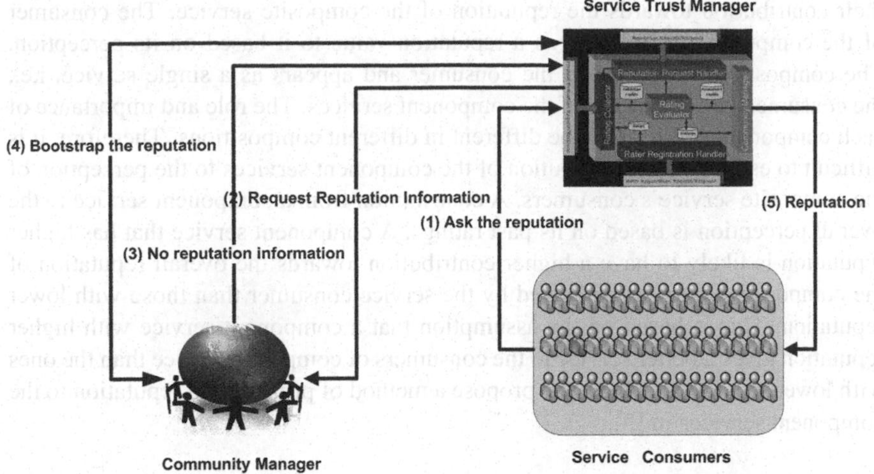

Fig. 14.7 Community based reputation bootstrapping model

2. The service trust manager does not have any reputation information. The reputation information belongs to the community manager. The service trust manager requests the reputation information from the community. In our example, the service trust manager requests the information from the job seeker's community (i.e., JSA community). It is important to mention that the service trust manager may reside within Centrelink or may be provided by a trusted third party.
3. Since the service provider is new, the community manager informs the service trust manager that there are no past usage information available for the given service. This requires the initiation of bootstrapping process. In our example, this means the JSA community does not have any feedback information associated with a particular JSA provider.
4. The trust manager requests the bootstrapping process. The process involves the execution of a bootstrapping algorithm and assigning the reputation value to the new service provider. The bootstrapping algorithm could be executed in either trust manager or community manager. The place of execution depends on how the algorithm is implemented. In our initial implementation, the bootstrapping algorithm simply assigns an average trust value (i.e., average of all ratings) of all members in the community to the newcomer. Therefore, the execution of bootstrapping algorithm takes place at the community manager.
5. The trust manager returns the reputation value to the consumer. The execution of the bootstrapping algorithm is transparent to the consumers.

Reputation Propagation Model: The reputation value received from the consumer for a composite service needs to be propagated to its component services. We propose a contribution-based distribution of reputation method for propagating reputation to component services. Each component service receives the reputation based on their contribution towards the reputation of the composite service. The consumer of the composite service assigns a reputation value to it based on its perception. The composition is opaque to the consumer and appears as a single service, i.e., the consumers are not aware of the component services. The role and importance of each component service may be different in different compositions. Therefore, it is difficult to estimate the contribution of the component services to the perception of the composite service's consumers. A contribution from a component service to the overall perception is based on its past ratings. A component service that has higher reputation is likely to have a higher contribution towards the overall reputation of the composite service as perceived by the service consumer than those with lower reputation. This is based on the assumption that a component service with higher reputation gives a better service to the consumers of composite service than the ones with lower reputation values. We propose a method of propagating reputation to the component services in [5].

14.5 Case Study

We illustrate how our trust management framework helps Alice (a citizen in need of help) to select the best service provider in assisting her to get employed. Alice is looking to re-enter employment after a gap of many years. Alice reports a new life event *looking for work* to the Human Services Department. The service selector maps a service request to the resources, processes and services registered in the Service Repository.. The Service Composer creates an integrated workflow by combining eligible employment services, processes and resources returned by the Service Selector. The composer generates an abstract composite service which includes a number of employment related services such as job capacity assessor and Employment Pathway Plan. The service selector selects the appropriate third party services and executes it. Once the registration process is completed, Alice has to answer a number of questions to classify her level of difficulties in finding job.

We assume that Alice has some difficulties and needs to have her job capacity assessed. This triggers the job capacity assessment service as well as job service provider services. This composite service is then passed on to the Service Optimiser. In our framework, we measure the quality of human services using some non-functional properties such as *reputation-based trust* computed on a defined set of QoHS parameters. The Service Optimiser is responsible for ensuring that these non-functional properties of the final integrated workflow presented to the customer are optimal within the resource and technology boundaries of the human services department. In the following, we explain how our trust management framework helps the service optimiser to produce the optimal solution for the customer. We explain it using an example of job service providers. However, the example scenario below is applicable to all component services in the abstract composite service if there are more than one corresponding concrete services.

The Department of Employment is registered in the *CommunityManagementService* as a community provider. The Australian government has contracted a wide range of organizations to provide employment services to its citizens. These organizations include small, medium and large enterprises operating in both profit and non-profit modes. These organizations are called job service providers and they are expected to deliver high quality services to the citizens. This means Department of Employment defines a community called *Job Community* using the *CommunityManagementService*. Within Job community, there are many employment service providers. Job providers are the members of the Job community that provides employment services. These concepts about community are stored in the ontology and are accessed using *OntologyAccessService*.

Alice lives in a small town. There are many Job Providers in her neighbourhood such as X, Y and Z (real names are removed). These providers offer employment services to customers under the contract with Department of Employment. Each of these service providers may have been used by a large number of customers. Their feedback is collected and managed by the *CommunityManagementService*. The optimizer invokes *GetTopK* method of the *TrustManagementService* to retrieve best Job providers for Alice. The *TrustManagementService* retrieves the history of all Job providers that meet Alice's requirements in terms of locality and the types of services provided. It then evaluates their trust and creates a ranked list of Job providers. The top K providers from the ranked list are returned to the optimizer along with their trust values. The optimizer/Alice may select one of the recommended service providers depending on the situation.

14.6 Conclusions

This chapter described a community based trust management framework for human services. Our approach is based on the consumers' experience on provider's past behaviour. We described the proposed approach, system architecture, algorithms and protocols using the motivation from the employment services model. We reported an initial implementation of the *Service Trust Management System* within the proposed holistic *Human Services Delivery System*. We then discussed the proposed model with a case study of a citizen looking for work. The initial implementation was demonstrated in the context of employment service.

References

1. Bouguettaya, A., Nepal, S., Sherchan, W., Zhou, X., Wu, J., Chen, S., Liu, D., Li, L., Wang, H., Liu, X. 2010. End-to-end service support for mashups. IEEE Transactions on Services Computing 3, 3, 250–263.

2. Li, L., Liu, D., Bouguettaya, A. 2009. Semantic weaving for context-aware web service composition. In International Conference on Web Information System, Engineering. 101–114.
3. Maximilien, E.M. and Singh, M.P. 2004. Toward autonomic web services trust and selection. In Proceedings of the 2nd international conference on Service oriented computing (ICSOC '04). ACM, New York, NY, USA, 212–221.
4. Medjahed, B., Atif, Y. 2007. Context-based matching for web service composition. Distributed and Parallel Databases 21, 1, 5–37.
5. Nepal, S., Malik, Z., Bouguettaya, A. 2009. Reputation Propagation in Composite Services. International Conference on Web Services, 295–302.
6. Ouzzani, M., Bouguettaya, A. 2004. Efficient access to web services. IEEE Internet Computing 8, 2, 34–44.
7. Ryu, S. H., Casati, F., Skogsrud, H., Benatallah, B., Saint-Paul, R. 2008. Supporting the dynamic evolution of web service protocols in service-oriented architectures. ACM Transactions on the Web 2, 2, 1–46.
8. Sherchan, W., Nepal, S., Hunklinger, J., Bouguettaya, A. 2010. "A Trust Ontology for Semantic Services," Services Computing, IEEE International Conference on, IEEE International Conference on Services Computing, pp. 313–320.
9. Sherchan, W., Nepal, S., Bouguettaya, A., Chen, S. 2012. Context-sensitive user interfaces for semantic services. ACM Transactions on Internet Technologies, 11, 3.
10. Wang, H., Zhou, X., Zhou, X., Liu, W., Li, W., Bouguettaya, A. 2010. Adaptive service composition based on reinforcement learning. In Proceedings of International Conference on Service Oriented, Computing (ICSOC). 92–107.
11. Zhou, X., Chen, S., Bouguettaya, A., Kai, X. 2009. Supporting Bioinformatic Experiments with a Service Query Engine. In Proceedings of the 2009 Congress on Services - I (SERVICES '09). 717–723.

Chapter 15
Trust-Oriented Service Provider Selection in Complex Online Social Networks

Guanfeng Liu and Yan Wang

Abstract In recent years, Online Social Networks (OSNs) with numerous participants have been used as the means for rich activities. For example, employers could use OSNs to investigate potential employees, and participants could use OSNs to look for movie recommendations. In these activities, trust is one of the most important indication of participants decision making, greatly demanding the evaluation of the trustworthiness of a service provider along certain social trust paths from a service consumer. In this chapter, we first analyze the characteristics of the current generation of functional websites and the current generation of online social networks based on their functionality and sociality, and present the properties of the new generation of social network based web applications. Then we present a new selection model considering both *adjacent* and *end-to-end* constraints, based on a novel concept Quality of Trust and a novel complex social network structure. Moreover, in order to select the optimal one from a lot of social trust paths yielding the most trustworthy trust evaluation result, this chapter presents an effective and efficient heuristic algorithm for optimal social trust path selection with constraints, which is actually an NP-Complete problem. Experimental results illustrate that our proposed method outperforms existing models in both efficiency and the quality of delivered solutions. This work provides key techniques to potentially lots of service-oriented applications with social networks as the backbone.

G. Liu (✉) · Y. Wang
Department of Computing, Macquarie University, Sydney, Australia
e-mail: guanfeng.liu@mq.edu.au

Y. Wang
e-mail: yan.wang@mq.edu.au

A. Bouguettaya et al. (eds.), *Advanced Web Services*,
DOI: 10.1007/978-1-4614-7535-4_15,

15.1 Introduction

Online Social Networks (OSNs) (e.g. Facebook[1] and MySpace[2]) have become increasingly popular recently and are being used as the means for a variety of rich activities. In service-oriented environment, OSNs can provide the infrastructure for the recommendation of service providers or services. According to a survey on 2600 hiring managers (i.e., service consumers) in 2008 by Career Builder[3] (a popular job hunting website), 22 % of them used social networking sites to investigate potential employees (i.e., service providers). The ratio increased to 45 % in June 2009, and 72 % in January 2010. In addition, participants (i.e., service consumers) could look for the service of movie recommendation at FilmTrust,[4] a movie recommendation OSN. In recent years, the new generation of social network based web application systems has drawn the attention from both academia and industry. The study in [1] has pointed out that it is a trend to build up social network based web applications (e.g., e-commerce or online recruitment systems). In October 2011, eBay[5] announced their strategic plan to deepen the relationship with Facebook[1] for creating a new crop of e-commerce applications with social networking features, integrating both their e-commerce platform and social networking platform seamlessly.[6] In such a situation, trust is one of the most important indications for service consumers decision making, greatly demanding approaches and mechanisms for evaluating the trustworthiness between a service consumer and a service provider who don't know each other.

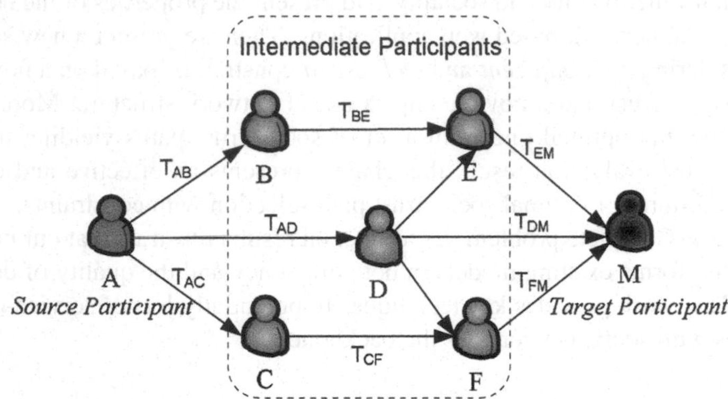

Fig. 15.1 social network structure

[1] http://www.facebook.com/

[2] http://www.myspace.com/

[3] http://www.careerbuilder.com/

[4] http://trust.mindswap.org/FilmTrust/

[5] http://www.ebay.com/

[6] refer to the Reuters news "eBay and Facebook unveil e-commerce partnership" at http://www.reuters.com/article/2011/10/12/ebay-facebook-idUSN1E79B22Y20111012

In OSNs, one participant can give a trust value to another based on their past interactions (e.g., T_{AB} in Fig. 15.1). If there exist a trust path (e.g, $A \rightarrow B \rightarrow E \rightarrow M$ in Fig. 15.1) linking two nonadjacent participants (there is no direct link between them), the source participant (i.e., the service consumer) can evaluate the trustworthiness of the target participant (i.e., the service provider) based on the trust information between the intermediate participants along the path. The path with trust information linking the source participant and the target participant is called a *social trust path* [2, 3].

In the literature, several methods have been proposed for trust evaluation in OSNs [2–5]. But these models have three main drawbacks: (1) As illustrated in social psychology [6, 7], the *social relationships* between participants (e.g., the one between an employer and an employee) and the *recommendation roles* of participants (e.g., a supervisor as a referee in his postgraduate's job application) have significant influence on trust and thus should be considered in the trust evaluation of participants. However, they are not considered by existing methods. (2) As there are usually many social trust paths between participants, existing methods evaluate the trustworthiness of a participant based on all social paths incurring huge computation time [2, 3]. Although a few methods [4, 5] have been proposed to address the path selection problem, they yet neglect the influence of social information on path selection. (3) In OSNs, a source participant may have different purposes in evaluating the trustworthiness of a target participant, such as *hiring employees* or *introducing products*. Therefore, a source participant should be able to set certain constraints on the *trust*, *social relationship* and *recommendation role* in trust path selection. However, existing methods do not support these selection criteria.

15.2 Related Work

The studies of social network properties can be traced back to 1960s when the small-world characteristic in social networks was validated by Milgram [8] (i.e., the average path length between two Americans was found to be about 6.6 hops). In recent years, sociologists and computer scientists investigated the characteristics of popular online social networks (OSNs) [9] (e.g., Facebook[1], MySpace[2] and Flickr[7]), and validated the small-world and power-law characteristics (i.e., the probability that a node has a degree k is proportional to k^{-r}, $r > 1$).

In the literature, the issue of trust becomes increasingly important in social networks. we review the existing approaches for evaluating the trustworthiness of participants in OSNs.

---

[7] http://flickr.com

15.2.1 Trust Network Discovery

As indicated in the disciplines of Social Psychology [10, 11] and Computer Science [2, 12], a trust network from a source to a target can provide the basis for evaluating the trustworthiness of the target as it contains some important intermediate participants, the trust relations between them and the social context under which their interactions happened, all of which have an important influence on trust relationships and trust evaluation. Extracting such a contextual trust network is an essential step before performing any trust evaluation between two participants in social networks. In addition, the results of trust network discovery can affect the trustworthiness of the trust evaluation [2, 13, 14]. To address the NP-Complete trust network discovery problem [15], in our previous work [16, 17], we have proposed a new social context-aware trust network discovery model which considers the influence of social context in trust network discovery. Furthermore, we have proposed two efficient and effective algorithms, i.e., an approximation algorithm, called SCAN, and a heuristic algorithm, called H-SCAN, to discover trust networks.

15.2.2 Trust Evaluation Based on Ratings Only

In this type of trust evaluation models, only ratings given to a target participant are considered. For example, at eBay[5], after each transaction, a buyer can give feedback with a rating of "positive", "neutral" or "negative" to the seller according to the seller's service quality. The overall positive feedback rate of the seller is calculated to reveal his/her trustworthiness, which is valuable to buyer. However, this type of trust evaluation model neglects the implicit social relationships between buyers and sellers that actually have significant influence on trust evaluation.

15.2.3 Trust Evaluation Based on All Social Trust Paths

In some other trust evaluation models, the trustworthiness of a target participant is evaluated based on all social trust paths between a source participant and the target participant. For example, in [2], the trust value of a target participant is computed by averaging all trust values along all social trust paths. In [5], Walter et al. propose a trust-based recommendation system. In their model, all social trust paths between a buyer and a seller selling the products preferred by the buyer are taken into account to evaluate the trustworthiness of the seller.

This type of trust evaluation methods neglects the social information with significant influence on trust evaluation. In addition, evaluating the trustworthiness of a target participant based on all social trust paths is very time consuming and thus they can not be applied in large-scale social networks.

15.2.4 Trust Evaluation Based on Selected Social Trust Path

In the literature, there are only a few works addressing the social path selection problem. In *SmallBlue* [4], an online social network constructed for IBM staff, between a source participant and a target participant, up to 16 social paths with no more than 6 hops are selected and the shortest one is taken as the optimal one that delivers the most trustworthy trust evaluation result. But this method neglects *trust information*, *recommendation roles* and *social relationships* between participants. In [3], the social trust path with the maximum of propagated trust value is selected as the most trustworthy one. Their model neglects recommendation roles and social relationships. In addition, none of these models considers different preferences of source participants.

15.2.5 Social Trust Influence on Service Selection

As indicated in Social Psychology [18, 19], in the reality of our society, a person prefers the recommendation from his/her trusted friends over those from others. In addition, in the discipline of Computer Science, based on statistics, Bedi et al., [20] has demonstrated that, given a choice between recommendations from trusted friends and those from recommender systems, trusted friends' recommendations are more preferred in terms of quality and usefulness. Furthermore, in several recent studies, some researchers [21, 22] have investigated how and to what extent a participant's service selection behavior (e.g., installing a specific application software) impacts on his/her friends' decision-making in service selection. These studies have indicated that the recommendations from trusted friends have significant influence on service or target selection, not only in the society in the real world, but also in OSNs.

Although a complete social network based trust-oriented service recommendation system does not yet exists, it has become an important research topic in recent years. Some researchers [23, 24] have proposed several models to provide more accurate recommendations of products and/or services by taking some social context information into consideration. In these studies, social trust path selection is a critical problem.

15.3 A New Categorization of OSNs

Golbeck et al. [25] propose the criteria of OSNs as follows. (1) OSNs could be accessible over the web with a web browser; (2) Users of OSNs must explicitly state their relationships with other people; (3) The web-based online social network system has explicit built-in support for users to make social connections, and (4) Each relationship is visible and browseable to users. Boyd et al. [26] propose the definition of social networking sites as Web-based services that allow individuals to

(1) construct public or semi-public profiles within a bounded system; (2) articulate a list of other users with whom they share connections; and (3) view and traverse their list of connections and those made by others with the system. Obviously, Facebook[1] and MySpace[2] are in accordance with these definitions.

However, many other Websites, like YouTube,[8] eBay[5], Blogs and online forums, where people can share their experience and carry out business. But relationships between participants on this type of Websites are implicit. Thus, it is still a puzzling problem whether these Websites belong to the scope of OSNs. In the following context, we first analyze the characteristics of these websites based on their functionality and sociality and present the properties of the new generation of OSNs [1].

15.3.1 The Current Generation of Functional Websites

The current generation of functional websites, like eBay[5], support rich functionality but do not contain explicit social relationships. For example, eBay[5] supports e-commerce activities and buying-selling relations. But it does not consider social relationships like a supervisor and his/her students, and a father and his son among the set of buyers and sellers. We summarize the characteristics of these functional websites as below.

1. They have weak sociality where the relationships between participants are implicit; and participants do not keep their friendship lists and thus they can not make new friends with friends of friends.
2. Then have rich functionality, such as email, Blogs, e-commerce, and video and photo sharing, etc.

15.3.2 The Current Generation of OSNs

As the sociality of the above websites is too weak for people to make rich social interactions, the current generation of OSNs, such as MySpace[2] and Facebook[1] emerged in 2003 and 2005 respectively. They can explicitly express simple social relations, but the functionality is limited to a very small scope, like information sharing. We summarize the characteristics of the current generation of OSNs as below.

1. They have medium sociality where the social relationships between participants are explicit and binary (friendship or non-friendship) which can be specified by participants; and participants can make new friends with a friend's friends, which is stronger than that of current functional website.

[8] http://www.youtube.com

2. They provide a platform where participants can make new friends and conduct some simple activities (e.g., sharing photos and videos) which are not as rich as those in current functional website.

15.3.3 The New Generation of OSNs

Technically, we can envisage that in the near future social networks can become the backbone to extend a number of traditional systems. For example, the traditional e-commerce system can have a social network of its buyers, and the friends' friends of buyers. Likewise, the traditional CRM (Customer Relation Management) systems can be extended to be supported by a social network of customers and other people with relations to these customers. Thus, the new generation of social network systems can be expected to support both rich social relations and rich functionality. In these systems, it would be easier to introduce products (e.g., by a retailer) or good sellers (e.g., by a buyer) to buyers, and the friends' friends of buyers. We summarize the characteristics of the new generation OSNs as below.

1. They have strong sociality where the social relationships are explicit and complex rather than the binary (friendship or non-friendship) in current generation OSNs.
2. They provide a platform where participants can conduct rich activities, such as, e-commerce, CRM system, recommendation systems.

15.4 Complex Social Networks

As the current functional website and OSNs can hardly illustrate real-world complex social information of social networks in real world scenarios [27], we present a complex social network structure, as depicted in Fig. 15.2, modeling well the social networks in real life. It contains the attributes of three impact factors, i.e., *trust*, *social intimacy degree* and *role impact factor*. Then have influence on trust evaluation and hence the decision making of participants.

15.4.1 A Complex Social Network Structure

15.4.2 Trust

In human societies, trust is a complex topic subject to a lot of factors, such as previous experience, and other people's recommendations [2]. Many different trust definitions have been proposed addressing different aspects. Alunkal et al. [28] define that "trust is the value attributed to a specific entity, including an agent, a service, or a person,

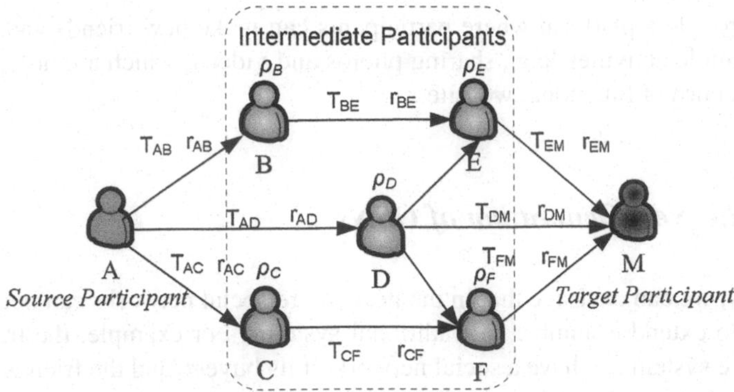

Fig. 15.2 Complex social network

based on the behaviors exhibited by the entity in the past". Golbeck et al. [2] define that "trust in a person is a commitment to an action based on a belief that the future action of that person will lead to a good outcome".

In the context of this paper, trust between participants in social networks can be defined as follows.

Definition 15.1 *Trust* is the belief of one participant in another, based on their interactions, in the extent to which the future action to be performed by the latter will lead to an expected outcome.

Let $T_{AB} \in [0, 1]$ denote the trust value that participant A assigns to participant B. If $T_{AB} = 0$, it indicates that A completely distrusts B while $T_{AB} = 1$ indicates A completely believes B's future action can lead to the expected outcome.

15.4.3 Social Intimacy Degree

As illustrated in social psychology [29], a participant can trust the participants with whom he/she has more intimate social relationships more than those with whom he/she has less intimate social relationships. Therefore, we introduce the social intimacy degree between participants into complex social networks structure, and give its definition as follows.

Definition 15.2 $r_{AB} \in [0, 1]$ is the *Social Intimacy Degree* between any given participants A and B in online social networks. $r_{AB} = 0$ indicates that A and B have no social relationship while $r_{AB} = 1$ indicates they have the most intimate social relationship.

15.4.4 Role Impact Factor

Rich activities of participants in social networks can be categorized into different domains (e.g., hiring employees or product sale) based on their characteristics [30]. As illustrated in social psychology [6], in a certain domain, the recommendation from a person who has expertise in the domain is more credible than the recommendation from a person who has no knowledge in that domain. Therefore, we introduce the role impact factor of a participant into the complex social network structure, and give its definition as follows.

Definition 15.3 $\rho_A \in [0, 1]$ is the value of the *Role Impact Factor*, illustrating the impact of participant A's recommendation role on trust propagation. $\rho_A = 1$ indicates that A is a domain expert while $\rho_A = 0$ indicates that A has no knowledge in the domain.

Though it is difficult to construct social relationships and comprehensive role hierarchies in all domains for the whole society, and obtain their global values, it is feasible to build them up in a specific social community.

For example, in the work by Mccallum et al. [31], through mining the subjects and contents of emails in *Enron* Corporation,[9] the social relationship between each email sender and receiver can be discovered and their roles can be known. Then the corresponding social intimacy degree and role impact factor values can be estimated based on probabilistic models. In addition, in academic social networks formed by large databases of Computer Science literature (e.g, DBLP[10] or ACM Digital Library[11]), the social relationships between two scholars (e.g., co-authors, a supervisor and his/her students) and the role of scholars (e.g., a professor in the field of data mining) can be mined from publications or their homepages. The social intimacy degree and role impact factor values can be calculated as an example by applying the PageRank model [32]. Furthermore, in addition to mine these values, the social position of a participant can be specified directly [33]. If the participant becomes a recommender, this social position information could illustrate his/her role impact factor in the recommendation of a specific domain.

Based on the above discussion, in addition to participants and the links between them, we propose a new structure for complex social networks that models trust, social intimacy degree and role impact factors, as depicted in Fig. 15.2.

15.5 Multiple QoT Constrained Social Trust Path Selection

To satisfy the different preferences of a source participant in social trust path selection, in this section, we introduce a novel concept Quality of Trust (QoT) and present a multiple QoT constrained social trust path selection model.

[9] http://www.cs.cmu.edu/~enron/

[10] http://www.informatik.uni-trier.de/~ley/db/

[11] http://portal.acm.org/

15.5.1 *Quality of Trust (QoT)*

Similar to the Quality of Service (QoS) in service-oriented computing, we present a new concept, *Quality of Trust* in social trust path selection.

Quality of Trust (QoT) is the ability to guarantee a certain level of trustworthiness in trust evaluation along a social trust path, taking trust (T), social intimacy degree (r), and role impact factor (ρ), as attributes.

15.5.2 *QoT Constraint*

To be adaptive to the rich activities in OSNs, a source participant should be able to set certain constraints of QoT attributes in selecting the optimal social trust path. They include two types: *Adjacent QoT Constraint (AQC)* and *End-to-End QoT Constraint (EEQC)*.

15.5.2.1 Adjacent QoT Constraint (AQC)

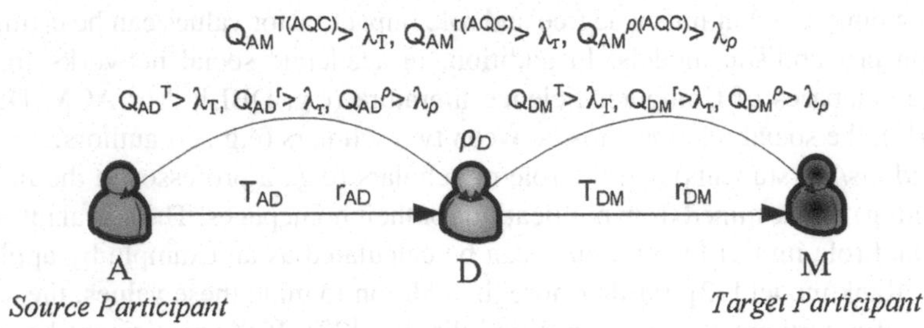

Fig. 15.3 Adjacent QoT constraints

An Adjacent QoT Constraint (AQC) is the constraint of a QoT attribute (i.e., T, r or ρ) between any two adjacent participants in a social trust path. In the complex social network depicted in Fig. 15.2, let $Q_{AM}^{\mu(AQC)}$ ($\mu \in \{T, r, \rho\}$) denote the AQC for the path between source participant A and target participant M. $Q_{AM}^{\mu(AQC)} > \lambda_\mu$ ($0 < \lambda_\mu < 1$) means that the value of QoT attribute μ between any two adjacent participants in a selected social trust path should be larger than λ_μ. For example, if the AQCs specified by A can be satisfied at $A \rightarrow D$, and $D \rightarrow M$, then social trust path $A \rightarrow D \rightarrow M$ satisfies the AQCs. In our model, a source participant can specify different AQCs. E.g., in *hiring employees*, A, a retailer manager specifies AQCs as $Q_{AM}^{T(AQC)} > 0.3$, $Q_{AM}^{r(AQC)} > 0.3$ and $Q_{AM}^{\rho(AQC)} > 0.8$. But when looking for new customers for *selling products*, A can specify $Q_{AM}^{r(AQC)} > 0.8$, if he/she believes the social relationships between participants are more important (Fig. 15.3).

15.5.2.2 End-to-End QoT Constraint (EEQC)

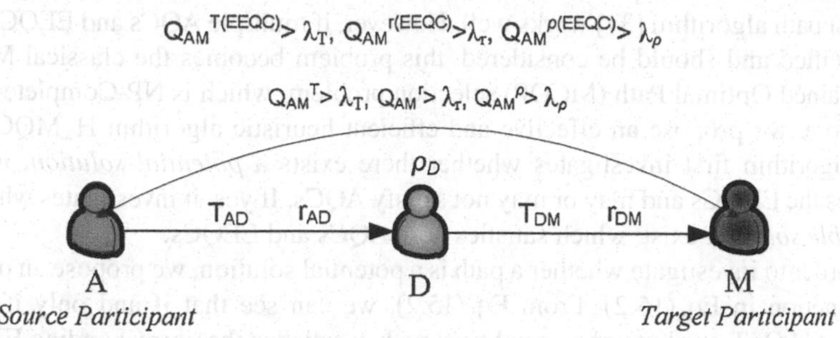

Fig. 15.4 End-to-End QoT constraints

An End-to-End QoT Constraint (EEQT) is the constraint of an aggregated QoT attribute value (i.e., T, r or ρ) between a source and a target in a social trust path. In Fig. 15.2, let $Q_{AM}^{\mu(EEQC)}$ ($\mu \in \{T, r, \rho\}$) denote the EEQC between source participant A and target participant M. $Q_{AM}^{\mu(EEQC)} > \lambda_\mu$ ($0 < \lambda_\mu < 1$) means the aggregated value of QoT attribute μ in a social trust path between A and M should be larger than λ. In addition to AQC, a source participant can also specify different EEQCs. E.g., in *hiring employees*, A can set EEQCs as $Q_{AM}^{T(EEQC)} > 0.3$, $Q_{AM}^{r(EEQC)} > 0.3$ and $Q_{AM}^{\rho(EEQC)} > 0.8$. But when looking for new customers for *selling products*, A can specify $Q_{AM}^{r(EEQC)} > 0.8$, if he/she believes the social relationships between participants are more important (Fig. 15.4).

15.5.3 Utility Function

Based on our proposed QoT attribute aggregation method [27], we define the utility (denoted as $\mathscr{F}$) in path $p(a_1, ..., a_n)$ as Eq. (15.1), which is the measurement of the trustworthiness of $p(a_1, ..., a_n)$ in trust evaluation.

$$\mathscr{F}_{p(a_1,\dots,a_n)} = \omega_T * T_{p(a_1,\dots,a_n)} + \omega_r * r_{p(a_1,\dots,a_n)} + \omega_\rho * \rho_{p(a_1,\dots,a_n)} \tag{15.1}$$

where $T_{p(a_1,\dots,a_n)}$, $r_{p(a_1,\dots,a_n)}$ and $\rho_{p(a_1,\dots,a_n)}$ are the aggregated value of trust, social intimacy degree and role impact factor of path $p(a_1, ..., a_n)$ respectively, ω_T, ω_r and ω_ρ are the weights of T, r and ρ respectively; $0 < \omega_T, \omega_r, \omega_\rho < 1$ and $\omega_T + \omega_r + \omega_\rho = 1$.

15.6 A Heuristic Algorithm for the MQCSTP Selection Problem

In optimal social trust path selection, if we consider trust values only, Dijkstra's shortest path algorithm [34] works well. However, if multiple AQCs and EEQCs can be specified and should be considered, this problem becomes the classical Multi-Constrained Optimal Path (MCOP) selection problem, which is NP-Complete [35]. Therefore, we propose an effective and efficient heuristic algorithm H_MQCSTP. This algorithm first investigates whether there exists a *potential solution*, which satisfies the EEQCs and may or may not satisfy AQCs. If yes, it investigates whether a *feasible solution* exist, which satisfies both AQCs and EEQCs.

In order to investigate whether a path is a potential solution, we propose an objective function in Eq. (15.2). From Eq. (15.2), we can see that if and only if each aggregated QoT attribute of a social trust path p satisfies the corresponding EEQC, $\delta(p) \leq 1$; otherwise $\delta(p) > 1$.

$$\delta(p) \triangleq max \left\{ \left(\frac{1 - T_p}{1 - Q_p^{T(EEQC)}} \right), \left(\frac{1 - r_p}{1 - Q_p^{r(EEQC)}} \right), \left(\frac{1 - \rho_p}{1 - Q_p^{\rho(EEQC)}} \right) \right\} \tag{15.2}$$

In addition, we adopt Dijkstra's shortest path algorithm [34] twice in both *backward* and *forward* search, together with our proposed novel heuristic search strategies to select the optimal social trust path.

Backward_Search: In the backward search, H_MQCSTP aims to identify the path p_s from the target v_t to the source v_s with the minimal δ based on Dijkstra's shortest path algorithm [34]. In this searching process, at each node v_k ($v_k \neq v_t$), the path from v_t to v_k with the minimal δ (denoted as p_k) is identified. Meanwhile T_{p_k}, r_{p_k} and ρ_{p_k} are aggregated and recorded.

The *Backward_Search* procedure can always identify the path with the minimal δ. If $\delta_{min} > 1$, it indicates that there is no potential solution in the sub-network. If $\delta_{min} \leq 1$, it indicates that there exists at least one potential solution and the identified path is a potential one.

Forward_Search: If there exists one potential solution in the sub-network, a heuristic forward search is executed from v_s to v_t. This process adopts the information provided by the above *Backward_Search* to investigate whether there is a feasible solution p_t. In this procedure, H_MQCSTP first searches the path with the maximal utility from v_s. Assume node $v_m \in \{neighboring\ nodes\ of\ v_s\}$ is selected based on Dijkstra's shortest path algorithm [35] as the utility of the path from v_s to v_m (denoted as path $p^{(f)}_{v_s \to v_m}$) is the maximal. Let $p^{(b)}_{v_m \to v_t}$ denote the path from v_m to v_t identified in the *Backward_Search* procedure. Then a *foreseen path* from v_s to v_t via v_m (denoted as $fp_{v_s \to v_m \to v_t} = p^{(f)}_{v_s \to v_m} + p^{(b)}_{v_m \to v_t}$) is identified. According to whether $fp_{v_s \to v_m \to v_t}$ is feasible, H_MQCSTP adopts the following searching strategies.

Situation 1: If $fp_{v_s \to v_m \to v_t}$ is a feasible solution, then H_MQCSTP chooses the next node from v_m with the maximal utility following Dijkstra's shortest path algorithm.

Situation 2: If $fp_{v_s \to v_m \to v_t}$ is not a feasible solution, then H_MQCSTP does not search any path from v_m and link $v_s \to v_m$ is deleted from the sub-network. Subsequently, H_MQCSTP performs the *Forward_Search* procedure to search other path from v_s in the sub-network.

Since H_MQCSTP adopts twice Dijkstra's shortest path algorithm, they have the same time complexity of $O(N^2)$ when implementing the priority queue with a disordered array, which can be optimized to $O(NlogN + E)$ by adopting a Fibonacci heap to store the priority queue [34] (N is the number of nodes and E is the number of links in the sub-network). H_MCOP [35] which is the most promising algorithm for the NP-Complete MCOP selection problem, has the same time complexity as H_MQCSTP. But our proposed heuristic algorithm adopts a better objective function and better searching strategies and thus can significantly outperform H_MCOP in both efficiency and the quality of selected social trust paths

15.7 Experiments

15.7.1 Experiment Settings

In order to validate our proposed algorithm, we need a dataset which contains social network structures. The *Enron* email dataset[9] has been proved to possess the small-world and power-law characteristics of social networks, it has been widely used in the studies of social networks [12–14, 31, 36]. Thus, we select *Enron* email dataset[9], containing 87,474 nodes (participants) and 30,0511 links (formed by sending and receiving emails) for our experiments. From this dataset, social intimate degree and role impact factor can be mined from the subjects and contents of emails [31], fitting our proposed complex social network structure well.

H_MCOP is the most promising algorithm for MCOP selection [35]. Based on it, several approximation algorithms [37, 38] have been proposed for quality-driven service selection. But as pointed in [27], they can not be applied in large-scale complex social networks. Thus, to study the performance of our proposed heuristic algorithm H_MQCSTP, we have a comparison with H_MCOP [35] in both execution time and the utilities of identified social trust paths. In our experiments, the T, r and ρ values are randomly generated. The EEQCs specified are set as $Q^{(EEQC)} = \{Q^{T(EEQC)} > 0.05,\ Q^{r(EEQC)} > 0.001,\ Q^{\rho(EEQC)} > 0.3\}$ and the adjacent QoT constraints are set as $Q^{(AQC)} = \{Q^{T(AQC)} > 0.1,\ Q^{r(AQC)} > 0.05,\ Q^{\rho(AQC)} > 0.1\}$. The weights of attributes in the utility function are set as $\omega_t = 0.25$, $\omega_r = 0.25$ and $\omega_\rho = 0.5$.

Each of H_MQCSTP and H_MCOP is implemented using Matlab R2008a running on an Lenovo ThinkPad SL500 laptop with an Intel Core 2 Duo T5870 2.00GHz CPU, 3GB RAM, Windows XP SP3 operating system and MySql 5.1.35 relational database. The results are plotted in Fig. 15.5, where the execution time and the utilities of the extracted trust network for each of the algorithms are averaged based on 5 independent runs.

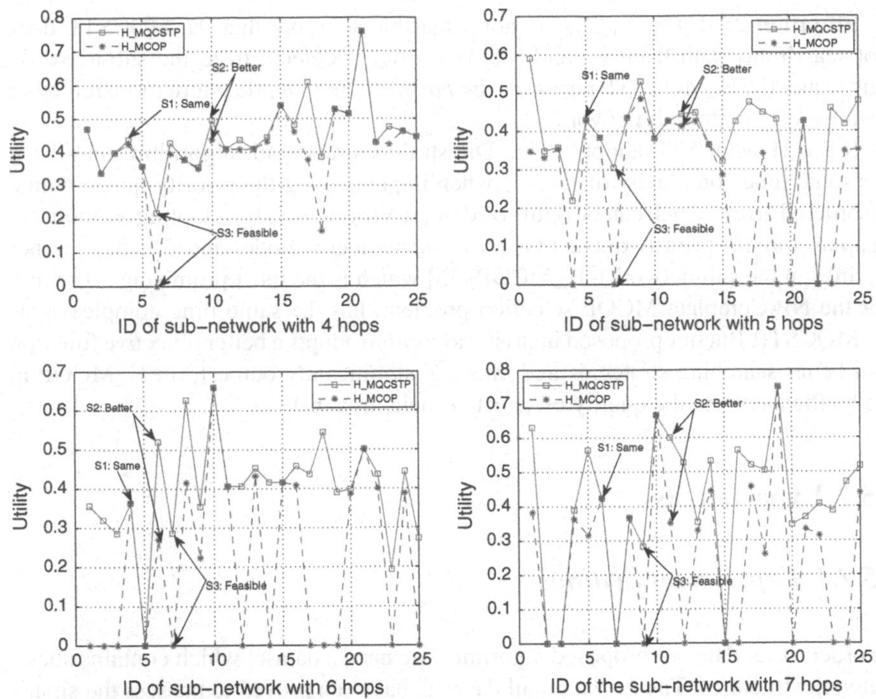

Fig. 15.5 Path utility of sub-networks

15.7.2 Performance in Social Trust Path Selection

In this experiment, we first randomly select 100 pairs of source and target participants from the *Enron* email dataset[9]. We then extract 100 corresponding sub-networks between them by using the exhaustive searching method, among which the maximal length of a social trust path varies from 4 to 7 hops following the *small-world* characteristic (i.e., the average path length between two nodes is about 6 hops in a social network [38]). The smallest case sub-network has 33 nodes and 56 links (4 hops), while the most complex sub-network has 1695 nodes and 11175 links (7 hops).

Figure 15.5 plots the utilities of the social trust paths identified by H_MQCSTP and H_MCOP respectively, ordered by the number of hops. From Fig. 15.5, we can observe that in any case, our H_MQCSTP does not yield any utility worse than that of H_MCOP (see case $S1$ in Fig. 15.5) while in most sub-networks (61 % of all sub-networks), the utilities of social trust paths identified by H_MQCSTP are better than those of H_MCOP (see case $S2$ in Fig. 15.5). In addition, H_MCOP sometimes returns an infeasible solution even when a feasible solution exists. In contrast, H_MQCSTP can identify a feasible solution if it exists, (see case $S3$ in Fig. 15.5). As illustrated in Table 15.1, the utility summarization of all social trust paths identified by our H_MQCSTP algorithms is greater than that of H_MCOP in

Table 15.1 The comparison in utility and execution time

Algorithm	Sum of utility				Sum of execution time (s)			
	4 hops	5 hops	6 hops	7 hops	4 hops	5 hops	6 hops	7 hops
H_MQCSTP	11.2014	9.7113	9.9469	10.1747	245.8564	871.8128	1.9528e + 003	4.3005e + 003
H_MCOP	10.3047	6.5274	6.6006	6.1979	340.4162	1.3571e + 003	3.0024e + 003	6.6996e + 003
difference	10.87 % more	14.88 % more	18.87 % more	16.42 % more	27.78 % less	35.76 % less	34.96 % less	35.81 % less

all 4 groups. This is because when a social trust path with the maximal utility is a feasible solution in a sub-network, both H_MCOP and H_MQCSTP can identify it as the optimal solution; however, when the social trust path with the maximal utility is not a feasible solution, since the objective function is not well defined, H_MCOP can hardly find a solution that is as good as that from H_MQCSTP and may even return an infeasible one even when a feasible solution exists.

Figure 15.6 plots the execution time of both H_MQCSTP and H_MCOP, each of which is average of 5 independent executions. From Table 15.1, we can see that our proposed heuristic algorithm is much faster than H_MCOP in all 4 groups. This is because that in the searching process of H_MQCSTP, the node leading to an infeasible solution is not regarded as a candidate to be selected for the next searching step, which can reduce much search space and thus significantly save execution time.

Through the above experiments, we can see that H_MQCSTP is much superior to H_MCOP in both efficiency and the quality of delivered solutions

15.8 Application Scenarios

Our proposed model and algorithm can provide key techniques to potential lots of applications with social networks as the backbone.

1. A New Generation of CRM System. Our proposed method can be applied into a new generation CRM (Customer Relation Management) system, which maintains a complex social network containing the social relationship between customers, and the recommendation roles of these customers. With this information, the new CRM system can help a retailer identify new trustworthy customers and introduce products to them, which can bring enormous commercial opportunities to retailers.
2. A New Generation Employment System. Our methods can also be applied in a new generation employment system which maintains a complex social network containing employees, their recommendation roles (e.g., a professor in computer science), and the social relationship between them (e.g., the relationship between a supervisor and his/her student). In such an application our methods can help a hiring manager evaluate the trustworthiness of all potential employees and find trustworthy persons to be employed, which in turn can bring great benefits for the employment of companies.

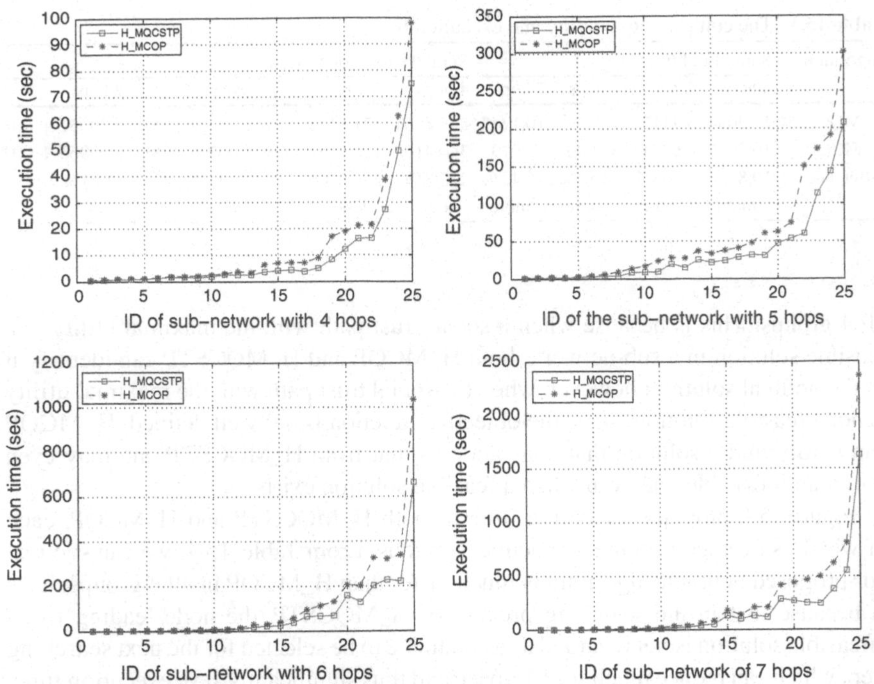

Fig. 15.6 Execution time of sub-networks

3. A New Generation Recommendation System. Our proposed method can be used in a new generation recommendation system, which maintains a social network of buyers, sellers and the complex social information, including social relationships and recommendation roles. In this system, our proposed method can be applied to help a buyer identify the most trustworthy seller from all those sellers selling the product preferred by the buyer.

15.9 Conclusions

In this chapter, we have analyzed the characteristic of current functional website and OSNs, and presented the properties in the new generation of OSNs. Our proposed new complex social network takes *trust*, *social relationships* and *recommendation roles* into account, and can reflect the real-world situations better. In addition, our proposed heuristic algorithm H_MQCSTP can solve the optimal social trust path selection problem with multiple both adjacent and end-to-end QoT constraints. The results of experiments conducted on a real dataset of social networks demonstrate that H_MQCSTP significantly outperforms existing methods in both efficiency and the quality of delivered solutions.

References

1. G. Liu, Y. Wang, and L. Li. Trust management in three generations of web-based social networks. In *Symposia and Workshops on Ubiquitous, Autonomic and Trusted Computing*, pages 446–451, 2009.
2. J. Golbeck and J. Hendler. Inferring trust relationships in web-based social networks. *ACM Transactions on Internet Technology*, 6(4):497–529, 2006.
3. C. Hang, Y. Wang, and M. Singh. Operators for propagating trust and their evaluation in social networks. In *AAMAS'09*, pages 1025–1032, 2009.
4. C. Lin, N. Cao, S. Liu, S. Papadimitriou, J. Sun, and X. Yan. Smallblue: Social network analysis for expertise search and collective intelligence. In *ICDE'09*, pages 1483–1486, 2009.
5. F. Walter, S. Battiston, and F. Schweitzer. A model of a trust-based recommendation system on a social network. *AAMAS Journal*, 16(1):57–74, February 2008.
6. P. S. Adler. Market, hierarchy, and trust: The knowledge economy and the future of capitalism. *Organization Science*, 12(12):215–234, 2001.
7. R. Miller, D. Perlman, and S. Brehm. *Intimate Relationships*. McGraw-Hill College, 4th edition, 2007.
8. S. Milgram. The small world problem. *Psychology Today*, 2(60), 1967.
9. A. Mislove, M. Marcon, K. Gummadi, P. Druschel, and B. Bhattacharjee. Measurement and analysis of online social networks. In *ACM IMC'07*, pages 29–42, 2007.
10. B. Christianson and W. S. Harbison. Why isn't trust transitivie? In *International Workshop on Security Protocols*, pages 171–176, 1996.
11. R. Mansell and B. Collins. *Trust and crime in information societies*. Edward Elgar Publishing, 2005.
12. G. Liu, Y. Wang, M.A. Orgun, and E-P. Lim. A heuristic algorithm for trust-oriented service provider selection in complex social networks. In *SCC*, pages 130–137, 2010.
13. G. Liu, Y. Wang, and Mehmet A. Orgun. Finding k optimal social trust paths for the selection of trustworthy service providers in complex social networks. In *ICWS'11*, pages 41–48, 2011.
14. G. Liu, Y. Wang, and Mehmet A. Orgun. Trust transitivity in complex social networks. In *AAAI'11*, pages 1222–1229, 2011.
15. Sara Baase and Allen Gelder. *Computer Algorithms Introduction to Design and Analysis*. Addision Wesley, 2000.
16. G. Liu, Y. Wang, and Mehmet A. Orgun. Social context-aware trust network discovery in complex contextual social networks. In *AAAI'12*, pages 101–107, 2012.
17. G. Liu, Y. Wang, Mehmet A. Orgun, and H. Liu. Discovering trust networks for the selection of trustworthy service providers in complex contextual social networks. In *ICWS'12*, pages 384–391, 2012.
18. E. Berscheid and H. T. Reis. *Attraction and close relationships, volume 2 of The Handbook of Social Psychology*. Oxford University Press, 4th edition, 1998.
19. S. Fiske. *Social Beings: Core Motives in Social Psychology*. John Wiley and Sons, 2009.
20. P. Bedi, H. Kaur, and S. Marwaha. Trust based recommender system for semantic web. In *IJCAI*, pages 2677–2682, 2007.
21. Y. Cho, G. Steeg, and A. Galstyan. Co-evolution of selection and influence in social networks. In *AAAI*, pages 779–784, 2011.
22. P. Cui and F. Wang. Item-level social influence prediction with probabilistic hybrid factor matrix factorization. In *AAAI*, pages 331–336, 2011.
23. S. Guo, M. Wang, and J. Leskovec. The role of social networks in online shopping information passing, price of trust, and consumer choice. In *EC'11*, pages 130–137, 2011.
24. H. Ma, T. Zhou, M. Lyu, and I. King. Improving recommender systems by incorporating social contextual informaiton. *ACM Transactions on Information Systems*, 29(2), 2011.
25. J. Golbeck. The dynamics of web-based social networks: Membership, relationships, and change. *First Monday*, 12:11, 2007.
26. D. Boyd and N. Ellison. Social network sites: Definition, history and scholarship. *Journal of Computer-Mediated Communication*, 13:1, 2007.

27. G. Liu, Y. Wang, and Mehmet A. Orgun. Optimal social trust path selection in complex social networks. In *AAAI'10*, pages 1397–1398, 2010.
28. B. Alunkal, I. Valjkovic, and G. Laszewski. Reputation-based grid resource selection. In *Proceedings of the Workshop on Adaptive Grid Middleware*, USA, September 2003.
29. R. Ashri, S. Ramchurn, J. Sabater, M. Luck, and N. Jennings. Trust evaluation through relationship analysis. In *AAMAS*, pages 1005–1011, 2005.
30. Y. Wang and V. Varadharajan. Role-based recommendation and trust evaluation. In *IEEE EEE'07*, pages 278–295, 2007.
31. A. Mccallum, X. Wang, and A. Corrada-Emmanuel. Topic and role discovery in social networks with experiments on Enron and academic email. *Journal of Artificial Intelligence Research*, 30(1):249–272, 2007.
32. J. Tang, J. Zhang, L. Yan, J. Li, L. Zhang, and Z. Su. Arnetminer: Extraction and mining of academic social networks. In *KDD'08*, pages 990–998, 2008.
33. J. Zhang S. Yang and I. Chen. Web 2.0 services for identifying communities of practice. In *SCC'07*, pages 130–137.
34. E. Dijkstra. A note on two problems in connexion with graphs. *Numerische Mathematik*, pages 269–271, 1959.
35. T. Korkmaz and M. Krunz. Multi-constrained optimal path selection. In *INFOCOM'01*, pages 834–843.
36. F. Lin S. Yoo, Y. Yang and I. Moon. Mining social networks for personalized email prioritization. In *KDD'09*, pages 967–976, 2009.
37. L. Li, Y. Wang, and E. Lim. Trust-oriented composite services selection and discovery. In *ICSOC'09*, pages 50–67, 2009.
38. T. Yu, Y. Zhang, and K. Lin. Efficient algorithms for web services selection with end-to-end qos constraints. *ACM Transactions on the Web*, 1(1), 2007.

Chapter 16
Analyzing Web Services Networks: Theory and Practice

Peep Küngas, Marlon Dumas, Shahab Mokarizadeh and Mihhail Matskin

Abstract This paper addresses the problem of applying the general network theory for analyzing qualitatively Web services networks. The paper reviews current approaches to analyzing Web services networks, generalizes the published approaches into a formal framework for analyzing Web services networks and demonstrates its applicability in practice. More specifically, two case studies are described where the presented framework has been applied. The first one considers identification of redundant data in large-scale service-oriented information systems, while the second one measures information diffusion between individual information systems.

16.1 Introduction

Network analysis has recently gained momentum in various areas, such as social networks, politics and media, just to mention a few. Network theory in these cases provides effective means to understand the dynamics within increasingly complex domains. Furthermore, it has been increasingly often recognized that analysing interactions between related domains will reveal more adequate insight into domain-specific phenomena compared to purely intra-domain studies.

P. Küngas (✉) · M. Dumas
University of Tartu, Tartu, Estonia
e-mail: peep.kungas@ut.ee

M. Dumas
e-mail: marlon.dumas@ut.ee

S. Mokarizadeh · M. Matskin
Royal Institute of Technology, Stockholm, Sweden
e-mail: shahabm@kth.se

M. Matskin
e-mail: misha@kth.se

A. Bouguettaya et al. (eds.), *Advanced Web Services*,
DOI: 10.1007/978-1-4614-7535-4_16,

For instance, network theory has been used for studying information diffusion between microblogs and weblogs [20], where it has revealed how rumors spread in the Web. The latter serves as a valuable input to online campaign planning. Additionally, application of network theory to computer science citation networks [17] has identified information diffusion patterns between computer science subdisciplines. For instance, it was showed that research results in algorithmics are applied in data mining and information retrieval. Finally, network theoretical metrics have been proposed to quantify information fluidity and to analyze the growth of the Semantic Web [5].

Network structures are present in the field of Web services as well making it possible to apply network theoretical approaches to study specific phenomena in the field. In the latter case links could be drawn between Web services, service providers, classes of Web services, compositions of Web services, data structures of Web services, just to mention a few cases. Based on particular topologies specific research problems can be studied.

In recent years several experiments have been made to construct a variety of Web services networks and to analyse them by first computing network metrics and then interpreting results. For instance, structural properties of a Web service networks have been studied [7] and resilience metrics have been identified for service-oriented networks based on the underlying network topology and distribution of services [15]. Also network theoretical analysis approaches have been adopted for service discovery and composition [3, 10] such that the link structure and density of underlying service network is considered. Additionally, service composition methods have been fine-tuned by taking into account characteristics of Web services networks [14]. Finally, information flow between categories of Web services has been analyzed for ensuring secure information flow in multi-domain systems [16] plus interaction and potential synergy between governmental and commercial Web services has been studied [9].

Despite the mentioned approaches Web services network analysis is still an isolated topic, which has not been thoroughly studied. Partly this is due to the lack of standardized datasets to validate the results. But also lack of a systematic framework for studying the problems has definitely affected the situation. Therefore one of the aims of the paper is to promote the topic by outlining potential network topologies, which could be studied together with interpretation of main metrics from network theory for these topologies. We also present two case studies, where network analysis has been applied for analysing Web services networks. The first study shows how to use simple network metrics, indegree and outdegree, for analysing redundancy in information systems exposing Web services, while the second study reveals how to analyse information diffusion between the same information systems with more complex metrics.

The rest of the paper is structured as follows. In Sect. 16.2 we define basic concepts and outline Web services network topologies. Section 16.3 presents two case studies—redundancy and information diffusion. In Sect. 16.4 related work is reviewed and, finally, Sect. 16.5 concludes the paper.

16.2 Fundamentals

16.2.1 Web Services Networks

The input for construction of Web services networks, as considered in this paper, is a collection of semantically annotated service interfaces. More specifically, we assume that we are given a collection of Web service interfaces described using WSDL and XML Schema, and a collection of semantic annotations on these interfaces. Semantic annotations are encoded as SA-WSDL *model references*. A model reference is an URI that refers to a concept in a semantic model. For example, a model reference may refer to a class or a property in an OWL ontology, but equally well it may refer to a class or attribute in an UML class diagram. In this paper, we do not deal with the issue of obtaining the semantic annotations. In the presented case studies we relied on a method for semi-automated annotation of Web services presented in our previous work [8, 11], but other annotation methods could be employed instead.

If multiple elements in an XML Schema are annotated with the same model references, these elements are deemed to encode the same datum. For example, if two XML Schema elements "client_address" and "customer_address" refer to the same class or property in an OWL ontology, they are considered to represent the same datum.[1]

In this paper we consider *entity attributes* the smallest pieces of Web services descriptions, which can be used to build Web services networks. By *entity attribute* we mean an atomic unit of information about an entity, like for example the address of a supplier or the salary of an employee. In the context of a service-oriented information system, an entity attribute corresponds to an XML element with no child elements or an XML attribute that appears in the schema of one of the messages produced or consumed by a Web service. We abstract away from the choice of granularity of an attribute. For example, one could either take "supplier address" to be an entity attribute, or "supplier address' street name" to be an entity attribute.

We define a (service-oriented) information system as a collection of service operations. A service operation takes as input a set of entity attributes and produces as output another set of entity attributes. As an alternative, we could have defined an information system as a set of services, each one providing a set of service operations, but the intermediate level of grouping (the "service") turns out not to be needed in our proposal. Anyway, it is possible to apply the same concepts and techniques presented in this chapter in order to analyze the network of relations between services and data types. This analysis at a higher level of granularity could be a direction for future work.

[1] Other notions of semantic equivalence between elements could be employed. For example, we could consider that two elements are equivalent if these elements are annotated with concepts that subsume one another according to a given ontology. For practical purposes, the notion of equivalence used to compare model references is orthogonal to the techniques proposed in this paper.

We write *input*(so) and *output*(so) to denote the set of inputs and the set of outputs of service operation so. Analogously we write *input*(IS) and *output*(IS) to denote the set of inputs and the set of outputs of all service operations of information system IS.

For a given information system IS, we define the set of attributes of IS as: $atts(IS) = \{d \in \mathscr{A} \mid \exists so \in IS, d \in input(so) \cup output(so)\}$, where $\mathscr{A}$ is the set of all possible attributes. In other words, the set of attributes of an information system IS is composed of all attributes that appear at least once as input or output of an operation in IS.

A federated (service-oriented) information system is a set of information systems whose schema are semantically annotated using a common vocabulary (either in OWL, UML or any other modelling language) or a reference system. Given a federated information system FIS, the set of attributes of a federated information system FIS is the union of the set of attributes of its contained information systems, i.e. $atts(FIS) = \cup_{IS \in FIS} atts(IS)$.

An attribute d may appear in multiple information systems within a federated information system. For a given FIS and a given attribute d, we define $occurs(FIS, d)$ as the number of information systems in which d appears, i.e. $occurs(FIS, d) = |\{IS \in FIS \mid d \in atts(IS)\}|$.

In order to derive the metric used for methods applied in the presented case studies, we start by abstracting a federated information system as a network. The network is modelled as a graph where each node represents either a service operation or a data attribute and the edges represent information flow. Each edge connects a service operation node and a data attribute node. An edge cannot connect two service operation nodes nor two data attribute nodes. Hence, the graph is bipartite. More specifically, the network is constructed by introducing an edge between each service operation and its inputs and outputs. An edge exists from an attribute to an operation if the attribute appears in the inputs of the operation, and an edge exists from an operation to an attribute if the attribute in question appears in the outputs of the operation. It is important to note that in the context of service networks, if we talk about inputs and outputs we mean conceptual representations of inputs and outputs. Formally:

Definition 16.1 (Web services network). A Web services network $\mathscr{N}$ is a bipartite graph $\{N, E\}$, where E and N represent respectively a set of edges and a set of nodes in the graph. Set N consists of service operation nodes N_{so} and entity attribute nodes N_d. Set E is defined as:

$$E = \bigcup_{IS \in FIS} \Big(\{(d, so) \mid so \in IS \wedge d \in inputs(so)\} \\ \cup \{(so, d) \mid so \in IS \wedge d \in outputs(so)\} \Big)$$

For analyzing Web services networks in more elaborated settings, such as for information diffusion as demonstrated in Sect. 16.3.3, the service network model given in Definition 16.1 has to be enriched with set of labels (e.g. category of an information system, quality of a service, popularity of a service, ...) depending on the requirements of a particular problem. This leads us to the definition of a labeled Web service network:

Definition 16.2 (Labeled Web services network). A labeled Web services network $\mathscr{N}_l = \{\mathscr{N}, \mathscr{L}\}$ is a Web service network, where each node has been assigned a set of labels. $\mathscr{L}$ is a label system consisting of a set of pairs (n, l) where $l \in L$ is a label, L is a set of all labels and $n \in N$ is a node of the Web services network $\mathscr{N}$.

The set of all labels of node n is denoted by *label*(n) and is defined as a set $\{l \mid l \in L \wedge (n, l) \in \mathscr{L}\}$. The set of all labels of information system *IS* is denoted with *label*(*IS*) and defined as: $label(IS) = \bigcup_{n \in N}(\{label(n) \mid n \in atts(IS)\})$.

The label system provides an effective mechanism for assigning specific attribute values (e.g. tags, information system classification, etc.) to Web services networks. Although the label system leverages a way to attach discrete attribute values to network nodes, for continuous values we take advantage of the concept of weights. We demonstrate here this case with a network, where weights are aggregated while contracting the network.

Definition 16.3 (Weighted labeled Web services network). A weighted labeled Web services network is an attribute-centric projection of a labeled Web service network model into classic (1-mode) loop-free directed graph $\{N_d, E_d\}$, where E_d is defined as:

$$E_d = \bigcup_{d \in atts(FIS)} (\{(d_i, d_j) \mid \exists IS \in FIS, \exists so \in IS, \exists d_i, d_j \in atts(FIS), d_i \in input(so) \wedge d_j \in output(so)\})$$

Each node $n \in N_d$ is associated with a weight vector $\overrightarrow{Q} = \{q_1, \ldots, q_u\}$, where every item q_i, $i = 1..u$ represents the weight of node n with respect to label $l_i \in L$.

The effectiveness of the weighted network model in capturing and preserving the structural properties of underlying Web services network is already studied in [7, 12]. The following definition defines how a weighted Web services network is transformed into a weighted label network. If a label identifies an information systems, as in one of our case studies, we end up with an information system network where weights identify relative attraction between information systems.

Definition 16.4 (Weighted label network). Weighted label network is a directed graph $\{N_l, E_l\}$, where each node in set N_l represents a label while edges in set E_l, represent inter-label relationships as constructed as follows:

$$E_l = \bigcup_{l \in L} (\{(l_i, l_j) \mid \exists IS_i, IS_j \in FIS, \exists d_i, d_j \in atts(FIS), d_i \in input(IS_i) \wedge d_j \in output(IS_j) \wedge l_i = label(IS_i) \wedge l_j = label(IS_j)\})$$

Each edge (l_i, l_j) is labeled with weight $\mathcal{W}_{ij}$ expressing the weight of which label l_i is attracted to label l_j. Unlike the previous models, loops are permitted in this model.

In the rest of the paper, we use also the following definitions for basic network theoretical metrics.

Definition 16.5 (Degree). The degree $deg(d)$ of an attribute node d in a service network $\mathcal{N}=(N, E)$ is the number of edges incident to that node (counting both incoming and outgoing edges), i.e. $deg(d) = |\{so \mid so \in N \wedge [(d, so) \in E \vee (so, d) \in E]\}|$. Meanwhile, the *degree of an attribute node in an information system IS* is the number of edges incident to d whose source or target is an operation in IS, i.e. $deg(d, IS) = |\{so \mid so \in IS \wedge [(d, so) \in E \vee (so, d) \in E]\}|$.

Definition 16.6 (Indegree). The indegree $deg^-(d)$ of an attribute node is the number of edges targeting d, i.e. $deg^-(d) = |\{so \mid so \in N \wedge (so, d) \in E\}|$. Meanwhile, the *indegree of an attribute node in an information system IS* is the number of edges targeting d whose source is an operation in IS, i.e. $deg^-(d, IS) = |\{so \mid so \in IS \wedge (so, d) \in E\}|$.

Definition 16.7 (Outdegree). The outdegree $deg^+(d)$ of an attribute node is the number of edges emanating from d, i.e. $deg^+(d) = |\{so \mid so \in N \wedge (d, so) \in E\}|$. Meanwhile, the *outdegree of an attribute node in an information system IS* is the number of edges emanating from d whose target is an operation in IS, i.e. $deg^+(d, IS) = |\{so \mid so \in IS \wedge (d, so) \in E\}|$.

16.2.2 Web Services Network Formation

As an example of Web services network construction, let us consider three information systems of the Estonian federated governmental information system: the Tax and Customs Board service, the Business Registry service and the Register of Economic Activities. Figures16.2, 16.3, 16.4 and 16.5 show message schema fragments for each of these services.

For the sake of understandability, element names have been translated to English and some irrelevant fragments have been deleted. The Business Registry service provides information about companies—their registration numbers (details_company/businessregistrycode in Fig. 16.4 and detailedQuery/businessregistrycode in Fig. 16.3)[2], names (details_business_name/content in Fig. 16.4 and detailedQuery/businessname in Fig. 16.3), and contact details (details_contact_medium/content in Fig. 16.4 and detailedQuery/address in Fig. 16.3). At the same time the Register of Economic Activities provides also business registration number (generalinfoBaseType/code in Fig. 16.5), name (generalinfoBaseType/name in Fig. 16.5) and contact details (generalinfoBaseType/{tel,fax,email,web} in Fig. 16.5). Furthermore, the Tax

[2] We use XPath-style references to refer to specific fragments of schema.

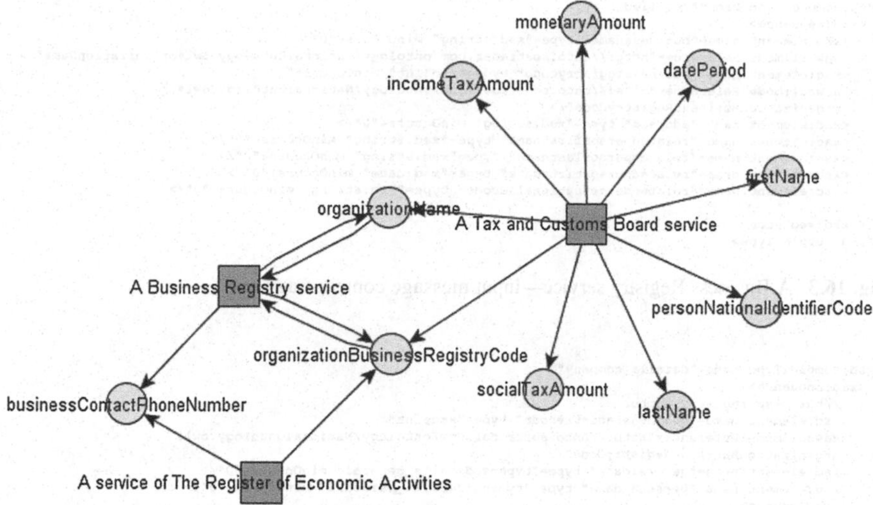

Fig. 16.1 Service network constructed from service interface fragments in Figs. 16.2, 16.3, 16.4 and 16.5

and Customs Board service also provides business registration numbers (employerTaxQueryAnswer/businessregistrycode in Fig. 16.2) and business names (employerTaxQueryAnswer/employername in Fig. 16.2).

```
<xsd:complexType name="employerTaxQueryAnswer">
  <xsd:all>
    <xsd:element name="nationalidcode" nillable="true" type="xsd:string"
     sawsdl:modelReference="http://onto.soatrader.com/ontology/NationalOntology.owl#
     personNationalIdentifierCode"/>
    <xsd:element name="personname" nillable="true" type="xsd:string"
     sawsdl:modelReference="http://onto.soatrader.com/ontology/NationalOntology.owl#firstName"
     sawsdl:modelReference="http://onto.soatrader.com/ontology/NationalOntology.owl#lastName"/>
    <xsd:element name="period" nillable="true" type="xsd:string"
     sawsdl:modelReference="http://onto.soatrader.com/ontology/TimeOntology.owl#datePeriod"/>
    <xsd:element name="businessregistrycode" nillable="true" type="xsd:string"
     sawsdl:modelReference="http://onto.soatrader.com/ontology/NationalOntology.owl#
    organizationBusinessRegistryCode"/>
    <xsd:element name="employername" nillable="true" type="xsd:string"
     sawsdl:modelReference="http://onto.soatrader.com/ontology/NationalOntology.owl#organizationName"/>
    <xsd:element name="sum" nillable="true" type="xsd:decimal"
     sawsdl:modelReference="http://onto.soatrader.com/ontology/FinanceOntology.owl#monetaryAmount"/>
    <xsd:element name="socialtax" nillable="true" type="xsd:decimal"
     sawsdl:modelReference="http://onto.soatrader.com/ontology/FinanceOntology.owl#socialTaxAmount"/>
    <xsd:element name="incometax" nillable="true" type="xsd:decimal"
     sawsdl:modelReference="http://onto.soatrader.com/ontology/FinanceOntology.owl#incomeTaxAmount"/>
  </xsd:all>
</xsd:complexType>
```

Fig. 16.2 A Tax and Customs Board service—output message content fragment

Based on SA-WSDL references in Figs. 16.2–16.5 we can construct a service network as seen in Fig. 16.1. Rectangular nodes in the figure represent service operations whose interface fragments were annotated with SA-WSDL references, while ellipsoidal nodes represent data attributes, which were annotated.

```
<xsd:complexType name="detailedQuery">
  <xsd:sequence>
    <xsd:element name="businessname" type="xsd:string" minOccurs="0"
     sawsdl:modelReference="http://onto.soatrader.com/ontology/NationalOntology.owl#organizationName"/>
    <xsd:element name="businessregistrycode" type="xsd:int" minOccurs="0"
     sawsdl:modelReference="http://onto.soatrader.com/ontology/NationalOntology.owl#
     organizationBusinessRegistryCode"/>
    <xsd:element name="address" type="xsd:string" minOccurs="0"/>
    <xsd:element name="relatedpersonfirstname" type="xsd:string" minOccurs="0"/>
    <xsd:element name="relatedpersonlastname" type="xsd:string" minOccurs="0"/>
    <xsd:element name="relatedpersonbirthdate" type="xsd:date" minOccurs="0"/>
    <xsd:element name="relatedpersonnationalidcode" type="xsd:string" minOccurs="0"/>
    ...
  </xsd:sequence>
</xsd:complexType>
```

Fig. 16.3 A Business Registry service—input message content fragment

```
<xsd:complexType name="details_company">
  <xsd:sequence>
    //business registry number
    <xsd:element name="businessregistrycode" type="xsd:int"
     sawsdl:modelReference="http://onto.soatrader.com/ontology/NationalOntology.owl#
     organizationBusinessRegistryCode"/>
    <xsd:element name="generaldata" type="typens:details_general" minOccurs="0"/>
    <xsd:element name="personaldata" type="typens:details_personal" minOccurs="0"/>
  </xsd:sequence>
</xsd:complexType>
...
<xsd:complexType name="details_contact_medium">
  <xsd:sequence>
    <xsd:element name="typecode" type="xsd:string" minOccurs="0" /> //phone, fax, e-mail, ...
    <xsd:element name="typename" type="xsd:string" minOccurs="0"/>
    //contact medium value
    <xsd:element name="content" type="xsd:string" minOccurs="0"
     sawsdl:modelReference="http://onto.soatrader.com/ontology/NationalOntology.owl#
     businessContactPhoneNumber"/>
    <xsd:element name="enddate" type="xsd:date" minOccurs="0"/>
  </xsd:sequence>
</xsd:complexType>
<xsd:complexType name="details_business_name">
  <xsd:sequence>
    ...
    <xsd:element name="entryno" type="xsd:int" minOccurs="0"/>
    // business name
    <xsd:element name="content" type="xsd:string" minOccurs="0"
     sawsdl:modelReference="http://onto.soatrader.com/ontology/NationalOntology.owl#organizationName"/>
    <xsd:element name="startdate" type="xsd:date" minOccurs="0"/>
    <xsd:element name="enddate" type="xsd:date" minOccurs="0"/>
  </xsd:sequence>
</xsd:complexType>
```

Fig. 16.4 A Business Registry service—output message content fragment

```
<complexType name="generalinfoBaseType">
  <sequence>
    <element name="name" type="string"/> // business name
// business registry code
    <element name="code" type="string" minOccurs="0"
     sawsdl:modelReference="http://onto.soatrader.com/ontology/NationalOntology.owl#
     organizationBusinessRegistryCode"/>
// contact phone
    <element name="tel" type="string" minOccurs="0"
     sawsdl:modelReference="http://onto.soatrader.com/ontology/NationalOntology.owl#
     businessContactPhoneNumber"/>
    <element name="fax" type="string" minOccurs="0"/> //contact fax
    <element name="email" type="string" minOccurs="0"/> // contact E-mail
    <element name="web" type="string" minOccurs="0"/> // contact WWW
  </sequence>
</complexType>
```

Fig. 16.5 A service of the Register of Economic Activities—output message content fragment

16.3 Applications

In this section we present two applications of Web services network analysis. The first application is redundancy detection in service-oriented systems. Network analysis in this case provides suggestions for redesigning services' interfaces to increase their reusability. The second application is analysis of information diffusion between large amounts of Web services. This application has practical impact for instance in "reverse-engineering" the initially intended usage of services and reducing the search space for service matching.

16.3.1 Dataset

As a dataset for both case studies we use Web services descriptions of the Estonian state information system [6], which is a federation of ca 200 information systems and is collectively called here as X-Road Web services. X-Road is a middle-tier data exchange layer enabling governmental databases to communicate with their clients. The system allows officials, as well as legal and natural persons, to search data from national databases over the Internet within the limits of their authority. An example

Table 16.1 Examined registries in X-Road dataset

Registry name	Registry name
1-Environment registry	23-Pension registry
2-Interpol personal registry	24-Messaging calendar
3-Communicable diseases registry	25-Central schengen information system
4-Health information database	26-Treasury ownership service
5-Alcohol movement database	27- Land information system
6-Customer support information system	28-TTY authorization system
7-Economic activity registry	29-Tallinn support activity system
8-Mobile infrastructure registry	30-Land registry
9-Citizens liable to military service registry	31-New business registry
10-CMB database	32-Mandatory funded pension registry
11-Visa registry	33-X-Road user rights management system
12-Agricultural support registry	34-National examination system
13-E-Mail service registry	35-Traffic registry
14-Police procedure information system	36-Messaging calendar registry
15-Registry of professions	37-PV system consulting interface
16-Unemployment insurance database	38-Tartu university user information system
17-Workplace database	39-Tax and custom database
18-Address database	40-Education information system
19-E-Notary database	41-Tallinn university user information system
20-Work planning information system	42-Estonia schengen information system
21-Police information system	43-Notification service
22-Criminal court registry	44-Research information system

of such national registries are *Land Information System*, *Pension Information System* and *Crime Court Information System*, just few to name. The system ensures sufficient security for the treatment of inquiries made to databases and responses received. Our dataset contains interfaces of 44 information systems exposing around 1000 Web service operations. The names of examined registries, translated to English, of the X-Road dataset are summarized in Table 16.1.

In previous work [8] we introduced a method to semantically annotate WSDL interfaces and we applied it to the above governmental information system. Altogether, there were 7757 leaf elements in the XML schemas in the repository from which we managed to annotate 5555 leaf elements. The remaining elements were too specialized to be annotated meaningfully, but since they each only occurred in one information system, they do not constitute a source of potential redundancy. The semantic annotations that we constructed refer to classes in an ontology that we built incrementally during the semantic annotation process.

From the semantically annotated Web service interfaces, we constructed a service network consisting of 928 service operation nodes (annotated WSDL operations), 466 entity attribute nodes (forming a unified data model used for covering about 72 % of XML Schema leaf node elements across all WSDL interfaces of the federated IS) and 17006 edges.

The ontology used to annotate the WSDL interfaces had taxonomic relations between classes. However, in order to reduce effects arising from semantic annotations with different granularity (such as "general identifier" vs. "person's national identifier code" vs. "child's national identifier code") we discarded annotations in the top-level of the taxonomy. In other words, we gave preference to more specific semantic annotations over more general ones. The rationale for this choice is the following: If we compared annotations at a higher level, we would immediately obtain a large number of false positives for the redundancy classifier. For example, every time we find an attribute containing an address we would say that this attribute is redundant. Yet, it is normal that a federated information system contains multiple address types (e.g. personal address versus work address, billing address versus shipping address). Thus, even though all these elements would have been annotated with the concept "address", this annotation was deleted during the pre-processing phase. Without this filtering step, the accuracy results of the statistical classifiers became meaningless.

16.3.2 Redundancy Detection

A major issue in large-scale information systems management is that of avoiding data redundancy, that is, ensuring that each fact is stored in a single location [19]. Data redundancy does not originate exclusively from duplicated records within a database [2], but perhaps more frequently, from a common practice to store partially overlapping entries in multiple databases or information (sub-)systems. For instance, it often happens that supplier contact addresses are stored in the procurement, billing, logistics and technical support subsystems, as opposed to storing this address at one subsystem and having the other subsystems retrieve it from this primary location. The reasons for such redundancy may range from performance, reliability or security concerns, to miscommunication between system architects, lack of documentation of existing systems, or lack of cooperation between independent business units. In some cases, data redundancy is deliberate and controlled, while in others it is highly problematic and may lead to inconsistency and poor data quality.

The practical relevance of data redundancy management has been highlighted in several previous works. Moody and Shanks [13] report on a technical review of a repository of data models of a large information system. This technical review surfaced a high degree of overlap between different application data models. Closer inspection showed that different project teams had independently decided to represent the same data in different ways, resulting in data redundancy and duplicated development effort. In a similar vein, Ventrone and Heiler [18] point to several cases where data model overlap in large federated information systems was up to 80 %. Our own previous research [8] identified a similar tendency in a governmental information system.

Ideally, each entity attribute is maintained in one information system and retrieved from other information systems if and when required. The information system in which an informed system architect would most likely place an attribute is called the *primary location* of the attribute. In some cases, replicas of the attribute exist in other information systems. Information systems where replicas of an attribute exist are called secondary locations of the attribute in question. The concept of primary location is purposefully left subjective since it is largely application-dependent. For example, an attribute *businessAddress* elaborated in Sect. 16.2.2 appears in two information systems: the *Business Registry* and the *Tax and Customs Information System*. Intuitively, this attribute belongs primarily in the business registry. We know this because we have some understanding of the functional scope of these two information systems.

Some attributes are used to link entities across multiple information systems. For example, a customer identifier can be used in one information system in order to refer to a customer entity in another information system. Such an attribute is called in this paper a *reference attribute*. The concept of reference attribute is akin to the concept of "key" in the database world. A reference attribute is a "(primary) key" from the perspective of the information system that is the primary location of the attribute, and a "foreign key" from the perspective of other information systems. However, it should be noted that reference and identifier attributes are different sets, although every reference attribute is related to an identifier attribute.

The key intuition of our redundancy detection method is the following: If an attribute appears in multiple information systems and it is not a reference attribute, then this attribute is redundant in some information systems. Reference attributes link different entities together so it is normal that they appear in multiple information systems. Since the definition of redundancy is based on two subjective definitions, it is itself subjective. It is also up the analysts and architects of a system to judge whether a given occurrence of an attribute in multiple information systems constitutes a redundancy or not. Our redundancy detection criterion is meant to approximate this subjective judgement.

In order to detect potential redundancy, we are looking for answers to the following questions:

1. Given a federated information system *FIS*, can we find a classification function $C(IS, d)$ that takes as input an information system $IS \in FIS$ and an attribute $d \in atts(FIS)$, and returns T (true) if *IS* is the primary location of d, and F (false) otherwise?
2. Given a federated information system *FIS*, can we find a classification function $C'(d)$ that takes as input an attribute $d \in atts(FIS)$ and returns T if d is a reference attribute in *FIS*, and F otherwise?

As an example, let us consider three information systems of the Estonian federated governmental information system from Sect. 16.2.2. In this example, it is clear that the business registry number is a reference attribute. Business names and business contact details fit most naturally in the Business Registry (i.e. this is their primary location). Therefore, elements referring to company names and contact details at the Register of Economic Activities and at the Tax and Customs Board service are redundant. However, the business registration number, which is stored in all three information systems, is not redundant since it is required in order to link company data stored across these information systems.

16.3.2.1 Redundancy Detection Method

In order to detect redundancy we start by constructing clusters representing entity attributes in different information systems (IS). Each cluster represents entity attributes within an information system, whereas entity attributes are collected from service descriptions of particular IS according to definitions in Sect. 16.2. An example of clusters and their overlappings is visualized in Fig. 16.6. The figure uses cluster map technology to represent overlappings of entity attribute clusters. The highlighted central area represents entity attributes that are potentially redundant, since they appear in multiple clusters at the same time.

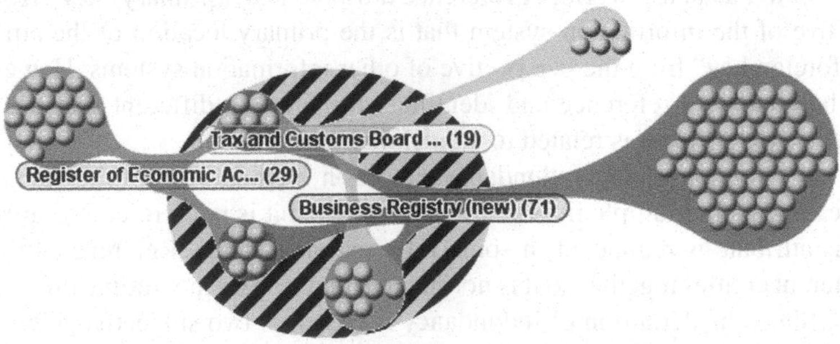

Fig. 16.6 A cluster map of data entities in different information systems

After clusters have been formed, we analyze in how many clusters an entity attribute occurs in. If an entity attribute occurs only in a single cluster, it is clearly not redundant. For instance, in Fig. 16.2 *socialtax* (paid social taxes) and *incometax* (paid income tax) are in this respect not redundant.

In the case of attributes occurring in multiple information systems, we start by determining the primary location. Primary location of an entity attribute is determined by measuring its degree in the constructed service network. An IS for which the entity attribute degree is highest, is most probably the attribute's primary location. The justification is based on the tendency that the majority of data processing services are normally provided at the same information system where the data originates from. Accordingly, the primary location classifier $C(IS, d)$ for information system *IS* and entity attribute *d* is defined as follows:

$$C(IS, d) = \begin{cases} T, \textbf{ if } S_r(IS, d) - S_m(d) \geq \rho \\ F, \textbf{ otherwise} \end{cases},$$

where relative score $S_r(IS, d) = deg(d, IS)/deg(d)$, average score $S_m(d)$ equals to $1/occurs(FIS, d)$ and $\rho \in [0, 1]$ is a threshold that can be used to tune the classifier.

We can interpret $deg(d, IS)/deg(d)$ as a metric indicating the "relative attachment" of attribute d to IS. A relative attachment of 1 means that the attribute exclusively belongs in that information system, an attachment of 0 means that the attribute does not appear at all in IS. The higher the attachment of an attribute to an IS, the higher the chances that this is the primary location of the attribute. If an attribute appears in multiple information systems (say n), and the attribute appears an equal amount of times in each system, then its relative attachment to each system is $1/n$. Thus a relative attachment above $1/n$ shows that an attribute is proportionally more strongly than average linked to an IS. In this light $S_m(d)$ can be interpreted as the "average attachment" of d to the information systems in which it is used.

When an attribute appears more times in one information system than in others, then the difference between relative attachment $S_r(IS, d)$ and $1/n$ becomes higher. For example, if an attribute d appears in two information systems X and Y and it is used 10 times in X and 5 times in Y, then the attachment of this attribute to X will be $10/15 = 0.66$ and $S_r(X, d) - 1/n = 0.16$. We can then say with some confidence that X is likely to be the primary location of d. Note that for a given attribute d, classifier $C(IS, d)$ might return true for multiple information systems. This may happen for example when the relative attachment of an attribute d is the same in all information systems in which this attribute appears—i.e. $S_r(IS, d) = S_m(d)$ for all *IS* such that $d \in atts(IS)$. In this case, the classifier is unable to assign attribute d to a single primary location.

To illustrate the primary location classifier, let us consider a selection of entity attributes (business registry code, business name, paid social tax, paid income tax, business contact phone number) from information system descriptions presented earlier. In Table 16.2 we summarize degrees of these entity attributes in considered information systems (Tax and Customs Board services (TCB), The Register of Economic Activities (REA), Business Registry (BR)). According to the classifier, the primary location of business registry code and business name is the Business Registry, while the primary location of "paid social tax" and "paid income tax" is the Tax and Customs Board services and the primary location of "business contact phone number" is the Register of Economic Activities.

Table 16.2 Example of entity attribute primary location detection with $\rho = 0$

Entity attribute d	Location is	$deg(d, is)$	$C(is, d)$
Business registry code	TCB	10	F
Business name	TCB	3	F
Paid social tax amount	TCB	1	T
Paid income tax amount	TCB	6	T
Business registry code	REA	6	F
Business name	REA	7	F
Business contact phone number	REA	5	T
Business registry code	BR	15	T
Business name	BR	13	T
Business contact phone number	BR	1	F

If an entity attribute appears in multiple information systems, it may be redundant, but only, if it is not a reference attribute. Symmetrically, an entity attribute occurring in more than one information system, is a potential reference attribute. In order to detect such reference attributes we use the following classifier:

$$C'(d) = \begin{cases} T, \textbf{ if } \exists IS : C(IS, d) \wedge \frac{deg^+(d,IS)}{deg^-(d,IS)} - \frac{deg^+(d)}{deg^-(d)} \leq \rho' \\ F, \textbf{ otherwise} \end{cases}$$

where $\rho' \in [-\infty, +\infty]$ is a threshold.

The hypothesis underpinning this definition is that the ratio between the number of times a reference attribute is used as input and the number of times it is produced as output can be used to characterize whether an attribute is a reference attribute. Especially in the attribute's primary location, we would expect that the reference attribute is used many times since such attributes are used to retrieve data about an entity and these data are normally located in the primary location. To illustrate the reference attribute detection classifier, let us elaborate further on the primary location suggestion results in Table 16.2. In Table 16.3 we list additional characteristics for

Table 16.3 Example of reference detection for attributes in Table 16.2 with $\rho' = 1$

Entity attribute d	Location IS	$deg^-(d, IS)$	$deg^+(d, IS)$	$deg^-(d)$	$deg^+(d)$	C'(d)
Paid social tax	TCB	0	1	0	3	F
Paid income tax	TCB	0	6	0	6	F
Business contact phone	REA	0	5	35	73	F
Business registry code	BR	7	8	38	52	T
Business name	BR	6	7	16	33	T

entity attributes whose primary location was proposed. According to Table 16.3 we see that both business registry code and business name serve as reference attributes, which would be used to link company records over multiple informations systems within a federated IS. One may argue that business name is not a reference attribute. If we adopt this view, we have here an example where the findings of the classifier do not always agree with the subjective judgement of informed users.

Given the above two classifiers, we define a third classifier, namely $R(IS, d)$, which determines whether or not an attribute d is redundant in an information system IS:

$$R(IS, d) = \begin{cases} T, \textbf{ if } occurs(d) > 1 \wedge C(IS, d) \wedge C'(d) \\ F, \textbf{ otherwise} \end{cases}$$

In other words, an attribute d is redundant in an information IS if it appears in multiple information systems, IS is not its primary location and d is not a reference attribute.

16.3.2.2 Evaluation Methodology

For evaluation purposes we use the dataset described in Sect. 16.3.1 and the classical notions of precision and recall defined for statistical classifiers. In a statistical classification task, the *precision* of a classifier for a given class is the number of true positives divided by the sum of true positives and false positives. Meanwhile, the *recall* of a classifier for a given task is defined as the number of true positives divided by the sum of true positives and false negatives.A *precision* score of 1.0 for a class c means that every item labeled by the classifier as belonging to class c does indeed belong to this class, whereas a *recall* of 1.0 means that every item of class c was labeled by the classifier as belonging to c. Finally, the evaluation also relies on the concept of F-score, which is defined as the harmonic mean of the precision and recall.

To evaluate the performance of the classifiers defined in Sect. 16.3.2.1, we manually inspected each entity attribute and we determined its primary location and whether it is a reference attribute or not. This manual judgement was made by the first author of the paper who is familiar with the overall information system, from involvements in previous projects. Based on these manual judgements, we computed redundancy as defined in Sect. 16.3.2.1 and we compared the resulting judgement to the one obtained with the automated redundancy classifier.

When evaluating the redundancy classifier, we discarded all entity attributes that occurred in a single information system, since these attributes are trivially non-redundant and including them in the evaluation of the redundancy classifier would have led to biased results (i.e. all these attributes would have been correctly classified, in a trivial manner).

16.3.2.3 Results and Discussion

We calculated precision, recall and F-score for every possible setting of parameters ρ and ρ', with ρ ranging from 0 to 1 in steps of 0.1 and ρ' ranging from −25 to 25 in steps of 5. The resulting F-scores for each setting are shown in Table 16.4, while precision and recall are summarized respectively in Table 16.5 and in Table 16.6.

Table 16.4 F-scores for redundancy detection with $\rho = [0.0, 1.0]$ and $\rho' = [-25, 25]$

r\r'	−25	−20	−15	−10	−5	0	5	10	15	20	25	min	max
0.0	0.765	0.766	0.766	0.766	0.752	0.746	0.664	0.665	0.665	0.665	0.666	0.664	0.766
0.1	0.849	0.849	0.849	0.849	0.838	0.830	0.765	0.765	0.765	0.765	0.767	0.765	0.849
0.2	0.882	0.883	0.883	0.883	0.872	0.869	0.813	0.813	0.813	0.813	0.815	0.813	0.883
0.3	0.885	0.885	0.885	0.885	0.876	0.875	0.823	0.823	0.823	0.823	0.825	0.823	0.885
0.4	0.885	0.887	0.887	0.887	0.877	0.878	0.828	0.829	0.829	0.829	0.830	0.828	0.887
0.5	0.886	0.888	0.888	0.888	0.878	0.880	0.833	0.834	0.834	0.834	0.836	0.833	0.888
0.6	0.890	0.891	0.891	0.891	0.882	0.883	0.837	0.838	0.838	0.838	0.840	0.837	0.891
0.7	0.890	0.891	0.891	0.891	0.881	0.883	0.838	0.840	0.840	0.840	0.842	0.838	0.891
0.8	0.887	0.888	0.888	0.888	0.878	0.881	0.836	0.837	0.837	0.837	0.840	0.836	0.888
0.9	0.887	0.888	0.888	0.888	0.878	0.881	0.836	0.837	0.837	0.837	0.840	0.836	0.888
1.0	0.887	0.888	0.888	0.888	0.878	0.881	0.836	0.837	0.837	0.837	0.840	0.836	0.888
min	0.765	0.766	0.766	0.766	0.752	0.746	0.664	0.665	0.665	0.665	0.666	0.664	
max	0.890	0.891	0.891	0.891	0.882	0.883	0.837	0.838	0.838	0.838	0.840		0.891

Table 16.5 Precision for redundancy detection with $\rho = [0.0, 1.0]$ and $\rho' = [-25, 25]$

r\r'	−25	−20	−15	−10	−5	0	5	10	15	20	25	min	max
0.0	0.852	0.853	0.853	0.853	0.851	0.873	0.917	0.919	0.919	0.919	0.925	0.851	0.925
0.1	0.850	0.852	0.852	0.852	0.851	0.872	0.926	0.928	0.928	0.928	0.932	0.850	0.932
0.2	0.839	0.841	0.841	0.841	0.840	0.869	0.922	0.924	0.924	0.924	0.928	0.839	0.928
0.3	0.822	0.823	0.823	0.823	0.823	0.854	0.904	0.906	0.906	0.906	0.909	0.822	0.909
0.4	0.810	0.812	0.812	0.812	0.811	0.842	0.893	0.894	0.894	0.894	0.898	0.810	0.898
0.5	0.804	0.806	0.806	0.806	0.806	0.837	0.889	0.892	0.892	0.892	0.896	0.804	0.896
0.6	0.804	0.806	0.806	0.806	0.806	0.837	0.889	0.892	0.892	0.892	0.897	0.804	0.897
0.7	0.801	0.803	0.803	0.803	0.802	0.834	0.888	0,891	0.891	0.891	0.895	0.801	0.895
0.8	0.797	0.799	0.799	0.799	0.798	0.829	0.883	0.886	0.886	0.886	0.891	0.797	0.891
0.9	0.797	0.799	0.799	0.799	0,798	0.829	0.883	0.886	0.886	0.886	0.891	0.797	0.891
1.0	0.797	0.799	0.799	0.799	0.798	0.829	0.883	0.886	0.886	0.886	0.891	0.797	0.891
min	0.797	0.799	0.799	0.799	0.798	0.829	0.883	0.886	0.886	0.886	0.891	0.797	0.891
max	0.852	0.853	0.853	0.853	0.851	0.873	0.926	0.928	0.928	0.928	0.932		0.932

We can note that the F-score is consistently high when $\rho > 0.2$. With lower value of ρ the F-score drops dramatically. Parameter ρ' has less influence on the F-score, although there is a trend that the F-score is better for negative values of ρ'. By inspecting the results closer, we noted that the problem when ρ' is positive is that

Table 16.6 Recall for redundancy detection with $\rho = [0.0, 1.0]$ and $\rho' = [-25, 25]$

r\r'	−25	−20	−15	−10	−5	0	5	10	15	20	25	min	max
0.0	0.695	0.695	0.695	0.695	0.673	0.651	0.520	0.520	0.520	0.520	0.520	0.520	0.695
0.1	0.847	0.847	0.847	0.847	0.825	0.792	0.651	0.651	0.651	0.651	0.651	0.651	0.847
0.2	0.929	0.929	0.929	0.929	0.907	0.869	0.726	0.726	0.726	0.726	0.726	0.726	0.929
0.3	0.958	0.958	0.958	0.958	0.936	0.875	0.898	0,755	0.755	0.755	0.755	0.755	0.958
0.4	0.976	0.976	0.976	0.976	0.954	0.917	0.772	0.772	0.772	0.772	0.772	0.772	0.976
0.5	0.987	0.987	0.987	0.987	0.965	0.928	0.783	0.783	0.783	0.783	0.783	0.783	0.987
0.6	0.995	0..995	0.995	0.995	0.973	0.936	0.791	0.791	0.791	0.791	0.791	0.791	0.995
0.7	1.000	1.000	1.000	1.000	0.976	0.939	0.794	0.794	0.794	0.794	0.794	0.794	1.000
0.8	1.000	1.000	1.000	1.000	0.976	0.939	0.794	0.794	0.794	0.794	0.794	0.794	1.000
0.9	1.000	1.000	1.000	1.000	0.976	0.939	0.794	0.794	0.794	0.794	0.794	0.794	1.000
1.0	1.000	1.000	1.000	1.000	0.976	0.939	0.794	0.794	0.794	0.794	0.794	0.794	1.000
min	0.695	0.695	0.695	0.695	0.673	0.651	0.520	0.520	0.520	0.520	0.520	0.520	
max	1.000	1.000	1.000	1.000	0.976	0.939	0.794	0.794	0.794	0.794	0.794		1.000

the recall drops significantly, meaning that we start getting many false negatives. These false negatives probably stem from the fact that for $\rho' \geq 0$, the method starts misclassifying some attributes as reference attributes and these misclassified attributes are not classified as redundant. After closer inspection of the method for values of $\rho' < 10$ we observed that the main reason why precision is negatively affected is because the method is unable to properly identify reference attributes and it reports majority of reference attributes as redundant. Anyway, it appears that a value of ρ' between -10 and 0 addresses this issue without overly affecting the precision. We therefore conclude that good settings can be obtained by simply setting ρ and ρ' to the middle of their ranges, i.e. $\rho = 0.5$ and $\rho' = 0$, although further work on other datasets would be needed to confirm this hypothesis.

The maximum F-score (0.89) was achieved with $\rho = 0.6$ and $\rho' \in (-20, -10)$. More detailed results for $\rho = 0.6$ are plotted in Fig. 16.7. We can observe from this figure the tradeoff that occurs between precision and recall when ρ' moves from negative to positive territory. Essentially, when $\rho' \in (-20, -10)$, the recall of the classifier is around 99 %. In other words, if an attribute could reasonably qualify as redundant, the classifier will find it. At around 80 %, the precision is not optimal, but arguably still acceptable. One could argue that higher precision (at close to 100 % recall) would be difficult to attain, given the subjectivity underpinning the notion of redundancy.

If an entity attribute does not satisfy this condition, we can assert almost for sure that considered entity attribute at a particular information system is not redundant. So the combined heuristic can correctly classify almost all entity attributes at given information systems that are not redundant and therefore it finds almost all entity attributes that are redundant at a given location (recall is close to 1). Precision is slightly worse compared to recall, but is still acceptable in certain applications by considering that 4 out 5 entity attributes classified as redundant are in fact redundant.

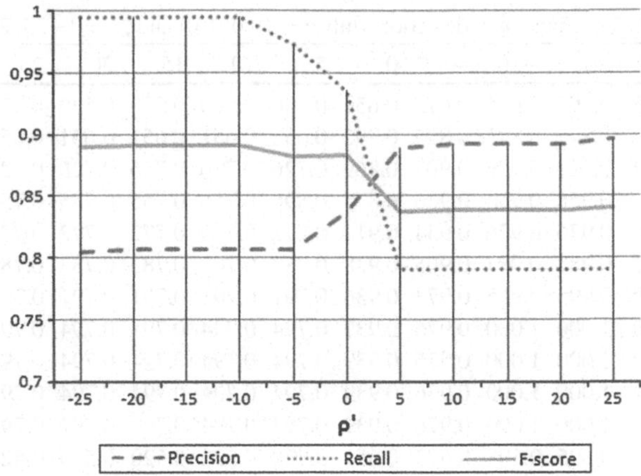

Fig. 16.7 Redundancy detection results for $\rho = 0.6$

Based on manually classified redundant data items, we analyzed also what percentage of data items occurring at multiple locations are redundant. It turned out that 79 % of such data items are redundant, which is consistent with findings of Ventrone and Heiler [18] who point to several cases where data model overlap in large federated information systems was up to 80 %.

The following threats to validity apply to our results:

- The evaluation of the classifiers proposed in the paper was made against our own judgement of the primary location of each attribute and its likelihood of it being a reference attribute. Some may argue that these judgements are subjective and possibly biased. To minimize the risk of bias, we made the manual classification of attributes before defining and evaluating the classifiers.
- The redundancy detection technique depends on the quality of the semantic annotations, so the conclusions we made might not be applicable if the quality of the semantic annotations is significantly lower (or higher), or if some semantic annotations are missing.
- There were large amounts of data redundancy in the federated information system considered in this study.

It is worth noting in this respect that although the level of data redundancy found is high, a large part of this redundancy is likely to be deliberate. Due to privacy concerns and IT governance decisions, information exchange between different information systems in the government sector is sometimes deliberately restricted. For example, the fact that a citizen can give multiple contact details for different engagements with government agencies is considered to be possible in certain scenarios and government agencies are sometimes restricted in their possibilities of exchanging these details.

16.3.3 Information Diffusion

Information diffusion is defined as the communication of knowledge over time among members of a social system [17]. This phenomenon has been studied between and within biosphere, microblogs [20], social networks [1] and other domains [17], where the network structure is present. These studies have turned to be useful for revealing intrinsic properties of particular real world phenomena. For instance, analysis of microblogs and blogosphere has provided an understanding on how rumours spread in the Web and valuable input to planning online campaigns.

Information diffusion has great potential in the context of Web services as well. For instance, the results of information diffusion patterns in the Web services networks can be exploited for *identifying adaptation spots*. Namely, substantial information flow between two Web service categories indicates a possibility for the potential applications interacting with the first category to adjust their interfaces in order to communicate with services of the second category. Also *security analysis of information flows* can be realized through analysis of information flows between categories of Web services similarly to the work done in security-aware service composition [16]. Finally, *introduction of new value-added services* can be leveraged by identifying isolated categories of Web services from the perspective of information diffusion.

In this case study we exploit the network structure of a set of Web services for discovering information diffusion patterns within a federated information system. Given a set of Web services' interfaces a category network, a specific case of weighted label network (Definition 16.4), is generated, which is then used to compute a diffusion matrix. The diffusion matrix captures the volume of potential information flow between groups of Web services, which in this case represent individual information systems within the federated information system.

The category network is constructed from the category projection of counterpart weighted labeled Web service network (Definition 16.4). Hence, first we describe the process of weighted labeled Web services network formation and then construction of the corresponding weighted label network is explained. As an illustrative example, we consider a fragment of the original Web service network of which categorized fragment is shown in Fig. 16.8.

16.3.3.1 Weighted Labeled Web Services Network Formation

In the Web service network, nodes are distinguished into attribute and operation sets and edges only occur between these two sets. To derive a monopartite projection with respect to attribute nodes, the vertices belonging to attribute set are connected by a directed edge if they are connected to at least one vertex of operation set. The direction of new edge is from attributes representing inputs of the operation toward those attributes modeling output of the operation. Next, self-loops are removed and redundant edges are eliminated such that there will be (maximum) only one edge connecting two nodes. We acknowledge that both the adopted monopartite projection of the network and the redundant edge removal are not without information loss. However, this reduction is performed to keep the computation model simple and traceable. Figure 16.9a illustrates the result of projection of the fragment of the example Web service network, Fig. 16.8, into weighted labeled network model. For the purpose of this case-study, the examined information systems are labeled with their associated categories. A category describes a general kind of a service that is provided [4], for example *Banking Information System* and *Health Information System*. Category of an information system is formally defined in the current case as $category(IS) = label(IS) \cap C$, where $C \subset L$ is a set of category labels.

Next, the associated categories of information systems in the Web services network are propagated to corresponding attribute nodes. Therefore it is possible that a node in this network model to be associated with several labels (categories in this case). We model the affiliated categories of a node d_u as a normalized category vector $\overrightarrow{Q_u} = \{q_{u,1}, \ldots, q_{u,n}\}$, where every item $q_{u,k}$ represents the weight of attribute d_u in the category $l_k \in C$. The node weights are calculated as follows:

$$q_{u,k} = \frac{frequency\ of\ d_u\ in\ l_k}{\sum_{i=1}^{n} frequency\ of\ d_u\ in\ l_i} \quad (16.1)$$

where n refers to the size of category set C. Returning back to the network presented in Fig. 16.9b, the normalized category vector for *businessContactPhoneNumber* according to (16.1) is {0.5, 0.5}, for *organizationName* is {0, 1} and for *organizationBusinessRegistryCode* is {0.33, 0.66}.

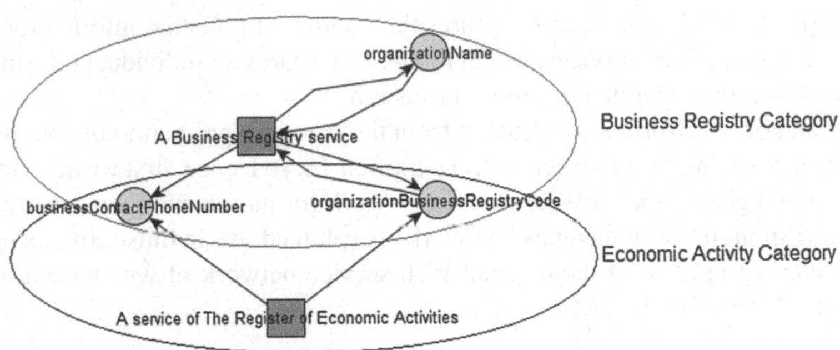

Fig. 16.8 Categorized fragment of a Web service network

16.3.3.2 Weighted Label Network Formation

The transformation mechanism as this step takes as an input a weighted labeled Web services network and generates a weighted labeled network where the labels denote the categories and weights refer to volume of data dependency between categories. The transformation starts with replacing attribute nodes with their affiliated category label nodes. Then category weights are propagated from attribute nodes to the corresponding edges in the category network. The category propagation mechanism works as follows. Let us assume that there exists a directed edge (d_u, d_v) in the weighted labeled Web services network such that node d_u is affiliated with category l_i with weight $q_{u,i}$ and similarly, d_v is affiliated with category l_j with weight $q_{v,j}$. By replacing the attribute nodes with respective categories, we obtain partial category weight for directed edge (l_i, l_j) as follows:

$$\mathsf{w}_{u,v(l_i,l_j)} = q_{u,i} \cdot q_{v,j} \tag{16.2}$$

We refer to $\mathsf{w}_{u,v(l_i,l_j)}$ as partial weight since the graph transformation step may result in multiple edges between the same pair of category nodes. Thus we need to merge identical nodes (the nodes with the same labels) and aggregate their category weights. In other words, for every directed edge (l_i, l_j) in the category network, the actual weight is computed as follows:

$$W_{(l_i,l_j)} = \sum_{\forall\, edge\ (d_u,d_v)\ in\ network} \mathsf{w}_{u,v(l_i,l_j)} \tag{16.3}$$

To illustrate application of the preceding, let us consider the previously constructed network in Fig. 16.9a. As result of the first step of transformation the attribute nodes *organizationName*, *businessContactPhoneNumber* and *organizationBusinessRegistryCode* are replaced with their affiliated category labels *Economic Activity Category* and *Business Registry Category* (abbreviated as *EAC* and *BRC*). As the category weights of attribute nodes are already computed in the previous example, we apply (16.3), which results in the following weights: $W_{(EAC,EAC)} = \frac{1}{6}$, $W_{(EAC,BRC)} = \frac{1}{2}$, $W_{(BRC,EAC)} = \frac{7}{6}$ and $W_{(BRC,BRC)} = \frac{13}{6}$. Next, by unifying the identical edges and augmenting the category weights, the category network presented in Fig. 16.9b is constructed.

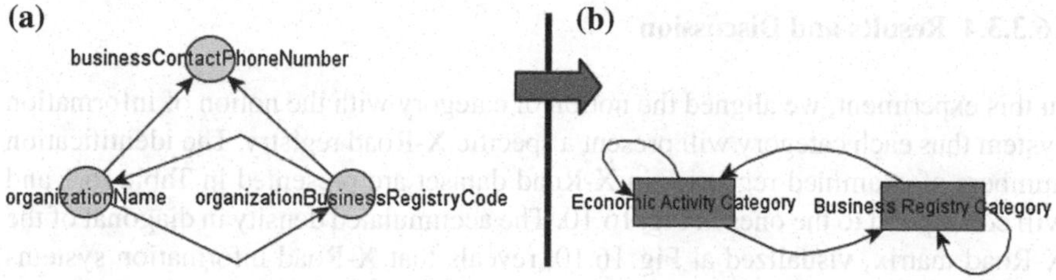

Fig. 16.9 Transformation of a weighted labeled Web services network (*left*) to a weighted label network structure (*right*)

16.3.3.3 Measuring Information Flow Between Web Service Categories

In order to measure density of information flow between different Web service categories, we adopt the approach exploited by Shi et al. [17], originally studied in the context of analyzing information diffusion in citation networks, to the category network structure. We regard category weights, associated to the edges of category network, as diffused information volume from source toward target category nodes. In order to make the information flow between different categories comparable, we normalize the weights and demonstrate the results as entries of a matrix. To this end, we compute the sum of all weights for all outgoing edges from each category in the network and populate information diffusion matrix A with these values. We then normalize (i.e. divide) the volume (i.e. sum) of weighted edges between any pair of nodes by the rate we would expect if the volume of weights of incoming and outgoing edges were the same.

Let us assume that $W_{(l_i,l_j)}$ is the actual weight of edge (l_i, l_j) obtained by utilization of (16.3), $W_{i*} = \sum_j W_{(l_i,l_j)}$ is the sum of all weights of all links from category i and $W_{*j} = \sum_i W_{(l_i,l_j)}$ is the sum of all weights of all links to category j and $W = \sum_{i,j} W_{(l_i,l_j)}$ is the sum of all weights of all links in matrix A. Then the expected volume of weights, assuming indifference to ones in their own category and others, from category i to category j is $E[W_{ij}] = W_{i*} \times W_{*j}/W$.

We define the category weight as a Z-score that measures standard deviations with respect to expected W_{ij}. Here we have learned that $W \gg W_{i*}$ and $W \gg W_{*j}$, hence we approximate the standard deviation by $\sqrt{E[W_{ij}]}$. In this way, for every entry in matrix A, we obtain a normalized value, which we refer to as *diffusion weight* (ϕ):

$$\phi_{ij} = (W_{ij} - \frac{W_{i*} \times W_{*j}}{W})/\sqrt{\frac{W_{i*} \times W_{*j}}{W}} \tag{16.4}$$

High proximity between categories i and j reveals a strong tendency for data associated with category i to be resulted from invocation of Web service operations which consume data associated with category j meaning that information flow from Web services of category j to Web services of category i is higher than average.

16.3.3.4 Results and Discussion

In this experiment, we aligned the notion of category with the notion of information system thus each category will present a specific X-Road registry. The identification numbers of examined registries in X-Road dataset are presented in Table 16.1 and will correspond to the ones in Fig. 16.10. The accumulated density in diagonal of the X-Road matrix, visualized at Fig. 16.10, reveals that X-Road information systems mainly provide output for their own services and consume mostly the information provided by the same information system. Closer inspection of the corresponding labeled Web service network reveals that services in these registries exploit frequently domain-specific concepts as input and output parameters (e.g. "engine type", "vehicle category" and "car model" in case of *Traffic Registry* information system). Moreover, since similar domain-specific concepts are mainly provided or consumed by services of the same information system, these information systems can be regarded as self-contained systems. We refer to this behavioral model as *self-referential* pattern. The following communities are identified to remarkably follow this pattern (i.e. those information systems where at least 50 % of their diffusion weight is accumulated on the main diagonal of the matrix): *E-Mail Service Registry, Estonian Research Information Systems, Criminal Court Registry, Traffic Registry, Estonian Business Registry, State Registry of Construction Works, Land Information System, Police Procedure Information System, Visa Registry and Pension Registry*.

On the other hand, there are some strongly connected pairs of information systems that can be identified outside of the main diagonal of matrix. For example pairs of: (*Tartu University User Information System* and *Workplace Information Registry*) and (*Tallinn University User Information System* and *Workplace Information registry*). A strong tie here means that there is a remarkable mutual information flow (at least 50 % of their average flow) between two parties. Emergence of this pattern is due to the fact these information systems feature symmetric set of services. This indicates that

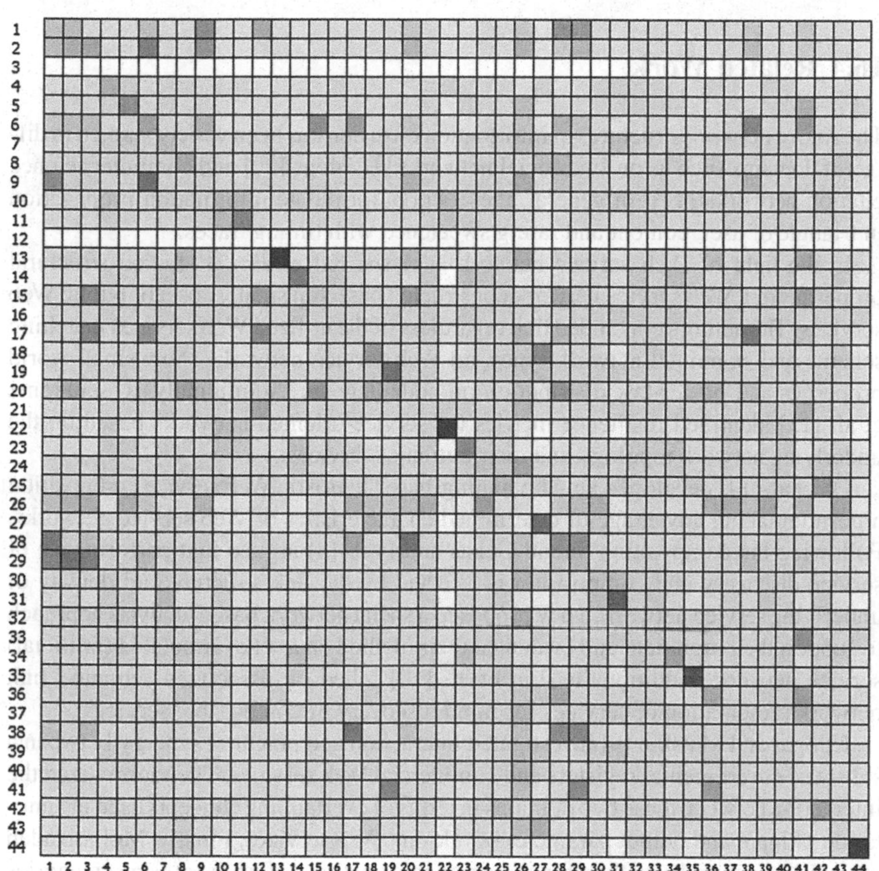

Fig. 16.10 Visualization of information flow among X-Road registries. Each entry is shaded according to a normalized Z-score representing whether the density of information flow is higher or less than expected at random. Darker shading indicates higher Z-scores. The diagonal represents information flow within same category

(1) these information systems expose similar functionality (2) the services exposed by these information systems have designed such that information, which can be inserted, can also be queried through public interfaces, which is not very common in practice. In addition, it can be concluded that these information systems are designed to interact with each other.

Finally, it appears to be considerable information flow from *Tallinn Sporting Activities Registry* to *Environmental Registry*, from *Estonian Citizens Liable to Military Service Registry* to *Support Register Information System*, and finally from *Address Database* to *Land Information System*, just few to name. One can also observe a noticeable information flow between *Tallinn Sporting Activities Registry* and a number of other X-Road registries. This is a quite expectable observation with respect to the need to collect information from surrounding organizations related to Tallinn's development activities.

16.4 Related Work

The role of network structures in information diffusion has been widely studied in different domains such as on-line social networks [1], blogs [20] and computer science citation networks [17]. In general, these works formulate information propagation in triangle of user, content and rating sweetened with timing traces.

In the light of Web service network analysis, Kil et al. [7] studied structural properties of a Web service network constructed based on small subset of public Web services. The authors concluded that regardless of the utilized Web services matching scheme and examined network types, all Web service networks show small world properties and power-law distribution on node degrees. Additionally, Rosenkrantz et al. [15] identified resilience metrics for service-oriented networks based on the underlying network topology and distribution of services.

Oh et al. [14] developed an AI planning-based heuristic Web service composition algorithm taking advantage of determined characteristics of Web service networks. Following the composition thread Gekas and Fasli [3] argued that performance of service discovery and composition is affected by the link structure and density of underlying service network. They proposed a social network based analysis approach to support their argument and evaluated their method on a set of simulated (artificial) service network. Additionally, Liu et al. [10] relied on associated semantic link network presentation of services for rapid discovery of composable services.

Küngas and Matskin [9] investigated interaction and potential synergy between a subset of governmental registers and commercial Web services. They formalized the interaction between these two domains in terms of overlapping concepts used in annotation of input and output parameter of relevant Web services. Finally, Mokarizadeh et al. [12] suggested a method for analyzing information diffusion between categories of data-centric Web services. The method operates on a Web services network constructed by linking interface descriptions of categorized Web services. The proposed method is evaluated on a case study of global Web services.

The analogy between semantic Web services and semantic networks opens potentially another gate for Web service network analysis. In this light, Jiang et al. [5] proposed metrics to measure information fluidity and suggested an analytical model based on small-world network theory. The emphasis of this work is to analyze interoperability in large-scale and their findings mainly concern the optimum quantity of required domain ontologies for annotating certain quantity of information system elements. Finally, research in security-aware service composition has addressing some issues in securing information flow in multi-domain systems [16].

16.5 Conclusion

In this paper we presented a basic formalism for modelling Web services networks and then extended it with a weighted label system. We presented specific schemes for computing the weights and transforming the network in the context of information diffusion. While the label system allows attaching arbitrary labels to nodes of Web services networks, the concept of weights facilitates assignment of specific values to the labels. The described weighted label network topology allows analysis of aggregated Web services networks with respect to specific phenomena. In this paper we used this network topology to measure information diffusion between information systems.

We also used the formalism for developing metrics for enabling discovery of data redundancy from WSDL descriptions of information system interfaces and evaluated them on a federated governmental information system. The results of the evaluation are encouraging, since consistently high precision and recall were achieved, both for identifying redundant attributes and for identifying the primary location of redundant attributes. Moreover, the evaluation unveiled that, although individual information systems might not have a lot of data redundancy, there can be considerable redundancy in federated information systems.

As a future work we plan to generalize the formalism to a wider range of Web services network topologies. More specifically, we are interested in analysing Web services networks from services provisioning perspective.

References

1. M. Cha, A. Mislove, and K. P. Gummadi. A measurement-driven analysis of information propagation in the flickr social network. In *Proc. of the 18th International Conference on World Wide Web*, WWW '09, pages 721–730, Madrid, Spain, 2009. ACM.
2. A. K. Elmagarmid, P. G. Ipeirotis, and V. S. Verykios. Duplicate record detection: A survey. *IEEE Transactions on Knowledge and Data Engineering*, 19(1):1–16, 2007.
3. J. Gekas and M. Fasli. Employing graph network analysis for web service composition. *International Journal of Information Technology and Web Engineering*, 2:21–40, 2007.
4. A. Heß and N. Kushmerick. Learning to attach semantic metadata to web services. In *Proc. of 2nd International Semantic Web Conference (ISWC2003)*, pages 258–273. Springer, 2003.

5. G. Jiang, G. Cybenko, and J. A. Hendler. Semantic interoperability and information fluidity. *Int. J. Cooperative Inf. Syst.*, 15(1):1–22, 2006.
6. A. Kalja, A. Reitsakas, and N. Saard. eGovernment in Estonia: Best practices. In *Technology Management: A Unifying Discipline for Melting the Boundaries*, pages 500–506. IEEE Press, 2005.
7. H. Kil, S.-C. Oh, E. Elmacioglu, W. Nam, and D. Lee. Graph theoretic topological analysis of web service networks. *World Wide Web*, 12:321–343, 2009.
8. P. Küngas and M. Dumas. Cost-effective semantic annotation of XML schemas and web service interfaces. In *Proc. of IEEE 2009 International Conference on Services Computing*, pages 372–379. IEEE Computer Society Press, 2009.
9. P. Küngas and M. Matskin. Interaction and potential synergy between commercial and governmental web services - a case study. In *Procedings of 2007 IEEE International Conference on Services Computing - Workshops (SCW 2007), 9–13 July 2007, Salt Lake City, Utah, USA*, pages 1–8. IEEE Computer Society, 2007.
10. F. Liu, Y. Shi, X. Luo, G. Liang, and Z. Xu. Discovery of semantic web service flow based on computation. In *Proceedings of the 2009 IEEE International Conference on Web Services*, ICWS '09, pages 319–326, Washington, DC, USA, 2009. IEEE Computer Society.
11. S. Mokarizadeh, P. Küngas, and M. Matskin. Ontology learning for cost-effective large-scale semantic annotation of web service interfaces. In *Proceedings of EKAW 2010*, pages 401–410. Springer, 2010.
12. S. Mokarizadeh, P. Küngas, and M. Matskin. Evaluation of a semi-automated semantic annotation approach for bootstrapping the analysis of large-scale web service networks. In *Proceedings of the 2011 IEEE/WIC/ACM International Conference on Web Intelligence, WI 2011, Lyon, France, August 22–27, 2011*, pages 388–395. IEEE Computer Society, 2011.
13. D. L. Moody and G. G. Shanks. Improving the quality of data models: empirical validation of a quality management framework. *Information Systems*, 28(6):619–650, 2003.
14. S.-C. Oh, D. Lee, and S. Kumara. Effective web service composition in diverse and large-scale service networks. *IEEE Transactions on Services Computing*, 1(1):15–32, 2008.
15. D. J. Rosenkrantz, S. Goel, S. S. Ravi, and J. Gangolly. Resilience metrics for service-oriented networks: A service allocation approach. *IEEE Trans. Serv. Comput.*, 2:183–196, July 2009.
16. W. She, I.-L. Yen, B. Thuraisingham, and E. Bertino. Policy-driven service composition with information flow control. In *The 8th International Conference on Web Services, ICWS 2010, Miami, Florida, USA, July 5–10, 2010*, pages 50–57. IEEE Computer Society, 2010.
17. X. Shi, B. L. Tseng, and L. A. Adamic. Information diffusion in computer science citation networks. *CoRR*, abs/0905.2636, 2009.
18. V. Ventrone and S. Heiler. Some practical advice for dealing with semantic heterogeneity in federated database systems. In *Proceedings of the Database Colloquium, San Diego, August 1994, Armed Forces Communications and Electronics Assc. (AFCEA)*, 1994.
19. G. C. Witt and G. C. Simsion. *Data Modeling Essentials: Analysis, Design, and Innovation*. The Coriolis, Group, 2000.
20. J. Yang and S. Counts. Comparing information diffusion structure in weblogs and microblogs. In *Proceedings of the Fourth International AAAI Conference on Weblogs and Social Media, ICWSM 2010, Washington, DC, USA, May 23–26, 2010*, pages 351–354. The AAAI Press, 2010.

Part III
Novel Perspectives and Future Directions

Chapter 17
Work as a Service

Daniel V. Oppenheim, Lav R. Varshney and Yi-Min Chee

Abstract Improving work within and among enterprises is of pressing importance. In this chapter we take a services-oriented view of both the doing and the coordinating of work by treating *work as a service*. We discuss how large work engagements can be decomposed into a set of smaller interconnected service requests and conversely how they can be built up. Encapsulation of work into a service request enables its assignment to any qualified work organization. As such, the encapsulation naturally lends itself to ongoing optimization of the overall engagement. A service request contains two distinct parts: coordination information for coordinating work and payload information for doing work. Coordination information deals with business concerns such as risk, cost, schedule, and value co-creation. Contrarily, payload information defines the deliverables and provides what is needed to do the work, such as designs or use-cases. This general two-part decomposition leads to a paradigm of work as a two-way information flow between service systems, rather than as a business process to be implemented. Treating work as information flow allows us to leverage extant web services technology using mainstream service-oriented architectures (SOA). Milestone structures may be used to formalize coordination and establish measurable outcomes. Benefits from the work-as-a-service approach include agility, visibility, responsiveness, and ongoing optimization.

Daniel V. Oppenheim · Lav R. Varshney (✉) · Yi-Min Chee
IBM Thomas J. Watson Research Center,
Yorktown Heights, NY, USA
e-mail: music@us.ibm.com

Lav R. Varshney
e-mail: lrvarshn@us.ibm.com

Yi-Min Chee
e-mail: ymchee@us.ibm.com

A. Bouguettaya et al. (eds.), *Advanced Web Services*, 409
DOI: 10.1007/978-1-4614-7535-4_17,

17.1 Introduction

The differences among labor pools globally and the rapid proliferation of capacious information technology infrastructures has disrupted the nature of work in many institutions, causing increased decentralization of workforces and increased leverage of communities, networks, and ecosystems of people and of firms to do work. These business, technological, and social trends have intensified interest in developing general ways of structuring the coordination and doing of work.

The fundamental problem of doing work is to transform inputs into outputs to meet specified requirements by leveraging resources. For human-based work, work systems can be individuals or groups of individuals that may be distributed within or between organizations. But most work required for businesses to reach their goals is complex. The fundamental problem then becomes how to translate a business need, perhaps expressed as a service request, into an optimal decomposition of units of required work and how to optimally coordinate the execution of all ongoing work. The latter is a problem of *coordination*.

The fundamental problem of coordinating work is to decompose a service request into units of work that can each be assigned to a work system, and then provide the necessary inputs and requirements to a set of work systems and to aggregate their outputs, while continuously responding to changing conditions. Often there are dependencies among work assigned to the several work systems. Different work systems may have local objectives beyond just meeting global requirements and moreover may perform work with differing costs, schedules, and reliabilities. Optimal coordination must take these factors into account.

In this chapter we treat *work as a service* (WaaS). That is, the doing of work is encapsulated as a service request and the coordination of work involves routing service requests to work systems. Within the WaaS paradigm, large work engagements can be decomposed into a set of smaller interconnected service requests and conversely larger work engagements can be built up from small service requests.

An encapsulated service request contains two distinct parts: coordination information for coordinating work and payload information for doing work. Coordination information deals with business concerns such as risk, cost, schedule, and value. Payload information defines the deliverables and provides what is needed to do the work, such as designs or use-cases. This general two-part decomposition leads to a paradigm of work as a two-way information flow between work systems, rather than as a business process that needs to be implemented or integrated between two organizations.

Encapsulation collects all necessary inputs in one place and explicitly specifies the requirements and format for outputs; this eliminates inefficiencies for work systems in searching for information or requirements. More importantly, however, encapsulation enables the assignment of a work request to any qualified work system, leading naturally to ongoing optimization of the overall work engagement in response to unpredictable system dynamics. Coordinating work becomes a problem of dynamically routing information flow. It is possible to use milestone-based structures to monitor progress and define measurables in the interaction between a service provider and a service requester.

By treating work as an information flow, several patterns of and organizational structures for doing work can be treated in a common framework. These include tearing work into smaller pieces for delegation, combining overlapping work to be done together, pausing and resuming to shift work in time, and reassignment to shift work to other providers when overloaded.

Since the need for work is encapsulated as service requests, mainstream service-oriented architectures (SOA) can be used to provide information technology support such as messaging infrastructures and client software.

As demonstrated in the sequel, significant benefits from this approach include agility in setting up large engagements to be carried out by distributed work systems, visibility into operations without violating providers' privacy or requiring changes to internal processes, responsiveness to unpredictability and change, and ongoing optimizations over competing system-level business objectives.

17.2 The Changing Nature of Work and Workforce

With the proliferation of information technologies that provide large-capacity communication at lightning speed, decentralized and globally distributed workforces are increasingly common. Moreover there are cultural changes afoot that are changing the nature of work and workforce; the millennial generation is project-based rather than jobs-based, and so there is a need to orchestrate work talent in an environment of churn [6].

The combined force of these technological and social trends has been the emergence of new models of work including: globally dispersed teams within the firm [27], outsourcing, crowdsourcing [29], informational work factories [8], virtual enterprises [21], cross-enterprise collaborations [25, 36], open source development, social production [5], and asset reuse in place of new creation [2]. There is a need for a common framework that can holistically operate with these several models.

With these new models of work, there is greater division of labor and therefore specialization of workforce [12, 20], but traditional coordination mechanisms such as mutual adjustment through informal communication [22] are no longer effective [14]. The work that is to be done must be defined with some specificity. It is well-known in economic theory that there is a tradeoff between the benefits provided by specialization and the costs of coordinating dispersed labor [4]. Formal mechanisms may be able to reduce coordination costs without reducing the benefits provided by specialization. The goal of the WaaS paradigm is precisely this.

As will become evident, encapsulation of work makes it procedurally equivalent to plug in any work system, whether it is a crowd or a partner organization or some combination of several work systems. Different work architectures can be constructed [11]. This is in contrast to business process management (BPM) approaches, where recombining the doing of work requires a new business process to connect the two pieces together, a provably complex undertaking [23]. Further, as detailed by Vergidis et al., BPM models do not lend themselves to too many optimizations [37]. Within the information flow paradigm herein, optimization is readily possible.

Notwithstanding, the doing of work by a work system may be carried out using a BPM approach for a single encapsulated work request; in particular an approach based on milestones may be appropriate [32]. Further, it is possible to use the fulfillment of encapsulated work requests as a signal to transition between states in business process models [18].

17.3 Application: Global Service Delivery

The WaaS encapsulation that will be described in the sequel arose from our experience in designing and implementing a new information technology framework for global service delivery: IBM's Application Assembly Automation (AAO). [1] Begun in 2006 and still ongoing, AAO has become a key component of IBM's Globally Integrated Capabilities [16]. Large software development projects that were once carried out by large colocated teams—often on the client's site—are now broken into pieces and executed in isolation by an interchangeable Technology Assembly Center (TAC). Different TACs specialize in different aspects of software development, such as design, packaged application implementation enhancements, SOA development, or testing, and are strategically located globally. Each piece of work is routed to a TAC through a construct called a work-packet, and the overall deliverables are integrated for delivery. A TAC is thus a virtual resource with a well-defined business capability and a work-packet a wrapper containing all information required for a TAC to produce its deliverable in relative isolation. Our framework enabled a high degree of automation and resulted in significant improvements in productivity, throughput, quality, and time-to-value.

17.3.1 Approach

Software development is considered most effective when carried out by a small team that works together in the same location. The dominant root cause for failure when breaking up complex projects across geographical boundaries has been unpredictability—both within a project and in its external environment. No matter how well planned a project, uncertainties arise that require ongoing adaptation [13]. In our view, managing uncertainty requires identification, coordination, and response; most projects that get into to trouble do poorly in at least one of the three.

[1] http://www.ibm.com/services/us/gbs/bus/html/gbs-application-assembly-optimization.html

1. *Identification*. It is desirable to detect problems early, or even better, to predict before symptoms become observable. Identification requires deep visibility into all aspects project internals and external environment, and can be achieved through the specification and collection of metrics. Since collecting extra metrics introduces a considerable overhead, we built a flexible metrics framework that not only automates collection but also allows dynamic adjustment of what is measured as the situation changes [26].
2. *Coordination*. When an issue is detected, a response must be taken. Since global delivery is a complex system with many interdependent stakeholders having possibly conflicting business objectives, a response must be coordinated between all stakeholders. The final decision will be some tradeoff between competing business concerns. The client, for example, may care about quality and cost; the delivery executive about schedule and service level agreement compliance; and the project manager about doing minimal work to meet the specified requirement. Our framework supports decision making by providing each stakeholder with all relevant data. This approach can support human decision making [24], computational tradeoffs [3, 18, 32] or any combination thereof.
3. *Response*. Effective response requires the ability to quickly change any aspect of ongoing and future work. In labor-intensive work this is difficult due to a sizable overhead in communication, coordination, and reallocation of human resources. However, if work can be encapsulated into atomic units, then a response can be fully automated and enacted in almost real-time: this is the core idea behind the work-packet as a container of information. Work-packets are used to assign work to a TAC as well as to manage the flow and coordination of work between TACs. To a TAC team, a work-packet is a one-stop source for all the information necessary for them to deliver the desired capability. This may include requirements, design, examples, normative guidance, and a clear definition of the desired output—the deliverable. To the team that governs the overall project, the work-packet is used to define and collect metrics that will be used to provide real-time visibility into any aspect of the ongoing work. As work-packets wrap work and coordination information, it is easy to enact an agile response.

With these insights, three key principles guided our work: enable work to be factored into atomic units that can be carried out in relative isolation; minimize the need for coordination, but maximize the ability to coordinate well when needed; and separate the doing of work from the coordination of work.

17.4 Work as a Service (WaaS) Encapsulation

In this section, we describe the essential aspects of the WaaS encapsulation for work requests and the information flow paradigm that it leads to.

As depicted schematically in Fig. 17.1, a work engagement consists of essentially three parts:

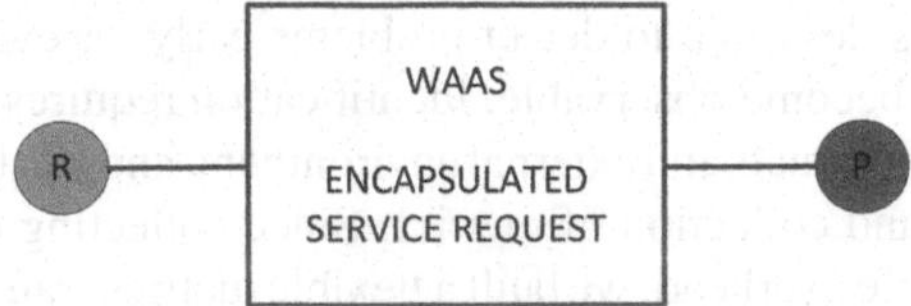

Fig. 17.1 Work as an encapsulated service request, where R represents the requestor and P represents the provider

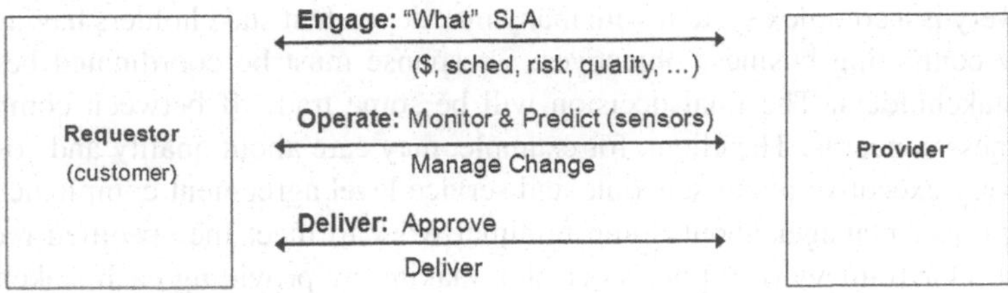

Fig. 17.2 The basic operation of a work request: engagement, operation, and delivery

1. A *requestor*, which is a service system that requests work to be done, provides inputs, and specifies the requirements.
2. A *provider*, which is a service system charged with fulfilling the work request to meet requirements.
3. An *encapsulated service request*, which captures the interaction between the requestor and provider, the two-way information flow among them.

As depicted in Fig. 17.2, there are three aspects of a work task that must be established between the requestor and the provider. First, a so-called service level agreement (SLA) must be reached. The SLA specifies the business-level properties of the work request, such as cost and schedule. Second, as the work is ongoing, there may be some monitoring by thc requestor of partial results produced by and checkpoints achieved by the provider, so as to have appropriate visibility. Third, at the conclusion of a work engagement, the provider sends deliverables to the requestor and the provider either confirms or rejects the efficacy of the delivered work. Note that all three of these involve two-way flows of information.

These two-way communications that arise in work should all be captured in the encapsulated work request. In formalizing and encapsulating, a general two-part decomposition of work into business concerns and domain concerns can be defined. These two parts are called *coordination information* and *payload information*, respectively, and are depicted schematically in Fig. 17.3. Coordination mechanisms can then restrict attention to coordination information whereas work systems can restrict attention to payload information.

In detailing the contents of coordination and payload information, it is easiest to first consider an *atomic service request*: an encapsulation of a unit of work so small that it cannot be broken into pieces. We will later see how to combine and recombine atomic service requests into *molecular service requests*.

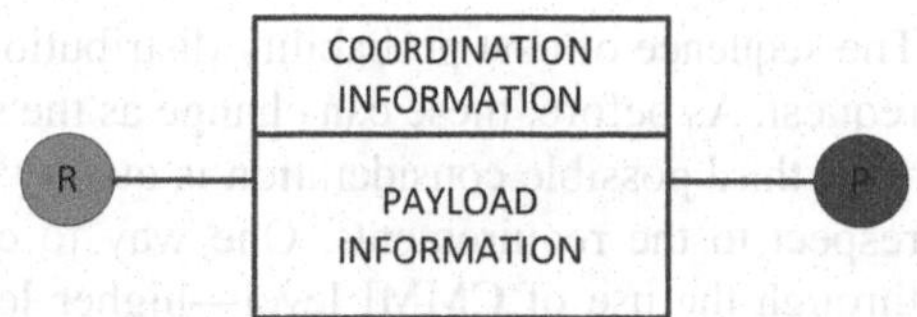

Fig. 17.3 The encapsulated work request partitioned into coordination information and payload information

17.4.1 Coordination Information

What information about an atomic service request is needed for coordination? To answer this question, we must enumerate several possible business concerns that arise in work. This is because the goal of coordination is to satisfy the business concerns faced by both requestors and providers, as well as perhaps larger systematic concerns. Negotiation among these different perspectives is possible through the coordination information. Note that coordination may be carried out by the requestors and providers themselves or by an external coordinating agent, and that concerns from the different perspectives of requestors and providers may conflict.

A first possible consideration is schedule: how long will it take for an atomic piece of work to be done. Since this varies across different work systems and is also potentially stochastic, there is a mapping from the Cartesian product of the possible set of work systems $\mathscr{S}$ and the possible set of work tasks $\mathscr{W}$ to the space of positive-valued random variables that represent time $\mathscr{T}$:

$$\mathscr{S} \times \mathscr{W} \mapsto \mathscr{T}.$$

The encapsulated service request carries the schedule probability distribution for each potential work system for the given work task, including the provider that is actually chosen. As milestones are reached and partial results are achieved, the schedule probability distributions can be updated with new information that is furnished by the provider. Exogenous perturbations to the system such as natural disasters might also change schedule distributions. These distributions can change not only based on intermediate results and exogenous effects, but also by changes in requirements imposed by the requestor.

A second possible consideration is cost: how much money will the provider charge the requestor to do work and whether there are bonuses or penalties associated with speed or quality [3]. Although the encapsulation formalism is eminently amenable to outcomes-based pricing [10, 30] rather than effort-based pricing, the cost may still have some variability. Hence, there is a mapping from the Cartesian product of the possible set of work systems and the possible set of work tasks to the space of random variables $\mathscr{C}$ (negative values might arise if the provider actually pays to do work):

$$\mathscr{S} \times \mathscr{W} \mapsto \mathscr{C}.$$

The sequence of cost probability distributions is included in the encapsulated work request. As before, these can change as the service request lifecycle progresses.

A third possible consideration is quality: how good with the deliverable be with respect to the requirements. One way to certify the quality of a work system is through the use of CMMI level—higher levels imply more stringent process and quality control. Again, there is a mapping from the Cartesian product of the set of work systems and the set of work tasks to the space of random variables $\mathscr{Q}$:

$$\mathscr{S} \times \mathscr{W} \mapsto \mathscr{Q}.$$

The evolving probability distributions are included in the encapsulated work request.

Additional business concerns may be similarly added to the coordination information to extend its range beyond $\mathscr{T} \times \mathscr{C} \times \mathscr{Q}$.

As presented so far, factors such as schedule, cost, and quality are independent, but in actuality they are very much intertwined. For example, loosening schedules may reduce costs or requiring higher quality may incur higher costs. These competing business concerns can be balanced through the notion of *value*. The overall value is what should be optimized. As we will see in the next section, the value-dominant logic of Vargo and Lusch brings this point out even further [33]. In terms of the encapsulated work request, joint probability distributions for business concerns such as schedule/cost/quality in the space $\mathscr{T} \times \mathscr{C} \times \mathscr{Q}$ should be stored rather than marginal probability distributions.

In discussing atomic service requests, we did not need to worry about the possibility of decomposition into smaller work requests. When considering molecular service requests, coordination information needs to also contain the interdependencies among its atomic constituents. Dependencies include not only things like the fact that one piece of work needs to be done before another, but also inertia effects on the doing of work, and other coordination-relevant factors, cf. [39]. In fact, operating on these dependencies will be crucial for defining valid ways of decomposing and recomposing work packets [32].

17.4.2 Payload Information

Switching gears to payload information, we now ask what information is needed by a work system to do work. In broad strokes, payload information should include the inputs that are to be transformed into outputs and the requirements that specify what is to be done. This should be the minimal sufficient information for doing work; if there is too much irrelevant information then it can cause information overload whereas if there is too little, then time and energy is wasted in acquisition.

Going into more specificity, however, requires specifying the kind of work itself. For global software development, it may include APIs, architectural diagrams, and requirements documents; for car engine design, it may include specifications of mechanical, hydraulic, and electrical interfaces, as well as performance requirements and CAD language specification. However, the WaaS encapsulation is designed to be general so it can support the needs of any specific domain.

The payload information of a molecular work request may have a natural construction from atomic payloads that reflects the architecture of the physical thing itself. For example in component-based software engineering, the atomic units of work may be the design of the atomic software components.

As the lifecycle of the work request proceeds, the payload information is updated based on partial results and milestones to its current state. If there are, say, technological developments that impact the doing of work, or if there are changes in requirements due to changing market conditions, these would also cause the payload information to evolve. If errors are made in the execution of work, fixes may also be incorporated into the payload information.

17.4.3 Information Flow

The WaaS paradigm may be interpreted as an information flow description. One can think of the encapsulated service request as a multidimensional variable that captures the current state of things, including the value being generated. As things happen, information flows to the service request for it to be updated. Updates to both payload and coordination information happen continuously: coordination information captures business concerns, whereas payload information captures domain concerns.

Coordination mechanisms can also be thought of in informational terms and in particular as routing. Essentially, coordination involves connecting the appropriate requestor and provider together to interact through an encapsulated service request. Moreover, as shown in Sect. 17.7, by appropriately routing several service requests within a work ecosystem, large work engagements can be constructed. Coordination, however must also consider issues of governance such as accountability, responsibility, and decision-making rights. Moreover, there may be different organizational structures for coordination. We discuss these in Sect. 17.8.

17.5 Value Co-Creation

In the service-dominant logic that has become a cornerstone of service science, value creation moves from the provider to a collaborative process between the requestor and provider. The value derived from this interaction is called *value co-creation* [34].

In further studying value, one can consider notions such as value-in-exchange, value-in-use, and value-in-context, depicted in Fig. 17.4. Value-in-exchange is the traditional goods-dominant view that one-time transfer from provider to requestor is all that provides value. Contrarily value-in-use and value-in-context—its enhancement to consider not just the value accrued by the requestor and provider but also the entire service ecosystem—specify that value is created by the interaction between the

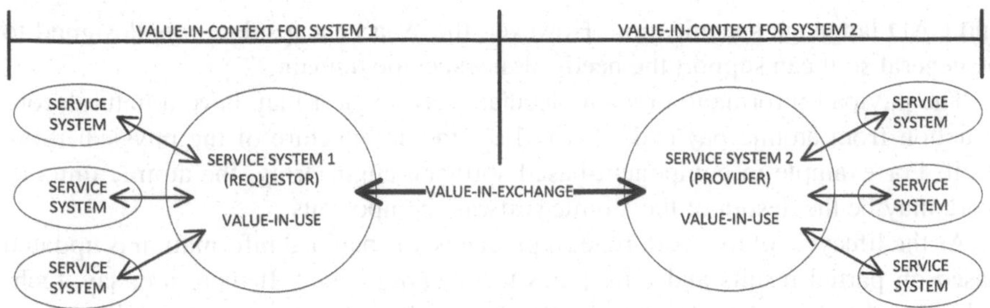

Fig. 17.4 The notion of value in services, redrawn following [34]

two parties [34]. In our view, depicted in Fig. 17.5, the encapsulated service request is the seat of value co-creation. It holds the current state of work as measurable milestones and also the various business concerns that determine value for either the requestor or the provider. Indeed value itself $V \in \mathscr{V}$ can be thought of as determined by business concerns such as schedule/cost/quality:

$$\mathscr{T} \times \mathscr{C} \times \mathscr{Q} \mapsto \mathscr{V}.$$

Further, the encapsulated work request provides the requestor with full visibility into the ongoing work and the mechanism for communication, collaboration, and negotiation that lead to value co-creation.

17.6 A Formal Milestone Mechanism

One way of defining coordination information for a given encapsulated service request is to include a formal coordination lifecycle using milestones [32] built from the guard-stage-milestone approach for specifying business entity lifecycles [15]. Here we briefly discuss the nature of this formalism.

A coordination lifecycle consists of stages, and composite stages may be built up from atomic ones. Atomic stages correspond to various tasks such as assignment, service invocation, human tasks, etc. Each stage has one or more milestones and one or more guards. A milestone represents a named business-relevant operational objective and is represented with a boolean attribute indicating if the milestone has been achieved or not. Similarly for a guard. Stages get activated by means of their guards and closed when certain milestones are achieved.

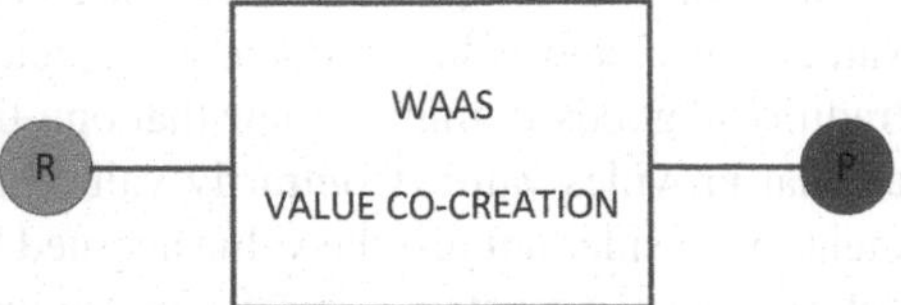

Fig. 17.5 The encapsulated service request is the seat of value co-creation

Triggering events for milestones and guards might originate from the external world such as from a human actor or an incoming service call, or from the internal processing of the lifecycle.

Milestones serve as a primary high-level coordination mechanism and may provide enough information for requesters and providers to assess/report the progress of a particular WaaS instance. When more detail is needed for coordination between the requestor and the provider, a set of domain-specific coordination information attributes may be defined to provide mechanisms for information exchange between service requestor and provider. Indeed, delivery of information attributes may be tied to milestone achievement and vice versa, achievement of milestones may depend on values of information attributes.

For instance, consider the case of a WaaS instance where the provider is performing test case execution for software components under development. In order to coordinate work appropriately, the requester wants to know when the work has progressed through several stages, corresponding to the setup of the test environment and actual testing of each component. The requestor defines milestones marking the completion of each stage, and uses business entities to capture the relevant lifecycle information for each the components being tested. As the provider completes its testing, it updates individual information attributes, such as the number of test cases executed, and the counts of successful and failed test cases. Milestones marking the completion of testing for each component are tied to the submission of these information attributes.

It should be emphasized that stages need not precisely represent how the provider will perform work. Typically, stages will only provide a high-level, loosely-defined specification of the basic WaaS breakdown structure according to which the provider should report progress to the requestor. Various combinations of milestones, coordination information attributes, and stage-based breakdown structures may be employed to faithfully model service agreements between requestors and providers to provide appropriate levels of visibility, coordination, and control.

17.7 Patterns and Structures

In this section, we discuss the structural building blocks that enable decomposition of large work engagements into several smaller encapsulated service requests and conversely building up small encapsulated service requests into larger work engagements. To do this, one can think of encapsulated service requests as service blocks. Several canonical patterns such as delegation, tearing, and merging emerge and they are tied to various organizational structures that arise in businesses; cf. Malone's notions of flow, sharing, and fit [19, p. 140]. See also related work in systems theory [38]. This section demonstrates that the WaaS paradigm applies to the problem space it is meant to address: possibly complicated work within or among multifarious organizations.

17.7.1 Emergence of Patterns

Consider work engagements in collaborative enterprise environments [36]. Due to the rapid pace in the modern business environment, there is a need for agile reconstitution of work to address new opportunities or disruptions and capture emerging efficiencies. In the context of WaaS, adaptation can take the form of modifications to both the structural and temporal characteristics of service requests that constitute the larger engagement.

Suppose that a project is initially parceled into encapsulated work requests and assigned to different providers for completion. Ideally, work will flow between the units as described by the initial project plan, and coordination will consist merely of ensuring that deliverables are made available and status is updated accordingly. However, experienced project managers understand that the ideal case is rarely encountered in practice [35]. One common issue that can arise during collaborative work is that one unit falls behind in the work that was assigned to it. Although there may be several underlying reasons, this situation needs to become visible through coordination information that flows through the encapsulated work request.

Coordination response can take one of many flavors. One possible response is simply to accept the delay and shift the scheduled end date further into the future, thereby impacting the start of other service requests depending on the delayed deliverables. Additionally, if the work must be combined with perishable outputs that are being produced by another provider, it may be necessary to pause other ongoing service requests and resume them later to ensure that they complete at the same time as the new scheduled end date of the tardy request. These temporal operations (pause and resume) allow shifting of work in time in order to accommodate schedule impacts on dependent work.

Another possible response to late work is to re-scope work that is to be done by the lagging provider. This can be accomplished by tearing the WaaS request into smaller pieces, and re-assigning some of the pieces to different providers. In this way, work can be done in parallel, resulting in schedule compression.

On the flip side, suppose a provider is operating extremely efficiently and is completing its assigned work faster than scheduled. This presents an opportunity for work to be delivered sooner than planned. To do this, some work may need to be shifted earlier (modeled as negative pause/resume).

In addition, it may be desirable to give the well-performing provider additional work. This can result in the merging of service requests that were originally assigned to this provider with requests that were assigned to other providers. Such merging can be particularly beneficial if it eliminates dependencies that existed between the original requests, or if it eliminates activities or milestones which are no longer needed after the merge.

The above issues and opportunities view coordination response from the perspective of managing work schedule. Issues and opportunities also arise from additional dimensions of value co-creation like quality or cost. For example, if a provider consistently produces defective deliverables, it may be desirable to re-scope or reassign work by tearing and merging, as described above, or it may simply be necessary to inject additional coordination information into the encapsulated work requests assigned to that provider.

Given this set of structural and temporal operations, we can then define the problem of coordination as one of determining when it is best to tear, merge, pause, or resume work in order to achieve certain value objectives. Next we delve deeper into the structures of these operations.

17.7.2 Structures

First consider delegating work from one work system to another, as in Fig. 17.6. This may be done, e.g. if the original provider is unexpectedly overloaded. In this case the original provider becomes a requestor for the downstream provider, and may be called a delegator. The service request is re-routed. The payload information and the interdependency portion of the coordination information are copied essentially unchanged to the newly instantiated encapsulated service request, perhaps adding some additional information useful to the new provider or specifying things further. The remaining coordination information, however, is written anew to capture the business concerns of the intermediate node and also to hide the business concerns of the original requestor, since they are not of direct relevance to the new provider and may be private. The delegator remains both accountable and responsible to the original requestor. The new provider, however, is only responsible and accountable to the delegator. Note that the originating requestor may specify that when is delegated some coordination information must also flow down to the sub-providers.

Another possible pattern of work is to tear a molecular encapsulated service request into pieces so as to assign it to several producers (Fig. 17.7). Tearing work into pieces involves both coordination and payload. The payload information is partitioned into (possibly overlapping) pieces that have the minimal sufficient information required for doing the newly reconstituted work. The interdependency portion of the coordination information is also partitioned. The remaining coordination information is written anew. After breaking up, re-routing is identical to delegating. Recursive hierarchical tearing can also be done.

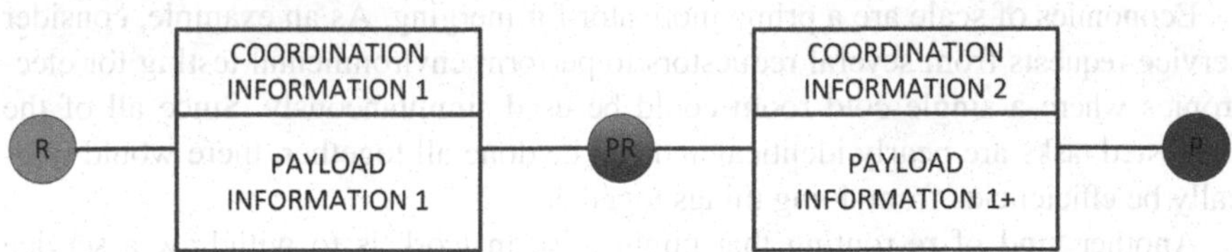

Fig. 17.6 Delegation of work by re-routing an encapsulated service request. The original provider becomes a requestor for the downstream provider

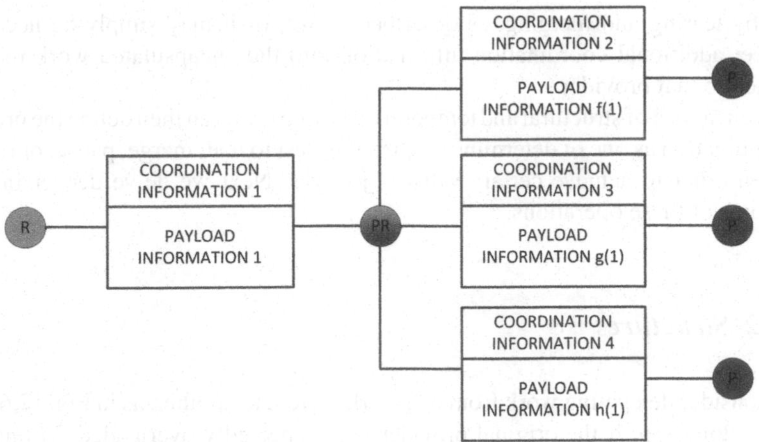

Fig. 17.7 Tearing work and delegating it by re-routing encapsulated service requests. The original provider becomes aggregates requests and becomes a requestor for the downstream provider

Tearing should be done when there are specialization gains to be had, in which case the new providers may each yield different outputs, or if there are underutilized work systems that can be brought into production, in which case each provider will yield a similar output that varies in quantity. For example, if a general service provider has several sourcing channels such as a crowd, a specialized work center, and a factory, different pieces might be routed to different places.

Note that decomposing a service request of the overall work into different aspects requires PR to monitor and eventually integrate or aggregate the completed work so as to be able to respond to R.

A third pattern is to merge several service requests (from a single requestor or from several requestors) into a single service request. Merging also involves both payload and coordination information. The payload information of the merged service request is simply the union of the payloads of the service requests being merged. The interdependencies must be combined while also including all new interdependencies that arise. The remaining coordination information is written afresh, but must typically meet the minimum specifications of the service requests being merged. Merging can also proceed hierarchically (Fig. 17.8).

Economies of scale are a prime motivator for merging. As an example, consider service requests from several requestors to perform environmental testing for electronics where a single cold room could be used simultaneously. Since all of the requested tasks are nearly identical and can be done all together, there would typically be efficiencies from doing things together.

Another kind of re-routing that might arise in work is to withdraw a service request from one provider and assign it to another, as in Fig. 17.9. This might happen when changing conditions prevent the original provider from reasonably completing the service request. As depicted, this pattern brings pluggability to the fore. Such

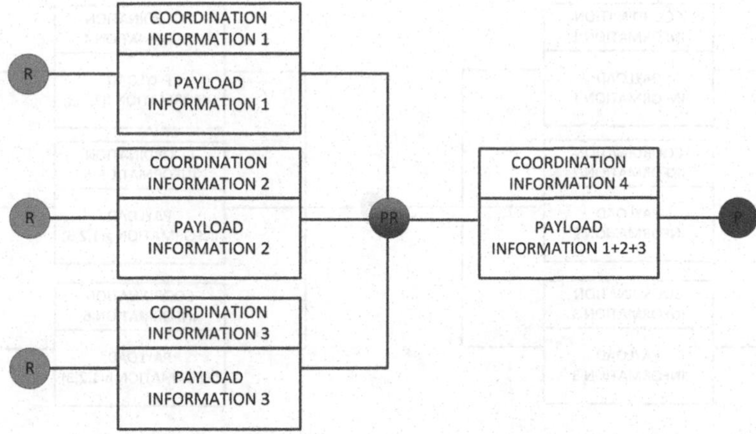

Fig. 17.8 Merging work and delegating it by re-routing encapsulated service requests. The original provider becomes a requestor for the downstream provider

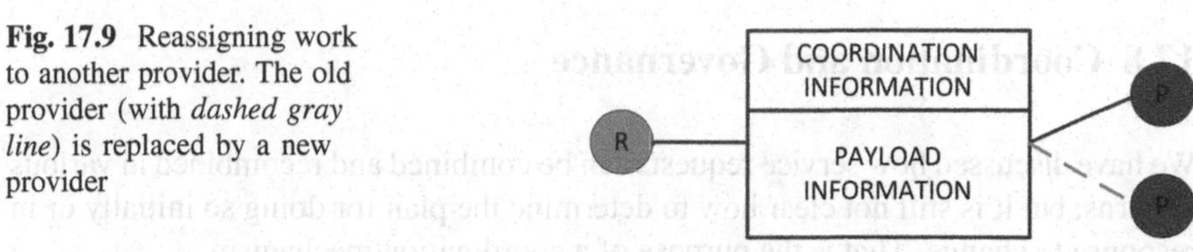

Fig. 17.9 Reassigning work to another provider. The old provider (with *dashed gray line*) is replaced by a new provider

reassignment can be thought of as two complementary operations: pause and resume. The work is paused by one provider and resumed by another. Formally, the resuming provider can be the same as the pausing provider, thereby providing a way to shift work in time.

The basic operations that have been discussed so far can be used in combination to generate other structures. As an example, consider a coordination hub [24], a centralized authority that is charges with coordinating the work in a large organization to derive maximal value, by taking in work from several requesters, tearing and merging, and then delegating to several providers, while also responding to changing conditions. As depicted in Fig. 17.10, a hub can be thought of as a kind of intermediate delegator. Note that cross-enterprise collaboration, when several organizations partner to do work, may take the form of a hub [3]. Robust supply chain collaboration may also take the same basic form [28].

Although this can be formally proven algebraically, it should be clear that arbitrary topologies of work can be constructed using the basic building block and the several operations that we have defined. In particular, it is possible to formalize what happens to coordination lifecycles under the various operations [32].

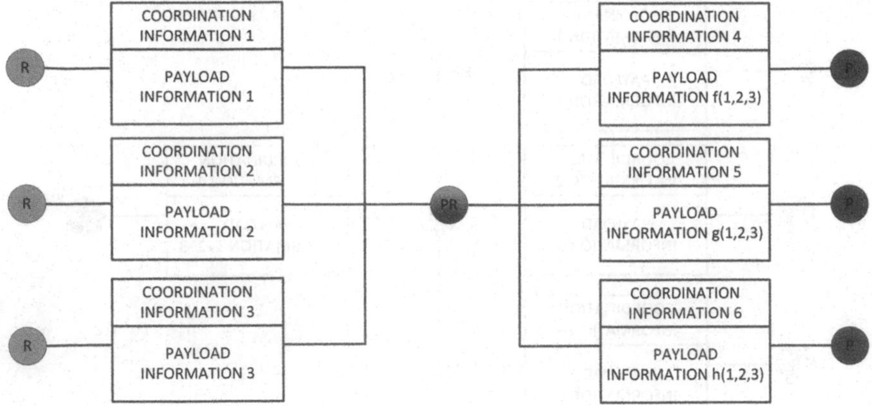

Fig. 17.10 A coordination hub is a delegator that matches work from several requestors to several other providers

17.8 Coordination and Governance

We have discussed how service requests can be combined and recombined in various patterns, but it is still not clear how to determine the plan for doing so initially or in response to change. That is the purpose of a coordination mechanism.

Initial coordination involves organizing the plan of work by appropriately tearing and merging, and then determining a route for work to be assigned to a provider that has sufficient capabilities; unlike communication networks the source and destination are not pre-specified. Negotiation between various parties on value may also be required.

As time goes on and more information becomes available, the initial work plan may need to be modified and service requests re-routed. As noted, there are three main interacting causes for change: updates in the work lifecycle itself; updates in interdependent tasks and systems; and environmental events.

There are several ways of implementing a coordination mechanism such as an automatic program in SOA built on a protocol like WS-coordination, a human program manager or program executive, or a governance council in cross-enterprise collaboration.

Any of these mechanisms, however, require access to the coordination information in the encapsulated work requests. Access control, as well as the ability to make re-routing decisions, is a matter of governance and organization. By requiring coordination information within each encapsulated service request to be freshly written, the WaaS paradigm naturally limits information to the two systems involved, which clearly must have it. Although the information flow is structured to limit visibility to its two endpoints, governance policies may provide a window to other systems upstream, downstream, or elsewhere.

In order to explicitly account for the coordination mechanism and its place in WaaS, we now introduce a coordinator role. The coordinator, as shown in Fig. 17.11, is an entity that has visibility to monitor a given WaaS information flow and power to make changes such as using the tear/merge/delay operations described above or changing the internals of the WaaS work flow.

Given this extended visual notation, we can illustrate several possible visibility and action governance policies, Fig. 17.12. If there is a centralized hub that is responsible for global coordination, with complete visibility, responsibility, and decision-making authority [25], a coordination scheme derived from global optimization can be used [3]. If there is hierarchical authority, visibility and decision-making authority is restricted to one level of depth in the tree and coordination mechanisms must respect this. In a fully decentralized governance structure, each pair of service systems is responsible for their own local coordination. Note that the coordination structure is orthogonal to the organizational structure of the work itself.

Due to these differences in visibility and authority for re-routing, the various forms of coordination have different abilities to react when conditions change.

Governance policies are intimately tied to observability of information and controllability through coordination actions. It should be noted however that WaaS readily leads to a metrics framework with measurables supporting any policy [26]. Indeed it is possible to utilize measureables at any level of work granularity.

17.8.1 WaaS and Web Services

Before moving on, let us further explicate how WaaS may be implemented using web services. WaaS requestors and providers naturally map to the service requestor and provider roles in web services enabled SOA. A WaaS encapsulated service request can be represented by a web service invocation, with the interface between the requestor and provider defined using WSDL. Operation input and output parameters provide the means to specify payload information.

Because of the long-running nature of human tasks, an asynchronous method of invocation is preferable, such as callbacks. Furthermore, the flow of information

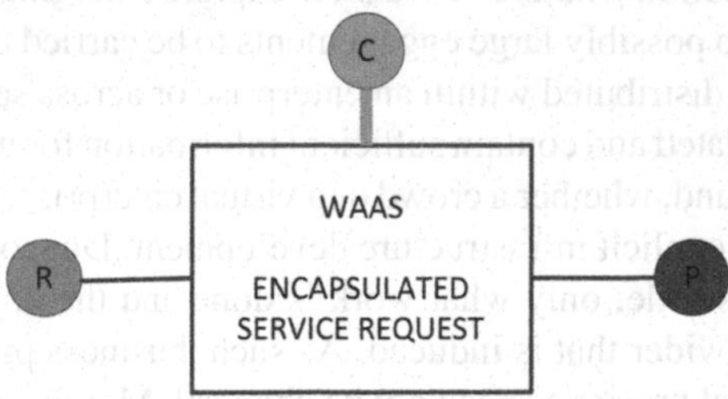

Fig. 17.11 An encapsulated service request with a coordinator role (C) that has visibility and control authority

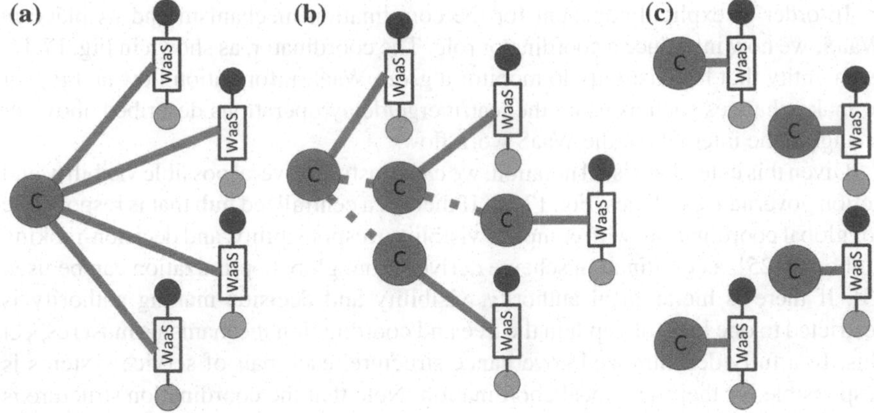

Fig. 17.12 WaaS can support various patterns of coordination; solid coordination lines depict full visibility/control flow whereas dashed coordination lines depict potentially limited flow. Note that the encapsulated work requests could have requester/provider relationships that are omitted. **a** Central coordinator with full visibility and authority into all encapsulated service requests. **b** Hierarchical visibility and authority. **c** Decentralized organization with localized visibility and authority

required by the coordination aspect of a WaaS request may additionally require a conversational or stateful approach to web services.

Extending beyond the interaction between a single requester and provider, coordination mechanisms can leverage enterprise service bus-like functionality in terms of handling mediation, transformation, routing, and other aspects of integration.

17.9 Benefits of WaaS: Agility, Visibility, Optimization, and Innovation

Having discussed the doing of work and the coordination of work within the WaaS framework, we discuss some beneficial attributes of this paradigm.

Due to the block-building nature of WaaS, to capture emerging opportunities, there is agility in setting up possibly large engagements to be carried out by work systems that may be globally distributed within an enterprise or across several. Since service requests are encapsulated and contain sufficient information for work, any admissible work system of any kind, whether a crowd or a virtual enterprise, can be plugged in as a provider with little explicit infrastructure development. Due to encapsulation, how work is done matters little; only what work is done and the collaboration between the requestor and provider that is induced. As such, business processes need not be integrated and internal processes need not be changed. Moreover, the agility extends to response to change; reconfiguration through re-routing is as easy as initial setup.

The recombinant nature of the encapsulated service requests further means that if there are n possible atomic service requests,

$$\sum_{k=1}^{n} \binom{n}{k} = 2^n$$

possible molecular service requests that can be created, providing exponential flexibility.

A second thing to note about the WaaS paradigm is that visibility is provided into operations without violating providers' privacy. Since the payload information in the encapsulated service request is the *minimal sufficient information* needed to do work, it is a minimal sufficient statistic and therefore by the data processing inequality in information theory [9], it minimizes information leakage. When service requests are delegated, the coordination information is not passed on to the new provider, again preserving privacy.

Within the WaaS paradigm, optimizing value becomes a partitioning and routing optimization question, but with destination also subject to choice. In particular, figuring out how to restructure service requests and then to determine which requestors to connect with which providers is rather similar to the routing problem faced by packet-switched communication networks like the internet. Centralized optimizations, e.g. as possible by a coordination hub, are essentially equivalent to nonlinear multicommodity flow problems, with a further optimization for balancing destinations, cf. [3]. Optimal nonlinear multicommodity flows can be found in polynomial time [7]. When performing distributed coordination, as in Fig. 17.12c, efficient routing algorithms developed for internet protocols can be adapted.

When BPM approaches are used, optimal coordination becomes a scheduling problem rather than a routing problem; optimal scheduling problems are often NP-hard [31]. Although routing and scheduling are rather similar, the computational complexity of finding an optimal solution can be different.

In construct to tightly designed business processes [37] but much like other modularized forms, the service request encapsulation and formalism may also lead to increased ease of innovation. When design complexity is low, e.g. as achieved through small loosely coupled service requests, then innovation has been found to be easier, since there are more opportunities to experiment [1].

Many of these benefits of the WaaS paradigm and several others have been seen in IBM's Application Assembly Optimization system [17], including accelerated response to changing business needs; improved visibility into all aspects of ongoing work; improved identification of issues and reduced response time to address them; reduction of time-to-value and time-to-market; improved productivity; improved quality; and ability to implement global governance with a transparent performance management system.

17.10 Concluding Remarks

We presented a new way for describing work as an information flow and then defined the underlying formalisms that enable the decomposition of requests into fine-grained units that can be coordinated and optimized over competing business, customer, provider, and resource objectives. We further demonstrated how this model generalizes over disparate models of work and can be utilized to support different patterns of organization, business, and governance.

In the context of IBM's Application Assembly Optimization, this has led to several paradigm shifts in global delivery [16]:

- *Workflow*: from location based delivery to virtual capabilities delivered by multiple centers and geographical locations;
- *Control*: from direct line of management to a more centralized pool of shared resources;
- *Metrics*: from utilization and productivity measures to performance-based value measures; and
- *Cost*: from an hourly, rate-based model to an outcome-based model.

Our approach in this chapter has been to describe the basic structural elements and decompositions in the WaaS paradigm. Moving forward, it is necessary to study in more detail the optimal coordination mechanisms that really make WaaS go. It may make sense to bring the role of uncertainty to greater prominence [35]. After all, "Uncertainty is what typifies projects. It's the nature of the beast" [13].

One of the biggest revolutions in the evolution of multi-cellular organisms occurred when neurons emerged. Before neurons, cells had to be very close to each other to coordinate their functions. After neurons, cells could communicate from a distance and ongoing two-way flow of information became central to complex life. This allowed cells to be rearranged and assigned different functions in a wide variety of life forms. The information flow paradigm for work developed herein may similarly allow an expansion in the variety of economic and organizational forms that are then able to efficiently fill a wide variety of niches.

References

1. Auerswald, P., Kauffman, S., Lobo, J., Shell, K.: The production recipes approach to modeling technological innovation: An application to learning by doing. Journal of Economic Dynamics and Control 24(3), 389–450 (Mar 2000)
2. Bacon, D.F., Bokelberg, E., Chen, Y., Kash, I.A., Parkes, D.C., Rao, M., Sridharan, M.: Software economies. In: Proceedings of the FSE/SDP Workshop on Future of Software Engineering Research (FoSER 2010). pp. 7–12 (Nov 2010)
3. Bagheri, S., Oppenheim, D.V.: Optimizing cross enterprise collaboration using a coordination hub. In: Proceedings of the SRII Global Conference 2011. pp. 565–571 (Mar 2011)
4. Becker, G.S., Murphy, K.M.: The division of labor, coordination costs, and knowledge. The Quarterly Journal of Economics 107(4), 1137–1160 (Nov 1992)

5. Benkler, Y.: The Wealth of Networks: How Social Production Transforms Markets and Freedom. Yale University Press, New Haven, CT (2006)
6. Bollier, D.: The Future of Work: What It Means for Individuals, Businesses, Markets and Governments. The Aspen Institute, Washington, DC (2011)
7. Cantor, D.G., Gerla, M.: Optimal routing in a packet-switched computer network. IEEE Transactions on Computers C-23(10), 1062–1069 (Oct 1974)
8. Chaar, J.K., Hamid, A.A., Harishankar, R., Huchel, J.P., Jobson, Jr., T.A., Oppenheim, D.V., Ratakonda, K.: Work packet delegation in a software factory (Feb 2010) This is United States Patent Application Publication 2010/0031226
9. Cover, T.M., Thomas, J.A.: Elements of Information Theory. John Wiley & Sons, New York (1991)
10. Dixit, A.: Incentives and organizations in the public sector: An interpretative review. The Journal of Human Resources 37(4), 696–727 (Autumn 2002)
11. Dorn, C., Taylor, R.N., Dustdar, S.: Flexible social workflows: Collaborations as human architecture. IEEE Internet Computing 16(2), 72–77 (March-April 2012)
12. Ehret, M., Wirtz, J.: Division of labor between firms: Business services, non-ownership-value and the rise of the service economy. Service Science 2(3), 136–145 (Fall 2010)
13. Goldratt, E.M.: Critical Chain. North River Press (1997)
14. Gumm, D.C.: Distribution dimensions in software development projects: A taxonomy. IEEE Software 23(5), 45–51 (September-October 2006)
15. Hull, R., Damaggio, E., Fournier, F., Gupta, M., III, Fenno, T.H., Hobson, S., Linehan, M., Maradugu, S., Nigam, A., Sukaviriya, P., Vaculin, R.: Introducing the guard-stage-milestone approach for specifying business entity lifecycles. In: Bravetti, M., Bultan, T. (eds.) Web Services and Formal Methods, Lecture Notes in Computer Science, vol. 6551, pp. 1–24. Springer, Berlin (2011)
16. IBM Global Business Services: Application assembly optimization: A new approach to global delivery (Aug 2009)
17. IBM Global Business Services: Application assembly optimization: A distinct approach to global delivery (Mar 2010)
18. Limonad, L., Varshney, L.R., Oppenheim, D.V., Fein, E., Soffer, P., Wand, Y., Gavish, M., Anaby-Tavor, A.: The WaaSaBE model: Marrying WaaS and business-entities to support cross-organization collaboration. In: Proceedings of the SRII Global Conference 2012. pp. 303–312 (Jul 2012)
19. Malone, T.W.: The Future of Work. Harvard Business School Press (2004)
20. Malone, T.W., Laubacher, R.J., Johns, T.: The age of hyperspecialization. Harvard Business Review 89(7/8), 56–65 (July-August 2011)
21. Mehandjiev, N., Grefen, P.: Dynamic Business Process Formation for Instant Virtual Enterprises. Springer, London (2010)
22. Mintzberg, H.: Mintzberg on Management. Free Press, New York (1989)
23. Norta, A.H.: Exploring Dynamic Inter-Organizational Business Process Collaboration. Ph.D. thesis, TU-Eindhoven (2007)
24. Oppenheim, D., Bagheri, S., Ratakonda, K., Chee, Y.M.: Coordinating distributed operations. In: Maximilien, E.M., Rossi, G., Yuan, S.T., Ludwig, H., Fantinato, M. (eds.) Service-Oriented Computing, Lecture Notes in Computer Science, vol. 6568, pp. 213–224. Springer, Berlin (2011)
25. Oppenheim, D.V., Bagheri, S., Ratakonda, K., Chee, Y.M.: Agility of enterprise operations across distributed organizations: A model of cross enterprise collaboration. In: Proceedings of the SRII Global Conference 2011. pp. 154–162 (Mar 2011)
26. Oppenheim, D.V., Chee, Y.M., Varshney, L.R.: Allegro: A metrics framework for globally distributed service delivery. In: Proceedings of the SRII Global Conference 2012. pp. 461–469 (Jul 2012)
27. Palmisano, S.J.: The globally integrated enterprise. Foreign Affairs 85(3), 127–136 (May-June 2006)

28. Tang, C.S.: Robust strategies for mitigating supply chain disruptions. International Journal of Logistics: Research and Applications 9(1), 33–45 (Mar 2006)
29. Tapscott, D., Williams, A.D.: Wikinomics: How Mass Collaboration Changes Everything. Portfolio Penguin, New York, expanded edn. (2006)
30. Tiwana, A.: Does technological modularity substitute for control? A study of alliance performance in software outsourcing. Strategic Management Journal 29(7), 769–780 (Jul 2008)
31. Ullman, J.D.: NP-complete scheduling problems. Journal of Computer and System Sciences 10(3), 384–393 (Jun 1975)
32. Vaculin, R., Chee, Y.M., Oppenheim, D.V., Varshney, L.R.: Work as a service meta-model and protocol for adjustable visibility, coordination, and control. In: Proceedings of the SRII Global Conference 2012. pp. 90–99 (Jul 2012)
33. Vargo, S.L., Lusch, R.F.: Evolving to a new dominant logic for marketing. Journal of Marketing 68(1), 1–17 (Jan 2004)
34. Vargo, S.L., Maglio, P.P., Akaka, M.A.: On value and value co-creation: A service systems and service logic perspective. European Management Journal 26(3), 145–152 (Jun 2008)
35. Varshney, L.R., Oppenheim, D.V.: Coordinating global service delivery in the presence of uncertainty. In: Proceedings of the 12th International Research Symposium on Service Excellence in Management (QUIS12). pp. 1004–1014 (Jun 2011)
36. Varshney, L.R., Oppenheim, D.V.: On cross-enterprise collaboration. In: Rinderle-Ma, S., Toumani, F., Wolf, K. (eds.) Business Process Management, Lecture Notes in Computer Science, vol. 6896, pp. 29–37. Springer, Berlin (2011)
37. Vergidis, K., Tiwari, A., Majeed, B.: Business process analysis and optimization: Beyond reengineering. IEEE Transactions on Systems, Man, and Cybernetics–Part C: Applications and Reviews 38(1), 69–82 (Jan 2008)
38. Willems, J.C.: The behavioral approach to open and interconnected systems. IEEE Control Systems Magazine 27(6), 46–99 (Dec 2007)
39. Wiredu, G.O.: A framework for the analysis of coordination in global software development. In: Proceedings of the 2006 International Workshop on Global Software Development for, the Practitioner. pp. 38–44 (May 2006)

Chapter 18
Virtualizing Software and Human for Elastic Hybrid Services

Muhammad Z. C. Candra, Rostyslav Zabolotnyi, Hong-Linh Truong and Schahram Dustdar

Abstract Human capabilities have been incorporated into IT systems for solving complex problems since several years. Still, it is very challenging to program human capabilities due to the lack of techniques and tools. In this paper, we will discuss techniques and frameworks for conceptualizing and virtualizing human capabilities under programmable units and for provisioning them using cloud service models. We will discuss how elastic composite applications can be built by combining programmable units of software-based and human-based services in the Vienna Elastic Computing Model.

18.1 Introduction

Utilization of human computation capabilities allows us to solve complex computational problems. This approach has been practiced at least since the middle of 80s, when Richard Dawkins presented an interactive evolution application in which preferences of user were used to lead evolution process [1]. To improve the quality and throughput of such human-enriched systems, in later approaches [2] this concept was extended by joining efforts from many people. However, the term "Human computation" in the modern meaning is believed to be coined out in 2005 [3].

M. Z. C. Candra (✉) · R. Zabolotnyi · H.-L. Truong · S. Dustdar
Distributed Systems Group, Vienna University of Technology,
Argentinierstrasse 8/184-1, 1040 Vienna, Austria
e-mail: m.candra@dsg.tuwien.ac.at

R. Zabolotnyi
e-mail: rstzab@dsg.tuwien.ac.at

H.-L. Truong
e-mail: truong@dsg.tuwien.ac.at

S. Dustdar
e-mail: dustdar@dsg.tuwien.ac.at

A. Bouguettaya et al. (eds.), *Advanced Web Services*,
DOI: 10.1007/978-1-4614-7535-4_18,

Recently, with the broad availability of Internet and the emergence of Internet-based technologies, techniques for human-based computation have been investigated intensively and developed rapidly. At the time of writing, a large number of people who are interested in contributing to complex problem solving can be found almost effortlessly [4]. This leads to the ever growing existence of the so-called collective intelligence which allows massive online human-based problem solving, such as wiki websites [5] and reCAPTCHA [6, 7]. This online human-based problem solving approach is usually associated with the term "crowdsourcing" [8]. On the other hand, professionals are also employed, as part of e-science and business workflows, for solving human-related tasks. They are utilized together with software in several complex workflows [9], using different technologies, such as BPEL4People [10] and WS-HumanTask [11].

While both crowdsourcing and workflows enable us to utilize human computing capabilities, they do not view human capabilities as a programmable unit that can be acquired, utilized and released in an elastic manner. Unlike software-based compute units (e.g., virtual machines and software services) that can be scaled in/out easily with today's cloud computing technologies, human efforts cannot be easily programmed in the way that they can be added, removed and interacted dynamically in parallel with quality, cost, and benefit control. In most cases, either workers are statically assigned to tasks based on their roles [10] or workers bid for suitable tasks that they can work on [12]. When workers bid on suitable tasks, elasticity of human computation capabilities is hindered as there is an uncertainty of whether someone will select a task or not. If the task has demanding requirements (e.g., workers with more than 10 years of image recognition experience), appropriate worker may not be available even in a large crowd of people [13]. Services where workers bid on suitable tasks make integration between humans and software in some composite applications more complicated because sometimes it is preferable to actively select a worker or to identify that such type of worker is not available, rather than to wait for the worker's initiative. To allow seamless integration of human into computation systems, it should be possible to use humans as programmable compute units, which are similar to other types of compute units [14], that can be scaled in/out based on quality, cost, and other benefits constraints.

Our aim in this chapter is to examine current techniques in virtualizing and programming human efforts in crowdsourcing and people-centric business processes in order to develop a novel way to program human capabilities for solving complex problems. In our view, human capabilities can be abstracted into programmable units and then can be provisioned under the service model, which can be easily specified and invoked in programs. To this end, we discuss challenges in supporting programming human capabilities and virtualizing human capabilities under human-based services. We will also present our approach in designing, deploying and executing human-based services.

The rest of this paper is organized as follows. Section 18.2 gives an overview of human computation approaches. Section 18.3 describes challenges and concepts for virtualizing human capabilities under programmable units. Section 18.4 studies existing techniques for realizing human capabilities as programmable units for elastic composite applications. Section 18.5 describes our solutions developed in the Vienna Elastic Computing Model. We conclude the paper and outline our future work in Sect. 18.6.

18.2 Overview of Human Computation Approaches

18.2.1 Crowdsourcing Platforms and Techniques

Several efforts have been done for mapping and building taxonomies from existing public crowdsourcing market [3, 15, 16]. According to [15], existing crowdsourcing scenarios can be categorized into three types:

- The first type is *"contest crowdsourcing"* where a contest is performed to obtain the best available solution for a certain problem, such as in *99designs* [17] and *Threadless* [18].
- The second type is *"task marketplace crowdsourcing"* in which typically simple and unrelated tasks are posted by clients, while registered workers will choose and solve the tasks. *Amazon Mechanical Turk* [19] and *CloudCrowd* [20] are some examples of this type.
- Finally, the third type is *"bid crowdsourcing"* where complex problems submitted by clients and the best bid from professionals will be chosen to solve the problems. Platforms such as *InnoCentive* [12] and *TopCoder* [21] support this model.

Several works focus on the enterprise crowdsourcing. Some elaborated lists of research agendas for enterprise crowdsourcing are presented in [22] and [23]. The distinction between public and enterprise crowdsourcing is discussed in [24], especially what factors affect the sustainability of the project's community. A sample crowdsourcing scenario in software development domain is discussed in [16]. An enterprise crowdsourcing solution is also provided by *CrowdEngineering* [25]. Using a proprietary crowdsourcing tools and infrastructure, it provides out-of-the-box vertical applications in the domain of customer care, sales, and survey.

Another interesting crowdsourcing approach that is actively developing nowadays are the human-based computation games [26] that present computation challenges to humans in an entertaining way. This approach presents great answers to human-based computation problems as game participants are motivated and interested in the task solving process because of game's entertainment. Also they try to get the highest score, which commonly represents the best solution of the stated problem. Foldit [27], a set of online challenges GWAP [28], and Phylo [29] belong to this category.

18.2.2 People-Centric Business Processes

With the growing popularity of Service-Oriented Computing (SOC), building of distributed systems by the means of service composition becomes more and more popular. We have been seeing many efforts done to integrate humans into business processes built atop Web services. In workflow-based systems, the Workflow Management Systems (WfMSs) manage the assignments and executions of tasks, which can be either software-based or human-based tasks. In the case of human-based tasks, each instance of the task is placed in the work-list of all eligible workers. The assignment of the task can be enforced by the WfMS, or the workers may be allowed to voluntarily select the task from the work-list [30]. In particular, BPEL4People [10] can be used as an extension for Web Services Business Process Execution Language (WS-BPEL) [31] to enable human interaction in business process.

However, these human-based task modeling approaches have several limitations. For seamless integration of human-based services into a Service-Oriented Architecture, we need a way to define, discover, and invoke human-based services in similar manner as we define, discover, and invoke Web services. Therefore, human tasks execution is no longer limited to a single organizational boundary.

18.2.3 Humans as Programmable Units

Conceptually, in crowdsourcing and people-centric business processes, human efforts can be considered as program elements, e.g., objects and statements in programs executing some instructions. However, the current way of programming human-related tasks is very different from that for software-related tasks. Very often, we have different design phases and techniques for specifying human-related tasks, using different tools [10, 32].

Consider, for example, a Web-service-based people-centric business process. Typically software-related tasks are programmed using a Web service composition technique [33]. It allows service providers to define interfaces to their services which the composed business process connects to [33]. Even though human-related tasks are also programmed and composed using service interfaces, the current techniques do not allow humans as service providers to define their own services. Also, the lack of capabilities for human-based service publication and discovery hinders some advance techniques such as automatic and adaptive service composition. Furthermore, in the approaches described above, humans as compute units have to adapt to the system and actively search for the tasks to solve [19]. Little effort has been spent for techniques to program applications to actively consider possibilities of human capabilities to decide how to use human computation.

AutoMan [34] is an example of the computation platform that allows integration of humans and software. AutoMan allows to specify a set of tasks to the workers in the form of function calls in a platform-independent manner. Additionally, AutoMan provides ability to specify required quality, time and price. However, AutoMan has some limitations that can be critical for some applications or might be limiting for others. For example, it defines only a limited list of task types and constrains specification allows to specify only upper limit. Also it forces application developers to specify human tasks in common crowdsourcing models.

Another platform worth mentioning is Jabberwocky [35]. Jabberwocky declares that humans and software have the same rights and programming possibilities. Jabberwocky provides a high level domain-specific language for task declaring, which is translated to the map-reduce pattern [36], what may be limiting or redundant for some applications.

Both AutoMan and Jabberwocky focus on the customer side, e.g., defining tasks utilizing human capabilities via crowd platforms, but they do not concentrate on developing techniques at the service provider side, e.g., developing human-based service provisioning models. Recently, techniques from SOC and cloud computing have been investigated for abstracting and provisioning human capabilities. One of the first approaches is to allow human capabilities to be described and published via Web services [37]. Furthermore, teams of people could be also established and provisioned under the service model, called Social Compute Unit (SCU) [38]. Overall, in this approach human capabilities can be categorized into Individual Compute Unit (ICU) and Social Compute Unit (SCU) and realized by service technologies. They can therefore be considered as programmable compute units [14] and belong to the so-called Human-based Service (HBS) built atop human-based computing elements, an analogy to software-based services (SBS), which is built atop machine-based computing elements [39]. This enables, for example, the possibility to unify HBS and SBS with the introduction of the virtualization layer [39] allows to simplify software development with HBS and SBS integration into scalable cloud-based service-oriented computing systems [3].

18.3 Incorporating Humans into Program Paradigms

18.3.1 Challenges

Thanks to the spread of the Internet, it becomes much easier and faster to find appropriate humans to perform the requested task. However, due to complexity and dynamicity of human possibilities and relations, it is still a huge challenge to proactively utilize human computation capabilities. In contemporary crowdsourcing platforms, it is common to put the tasks in a form of open call [8], but this approach assumes that appropriate workers will find the task and solve it within time constraints, what might be a challenge for a new and not popular type of tasks. Even more, people participating in a specific project are often homogeneous and, despite the size, the required person for a rare and unusual task might be missing. This problem can be solved either by popularization of the project or by active searching of an expert for a specific task, which goes beyond existing crowdsourcing models and requires additional efforts from the project's developers or supporters.

An active expert search approach, similar to the SBS invocation behavior, is that the worker plays only a passive role by presenting her possibilities and capabilities and waiting for incoming tasks. Active service search techniques are widely used for SOA-based systems [10, 40], but for HBS selection they have some major drawbacks that will be discussed in the following.

- First of all, this approach usually assumes that characteristics of the provided service are either static or changing only occasionally. It contradicts with the fact that human abilities can be very dynamic and even change during the day.
- Also, even when human worker is rated with respect to quality of the results, usual active service selection ignores the fact that selected human workers may consult with other experts for challenging tasks or even use solution of others. Currently it is also complicated (if it is possible at all) for a selected worker to redirect the task to another expert or worker who might be more experienced or has better chances to solve the specified task.
- Furthermore, for conceptual business tasks, problem description can be very complicated and challenging. Worker may have difficulties understanding the task, require some additional clarification, or perform the task incorrectly.

Another issue in programming human capabilities is that the task might be given not to a single person, but to a closely-connected group or a team of people. Such a group or team can be modeled as SCU and it cannot be referenced in the same way for separate workers, as abilities and characteristics of such a group/team are completely different from that of the separate worker. Nowadays the target worker type is selected at the stage of task generation, but there might be situations when it is impossible to do so. Required worker type may depend on the content of the task, quality, or cost constraints, which are known only in runtime. In such cases we must be able to develop abstract compute units and select appropriate humans for tasks right before the task assignment.

Summarizing what have been said above, integration of human worker into SOA-based system faces challenges such as the following:

1. the dynamic nature of non-functional properties of HBS
2. the need to consult with others or to redirect tasks to expert in the field
3. the need to support clarifying the task or receiving additional information interactively at runtime
4. the need to support different task structure depending on whether tasks will be processed by a single person or teams

We will discuss these challenges and present our approach to handle these challenges. We will focus on the first and the last one. Additionally, we will provide appropriate infrastructure that will allow solving other challenges on the level of the communication protocol.

18.3.2 Virtualizing Humans as Programmable Compute Units

Nowadays, the SOC model has been flourishing and widely used to model the hardware and software functionalities of machine-based computing elements (MCEs). Through standardized service interfaces, these functionalities can be accessed and composed for solving particular problems. However, for complex computational problems, we need to include human-based computing elements (HCEs) into the ecosystem for solving particular steps of the complex problem. Therefore, it is of paramount importance to have conceptual frameworks and tools for integrating HCE into service-based systems. If the HCE will be accessible in the same way as MCE, it will allow selecting the actual processing unit dynamically, depending on the current preferences in processing duration, cost, or results quality. To allow this, actual workers should be hidden behind another abstract layer, which would allow unification of task assignment information provision about the processing unit.

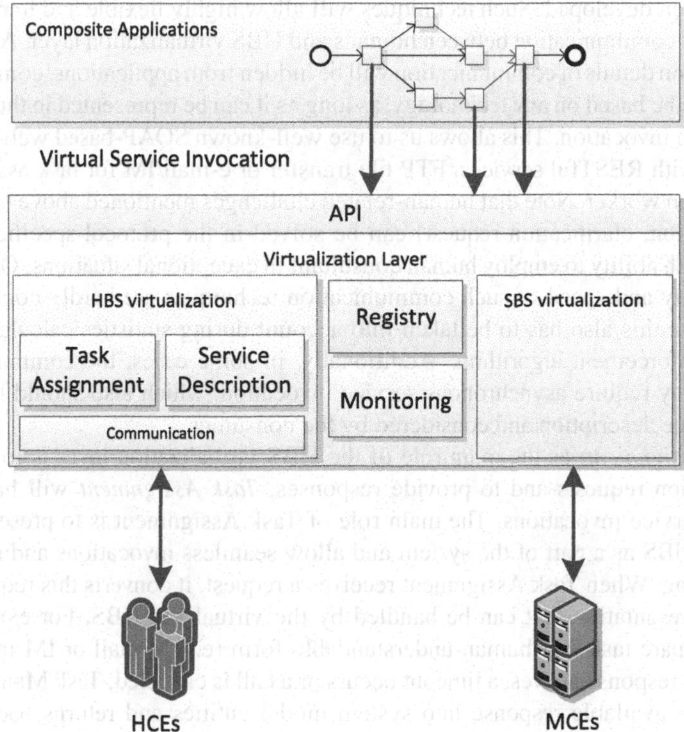

Fig. 18.1 Virtualizing and provisioning humans using SOC

One way to do this is to virtualize and unify HCE and MCE functionality to access them through a well-defined service interface just like it is traditionally done in SOC. Under the service model, everything is a service. Therefore, a distributed application may invoke available distributed services regardless of the underlying service type (MCE or HCE). Virtualizing HCEs under the same service model as MCEs also allows service providers (e.g., human workers) to offer their services through a standardized/common service description. This way, HBS discovery and negotiation become easier. This virtualization layer can also solve some of the aforementioned problems: it will provide unified interface that allows processing units to provide feedback to the system, calculate worker's qualities and preferences in run-time, or provide additional task context on request.

Furthermore, as with MCEs, application developers should be able to compose services involving HCEs. Through this virtualized services, application developers can compose mixed SBS and HBS either statistically during design-time or dynamically during run-time. Figure 18.1 depicts this concept of mixed service compositions using virtualized HBS and SBS. Since the virtualization and provisioning of SBS are known, we discuss possible approaches for virtualizing HBS:

- *Communication*: well-known techniques for communicating humans input/output have been developed. Such techniques will allow highly flexible and unrestricted types of communication between humans and HBS virtualization layer. All implementation details of communication will be hidden from applications, communication can be based on any technology, as long as it can be represented in the form of function invocation. This allows us to use well-known SOAP-based web-services along with RESTful services, FTP file transfer or e-mail/IM for task assignment to human worker. Note that human-related challenges mentioned above (e.g., task redirection, clarification request) can be solved in the protocol-specific way or even with ability to employ human consultant in exceptional situations. Of course, reliability and speed of such communication techniques are hardly comparable, therefore this also has to be taken into account during statistics calculation and SLA enforcement algorithms. Additionally, in some cases, the communication layer may require asynchronous service invocation, which also should be stated in service description and considered by the consumer.
- *Task Assignment*: as the main role of the HBS virtualization layer is to forward invocation requests and to provide responses, *Task Assignment* will handle all HBS service invocations. The main role of Task Assignment is to present virtualized HBS as a part of the system and allow seamless invocations and response retrieving. When Task Assignment receives a request, it converts this request into the representation that can be handled by the virtualized HBS. For example, it can prepare task in a human-understandable form (e.g., e-mail or IM message). When a response arrives, a timeout occurs or a call is canceled, Task Management converts available response into system model entities and returns back to the component that requested HBS. One important feature of Task Assignment is that it should allow composite applications to acquire, invoke and release HBS in an elastic manner, based on their specific constraints.
- *Service Description*: we need to develop models for describing HBS to allow HBS consumers to select appropriate HBS in runtime. *Service Description* provides existing services descriptions and functionality in a unified format. This component

allows getting all static service information, which includes also invocation cost, SLA agreement and allowed input data. All this information can be used to select the set of services that can handle requests.

- *Monitoring*: as discussed, human capabilities are very dynamic and cannot be described statically. For these needs, *Monitoring* is responsible for gathering and providing such dynamic information as average invocation duration, invocation jitter, communication problems and results quality/completeness. These properties can be used to validate SLA restrictions, rank available alternative services or balance request load, if one of the services is overloaded or has too long response time. Additionally, *Monitoring* manages list of assigned tasks and allows calculating current service load or billing information.
- *Registry*: we also need the *Registry* for storing, searching, filtering and providing the set of available HBS that can be searched based on the specified restrictions. The *Registry* would support *Service Description* models for HBS and SBS.

Finally, all features of the virtualization layer can be exposed via a set of APIs, designed in a similar fashion to APIs for contemporary cloud systems, to allow different applications to select and invoke HBS on-demand based on elasticity constraints.

18.4 State of the Art

In this section we discuss the state of the art of the technologies, which can be used to implement virtualization of SBS and HBS. To make discussion clear, we center the discussion around an example scenario to show how a composite application utilizes HBS and SBS. The scenario shown in Fig. 18.2 represents an application system used for mitigating and handling natural disasters. This application system mainly consists of 3 components: the data analysis workflow, the decision support system, and the disaster response workflow.

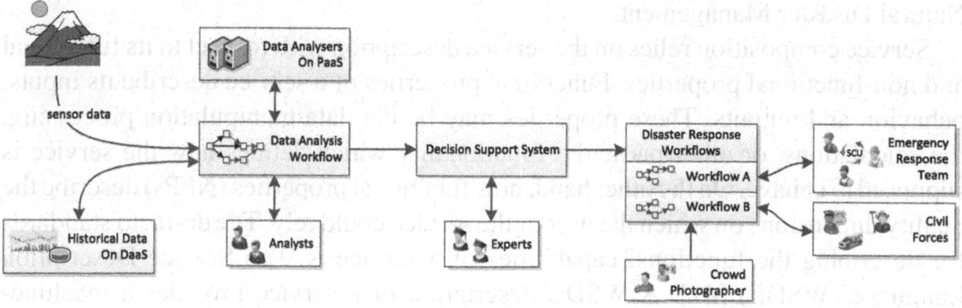

Fig. 18.2 Natural disaster management application

The data analysis workflow received data from sensors which capture nature activities such as earth vibration, rain and snow precipitation, wind speed, and so on.

Upon analyzing the data the workflow will generate signals to indicate whether certain activities may lead to a disaster and require further investigation. This workflow utilizes a Data-as-a-Service (DaaS) for storing and retrieving historical data through a defined SBS. A data analysis algorithm software running on a PaaS also provides services for analysis tasks. Furthermore, depending on the nature of the sensor data, the workflow may also invoke an HBS for manual data analysis provided by professional analysts.

Analysis results sent to the decision support system (DSS) will be used by the decision maker to decide whether a disaster warning should be declared. In situation where further consultation is required, the DSS may invoke an HBS to start expert's consultation service. When a disaster warning is declared, the disaster response workflow is initiated.

The disaster response workflow provides control over the disaster response and recovery activities. An SCU consisting of emergency response teams automatically assembled when necessary. The workflow may also invoke external workflows which control external team such as civil forces. Furthermore, the workflow may also initiate tasks to crowdsourcing platforms for obtaining pictures of the disaster location.

18.4.1 Composition Techniques

18.4.1.1 Syntax and Semantic for HBS

In SOA, applications are built by the means of composition of distributed services. Each application component is a service providing a particular set of functionalities. For example, on the aforementioned Natural Disaster Management application, the Data Analyzers component can be realized as external service which provides capability to analyze streams of sensor data for monitoring nature activities. Furthermore, we can also wrap the functionalities of human analysts and experts as services. Once we compose this various services properly, we obtain a composite application for Natural Disaster Management.

Service composition relies on the service description with respect to its functional and non-functional properties. Functional properties of a service describe its inputs, behavior, and outputs. These properties may be the data manipulation processing, the calculations, or other particular functionality which defines how the service is supposed to behave. On the other hand, non-functional properties (NFPs) describe the quality dimensions on which the user of the service could rely. The de-facto standards for describing the functional capabilities of a service is Web Service Description Language (WSDL) [41]. A WSDL description of a service provides a machine-readable definition so that users know how the service should be called. By evaluating a WSDL description of a service, users can decide whether the service matches with the functional requirements of the application. The quality descriptions of the services, also known as Quality of Services (QoS), are normally defined in Service Level Agreement (SLA) document. SLA provides formal definition of quality level in the form of a contract on which the user and provider of a service agree. Several standards for defining SLA are widely used. Some of the standards are *Web Services Agreement (WS-Agreement)* [42], *Web Service Level Agreement (WSLA)* [40], and *Web Services Policy (WS-Policy)* [43].

Syntax used in the aforementioned specification languages for defining functional and non-functional properties of services may be applicable for both SBS and HBS. A work was done to allow the usage of WSDL as HBS description language [44]. This allows us to describe the interface to services provided by human. For example, on our example scenario, the Data Analyzer service (an SBS) and Analyst service (an HBS) may offer similar service, i.e., analyzing sensor data. However, different interfaces can be defined for both type of services; the Analyst HBS may have a human collaborative platform such as Dropbox as interface.

While defining syntax for describing HBS may be straightforward, defining semantic of HBS description can be much more challenging compared to SBS description semantic. Human services functionality contains intangible aspects which are hard to define formally. HBS and SBS have different NFPs and the semantics of their similar NFPs can be different (Fig. 18.3 lists some examples of NFPs for HBS and SBS). For example, the SBS Data Analyzer service may be described to have 99 % availability. The interpretation of this value is widely understood. However, how would we define an HBS Analysis service that has 99 % availability? What does 100 % availability of human services entitle? This aspect HBS properties interpretation currently remains as an interesting research challenge in the service engineering area.

Metric Dimension	*MCEs Metrics*	*HCEs Metrics*
Resources	Number of resources, utilization, storage capacity, bandwidth capacity	Number of resources, utilization
Quality	Response time, throughput, availability	Response time, rating, availability, throughput, task acceptance rate
Cost and Benefit	Cost / API calls, virtual instance / hours	Task price, hourly price, reputation point

Fig. 18.3 Example of metrics for HBS and SBS

The SLA standards used above, for example WSLA, are designed to deal with virtually any types of QoS metrics. Therefore, theoretically it should be possible to use such standards to define SLA of HBS. However, there are two most important challenges that we should deal with: the *definition* and the *measurement* of the HBS metrics. For example, how can we model the expertise metric and how do we measure it. The quality of SBS, such as computing power, response time, and so on, can be defined and measured easier. But that is not the case for HBS. In most cases, the definition and measurement of HBS metrics is domain specific. Therefore, once we could address these two important challenges, at least for a particular domain we are interested in, we could use similar methodology for defining SLA mentioned above.

18.4.1.2 Design-Time and Run-Time Composition

Once we have a formal description of services, the composition of those services becomes possible. There are various service composition tools available [33]. In the business domain, some of the prominent examples are Business Process Execution Language for Web Services (BPEL) [31] and Business Process Modeling Notation (BPMN) [52]. Petri-Net is also a common tool used for composing services [53]. These composition tools are used during design-time by developers to compose workflow-based applications containing various invocations of services.

Many attempts have been undertaken to address run-time flexible composition issues in workflow systems and Process-Aware Information System (PAIS) in general. Organizations may need to refine their processes to adapt to changing environments due to new requirements, competitions, and laws. Papers, such as [54] and [55], propose methodologies to deal with flexibility issues in workflows, especially to manage running instances while evolving the workflow to a new schema. Those techniques discussed above traditionally deal only with SBS. There are some efforts to allow integration of human in service composition. BPEL4People [10] and WS-HumanTask [11] are some prominent examples. However, these approaches do not see human task in term of human as a *service* provider. Hence, it cannot utilize human capabilities when they are described as *services* such as discovering services just like we normally do in SBS.

The aforementioned service composition techniques deal with the functional requirement of the application. Other techniques are introduced to obtain a QoS-aware service composition. Consider we have a workflow as described in our Natural Disaster Management application. Each component, either human-based or software-based, is described as a service. Functional properties of those services are defined in a Web service description document, such as using WSDL, and the NFPs are defined in SLA specification, such as in WSLA. The service functionalities are orchestrated using BPMN tool. Furthermore, there are some service providers offering same service for each functionalities with different QoS. The SBS Data Analyzers service is provided by some SaaS providers. The HBS Analysis service is provided by a pool of human analysts, and so on. The next question is, how would we select which particular service providers to use in the application? This QoS-aware composition problem is an optimization problem; i.e., which service providers should be invoked so that we get an optimized (or satisfied) solution without violating the constraints.

Finding an optimized QoS-aware composition of services is known as NP-hard problem [56]. Some approaches based on integer programming [57], heuristics [58], and genetic algorithm [59, 60] have been proposed. These approaches can be applied during design-time, to help the developer choosing appropriate services for the application. They can also be used during run-time to allow late-binding of services. Optimizing service composition during run-time is more challenging. It requires an acceptable performance so that the optimization can be done in real-time. It should also consider interdependencies between services and how changes on one service may affect others or even stop the entire process instance. These approaches are currently available only for SBS. Addressing this composition service issues for HBS presents interesting open challenges for the service computing community.

Furthermore, some works have been done for more advance composition tools. Approaches to compose services in non-procedural ways are introduced in SELF-SERV [45] and SWORD [46]. Several tools such as CPM [47], Mentor [48], SELF-SERV [45], and OSIRIS [49] provide distributed workflow engine which allow web services to be composed and executed in distributed or peer-to-peer environment. To obtain an autonomic service composition, JOpera [50] provides an advance tool for composing services and a run-time environment with self-configuring, self-healing, and self-tuning capabilities. MarcoFlow [51] goes beyond the orchestration of human actors into a service composition by allowing distributed orchestration of user interfaces the users need to participate in the process. However, mostly, these tools focus on software-based services; and further works are required to integrate human-based services to the systems.

18.4.1.3 Services Matching and Discovery

On the famed *SOA triangle*, a service-based system not only consists of service providers and service clients, but also service discovery agents. Theoretically, the discovery agent functions as a bridge so that providers may publish their offered services and clients may find suitable services. Service discovery is done through a matching algorithm to find services with appropriate functional and non-functional properties.

The simplest service matching algorithm is keyword based searching. Other advance matching approaches were also proposed. Semantic, ontology, and similarity based matching have been employed to enhance the service matching [61–63]. Those matching algorithms focus on service functionality matching. To take NFPs into account, many works have been done for obtaining QoS-aware service discovery [64–66]. The aforementioned techniques for service discovery are designed for SBS. Service discovery for HBS is a new and challenging area for research. Human factors, such as skills, expertise, and reputations should be taken into account for effective discovery of HBSs. Several works, such as [67] and [68], have been done to address those issues. Trust network such as friend-of-a-friend (FOAF) network also provides important information about the HBS providers. In [69], a Broker Query and Discovery Language (BQDL) is proposed to discover suitable brokers who connect independent subgroups in professional virtual communities, such as normally found in social networks.

Although some standards for service registry exists, many providers prefer to use ad-hoc mechanisms for informing clients about their services. The situation is similar in the case of HBS. Currently there are no formal registries used for HBS discovery. We can consider task-based crowdsourcing marketplaces such as Amazon Mechanical Turk [19] as ad-hoc HBS registries. These crowdsourcing marketplaces have been flourishing dramatically in the recent years. However, the lack of formal service publications in these registries has been hindering automatic services matching and discovery for HBS.

18.4.2 Virtualization Techniques

18.4.2.1 Communication Interface to HCEs

The communication layer is responsible for delivering tasks and retrieving results from external service and handling other types of communication in a transparent way for the rest of the system. This part is already well-known for SBS, but for HBS it is only developing. For example, Amazon Mechanical Turk [19] provides a web-site with available jobs for a registered workers where they can select jobs they like from the set of available tasks (named HIT, Human Intelligence Task). But the set of operations available to the workers is limited: they are only allowed to select HITs and submit results, which often satisfies neither workers nor the creators of the task. To solve these problems, different companies present their own solutions that extend Amazon Mechanical Turk functionality and provide additional features required by participants. For example, Scalable Workforce [32] allows workers to subscribe on some subset of the HITs, extend worker's profile and allows workers to deliver feedback or clarification requests [70]. But the web-site is not the best way to communicate with the human workers. For example, Aardvark [67] tries to use existing human communication channels like Instant Messaging (IM), e-mail, SMS, Twitter, or others. Furthermore, this allows the worker to ask additional questions or to forward request to another person in case the worker cannot solve the task.

18.4.2.2 Task Assignment

Several systems provide SOAP or RESTful APIs for task assignment. For example, Amazon Mechanical Turk provides a SOAP or RESTful web-service, what makes it easy to integrate in the system that needs some work to be performed by the human. Furthermore, to simplify understanding and interaction with corresponding web-service, Amazon also provides set of API libraries for popular programming languages. Similar APIs are provided by other platforms, such as CrowdFlower [71] or CloudCrowd. However, Web service interface is not the only interface for creating and assigning a task. Some systems have provided few different interfaces to interact with different customers. For example, search engine and question answering service ChaCha [72] additionally provides ability to state tasks for a people through web-site, SMS, or phone applications. In most systems, it is the worker who selects tasks: if the required parameters are met, the worker is allowed to take any task, assuming that the worker takes only interesting and feasible tasks. However, this approach oversimplifies task assignment. It introduces situations when some tasks are not handled by anyone or handled with a huge delay. Instead, to guarantee fast and still correct response, some systems (e.g., Aardvark) tries to assign tasks themselves. With this way, systems have to know workers' profiles, current load, and availability.

Besides the capabilities of APIs, by relying on specific APIs of particular crowdsourcing platforms, such as Amazon Mechanical Turk or CrowdFlower, for utilizing human capabilities, we cannot easily program and scale in/out human capabilities from different platforms, as the API provided by different platforms is usually completely incompatible and often crowd workers do not know anything about the task source company. Therefore, the standardization and unification of the APIs for acquiring and invoking human capabilities is important, which would allow customers to select crowdsourcing platforms without carrying about future changes or even to use more than one platform to diverse risks and improve results speed and quality.

18.4.2.3 Service Description

Service description models, which allows collecting, generation and representation of available information about the underlying service, are not well studied for HBS. Amazon Mechanical Turk stores information about worker's qualifications and result acceptance rate. Scalable Workforce proposes to create full worker profile with photo, areas of expertise, interests and last activity and efficiency [70]. Such description system is usually good enough, but it hardly allows comparing different human-based services to detect who could do the specific task better. To allow this, service description models should analyze which similar tasks were already assigned to workers and how they managed to solve these tasks. Also it might be good to know the current load, non-functional properties of the workers, and current interests in this type of tasks, as these factors can influence results quality and service selection strategy.

18.4.2.4 Registry

Registry systems for SBS have been well developed. For example, Amazon AWS Marketplace[1] allows to find different virtual machines and software, while Microsoft Azure Marketplace[2] enables the search for data assets. For HBS, *Registry* is usually implemented by the database of registered users and their last activity information. In the systems where tasks are selected by workers, the role of the Registry is not large: usually it is just statistical information. Aardvark used to store and regularly verify a lot of additional information about users (e.g., last activities, last response time, and current task load). To allow fast service searching and query processing, access to such registry has to be optimized and important fields have to be indexed. Additionally, such systems require more information from users during the registration

---

[1] https://aws.amazon.com/marketplace/

[2] https://datamarket.azure.com/

and often might have difficulties in assigning tasks to the new human-based services, as information about them is not known yet and they are least preferable than older ones. This issue can be partially solved with the help of qualification tests or assigning previously solved tasks, but still this is an open challenge.

18.4.2.5 Monitoring

Monitoring service is responsible for gathering statistical information and verification of the task solution. As the tasks for human-based services are challenging, often it is hard to validate results' quality and speed. For example, Amazon Mechanical Turk leaves this to the requesting companies, which usually try to either estimate efforts or compare results to another worker. To introduce more intellectuality to this process, some companies invented algorithms that could be used to validate how fast and carefully workers were performing the task. For instance, CrowdControl proposed few interesting techniques that dramatically raise the quality of results [73]: it proposed more than 15000 rules to determine whether the solution is correct and worker performed job carefully and whether it is better to check solution again. Based on task validation results, CrowdControl changes the rating of the workers, what also influences on how much they will be paid now and how often validated in the future. In Yahoo! Answers tasks and solutions are usually unstructured, but readers rate the answers and select the best result. Another approach to solve the tasks with the appropriate quality of results is that tasks are usually split on the small slices that are sent to the few people to compare their results to each other [73]. But this approach also does not work well due to the fact that there are quite a few tasks that can be divided and results merged automatically. Correct results for several types of tasks, such as translation, pattern recognition or content generation, often are impossible without knowledge of the whole goal.

18.5 Programming Elastic Composite Applications in the Vienna Elastic Computing Model

The complexity of executing and managing elastic applications becomes even higher when we have to deal with clouds containing SBS and HBS. In this section, we outline steps in designing, deploying and executing composite applications consisting of HBS and SBS in our Vienna Elastic Computing Model (VieCOM), which offers techniques and frameworks to support multi-dimensional elastic processes of hybrid services represented under programmable units. Our approach addresses issues related during *design*, *deployment*, and *runtime* stage of composite applications. Figure 18.4 depicts the overall flow of our steps.

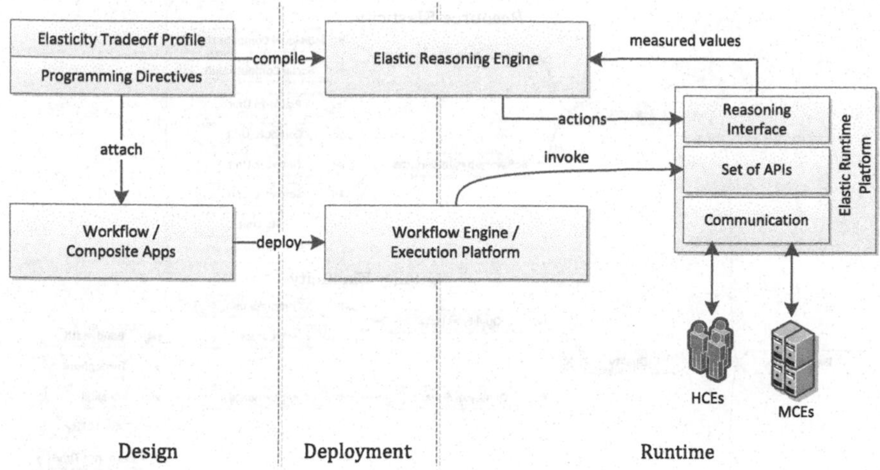

Fig. 18.4 Steps in programming and executing hybrid services in VieCOM

18.5.1 Multi-Dimensional Elastic Application

An elastic application should be able to address issues from two standpoints: it should consider resource provisioning constraints from its resource providers, and it must satisfy its own customers' demand at the same time. Therefore, it is important for an application designer to consider not only the resources but also the trade-off between cost and quality. Consider, for example, a Software as a Service (SaaS) which consists of many application components; each component with its own quality metrics such as performance, availability, throughput, and so on. These quality metrics may be dynamically specified by the customers and affect the SaaS provider's decision to scale-up or down resources. These changes will eventually affect cost needed for resource provisioning and cost charged to customers.

Traditionally, we have seen this elastic computing model being applied to cloud of SBS. However, the concept of elasticity can also be applied to hybrid cloud consisting of SBS and HBS. The principles of elastic processes [74] define various facets of elasticity that capture process dynamics. The elastic properties of applications are multi-dimensional. Figure 18.5 depicts our concept of multi-dimensional elasticity, classified into resource, quality, and cost and benefits. In these classes, several subclasses exist. During run-time, these elastic metrics are measured. The measured metrics can then be used to reason about adaptive actions needed to achieve a certain degree of required elasticity. A typical example for scaling Infrastructure-as-a-Service (IaaS) can be used to explain this reasoning process: when average utilization of running machines exceeds certain threshold, then start another machine.

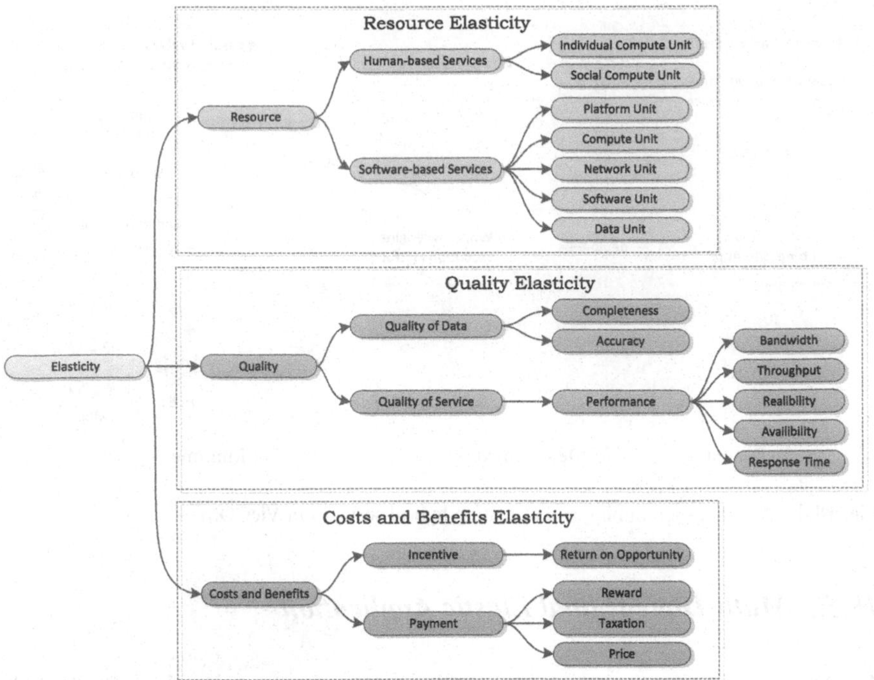

Fig. 18.5 Multi-dimensional elasticity

18.5.2 Modeling Process Elasticity

In our framework, elasticity is modeled by the notion of *Elasticity Profiles* which can be attached to workflows or distributed applications. An elasticity profile contain constructs to define elastic *objects*, *metrics*, and *rules*. The objective of modeling elastic processes is essentially to define the behavior of the process in response to the changing properties of the process' objects.

In an elastic process, we deal with objects and manipulation of the objects. These *elastic objects* are tasks (such as in workflows/processes), or software components (such as in distributed applications) that can be elastic by utilizing software-based or human-based cloud resources. Elastic objects of processes can be either individual tasks or process fragments. In order to make process' objects become elastic objects, two steps are needed: first, elastic properties must be associated with the objects during the modeling phase; and second, at runtime, the elastic reasoning engine decides elastic strategies for these objects based on their properties and runtime information.

Our framework uses a collection of rules describing the elastic aspects of the system. A process designer specifies these rules to model the dynamic changes of resources, quality, and cost of the system. Below are some examples of rules for expressing dynamic behavior of resources:

- When the average utilization of the human workers on the active pool is above 8 hours per day then add additional workers to the pool.
- A human-task requester wants to pay a cheaper price if the worker takes more than 1 hour to finish the task.

An elasticity profile will be deployed to our Elastic Reasoning Engine (ERE) and the application deployed to an execution engine. The elasticity profiles deployed to the ERE contain all definitions required to achieve the desired elasticity. The ERE is a *production rule system* which consists primarily of a set of rules about elastic behavior. The core element of this engine is a *forward-chaining inference engine* used to reason about adaptability actions required to achieve the desired elasticity.

The Elastic Runtime Platform (ERP) manages resources required for process executions. This underlying runtime layer provides the execution platform and resource management for elastic processes. This platform can be in the form of a cloud infrastructure, a scientific or business workflow engine, or it can also be a crowdsourcing platform as a human task execution environment. The monitor component of the ERP is responsible for capturing events of elastic objects and monitors their data. When a task is created, its corresponding elastic object is asserted to the ERE. Using the deployed set of rules, ERE decides which actions are necessary to obtain the desired behavior.

18.5.3 Executing Hybrid Services on the Cloud

Existing approaches exploiting human capabilities via crowds do not support well on-demand, proactive, team-based human computation. In VieCOM, we have proposed a novel method for invoking HBS in a similar manner as invoking SBS [75]. In our model, we present common APIs, similar to APIs for software services, to access individual and team-based compute units in clouds of human-based services. For example, Table 18.1 presents some APIs for provisioning HBS. Such APIs are provided at the cloud service level by HBS cloud providers. Therefore, they can be utilized by workflow engines and any application. The key idea is that based on elastic profiles, the ERE can utilize the APIs to find suitable HBS and depending on the elasticity constraints/rules, the ERE can invoke suitable HBS using these APIs. Furthermore, the ERE can use similar APIs for SBS, e.g., based on JCloud,[3] to invoke corresponding SBS.

[3] http://www.jclouds.org/

18.6 Conclusions and Future Work

In this paper, we discussed the challenges of programming human capabilities as programmable compute units. We have studied techniques for virtualizing human capabilities and how to incorporate humans into program paradigms. As we show in the paper, several techniques developed for crowdsourcing platforms and people workflows are not flexible enough to support the concept of program "humans" in complex, elastic applications. We have discussed our approach in virtualizing human capabilities as programmable compute units, realized and provisioned under the service model, to allow seamless integration between humans and software.

We have presented steps in designing, deploying and executing elastic composite applications in our Vienna Elastic Computing Model. We are currently prototyping an integrated development environment to support these steps, thus we will concentrate on integration aspects of HBS modeling, reasoning and execution by exploiting proposed APIs for clouds of HBS. Furthermore, our future work will focus on intelligent task assignment based on elasticity trade-offs in hybrid systems of software and humans.

Table 18.1 Main APIs for provisioning HBS [75]

APIs	Description
listSkills ();listSkillLevels()	list all pre-defined skills and skill levels of clouds
listICU();listSCU()	list all ICU and SCU instances that can be used.
negotiateHBS()	negotiate service contract with an HBS
startHBS()	start an HBS
suspendHBS ()	suspend the operation of an HBS
resumeHBS ()	resume the work of an HBS
stopHBS()	stop the operation of an HBS
reduceHBS()	reduce the capabilities of HBS
expandHBS()	expand the capabilities of HBS
runRequestOnHBS()	execute a request on an HBS
receiveResultFromHBS()	receive the result from an HBS
sendMessageToHBS()	send (support) messages to HBS
receiveMessageFromHBS()	receive messages from HBS

References

1. The blind watchmaker. Website http://en.wikipedia.org/wiki/The_Blind_Watchmaker.
2. Johnston, V., Caldwell, C.: Tracking a criminal suspect through face space with a genetic algorithm. Handbook of, Evolutionary Computation (1997) G8
3. Quinn, A., Bederson, B.: Human computation: a survey and taxonomy of a growing field. In: Proceedings of the 2011 annual conference on Human factors in computing systems, ACM (2011) 1403–1412
4. Howe, J.: The rise of crowdsourcing. Wired magazine **14**(6) (2006) 1–4

5. Leuf, B., Cunningham, W.: The wiki way: quick collaboration on the web. (2001)
6. recaptcha: Stop spam, read books. Website (2012) http://recaptcha.net/.
7. Von Ahn, L., Maurer, B., McMillen, C., Abraham, D., Blum, M.: recaptcha: Human-based character recognition via web security measures. Science **321**(5895) (2008) 1465–1468
8. Howe, J.: The rise of crowdsourcing. Website http://crowdsourcing.typepad.com/cs/2006/06/crowdsourcing_a.html.
9. Reiter, M., Breitenbücher, U., Dustdar, S., Karastoyanova, D., Leymann, F., Truong, H.L.: A novel framework for monitoring and analyzing quality of data in simulation workflows. In: eScience, IEEE Computer Society (2011) 105–112
10. Kloppmann, M., et al.: WS-BPEL extension for people-bpel4people. Joint white paper, IBM and SAP (2005)
11. Agrawal, A., et al.: Web Services Human Task (WS-HumanTask), version 1.0. (2007)
12. Home — innocentive. Website (2012) http://www.innocentive.com/.
13. Amatriain, X., Lathia, N., Pujol, J., Kwak, H., Oliver, N.: The wisdom of the few: a collaborative filtering approach based on expert opinions from the web. In: Proceedings of the 32nd international ACM SIGIR conference on Research and development in information retrieval, ACM (2009) 532–539
14. Tai, S., Leitner, P., Dustdar, S.: Design by units - abstractions for human and compute resources for elastic systems. IEEE Internet Computing (2012)
15. La Vecchia, G., Cisternino, A.: Collaborative workforce, business process crowdsourcing as an alternative of bpo. Current Trends in Web, Engineering (2010) 425–430
16. Vukovic, M.: Crowdsourcing for enterprises. In: Services-I, 2009 World Conference on, Ieee (2009) 686–692
17. Logo design, web design and more. design done differently — 99designs. Website (2012) http://www.99designs.com/.
18. Threadless graphic t-shirt designs: cool funny t-shirts weekly! tees designed by the community. Website (2012) http://www.threadless.com/.
19. Amazon mechanical turk. Website (2012) http://www.mturk.com/.
20. Work from home — cloudcrowd - we're working on it. lots of us. Website (2012) http://www.cloudcrowd.com/.
21. Topcoder, inc. — home of the world's largest development community. Website (2012) http://www.topcoder.com.
22. Brabham, D.: Crowdsourcing as a model for problem solving. Convergence: The International Journal of Research into New Media Technologies **14**(1) (2008) 75
23. Vukovic, M., Bartolini, C.: Towards a research agenda for enterprise crowdsourcing. Leveraging Applications of Formal Methods, Verification, and Validation (2010) 425–434
24. Stewart, O., Huerta, J., Sader, M.: Designing crowdsourcing community for the enterprise. In: Proceedings of the ACM SIGKDD Workshop on Human Computation, ACM (2009) 50–53
25. Crowdengineering - crowdsourcing customer service. Website (2012) http://www.crowdengineering.com/.
26. von Ahn, L.: Games with a purpose. Computer **39**(6) (june 2006) 92–94
27. Solve puzzles for science — foldit. Website (2012) http://fold.it/.
28. gwap.com - home. Website (2012) http://www.gwap.com.
29. Phylo. Website (2012) http://phylo.cs.mcgill.ca.
30. Salimifard, K., Wright, M.: Petri net-based modelling of workflow systems: An overview. European journal of operational research **134**(3) (2001) 664–676
31. Jordan, D., et al.: Web Services business Process Execution Language (WS-BPEL) 2.0. OASIS Standard **11** (2007)
32. Scalable workforce - mechanical turk software. Website (2012) http://www.scalableworkforce.com/.
33. Milanovic, N., Malek, M.: Current solutions for web service composition. Internet Computing, IEEE **8**(6) (2004) 51–59
34. Barowy, D., Berger, E., McGregor, A.: Automan: A platform for integrating human-based and digital computation. Technical report, Technical report, University of Massachusetts, Amherst (2012)

35. Ahmad, S., Battle, A., Malkani, Z., Kamvar, S.: The jabberwocky programming environment for structured social computing. In: Proceedings of the 24th annual ACM symposium on User interface software and technology, ACM (2011) 53–64
36. Dean, J., Ghemawat, S.: Mapreduce: Simplified data processing on large clusters. Communications of the ACM **51**(1) (2008) 107–113
37. Schall, D., Truong, H.L., Dustdar, S.: Unifying human and software services in web-scale collaborations. IEEE Internet Computing **12**(3) (2008) 62–68
38. Dustdar, S., Bhattacharya, K.: The social compute unit. Internet Computing, IEEE 15(3) (2011) 64–69
39. Dustdar, S., Truong, H.L.: Virtualizing software and humans for elastic processes in multiple clouds-a service management perspective. International Journal of Next-Generation Computing (IJNGC) (2012)
40. Keller, A., Ludwig, H.: The WSLA framework: Specifying and monitoring service level agreements for web services. Journal of Network and Systems Management **11**(1) (2003) 57–81
41. Christensen, E., Curbera, F., Meredith, G., Weerawarana, S., et al.: Web Services Description Language (wsdl) 1.1 (2001)
42. Andrieux, A., et al.: Web Services Agreement specification (WS-Agreement). In: Global Grid Forum. Number GFD. 107 (2004) 1–47
43. Vedamuthu, A.S., Orchard, D., Hirsch, F., Hondo, M., Yendluri, P., Boubez, T., Yalçınalp, U.: Web Services Policy framework 1.5. W3C Recommendation (September 2007)
44. Schall, D., Truong, H., Dustdar, S.: The human-provided services framework. In: 10th IEEE Conference on E-Commerce Technology, IEEE (2008) 149–156
45. Benatallah, B., Sheng, Q., Dumas, M.: The self-serv environment for web services composition. Internet Computing, IEEE 7(1) (2003) 40–48
46. Ponnekanti, S., Fox, A.: Sword: A developer toolkit for web service composition. In: Proc. of the Eleventh International World Wide Web Conference, Honolulu, HI. (2002)
47. Chen, Q., Hsu, M.: Inter-enterprise collaborative business process management. In: Data Engineering, 2001. Proceedings. 17th International Conference on, IEEE (2001) 253–260
48. Muth, P., Wodtke, D., Weissenfels, J., Dittrich, A., Weikum, G.: From centralized workflow specification to distributed workflow execution. Journal of Intelligent Information Systems **10**(2) (1998) 159–184
49. Schuler, C., Weber, R., Schuldt, H., Schek, H.: Peer-to-peer process execution with osiris. Service-Oriented Computing-ICSOC 2003 (2003) 483–498
50. Heinis, T., Pautasso, C., Alonso, G.: Design and evaluation of an autonomic workflow engine. In: Autonomic Computing, 2005. ICAC 2005. Proceedings. Second International Conference on, IEEE (2005) 27–38
51. Daniel, F., Soi, S., Tranquillini, S., Casati, F., Heng, C., Yan, L.: From people to services to ui: distributed orchestration of user interfaces. Business Process Management (2010) 310–326
52. White, S.: Introduction to BPMN. (2004)
53. Hamadi, R., Benatallah, B.: A petri net-based model for web service composition. In: Proceedings of the 14th Australasian database conference-Volume 17, Australian Computer Society, Inc. (2003) 191–200
54. Casati, F., Ceri, S., Pernici, B., Pozzi, G.: Workflow evolution. Data & Knowledge Engineering **24**(3) (1998) 211–238
55. Reichert, M., Rinderle-Ma, S., Dadam, P.: Flexibility in process-aware information systems. Transactions on Petri Nets and Other Models of Concurrency II (2009) 115–135
56. Canfora, G., Di Penta, M., Esposito, R., Villani, M.: An approach for qos-aware service composition based on genetic algorithms. In: Proceedings of the 2005 conference on Genetic and evolutionary computation, ACM (2005) 1069–1075
57. Zeng, L., Benatallah, B., Ngu, A., Dumas, M., Kalagnanam, J., Chang, H.: Qos-aware middleware for web services composition. Software Engineering, IEEE Transactions on **30**(5) (2004) 311–327
58. Berbner, R., Spahn, M., Repp, N., Heckmann, O., Steinmetz, R.: Heuristics for qos-aware web service composition. In: Web Services, 2006. ICWS'06. International Conference on, IEEE (2006) 72–82

59. Wada, H., Champrasert, P., Suzuki, J., Oba, K.: Multiobjective optimization of sla-aware service composition. In: Services-Part I, 2008. IEEE Congress on, Ieee (2008) 368–375
60. Canfora, G., Di Penta, M., Esposito, R., Villani, M.: A lightweight approach for qos-aware service composition. In: Proceedings of 2nd international conference on service oriented, computing (ICSOC04). (2004)
61. Benatallah, B., Hacid, M., Leger, A., Rey, C., Toumani, F.: On automating web services discovery. The VLDB Journal **14**(1) (2005) 84–96
62. Wu, J., Wu, Z., Li, Y., Deng, S.: Web service discovery based on ontology and similarity of words. Jisuanji Xuebao(Chin. J. Comput.) **28**(4) (2005) 595–602
63. Pathak, J., Koul, N., Caragea, D., Honavar, V.: A framework for semantic web services discovery. In: Proceedings of the 7th annual ACM international workshop on Web information and data management, ACM (2005) 45–50
64. Ran, S.: A model for web services discovery with qos. ACM Sigecom exchanges **4**(1) (2003) 1–10
65. Xu, Z., Martin, P., Powley, W., Zulkernine, F.: Reputation-enhanced qos-based web services discovery. In: Web Services, 2007. ICWS 2007. IEEE International Conference on, Ieee (2007) 249–256
66. Ali, R., Rana, O., Walker, D., Jha, S., Sohail, S.: G-qosm: Grid service discovery using qos properties. Computing and Informatics **21**(4) (2012) 363–382
67. Horowitz, D., Kamvar, S.: Searching the village: models and methods for social search. Communications of the ACM **55**(4) (2012) 111–118
68. Schall, D., Skopik, F., Dustdar, S.: Expert discovery and interactions in mixed service-oriented systems. Services Computing, IEEE Transactions on (99) (2011) 1–1
69. Schall, D., Skopik, F., Psaier, H., Dustdar, S.: Bridging socially-enhanced virtual communities. In: Proceedings of the 2011 ACM Symposium on Applied Computing, ACM (2011) 792–799
70. Turker communication. Website (2012) http://www.scalableworkforce.com/software-features-and-benefits/turker-communication/.
71. Crowdsourcing, labor on demand - crowdflower. Website (2012) http://crowdflower.com/.
72. Questions and answers chacha. Website (2012) http://www.chacha.com/.
73. Harris, D.: Exclusive: Crowdcontrol launches, brings ai to crowdsourcing. Website (2011) http://gigaom.com/cloud/exclusive-crowdcontrol-launches-brings-ai-to-crowdsourcing/.
74. Dustdar, S., Guo, Y., Satzger, B., Truong, H.: Principles of elastic processes. Internet Computing, IEEE **15**(5) (2011) 66–71
75. Truong, H., Dustdar, S., Bhattacharya, K.: Programming hybrid services in the cloud. In: 10th International Conference on Service-oriented Computing (ICSOC 2012), Shanghai, China (Nov 12–16 2012)

Chapter 19
Realizing a Social Ecosystem of Web Services

Zakaria Maamar, Youakim Badr, Noura Faci and Quan Z. Sheng

Abstract The success in Web services goes well beyond the building of loosely-coupled, interoperable software components. Nowadays, large-scale collaboration through social media (e.g., social networks) and new generation of service-oriented software have spurred the growth of Web service ecosystems. This chapter discusses how a social ecosystem of Web services can be realized by defining first, the necessary actors that take part in this ecosystem formation and second, the interactions that occur between these actors during this ecosystem management. Such ecosystem permits to track who does what and where and when it is done. Compared to (regular) Web services, Web services in a social ecosystem take different actions that allow them, for instance to establish and maintain networks of contacts with other peers and to form with some peers strong and long lasting collaborative groups. The actors in the ecosystem are referred to as providers of Web services, providers of social networks of Web services, consumers of Web services, and providers of social networks of consumers. They all engage in different types of interactions like making Web services sign up in social networks of Web services, supporting users seek advices from existing members in a social network of consumers, and combining social networks of consumers and of Web services to achieve users' requests. Existing

Z. Maamar (✉)
Zayed University, Dubai, U.A.E
e-mail: zakaria.maamar@zu.ac.ae

Y. Badr
INSA de Lyon, Villeurbanne 69621, France
e-mail: youakim.badr@insa-lyon.fr

N. Faci
Claude Bernard Lyon 1 University, Lyon, France
e-mail: noura.faci@univ-lyon1.fr

Q. Z. Sheng
The University of Adelaide, Adelaide, Australia
e-mail: qsheng@cs.adelaide.edu.au

A. Bouguettaya et al. (eds.), *Advanced Web Services*,
DOI: 10.1007/978-1-4614-7535-4_19,

research initiatives on social Web services as well as open issues in the development of a social ecosystem of (social) Web services are also discussed in this chapter.

19.1 Introduction

The IT community regularly hails Web services for their capacity of implementing loosely-coupled, cross-organization business applications. This is primarily due to the properties that characterize Web services [2]: (*i*) independent as much as possible from specific platforms and computing paradigms; (*ii*) primarily developed for inter-organization situations; and (*iii*) easy to integrate into existing applications so that developing complex adapters for composition needs is not required. Composition is one of Web services' attractive features. It allows to put several Web services together in response to complex users' requests.

In previous work (e.g., [12] and [13]) we designed and developed social Web services in response to certain limitations that undermine (regular) Web services efficient operation. Among these limitations we cite the following: (*i*) Web services know about themselves only, not about their users or peers; (*ii*) Web services cannot reconcile ontologies among each other or with their users; and (*iii*) Web services cannot delegate their invocation requests to other peers. Contrarily social Web services can establish and maintain networks of contacts; count on their (privileged) contacts when needed; form with other peers strong and long lasting collaborative groups; and know with whom to partner so that effort reconciliation due to disparities like semantics is minimized. Web services operation illustrates perfectly how people behave when it comes to *offering services that somebody else may need* and *requiring services that somebody else may offer*. Service offering and requiring permit to connect Web services together (this connection leads into labeling Web services as social), and hence to enrich them with social elements like collaboration and coordination.

Social Web services' operations (e.g., count on their contacts when needed) are made possible because of various details (e.g., collaboration level between peers) that are extracted from the social networks that have these social Web services as members. Networks (e.g., competition, collaboration, and substitution) are developed in order to support social Web services operation. For instance, a social Web service maintains its own network of collaborators, so that it decides if working with certain peers is rewarding based on previous experiences. A social Web service can, also, recommend peers to join its underdeveloped compositions so that additional details are returned to users. Last but not least, a social Web service learns about its competitors, so that it can attempt to improve its non-functional properties.

In this chapter, we identify the necessary actors related to social Web services management in terms of description, announcement, discovery, and connection. We expect that all these actors will form a social digital ecosystem. In this ecosystem the social Web services will be described, discovered, offer services (*a.k.a* functionalities) to users and other peers, tested prior to their use, held accountable for their actions, to cite just a few. A general definition of ecosystem states that "*it is a natural system consisting of all plants, animals and microorganisms (biotic factors) in an area functioning together with all the non-living physical (abiotic) factors of the environment*" [3]. Our work on social Web services does not include a complete compilation of all these actors and thus, questions like who are these actors, what are their roles, and how do they interact need to be addressed.

The main contributions of this chapter are manifold: (*i*) a definition of what a social ecosystem of (social) Web services is; (*ii*) a list of all actors contributing to the management of this ecosystem along with their specific roles; (*iii*) a list of existing research initiatives that study social Web services; and (*iv*) a list of open issues that need to be addressed in order to make this ecosystem operational. The rest of this chapter is organized as follows. Section 19.2 discusses the blend of social computing with service computing and provides a literature review of the Web services ecosystems field. Section 19.3 presents an ecosystem of social Web services in terms of architecture, actors in this ecosystem, interactions between these actors, and finally open issues. Conclusions are drawn in Sect. 19.4.

19.2 Background

This section discusses how social computing meets service computing and then, provides an overview of some initiatives on Web services ecosystems.

19.2.1 When Social Computing Meets Service Computing

Current research on blending social computing (Web 2.0) with service computing (Web services) sheds the light on two categories of social networks: those connecting users and those connecting Web services.

On the one hand, social networks of users record users' experiences interacting with Web services over time so that these experiences are captured and shared later with other members of these networks. Assuming that users' feedbacks on these interactions are fair (i.e., unbiased), it becomes possible to advise users on where to look for Web services, how to select Web services, and what to expect out of Web services. A good number of approaches that study Web services-based social networks of users are reported in the literature. Xie et al. propose a composition framework that relies on social based recommendations of semantic Web services [33]. Wu et al. rank Web services using run-time non-functional properties and invocation requests [32]. Ranking takes into account the popularity of a Web service is the social element analyzed by users. Al-Sharawneh and Williams mix semantic Web, social networks, and recommender systems technologies to help users select Web services with respect to their functional and non-functional requirements [1]. Besides the market-leader concept that refers to the best Web service, Al-Sharawneh and Williams use two ontologies that are (*i*) follow-leader ontology to classify users and (*ii*) preference ontology to specify users' preferences. Maaradji et al. propose an event-driven social composer to assist users take actions in response to events such as selecting a given Web service [22]. Finally, Nam Ko et al. discuss the way the social Web (exemplified by well-known networking sites such as Facebook) contributes to create social applications without having to build social networks [25].

On the other hand, social networks of Web services record the situations that Web services come across at run time [18]. These situations known as collaboration, competition, and substitution permit to tell users which Web service peers can or like to collaborate with a Web service, which Web service peers compete in case of selection, and which Web service peers can replace a failing Web service. Different approaches that study social networks of Web services are reported in the literature. In [14] Maamar et al. introduce a method for engineering social Web services. This engineering requires identifying relationships between Web services, mapping these relationships onto social networks, building social networks of social Web services, and setting the social behaviors of social Web services. In [20] the same authors inject social networks' elements into Web services discovery process. Indeed Web services are not "isolated" components that respond to user queries, only. They compete and collaborate permanently during selection and composition, respectively. In [21] Maamar et al. also discuss the different social networks in which Web services can sign up, for instance supervision, competition, substitution, collaboration, and recommendation. The mining of these networks results in identifying social qualities like selfishness, fairness, and unpredictability that Web services exhibit at run time. Finally, in [7] and [15], Maamar et al. propose a set of quality criteria that help Web services assess the pros and cons of signing-up in these networks. This set includes, but is not limited to, privacy, trust, fairness, and traceability. Policies for managing the sign up are also provided in this paper. The adoption and efficiency of these policies are monitored and assessed with respect to the values that these criteria take.

19.2.2 Literature Review

A search of the Web services ecosystems field identifies an exhaustive list of research initiatives [6, 11, 26–28, 31]. In the following we summarize some and discuss how and why they fall short of meeting the intrinsic characteristics of social Web services.

In [11] Li and Chen consider that the overlap between social computing, Internet of things, service computing, and cloud computing disciplines result in a new discipline that is social services computing. This overlap means that the respective constituents in these disciplines interact with each other to form social networks. Social services computing needs to carefully look into service management in terms of classification, clustering, migration, recommendation, composition, discovery, and publication all from a social perspective. The social services ecosystem of Li and Chen consists of service computing infrastructure, social consumers, social providers, and social networks. In this ecosystem services can be shared, partially shared, leased, or sold.

In [26] Riedl et al. propose a framework to analyze service ecosystem capabilities. This ecosystem includes repositories of services that can be re-used, re-combined, and re-purposed to create new, innovative services. The actors populating this ecosystem are: providers, users/customers, brokers that bring service providers and consumers together, mediators that offer translation between different service formats and other routine functions and support brokers in their operation, and specialist intermediaries that offer service delivery components used by others.

In [27] Scheithauer et al. propose a set of necessary properties to describe services in service ecosystems. These latter are electronic marketplaces where services can be traded over the Internet. Two obstacles impede this type of trade: lack of adequate properties for service description and lack, also, of a clear classification for service description notations. Scheithauer et al.'s proposed properties and classifications are as follows: functionality properties namely capability and classification, financial properties namely price, payment, and discount, legal properties namely rights, obligations, and penalty, marketing properties namely certification, expert test rating, and benefit, and finally quality of service properties namely latency, throughput, availability, and reliability.

In [31] Wu and Chang discuss the limitations of the centralized Web services client/service architecture in terms of performance, bottleneck, and scalability and propose DWSASE, standing for Distributed Web Services Architecture for Service Ecosystem, to address these limitations. The components upon which DWSASE is built upon are service peer, domain peer, alliance peer, super peer, domain broker, domain UDDI, global broker, and global UDDI. For instance a service peer is an ordinary service provider and/or service consumer available in an area that does not belong to any domain known as global space. In addition, a super peer initiates the formation of a particular dynamic alliance by sending invitation messages to selected partner peers. The DWSASE components interact according to different protocols that are Web service community protocol, broker protocol, alliance P2P protocol, super-peer protocol, WS business protocol, and domain protocol.

The aforementioned paragraphs offer a glimpse of existing ecosystems for managing Web services. However social Web services' intrinsic features raise other challenges that these ecosystems do not consider for instance, what types of networks social Web services can sign up in, how social Web services get to know about available networks, what billing means can networks adopt for the resource offered to social Web services, how to assist social Web services select the best networks, and how to assess the quality of services that networks offer. The next section proposes a dedicated ecosystem for social Web services.

19.3 Social Web Services Ecosystem

This section begins by proposing a set of components (called actors later) upon which a dedicated social ecosystem of (social) Web services is built. Afterwards it discusses the interactions that occur between these components as well as the existing research initiatives that look into these interactions.

19.3.1 Architecture of the Ecosystem

Figure 19.1 illustrates an architecture for an ecosystem of social Web services. Four different clusters hosting each similar actors populate this ecosystem. These clusters are **P**roviders of **W**eb **S**ervices ($\mathbf{P}_{ws}$), **P**roviders of **S**ocial **N**etworks of social Web services ($\mathbf{PSN}_{sws}$), **C**onsumers of **W**eb **S**ervices ($\mathbf{C}_{ws}$), and **P**roviders of **S**ocial **N**etworks of consumers ($\mathbf{PSN}_c$). Consumers and providers refer here to both persons and organizations. Web services turn out social when they sign up in at least a $\mathbf{PSN}_{sws}$'s social network. In the same figure discontinued lines represent cross-cluster interactions that are detailed in Sect. 19.3.3. In this ecosystem there is no central authority in charge of managing the social networks of social Web services or of consumers. Therefore mechanisms that allow to identify who does what are critical and constitutes an open issue to address in the ecosystem. The different networks are completely independent from each other, though bridges connecting social networks of users (i.e., consumers) may exist like discussed in [4].

The actors populating the four clusters are briefly discussed below:

- **$\mathbf{P}_{ws}$ cluster** identifies all providers who develop and make Web services available for invocation. The providers rely on regular means like service registries (e.g., UDDI) or $\mathbf{PSN}_{sws}$ to announce their Web services to potential consumers. Registries are excluded from the architecture since the ecosystem relies on social networks to expose Web services to the external world.
- **$\mathbf{C}_{ws}$ cluster** identifies all consumers who invoked Web services and recorded their experiences of using these Web services. Records concern for instance, the quality of response and reliability level (aka QoS). The consumers consult service registries or rely on the $\mathbf{PSN}_c$ to identify the Web services that they will invoke. Registries are, also, excluded from the architecture.
- **$\mathbf{PSN}_{sws}$ cluster** hosts different types of social networks of social Web services that independent providers set up. The value added of these networks to users varies depending on the nature of needs to satisfy such as building a new composite Web service, replacing a failing Web service, etc. Collaboration and competition are examples of social networks of social Web services [13].
- **$\mathbf{PSN}_c$ cluster** hosts different types of social networks connecting consumers together. Facebook, LinkedIn, or any other private social network are examples of social networks of consumers that independent providers set up so that consumers sign up in to report their feedbacks and seek feedbacks on the Web services invoked/to invoke.

The four clusters engage in different interactions that are briefly discussed below. Some interactions are already part of the ecosystem (plain lines in Fig. 19.1) while the rest are recommended for inclusion in the ecosystem (discontinued lines in Fig. 19.1):

- **Interaction 1** ($\mathbf{P}_{ws}$:$\mathbf{PSN}_{sws}$) corresponds to the chronology of operations that allows Web services to be members of social networks of social Web services.
- **Interaction 2** ($\mathbf{C}_{ws}$:$\mathbf{PSN}_c$) corresponds to the chronology of operations that allows consumers to be members of social networks of consumers.

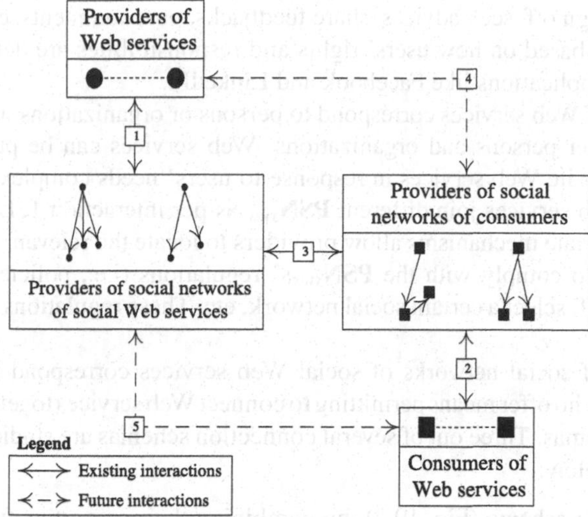

Fig. 19.1 Proposed architecture for a social Web services ecosystem

- **Interaction 3 ($\mathbf{PSN}_c$:$\mathbf{PSN}_{sws}$)** corresponds to the collaborative actions between the social networks of social Web services and of consumers to help consumers identify the Web services to invoke.
- **Interaction 4 ($\mathbf{P}_{ws}$:$\mathbf{PSN}_c$)** corresponds to the actions that providers take to expose their Web services to future consumers by relying on social networks of consumers. This interaction is detailed in Sect. 19.3.4.
- **Interaction 5 ($\mathbf{C}_{ws}$:$\mathbf{PSN}_{sws}$)** corresponds to the actions that consumers take to look for the Web services they need by screening social networks of social Web services. This interaction is detailed in Sect. 19.3.4.

19.3.2 Actors in the Ecosystem

Three types of providers and one type of consumers operate in the ecosystem of social Web services. They perform multiple operations according to their roles, needs, interests, and objectives.

Consumers of Web services correspond to persons or organizations who require Web services to satisfy their requests. Requests vary from basic like currency conversion to complex like travel planning. Consumers can sign up in different $\mathbf{PSN}_c$ as per interaction 2. It is assumed the existence of mechanisms (e.g., search engines) permitting consumers to locate the relevant $\mathbf{PSN}_c$. Being a member of $\mathbf{PSN}_c$s gives consumers the opportunity of sharing their experiences of using Web services with other members as well as seeking these members' recommendations on potential Web services to use. Consumers have to comply with the $\mathbf{PSN}_c$s' regulations when they sign up, sign off, seek advices, share feedbacks, post comments, etc. This compliance can be based on how users' rights and responsibilities are defined in some online social applications like Facebook and LinkedIn.

Providers of Web services correspond to persons or organizations who offer Web services to other persons and organizations. Web services can be put together to develop composite Web services in response to users' needs complexity. Providers make their Web services join different $\mathbf{PSN}_{sws}$ as per interaction 1. Like with consumers appropriate mechanisms allow providers to locate the relevant $\mathbf{PSN}_{sws}$. Web services have to comply with the $\mathbf{PSN}_{sws}$s' regulations (i.e., policies) when they sign up, sign off, select a certain social network, etc. These regulations are explained in Sect. 19.3.3.

Providers of social networks of social Web services correspond to persons or organizations who offer means permitting to connect Web services together according to specific schemas. Three out of several connection schemas are studied in [13] and summarized below:

- Collaboration schema (Fig. 19.2): by combining their respective functionalities, social Web services have the capacity to work together on complex user requests. Consequently, a social Web service has its own network of collaborators, so that it decides if it likes collaborating with peers based on previous experiences. A social Web service can, also, recommend peers to join underdeveloped compositions.

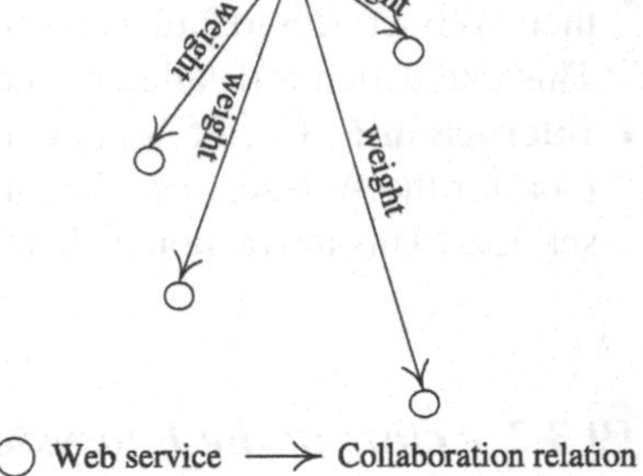

Fig. 19.2 Example of a collaboration social network connecting Web services

- Substitution schema: although social Web services compete against each other, they can still help each other when they fail as long as they offer similar functionalities. Consequently, a social Web service manages its own networks of substitutes, so that it can meet its Service Level Agreements (SLA) when it encounters a potential failure. It can then identify its own best substitutes in response to users' non-functional requirements.
- Competition schema: social Web services compete against each other when they offer similar functionalities. Their non-functional properties differentiate them when users non-functional requirements must be satisfied. Consequently, a social

Web service learns about its own network of competitors, so that it can attempt to improve its non-functional properties with respect to other peers.

Providers of social networks of consumers correspond to persons or organizations who offer means permitting to connect consumers of Web services together according to specific schemas. Recommendation is possibly the most appropriate connection schema between consumers allowing consumers to indicate potential Web services to other peers.

19.3.3 Interactions in the Ecosystem

19.3.3.1 Web Services/Social Networks Interactions (1)

In [16] we study the interactions that take place between Web services and $\mathbf{PSN}_{sws}$ and adopt commitments to guarantee the compliance of the future social Web services (that act on behalf of Web services) with the regulations of these $\mathbf{PSN}_{sws}$ in terms of privacy, content sharing, payment, pricing, etc. Singh et al. seem to be the first who advocate for examining service-oriented architecture principles from a commitment perspective [30]. The traditional service-oriented architecture is built upon low-level abstractions that are inappropriate for capturing the intrinsic characteristics of business services such as autonomy, complexity, and adaptability. Contrarily a commitment-based service-oriented architecture allows to judge the correctness of a service enactment as long as commitments are not violated and to support business compliance without dictating specific operationalization.

When Web services join a $\mathbf{SN}_{sws}$ (led by an authority component (sn_{auth}) and illustrated with Fig. 19.3) the social Web services perform actions whose outcomes might "harm" peers in the same network (e.g., revealing their private details), or even slowdown the operation of the network (e.g., broadcasting irrelevant details). Thus the social Web services are responsible for these actions' outcomes. A Responsibility (*Resp*) is structured as a triple: either an obligation or a permission, actions to perform, and possible conditions that authorize the execution of actions. Below is an example of responsibility.

- $Resp_1$. Collecting any detail (d) in a social network would require indicating the purpose (p) of this collection to this detail's owner (o).
  Representation: `Permission(Collect(`$d, o, valid(p)$`))`.
  `Collect` is the action; d, for instance is a non-functional property like response time and is either public (made available to all members of a social network), protected (made available to the social network's authority component, only), or private (not available); o is the owner of d for instance social Web service; p is the rationale of collecting d; and *valid* is a function that checks p. Two purposes exist: collaboration (*col*) to support the development of composite Web services and substitution (*sub*) to support the execution continuity of Web service-based business processes in case of failure.

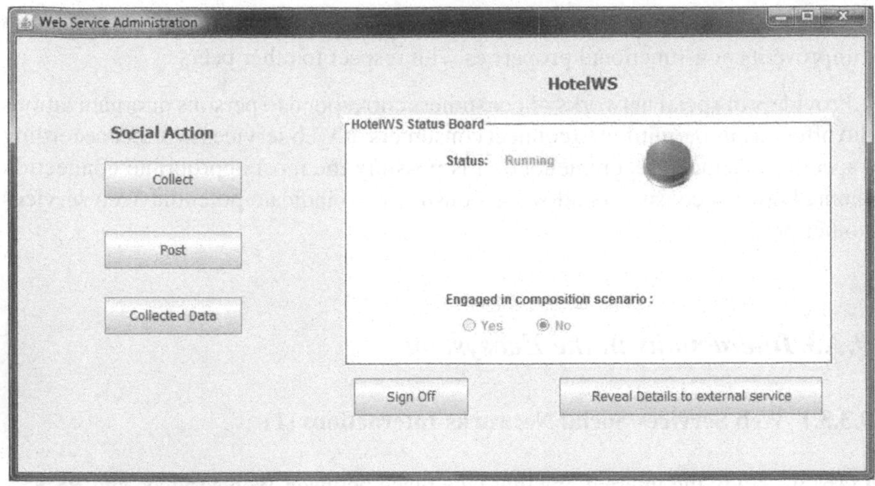

Fig. 19.3 *HotelWS* administration module

Representation: `Obligation(Post(`d, *true*`))`.
`Post` is the action and *true* is the veracity of d.
Representation: `Obligation(not-Tamper(`d, o, *collection*(d)`))`.
`not-Tamper` is the action and *collection* is a function that checks if collecting d is approved in compliance with $Resp_1$.

Afterwards the responsibilities are mapped onto commitments. The formalism of Fornara and Colombetti is adopted to structure the commitments [8]:
$C_{Resp_i}(debtor, creditor, content[|condition])$ where sws_i is a social Web service, C_{Resp_i} is a commitment associated with $Resp_i$, and [ ] means optional.

- $C_{Resp_1}(sws_i, sws_j, Collect(d, sws_j)|valid(p_d))$ is a conditional commitment by sws_i to sws_j, that if $valid(p_d)$ holds then $Collect(d, sws_j)$ will be satisfied.

When a social Web service violates commitments for reasons like being malicious or temporary shortage of computation resources this requires continuous monitoring so that corrective actions are taken [24]. Besides commitment violation, it may happen that social Web services carry out actions that are prohibited calling for setting sanctions like decrementing reputation level and revoking some access privileges.

- C_{Resp_1}: violation arises when collection occurs over a non-public detail. And prohibition arises when the purpose of a detail collection is neither composition nor substitution.
  - Violation monitoring requires that sws_j reports to sn_{auth} recurrent, tentative accesses to its non-public details from sws_i. If these tentatives are confirmed using logs for example, this will be a violation to accessing non-public details of sws_j. Sanctions consist of reviewing the trust/reputation levels of sws_i if first

time. Otherwise, eject sws_i from the social network if these levels go below a threshold.

– Prohibition monitoring requires that sn_{auth} checks if sws_j was really used either as a component in an underdeveloped composition or as a substitute in an under-execution composition for the purpose that sws_i mentioned to sn_{auth} so that it collects details on sws_j. If sws_j was not used as expected, this would be a prohibition to collecting details on sws_j. Compensations include informing sws_j of what happened as well as giving it more access privileges like tracking all the peers that request its details.

19.3.3.2 Consumers/Social Networks Interactions (2)

The ecosystem of social Web services treats consumers as not mere end-users but active and trusted co-creators of new composite services. Grouping persons or organizations together into specific social networks may have an important effect on the overall ecosystem. Consumers build trust in their social networks and develop friendships, professional alliances or even cooperate to achieve business-to-business activities. Social networks are, also, important incentive factors for many consumers to organize themselves into communities, assign different roles, and share common interests. This social environment requires basic mechanisms to support consumer-driven activities and enable them to co-operate as well as re-use, combine, and share their Web services. The mechanisms (or services) that facilitate interactions between consumers and social networks of consumers are follows:

- Profile mechanism consists of creating a profile (including private and public data) for each consumer and allowing peers to discover it. Any consumer can belong to one or several social networks. Each network may have at least one or more membership groups (e.g., owners, mediators, and casual members).
- Search mechanism allows members to search social networks based on criteria like names, business domains, and location, and pro-actively recommend interesting Web services to peers to enrich their businesses.
- Contact mechanism provides basic mechanisms to maintain personal contact list, tag members and manages granting access control to profiles maintained by each member.

19.3.3.3 Social Networks Interactions (3)

The interactions between $\mathbf{PSN}_{sws}$ and $\mathbf{PSN}_c$ permit to compose, execute, and monitor Web services while taking into account both consumers' experiences in using Web services and social Web services' connections to other peers. $\mathbf{SN}_c$ and $\mathbf{SN}_{sws}$ interleave during composition, execution, and monitoring requires developing a *social composer*, a *social executor*, and a *social monitor*, respectively (Fig. 19.4, [17]).

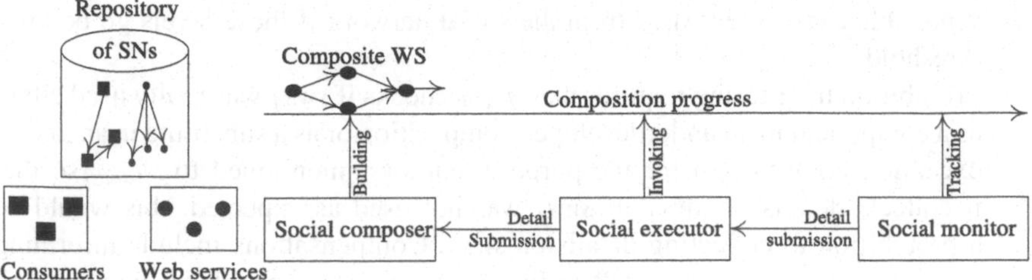

Fig. 19.4 Composer, executor, and monitor social components in action

The social composer relies on $\mathbf{SN}_c$ and $\mathbf{SN}_{sws}$ to advise users on how to build compositions (or composite Web services). These advices concern (*i*) which Web services to include in these compositions [22], (*ii*) which Web services to check in case the contacted ones decline to participate in these compositions [19], and (*iii*) which Web services to select to ensure a better compatibility level of these compositions [29].

The social executor assesses the impact of the social composer's advices (when these advices are considered) on composition execution progress. The social executor feeds the social composer with details so that the social composer updates the necessary social networks. These details include (*i*) how the Web services that were suggested through $\mathbf{SN}_c$ and $\mathbf{SN}_{sws}$ performed and (*ii*) which Web services that were also suggested did not join the compositions.

The social monitor relies on $\mathbf{SN}_{sws}$ to advise users on which Web services to check in case those that are already taking part in their respective ongoing compositions fail. The social monitor feeds the social executor with details so that this latter updates the $\mathbf{SN}_{sws}$ for the benefit of the social composer. These details include (*i*) which Web services failed, (*ii*) which Web services replaced them, (*iii*) how the replacing Web services performed, and (*iv*) how the Web services that are already in compositions reacted to the replacing Web services. Out of these details, the social monitor does more than a simple monitoring but puts forward different solutions for the social composer like assessing Web services performance.

The aforementioned social components are supported by four types social networks: recommendation [22], collaboration, competition, and substitution [13]. The former network ($\mathbf{SN}_c$) is developed to support consumers develop composite Web services. This network suggests Web services according to the current status of the composition process. The Recommendation Confidence (**RC**) as discussed in [22] is defined in Eq. 19.1.

$$\mathbf{RC}(ws_k, ws_l) = \sum_{j=1}^{n} \mathbf{NC}_{v_j}(ws_k, ws_l) \times \mathbf{Fit}(v_j, ws_l) \times \mathbf{SP}(v_i, v_j) \qquad (19.1)$$

where $\mathbf{NC}_{vj}(ws_k, ws_l)$ represents how many times a user v_j used Web service ws_l following the use of Web service ws_k in compositions, $\mathbf{F}it(v_j, s_l)$ quantifies the expertise of user v_j in using service ws_l, and $\mathbf{SP}(v_i, v_j)$ defines v_i's social proximity to v_j in the recommendation network.

The collaboration, competition, and substitution social networks ($\mathbf{SN}_{sws}$) are built to support the development of composite Web services. They are established based on the functionality that Web services offer to the external community. Different techniques permit assessing either the similarity or the complementarity of Web services' functionalities, but this is outside this chapter's scope. Interested readers are referred to [5, 23]. For illustration purposes the competition social network $\mathbf{SN}_{sws}$ is analyzed. Since this network involves social Web services that act on behalf of Web services with similar functionalities, they are all in competition against each other and hence, all connected to each other through bidirectional edges. To evaluate the weight of a competition edge, which we refer to as *Competition Level* ($\mathbf{L}_{Comp}$, Eq. 19.2) between two social Web services (sws_i, sws_j), we use the Functionality Similarity Level ($\mathbf{L_{FS}}$) to compare the functionalities of their respective Web services (ws_i, ws_j) and Non-Functionality Similarity Level ($\mathbf{L_{NFS}}$) to compare the ws_i's and ws_j's non-functional properties (e.g., reliability level and response time). We assume that the non-functional properties of Web services are defined with the same taxonomy.

$$\mathbf{L}_{Comp}(sws_i, sws_j) = \mathbf{L_{FS}}(ws_i, ws_j) \times (1 - \mathbf{L_{NFS}}(ws_i, ws_j)) \qquad (19.2)$$

where

- $\mathbf{L_{FS}}(ws_i, ws_j)$ corresponds to the similarity level between the respective functionalities of ws_i and ws_j.
- $\mathbf{L_{NFS}}(ws_i, ws_j) = \omega_1 \times (|\mathbf{P}(ws_{i,1}) - \mathbf{P}(ws_{j,1})|) + \cdots + \omega_n \times (|\mathbf{P}(ws_{i,n}) - \mathbf{P}(ws_{j,n})|)$ with $\mathbf{P}(ws_{i,k})$ is the value of the kth non-functional property of the ith Web service (assumed to be between 0 and 1), ω_k is a weighting factor representing the importance of a non-functional property, and $\sum_{k=1}^{n} \omega_k = 1$.

As per Eq. 19.2 the more the competition level is close to one, the closer sws_i is to sws_j. As a result, ws_i threatens the competitiveness capacity of ws_j. Only one Web service can be selected at a time to complete a task in a composition.

To illustrate how the composer, executor, and monitor components operate so that the interleaving of social networks of consumers and of Web services happens (Fig. 19.5), we suggest the following scenario. A business woman who has a stop over in a city on her way back from a business trip, decides to visit some museums among other sightseeing activities. She logs into a Web site and invokes `museumVisitWS` submitting the museums that she is interested in and her budget. Different cases are listed hereafter to illustrate the role of the composer, executor, and monitor components.

1. Prior to executing `museumVisitWS`, the social composer consults the businessman's social networks of consumers. It finds out that some colleagues at work visited the same city in the past and recommend riding taxis during this time of the year due to heavy rains falling sometimes unexpectedly.

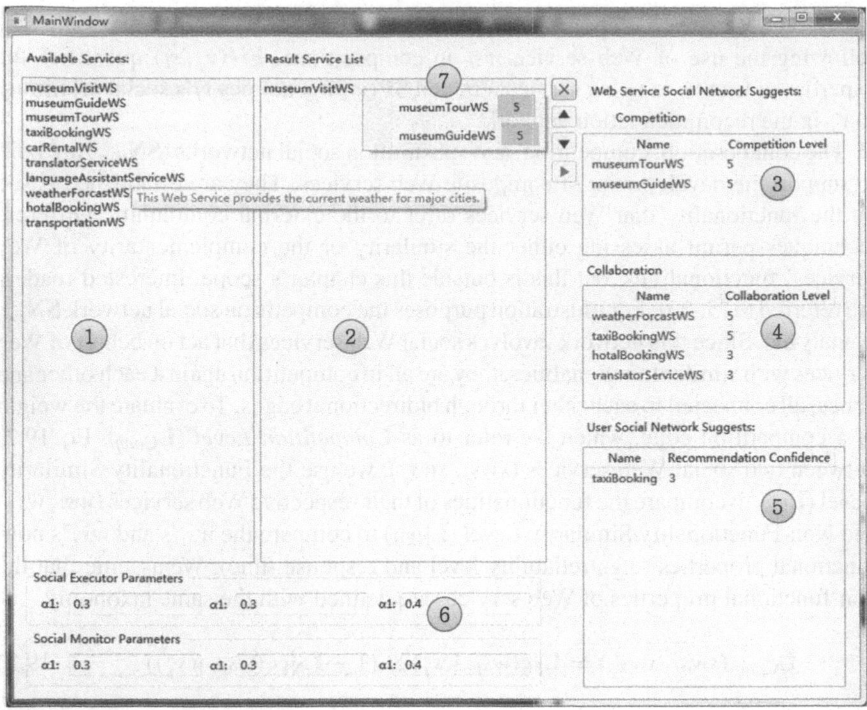

Fig. 19.5 The system frontend

2. To identify a Web service for taxi booking, the social composer consults `museumVisitWS`'s social networks of social Web services to find out that `museumVisitWS` has frequently and successfully collaborated with `taxiBookingWS`, which is subsequently selected to arrange taxi booking. Another Web service called `translatorServiceWS` is also advised by the social composer as reported in the social networks of `museumVisitWS`, but this time the businessman declines the advice since she is familiar with the language spoken in the city.
3. When the selection of `taxiBookingWS` and `museumVisitWS` is complete, the social executor invokes both while keeping an eye on all the Web services that were added to the composition through the social networks of consumers and of social Web services. The objective is to reflect the performance of these Web services on the different networks.

The aforementioned cases offer a glimpse of the advantages of each type of social networks brought to the cycle of Web services composition, execution, and monitoring. It is for sure that some of these cases can be handled by screening registries, but Web services' previous experiences and users' advices are not captured and hence, overlooked during this screening.

19.3.4 Open Issues

19.3.4.1 Interactions (4) and (5)

Providers of and consumers of Web services should be given the opportunity of interacting directly with the providers of consumers and of social Web services, respectively. Providers of Web services could develop and offer new Web services based on consumers' needs and feedbacks on existing Web services. These details can be made available through the social networks of consumers subject to guaranteeing consumers' privacy. The same applies to consumers who could express their requirements and expectations in advance to providers of social networks of social Web services so these latter offer better services like showing the collaborating Web services using graphs, for example. The questions that interaction (4) raise include the following: do providers of Web services have to sign up in social networks of consumers, how is consumers' privacy maintained, how are these providers held accountable for their actions, and how are consumers notified about providers' requests? Interaction (5) raises almost the same set of questions.

19.3.4.2 Payment and Pricing

To create a sustainable social Web services ecosystem, all actors should interact, reuse Web services, and make them available for others. In addition to these basic actions, the ecosystem should provide incentives like financial for providers to offer a large spectrum of Web services for a variety of domains (e.g., business, education, and entertainment). Accessing $\mathbf{SN}_{sws}$ requires mechanisms for electronic payments and online transactions.

Some factors that help encourage or discourage demands of Web services and regulate their usage are pricing strategies and pricing models. This regulation involves to collect and analyze "service" metrics for purposes such as billing and auditing. It requires that "service" consumption be measured and the charging information be communicated between appropriate actors. To obtain viable business models, non-standard pricing mechanisms have to be taken into consideration. Most common pricing models are based on fixed prices. For example, Günther et al. discuss the challenges associated with pricing Web services [10]. They argue that the usage-based pricing model, combined with an option to switch to a flat subscription, is a suitable strategy to penetrate the market of Web services. Bitran et al. advocate that dynamic price models are particularly useful for short selling horizons and demands that are both stochastic and price sensitive [9]. Airline companies and hotels are good examples where dynamic pricing strategies are key drivers for increasing their revenues.

In recent years, a good number payment systems are available for online transactions, such as the traditional credit card but, also, new payment systems such as Google Checkout and Paypal Check-out, which are mainly geared toward selling goods. These systems can be easily adapted to support selling Web services online. Companies that enable financial transactions, a.k.a Payment Service Providers (PSP), are viewed as important actors in the social Web services ecosystem. They do not only allow customers of Web services to transfer funds from their traditional bank accounts into providers' accounts but they establish trust relationships among all actors to collaborate within the social Web services ecosystem.

Interactions among consumers, social networks, Web services and providers, and how they are related to payment mechanisms have the following characteristics.

- Applying payment mechanisms, pricing models and strategies to social Web service ecosystems is particularly interesting since it becomes possible to collect valuable information about Web services, social networks, and actors and process them in real time. As a result, providers can act and react dynamically to changes by adjusting any variable under control, specifically prices.
- Incorporating consumers in the social Web services ecosystem offers them the ability to inquiry prices and keep track of the evolution of the selling process.
- Supporting different payment service providers and pricing models need to be reflected on the infrastructure. Existing service registries needs for example to be extended to support the social Web services ecosystem by including more complex transactions such as negotiations and auctioning.

Emerging potential applications for pricing and payment can be useful for the social Web service ecosystem. Although different in many respects, these applications have to support all actors and deal with the complexity that comes from perishability of Web services and social networks, short selling horizons, and price sensitivity and unpredictable demand of consuming Web services.

19.4 Conclusion

The social Web services ecosystem initiative as a novel approach for fostering development, discovery and, usage of Web services provides a sustainable environment by which all actors share and recommend trustworthy Web services. This chapter discussed the realization of an ecosystem of social Web services. This realization identified the necessary actors upon which this ecosystem is built namely providers of Web services who correspond to persons or organizations offering Web services to other persons and organizations, consumers of Web services who correspond to persons or organizations requiring Web services to satisfy their requests, providers of social networks of social Web services who offer means that permit to connect Web services together according to specific schemas like collaboration and substitution, and last but not least providers of social networks of consumers who offer means permitting to connect consumers of Web services together according to specific schemas like recommendation. Different types of interactions occurred between all these actors such as making Web services sign up in a social network of social Web services, supporting users seek advices from other members in a social network of consumers, and combining social networks of consumers and of Web services to achieve users' requests. Some interactions between these actors are already investigated from different perspectives for instance making Web services sign up in a social network of social Web services requires the compliance of these Web services with this social network's internal regulations to avoid privacy issues. This compliance is being handled through commitments. The rest of interactions that correspond to providers of and consumers of Web services interacting directly with the providers of social networks of social Web services and of consumers are still pending and hence, further investigation is required.

Acknowledgments The authors acknowledge the contributions of Khouloud Boukadi (Sfax University, Tunisia), Salahdine Hachimi (Claude Bernard Lyon 1 University, France), and Lina Yao (The University of Adelaide, Adelaide, Australia) to the social Web services research initiative.

References

1. J. Al-Sharawneh and M.-A. Williams. A Social Network Approach in Semantic Web Services Selection using Follow the Leader Behavior. In *Proceedings of the 13th Enterprise Distributed Object Computing Conference Workshops (EDOCW'2009)*, Auckland, New Zealand, 2009.
2. B. Benatallah, Q. Z. Sheng, and M. Dumas. The Self-Serv Environment for Web Services Composition. *IEEE Internet Computing*, 7(1), January/February 2003.
3. R. W. Christopherson. *Elemental Geosystems*. Prentice Hall, 1997.
4. D. Dasgupta and R. Dasgupta. Social Networks using Web 2.0, Part 2: Social Network as a Service (SNaaS). Technical report, IBM, developerWorks, http://www.ibm.com/developerworks/webservices/library/ws-socialpart2/index.html?ca=drs, 2010.
5. B. Di Martino. Semantic Web Services Discovery based on Structural Ontology Matching. *International Journal of Web and Grid Services*, 5(1), 2009.
6. H. Dong, F. K. Hussain, and E. Chang. A Human-Centered Semantic Service Platform for the Digital Ecosystems Environment. *World Wide Web*, 13(1-2), 2010.
7. N. Faci, Z. Maamar, and P. Ghodous. Which Social Networks Should Web Services Sign-Up In? In *AAAI Spring Symposium on Intelligent Web Services Meet Social Computing (IWEBSS'2012)*, Palo Alto, USA, 2012.
8. N. Fornara and M. Colombetti. Operational Specification of a Commitment-based Agent Communication Language. In *Proceedings of the First International Joint Conference on Autonomous Agents & Multiagent Systems (AAMAS'2002)*, Bologna, Italy, 2002.
9. Bitran G. and R. Caldentey. An Overview of Pricing Models for Revenue Management. Technical report, MIT Sloan Working Paper No. 4433-03, December 2002.
10. O. Günther, G. Tamm, and F. Leymann. Pricing Web Services. *International Journal of Business Process Integration and Management*, 2(2), 2007.
11. S. Li and Z. Chen. Social Services Computing: Concepts, Research Challenges, and Directions. In *Proceedings of the 2010 IEEE/ACM International Conference on Green Computing and Communications (GreenCom'2010) & 2010 IEEE/ACM International Conference on Cyber, Physical, and Social Computing (CPSCom'2010)*, Hangzhou, China, 2010.
12. Z. Maamar, F. Faci, L. Krug Wives, P. Bispo dos Santos, Y. Badr, and J. Palazzo Moreira de Oliveira. Using Social Networks for Web Services Discovery. *IEEE Internet Computing*, 15(4), 2011.
13. Z. Maamar, N. Faci, Y. Badr, L. Krug Wives, P. Bispo dos Santos, D. Benslimane, and J. Palazzo Moreira de Oliveira. Towards a Framework for Weaving Social Networks Principles into Web Services Discovery. In *Proceedings of the International Conference on Web Intelligence, Mining, and Seantics (WIMS'2011)*, Sogndal, Norway, 2011.

14. Z. Maamar, N. Faci, L. Krug Wives, H. Yahyaoui, and H. Hacid. Towards a Method for Engineering Social Web Services. In *Proceedings of the IFIP WG8.1 Working Conference on Method Engineering (ME'2011)*, Paris, France, 2011.
15. Z. Maamar, N. Faci, A. Loo, and P. Ghodous. Towards a Quality of Social Network (QoSN) Model in the Context of Social Web Services. In *Proceedings of the 3rd International Conference on Exploring Services Science (IESS'2012)*, Geneva, Switzerland, 2012.
16. Z. Maamar, N. Faci, M. Luck, and S. Hachimi. Specifying and Implementing Social Web Services Operation using Commitments. In *Proceedings of the 27th Annual ACM Symposium on Applied Computing (SAC'2012)*, Riva del Garda, Trento, Italy, 2012.
17. Z. Maamar, N. Faci, Q. Z. Sheng, and L. Yao. Towards a User-Centric Social Approach to Web Services Composition, Execution, and Monitoring. Technical report, Zayed University Working Paper, January 2012.
18. Z. Maamar, H. Hacid, and M. N. Huhns. Why Web Services Need Social Networks. *IEEE Internet Computing*, 15(2), March/April 2011.
19. Z. Maamar, S. Kouadri Mostéfaoui, and H. Yahyaoui. Towards an Agent-based and Context-oriented Approach for Web Services Composition. *IEEE Transactions on Knowledge and Data Engineering*, 17(5), May 2005.
20. Z. Maamar, L. Krug Wives, Y. Badr, S. Elnaffar, K. Boukadi, and N. Faci. `LinkedWS`: A Novel Web Services Discovery Model Based on the Metaphor of "Social Networks". *Simulation Modelling Practice and Theory, Elsevier Science Publisher*, 19(10), 2011.
21. Z. Maamar, H. Yahyaoui, E. Lim, and P. Thiran. Social Engineering of Communities of Web Services. In *Proceedings of the 11th Annual International Symposium on Applications and the Internet (SAINT'2011)*, Munich, Germany, 2011.
22. A. Maaradji, H. Hacid, J. Daigremont, N. Crespi. Towards a Social Network Based Approach for Services Composition. In *Proceedings of the 2010 IEEE International Conference on Communications (ICC'2010)*, 2010.
23. L. Min, S. Weiming, H. Qi, and Y. Junwei. A Weighted Ontology-based Semantic Similarity Algorithm for Web Services. *Expert Systems with Applications*, 36(10), December 2009.
24. S. Modgil, N. Faci, F. Rech Meneguzzi, N. Oren, S. Miles, and M. Luck. A Framework for Monitoring Agent-based Normative Systems. In *Proceedings of the 8th International Conference on Autonomous Agents and Multiagent Systems (AAMAS'2009)*, Budapest, Hungary, 2009.
25. M. Nam Ko, G. P. Cheek, M. Shehab, and R. Sandhu. Social-Networks Connect Services. *IEEE Computer*, 43(8), August 2010.
26. C. Riedl, T. Böhmann, J. M. Leimeister, and H. Krcmar. A Framework for Analysing Service Ecosystem Capabilities to Innovate. In *Proceedings of the 17th European Conference on Information Systems (ECIS'2009)*, Verona, Italy, 2009.
27. G. Scheithauer, S. Augustin, and G. Wirtz. Describing Services for Service Ecosystems. In *Proceedings of the ICSOC 2008 Workshops held in conjunction with the 6th International Conference on Service Oriented Computing (ICSOC'2008)*, Sydney, Australia, 2009.
28. J. Schulz-Hofen. Web Service Middleware - An Infrastructure For Near Future Real Life Web Service Ecosystems. In *Proceedings of the IEEE International Conference on Service-Oriented Computing and Applications (SOCA'2007)*, Newport Beach, California, USA, 2007.
29. Q. Z. Sheng, J. Yu, Z. Maamar, W. Jiang, and X. Li. Compatibility Checking of Heterogeneous Web Service Policies Using VDM++. In *Proceedings of the IEEE Workshop on Software and Services Maintenance and Management (SSMM'2009) held in conjunction the 2009 IEEE Congress on Services, Part I (SERVICES I'2009)*, 2009.
30. M. P. Singh, A. K. Chopra, and N. Desai. Commitment-Based Service-Oriented Architecture. *Computer*, 42(11), November 2009.
31. C. Wu and E. Chang. A Conceptual Architecture of Distributed Web Services for Service Ecosystems. In *Proceedings of the 18th International Conference on Computer Applications in Industry and Engineering (CAINE'2005)*, Hawaii, USA, 2005.
32. Q. Wu, A. Iyengar, R. Subramanian, I. Rouvellou, I. Silva-Lepe, and T. Mikalsen. Combining Quality of Service and Social Information for Ranking Services. In *Proceedings of ServiceWave*

2009 Workshops held in conjunction with the 7th International Conference on Service Service-Oriented Computing (ICSOC'2009), Stockholm, Sweden, 2009.
33. X. Xie, B. Du, and Z. Zhang. Semantic Service Composition based on Social Network. In *Proceedings of the 17th International World Wide Web Conference (WWW'2008)*, Beijing, China, 2008.

Chapter 20
*ubi*REST: A RESTful Service-Oriented Middleware for Ubiquitous Networking

Mauro Caporuscio, Marco Funaro, Carlo Ghezzi and Valérie Issarny

Abstract The computing and networking capabilities of today's wireless mobile devices allow for seamlessly-networked, ubiquitous services, which may be dynamically composed at run-time to accomplish complex tasks. This vision, however, remains challenged by the inherent mobility of such devices, which makes services highly volatile. These issues call for a service-oriented middleware that should (*i*) deal with the run-time growth of the application in terms of involved services (*flexibility*), (*ii*) accommodate heterogeneous and unforeseen services into the running application (*genericity*), and (*iii*) discover new services at run time and rearrange the application accordingly (*dynamism*). This chapter discusses the design and implementation of *ubi*REST, a service-oriented middleware that leverages REST principles to effectively enable the ubiquitous networking of Services. *ubi*REST specifically defines a layered communication middleware supporting RESTful Services while exploiting nowadays ubiquitous connectivity.

M. Caporuscio (✉) · M. Funaro · C. Ghezzi
Dipartimento di Elettronica e Informazione, Politecnico di Milano, Piazza L. da Vinci 32, 20133 Milan, Italy
e-mail: mauro.caporuscio@polimi.it

M. Funaro
e-mail: funaro@elet.polimi.it

C. Ghezzi
e-mail: carlo.ghezzi@polimi.it

V. Issarny
INRIA Paris-Rocquencourt, Domaine de Voluceau, Le Chesnay 78153, France
e-mail: valerie.issarny@inria.fr

A. Bouguettaya et al. (eds.), *Advanced Web Services*,
DOI: 10.1007/978-1-4614-7535-4_20,

20.1 Introduction

With network connectivity being embedded in most computing devices, any device may seamlessly consume, but also provide, software applications over the network. Service-Oriented Computing (SOC) is a natural design abstraction to deal with ubiquitous networking environments [3]. Applications may conveniently be abstracted as autonomous loosely-coupled services, which may be composed to accomplish complex tasks. A service composition forms into a *network-based application*, which relies on the explicit distribution of services interacting by means of message passing. *Network-based applications* differ from *distributed applications* because the involved networked resources are independent and autonomous, rather than viewed as integral part of a conceptually monolithic system [47].

Issues related to the design/development of network-based systems have been largely discussed in literature, and several middleware solutions, providing different types of resource's abstraction (e.g., remote procedure, object, component, service), have been proposed to deal with them. However, such middleware solutions rely on the assumption that the underlying network is stable. Whereas, concerning ubiquitous networking, such assumption is no longer valid due to the intrinsic dynamism and resource mobility (both physical and logical) [42]. Indeed, ubiquitous applications emerge from the spontaneous aggregation of the resources available (within the environment) at a given time, and thus are characterized by a highly dynamic software architecture where both the resources that are part of the architecture and their interconnections may change dynamically, while applications are running. In these settings, two main problems must be faced: (*i*) achieving the ubiquitous networking environment on top of heterogeneous communication media, and (*ii*) providing a flexible architectural style, which allows for designing and developing applications resilient to such an extreme variability.

In ubiquitous networking environments applications run on devices (e.g., tablets and smartphones), which are usually interconnected through one or more heterogeneous wireless links, which are characterized by lower bandwidth, higher error rates, and frequent disconnections. Hence, key feature of ubiquitous networking environments is the diversity of radio links available on portable devices, which may be exploited towards ubiquitous connectivity. While computationally suitable for ubiquitous applications, such devices usually have serious issues with battery life when the computational burden grows. Thus, the middleware should be able to energetically optimize the communication through scheduling and handover across different radio links [41, 44]. This requires services to be network-agnostic [45], while the underlying middleware is in charge of exchanging messages over the network links that best matches Quality of Service (QoS) requirements [10], and further ensuring service continuity through vertical handover (handover between different protocols) [21]. In this setting, a primary requirement for supporting service-oriented middleware is to provide a comprehensive *networking abstraction* that allows applications to be unaware of the actual underlying networks while exploiting their diversities in terms of both functional and extra-functional properties.

As for the architectural layer, applications should support adaptive and evolutionary situation-aware behaviors. *Adaptation* refers to the ability to react to environmental changes to keep satisfying the requirements, whereas *evolution* refers to the ability of satisfying new or different requirements [6]. In order to be self-adaptable and easily evolvable, applications should exploit design models able to: (*i*) deal with the run-time growth of the application in terms of involved resources (*flexibility*), (*ii*) accommodate heterogeneous and unforeseen functionalities into the running application (*genericity*), and (*iii*) discover new functionalities at run time and rearrange the application accordingly (*dynamism*).

This chapter presents the *ubi*REST middleware, which enhances the *ubi*SOAP approach [9] by providing RESTful access to services. Specifically, *ubi*REST adopts the P-REST architectural style [7], a refinement of the REST style [14] that we have introduced to fulfill the aforementioned requirements, namely *flexibility*, *genericity*, and *dynamism*.

The chapter is organized as follows: Sect. 20.2 summarizes related work. Section 20.3 discusses the design rationale for *ubi*REST, whereas Sects. 20.4, 20.5, and 20.6 detail the core functionalities of *ubi*REST, namely *network-agnostic connectivity*, *ubi*REST *communication*, and *ubi*REST *programming model*, respectively. Section 20.7 presents an example showing how to develop a simple RESTfull ubiquitous application. Finally, Sect. 20.8 concludes the chapter, and sketches our perspectives for future work.

20.2 Related Work

Work related to *ubi*REST ranges different research areas from multi-radio networks integration to ubiquitous computing and service technologies.

*ubi*REST aims at providing a communication layer enabling RESTful services within ubiquitous networking environments. To effectively enable mobile RESTful services, *ubi*REST comprehensively exploits the ubiquitous networking environment by dealing with multi-radio networking on the mobile device. Concerning this issue, the Third Generation Partnership Project (3GPP) defines a standard layered architectures (decomposing into the network, control and service layers) enabling service-oriented applications in the B3G network [2]. In that direction, recent proposal that aims at interconnecting various networks at once, has been published by the ITU under the name of IMT-Advanced (also known as 4G) [22]. Main goal of IMT-Advanced is to achieve "Always Best Connected" property by embedding broadband in all types of consumer devices. Interactions among networks include horizontal (intra network) and vertical (inter network) handover for service continuity, and encompass complex functions such as billing and QoS. This de-facto eliminates the need for the user to know anything about the network (e.g., topology, radio). However, both systems require the network operator to deploy new entities within the network that allow the native infrastructures to work together. Contrary to this closed, network-controlled approach, *ubi*REST provides a set of abstractions enabling clients to autonomously adapt to the available networks, and to benefit from networks characteristics. This requires neither to modify the network infrastructure nor to establish contracts with a predetermined network operator.

Concerning ubiquitous computing at large, the literature proposes different middleware classes, each addressing a specific issue: (*i*) Context-aware middleware [13] deal with leveraging context information to provide user-centric computation, (*ii*) Mobile computing middleware [34] aim at providing communication and coordination of distributed mobile-components, (*iii*) Adaptive middleware [35] enable software to adapt its structure and behavior dynamically in response to changes in its execution environment. However, each middleware provides an ad hoc approach, whereas standards-compliant solutions are still missing.

Moreover, many middleware proposals aim at supporting the development of ubiquitous applications through the provision of different abstractions—e.g., objects, components, and services. The Obje framework [12] is an object-oriented framework where networked devices appear to applications as objects that implement specific "meta-interfaces". Such "meta-interfaces" are further used by applications to exchange the behaviors needed to achieve compatibility at run time. The methods of such interfaces make use and return objects that themselves implement well-known interfaces. Hence, the loading of objects is made transparent to user applications, which simply see them as new implementations of already-known interfaces. The framework described in [20], addresses the distribution and deployment of components throughout the ubiquitous networking environment. It provides developers with an architecture description language to specify constrains on components, which can be considered at deploy time to find a distribution scheme satisfying all constraints. Service-Oriented Computing (SOC) provides natural design abstractions to deal with ubiquitous environments. Networked applications are abstracted as autonomous loosely-coupled services, which may be dynamically combined to accomplish complex tasks [3]. ReMMoC [15] and *ubi*SOAP [9] provide middleware functionalities supporting service provision over ubiquitous networks.

In particular, focusing on Service-Oriented Computing, the widespread adoption of WS technologies combined with mobile networking has led to investigating the definition of architectures dedicated to mobile Web services [19, 23]. Overall, existing efforts towards enabling mobile Web services platforms address the development of service-oriented applications on mobile, wireless devices that act mostly as Web service clients. However, todays device technologies enable mobile devices to act as Web services providers. To this extent, many optimizations for SOAP have been proposed to improve memory and CPU usage [49], as well as to improve the bandwidth requirement of SOAP communication [43, 51, 52].

The idea of exploiting RESTful principles beyond the Wed is not new, and some research projects have been investigating how to apply the REST architectural style to different fields—e.g., ubiquitous computing and web of things. For example, [26, 33] leverage RESTfulness in the context of Ambient Computing, whereas [16, 18] exploit REST principles to achieve the Internet of Things. However, these approaches rely on Web standards to achieve interoperation, and therefore they suffer from the Web's limitations, e.g., lack of mobility management, point-to-point communication, and client-server interaction style. To this end, the XWeb [37] project presents a web-oriented architecture relying on a new transport protocol, called XTP, which provides mechanisms for finding, browsing, and modifying information.

Furthermore, in [4] RESTfulness has been exploited to achieve scalability, by means of replication of resources, in the context of Web Services. In particular, the REactor (RESTful Actor) framework provides a RESTful Web service interface and a composable architecture which is capable of delivering scalability and high performance independently from the underlying deployment infrastructure. Moreover, due to its scalability and the flexibility, REST architectural style has been employed also for monitoring and controlling data- and computationally-intensive tasks, such as in the context of Grid [30].

However, even thought REST has been gaining wide popularity as well suited solution for a large class of problems, to the best of our knowledge, *ubi*REST is the first attempt to design and develop a resource-oriented middleware, which specifically supports the development of ubiquitous RESTful services by addressing all the above aspects together.

20.3 *ubi*REST Design Rationale

*ubi*REST has been conceived and designed to provide RESTful access to services over ubiquitous-networking environments. To this extent, *ubi*REST aims at effectively exploiting all the diverse network technologies at once to create an integrated multi-radio networking environment, hence offering *network-agnostic connectivity* to services. On the other hand, *ubi*REST aims to provide proper programming abstractions enabling service-oriented applications to adapt and evolve at run time.

Achieving the network-agnostic connectivity requires addressing a number of critical issues such as *network availability*, *user and application QoS requirements* and *vertical handover*. *Vertical handover* [50] is particularly important with respect to the *service continuity* requirement. Indeed, when a host changes its point of attachment (vertical handover between two networks), the IP address is modified accordingly in order to route packets to the new network. Hence, since the IP address is the base of any Internet transmission [36], all the ongoing connections break. Moreover, as devices can bind various networks at the same time, two interacting parties might communicate through multiple paths. Hence, choosing the best connection to serve a given interaction is a key issue to deal with in ubiquitous networks, as this significantly affects the QoS at large (e.g., availability, performance with respect to both resource consumption and response time, security) [5].

Pervasive applications are composed as composition of (heterogeneous) independent services, forming into a *network-based application*. Since mobility makes services available/unavailable suddenly, ubiquitous applications emerge de-facto from the spontaneous aggregation of the services available (within the environment) at a given time. As result, ubiquitous applications are characterized by a highly dynamic software architecture where both the services that are part of the architecture and their interconnections may change dynamically, while applications are running.

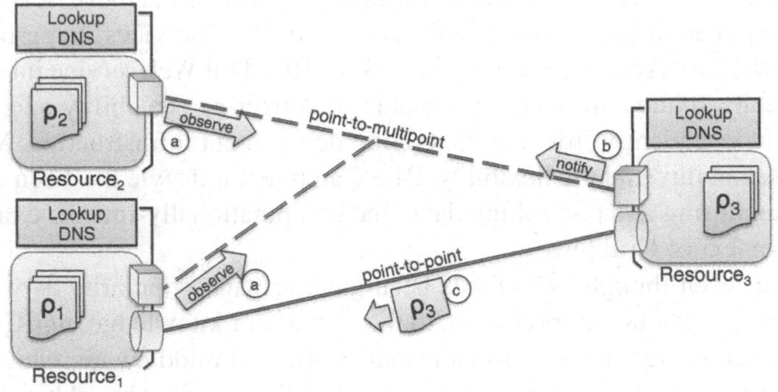

Fig. 20.1 P-REST architectural style

Issues related to the design/development of ubiquitous systems have been largely discussed in literature, and many middleware, providing different types of abstraction—e.g., objects [12], components [20], and services [9]—have been proposed to deal with them. Departing from these approaches, *ubi*REST tackles the problem by adhering to REST principles [14]: *addressability*, *statelessness*, *connectedness*, and *uniformity*. However, due to the inherent complexity of ubiquitous environments, the REST architectural style cannot be directly applied to them. Hence, we enhanced it by creating the P-REST (Pervasive REST) architectural style, which refines REST to specifically address ubiquitous networking environments, while keeping REST principles unaltered.

P-REST (see Fig. 20.1) promotes the use of *Resource* as first-class object that plays the role of "prosumer" [40], i.e., fulfilling both roles of producer and consumer. To support coordination among resources, P-REST extends REST with a set of new facilities: (*i*) a *Lookup* service enabling the run-time discovery of new resources, (*ii*) a distributed *Domain Name System* (DNS) service mapping resource URIs to actual location in case of mobility, and (*iii*) a coordination model based on the *Observer* pattern [25] allowing a resource to express its interest in a given resource and to be notified whenever changes occur in it.

Following the P-REST style, resources interact with each other by exchanging their representations. Referring to Fig. 20.1, both Resource_1 and Resource_2 observe Resource_3 (messages 1). When a change occurs in Resource_3, it notifies (message 2) the observer resources. Upon receipt of such notification, Resource_1 issues a request for the Resource_3 and obtains as a result the representation ρ_3 (message 3). Note that, while observe/notify interactions take place through the *point-to-multipoint* connector (represented as a cube), REST operations exploit *point-to-point* connector (represented as a cylinder). All the resources exploit both the *lookup* operation to discover the needed resources, and the DNS service to translate URIs into physical addresses.

P-RESTful applications are built following the P-REST conceptual model [7], which defines: (1) a *environment* as a resource container providing infrastructural facilities (i.e., *lookup* and *observe/notify*); (2) a *resource* as a first-class object that, according to the REST *uniformity* [14], implements a fixed set of well-defined operations (i.e., `PUT`, `DELETE`, `POST`, `GET`, and `INSPECT`); (3) a semantics-aware *description* specifying both functional and non-functional properties of resources with respect to given ontologies.

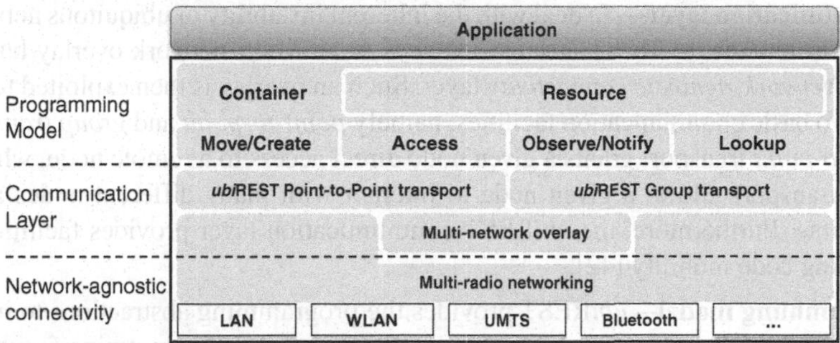

Fig. 20.2 *ubi*REST software architecture

Resources interact with each other by exchanging their *representation*s, which capture the current state of a resource. Furthermore, every Resource is bound to at least one *concrete URI* (CURI). P-REST enhances the concept of URI by introducing *abstract URI*s (AURI). An AURI is a URI identifying a group of resources. Indeed, a CURI allows for point-to-point communication, whereas an AURI allows for group communication. Resources can be used as building-blocks for composing complex functionalities. A *composition* is a resource that can, in turn, be used as a building-block by another composition. Resources involved in a composition are handled by means of a *composition logic*.

20.3.1 Run-Time Support

The *ubi*REST middleware provides the run-time support for the development of P-RESTful service-oriented applications by realizing P-REST at the infrastructure level, and providing developers with effective P-RESTful abstractions. Note that *ubi*REST cannot enforce REST principles at the application level, which is totally entrusted to the designer.

Referring to Fig. 20.2, the *ubi*REST architecture exploits a three-layer design where each layer deals with a specific issue.

Network-agnostic connectivity—Providing network-agnostic connectivity within ubiquitous networks relates to abstracting the rich and heterogeneous networking environment for reasoning about the networks characteristics and seamlessly manage them. To this extent, *ubi*REST goal is to support: (*i*) network abstractions to provide connectivity regardless of the actual underlying network technology, (*ii*) the selection of the best possible network matching the QoS needs expressed by the end user, and (*iii*) the unique identification and addressing of users applications within the networking environment irrespectively of their physical location.

Communication layer—To deal with the inherent instability of ubiquitous networking environments, *ubi*REST arranges devices in an Multi-network overlay built on top of *Network-agnostic connectivity* layer. Such an overlay is then exploited to provide two basic communication facilities, namely *point-to-point* and *group transport*. *Point-to-point* transport grants a given node direct access to a remote node, whereas *group* transport allows a given node to interact with many different nodes at the same time. Furthermore, the *ubi*REST communication layer provides facilities for managing code mobility [42].

Programming model—*ubi*REST provides the programming abstractions to implement P-RESTful applications by leveraging the functional programming features of the Scala language [48] and the Actor Model [1]. In particular, *ubi*REST defines two main abstractions and a set of operations to be performed on them. *Resource* represents the computation unit, whereas *Container* handles both the life-cycle and the provision of resources. The set of operations allowed on resources defines the message-based *ubi*REST *interaction protocol* and includes: (*i*) *Access*, which gathers the set of messages to access and manipulate resources, (*ii*) *Observe/Notify*, which allows resources to declare interest in a given resource and to be notified whenever changes occur, (*iii*) *Create*, which provides the mechanism for creating a new resource at a given location, and *Move*, which provides the mechanism to relocate an existing resource to a new location, and (*iv*) *Lookup*, which allows for discovering new resources on the basis of a given semantics-aware description.

*ubi*REST fulfills the set of requirements introduced above. *Flexibility* is achieved by exploiting the Actor Model, which in turn relies on the *ubi*REST *communication* to provide message-passing interaction among actors. *Genericity* arises from the uniformity principle exploited in conjunction with both code mobility and functional programming capabilities (e.g., high-order functions). *Dynamism* is provided by means of semantic lookup, uniformity and resource composition. The following sections clarify these aspects, and detail *network-agnostic connectivity* (Sect. 20.4), *ubi*REST *communication* (Sect. 20.5), and *ubi*REST *programming model* (Sect. 20.6), respectively.

20.4 Network-Agnostic Connectivity

In this section, for the sake of self-containment, we report an excerpt of the *network-agnostic connectivity* layer implementation [9].

The *network-agnostic connectivity* layer offers the core functionalities to effectively manage the underlying multi-radio environment through: (*i*) a network-agnostic addressing scheme together with (*ii*) QoS-aware network link selection and (*iii*) base unicast and multicast communication schemes.

Such Multi-Radio Networking (MRN) functionality are provided by means of two modules (see Fig. 20.3): (*i*) a Multi-Radio Networking Daemon (MRN-Daemon) that implements the provided features, and (*ii*) a Multi-Radio Networking API (MRN-Api) that allows for an easy and transparent access to the functionalities offered by MRN-Daemon. Furthermore, a *ubi*LET is any entity (e.g., application) that exploits the *network-agnostic connectivity* layer by accessing the functionalities provided by MRN-Daemon through MRN-Api.

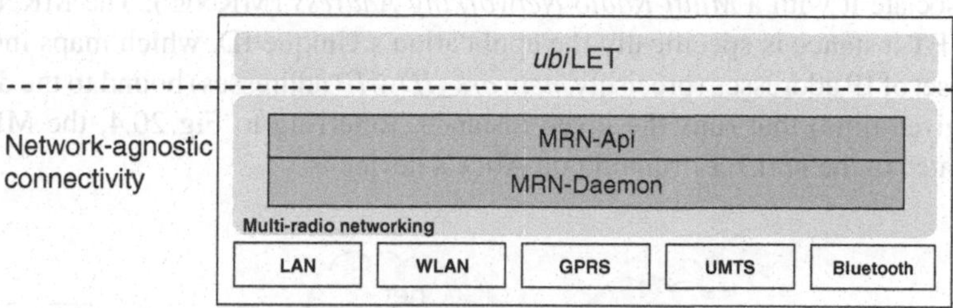

Fig. 20.3 Network-agnostic connectivity layer software architecture

In particular, MRN-Daemon is in charge of managing the entire communication between two devices through the underlying radio networks. It runs on each device and is accessible by many applications at the same time. It is also in charge of managing the *ubi*REST addressing scheme as well as its mapping to the actual set of IP addresses. On the other hand, MRN-Api is a component, embedded in the application, used to interact with the MRN-Daemon. It offers a set of high-level API allowing for an easy and transparent access to the services offered by he MRN-Daemon. Indeed, in order to communicate with each other, services deployed on *ubi*REST-enabled devices must use the functionalities provided by the MRN-Daemon through the MRN-Api.

Since *ubi*REST aims at running on resources-scarce platforms (e.g., PDA and mobile phones), which have limited CPU power, memory, and battery life, to best fit the resources available on the hosting device, *ubi*REST provides two different (but equivalent and fully compatible) implementations of the *network-agnostic connectivity* layer, namely *shared* and *embedded*.

A *shared network-agnostic connectivity* layer is implemented as a "shared" instance of MRN-Daemon, which is simultaneously accessed by multiple *ubi*LETs (through the API provided by MRN-Api). Since all the *ubi*LETs access the same instance, possible conflicts can be solved in an automated way (i.e., two *ubi*LETs expressing conflictual QoS requirements over the interface activation).

On the other hand, an *embedded network-agnostic connectivity* layer is implemented by "embedding" the MRN-Daemon into the MRN-Api. In this case, each *ubi*LET accesses a different, and standalone, instance of MRN-Daemon. This solution is lighter than the *shared* one, and is obviously appropriate when there exists only one *ubi*LET per device. In fact, the *shared* MRN-Daemon interacts with MRN-Api by means of a TCP socket bound to the loopback interface. This requires for having a synchronized thread-pool managing the incoming concurrent requests. It thus implies both larger memory footprint and computational needs. However, *embedded* MRN-Daemons cannot communicate with each other and then, they cannot synchronize to solve possible conflicts.

Network-agnostic addressing—Devices embedding multiple network interfaces (e.g., WLAN and Bluetooth) may have multiple IP addresses, at least one for each active interface. Thus, in order to identify uniquely a given *ubi*LET in the network we associate it with a *Multi-Radio Networking Address* (MRN@). The MRN@ of a *ubi*LET instance is specifically the application's Unique ID, which maps into the actual set of IP addresses (precisely, *network_ID*⊕*IP* addresses) bound to the device (at a given time) that runs the given instance. Referring to Fig. 20.4, the MRN@ associated to the *ubi*LET$_j$ running on Alice's device is:

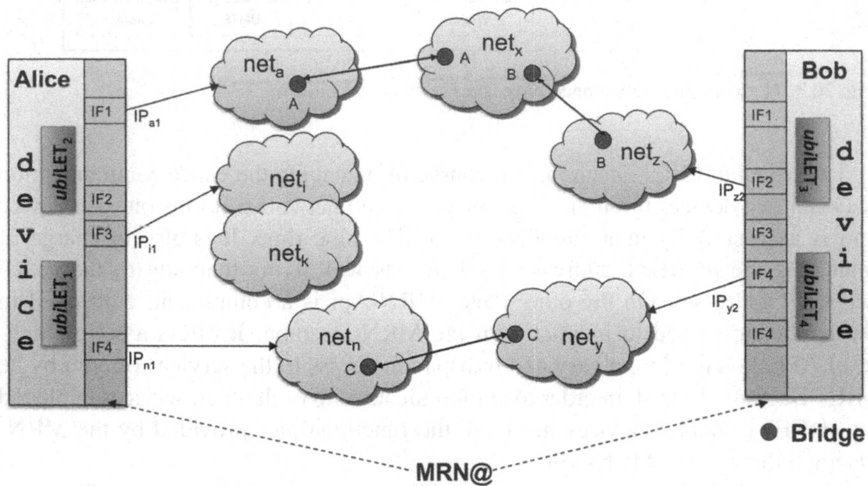

Fig. 20.4 Network-agnostic addressing over Multi-network overlay

$$MRN@_{ubiLET_j} \mapsto \{net_a \oplus IP_{a_1}, net_i \oplus IP_{i_1}, net_n \oplus IP_{n_1}\}$$

where $\forall j \in \{1, 2\}$, $MRN@_{ubiLET_j}$ is the ID of *ubi*LET$_j$ and, $\{net_a \oplus IP_{a_1}, net_i \oplus IP_{i_1}, net_n \oplus IP_{n_1}\}$ is the set of *network_ID*⊕*IP* addresses denoting the actual location of the device.[1] Then, upper layers shall use MRN@ as part of their addressing scheme (e.g., through WS-addressing in the case of Web services), which replaces the traditional IP-based addressing scheme. MRN@s are automatically generated and managed by multi-radio networking. Furthermore, multi-radio networking allows for performing a lookup operation that, starting from an MRN@, returns the set of IP addresses actually bound to it. The basic operations provided by network-agnostic connectivity are as follows. First, *Registration* allows the *ubi*LET to register within the network-agnostic connectivity layer and generates the MRN@ that uniquely identifies it. In particular, the *ubi*LET (i.e., user application) provides as input an identifier (locally unique), which is used to generate the MRN@ to be returned. Then, *Lookup* allows user applications to retrieve the actual set of IP addresses related to a given MRN@. If the resolution of MRN@ is not cached or needs to be updated, a request is multicasted to all the networks currently accessible and, if the device related to such MRN@ is reached, it will directly reply to the requester by supplying the actual set of IP addresses.

QoS-aware network link selection—Next to MRN@ addressing, it is crucial to activate and select the best possible networks (among those available) with respect to required QoS, which is defined as a set of pairs $< QoS_{attr}, QoS_{value} >$. Attributes are grouped in two subsets: (*i*) *quantitative* attributes that describe the performance provided by the networks—e.g., bitrate, packet loss transfer delay and signal strength—and allows for networks ranking, and (*ii*) *qualitative* attributes that describe those characteristics of the network that do not affect the network performance but should be considered—e.g., power consumption, price, coverage area. Departing from WS-oriented approaches (e.g., WS-Policy) that are "asymmetric" and they do not allow service consumers to specify their requirements, *ubi*REST strives to enable network QoS negotiation by trying to meet both provider and consumer requirements (expressed in terms of network QoS). To this extent, *ubi*REST provides two functionality, namely *interface activation* and *network selection. Interface activation* allows the user application to activate the best possible interfaces (among those available) with respect to the required QoS. In particular, the application submits its QoS requirement (a set of pairs $< QoS_{attribute}, QoS_{value} >$) to multi-radio networking, which in turn compares it with the QoS of each available interface (Network-side QoS and Context). In this case, since the interface is switched off, QoS refers to the theoretic values of a network interface declared by the manufacturer (e.g., GPRS maximum bitrate = 171.2 Kb/s). If the interface satisfies the requirement posed by the application, within a given approximation expressed in percentage, it is activated. It is also possible to define priorities upon the various quantitative parameters, in order to specify if a given parameter is more important than the others. On the other hand, *network selection* is performed during the establishment of the communication and takes into account the QoS attributes required by the client application that is initiating the connection, as well as the networks active on the server listening for incoming connections, as given by the servers MRN@. If the client and

[1] For the sake of simplicity we refer to IP address, but it is actually implemented as IP address and port number, e.g., `128.131.10.1:90`.

the server share only one network that satisfies the requirements, it is used to carry on the interaction. On the other hand, when the two parties share more than one network, the selection algorithm selects the one that best meets the required QoS.

Multi-radio unicast and multicast—Once defined the MRN@ addressing scheme and the operations enabling the network link selection, the *network-agnostic connectivity* layer provides two base communication facilities: *synchronous unicast* and *asynchronous multicast*.[2] *ubi*REST *synchronous unicast* allows for messaging communication between two *ubi*LETs sharing at least one network. Specifically, it is provided by means of a logical stream channel that is used by the *ubi*LETs to read/write the packets belonging to the ongoing communication. Whereas, *ubi*REST *asynchronous multicast* allows for multicast messaging communication within a group of *ubi*LETs sharing at least one network. Specifically, it is provided by means of multicast packets that are sent to all members of a given group.

20.5 *ubi*REST Communication Layer

Providing communication within ubiquitous networks relates to comprehensively exploiting the rich, heterogeneous networking environment for message handling. In particular, *ubi*REST goal is to support: (1) *Mobility* so that active connections are maintained transparently to the application layer despite the mobility of nodes, as long as a network path exists, (2) efficient *messages routing* in multi-paths configurations (i.e., when multiple network paths exist between the consumer and the provider), (3) both *point-to-point* and *group* communications using the same abstractions (i.e., MRN@), and (4) *multi-network routing* so that access to resources in distant networks is enabled as long as there exists a path bridging the heterogeneous networks between the consumer and target resource provider.

To meet the above, *ubi*REST arranges devices in a multi-network overlay, a virtual network of nodes and logical links built on top of existing actual networks [11] and meant to augment the native network with new services. The *ubi*REST overlay network manages the logical links between nodes (i.e., resources) and enables message exchange. In particular, *ubi*REST embeds (*i*) the protocols that keep the overlay network connected when the topology of the underlying native network changes (e.g., as a consequence of mobility), and (*ii*) the routing algorithms that regulate the message flow between nodes according to the specific coordination model used, namely point-to-point communication and group communication. In pervasive environments, a key requirement for the overlay is the ability to self-organize itself into a flexible topology, as well as to maintain it. To this extent, *ubi*REST defines a custom transport layer that leverages *network-agnostic connectivity* and provides: (*i*) the multi-network overlay in charge of forwarding messages across independent networks, and (*ii*) two transports for point-to-point and group communication in ubiquitous networking.

[2] The interested reader is referred to [9] for further details.

Multi-network overlay—Thanks to the *ubi*REST *network-agnostic connectivity* layer, communication among nodes exploits the various network links that the nodes have in common by selecting the links that provide the required QoS. However, in some cases, it might also be desirable for nodes to be able to access resources that are hosted in *distant* networks to which the requesting node is not directly connected to (e.g., to provide continuity of service despite node mobility). For example, in Fig. 20.4, the device of Alice is connected to networks `a`, `i`, and `n`, through its various network interfaces. Clearly, the device can trivially access resources hosted in these networks. However, it cannot access resources hosted by Bob's device that is located in the distant networks `x`, `y`, and `z`. In fact, the *network-agnostic connectivity* layer does not provide neither an overlay IP network nor multi-network routing.

However, relying on the MRN@, together with both *unicast* and *multicast communication* schemes, *ubi*REST introduces an overlay network that is able to bridge heterogeneous networks, thus enhancing overall connectivity. In particular: (*i*) MRN@ addressing provides a two-layer identification scheme (i.e., $network\_ID \oplus IP$) allowing for uniquely identifying a device irrespectively of the network it belongs to, and (*ii*) *unicast* and *multicast communication* support allows for MRN@ management across the networks. Specifically, nodes that are connected to two (or more) different networks through their network interfaces can assume the role of *bridge* nodes. *Bridge* nodes quite literally "bridge" between two separate networks, relaying *ubi*REST *point-to-point* and *group* messages across those networks. Still, we assume that nodes will not access resources that would require the consecutive traversal of more than five wireless networks (see [17, 31] for a detailed analysis on wireless communication) in order to access them. Hence, still referring to Fig. 20.4, Alice has to route its request through an appropriate bridge node (i.e., bridges *A*, *B* and *C*, noting that each bridge node is displayed in each network it is part of).

Specifically, *bridges* are in charge of routing messages within the multi-network overlay by determining the best route to reach a distant network. To achieve these tasks, bridges nodes run an instance of OLSR [24] among each other, and exchange routing messages using the specific asynchronous multicast transport provided by the *network-agnostic connectivity* layer. Instead of concrete node addresses, however, bridges store as destinations the identifiers of the various present networks (i.e., *network_ID*) and as next hop the bridge that needs to be contacted next to eventually reach the target network. The, whenever a non-bridge node wants to access a resource outside one of the networks it is itself connected to, it simply routes the request to any bridge of choice that will then forward the request accordingly.

Point-to-point transport—The *ubi*REST *point-to-point transport* is a connection-oriented transport for supporting resource access. The *ubi*REST *point-to-point transport*: (*i*) leverages the *network-agnostic connectivity* layer to send and receive messages relying on the MRN@ addressing scheme, and (*ii*) delivers the message to the appropriate resource. When the CURI of the destination resource is specified (e.g., mrna://dd3ef7e3-5f50-3800-982d-62095c6e8075/cart), *ubi*REST selects *point-to-point* as transport layer and extracts the MRN@ from the CURI. Note that, when both the consumer and the provider simultaneously change the complete set of IP addresses associated to their MRN@ (and no direct link exists) the session will break and the consumer needs to perform a resource discovery to find the same resource again and reestablish the communication.

Group transport—In ubiquitous networking environments, it is crucial to support point-to-multipoint interactions since it is central to advanced middleware services like dynamic discovery [53]. We thus introduce the *ubi*REST *group transport* over *multi-network overlay*, building upon the *asynchronous multicast* facilities provided by *network-agnostic connectivity* layer. Specifically, the *ubi*REST *group transport* is a connectionless transport for one-way communication between multiple peers in multi-network configurations. The *ubi*REST *group transport* interacts with the *network-agnostic connectivity* layer to send multicast messages based on an MRN@ identifying the group (i.e., AURI), and to deliver messages to the registered resources.

20.5.1 Code Mobility

Concerning the *genericity* requirement, *ubi*REST is able to accommodate heterogeneous and unforeseen functionalities into the running application. Unknown Java classes can be dynamically deployed in the overlay by leveraging code mobility [42]. *ubi*REST code mobility mechanism directly relies on the *ubi*REST communication facilities, then different coordination mechanisms impose different code mobility approaches. For point-to-point communication, *ubi*REST implements an end-to-end strategy that enables two *ubi*REST nodes to exchange executable code, whereas for group communication, *ubi*REST adopts a hop-by-hop strategy that, starting from the origin node, spreads the executable code towards multiple destinations.

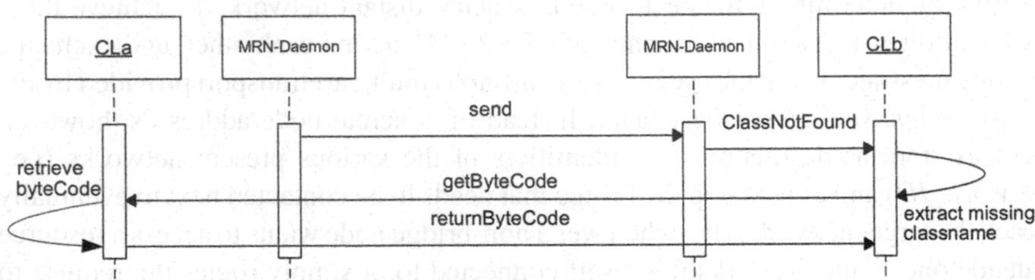

Fig. 20.5 Sequence diagram for point-to-point code mobility

Independently of the specific strategy, *ubi*REST implements an ad-hoc classloader hierarchy to cope with the "missing class" problem. In fact, when sending a message containing a Java object, such an object is serialized into a byte array and delivered towards the destination, which in turn deserializes the object before using it. However, if the object is unknown to the destination (i.e., the destination node does not hold the class bytecode for the received object), the object cannot be deserialized. To this extent, *ubi*REST implements a custom *classloader*, which is in charge of retrieving the bytecode for the missing classes, and loading them at run time in the local JVM to allow for a correct deserialization. The JVM specification [32] allows for creating a tree-like hierarchy of classloaders to load classes from different sources. When a classloader in the hierarchy is asked to load a class, it asks its parent classloader to load it. If the parent classloader cannot find the class, the child classloader then tries to load it itself. If also the child classloader fails, an exception is thrown. *ubi*REST exploits such a feature by defining a custom *ubi*REST *classloader* as child of the standard Java Bootstrap classloader. When loading classes, the *ubi*REST *classloader* delegates its parent classloader (i.e., Bootstrap). If the Bootstrap classloader fails, then the bytecode is not available within the node and should be retrieved remotely. Thus, the *ubi*REST classloader contacts the origin *ubi*REST node asking for the missing bytecode. The origin side retrieves the bytecode from its classpath and sends it back to the requesting node. At this point, the *ubi*REST *classloader* holds the needed bytecode and can load the class and deserialize the incoming object. If other classes are missing, then such a procedure is iterated until the entire class closure is retrieved.

*ubi*REST implements an end-to-end strategy to achieve point-to-point code mobility among nodes. Referring to Fig. 20.5, let A be an *ubi*LET sending a message to an *ubi*LET B, and let CL_a, CL_b be the classloader of A and B, respectively. Whenever B receives a message containing an object of an unknown type from A, an Exception is thrown, and the control is passed to CL_b, which in turn asks for the missing class to CL_a. CL_a processes the request, encapsulates the needed bytecode into a message, and sends it back to B. Once the bytecode is available at CL_b, it can be loaded into the JVM. The whole procedure is recursively applied until the whole closure of the original class is available on B. The retrieved bytecode is now stored on B and made available for further instantiations.

As for the group communication, this solution is not applicable. In fact, *ubi*REST group communication relies on the underlying *Multi-radio multicast* where message sender and receiver are completely decoupled, and do not have any knowledge about each other. Moreover, applying the end-to-end strategy to group communication would flood the overlay network with requests for bytecode retrieval towards the origin node, which become overloaded. To prevent this problems, *ubi*REST *communication* adopts a hop-by-hop strategy, which spreads the bytecode across the Multi-network overlay towards all the destinations: *ubi*REST applies the end-to-end strategy at each *bridge* along the path between the origin node and each recipient.

20.6 The *ubi*REST Programming Model

As already introduced, P-REST defines systems that comply with the "network-based" paradigm, which rely on the explicit distribution of resources interacting by means of (asynchronous) message passing. Network-based applications can be easily modeled and developed as a set of interacting actors [29], a computational resource reacting to external stimuli (e.g., messages) by either (*i*) sending messages to other actors, or *(ii)* creating new actors, or *(iii)* designating the behavior for the next stimulus.

The *ubi*REST programming model exploits the Scala [48] programming language, which *(i)* natively provides the Actor system, *(ii)* provides functional features (e.g., high-order functions), and *(iii)* is a JVM language, then allowing for Java libraries reuse (e.g., Multi-radio Networking), and for benefiting from JVM facilities (e.g., security manager for sandboxing). According to both the P-REST model and the *ubi*REST software architecture (Sect. 20.3), the *ubi*REST programming model revolves around the *resource* and *container* abstractions. A *resource* represents the computational unit, whereas *container* handles both the life-cycle and the provision of resources. The *ubi*REST programming model exploits the Scala Actor System [1] by benefiting from its intrinsic qualities: i.e., functional programming paradigm, event-based computation and shared-nothing concurrency, as well as Java interoperability. Hence, the set of *ubi*REST's abstractions is fully implemented in Scala and exploits the actor model.

Resource—The resource abstraction is directly mapped to a Scala actor. A `Resource` actor is defined as a Scala abstract class, which is further extended by any resource to be deployed within *ubi*REST. When extended and instantiated, a `Resource` object is initialized by specifying: *(i)* the CURI address, *(ii)* the set of operations available for the specific resource, and *(iii)* the resource's *Description* specifying the actual semantic concept implemented by a resource, defined as AURI.

According to the Scala Actor Model, `Resource` implements the `act()` method, which defines the resource's passive behavior, i.e., how the resource responds to external stimuli encoded as received messages. `act()` removes messages from its mailbox and, processes them accordingly. To prevent overriding, and then enforcing resources to conform to the REST uniformity principle, `act()` is defined as final, and accepts only messages defined by the P-REST uniform interface. Moreover, PUT, DELETE, and GET methods are declared as `final` and implement the well known semantics defined by HTTP. Further, *ubi*REST defines a new method INSPECT, which allows for retrieving meta-information about the resource (e.g., Description). Rather, the POST method is declared as `abstract` to allow developers to implement their own semantics. Furthermore, according to the Observer pattern defined by P-REST, a resource notifies the observers whenever its internal state changes. That is, when executing either a PUT, a DELETE or a POST operation, the resource actor exploits the underlying *ubi*REST *communication* to send a group message notifying the occurred changes.

According to P-REST, a resource plays a *prosumer* role, i.e., it is able to fulfill both roles of producer and consumer. In order to access external resources and consume their artifacts, a given resource sends request messages to the resources of interest and receives response messages. To this extent, *ubi*REST defines a `workflowEngine` function to be instantiated with the desired behavior by any `Resource` that wants to consume external resources. Indeed, the active behavior is specified by a `workflow` implementing the composition logic defined by P-REST. Specifically, *ubi*REST defines `workflowEngine` as a Scala higher-order function, which takes a `workflow` as input and executes it:

$$\texttt{workflowEngine} : (\texttt{workflow} : Unit \Rightarrow Unit) \Rightarrow Unit$$

The definition of `workflowEngine` as a higher-order function provides *ubi*REST with the ability of accomplishing hot deployment of new active behaviors at run time. This feature, in turn, supports dynamic situation-aware evolution.

Furthermore, also *ubi*REST provides developers with a high-level domain specific data-flow language for coordinating resources, namely the PaCE (*ubi*REST Coordination languagE) [8]. Specifically, PaCE (*i*) allows developers to specify the active behavior (composition logic) of a composite resource in terms of the set of operations defined by the *ubi*REST programming model, and (*ii*) achieves both adaptation and evolution of compositions in terms of *resource addition*, *resource removal*, *resource substitution*, and *resource rewiring* [38].

Representation—Resources interact with each other by exchanging their representations. *ubi*REST provides a resource representation by serializing the resource instance into a byte array. All the fields specifying the internal state of a resource are serialized into the array. However, since a *ubi*REST resource is implemented as a actor, it is not directly serializable. In fact, actors inherit from threads, which are not serializable as well. To cope with this issue *ubi*REST exploits the *trait* mechanism provided by the Scala language. In Scala, traits are used to define object types by specifying the signature of the supported methods, similarly to interfaces in Java. However, unlike Java interfaces, traits can be partially implemented, i.e., it is possible to define default implementations for some methods. Thus, *ubi*REST defines a special Scala trait, which implements custom serialization/deserialization mechanisms through two methods, namely `writeExternal` and `readExternal`. Both methods are automatically invoked by the JVM when the object is serialized and deserialized, respectively.

The `writeExternal` method makes use of the Java reflection mechanism to (*i*) discover the names and the values of the attributes of a class extending `Resource`, (*ii*) filter out the attributes inherited by `Actor`,[3] and (*iii*) serialize the remaining attributes using standard serialization. On the other hand, when the JVM deserializes a `Resource`, it instantiates an empty object and invokes the `readExternal` method, which in turn reads serialized attributes from the input stream, and makes use of the reflection mechanism to properly assign values to resource's attributes. This mechanism allows for the automatic generation of resource representations. `Representation` stores the byte array generated by the `writeExternal` method.

It is important to note that, designers are entrusted with preserving information hiding in `Representation`, i.e., avoiding the serialization of internal state information. For example, given a resource abstracting an algorithm, it should not return

[3] Scala Actors are not serializable and do not contain information regarding the resource internal state.

the representation of the algorithm. Rather, it should return the representation of the resource abstracting the results computed by the algorithm.

Description—As introduced in Sect. 20.3, resource descriptions are semantics-aware and play a key role in *ubi*REST. In fact, since all resources implement the same interface, descriptions result to be the only discriminant. To this extent, *ubi*REST provides developers with a Resource Description Language (RDL) defined by means of a XML Schema (see Figs. 20.6, 20.7). In particular, a *Description* is composed of two entities: (*i*) the *functional* description, which describes the functionalities provided by the given resource, and (*ii*) the SURI and CURI attributes, which define the semantic concept implemented by the given resource and its concrete identifier (i.e., the actual resource URI), respectively. The *functional* description aims at specifying "what" capabilities are actually provided through the uniform interface. To this end, it describes, for each implemented operation, the semantic concept it refers to (i.e., *semanticRef*), the data expected as output, and the input parameters if required (e.g., POST and PUT operations require for an input parameter, whereas the others do not).

Container—*ubi*REST handles resources' life-cycle and provisioning through the `Container` actor, which is implemented as an *ubi*LET. Indeed, the `Container` stores references to the hosted resources into a *resource repository* built as a mapping

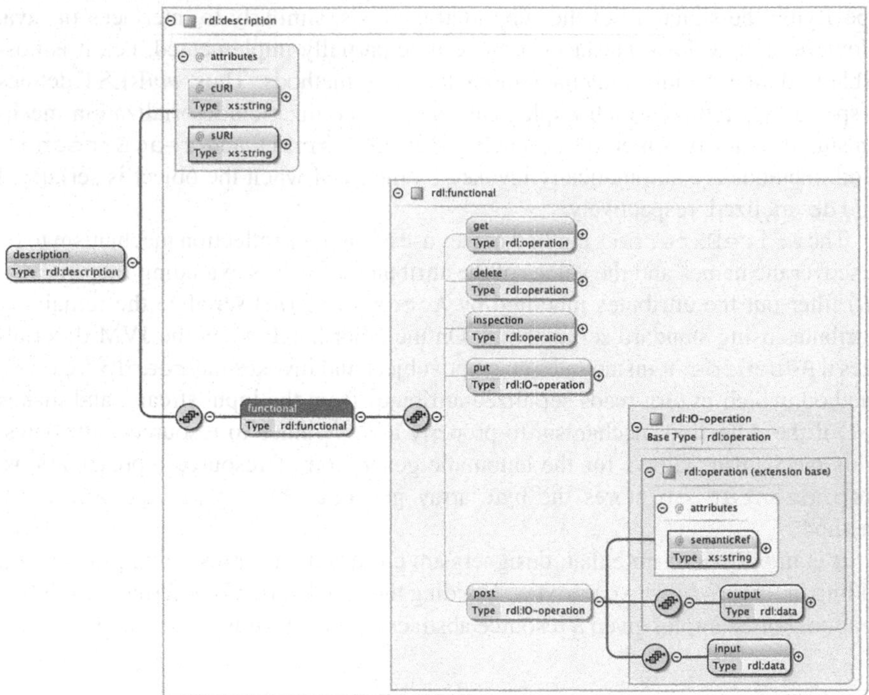

Fig. 20.6 Resource Description Language

from resources CURI to the respective `Resource` instance. Since a container is an active party in *ubi*REST, it also holds a CURI address, which is used to access a container's services. Hence, the container is in charge of handling three classes of incoming messages: (*i*) messages addressed to a specific resource hosted by the container, (*ii*) messages directly addressed to the container itself, and (*iii*) broadcast messages. In the first case, the container simply forwards the message payload to the right `Resource` actor. Messages addressed to the container are directly handled and processed. Finally, broadcast messages are received by the *ubi*REST node either as result of an active subscription within the Group-based communication submitted by a local resource (see Sect. 20.5), or as a *lookup* request. Notifications are delivered to subscribed resources, whereas lookup messages are processed by the container itself.

Concerning the outgoing messages issued by hosted resources, the container is in charge of forwarding such messages towards their destination by means of the proper communication protocol. `Lookup` messages are broadcast throughout the overlay; `Notify` messages are multicasted by means of the Group-based communication; `Observe` messages are encoded as subscriptions to a specific Group; the other messages are simply forwarded towards the final destination by exploiting the point-to-point communication facility.

As already pointed out, the container is in charge of managing resources' life-cycles and provision. In particular, a container creates and moves resources, provides support for resource lookup, as well as grants for resource access. While resource access is managed by the resource itself through its interface, creation, relocation and lookup operations are managed by containers.

```
<?xml version="1.0" encoding="UTF-8"?>
 <rdl:description aURI="presenter"
                 CURI="dd3ef7e3-5f50-3800-982d-62095c6e8075/Projector">
  <functional>
    <put semanticRef="display">
  <output xsi:type="rdl:simpleData"
      name="ack" type="bool" semanticRef="response"/>
     <input xsi:type="rdl:simpleData"
          name="PNG" type="bin" semanticRef="slide"/>
    </put>
  </functional>
 </rdl:description>
```

Fig. 20.7 A resource description example using RDL

To create a resource, the container must be provided with information concerning (*i*) the `Representation` of the resource to be created, and (*ii*) an optional CURI to be assigned to the resource. When creating a new resource, the container checks whether the CURI has been specified or not (if not a CURI is automatically generated), and extracts the `Resource` instance from the provided `Representation`. The newly created `Resource` is then deployed within the container and a new entry is added to the *resource repository*. Finally, the new `Resource` is initialized and started.

When moving a resource r from a container C_A to a container C_B, *ubi*REST needs to coordinate the two containers in order to guarantee both the correct deployment of r within the container C_B, and the delivery of messages to the r's new location (to avoid packet loss). Specifically, C_A buffers all the incoming messages addressed to r. *ubi*REST performs the move operation in three steps: (*i*) C_A waits until r consumes all the messages already in its mailbox and reaches a quiescent state [28]; (*ii*) C_A generates a representation ρ for r; (*iii*) C_A invokes a `Create` operation on C_B by passing both ρ and the CURI of r; r is then created in C_B and kept quiescent. Once these steps are successfully accomplished, *ubi*REST updates the naming system with the new location of r, and activates it. Finally, C_A removes r from its *resource repository*, and forwards all the buffered messages towards C_B, where r is now able to consume old messages, as well as the new ones that are directly delivered to the new location.

Finally, a *lookup* operation is used to query the *ubi*REST overlay for resources of interest on the basis of their descriptions. In particular, *lookup* takes advantage of Scala functional features by allowing developers to specify their own lookup strategy as a `filter` function, which is used to filter out results to be returned to requesters:

$$\texttt{lookup:}\,(\texttt{filter:}\,RDL \Rightarrow Boolean, \texttt{d} : RDL) \Rightarrow \texttt{cURI[ ]}$$

Lookup is a high-order function that evaluates the function `filter` with all the RDL descriptions stored by the resource repository, and returns the list of CURI identifying those resources evaluated *true*. *ubi*REST provides a default implementation for `filter`, which exploits well known signature matching algorithm [39, 46]. Indeed, the `lookup` function matches a requested AURI, against the set of AURI implemented by the resources stored within the *resource repository*. Then, `filter` checks if provided and required AURIs, specified by means of ontology concepts, satisfy one of the following subsumption relationships: (*i*) the concepts are equivalent (*exact matching*), (*ii*) the provided concept subsumes the required one (*plugin matching*), (*iii*) the required concept subsumes the provided one (*subsume matching*), and (*iv*) there does not exist any subsumption relation between the two concepts (*fail*). If the result is not *fail*, then CURI of the matching resource(s) is returned to the requesting node.

20.7 *ubi*REST in Action: An Example

This section shows how *ubi*REST abstractions can be easily and intuitively exploited to develop a ubiquitous application, namely *Ubiquitous Slide Show* (USS).

To this extent, we introduce a simple scenario describing a USS use case: *Carl, a university professor, is going to give a talk at the conference room, and carries his laptop storing both the slides and related handouts. The conference room provides speakers with a smart-screen available on the local wireless network, whereas the audience is supposed to be equipped with devices (e.g., laptop, smartphone, tablet), which can be used for displaying either the slide currently projected on the screen or the related handouts. The audience and the speaker always refer to the same slide, and to the same page of the handouts. All the devices are supposed to have a* ubi*REST instance running on them.*

USS conforms to the P-REST conceptual-model and specifies the following resources: `CurrentSlide` and `CurrentPage` represent the slide currently projected, and the corresponding handout page, respectively; `Remote` models the remote controller used by Carl to browse the slide show represented as an ordered list of slides; `PresReader` and `HoReader` visualize the slide show and the handout on the audience's devices, respectively; `Projector` handles the smart-screen of the conference room. The `Projector` resource is deployed within the smart-screen *ubi*REST container. `CurrentSlide`, `CurrentPage`, `Remote`, `PresReader` and `HoReader` are initially deployed on Carl's container, and made available to the devices in the audience which join the slide show.

Figure 20.8 shows a sequence diagram defining how such resources interact with each other to implement USS. `Remote` broadcasts a `Lookup` messages searching

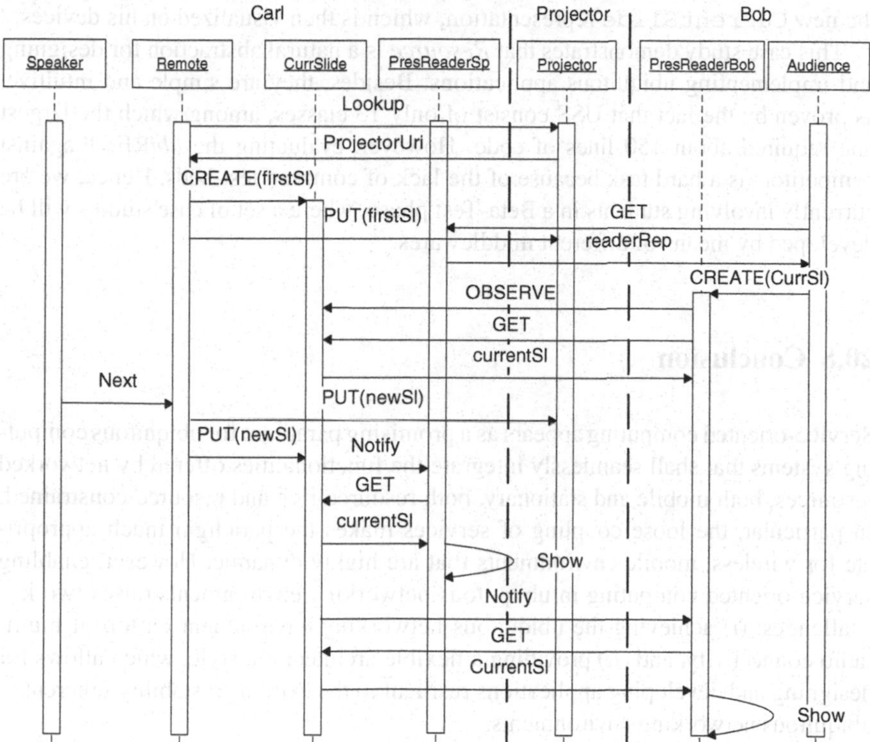

Fig. 20.8 Behavioral specification of the USS application

for a resource that implements the *presenter* concept, as defined by the `Projector` RDL description (see Fig. 20.7). As a result, it obtains the projector CURI that, in our example, matches the lookup request. Once the projector CURI's has been retrieved, Carl starts the slide show: `Remote` sends a `PUT` message, containing the representation of the first slide, to the projector, and then creates the `CurrentSlide` resource also initialized with the representation of the first slide.

On the other side, when a participant (say, Bob) enters the conference room, he uses the *ubi*REST *resource finder* built-in tool, which lists all the resources available within the overlay, to explore the environment and find the `PresReader` resource. Hence, selecting `PresReader` from the list, the *ubi*REST node issues a `GET` operation to retrieve a representation of `PresReader`, which, in turn, is used to create the `PresReaderBob` resource. Once this resource is created, it performs two actions: (1) it gets the state of `CurrentSlide` to initialize itself, and (2) it declares interest on observing the `CurrentSlide` resource (i.e., `OBSERVE` message).

When Carl needs to show the next slide of his presentation, he generates a `next` event that is handled by the `Remote`'s `workflowEngine` by performing a `PUT` operation on both `Projector` and `CurrSlide`. Modifying the `Projector` resource causes the projected slide to change, whereas modifying `CurrSlide` generates notifications towards all the resources that are observing `CurrSlide`. Then, `PresReaderBob` receives such a notification and retrieves the new `CurrentSlide` representation, which is then visualized on his devices.

This case study demonstrates that *Resource* is a natural abstraction for designing and implementing ubiquitous applications. Besides, they are simple and intuitive, as proven by the fact that USS consist of only 13 classes, among which the largest one required about 150 lines of code. However, evaluating the *ubi*REST against competitors is a hard task because of the lack of common test-beds. Hence, we are currently involving students in a Beta-Test phase, where a set of case studies will be developed by means of different middlewares.

20.8 Conclusion

Service-oriented computing appears as a promising paradigm for ubiquitous computing systems that shall seamlessly integrate the functionalities offered by networked resources, both mobile and stationary, both resource-rich and resource-constrained. In particular, the loose coupling of services makes the paradigm much appropriate for wireless, mobile environments that are highly dynamic. However, enabling service-oriented computing in ubiquitous networking environments raises two key challenges: (*i*) achieving the ubiquitous networking environment on top of multi-radio connectivity, and (*ii*) providing a flexible architectural style, which allows for designing and developing applications resilient to the extreme instability inherent to ubiquitous networking environments.

Exploiting multi-radio connectivity has led to the definition of various algorithms for optimizing the scheduling of communications over multiple radio interfaces, e.g., [10, 27, 41]. Building on this effort, this paper has introduced a *network-agnostic connectivity* layer, which leverages multi-radio networking by means of a special addressing scheme for networked services, namely MRN@, a QoS-aware network selection mechanism and both *unicast* and *multicast* communication facilities. In particular, this layer is in charge of managing the low-level heterogeneity inherent to multi-radio networking environments, by allowing for the exploitation of different application-level communication protocols. Building upon these functionalities, the *ubi*REST *communication* layer implements two different transports, namely *ubi*REST *point-to-point* and *ubi*REST *group*, which leverage *network-agnostic connectivity* to enable the ubiquitous networking of RESTful services deployed on various devices—e.g., Tablets and smartphones—embedding multiple radio interfaces.

On the other hand, *ubi*REST strives to satisfies the *flexibility*, *genericity* and *dynamism* requirements by adhering to the P-REST principles and exploiting both functional programming and code mobility. Specifically, *(i) ubi*REST achieves *flexibility* by exploiting the Actor Model and relying on the *ubi*REST overlay network to provide message-passing interaction, *(ii) ubi*REST provides *genericity* through the exploitation of a uniform interface in conjunction with both code mobility and functional programming capabilities (i.e., high-order functions), and *(iii) ubi*REST provides *dynamism* by allowing resource composition.

Ongoing and future work is manyfold and proceed towards different lines of research. First of all, we are currently defining an high-level *composition language* allowing developers to specify their own resource compositions in an agile and asynchronous way. Further evolution of *ubi*REST is towards the satisfaction of extra-functional requirements. In particular, we want extend the Resource Description Language, and the *lookup* service as well, to consider extra-functional concerns (e.g., quality of service, security), and contextual information (e.g., physical location) while specifying and search for resources of interest, as well as when composing them. Concurrently, we aim at improving *ubi*REST performances in terms of network load by investigating different types of overlay networks (e.g., peer-to-peer and hybrid).

Acknowledgments This research has been partially funded by the European Commission, Programme IDEAS-ERC, Project 227077-SMScom (http://www.erc-smscom.org), and by European Community's Seventh Framework Programme FP7/2007-2013 under grant agreement number 257178 project CHOReOS—Large Scale Choreographies for the Future Internet—http://www.choreos.eu.

References

1. Agha, G.: Actors: a model of concurrent computation in distributed systems. MIT Press, Cambridge, MA, USA (1986)
2. Asprino, P., Fresa, A., Gaito, N., Longo, M.: A layered architecture to manage complex multimedia services. In: Proc. of 15th International Conference on Software Engineering and Knowledge Engineering (2003)

3. Bellur, U., Narendra, N.C.: Towards service orientation in pervasive computing systems. In: Proc. of the International Conference on Information Technology: Coding and Computing (2005)
4. Bonetta, D., Pautasso, C.: An architectural style for liquid web services. In: Proceedings of the Ninth Working IEEE/IFIP Conference on Software Architecture. Washington, DC, USA (2011)
5. Caporuscio, M., Charlet, D., Issarny, V., Navarra, A.: Energetic performance of service-oriented multi-radio networks: issues and perspectives. In: Proc. of the 6th international workshop on software and performance (2007)
6. Caporuscio, M., Funaro, M., Ghezzi, C.: Architectural issues of adaptive pervasive systems. In: G. Engels, C. Lewerentz, W. Schfer, A. Schrr, B. Westfechtel (eds.) Graph Transformations and Model-Driven Engineering, *Lecture Notes in Computer Science*, vol. 5765, pp. 492–511. Springer Berlin/Heidelberg (2010)
7. Caporuscio, M., Funaro, M., Ghezzi, C.: RESTful service architectures for pervasive networking environments. In: E. Wilde, C. Pautasso (eds.) REST: From Research to Practice, pp. 401–422. Springer New York (2011)
8. Caporuscio, M., Funaro, M., Ghezzi, C.: PaCE: A Data-Flow Coordination Language for Asynchronous Network-Based Applications. In: T. Gschwind, F. Paoli, V. Gruhn, M. Book (eds.) Software Composition, *Lecture Notes in Computer Science*, vol. 7306, pp. 51–67. Springer Berlin Heidelberg (2012)
9. Caporuscio, M., Raverdy, P.G., Issarny, V.: ubiSOAP: A service-oriented middleware for ubiquitous networking. IEEE Transactions on Services Computing **5**(1), 86–98 (2012)
10. Charlet, D., Issarny, V., Chibout, R.: Energy-efficient middleware-layer multi-radio networking: an assessment in the area of service discovery. Comput. Netw. **52**(1) (2008)
11. Doval, D., O'Mahony, D.: Overlay networks: A scalable alternative for P2P. IEEE Internet Computing **7**(4), 79–82 (2003)
12. Edwards, W.K., Newman, M.W., Sedivy, J.Z., Smith, T.F.: Experiences with recombinant computing: Exploring ad hoc interoperability in evolving digital networks. ACM Trans. Comput.-Hum. Interact. **16**, 3:1–3:44 (2009)
13. Ellebaek, K.K.: A survey of context-aware middleware. In: Proc. of the 25th conference on IASTED International Multi-Conference (2007)
14. Fielding, R.T.: REST: Architectural styles and the design of network-based software architectures. Ph.D. thesis, University of California, Irvine (2000)
15. Grace, P., Blair, G.S., Samuel, S.: A reflective framework for discovery and interaction in heterogeneous mobile environments. SIGMOBILE Mob. Comput. Commun. Rev. **9**, 2–14 (2005)
16. Guinard, D., Trifa, V., Wilde, E.: A resource oriented architecture for the Web of Things. In: Proceedings of Internet of Things (IOT). Japan (2010)
17. Gupta, P., Kumar, P.: The capacity of wireless networks. IEEE Transactions on information theory **46**(2) (2000)
18. Gupta, V., Goldman, R., Udupi, P.: A network architecture for the web of things. In: Proceedings of the Second International Workshop on Web of Things. New York, NY, USA (2011)
19. Hirsch, F., kemp, J., Ilkka, J.: Mobile Web Services: Architecture and Implementation. John Wiley & Sons (2006)
20. Hoareau, D., Mahéo, Y.: Middleware support for the deployment of ubiquitous software components. Personal Ubiquitous Comput. **12**, 167–178 (2008)
21. Huang, H., Cai, J.: Improving TCP performance during soft vertical handoff. In: Proc. of the 19th international conference on advanced information networking and applications (2005)
22. International Telecommunication Union (ITU): Global standard for International Mobile Telecommunications - IMT-Advanced. http://www.itu.int/
23. Issarny, V., Sacchetti, D., Tartanoglu, F., Sailhan, F., Chibout, R., Levy, N., Talamona, A.: Developing ambient intelligence systems: A solution based on web services. Automated Software Engg. **12**(1), 101–137 (2005)

24. Jacquet, P., Muhlethaler, P., Clausen, T., Laouiti, A., Qayyum, A., Viennot, L.: Optimized link state routing protocol for ad hoc networks. In: Proc. of the IEEE international multi topic conference: technology for the 21st century (2001)
25. Khare, R., Taylor, R.N.: Extending the representational state transfer (rest) architectural style for decentralized systems. In: Proceedings of the 26th International Conference on Software Engineering, pp. 428–437. Edinburg, UK (2004)
26. Kindberg, T., Barton, J.: A web-based nomadic computing system. Computer Networks **35**(4), 443–456 (2001)
27. Klasing, R., Kosowski, A., Navarra, A.: Cost minimisation in wireless networks with bounded and unbounded number of interfaces. Networks **53**(3), 266–275 (2009)
28. Kramer, J., Magee, J.: The evolving philosophers problem: Dynamic change management. IEEE Tran. Soft. Eng. **16**(11), 1293–1306 (1990)
29. Kuuskeri, J., Turto, T.: On actors and the rest. In: Web Engineering, *Lecture Notes in Computer Science*, vol. 6189, pp. 144–157. Springer Berlin/Heidelberg (2010)
30. Lelli, F., Pautasso, C.: Controlling and monitoring devices with REST. In: Proceedings of the 4th International Workshop on Distributed Cooperative Laboratories: "Instrumenting" the Grid (INGRID 2009). Italy (2009)
31. Li, J., Blake, C., De Couto, D.S.J., Lee, H.I., Morris, R.: Capacity of ad hoc wireless networks. In: Proc. of the 7th ACM international conference on mobile computing and networking (2001)
32. Lindholm, T., Yellin, F.: Java virtual machine specification. Addison-Wesley Longman Publishing Co., Inc. (1999)
33. Mancinelli, F.: Leveraging the web platform for ambient computing: An experience. IJACI **2**(4), 33–43 (2010)
34. Mascolo, C., Capra, L., Emmerich, W.: Middleware for mobile computing (a survey). In: Networking 2002 Tutorial Papers (2002)
35. McKinley, P., Sadjadi, S., Kasten, E., Cheng, B.: Composing adaptive software. Computer **37**(7), 56–64 (2004)
36. Network Working Group: RFC675 - Specification of Internet Transmission Control Program. http://www.ietf.org/rfc/rfc0675.txt (1974)
37. Olsen Jr., D.R., Jefferies, S., Nielsen, T., Moyes, W., Fredrickson, P.: Cross-modal interaction using XWeb. In: 13th annual ACM symposium on User interface software and technology, UIST '00, pp. 191–200 (2000)
38. Oreizy, P., Medvidovic, N., Taylor, R.N.: Architecture-based runtime software evolution. In: Proceedings of the 20th international conference on Software engineering, pp. 177–186. IEEE Computer Society, Washington, DC, USA (1998)
39. Paolucci, M., Kawamura, T., Payne, T., Sycara, K.: Semantic matching of web services capabilities. In: First International Semantic Web Conference (2002)
40. Papadimitriou, D.: Future Internet - the Cross-ETP Vision Document. http://www.future-internet.eu/news/view/article/the-cross-etp-vision-document.html (2009). Ver. 1.0
41. Qureshi, A., Guttag, J.: Horde: separating network striping policy from mechanism. In: Proc. of the 3rd international conference on mobile systems, applications, and services (2005)
42. Roman, G.C., Picco, G.P., Murphy, A.L.: Software engineering for mobility: a roadmap. In: FOSE '00, pp. 241–258. ACM, New York, NY, USA (2000)
43. Sakr, S.: Xml compression techniques: A survey and comparison. J. Comput. Syst. Sci. **75**(5), 303–322 (2009)
44. Sorber, J., Banerjee, N., Corner, M.D., Rollins, S.: Turducken: hierarchical power management for mobile devices. In: Proc. of the 3rd international conference on mobile systems, applications, and services (2005)
45. Su, J., Scott, J., Hui, P., Crowcroft, J., de Lara, E., Diot, C., Goel, A., Lim, M., Upton, E.: Haggle: seamless networking for mobile applications. In: Proc. of the 9th international conference on ubiquitous computing (2007)
46. Sycara, K., Paolucci, M., Ankolekar, A., Srinivasan, N.: Automated discovery, interaction and composition of semantic web services. Journal of Web Semantics **1**(1), 27–46 (2003)

47. Tanenbaum, A.S., Van Renesse, R.: Distributed operating systems. ACM Comput. Surv. **17**, 419–470 (1985)
48. The Scala language. http://www.scala-lang.org/
49. van Engelen, R.A., Gallivan, K.: The gSOAP toolkit for web services and peer-to-peer computing networks. In: Proc. of the 2nd International Symposium on Cluster Computing and the Grid (2002)
50. Wang, H.J., Katz, R.H., Giese, J.: Policy-enabled handoffs across heterogeneous wireless networks. In: Proc. of the 2nd IEEE workshop on mobile computer systems and applications (1999)
51. Wolff, A., Michaelis, S., Schmutzler, J., Wietfeld, C.: Network-centric middleware for service oriented architectures across heterogeneous embedded systems. In: Proc. of the 11th International EDOC Conference Workshop (2007)
52. XML Protocol Working Group: SOAP message transmission optimization mechanism. http://www.w3.org/TR/soap12-mtom/
53. Zhu, F., Mutka, M.W., Ni, L.M.: Service discovery in pervasive computing environments. IEEE pervasive computing **4**(4) (2005)

Chapter 21
Mobile Web and Cloud Services

Satish Narayana Srirama

Abstract The developments in the web services domain, the improved device capabilities of the smart phones, the increased transmission rates of the cellular networks and the ubiquity of the wifi networks have lead to the mobile web services (MWS). In MWS domain, the resource constrained smart phones can act as both web service clients and providers (Mobile Host), thus forming a Mobile Enterprise. Simultaneously, with the advent of cloud computing, mobiles tried to utilize cloud services which, most often, provide web service interfaces. The benefits of offloading tasks to the cloud include extended battery lifetime, improved storage capacity and increased processing power, for the mobile devices. This paper summarizes the research associated with mobile web and cloud services. The QoS aspects of the Mobile Host, like providing proper security and scalability, the discovery of the provided services, the integrational aspects of the different technological solutions and their migration to the cloud are thoroughly discussed. The paper also discusses Mobile Cloud Middleware (MCM), which eases the invocation of multiple cloud services from mobiles. MCM raises the necessity for an asynchronous notification mechanism and with the Mobile Host feature; this is as simple as providing one more service from the device.

21.1 Introduction

Mobile data services in tandem with web services [21] are seemingly the path breaking domain in current information systems research. In mobile web services domain, the resource constrained smart phones are used as both web service clients and providers (Mobile Host). Mobile terminals accessing the web services cater for anytime and anywhere access to services. Some interesting mobile web

S. N. Srirama (✉)
Mobile Cloud Lab, Institute of Computer Science, University of Tartu,
J Liivi 2, Tartu 50409, Estonia
e-mail: srirama@ut.ee

A. Bouguettaya et al. (eds.), *Advanced Web Services*,
DOI: 10.1007/978-1-4614-7535-4_21,

service applications are the provisioning of services like information search, language translation, company news etc. for employees who travel regularly. There are also many public web services like the weather forecast, stock quotes etc. accessible from smart phones. Mobile web service clients are also significant in the geospatial and location based services [9].

Similarly, with the advent of cloud computing, the mobile applications also started using cloud services, which most often have web service interfaces. Mobile computing and cloud computing [6] domains are converging as the prominent technologies that enable developing the next generation of ubiquitous services based on data-intensive processing. Cloud computing is a style of computing in which, typically, resources scalable on demand are provided "as a service (aaS)" over the Internet to users who need not have knowledge of, expertise in, or control over the cloud infrastructure that supports them. The provisioning of cloud services can occur at the Infrastructural level (IaaS) or Platform level (PaaS) or Software level (SaaS). Cloud computing mainly forwards the utility computing model, where consumers pay on the basis of their usage. Mobile technologies are drawing the attention to the clouds due to the demand of the applications, for processing power, storage space and energy saving. This has lead to the Mobile Cloud Computing (MCC) domain.

While mobile web service clients are common, the scope of mobile web service provisioning (MWSP) was studied at RWTH Aachen University since 2003 [50], where Mobile Hosts were developed, capable of providing basic web services from smart phones. Mobile web service clients and the Mobile Hosts in a cellular network, together form a Mobile Enterprise.

Mobile Hosts enable seamless integration of user-specific services to the enterprise, by following standard web service interfaces and standards also on the radio link. Moreover, services provided by the Mobile Host can be integrated with larger enterprise services bringing added value to these services. For example, services can be provided to the mobile user based on his up-to-date user context. Context details like device and network capabilities, location details etc. can be obtained from the mobile at runtime and can be used in providing most relevant services like maps specific to devices and location information. Besides, Mobile Hosts can collaborate among themselves in scenarios like Collaborative Journalism and Mobile Host Co-learn System and bring value to the enterprise [43, 46].

Once the Mobile Host was developed, an extensive performance analysis was conducted to prove its technical feasibility [44, 50]. While service delivery and management from Mobile Host were thus shown technically feasible, the ability to provide proper quality of service (QoS), especially in terms of security and reasonable scalability, for the Mobile Host is observed to be very critical. Similarly, huge number of web services possible, with each Mobile Host providing some services in the wireless network, makes the discovery of these services quite complex. Proper QoS and discovery mechanisms are required for successful adoption of mobile web services into commercial environments. Moreover, the QoS and discovery analysis of mobile web services [46] has raised the necessity for intermediary nodes helping in the integration of Mobile Hosts with the enterprise. Based on these requirements a Mobile Web Services Mediation Framework (MWSMF) [51] is designed as an intermediary between the web service clients and the Mobile Hosts within the Mobile Enterprise, using the Enterprise Service Bus (ESB) technology.

While MWSMF is shown to scale well, we could achieve much better horizontal scalability and elasticity, by moving some of the components of the mediation framework to the cloud. We also have observed that load balancing is another key factor in successful deployment of Mobile Enterprise in commercial environments. So, we established the mediation framework on a public cloud infrastructure so that the framework can adapt itself to the loads of the mobile operator proprietary networks, thus mainly helping in horizontal scaling and load balancing the MWSMF and its components and consequently the Mobile Enterprise.

Cloud computing not only helps in scaling the components of Mobile Enterprise and MWSMF, it also helps in increasing the scope of mobile applications. However, accessing cloud services from mobiles poses several challenges like platform restrictions and interoperability across multiple clouds. To address these challenges, Mobile Cloud Middleware (MCM) is introduced as an intermediary between the mobile phones and the cloud. MCM hides the complexity of dealing with multiple cloud providers and enables the development of customized services based on service composition. The remaining sections of the paper are ordered as follows.

Section 21.2 discusses the mobile web services in detail. Section 21.3 discusses the cloud computing and mobile cloud services in general. Section 21.4 discusses the mobile web service provisioning and Sect. 21.5 address the challenges associated with establishing the Mobile Enterprise. Section 21.6 later discusses the MWSMF and Sect. 21.7 addresses the benefits with migrating MWSMF and its components to the public cloud. Section 21.8 discusses the Mobile Cloud Middleware designed and developed to ease the invocation of mobile cloud services from smart phones. Section 21.9 discusses the related work and Sect. 21.10 provides a conclusion for the discussion.

21.2 Mobile Web Services

Service Oriented Architecture (SOA) is a component model that delivers application functionality as services to end-user applications and other services, bringing the benefits of loose coupling and encapsulation to the enterprise application integration. Services encapsulate reusable business function and are defined by explicit, implementation-independent interfaces. SOA is not a new notion and many technologies like CORBA (Common Object Request Broker Architecture) and DCOM (Distributed Component Object Model) at least partly represent this idea. Web services are recent of these developments and by far the best means of achieving SOA. Using web services for SOA provides certain advantages over the other technologies like CORBA, Jini etc. Specifically, web services are based on a set of still evolving, though well-defined W3C standards that allow much more than just defining interfaces. Web services have wide range of applications and range from simple stock quotes to pervasive applications using context-awareness like weather forecasts, map services etc. The biggest advantage of web service technology lies in its simplicity in expression, communication and servicing.

Concurrent to the SOA developments, the capabilities of today's smart phones have increased significantly. In terms of hardware, now they have embedded sensors, better memory and power consumption, touchscreen, better ergonomic design, etc. In terms of software, more and sophisticated applications are possible with the release of iPhone and Android platforms. The data transmission rates also have increased significantly with 3G and 4G technologies and ubiquity of Wifi networks. These developments have contributed towards having higher mobile penetration and better services provided to the customers. Moreover, smart phones are becoming pervasive and are being used in wide range of applications like location based services, mobile banking services, ubiquitous computing, community and social networking etc. The main driving force for the rapid acceptance of such small mobile devices is the capability to get services and run applications at any time and at any place, especially while on the move. The experience from Japanese market shows that the most important factor in this development is that the terminals are permanently carried around, and thus people can use so-called "niche-time" to use the devices for various things [23].

These developments have brought out a large scope and demand for software applications for smart phones in high-end wireless networks. Many software markets have evolved like NTT DoCoMo [23] capturing this demand of this large mobile user base. Many nomadic services were provided to the mobile phone users. For Example, DoCoMo provides phone, video phone, i-mode (internet), and mail (i-mode mail, Short Mail, and SMS) services. i-mode is NTT DoCoMo's proprietary mobile internet platform. With i-mode, mobile phone users can get easy access to thousands of Internet sites, as well as specialized services such as e-mail, online shopping, mobile banking, ticket reservations, and restaurant reviews [41]. Similarly, a free mapping, search and navigation application for mobile phones is being provided by LocatioNet Systems. The company's free service called Amaze looks like a hybrid between the popular TomTom GPS (Global Positioning System) system and Google Maps. Apart from these services many location based services (LBS) have been developed in improving the general tourism experience.

These nomadic services bring benefits to all the participants of the mobile web. The mobile users benefit from these mobile services and the mobile phone becomes the network computer and wallet PC (Personal Computer) for him. The enterprises can benefit as they can support technologies and services that allow for anywhere and anytime connectivity of the office information sources. The mobile operator networks can increase their revenues with "open" models. For example NTT DoCoMo with its i-mode portal has proved this success, where the operator provides a framework and environment in which third party content developers can deploy their services. The content providers can in turn get incentives from these open models.

From the analysis of most of these nomadic mobile services; each operator provided some set of services, applicable to specific group, over specific platforms. But most of these approaches were proprietary and followed specific protocols. For example if we consider a company trying to advertise itself, it can use the mobile push services that are run over the GSM (Global System for Mobile communications) network. Then the advertisement has to be shaped in such a way that it fits the terminals and platforms by the mobile operators and vendors. This makes the services un-interoperable and the integration of services becomes highly impossible. In order to overcome the interoperability issues and to reap the benefits of the fast developing web services domain and standards, mobile web services domain came to the picture. In the mobile web services domain, the resource constrained mobile devices are used as both web service clients and providers, still preserving the basic web services architecture in the wireless environments.

Mobile terminals accessing the web services are common these days [9] and mobile web service clients cater for anytime and anywhere access to services. Some interesting mobile web service applications are the provisioning of services like e-mail, information search, language translation, company news etc., for employees who travel regularly. There are also many public web services accessible from smart phones like the weather forecast, stock quotes etc. They are also significant in geospatial and location based service applications. Moreover, there exists significant support for mobile web service clients, from several organizations such as Open Mobile Alliance (OMA), Liberty Alliance (LA) on the specifications front; and SUN, IBM toolkits on the development front. In parallel, with the advent of cloud computing, the mobile applications also started using cloud services, which most often have web service interfaces.

21.3 Mobile Cloud Services

In the emerging world of mobile computing, a rich mobile application is one, in which through a real-time interactivity, huge amounts of information is processed and presented to the user as a single result. Performing such tasks in a mobile phone is difficult due to the limitations in energy and storage. Thus, computation offloading is needed for extending the capabilities of the mobile applications in order to cover high user demands in functionality. Latest developments in cloud computing offer an appealing platform for pushing these process intensive tasks to the cloud.

Mobile cloud services use the shared pool of computing resources provided by the clouds to get the process and storage intensive tasks done. Some of the well known mobile cloud services are the services provided by the social network sites like the facebook mobile, twitter mobile etc. facebook claims to have 350 million users accessing their services from mobile devices every month. It provides SDKs for iOS and Android and a REST API/Dialogs for accessing the facebook Open Graph, the mechanism for accessing user's profile.

More examples of SaaS are those that help in building collaboration and data sharing applications such as Google Docs and Zoho suite. These services provide suits of applications for collaboration (chat, docs, wiki etc.), business (CRM, reports, market places etc.), and productivity (calendars, planners etc.). Other SaaS, such as Picasa and flickr, offer services for storing and tagging media files (pictures/videos).

All these services are accessible from mobile devices through applications usually owned by the service providers. Similarly, Google Analytics services are accessible through GAnalyticz for Android and iSpy Analytics for iPhone.

Another prominent domain with lot of mobile cloud services being developed is the Mobile sync. Mobile sync refers to the synchronization of data in the handset, like contacts, calendar, email, photos and media files, with that of the cloud, dynamically. Services such as Google sync, Microsoft MyPhone and Apple MobileMe are few examples that provide such functionality. The applications, most of them based on SyncML protocol, connect to a storage server within the cloud and a portal also located in the cloud that helps in managing the data. Alternatively, Funambol [34] is an enterprise solution for data synchronization that has released an open source version of its synchronization server. This server can be deployed within any cloud provider and consists of a synchronization engine, a server administration GUI and a Web interface for managing basic synchronization data. Funambol allows handsets to consume cloud services from any vendor, using the Funambol client application developed for each mobile platform.

At the core level (IaaS), the main services provided by cloud infrastructure are, generally, the storage service and the processing service. These services are basic in the creation of composite services which are delivered as SaaS. In addition, accessing these basic services from different cloud providers implies new types of applications, in which data saved on one storage service can be processed using a different cloud processing service, given as a result, a truly mashup application. Some of the popular IaaS providers are Amazon Elastic Compute Cloud (Amazon EC2) [3] and Rackspace [40]. There are also numerous private clouds based on free implementations of cloud infrastructure like Eucalyptus [17], which are compatible with Amazon EC2. Applications can access these IaaS using APIs provided by the cloud vendors directly or by the open source community. However, most of the APIs are not suitable for directly deploying them into a mobile phone. The integration issues with the compiler or other libraries which are required by the cloud API, may not be compatible for mobiles. For example in jclouds [24] API when some dependencies are included within Android, various runtime issues emerge (with the Dalvik Virtual Machine) which are not supported by the platform compiler.

The problem intensifies further as cloud vendors are generally observed to be slow in providing APIs for multiple mobile platforms, since it is not in their main agenda. Even if they do, they provide proprietary APIs and routines to consume the cloud services. Therefore, cloud interoperability is not possible and when a lighter mobile application is to be created, it has to be developed for a specific cloud provider and specific mobile platform. Moreover, for developing mashup applications using hybrid cloud services, the device must store all the different APIs. Subsequently, the mobile applications become heavy and inefficient. To address most of these problems, a Mobile Cloud Middleware (MCM) is proposed, which is discussed in Sect. 21.8.

21.4 Mobile Web Service Provisioning

While mobile web service clients are common these days, and many software tools already exist in the market, easing their development and adoption, the research with providing web services from smart phones is still sparse. A mobile device in the role of a service provider enables, amongst others, entirely new scenarios and end-user services. Moreover, the paradigm shift of smart phones from the role of service consumer to the service provider is a step towards practical realization of various computing paradigms such as pervasive computing, ubiquitous computing, ambient computing and context-aware computing. For example, the applications hosted on a mobile device provide information about the associated user (e.g. location, agenda) as well as the surrounding environment (e.g. signal strength, bandwidth). Mobile devices also support multiple integrated devices (e.g. camera) and auxiliary devices (e.g. Global Positioning Systems (GPS) receivers, printers). For the hosted services, they provide a gateway to make available their functionality to the outside world (e.g. providing paramedics assistance). In the absence of such provisioning functionality the mobile user has to regularly update the contents to a standard server, with each update of the device's state.

The scope of mobile web service provisioning was studied by two projects at RWTH Aachen University since 2003 [19, 46, 50], where Mobile Hosts were developed, capable of providing basic web services from smart phones. Figure 21.1 shows the basic mobile web services framework with web services being provided from the Mobile Host. Mobile Host is a light weight web service provider built for resource constrained devices like cellular phones. It has been developed as a web service handler built on top of a normal Web server. Mobile web service messages can be exchanged using the SOAP over different transportation protocols like HTTP, BEEP (Block Extensible Exchange Protocol), UDP (User Datagram Protocol), and WAP (Wireless Application Protocol) etc. In the Mobile Host's implementation, the SOAP based web service requests sent by HTTP tunneling are diverted and handled by the web service handler component. The Mobile Host was developed in PersonalJava on a SonyEricsson P800 smart phone. The footprint of the fully functional prototype is only 130 KB.

Open source kSOAP2 [27] was used for creating and handling the SOAP messages. kSOAP2 is thin enough to be used for resource-constrained devices and provides a SOAP parser with special type mapping and marshalling mechanisms. Considering the low-resource constraints of smart phones, no deployment environment can be easily provided. Hence, all services have to be deployed at the installation of the Mobile Host. Alternatively, the Mobile Host can be configured to look for services at other locations apart from the main JAR location, where the services could then be deployed at runtime. There is also support for Over the Air (OTA) and dynamic deployment of new services to the Mobile Host. Along with these basic features, a light weight Graphic User Interface (GUI) was provided to activate and deactivate the deployed services as and when necessary, so as to control the load on the Mobile Host. The GUI also has support for providing memory usage details of

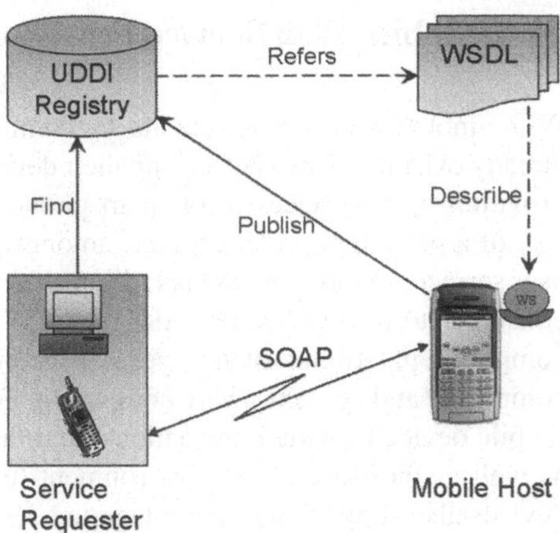

Fig. 21.1 Basic mobile web services framework with the Mobile Host

the smart phone and the basic server operations like start, stop and exit, thus helping in evaluating the performance analysis of the Mobile Host.

The key challenges addressed in Mobile Host's development are threefold: to keep the Mobile Host fully compatible with the usual web service interfaces such that clients will not notice the difference; to design the Mobile Host with a very small footprint that is acceptable in the smart phone world; and to limit the performance overhead of the web service functionality such that neither the services themselves nor the normal functioning of the smart phone for the user is seriously impeded. Even though the web service provider is implemented on the smart phone, the standard WSDL can be used to describe the services, and the standard UDDI (Universal Description, Discovery and Integration) registry [8] can be used for publishing and un-publishing the services. Figure 21.1 basically illustrates this idea of advertising mobile web services to a UDDI registry. An alternative for the UDDI-based discovery [53] is also studied, where the study tried to realize Mobile Host in a Peer to Peer (P2P) network [32], there by leveraging the advertising and searching of WSDL documents to the P2P network. The approach is addressed in detail in Sect. 21.5.3, while discussing the discovery issues of mobile web services.

The detailed performance evaluation of this Mobile Host clearly showed that service delivery as well as service administration can be done with reasonable ergonomic quality by normal mobile phone users. As the most important result, it turns out that the total web service processing time at the Mobile Host is only a small fraction of the total request-response time (<10 %) and rest all being transmission delay. This makes the performance of the Mobile Host directly proportional to achievable higher data transmission rates. Further, the regression analysis of the Mobile Host showed that the Mobile Host can handle up to 8 concurrent requests for reasonable services of message sizes approximately 2 Kb. Mobile Host is also possible with other Java variants like Java 2 Micro Edition (J2ME) [55], for smart phones. We also have developed a J2ME based Mobile Host and its performance was observed to be not so significantly different from that of the PersonalJava version.

21.4.1 Alternatives for Nomadic Mobile Service Provisioning

Nevertheless, web services are not the only studied means of providing services from devices like smart phones and PDAs. The provisioning can also be based on any distributed communication technology like Java Remote Method Invocation (RMI) or Jini, if the device supports the respective platform. Van Halteren et al have addressed nomadic mobile service provisioning, based on Jini technology [61]. The approach proposes the Mobile Service Platform (MSP) as a supporting infrastructure, which extends the SOA paradigm to the mobile device. The MSP design is based on the Jini Surrogate Architecture Specification which enables a device which can not directly participate in a Jini Network to join a Jini network with the aid of a third party. Using this architecture a service provided from the device is composed of two components: (1) A service running on the mobile device (referred to as a device service (DS)); and (2) A surrogate service (SS), which is the representation of the device service in the fixed network. The surrogate functions as a proxy for the device service and is responsible for providing the service to the clients. The MSP supports the communication between the device service and the surrogate service. Thus using mobile service platform, a service hosted on a mobile device, can participate as a Jini service in the Jini network.

However, splitting a service into a device service and surrogate introduces a state synchronization problem. The surrogate must be aware of the change in the state of a device service. Most serious limitation of this approach is that, it is based on a proprietary protocol. The technology (Jini) is also fixed. So the client should be aware of Jini technology. Moreover the services are to be developed both for the surrogate and the device, and changes are not propagated. The approach thus tightly fixes the service provided by the mobile device to platform (Java), protocol (HTTPInterconnect), technology (Jini) and surrogate host, thus seriously affecting the interoperability of the provided services. The main benefit with our developed Mobile Host is the achieved integration and interoperability for the mobile devices. It allows applications written in different languages and deployed on different platforms to communicate with Mobile Hosts over the cellular network, of course the benefits it acquired from the web services domain in general [46].

21.4.2 Mobile Host in Current Generation Technologies

In the meanwhile, the shift in web services has moved from SOAP to REST. Moreover, as the popularity of Android rose and with the upcoming of standards like Open Services Gateway initiative (OSGi) framework [1], we have upgraded the research to the current generation mobile devices and technologies. The OSGi framework is a module system and service platform for the Java programming language. With OSGi, applications or components can be remotely installed, started, stopped, updated and uninstalled without requiring a reboot. Application life cycle management (start, stop, install, etc.) is done via APIs that allow for remote downloading of management policies. Mobile Host for Android is realized using Apache Felix, an OSGI implementation for Android. The services run as bundles within Felix and the invocation of the services is through REST protocol. So the services are considered as resources that can be accessed via HTTP requests. Android SDK provides a mechanism to establish Server Sockets communication between the device and the clients; consequently, the HTTP request can be handled from the device.

Mobile Host exposes itself and its services to external devices through ZeroConf [22]. It consists of a set of techniques for automatic configuration and creation of a usable local Internet protocol network. ZeroConf dynamically configures the host in the network assigning them an IP address and also a domain name. Furthermore, ZeroConf provides a mechanism for service discovery and domain resolution. Mobile Host uses JmDNS, a service discovery protocol which is an implementation of ZeroConf. JmDNS assigns a local domain name to Mobile Host which can be used by other devices to access the services exposed by the host. JmDNS is also totally compatible with other implementations of ZeroConf for other platforms such as Bonjour for Apple. In addition, Mobile Host also includes Wide Area Bonjour support based on DNS Service Discovery. The DNS Service Discovery enables the service discovery via DNS records in the wide area network and also the self-configuration of devices in order to be accessible from other devices. The mobile device updates its IP in the DNS Service Discovery records every time it moves from one wireless network to another. When a request comes the DNS routes it to the most recent address updated by the mobile device. This way, the dynamic nature of the devices is addressed and the services can be invoked from other devices in the network.

Mobile Host opens up a new set of applications and it finds its use in several domains like mobile community support, collaborative learning, social systems etc. Primarily, the smart phone can act as a multi-user device without additional manual effort on part of the mobile carrier. Several applications were developed and demonstrated with the Mobile Host, for example in a remote patient tele-monitoring scenario, the Mobile Host can collect remote patient's vital signs like blood pressure, heart rate, temperature etc. from different sensors and provide them to the doctors in real time. In the absence of such Mobile Host the details are to be regularly updated to a server, where from the doctor can access the details. The latter scenario causes problems with stale details and increased network loads. A second example is that in case of a distress call; the mobile terminal can provide a geographical description of its location (as pictures) along with location details. Another interesting application scenario involves the smooth co-ordination between journalists and their respective organizations while covering events like Olympics. Besides, Mobile Hosts can collaborate among themselves in scenarios like Collaborative Journalism and MobileHost CoLearn System and bring value to the enterprise [43, 46].

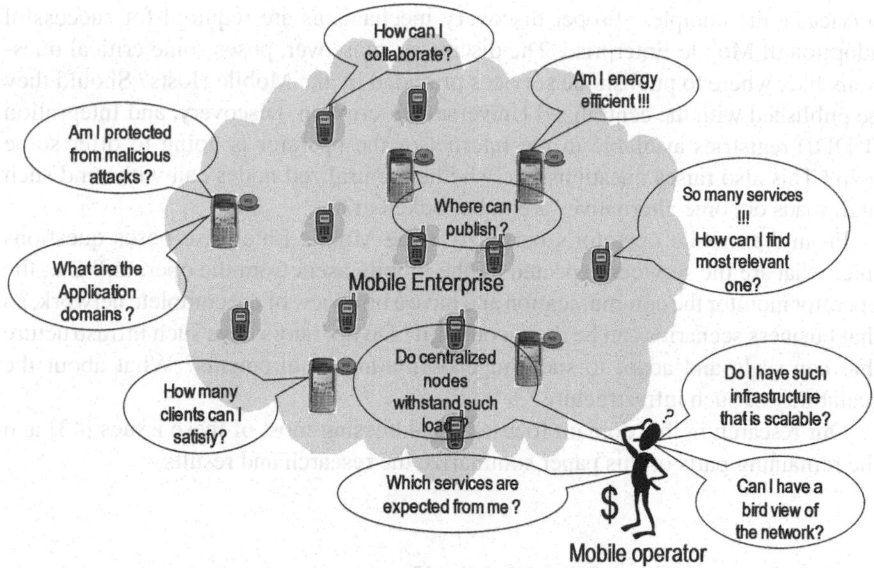

Fig. 21.2 Mobile Enterprise and the critical challenges posed to the mobile phone users and the operator

21.5 Mobile Enterprise

A Mobile Enterprise [43, 49] can be established in a cellular network by participating Mobile Hosts and their clients, where the hosts provide user-specific services to the clients as per the WS* standards. However, such a Mobile Enterprise established, poses many technical challenges, both to the service providers and to the mobile operator. Some of the critical challenges and associated research are addressed in this section.

21.5.1 Challenges for Establishing Mobile Enterprise

Figure 21.2 shows the Mobile Enterprise and hints the critical challenges posed to the mobile phone users and the operators. As the Mobile Host provides services to the Internet, devices should be safe from malicious attacks. For this, the Mobile Host has to provide only secure and reliable communication in the vulnerable and volatile mobile ad-hoc topologies. In terms of scalability, the Mobile Host has to process reasonable number of clients, over long durations, without failure and without seriously impeding normal functioning of the smart phone for the user.

Similarly, huge number of available web services, with each Mobile Host providing some services in the wireless network, makes the discovery of the most relevant services quite complex. Proper discovery mechanisms are required for successful adoption of Mobile Enterprise. The discovery, moreover, poses some critical questions like: where to publish the services provided by the Mobile Hosts? Should they be published with the centralized Universal Description, Discovery, and Integration (UDDI) registries available in the Internet or the operator is going to offer some help? This also raises questions like whether centralized nodes can withstand such high loads or some alternatives are to be looked at?

From the mobile operator's perspective the Mobile Enterprise poses questions like: what are the services expected by the mobile users from the operator? Can the operator monitor the communication and have a bird view of the complete network, so that business scenarios can be drawn out of it? Do operators have such infrastructure that can scale and adapt to such huge oscillating requirements? What about the scalability of such infrastructure?

Our research in this domain focused at addressing most of these issues [43] and the remaining parts of this paper summarize the research and results.

21.5.2 QoS Aspects of the Mobile Host

Providing proper QoS, especially, appropriate security and reasonable scalability, for mobile web service provisioning domain was observed to be very critical. The security analysis of the Mobile Host studied the adaptability of WS-Security specification to the MWSP domain and concludes that not all of the specification can be applied to the Mobile Host, mainly because of resource limitations. The results of our analysis suggest that the mobile web service messages of reasonable size, approximately 2–5 kb, can be secured with web service security standard specifications. The security delays caused are approximately 3–5 s. We could also conclude from the analysis that the best way of securing messages in a Mobile Enterprise is to use AES (Advanced Encryption Standard) symmetric encryption with 256 bit key, and to exchange the keys with RSA 1024 bit asymmetric key exchange mechanism and signing the messages with RSAwithSHA1. But there are still high performance penalties when messages are both encrypted and signed. So we suggest encrypting only the parts of the message, which are critical in terms of security and signing the message. The signing on top of the encryption can completely be avoided in specific applications with lower security requirements [45].

In terms of scalability, the layered model of web service communication, introduces a lot of message overhead to the exchanged verbose XML based SOAP messages. This consumes a lot of resources, since all this additional information has to be exchanged over the radio link. Thus for improving scalability the messages are to be compressed without effecting the interoperability of the mobile web services. Message compression also improves the energy efficiency of the devices as there will be less data to transmit.

In the scalability analysis of the Most Host [52], we have adapted BinXML [16] for compressing the mobile web service messages. BinXML is a light-weight XML compression mechanism, which replaces each XML tag and attribute with a unique byte value and replaces each end tag with 0xFF. By using a state machine and 6 special byte values including 0xFF, any XML data with circa 245 tags can be represented in this format. The approach is specifically designed to target SOAP messages across radio links. So the mobile web service messages are exchanged in the BinXML format, and this has reduced the message of some of the services by 30 %, drastically reducing the transmission delays of mobile web service invocation. The BinXML compression ratio is very significant where the SOAP message has repeated tags and deep structure. The binary encoding is also significant for the security analysis as there was a linear increase in the size of the message with the security incorporation. The variation in the WS-Security encrypted message size for a typical 5 Kb message is approximately 50 % [46].

21.5.3 Discovery Aspects of the Mobile Enterprise

In a commercial Mobile Enterprise with Mobile Hosts, and with each Mobile Host providing some services for the Internet, expected number of services to be published could be quite high. Generally web services are published by advertising WSDL (Web Services Description Language) descriptions in a UDDI registry. But with huge number of services possible with Mobile Hosts, a centralized solution is not the best idea, as they can have bottlenecks and can introduce single points of failure. Besides, mobile networks are quite dynamic due to the node movement. Devices can join or leave network at any time and can switch from one operator to another operator. This makes the binding information in the WSDL documents, inappropriate. Hence the services are to be republished every time the Mobile Host changes the network.

Dynamic service discovery is one of the most extensively explored research topics in the recent times. Most of these service discovery protocols are based on the announce-listen model like in Jini. In this model periodic multicast mechanism is used for service announcement and discovery. But these mechanisms assume a service proxy object that acts as the registry and it is always available. For dynamic ad hoc networks, assuming the existence of devices that are stable and powerful enough to play the role of the central service registries is inappropriate. Hence services distributed in the ad-hoc networks must be discovered without a centralized registry and should be able to support spontaneous peer to peer (P2P) connectivity [15] proposes a distributed peer to peer Web service registry solution based on lightweight Web service profiles. They have developed VISR (View based Integration of Web Service Registries) as a peer to peer architecture for distributed Web service registry. Similarly Konark service discovery protocol [28] was designed for discovery and delivery of device independent services in ad hoc networks.

Considering these developments and our need for distributed registry and dynamic discovery, we have studied alternative means of mobile web service discovery and realized a discovery mechanism in the P2P network [42]. In this solution, the virtual P2P network also called the mobile P2P network is established in the mobile operator network with one of the nodes in operator proprietary network, acting as a JXTA super peer. JXTA (Juxtapose) is an open source P2P protocol specification. Once the virtual P2P network is established, the services deployed on Mobile Host in the JXME virtual P2P network are to be published as JXTA advertisements, so that they can be sensed as JXTA services among other peers. JXTA specifies Modules as a generic abstraction that allows peers to describe and instantiate any type of implementation of behavior representing any piece of "code" in the JXTA world. So the mobile web services are published as JXTA modules in the virtual P2P network. Once published to the mobile P2P network, the services can later be discovered by using the keyword based search provided by JXTA. This approach also considered categorizing the services and the advanced features like context aware service discovery. We address the discovery solution as mobile P2P discovery mechanism. The evaluation of the discovery approach suggested that the smart phones are successful in identifying the services in the P2P network, with reasonable performance penalties for the Mobile Host [53].

Recently we have extended the mobile web service discovery mechanism to also include a Semantic Mobile Web Services Discovery over JXTA networks for the discovery but also over ZeroConf networks for the local discovery and global addressing. The current discovery mechanism considers challenges such as the mobility of the networks and the size of the networks. The mechanism addresses these issues by supporting the service discovery in small and medium size networks with low and medium mobility, with the aid of ZeroConf and by supporting the service discovery in large networks such as the wide area network with high mobility of devices, with the aid of JXTA and ZeroConf technologies. So the Mobile Host supports two discovery mechanisms: a directory-based with overlay support discovery mechanism for large networks with high mobility; and a directory-less with overlay support discovery mechanism for small networks with low mobility [35].

Apart from these discovery mechanisms, we also have looked at the context-aware proactive mobile service discovery, within our Mobile Social Network in Proximity (MSNP) [10]. MSNP represents a new form of social network in which users are capable of interacting with their surroundings via their mobile devices in public mobile peer-to-peer (MP2P) environments. MSNP brings opportunity to people to meet new friends, share device content, and perform various social activities. The concept of Mobile Host makes such resource-aware social networks feasible.

21.6 Mobile Web Services Mediation Framework

Mobile Hosts with proper QoS and discovery mechanisms, enable seamless integration of user-specific services to the Mobile Enterprise. Moreover services provided by the Mobile Host can be integrated with larger enterprise services bringing added value to these services. However, enterprise networks deploy disparate applications, platforms, and business processes that need to communicate or exchange data with each other or in this specific scenario addressed by the paper, with the Mobile Hosts.

The applications, platforms and processes of enterprise networks generally have non-compatible data formats and non-compatible communications protocols. Besides, within the domain of our research, the QoS and discovery study of the Mobile Host offered solutions in disparate technologies like JXTA. This leads to serious integration problems within the networks. The integration problem extends further if two or more of such enterprise networks have to communicate among themselves. We generally address this research scope and domain, as the Enterprise Service Integration.

The mobile web services mediation framework (MWSMF) [51] is established as an intermediary between the web service clients and the Mobile Hosts in mobile enterprise. ESB is used as the background technology in realizing the mediation framework. Similar mediation mechanisms for mobile web services are addressed in [26]. Especially, [26] describes the status of research with provisioning services from resource constrained devices. When considering mediation within semantic web services, Web Service Modeling Ontology (WSMO) has significant contributions [33]. However, we went with the ESB approach, due to the availability of several open source implementations.

Figure 21.3 shows the Mobile Enterprise and the basic components of the mediation framework. For realizing the mediation framework we relied on ServiceMix [4], an open source implementation of ESB, based on the JBI specification [58]. JBI architecture supports two types of components Service Engines and Binding Components. Service engines are components responsible for implementing business logic and they can be service providers/consumers. Service engine components support content-based routing, orchestration, rules, data transformations etc. Service engines communicate with the system by exchanging normalized messages across the normalized message router (NMR). The normalized messaging model is based on WSDL specification. The service engine components are shown as straight lined rectangles in the figure. Binding components are used to send and receive messages across specific protocols and transports. The binding components marshal and unmarshal messages to and from protocol-specific data formats to normalized messages. The binding components are shown as dashed rectangles in the Fig. 21.3.

The HttpReceiver component shown in Fig. 21.3 receives the web service requests (SOAP over HTTP) over a specific port and forward them to the Broker component via NMR. The main integration logic of the mediation framework is maintained at the Broker component. For example, in case of the scalability maintenance, the messages received by Broker are verified for mobile web service messages. If the messages are normal Http requests, they are handled by the HttpInvoker binding component. If they comprise mobile web service messages, the Broker component further ensures the QoS of the mobile web service messages and transforms them as and when necessary, using the QoSVerifier service engine component, and routes the messages, based on their content, to the respective Mobile Hosts. The framework also ensures that once the mobile P2P network is established, the web service clients can discover the services using mobile P2P discovery mechanism and can access deployed services across MWSMF and JXTA network [46].

Apart from security and improvements to the scalability, QoS provisioning features of the MWSMF also include message persistence, guaranteed delivery, failure

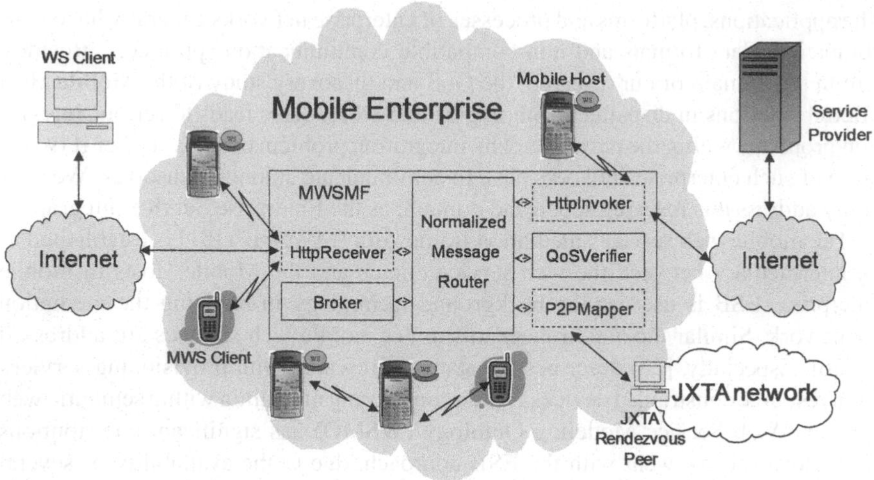

Fig. 21.3 Mobile Enterprise setup with Mobile Hosts, MWS clients and MWSMF

handling and transaction support. External web service clients, that do not participate in the mobile P2P network, can also directly access the services deployed on the Mobile Hosts via MWSMF, as long as the web services are published with any public UDDI registry or the registry deployed at the mediation framework and the Mobile Hosts are provided with public IPs. This approach evades the JXME network completely. Thus the mediation framework acts as an external gateway from Internet to the Mobile Hosts and mobile P2P network. The framework also provides a bird view of the mobile enterprise to the cellular operator, so that business scenarios can be drawn out of it. Preliminary analysis of the mediation framework is available at [43].

21.7 MWSMF on the Cloud

While the MWSMF was successful in achieving the integrational requirements of the Mobile Host and the Mobile Enterprise, a standalone framework again faces the troubles with heavy loads. The problems with scalability are quite relevant in such scenarios and the system should scale on demand. For example number of Mobile Hosts providing the services and the number of services provided by the Mobile Hosts can explode while some events are underway; like Olympics or national elections etc. Some of these application scenarios are addressed in [43]. This increases the number of MWS clients the framework has to support. Elasticity of the framework can be defined as its ability to adjust according to the varying number of requests, it has to support. As the study targets the scales of mobile operator proprietary networks, to achieve elasticity, horizontal scaling (scaling by adding more nodes to the cluster, rather than increasing performance of a single node) and load balancing for the MWSMF, the mediation framework was installed on the Amazon EC2 cloud. Once the Amazon Machine Images (AMI) are configured, stateless nature of the MWSMF allows, fairly easy horizontal scaling by adding more MWSMF nodes and distributing the load among them with the load balancer.

There are several load balancing techniques that can be used in this scenario. One approach is to use DNS based load balancing, where each call to the DNS server will result in different IP address. This means that each MWSMF node will be accessed by certain subset of clients directly, without an intermediary load balancing proxy as discussed below. This approach is not fault tolerant in case the framework node would crash but its IP would be cached on the client's DNS cache. However, this approach is inevitable, if loads on the single proxy based load balancer will grow to a level that a single load balancer itself will become a bottleneck. Another approach is to use load balancing proxy server in front of MWSMF nodes. Among other options, Apache HTTPD server with mod_proxy and mod_load_balancer is probably most commonly used configuration. It has one major drawback in elastic environment, as it doesn't allow dynamic reconfiguration of worker nodes. If we add or remove some MWSMF nodes we are required to restart load balancer as well, which is not convenient and potentially introduces some failed requests during restart. Alternative http proxy load balancer HAProxy [57] allows such dynamic behavior.

In the load test of the MWSMF, we measured how success rate of the requests depends on a number of worker nodes depending on a number of concurrent requests. Success means that a request will get a response before connection or response time-out occurs and success rate shows how many requests from all performed requests succeeded. The results of the experiment are shown in Fig. 21.4. From the diagram it can be clearly seen that the percentage of succeeded requests grows logarithmically with the number of nodes and degrades exponentially as load grows. Each node is an Amazon small instance that has 1.7 GB of memory, CPU power of 1 EC2 Compute unit, which is equivalent to CPU capacity of a 1.0–1.2 GHz 2007 Opteron or 2007 Xeon processor as of 07.12.2009 (CPU capacity of an EC2 compute unit do change in time). Performance of a single node drops rapidly already after 300 concurrent requests and even with 300 concurrent requests success rate is only 77 %, however 3 nodes can handle this load with 100 % success rate. It can be also seen, that with current setup adding more nodes does not show any visible effect after 6 nodes and performance is improved by an insignificant fraction in contrast to difference between 1, 2 and 3 nodes.

In summary we observed that, with current MWSMF implementation one single node can handle around 100–130 concurrent MWS requests with 100 % success rate. Adding an additional node adds roughly 100 new concurrent requests to the total capability until the load grows up to 800 concurrent requests, when load balancer itself becomes a bottleneck and adding any additional nodes do not give desired effect. This analysis showed mediation framework to be horizontally scalable. However, certain loads demand more advanced load balancing techniques. The elastic cloud environment helps to achieve this required setup very quickly [47].

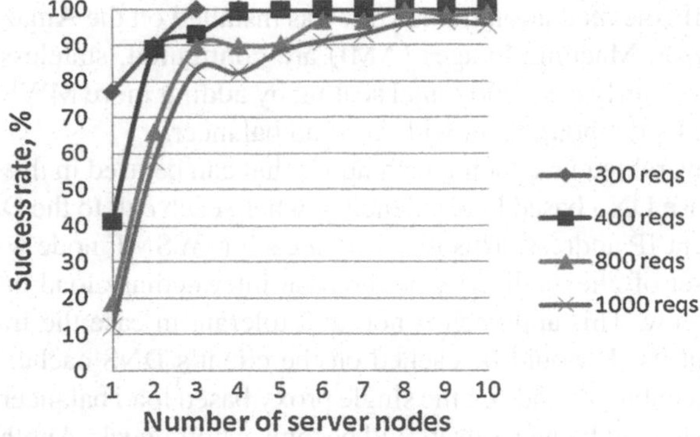

Fig. 21.4 Success rate of concurrent requests over multiple server nodes

21.8 MCM Architecture and Realization

Cloud computing not only helps in scaling the components of MWSMF, it also helps in increasing the scope of mobile applications, as discussed in Sect. 21.3. However, as already mentioned, accessing cloud services from mobiles poses several challenges. To address these challenges, Mobile Cloud Middleware (MCM) [18] is introduced as an intermediary between the mobile phones and the cloud. MCM hides the complexity of dealing with multiple cloud providers and enables the development of customized services based on service composition. The architecture is shown in Fig. 21.5. When an application tries to connect to a basic cloud service, it sends a request to the TP-Handler component of the middleware. The request is immediately followed by an acknowledgement from MCM, freeing the mobile. The request consists of a URL with the name of the server and the service being requested. For example, http://ec2-107-22-125-227.compute-1.amazonaws.com:8080/MessageServer/VideoProcessor represents a video processing service on an Amazon cloud instance. The request can be sent based on several protocols like the Hypertext Transfer Protocol (HTTP) or the Extensible Messaging and Presence Protocol (XMPP).

When the request is forwarded to the MCM-Manager, it first creates a session assigning a unique identifier for saving the system configuration of the handset (OS, clouds' credentials, etc.) and the service configuration (list of services, cloud providers, types of transactions, etc.) requested. The identifier is used for handling different requests from multiple mobile devices and for sending the notification back when the process running in the cloud is finished. Later, the Interoperability-API-Engine verifies the service configuration for selecting the suitable API, depending on the cloud vendor. A transactional space is also created for exchanging data between the clouds, so as to avoid offloading the same information from the mobile, again and again.

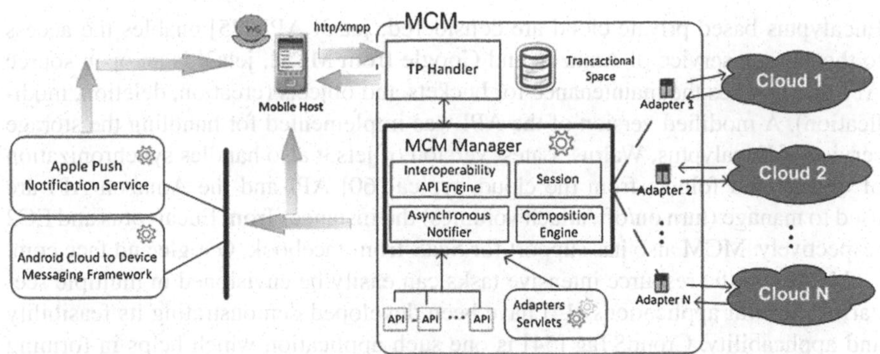

Fig. 21.5 Architecture of the Mobile Cloud Middleware

The selection of the API is based on querying a list that contains the specifications of each API (previously registered) and matching that information with the existent routines (classes) of the Adapter-Servlets component. Once the Interoperability-API-Engine decides which API set it is going to use, the MCM-Manager requests for the specific routines from the Adapter-Servlets. The servlets contain the set of functions for the consumption of the cloud services. Finally, MCM-Manager encapsulates the API and the routine in an adapter for performing the transactions and accessing the SaaS. The result of each cloud transaction is sent back to the handset in a JSON (JavaScript Object Notation) format, based on the application design. If the request is for a composite service, the Composition-Engine interprets the service schema and acquires the adapters needed for executing the services from the Interoperability-API-Engine. Each adapter keeps the connection alive between MCM and the cloud and monitors the status of each task running within the cloud.

When all the cloud services are completed, MCM-Manager uses the asynchronous notification feature to push the response back to the handset. Asynchronicity is added to the MCM by implementing the Android Cloud to Device Messaging Framework (AC2DM) [20] and the Apple Push Notification Services (APNS) [5] protocols for Android and iOS respectively. APNS messages are sent through binary interface that uses streaming TCP socket design. Forwarding messages to device happens through constantly open IP connection. Similarly, AC2DM is a lightweight mechanism which lets to push a message into a queue of a third party notification service, which is later sent to the device. Once the message is received, the system wakes up the application via Intent Broadcast, passing the raw message data received straight to the application. Alternatively, MCM also has support for the Mobile Host concept. With Mobile Host the device acts as a Web service provider. So the mobile cloud service response can directly be sent to the device. Currently we have Mobile Host implementations for PersonalJava, J2ME and Android platforms.

MCM is implemented in Java as a portable module based on Servlets 3.0 technology, which can easily be deployed on a Tomcat Server or any other application server such as Jetty or GlassFish. Hybrid cloud services from Amazon EC2, S3, Google and

Eucalyptus based private cloud are considered. jets3t API [25] enables the access to the storage service of Amazon and Google from MCM. jets3t is an open source API that handles the maintenance for buckets and objects (creation, deletion, modification). A modified version of the API was implemented for handling the storage service of Eucalyptus, Walrus. Latest version of jets3t also handles synchronization of objects and folders from the cloud. typica [60] API and the Amazon API are used to manage (turn on/off, attach volumes) the instances from Eucalyptus and EC2 respectively. MCM also has support for SaaS from facebook, Google and face.com.

MCM and the resource intensive tasks can easily be envisioned in multiple scenarios. Several applications [14] have been developed demonstrating its feasibility and applicability. CroudSTag [54] is one such application which helps in forming a social group with people identified in a set of media files, using face recognition cloud services. Zompopo [48] is another application which processes the accelerometer sensor data for creating an intelligent calendar. With MCM we can also think of applications which can help in managing the cloud resources themselves, like our Bakabs [36] application.

21.9 Related Work

Web services are not the only means of providing services from smart phones. van Halteran and Pawar [61] proposed a proxy based middleware using Jini surrogate architecture, which is discussed in Sect. 21.4.1 [37] gives a comparison of the nomadic mobile service provisioning technologies at the time. Similarly, Kim and Lee [26] mention several mobile web service provisioning approaches, along with our Mobile Host [50]. Subsequently, with the advent of Android and Apple iOS phones, the technologies are ripe and the devices are capable enough to envision Mobile Hosts in better application scenarios, and several publications [2, 30] have dealt with the issues recently. While most of the approaches have targeted at particular issues of providing services from smart phones, our research focused at service provisioning, Mobile Host access in different environments, QoS (Security, Scalability, battery life etc.) issues, mobile web service discovery and enterprise service integration issues for the mobile web services provisioning domain [46].

Regarding QoS analysis of the mobile web services is concerned; performance evaluation of WS-Security for network computers is provided at [29, 56]. Following these studies, we tried to adapt the WS-Security for mobile web service provisioning domain [45]. Asif et al. later proposed a lightweight toolkit for providing services from smart phones along with a security subsystem for mobile web services [7]. Regarding, XML compression technologies for smart phones, Tian et al. have proposed an end-to-end compression mechanism for mobile web services with detailed analysis [59]. Ericsson and Levenshteyn also have done a detailed study of the compression technologies available at the time [16]. From this analysis, we identified BinXML to be very efficient for SOAP messages, and adapted BinXML for the mobile web service provisioning domain.

To come up with the mobile web service discovery mechanism, we have studied several approaches like Konark service discovery protocol [28], VISR (View based Integration of Web Service Registries) [15] etc. Similarly, Qu and Nejdl [39] with their Edutella product, discuss exposing existing JXTA services as web services; and also integrating web service enabled content providers into JXTA, using the proxy model. We have studied all these works and tried to adapt the best practices to the mobile web services domain.

Regarding integration of the different subsystems is concerned, MWSMF [51] is the first study which proposed a middleware framework in the mobile web services domain [26]. We have observed several other studies like [13], continuing the work in this domain. Chang et al. [10] is studying the scope of implementing ESB on mobile devices. Meads et al. [31] employs the middleware technique to provide a communication interface for ubiquitous devices to communicate with mobile providers in heterogeneous networks. Similarly, IST EU project PLASTIC [38] designed a service-oriented middleware supporting service deployment on mobile multi-radio devices and multi-network environments.

Regarding mobile cloud domain, [14] provides a survey of mobile cloud computing and applications. Multiple approaches [11, 12] have focused on offloading code components from the mobile to nearby server as processing is needed [12] proposes MUAI, a framework that enables offloading mobile code of game applications to the cloud, based on the energy requirements of the code components. Similarly, Chun et al. [11] introduces CloneCloud that enables execution of the mobile platform on a virtual machine (VM) on the cloud. The VM handles the resource intensive tasks, once a real handset is synchronized with it. However, these approaches do not consider that a mobile application can benefit from multi-cloud operations, which was the main target of the MCM.

21.10 Conclusions

The developments in the web services domain, the improved device capabilities of the smart phones and the improved transmission capabilities of the cellular networks have lead to the mobile web services domain. In mobile web services domain, the resource constrained smart phones are used as both web service clients and providers (Mobile Host). Mobile terminals accessing the web services cater for anytime and anywhere access to services. With the advent of cloud computing, the mobile applications also started using cloud services, which most often have web service interfaces, leading to new domain of applications, Mobile Cloud. Mobile technologies are drawing their attention to the clouds due to the demand of the applications, for processing power, storage space and energy saving.

While mobile web service clients are common, this paper also addressed mobile web service provisioning and summarized the challenges and research associated in this domain. Mobile Hosts enable seamless integration of user-specific services to the enterprise, by following standard web service interfaces and standards also on the radio link. Moreover, services provided by the Mobile Host can be integrated with larger enterprise services bringing added value to these services. The QoS aspects of the developed Mobile Host, like providing proper security and scalability, and the discovery of the provided services are addressed briefly. Further, the QoS and discovery analyses of the Mobile Host have raised the necessity for a middleware framework and the features and realization details of the MWSMF in establishing the Mobile Enterprise are discussed.

While the MWSMF was successful in achieving the integrational requirements of the Mobile Host and the Mobile Enterprise, a standalone framework again faces the troubles with heavy loads. Hence, to scale the Mobile Enterprise to the loads possible in mobile networks, we shifted some of its components to the cloud computing paradigm. The mediation framework was established on the Amazon cloud infrastructure thus mainly helping in horizontal scaling and load balancing the MWSMF and its components and consequently the Mobile Enterprise. The study showed that MWSMF is horizontally scalable, thus allowing to utilize cloud's elasticity to meet load requirements in an easy and quick manner.

Cloud computing not only helps in scaling the components of Mobile Enterprise and MWSMF, it also helps in increasing the scope of mobile applications. However, accessing cloud services from mobiles poses several challenges like platform restrictions and interoperability across multiple clouds. To address these challenges, Mobile Cloud Middleware (MCM) is introduced as an intermediary between the mobile phones and the cloud. MCM hides the complexity of dealing with multiple cloud providers and enables the development of customized services based on service composition. The architecture and realization details of the MCM are mentioned in detail. MCM and the resource intensive tasks can easily be envisioned in multiple scenarios. However, most of the tasks deleted to the cloud from the mobiles will be time consuming. So MCM needs to send the response asynchronously to the device. With the mobile device acting as a Mobile Host, this is as easy as providing one more service from the mobile, the push notification service. The response from the cloud can be sent to the mobile, via MCM, by just invoking the push notification service on the device.

Acknowledgments The research is supported by the European Social Fund through Mobilitas program, the European Regional Development Fund through the Estonian Centre of Excellence in Computer Science and Estonian Science Foundation grant ETF9287. Special thanks go to Prof. Matthias Jarke of RWTH Aachen University, under whose valuable guidance, most of the research addressed in this paper is performed.

References

1. Alliance, O.S.G.: Osgi service platform, release 3. IOS Press, Inc. (2003)
2. AlShahwan, F., Moessner, K.: Providing soap web services and restful web services from mobile hosts. In: 2010 Fifth International Conference on Internet and Web Applications and Services, pp. 174–179. IEEE (2010)

3. Amazon Inc.: Amazon elastic compute cloud (amazon ec2) (2012). URL http://aws.amazon.com/ec2/. Accessed 12 Sep 2012
4. Apache Software Foundation: Apache ServiceMix (2007). URL http://incubator.apache.org/servicemix/home.html. Accessed 12 Sep 2012
5. Apple, Inc: APNS. URL http://developer.apple.com/library/ios/. Accessed 12 Sep 2012
6. Armbrust, M., Fox, A., Griffith, R., et al.: Above the clouds: A Berkeley view of cloud computing. EECS Department, University of California, Berkeley, Tech. (2009)
7. Asif, M., Majumdar, S., Dragnea, R.: Hosting web services on resource constrained devices. In: Web Services, 2007. ICWS 2007. IEEE International Conference on, pp. 583–590. IEEE (2007)
8. Bellwood, T.: UDDI Version 2.04 API Specification. Tech. rep., UDDI Committee Specification (2002). URL http://uddi.org/pubs/ProgrammersAPI_v2.htm. Accessed 12 Sep 2012
9. Benatallah, B., Maamar, Z.: Introduction to the special issue on m-services. IEEE transactions on systems, man, and cybernetics - part a: systems and humans **33**(6), 665–666 (2003)
10. Chang, C., Srirama, S.N., Ling, S.: An adaptive mediation framework for mobile p2p social content sharing. In: 10th International Conference on Service Oriented Computing (ICSOC 2012). Springer (2012)
11. Chun, B., Maniatis, P.: Augmented smartphone applications through clone cloud execution. In: Proceedings of the 12th conference on Hot topics in operating systems, pp. 8–8. USENIX Association (2009) URL http://www.usenix.org/event/hotos09/tech/full_papers/chun/chun_html/
12. Cuervo, E., Balasubramanian, A., Cho, D., Wolman, A., Saroiu, S., Chandra, R., Bahl, P.: Maui: making smartphones last longer with code offload. In: Proceedings of the 8th international conference on Mobile systems, applications, and services, pp. 49–62. ACM (2010)
13. de Spindler, A., Grossniklaus, M., Lins, C., Norrie, M.: Information Sharing Modalities for Mobile Ad-Hoc Networks. On the Move to Meaningful Internet Systems: OTM 2009, pp. 322–339 (2009)
14. Dinh, H., Lee, C., Niyato, D., Wang, P.: A survey of mobile cloud computing: architecture, applications, and approaches. Wireless Communications and Mobile Computing (2011)
15. Dustdar, S., Treiber, M.: Integration of transient web services into a virtual peer to peer web service registry. Distributed and Parallel Databases **20**, 91–115 (2006)
16. Ericsson, M., Levenshteyn, R.: On optimization of XML-based messaging. In: Second Nordic Conference on Web Services (NCWS 2003), pp. 167–179 (2003)
17. Eucalyptus Systems Inc.: Eucalyptus. Online. URL http://www.eucalyptus.com. Accessed 12 Sep 2012
18. Flores, H., Srirama, S., Paniagua, C.: A Generic Middleware Framework for Handling Process Intensive Hybrid Cloud Services from Mobiles. In: The 9th International Conference on Advances in Mobile Computing & Multimedia (MoMM-2011), pp. 87–95. ACM (2011)
19. Gehlen, G.: Mobile web services - concepts, prototype, and traffic performance analysis. Ph.D. thesis, RWTH Aachen University (2007)
20. Google Inc.: Google code labs - Android Cloud to Device Messaging Framework. URL http://code.google.com/intl/es-ES/android/c2dm/index.html. Accessed 12 Sep 2012
21. Gottschalk, K., Graham, S., Kreger, H., Snell, J.: Introduction to web services architecture. IBM Systems Journal: New Developments in Web Services and E-commerce **41**(2), 178–198 (2002). URL http://researchweb.watson.ibm.com/journal/sj/412/gottschalk.html
22. Günes, M., Reibel, J.: An IP address configuration algorithm for zeroconf. Mobile multi-hop ad-hoc networks. In: Proceedings of the International Workshop on Broadband Wireless Ad-Hoc Networks and Services. Citeseer (2002)
23. Ichikawa, K.: The View of NTT DoCoMo on the Further development of Wireless Internet. In: Tokyo Mobile Round Table Conference (2002)
24. jclouds: jclouds - multi cloud library. URL http://code.google.com/p/jclouds/. Accessed 12 Sep 2012
25. jets3t: jetS3t - An open source Java toolkit for Amazon S3 and CloudFront. URL http://jets3t.s3.amazonaws.com/toolkit/guide.html. Accessed 12 Sep 2012

26. Kim, Y., Lee, K.: A lightweight framework for mobile web services. Journal on Computer Science - Research and Development **24**(4), 199–209 (2009)
27. kSOAP2: kSOAP2 - An efficient, lean, Java SOAP library for constrained devices. SourceForge.net (2012). URL http://sourceforge.net/projects/ksoap2. Accessed 12 Sep 2012
28. Lee, C., Helal, A., Desai, N., Verma, V., Arslan, B.: Konark: A system and protocols for device independent, peer-to-peer discovery and delivery of mobile services. IEEE transactions on systems, man, and cybernetics - part a: systems and humans **33**(6), 682–696 (2003)
29. Liu, H., Pallikara, S., Fox, G.: Performance of web service security. In: Proceedings of 13th Annual Mardi Gras Conference (2005)
30. Lomotey, R., Deters, R.: Using a cloud-centric middleware to enable mobile hosting of web services. Procedia Computer Science **10**, 634–641 (2012)
31. Meads, A., Roughton, A., Warren, I., Weerasinghe, T.: Mobile service provisioning middleware for multihomed devices. In: Wireless and Mobile Computing, Networking and Communications, 2009. WIMOB 2009. IEEE International Conference on, pp. 67–72. IEEE (2009)
32. Milojicic, D.S., Kalogeraki, V., Lukose, R., Nagaraja, K., Pruyne, J., Richard, B., Rollins, S., Xu, Z.: Peer-to-peer computing. Tech. rep., HP Laboratories Palo Alto (2003). URL http://www.hpl.hp.com/techreports/2002/HPL-2002-57R1.pdf. Accessed 12 Sep 2012
33. Mocan, A., Cimpian, E., Stollberg, M., Scharffe, F., Scicluna, J.: WSMO mediators. Online (2005). URL http://www.wsmo.org/TR/d29/. Accessed 12 Sep 2012
34. Onetti, A., Capobianco, F.: Open source and business model innovation. The funambol case. In: International Conference on OS Systems Genova, 11th-15th July, pp. 224–227 (2005)
35. Paniagua, C.: Discovery and push notification mechanisms for mobile cloud services. Master's thesis, University of Tartu (2012)
36. Paniagua, C., Srirama, S.N., Flores, H.: Bakabs: Managing Load of Cloud-based Web Applications from Mobiles. In: The 13th International Conference on Information Integration and Web-based Applications & Services (iiWAS-2011), pp. 489–495. ACM (2011)
37. Pawar, P., Srirama, S., van Beijnum, B., van Halteren, A.: A comparative study of nomadic mobile service provisioning approaches. In: Next Generation Mobile Applications, Services and Technologies, 2007. NGMAST'07. The 2007 International Conference on, pp. 277–286. IEEE (2007)
38. PLASTIC Consortium: A B3G Service Platform: The IST PLASTIC Project (2012). URL http://plastic.paris-rocquencourt.inria.fr/plasticwhitepaper.pdf. Accessed 12 Sep 2012
39. Qu, C., Nejdl, W.: Interacting the Edutella/JXTA peer-to-peer network with web services. In: Proceedings of the 2004 International Symposium on Applications and the Internet (SAINT'04) (2004)
40. Rackspace Inc.: The rackspace open source cloud (2012). URL http://www.rackspace.com/. Accessed 12 Sep 2012
41. Ratliff, J.: NTT Docomo and its i-mode success: origins and implications. California Management Review **44**(3) (2002)
42. Srirama, S.: Publishing and discovery of mobile web services in peer to peer networks. In: Proceedings of First International Workshop on Mobile Services and Personalized Environments (MSPE'06), vol. P-102, pp. 15–28. Lecture Notes in Informatics, GI (2006)
43. Srirama, S., Jarke, M.: Mobile hosts in enterprise service integration. International Journal of Web Engineering and Technology (IJWET) **5**(2), 187–213 (2009)
44. Srirama, S., Jarke, M., Prinz, W.: Mobile Host: A feasibility analysis of mobile Web Service provisioning. In: 4th International Workshop on Ubiquitous Mobile Information and Collaboration Systems, UMICS 2006, a CAiSE'06 workshop (2006)
45. Srirama, S., Jarke, M., Prinz, W.: Security analysis of mobile web service provisioning. International Journal of Internet Technology and Secured Transactions (IJITST) **1**(1/2), 151–171 (2007)
46. Srirama, S.N.: Mobile hosts in enterprise service integration. Ph.D. thesis, RWTH Aachen University (2008)
47. Srirama, S.N.: MWSMF: A Mediation Framework for Mobile Hosts and Enterprise on Cloud. International Journal of Pervasive Computing and Communications **7**(4), 316–338 (2011)

48. Srirama, S.N., Flores, H., Paniagua, C.: Zompopo: Mobile Calendar Prediction based on Human Activities Recognition using the Accelerometer and Cloud Services. In: 5th Int. Conf. On Next Generation Mobile Applications, Services and Technologies (NGMAST), pp. 63–69. IEEE CS (2011)
49. Srirama, S.N., Jarke, M.: Mobile enterprise - a case study of enterprise service integration. In: 3rd International Conference and Exhibition on Next Generation Mobile Applications, Services and Technologies (NGMAST 2009), pp. 101–107. IEEE Computer Society (2009)
50. Srirama, S.N., Jarke, M., Prinz, W.: Mobile web service provisioning. In: AICT-ICIW '06: Advanced Int. Conf. on Telecommunications and Int. Conf. on Internet and Web Applications and Services, p. 120. IEEE Computer Society (2006)
51. Srirama, S.N., Jarke, M., Prinz, W.: Mobile web services mediation framework. In: Middleware for Service Oriented Computing (MW4SOC) Workshop @ 8th Int. Middleware Conf. 2007. ACM Press (2007)
52. Srirama, S.N., Jarke, M., Prinz, W.: MWSMF: A mediation framework realizing scalable mobile web service provisioning. In: International Conference on MOBILe Wireless MiddleWARE, Operating Systems, and Applications (Mobilware 2008). ACM Press (2008)
53. Srirama, S.N., Jarke, M., Prinz, W., Zhu, H.: Scalable mobile web service discovery in peer to peer networks. In: IEEE Third International Conference on Internet and Web Applications and Services (ICIW 2008), pp. 668–674. IEEE Computer Society (2008)
54. Srirama, S.N., Paniagua, C., Flores, H.: CroudSTag: Social Group Formation with Facial Recognition and Mobile Cloud Services. Procedia Computer Science **5**, 633–640 (2011)
55. Sun Microsystems: Java^{TM} 2 Platform, Micro Edition (J2ME^{TM}) Web Services Specification - Datasheet. Tech. rep., Sun Microsystems, Inc. (2007)
56. Tang, K., Chen, S., Levy, D., Zic, J., Yan, B.: A performance evaluation of web services security. In: 10th IEEE International Enterprise Distributed Object Computing Conference (EDOC'06), pp. 67–74 (2006)
57. Tarreau, W.: Haproxy architecture guide, version 1.1.34. Online (2006). URL http://haproxy.1wt.eu/download/1.3/doc/architecture.txt. Accessed 12 Sep 2012
58. Ten-Hove, R., Walker, P.: Java^{TM} Business Integration (JBI) 1.0 -JSR 208 Final Release. Tech. rep., Sun Microsystems, Inc. (2005)
59. Tian, M., Voigt, T., Naumowicz, T., Ritter, H., Schiller, J.: Performance considerations for mobile web services. Computer communications **27**(11), 1097–1105 (2004)
60. typica: typica - A Java client library for a variety of Amazon Web Services. URL http://code.google.com/p/typica/. Accessed 12 Sep 2012
61. van Halteren, A., Pawar, P.: Mobile Service Platform: A Middleware for Nomadic Mobile Service Provisioning. In: 2nd IEEE International Conference On Wireless and Mobile Computing, Networking and Communications (WiMob 2006) pp. 292–299 (2006)

57. [illegible]: The Hadoop distributed file system architecture and design [illegible] Online (2009). URL http://hadoop.apache.org/[illegible]. Accessed 12 Sep 2012

Chapter 22
TOSCA: Portable Automated Deployment and Management of Cloud Applications

Tobias Binz, Uwe Breitenbücher, Oliver Kopp and Frank Leymann

Abstract Portability and automated management of composite applications are major concerns of today's enterprise IT. These applications typically consist of heterogeneous distributed components combined to provide the application's functionality. This architectural style challenges the operation and management of the application as a whole and requires new concepts for deployment, configuration, operation, and termination. The upcoming OASIS Topology and Orchestration Specification for Cloud Applications (TOSCA) standard provides new ways to enable portable automated deployment and management of composite applications. TOSCA describes the structure of composite applications as topologies containing their components and their relationships. Plans capture management tasks by orchestrating management operations exposed by the components. This chapter provides an overview on the concepts and usage of TOSCA.

22.1 Introduction

The increasing use of IT in almost any part of today's enterprises leads to a steadily increasing management effort, a challenge for enterprises as each new system or technology increases the degree of complexity [11]. This can be tackled by automation of

---

T. Binz (✉) · U. Breitenbücher · O. Kopp · F. Leymann
University of Stuttgart, IAAS,
Universitätsstr. 38, 70569 Stuttgart, Germany
e-mail: binz@iaas.uni-stuttgart.de

U. Breitenbücher
e-mail: breitenbuecher@iaas.uni-stuttgart.de

O. Kopp
e-mail: kopp@iaas.uni-stuttgart.de

F. Leymann
e-mail: leymann@iaas.uni-stuttgart.de

A. Bouguettaya et al. (eds.), *Advanced Web Services*,
DOI: 10.1007/978-1-4614-7535-4_22,

IT management or by outsourcing to external providers [18], which are both enabled and supported by cloud computing.

In recent years, cloud computing introduced a new way of using and offering IT software, platforms, and infrastructure services [21]. The "utility-like" offering of these services and flexible "pay-per-use" pricing are similar to how resources such as electricity and water are offered today [18]: Applications and other IT resources such as compute and storage must not be bought upfront and managed by the enterprise on its own, but can be simply requested when the respective functionality is actually needed—without dealing with the complexity of management, configuration, and maintenance. Therefore, enterprises move from a model of capital expenditure (CAPEX) to operational expenditure (OPEX) [1]. These approaches are expected to change the way how enterprises use and think about IT and may even relieve them from owning their own IT environment, which could be seen as the "next revolution in IT" [17]. Not only Gartner considers the efficient use of cloud computing as one of the key success factors for enterprises [12]. From a provider's perspective, automating the management of the offered services is of vital importance, because management and operation of IT is one of the biggest cost factors today—in terms of money and time. The ability to offer services which are elastic, self-serviced, rapidly provisioned, and priced based on actual consuption (pay-as-you-go) depends on the degree of automation of management. Thus, the management has to be organized in an industrial manner, i.e., shared throughout a number of customers and tenants [18].

Enterprise applications are typically complex composite applications, which consist of multiple individual components, each providing a clearly distinguishable piece of functionality. The functionality of the involved components is aggregated and orchestrated into a composite application providing a higher-level of functionality. Components typically have relationships to other components. For instance, a Web server component runs on an operating system component or an application connects to a database and external services. These composite enterprise applications typically rely on modular, component based architectures, which benefit from cloud technologies and properties such as elasticity, flexibility, scalability, and high availability [1, 5, 33, 34]. The different components involved need to be managed in terms of deployment, configuration, quality of service, and their communication to other components. The management becomes time-consuming and error-prone if the application structure, i.e., its components and relations, are not documented in a well-defined, machine-readable format. The management is often done manually by executing scripts or even completely manual work, which hinders automation, repeatability, and self-service.

To enable the creation of portable cloud applications and the automation of their deployment and management, the application's components, their relations, and management must be modeled in a portable, standardized, machine-readable format. This is where TOSCA—the Topology and Orchestration Specification for Cloud Applications [24]—proposes an XML-based modeling language tackling these issues by formalizing the application's structure as typed topology graph and capturing the management tasks in plans. In the scope of IT service management in general and cloud computing in particular, three problems are addressed by TOSCA: (1) automated application deployment and management, (2) portability of applications and their management, and (3) interoperability and reuseability of components. An overview on TOSCA and how TOSCA addresses these challenges is provided in Sect. 22.2. After presenting the details of TOSCA in Sect. 22.3, we describe the supporting ecosystem in Sect. 22.4. In Sect. 22.5, we discuss how TOSCA achieves portability of composite cloud applications and what to do to improve portability of a TOSCA application. Finally, we close with our conclusions in Sect. 22.6.

22.2 Overview on TOSCA

TOSCA is an upcoming OASIS standard to describe composite (cloud) applications and their management. It provides a standardized, well-defined, portable, and modular exchange format for the structure of the application's components, the relationships among them, and their corresponding management functionalities. In this section, we provide a brief overview on the main concepts (Sect. 22.2.1) and which challenges in the are of cloud computing are addressed by TOSCA (Sect. 22.2.2).

22.2.1 Main Concepts of TOSCA

TOSCA enables full automated deployment, termination, and further management functionalities, such as scaling or backing up applications through the combination of the two TOSCA main concepts: (1) Application topologies and (2) management plans. Application topologies provide a structural description of the application, the components it consists of and the relationships among them. Each node is accompanied with a list of operations it offers to manage itself. Thus, the topology is not only a description of the application's components and their relations, but also an explicit

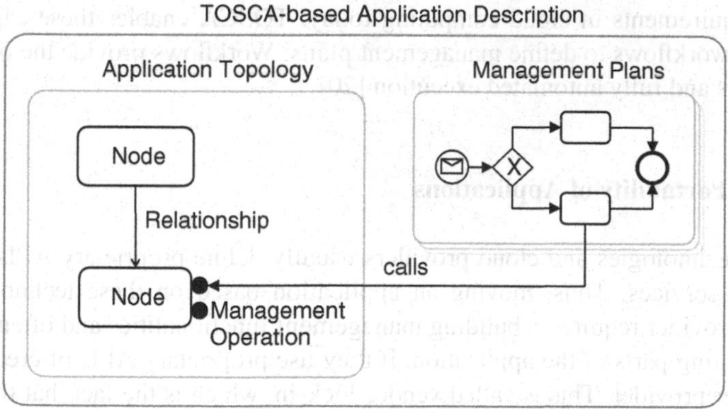

Fig. 22.1 Relation of TOSCA concepts

declaration of its management capabilities. Management plans combine these management capabilities to create higher-level management tasks, which can then be executed fully automated to deploy, configure, manage, and operate the application. Figure 22.1 presents an abstract TOSCA-based application description, showing the two TOSCA main concepts and their relation: The application topology contains nodes, which are connected by relationships. Management plan are started by an external message and call management operations of the nodes in the topology.

22.2.2 Challenges Addressed by TOSCA

In the area of cloud computing, there is a number of research challenges (cf. [9, 14]). This section discusses three major challenges and how TOSCA addresses them, namely ensure the portability of applications (Sect. 22.2.2.1), enable the automated management of applications (Sect. 22.2.2.2), and allow interoperability and re-usability of application components (Sect. 22.2.2.3).

22.2.2.1 Automated Management

The management of applications plays an important role in enterprise IT (see Sect. 22.1). Especially external solutions impose the problem that the respective management knowledge must be acquired by each user, which usually results in slow and error prone manual management. TOSCA aims to formally capture the knowledge of the creator of the IT solution, who has all the knowledge of the solution's internals and proven best practices, in management plans [2]. These plans make the management of complex enterprise applications automated, repeatable, traceable, and less error prone. Users can easily fulfil management tasks without deep knowledge on how to manage the IT solution.

Management plans are portable between various environments and can be executed fully automated to support self-service management and rapid elasticity, both major requirements in cloud computing today. TOSCA enables these capabilities by using workflows to define management plans: Workflows provide the properties portability and fully automated execution [20].

22.2.2.2 Portability of Applications

Current technologies and cloud providers usually define proprietary APIs to manage their services. Thus, moving an application based on these technologies to another provider requires rebuilding management functionalities and often even re-implementing parts of the application, if they use proprietary APIs offered only by the former provider. This is called vendor lock-in, which is the fact that the investment to switch from one provider to another provider is too expensive for a customer to be done economically. There is current research on technologies abstracting from concrete APIs towards a unified interface for different APIs in order to reduce the problem of vendor lock-in, for example the work by Petcu et al. [29]. This may prevent vendor lock-in on the lower level but the user is then locked into this unified API, if, for instance, the unified API does not support certain providers. Research on this issue has already proposed solutions for supporting movability and migration of applications on a functional level, but especially application portability in terms their (automated) management is still a big problem [3, 19, 30]. TOSCA achieves portability by fomalizing the application topology as well as its management in a self-contained way. Each component defines and implements its management functionality in a portable way. How TOSCA achieves portability is discussed in detail in Sect. 22.5.

22.2.2.3 Interoperability and Reusability of Application Components

TOSCA aims to enable the interoperability and reusability of application components such as Web servers, operating systems, virtual machines, and databases. These components are defined in a reusable manner by the developers, providers, or third parties together with their executables. Components of different providers do not stand on their own, as TOSCA enables combining them into new composite applications. Thus, TOSCA enables defining, building, and packaging the building blocks of an application in a completely self-contained manner. This allows a standardized way to reuse them in different applications.

22.3 TOSCA in Detail

TOSCA conceptually consists of two different parts: (1) The structural description of the application, called topology, and (2) the standardized description of the application's management by plans. These concepts are explained in Sects. 22.3.1 and 22.3.2 in detail. Instantiating the topology requires software files such as installables. In TOSCA, required software files, the topology and the management plans are packaged into one TOSCA archive. Section 22.3.3 describes this packaging. Section 22.3.4 describes an application topology example with a respective management plan for deploying the exemplary application.

22.3.1 TOSCA Application Topologies

In TOSCA, the structure of a composite application is explicitly modeled by a colored graph called "application topology". Vertices represent the components of a composite application, edges represent different kinds of relations between these components. Relations may be, for example, one component is *hosted on*, *depends*

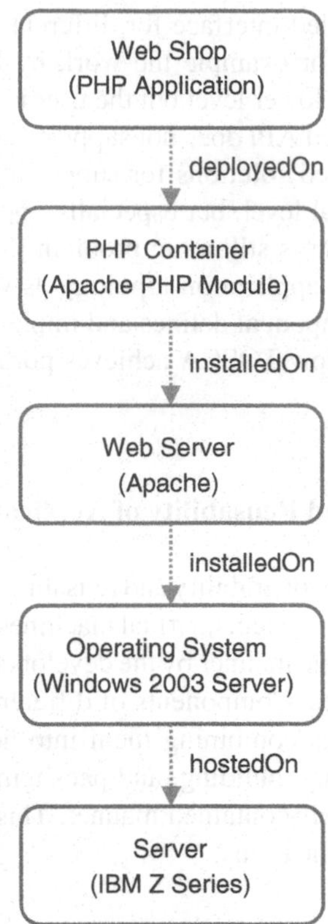

Fig. 22.2 Conceptual layers of TOSCA-based applications

on, or *communicates with* another component. Figure 22.2 shows a PHP example topology delivering a PHP Web shop: A Windows 2003 Server operating system is hosted on an IBM server. Thereon, an Apache Web server is installed together with the PHP module on which the PHP application is deployed.

Vertices and edges in the topology may define additional properties, the management operations they offer, the artifacts required to run the component, or non-functional requirements. It is important to note that TOSCA does not only define the functional aspects of vertices and edges, i.e., providing a certain business functionality such as a Web service implementation, but in addition defines their management operations, for example, how to setup the component, establish a relation, deploy artifacts, scale-up, or backup. These management functionalities are reflected in the topology model and are the basis for the automated management concept of TOSCA, which is described in Sect. 22.3.2.

Figure 22.3 presents the structural elements of a Service Template: The Topology Template, Node Templates, Relationship Templates, and their types. The term *template* is used to indicate that it may be instantiated more than once and does not

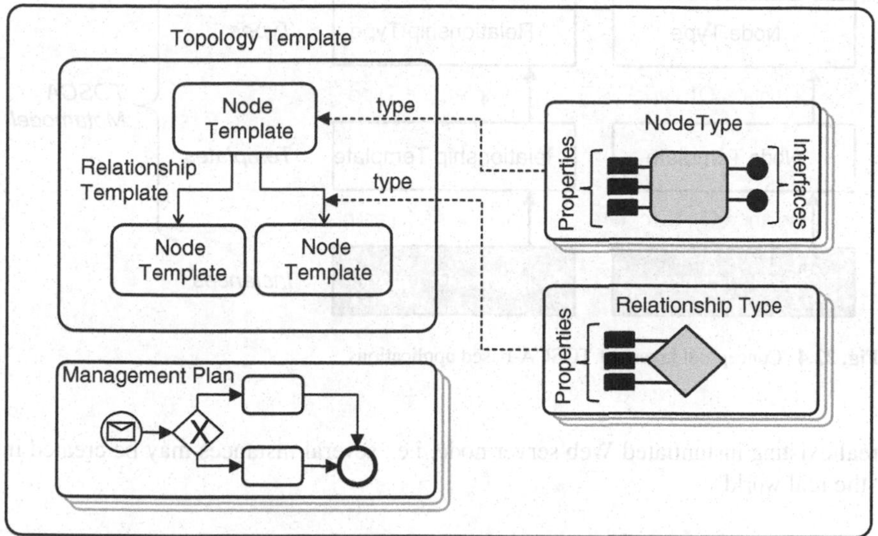

Fig. 22.3 General structure of TOSCA service template (adapted from [24])

reflect the existing infrastructure. Each template is associated with a type, which defines the semantics of the template.

The layers of the topology are discussed in detail in Sect. 22.3.1.1. Section 22.3.1.2 details Node Types and Relationship Types. Node Templates and Relationship Templates are detailed in Sect. 22.3.1.3.

22.3.1.1 Conceptual Layers of TOSCA

To enable a clear understanding of TOSCA it is important to distinguish three conceptual layers as shown in Fig. 22.4: TOSCA defines a metamodel and exchange format for (1) types and (2) templates, which results in a third layer, the (3) instance layer, which depends on the TOSCA runtime (discussed in Sect. 22.4.2).

The metamodel layer defines Node Templates, which represent components, and Relationship Templates, representing the relations among the components, e.g., a *hosted on* relationship is used to define that a Web server component is hosted on an operating system component. These templates are typed with reusable types, i.e., Node Type for Node Templates and Relationship Type for Relationship Templates, respectively. These types are conceptually comparable to abstract classes in Java, whereas the templates are comparable to concrete classes extending these abstract classes.

The instance-layer represents the real instances of the components and relationships defined by templates. Thus, an instance of a Web server Node Template is a

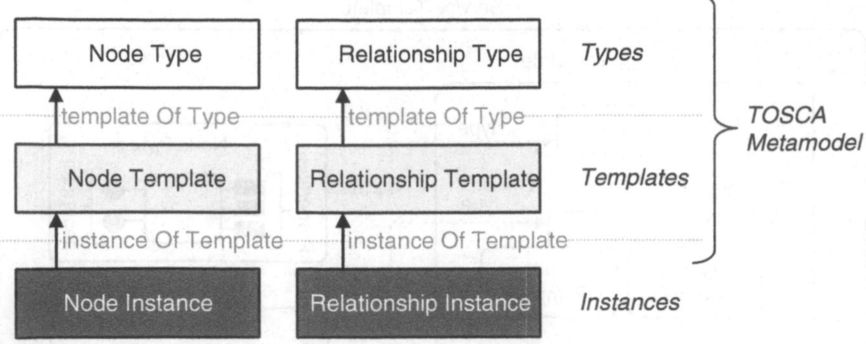

Fig. 22.4 Conceptual layers of TOSCA-based applications

real existing instantiated Web server node, i.e., several instances may be created in "the real world".

22.3.1.2 Node Types and Relationship Types

This section describes the information TOSCA offers to specify at Node Types and Relationship Types.

Properties of Node Instances. A node instance may have properties. Therefore, the respective Node Type references an XSD element (or type, [35]) declaring the schema for the actual property document. Properties are runtime information such as IP address, username, configuration, ports, and all other information required for deployment and management of the application. XSD supports lists and other complex structures, which basically allows to store all kind of information. In addition, XSD defines a strict schema for the resulting properties which can be used for validation. Templates are capable to define property defaults used at instantiation, for instance, the default port or username of the administrative interface. Support for reading and writing the properties is offered by a TOSCA container, which is explained in Sect. 22.4.2.

Deployment Artifacts. Deployment Artifacts specify the actual implementation of a Node Type. For example, an operating system type may have an image as Deployment Artifact and a Web server Node Type a Tomcat servlet container installable. During deployment of the application, the Deployment Artifacts are put onto the respective node. The concrete deployment procedure is not defined in the TOSCA topology. It is up to the management plans and management operations of the nodes.

Lifecycle Definition. Relationship instances and node instances may be in different states which aggregate the complex internal state of the instance. Example states are starting, running, stopping, and error. During runtime, each instance is in one of these states. The transition between the states is not described in a TOSCA model itself: The management plans and management operations trigger transitions between the states. A TOSCA model defines, however, which states are possible in general: The possible states are defined as URIs in the respective types.

Management and Implementation Artifacts. Each hardware and software component offers explicit and implicit management capabilities. Explicit capabilities are startup parameters, configuration files, management interfaces, hardware buttons and so on. Implicit capabilities are descriptions of how to backup the application by copying a certain file, for instance. Offered operations include deployment operations, which are the deployment of an application on an application server or instantiating a new virtual machine, for instance. Further operations are offered for the *management* of an application, for example, upgrade, backup, scale up, and configure. A new concept introduced by TOSCA is that management capabilities of Node Types and Relationship Types are explicitly defined as REST-Service [10], WSDL-service [6], or scripts [26]. However, not all management capabilities of nodes are accessible that way. This is either because of technical reasons, such as incompatible protocols, or due to logical reasons, such as the operation being part of a composed operation. Management plans require standardized interface descriptions to be able to access management operations (see Sect. 22.3.2). Offering management capabilities not directly accessible by TOSCA plans is done by *Implementation Artifacts*. They are basically small management applications delivered together with the TOSCA application (cf. Sect. 22.3.3). Implementation Artifacts expose management capabilities of a Node Type via REST, WSDL, or script interfaces. Internally, they can do anything required to provide this functionality, including the invokation of management capabilities not compatible with TOSCA before. This ensures that all management operations are either offered by the node itself, an external service, a script, or an Implementation Artifact. Therefore, each Node Type or Relationship Type is self-contained with respect to its management. These basic management operations are then orchestrated by management plans into higher level management functionality spanning the whole application and, therefore, making the application self-contained with respect to its management.

Policies. TOSCA provides a generic container for attaching policies, for example, using WS-Policy [36] or the Rei Ontology [13], to nodes and relationships. The TOSCA specification does not state how and when policies are evaluated; it is only expected that a TOSCA-compliant environment respects these policies. Two examples for using policies are a connection (represented by a Relationship Template) with a policy that this connection must be encrypted and a server (represented by a Node Template) with a policy that a certain power consumption must not be exceeded during operation.

Standardized and Derivation Types. Node Types and Relationship Types can be refined through derivation [24, Sect. 4.3]. For instance, the Node Type `Tomcat` may be derived from Node Type `JavaApplicationServer` and the Relationship Type `JDBCConnection` may be derived from Relationship Type `connectsTo`. Each type may be derived from exactly one or no other type, which structures the types as trees.

Derivation enables groups of subject matter experts to standardize selected Node Types and Relationship Types. For instance, a generic virtual machine with its properties and operations may be offered as standardized Node Type. Vendors extend these standardized Node Types to offer their specific implementations. Besides offering standardized functionality, they might add proprietary functionality representing their competitive advantage. Offering different solutions under a common interface simplifies the creation of applications suitable for multiple environments and fosters portability.

From the ecosystem perspective (cf. Sect. 22.4), cloud and application providers may create and distribute libraries containing the Node Types and Relationship Types for their services and products to enable frictionless usage of them when building new applications.

22.3.1.3 Node Templates and Relationship Templates

Node Templates and Relationship Templates, which are typed with exactly one Node Type or Relationship Type respectively, are composed to create the Topology Template of a TOSCA application. Templates define how the respective type is instantiated for use in the application. Templates allow defining the start values of the properties by specifying defaults for the properties. Deployment Artifacts, Implementation Artifacts, and policies may be overwritten and extended to adjust the types for the usage in the respective application, for example, an *Web Shop Application* Node Template of Node Type *PHP Application* defines a Deployment Artifact, which contains the respective PHP application files. Additionally, constraints may be put on properties to ensure that the properties fit to the overall application. For instance, the IP range of an application might be restricted to internal IPs of the company.

A Node Template may be instantiated multiple times. For instance, this is the case when there are multiple cluster nodes of an application or database cluster. Instead of requiring to put multiple Node Templates into the Topology Template, the properties `minInstances` and `maxInstances` are offered to set the range of the number of instances. This concept also supports Node Templates having a variable number of instances during runtime. For instance, the number of cluster nodes may be scaled up and down between 2 and 10. During runtime, for each instance of a Topology Template, each Node Template instance has its own identity and properties. This is obviously required, for example, to have multiple cluster nodes being equal besides the properties IP address and average load.

Grouping subgraphs of the Topology Template is possible by using Group Templates, which can be nested, but not overlapping. Group Templates can be used to separate nodes technically. For instance, a database cluster may be scaled independently of the other parts of the application. Either physically, e.g., by hosting all nodes of the database cluster in one dedicated data center, or logically, e.g., by assigning all database cluster nodes to a certain operations department.

22.3.2 TOSCA Management Plans

Section 22.3.1.2 showed how nodes and relationships offer their management capabilities. Based on the brief introduction to the concepts of management plans in Sect. 22.2, this section discusses details of the management plan concept. Management plans are not restricted to management operations of one node or relationship, but can also invoke a series of operations from different nodes, relationships, and also external services, including a human task interface [23]. Therefore, they are able to cover all kind of management tasks required by a TOSCA application.

Without TOSCA, the deployment and management of composite applications requires extensive, mostly manual, effort by the administrator, e.g., installing software on servers by using installation software provided on a DVD, logging onto servers updating applications, or creating backups. Each user has to learn on its own how to manage and operate the application, most of them making the same experiences and encounter the same difficulties, acquire management knowledge, and sometimes automate some management aspects through scripts. This is even more complicated for complex composite applications involving a large number of components by different vendors, which are combined to provide a certain business functionality. It requires significant knowledge and effort to provision, deploy, configure, manage, and, finally, terminate the components and their relationships [31]. TOSCA tackles these issues by enabling application developers and operators to capture reoccurring management tasks as management plans, which can be executed fully automated and thus decrease manual effort for application management and operation. Plans formalize the management knowledge and best practices implicitly for everyone to reuse. The management cost of applications described using TOSCA, including management plans, is significantly lower, especially because enterprises executing these management plans must not know all the details behind the management best practices. Figure 22.5 presents a simplified management plan used to deploy a PHP-based application: The plan installs an Apache Web server on a Windows operating system, installs the PHP module on that Web server, and finally deploys the PHP application thereon.

Automation of application management is a prerequisite to realize key cloud properties. Most important are self-service and rapid elasticity. Self-service means that a customer can instantiate and manage his application instance himself, e.g., add a new email account. Rapid elasticity enables on demand growing and shrinking of resources depending on the user needs, e.g., extending the storage of an email account. When going beyond cloud computing, automation has always been a key goal in IT service and application management. We want to stress that, despite its name, TOSCA is by no means restricted to cloud applications.

TOSCA does not introduce a new language for modeling and executing plans. Instead, TOSCA includes plans by using existing workflow languages such as the Business Process Model and Notation (BPMN, [25]) or the Business Process Execution Language (BPEL, [22]). By using workflow technology to automate management tasks, TOSCA benefits from all the capabilities and properties of workflow languages and workflow execution environments. These properties include parallel

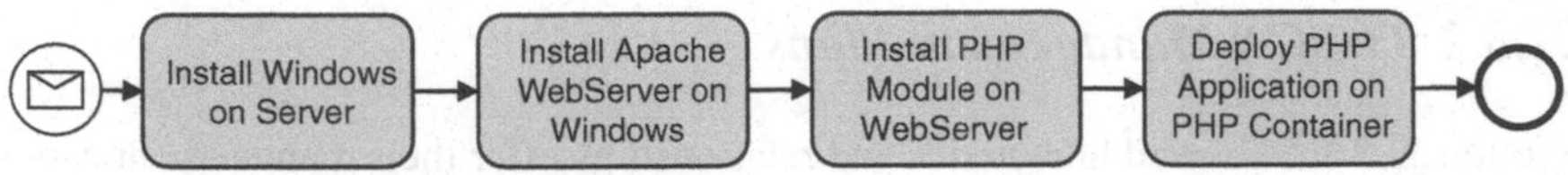

Fig. 22.5 Example management plan for deploying a PHP-based application

execution, monitoring, compensation, recovery, auditing, and tracing functionalities [20]. In addition, established workflow languages and environments also support human tasks to include manual work into the management plans. A typical example for a manual task, which cannot be executed automatically without human intervention, is installing physical infrastructure such as servers, network components, or storage as basis for virtualized environments. Using workflow technology moves the low level management tasks onto business processes level and makes them accessible to people or software not aware of the technical management details.

To ensure portability of management plans, TOSCA relies on the portability of standardized workflow languages such as BPEL and BPMN. The recommended workflow language for TOSCA management plans is BPMN. However, TOSCA allows plans to be defined in any workflow language providing clear execution semantics required for automated execution. Unfortunately, not all existing languages are suitable as many process modeling languages focus either on modeling or on execution [16, 28, 32].

22.3.2.1 Scripts and Plans

Today, many tasks in systems and operations management of applications are already automated by using scripts. These scripts are typically—often manually—copied to the target system on which they are executed. In comparison to plans, these scripts can be seen as microflows: small isolated pieces of work which can be executed fast and do not require transactional support, called micro script stream without transactions by Leymann and Roller [20]. In TOSCA, scripts are used for small management tasks such as setting up databases on a single component, whereas plans are used for large management tasks typically involving multiple components such as deploying a Tomcat servlet container on a Linux operating system followed by the configuration of both components. Of course, both concepts can be combined to provide the ability of specifying management operations on different layers of granularity. Then, plans represent workflows orchestrating several microflows represented by scripts.

A main benefit of this separation of concerns is provided by the combination of both concepts: Plans can use scripts to do more fine grained work directly on the target components while all problems of script handling such as data passing from and to other tasks, error handling, compensation, and recovery can be done by the workflow technology, which is on a much more coarse grained layer. Thus, wrapping script handling through workflow technology increases the level of abstraction for the operators as they do not have to deal with the deep technical details of script handling [15]. This is in line with the programming-in-the-large idea by DeRemer and Kron [8], which is applied by the workflow technology, too [20].

22.3.2.2 Plan Usage of the Application Topology Model

Management plans may inspect the application topology to retrieve nodes and relationships in order to manage them. This may be necessary for flexible plans not developed for one specific application topology to manage, but for multiple different topologies consisting of similar structures, or at least similar components. Thus, the plan needs information about the concrete structure of the considered topology to find the respective components and relationships therein the plan is supposed to manage. One example is a large topology consisting of multiple software stacks and a plan which updates the operating system components of each stack.

Management plans are executed on external workflow engines and may do various kinds of manipulations on the node and relationship instances. During operation, the state of node and relationship instances may change. For instance, the patch level of an operating system changes after installing a patch on an operating system node. To transfer this state information between different management plans, they need to store this information externally of the workflow context to make them accessible by various stakeholders. Therefore, the possible properties of nodes are explicitly defined by a schema to standardize accessing them. This information is included in the application topology model (see Sect. 22.3.1.2) and plans may read and write these service instance state information [2].

22.3.3 Packaging

A TOSCA Service Template defines application topologies and corresponding management plans. The physical associated files such as Implementation Artifacts and Deployment Artifacts, scripts, or XML schema files are packaged together with the actual Service Template into a TOSCA archive, called "Cloud Service Archive (CSAR)" [24, Sect. 3.3]. This standardized archive format provides a way to package applications fully self-contained, with all required management functionalities into one single file used for installing the application. Thus, the archive can be seen as single installable for complex composite applications including their management. A TOSCA archive can be deployed on a TOSCA runtime environment (see Sect. 22.4.2) which is responsible for installing the application package, i.e., processing the archive. TOSCA archives follow a standardized format ensuring portability between different TOSCA runtime environments and thus provide an exchange format for complex composite applications including their management functionalities. Figure 22.6 shows the conceptual structure of a TOSCA archive.

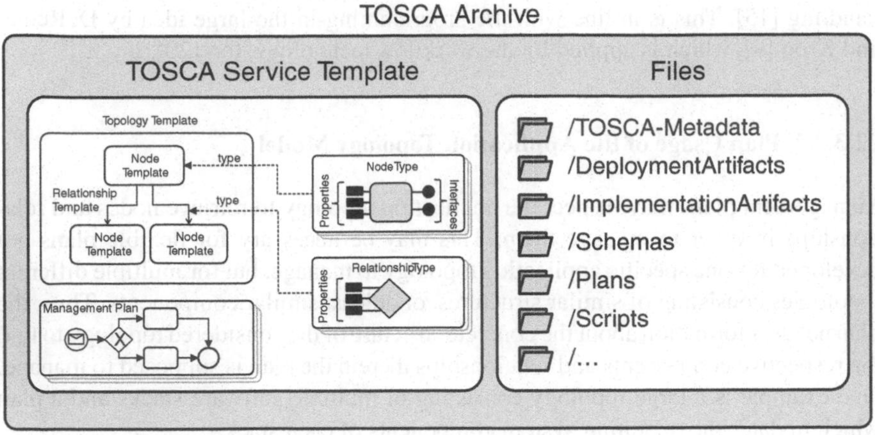

Fig. 22.6 Conceptual structure of TOSCA archives

22.3.4 TOSCA-Based Example Application

In this section we describe a TOSCA application example and a corresponding build plan, which deploys and instantiates the application. The example implements an online Web shop which consists of two functionally different software stacks: The first stack provides a Web-based GUI for the Web shop application, the second stack provides product information data stored in a MySQL database accessible through a REST API which is called by the Web-based GUI.

The complete application topology is presented in Fig. 22.7. The stack providing the GUI is presented on the left side of the figure. The infrastructure layer of this stack consists of a *Server* Node Template of Node Type IBM Z Series. This represents a physical server node. Thereon runs a Windows operating system represented by an Operating System Node Template of Node Type Windows 2003 Server. On this OS, a Web server Node Template of Node Type Apache runs with an installed PHP Module, which in turn is represented as a PHP Container Node Template of Node Type Apache PHP Module. This container is able to run PHP-based applications. The Web Shop Node Template of Node Type PHP Application implements the GUI of the Web shop software and is hosted on the PHP Container.

The infrastructure layer of the second topology stack providing product data for the Web-based GUI consists of a Virtual Server Node Template of Node Type AWS EC2 Server. This is an Infrastructure-as-a-Service (IaaS, [21]) offering provided by Amazon.[1] On this virtualized infrastructure an operating system of Node Type Windows 7 runs in a VM which is represented by an Operating System VM Node Template. On this operating system, there are two components hosted on: A Servlet Container Node Template of Node Type Tomcat and the Product Database Node

[1] http://aws.amazon.com/ec2/

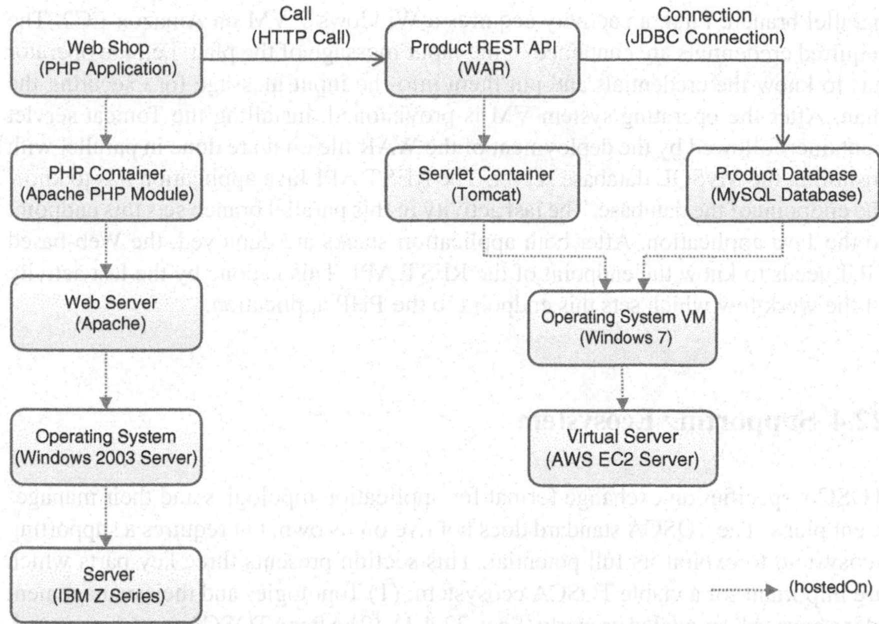

Fig. 22.7 Example TOSCA application topology

Template of Node Type MySQL Database, which represents the database in which the product data are stored. On the servlet container, there is a REST API providing access to the product data stored in the database. The API is implemented as Java application, which is deployed as Web Archive (WAR) file. This Java application is hosted on the Tomcat servlet container and is represented as Product REST API Node Template of Node Type WAR hosted on the servlet container node. For simplification reasons, we modeled all runsIn, deployedOn, and installedIn relations as hostedOn relation, which is the parent Relationship Type for all these Relationship Types.

The Build Plan shown in Fig. 22.8 is responsible for deploying both software stacks. We simplified the plan in some points to reduce the degree of complexity. For instance, handling of security issues (e.g., password generation and storage) are hidden. BPMN supports parallel execution of tasks. Therefore, the two software stacks are deployed in parallel. First, the deployment of the Web-based GUI is described. The first activity installs the Windows 2003 Server operating system on a physical server whose IP-address is given by the input message of the Build Plan. Thus, for executing the plan, the IP-address of the server has to be known by the operator and written into the input message. After the OS is installed, the subsequent activity configures the operating system such as setting the correct firewall rules. After that, the Apache Web server is installed on the Windows 2003 operating system, the PHP Module is installed on the Apache Web server and the PHP Application is deployed into the PHP Container. The second software stack is deployed in the parallel branch. First, an activity acquires a Windows 7 VM on Amazon EC2. The required credentials are contained in the input message of the plan, i.e., the operator has to know the credentials and put them into the input message for executing the plan. After the operating system VM is provisioned, installing the Tomcat servlet container followed by the deployment of the WAR file on it are done in parallel with installing the MySQL database server. The REST API Java application has to know the endpoint of the database. The last activity in this parallel branch sets this endpoint to the Java application. After both application stacks are deployed, the Web-based GUI needs to know the endpoint of the REST API. This is done by the last activity of the workflow which sets this endpoint to the PHP application.

22.4 Supporting Ecosystem

TOSCA specifies an exchange format for application topologies and their management plans. The TOSCA standard does not live on its own, but requires a supporting ecosystem to exploit its full potential. This section presents three key parts which are important for a viable TOSCA ecosystem: (1) Topologies and their management plans have to be modeled properly (Sect. 22.4.1). (2) After a TOSCA model is created, it has to be interpreted by a TOSCA-compliant runtime environment to enable automatic deployment and management (Sect. 22.4.2). (3) Finally, Sect. 22.4.3 presents how an application marketplace could benefit from the new possibilities enabled by TOSCA.

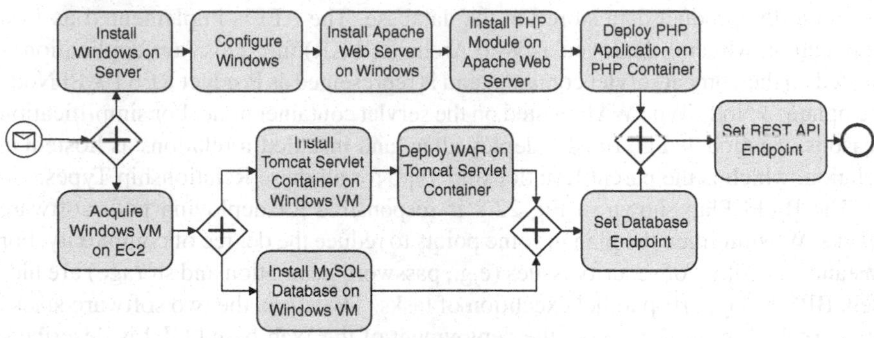

Fig. 22.8 Build plan for the example application

22.4.1 Modeling Tool Support

As TOSCA's representation format is XML, modeling TOSCA-based applications and their management plans, typically also having a textual XML representation, may be time-consuming when using text editors only. XML editors may be helpful as TOSCA defines a schema which can be used by the editor to provide features such as auto-completion and tag-proposals. These tools might help avoiding syntactic errors and improve the speed of creating models compared to pure text editors. Nevertheless, they are still uncomfortable as manual typing is error prone and semantical dependencies are hard to recognize textually by the user or the tool.

Therefore, graphical modeling tools tailored towards TOSCA could reduce the effort significantly as topologies as well as plans can be represented visually easily. For example, modeling topologies can be enriched with graphical details, such as icons for nodes, which supports a faster recognition of the semantics. Thus, semantic errors, such as wrong hostedOn-relationships, can be recognized faster by the user. In addition, the speed of modeling increases noticeably as a lot of unnecessary typing is spared. As modeling of topologies as well as modeling of plans can be done graphically, some modeling tools combine both activities. This is an important advantage as bringing together modeling of topologies and corresponding management plans might be cumbersome—especially for annoying frequently reoccurring tasks such as copying IDs, creating boilerplate code, and so on. Enhancing a BPMN modeling tool to provide a tight integration with TOSCA has been presented by Kopp et al. [15]. TOSCA-tailored graphical modeling tools also may support reusability of Node Types by providing existing Node Types in a palette for dragging them into the topology, for example. Automated management of a variety of artifacts and exporting them into a TOSCA archive as described in Sect. 22.3.3 additionally reduces the complexity and assists the user.

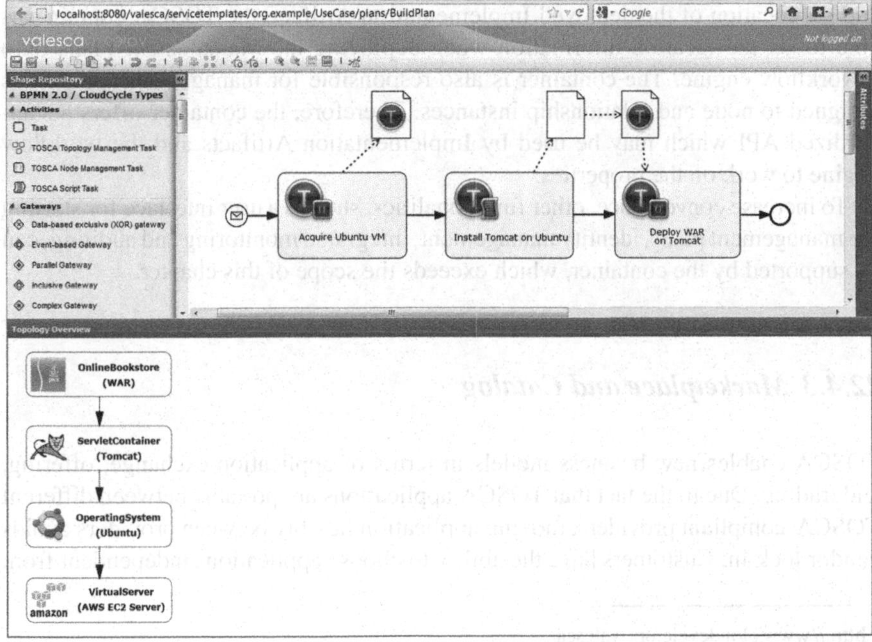

Fig. 22.9 Screenshot of Valesca

One open source implementation of a TOSCA-tailored graphical tool combining the modeling of TOSCA application topologies and associated management plans is "Valesca".[2] It implements "Vino4TOSCA" [4], a visual notation for TOSCA topologies. Valesca uses the Signavio Core Components,[3] which are the commercially-supported enhancements of Oryx [7]. Figure 22.9 shows a screenshot. Valesca supports all the advantages mentioned above and is provided under the Apache 2.0 license.

22.4.2 TOSCA Container

To use all the features of TOSCA—especially automation of application management—a TOSCA-compliant runtime is required. Without such a container, TOSCA could be used as pure exchange format and manually operated according to the definitions in the Service Template. However, a bare-minimum TOSCA container stores and serves the files contained in the TOSCA archive, installs and operates Implementation Artifacts and Management Plans, and manages the instance data of the application: The container is the glue between these functionalities. During modeling the management plans are written without knowing the exact location of the Implementation Artifacts, only referencing the abstract service description (port type and operation in case of WSDL services). Implementation Artifacts are deployed by the TOSCA container to the respective runtime, for example, Java Web services to an Apache Tomcat known and managed by the TOSCA container. Knowing the runtime and the location of the deployed Implementation Artifact, the TOSCA container is able to set the location information when deploying the Management Plans onto a workflow engine. The container is also responsible for managing the properties assigned to node and relationship instances. Therefore, the container offers a standardized API which may be used by Implementation Artifacts and the workflow engine to work on the properties.

To increase convenience, other functionalities, such as a user interface for starting the management plans, identity management, integrated monitoring and auditing, can be supported by the container, which exceeds the scope of this chapter.

22.4.3 Marketplace and Catalog

TOSCA enables new business models in terms of application exchange, offering, and trading. Due to the fact that TOSCA applications are portable between different TOSCA-compliant providers, moving application flexibly between providers avoids vendor lock-in: Customers have the ability to choose applications independent from

---

2 http://www.cloudcycle.org/valesca/

3 http://code.google.com/p/signavio-core-components/

the cloud provider which hosts the application later on. This enables a new kind of marketplaces for trading manageable and portable applications which can be hosted by any TOSCA-compliant provider, as shown in Fig. 22.10. Inside enterprises, the TOSCA ecosystem enables offering self-service catalogs which allow flexible and rapid deployment of business applications.

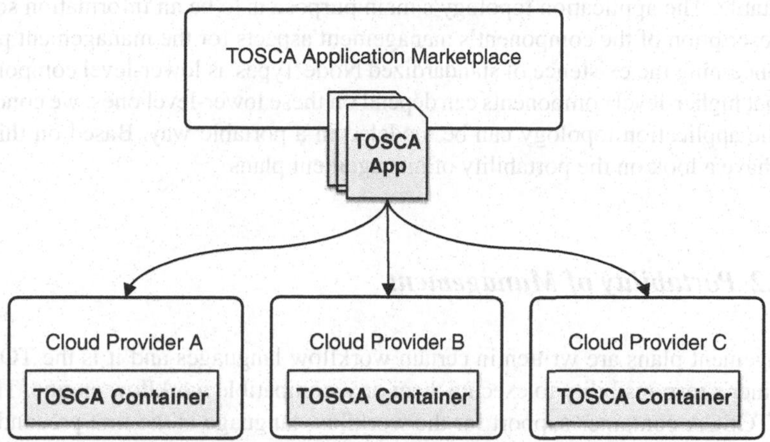

Fig. 22.10 Sketch of an TOSCA application marketplace

22.5 Portability

As portability is a central goal of TOSCA, this section discusses in detail how TOSCA supports portability (Sects. 22.5.1 and 22.5.2) and propose how modelers can increase the portability of their TOSCA applications (Sect. 22.5.3).

22.5.1 Portability of Applications

TOSCA addresses the portability of application descriptions and their management, not the portability of the application components themselves. That means, TOSCA does not make Deployment Artifacts portable, e.g., to run a .net application on Apache Tomcat or to migrate one flavor of relational database system to another.

The application topology may have some prerequisites concerning the environment it is deployed on. For instance, it might require an external service such as Amazon EC2 or inhouse infrastructure such as VMware. However, there are ways to abstract from concrete providers and increase portability between different environments, for example, by using software such as Deltacloud,[4] which unifies the APIs of

[4] http://deltacloud.apache.org/

different cloud infrastructure providers into a common interface or by using a generic and standardized virtual machine Node Type as described in Sect. 22.3.1.2, which can be bound to different implementations. The remaining parts of the application topology are built on top of these lower-level infrastructure and, therefore, are basically self-contained inside this application topology. Thus, they only depend on the lower-level infrastructure components. If these are portable, the whole application is portable. The application topology's main purpose is to be an information source and description of the component's management aspects for the management plans. By concerning the existence of standardized Node Types as lower-level components and that higher-level components can depend on these lower-level ones, we conclude that the application topology can be modeled in a portable way. Based on this we must have a look on the portability of management plans.

22.5.2 Portability of Management

Management plans are written in certain workflow languages and it is the TOSCA container's responsibility to execute them on a compatible workflow engine. Therefore, TOSCA container support for the workflow language is the first precondition for TOSCA portability, which is, however, softened to some extend by the fact that BPMN is the recommended workflow language in TOSCA. Management plans are orchestrations of three types of services: (1) External services, which are portable, because services are, by definition, accessible from everywhere [6], (2) management operations offered by Node Types and Relationship Types, and (3) APIs of the TOSCA container, for example, to access the instance data of the application instance. As discussed in Sect. 22.3.1.2, the management operations can be provided as Implementation Artifacts, whose execution is also the TOSCA container's responsibility. The API of the TOSCA container will be standardized. Therefore, support for the language of the Implementation Artifact by the TOSCA container is the second precondition for TOSCA portability.

Consequently, the portability of TOSCA applications only fails if the type of management plan or Implementation Artifact is not known and supported by the TOSCA container. We want to highlight that both of them, management plans and Implementation Artifacts, represent the management part of TOSCA and are not the actual application. Moreover, we expect most TOSCA containers to provide some kind of extensibility mechanism to add plugins supporting additional plan types and additional Implementation Artifact types. A couple of basic types will then be offered by most of the TOSCA containers, which will provide a solid basis for portable TOSCA applications.

22.5.3 Improving Portability of TOSCA Applications

The conclusions of the previous two sections lead to the following recommendations on how to increase the portability of a TOSCA application: For Implementation Artifacts, the goal is to provide them in programming languages, which are widely supported by TOSCA containers. Due to the fact that Implementation Artifacts are bound to Node Types and Relationship Types, they are widely reused so it may be worth the effort to do multiple implementations. Management plans are tied to the actual application and, therefore, their level of reusability is lower than reusability for Implementation Artifacts. Providing them in multiple workflow languages would also increase their portability, but doing this manually might not be worth the effort. Fortunately, there are existing approaches to transform workflow languages [32], for example, transforming BPMN to BPEL by using the approach by Ouyang et al. [27]. In addition, due to the fact that BPMN is the recommended workflow language for management plans, a wide variety of TOSCA containers will presumably support BPMN.

22.6 Conclusions

This chapter presented the upcoming OASIS standard Topology and Orchestration Specification for Cloud Applications (TOSCA). We highlighted that TOSCA distinguishes between the application topology and management plans. The application topology declares the components of the application and their relationships as a graph. We discussed that each vertex in the graph represents a Node Template, which has a Node Type and is instantiated as node instance. The management plans invoke management operations on these node instances.

TOSCA is a standard not providing any software and, therefore, requires an ecosystem. We gave a short overview on possible modeling tool support and runtime support. TOSCA packages may be distributed directly by a software vendor or available through dedicated marketplaces.

At the point of writing this chapter, the TOSCA specification was not finally released. However, we expect no fundamental changes going beyond what we described. One can follow the current development of the TOSCA specification on the OASIS TC website[5] and the development of the OpenTOSCA ecosystem of the University of Stuttgart on the OpenTOSCA website[6].

Acknowledgments This work was partially funded by the BMWi project CloudCycle (project 01MD11023).

5 http://www.oasis-open.org/committees/tc_home.php?wg_abbrev=tosca

6 http://www.opentosca.org

References

1. Armbrust, M., Fox, A., Griffith, R., Joseph, A., Katz, R., Konwinski, A., Lee, G., Patterson, D., Rabkin, A., Stoica, I., et al.: Above the Clouds: A Berkeley View of Cloud Computing. Tech. Rep. UCB/EECS-2009-28, EECS Department, University of California, Berkeley (2009)
2. Binz, T., Breiter, G., Leymann, F., Spatzier, T.: Portable Cloud Services Using TOSCA. IEEE Internet Computing **16**(03), 80–85 (2012). doi:10.1109/MIC.2012.43
3. Binz, T., Leymann, F., Schumm, D.: CMotion: A Framework for Migration of Applications into and between Clouds. In: Proceedings of the 2011 IEEE International Conference on Service-Oriented Computing and Applications (SOCA). IEEE Computer Society Conference Publishing Services (2011). doi:10.1109/SOCA.2011.6166250
4. Breitenbücher, U., Binz, T., Kopp, O., Leymann, F., Schumm, D.: Vino4TOSCA: A Visual Notation for Application Topologies based on TOSCA. In: Proceedings of the 20th International Conference on Cooperative Information Systems (CoopIS 2012), Lecture Notes in Computer Science. Springer-Verlag (2012) doi:10.1007/978-3-642-33606-5_25
5. Buyya, R., Yeo, C.S., Venugopal, S., Broberg, J., Brandic, I.: Cloud computing and emerging it platforms: Vision, hype, and reality for delivering computing as the 5th utility. Future Generation Computer Systems **25**(6), 599–616 (2009). doi:10.1016/j.future.2008.12.001
6. Curbera, F., Leymann, F., Storey, T., Ferguson, D., Weerawarana, S.: Web Services Platform Architecture: SOAP, WSDL, WS-Policy, WS-Addressing, WS-BPEL, WS-Reliable Messaging and More. Prentice Hall PTR (2005).
7. Decker, G., Overdick, H., Weske, M.: Oryx - An Open Modeling Platform for the BPM Community. In: Proceedings of the 6th International Conference on Business Process Management (2008). doi:10.1007/978-3-540-85758-7_29
8. DeRemer, F., Kron, H.: Programming-in-the-Large Versus Programming-in-the-Small. Software Engineering, IEEE Transactions on **SE-2**(2), 80–86 (1976). doi:10.1109/TSE.1976.233534
9. Dillon, T., Wu, C., Chang, E.: Cloud Computing: Issues and Challenges. In: Advanced Information Networking and Applications (AINA), 2010 24th IEEE International Conference on, pp. 27–33 (2010). doi:10.1109/AINA.2010.187
10. Fielding, R.: Architectural styles and the design of network-based software architectures. Ph.D. thesis, University of California (2000)
11. Garbani, J., Mendel, T., Radcliffe, E.: The Writing on ITs Complexity Wall (2010). Forrester Research
12. Gartner: Gartner Identifies the Top 10 Strategic Technologies for 2011 (2010). Press Release
13. Kagal, L.: Rei Ontology Specifications, Ver 2.0 (2012). http://www.csee.umbc.edu/~lkagal1/rei/
14. Khajeh-Hosseini, A., Sommerville, I., I, S.: Research Challenges for Enterprise Cloud Computing. Tech. rep., LSCITS (2010)
15. Kopp, O., Binz, T., Breitenbücher, U., Leymann, F.: BPMN4TOSCA: A Domain-Specific Language to Model Management Plans for Composite Applications. In: 4th International Workshop on the Business Process Model and Notation. Springer (2012) doi:10.1007/978-3-642-33155-8_4
16. Kopp, O., Martin, D., Wutke, D., Leymann, F.: The Difference Between Graph-Based and Block-Structured Business Process Modelling Languages. Enterprise Modelling and Information Systems **4**(1), 3–13 (2009)
17. Leymann, F.: Cloud Computing: The Next Revolution in IT. In: Proc. 52th Photogrammetric Week, pp. 3–12. Wichmann Verlag (2009)
18. Leymann, F.: Cloud Computing. it - Information Technology **53**(4) (2011) doi:10.1524/itit.2011.9070
19. Leymann, F., Fehling, C., Mietzner, R., Nowak, A., Dustdar, S.: Moving Applications to the Cloud: An Approach based on Application Model Enrichment. International Journal of Cooperative Information Systems (IJCIS) **20**(3), 307–356 (2011). doi:10.1142/S0218843011002250

20. Leymann, F., Roller, D.: Production Workflow - Concepts and Techniques. Prentice Hall PTR (2000)
21. Mell, P., Grance, T.: Cloud Computing Definition. National Institute of Standards and Technology (2009)
22. OASIS: Web Services Business Process Execution Language Version 2.0 - OASIS Standard (2007). https://www.oasis-open.org/committees/wsbpel/
23. OASIS: WS-BPEL Extension for People (BPEL4People) Specification Version 1.1 (2010). http://docs.oasis-open.org/bpel4people/bpel4people-1.1.html
24. OASIS: Topology and Orchestration Specification for Cloud Applications Version 1.0 Committee Specification Draft 03 (2012). http://docs.oasis-open.org/tosca/TOSCA/v1.0/csd03/TOSCA-v1.0-csd03.html
25. OMG: Business Process Model and Notation (BPMN) Version 2.0 (2011). http://www.omg.org/spec/BPMN/2.0/. OMG Document Number: formal/2011-01-03
26. Ousterhout, J.: Scripting: Higher level programming for the 21st century. Computer 31(3), 23–30 (1998)
27. Ouyang, C., Dumas, M., ter Hofstede, A., van der Aalst, W.: Pattern-based Translation of BPMN Process Models to BPEL Services. International Journal of Web Services Research **5**(1), Idea Group Publishing (2008)
28. Palmer, N.: Understanding the BPMN-XPDL-BPEL Value Chain. Business Integration Journal **November/December**, 54–55 (2006)
29. Petcu, D., Craciun, C., Rak, M.: Towards a Cross Platform Cloud API - Components for Cloud Federation. In: CLOSER. SciTePress (2011)
30. Petcu, D., Macariu, G., Panica, S., Crciun, C.: Portable Cloud applications–From theory to practice. Future Generation Computer Systems (2012). doi:10.1016/j.future.2012.01.009
31. Rus, I., Lindvall, M.: Knowledge management in software engineering. Software, IEEE 19(3), 26–38 (2002)
32. Stein, S., Kühne, S., Ivanov, K.: Business to IT Transformations Revisited. In: 1st International Workshop on Model-Driven Engineering for Business Process Management (2008). doi:10.1007/978-3-642-00328-8_18
33. Varia, J.: Architecting for the Cloud: Best Practices. Tech. rep., Amazon (2010). http://media.amazonwebservice.com/AWS_Cloud_Best_Practices.pdf
34. Varia, J.: Cloud Architectures. Tech. rep., Amazon (2010). http://jineshvaria.s3.amazonaws.com/public/cloudarchitectures-varia.pdf
35. W3C: XML Schema Part 1: Structures Second Edition (2004). http://www.w3.org/TR/xmlschema-1/
36. W3C: Web Services Policy 1.5 - Framework (2007). http://www.w3.org/TR/ws-policy/

Chapter 23
A V-Model Approach for Business Process Requirements Elicitation in Cloud Design

Nuno Ferreira, Nuno Santos, Ricardo J. Machado, José Eduardo Fernandes and Dragan Gasević

Abstract The benefits of cloud computing approaches are well known but designing logical architectures for that context can be difficult. When there are insufficient inputs for a typical (product) approach to requirements elicitation, a process-level perspective is an alternative way for achieving the intended logical design. We present a V-Model based approach to derive logical architectural models to execute in the different cloud layers from a process-level perspective, instead of the traditional product-level perspective. This V-Model approach encompasses the initial definition of the project goals and the process-level perspective of the systems intended logical architecture. The approach application results in the creation of a validated process-level structure and behavior architectural models that create a context for eliciting requirements for a cloud product. Throughout this process, we assess our decisions

N. Ferreira (✉)
I2S Informática, Sistemas e Serviços S.A., Porto, Portugal
e-mail: nuno.ferreira@i2s.pt

N. Santos
CCG—Centro de Computaao Gráfica,
Campus de Azurm, Guimaraes, Portugal
e-mail: nuno.santos@ccg.pt

R. J. Machado
Centro ALGORITMI, Escola de Engenharia,
Universidade do Minho, Guimaraes, Portugal
e-mail: rmac@dsi.uminho.pt

J. E. Fernandes
Bragança Polytechnic Institute, Bragança, Portugal
e-mail: jef@ipb.pt

D. Gasević
School of Computing and Information Systems,
Athabasca University, Alberta, Canada
e-mail: dgasevic@acm.org

A. Bouguettaya et al. (eds.), *Advanced Web Services*,
DOI: 10.1007/978-1-4614-7535-4_23,

based on the ARID method to identify process vulnerabilities and evaluate the quality of the derived logical architecture. We introduce a case study where our approach was applied and the resulting logical architectural model is presented.

23.1 Introduction

One of the top concerns of Information Technology (IT) managers for almost thirty years relates to IT and business alignment [27]. The importance of aligning IT with business needs for the purpose of attaining synergies and improvements in all the organization is a long-running problem with no visible or deterministic solution. There are many questions concerning this subject, going from how to align several strategic components of an organization with the necessary maturity or how business and IT are aligned with each other. Designing software architectures for a system to be executed in a cloud environment that ensures a proper alignment with the business needs and the possible IT solution is a difficult task. Typical software design approaches are based on a product-level perspective, that is, are based on the intended final product design characteristics. These approaches are not always feasible, namely when there is not enough information for eliciting the product requirements. Our proposed solution is based on a process-level perspective for designing a cloud computing architecture, with the purpose of contributing to a more accurate definition of product requirements and understanding of the development project scope.

We chose to represent an IT solution by its logical architecture in order to achieve a structured view of the system functionalities, resulting from a process of transforming business-level and technological-level decisions and requirements into a representation (model). This representation is fundamental to analyze and validate a system but is not enough for achieving a full transformation of the requirements into a model able to implement business stakeholders decisions. Therefore, to achieve such representativeness, we add artifacts that represent requirements at different levels of abstraction and promote an alignment between them and with the logical architecture. Those artifacts are, for instance, organizational configurations, processes or behavior representations.

Our approach requires the definition of information regarding the business context domain of an organization. This information concerns people, namely stakeholders, and also the processes they are involved in. Stakeholders are responsible for the decision making processes that influence the organizations strategy at any given level under analysis [10]. At the same time, the organization's software architecture and systems are also influenced by the decisions of the stakeholders regarding their own technical and business background.

We propose in this chapter a "Vee" Model-based adaptation (V-Model) [20], which suggests a roadmap for product design based on business needs. The model requires the identification of business needs and then, by successive artifact derivation it is possible to transit from a business-level perspective to an IT-level perspective and at the same time, assure the alignment of the requirements with the derived IT artifacts. This chapter also describes the extensions introduced into the Four-Step-Rule-Set (4SRS) method to be adopted at the process-level perspective in large-scale projects. The 4SRS method was first defined and detailed in [29]. The described extensions are focused on a process-level perspective to deliver a logical architectural model. This logical architectural model contributes to support the creation of context for the elicitation of requirements of the product to be developed. This chapter additionally illustrates a case study to present the applicability of the proposed approach in a real industrial project: ISOFIN—Interoperability in Financial Software, architecture capable to be implemented in the three typical cloud-layers: Infrastructure-as-a-Service (IaaS), Platform-as-a-Service (PaaS), and Software-as-a-Service (SaaS), as defined in [32]. The transformation of such context into product-level requirements does not belong to the scope of the present work.

This chapter is structured as follows: in Sect. 23.2 we present the core topics concerning business process requirements modeling through multiple views; Sect. 23.3 contains our V-Model representations (pictographic and SPEM) that is the basis of our work for business requirements, along with the derived artifacts and the alignment between them; Sect. 23.4 details the artifacts regarding organizational configurations and interactions; Sect. 23.5 describes the rationale for executing the 4SRS method in the process-level perspective rather than the traditional product-level perspective; Sect. 23.6 details the derivation of logical architectures as context for elicitation in cloud design and the assessment of the V-Model approach through ARID; and in Sect. 23.7 we present our work conclusions.

23.1.1 The ISOFIN Project

We assess the applicability of the proposed approach using a case study which results from the process-level requirements elicitation in a real project: the ISOFIN project [21]. This project aimed to deliver a set of coordinating services in a centralized infrastructure, enacting the coordination of independent services relying on separate infrastructures. The resulting ISOFIN platform contributes for the semantic and application interoperability between enrolled financial institutions (Banks, Insurance Companies and others), as depicted in Fig. 23.1. The global ISOFIN architecture relies on two main service types: Interconnected Business Service (IBS) and Supplier Business Service (SBS). IBSs concern a set of functionalities that are exposed from the ISOFIN core platform to ISOFIN Customers. An IBS interconnects one or more SBSs and/or IBSs exposing functionalities that relate directly to business needs. SBSs are a set of functionalities that are exposed from the ISOFIN Suppliers production infrastructure. Figure 23.1 encompasses the primary constructors (IBS, SBS and the ISOFIN Platform) available in the logical representations of the system: in the bottom layer there are SBSs that connect to IBSs in the ISOFIN Platform layer and the later are connected to ISOFIN Customers.

23.1.2 Roadmap from Process- to Product-Level Requirements Elicitation

Our proposed approach intended usage is for cases with insufficient inputs for the traditional product-level requirements elicitation. We propose an approach that begins with eliciting process-level requirements and later evolving to properly aligned product-level requirements. Our proposal, a V + V process, is based on the execution of two V-Model based approaches, one executed in a process-level perspective and the other executed in a product-level perspective. In this chapter we only present the process-level V-Model execution, which will allow for creating context for executing the product-level V-Model.

The process-level V-Model need is based on the premise that there is no clearly defined context for eliciting product requirements. As an example for a situation where there is no clearly defined context, we use the case study presented in the previous section, the ISOFIN project. This project is executed in a consortium comprising eight entities (private companies, public research centers and universities), making the requirements elicitation and the definition of a development roadmap difficult to agree. The initial request for the project requirements resulted in mixed and confusing sets of misaligned information. Our proposal of adopting a process-level perspective was agreed on and, based on the knowledge that each consortium member had of the intended project results, the major processes were elicited and a first approach to a logical (process-level) architecture was made. After execution of the process-level perspective, it was possible to gather a set of information that the consortium is sustainably used to evolve to the traditional (product-level) development scenario. Elicited requirements in a process level perspective describe the processes in a higher level of abstraction, making them understandable by the consortium key decision-taking members (business stakeholders).

Due to the lack of consensus in the requirements elicitation in this “newfound” paradigm of IT solutions (Cloud Computing), our approach changed the traditional

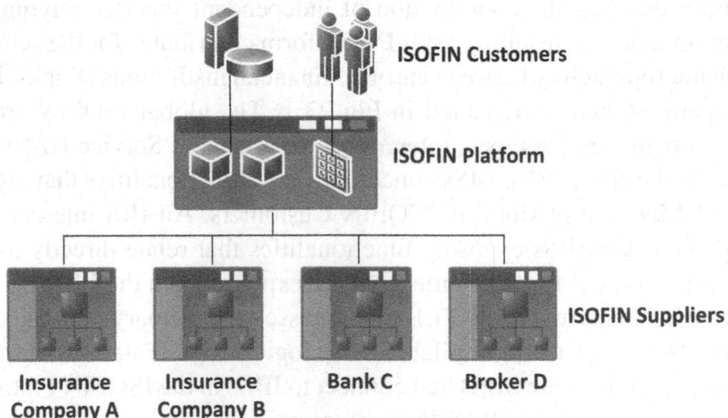

Fig. 23.1 Interoperability in ISOFIN

product-level perspective to the described process-level perspective. This new perspective allows the proper elicitation of requirements in Cloud Computing projects. The rationale for the design of the models proposed in the approach (to be presented in Sect. 23.3), in the case of this project, was based on specifying processes that intent to execute in a cloud-based software solution. Also, the execution of non-automatic micro-steps of the 4SRS method relate to cloud-issues. However, our approach is generic enough to be independently used from the type of solution decided from by the project consortium.

The intended cloud solution is able to be deployed in an IaaS layer. That layer supports the execution of a set of services that will allow suppliers to specify the behaviour of the services they intend on supplying, in a PaaS layer. This will allow customers, or third-parties, to use the platform's services, in a SaaS layer and be billed accordingly.

23.2 Multiple View Requirements Modeling

It is acknowledged in software engineering that a complete system architecture cannot be represented using a single perspective [25, 38]. Using multiple viewpoints, like logical diagrams, sequence diagrams or other artifacts, contributes to a better representation of the system and, as a consequence, to a better understanding of the system. Krutchen's work [25] refers that the description of the architecture can be represented into four views: logical, development, process and physical. The fifth view is represented by selected use cases or scenarios. Zou and Pavlovski [41] add an extra view, the control case view, that complements the use case view to complete requirements across the collective system lifecycle views.

Our method is executed in a process-level perspective, but how the term *process* is applied in this approach can lead to inappropriate interpretations. For scope definition of our work, we characterize the process-level perspective by: (1) being related to real world activities, including business; and (2) when related to software those activities encompass the typical software development lifecycle. Activities and their interface in a process can be structured or arranged in a process architecture [9].

We typically characterize product-level approaches with functional decomposition of systems models. The process architecture represents a fundamental organization of service development, service creation, and service distribution in the relevant enterprise context [40]. In this context, we believe that the process-level 4SRS method can be used when there is no agreed on or defined context for requirements elicitation. Requirements elicitation is concerned with where software requirements come from and how they are collected [1] within the Requirements Engineering area. The objective of a requirements elicitation task is to communicate the needs of users and project sponsors to system developers [42]. A proper requirements elicitation task must encompass an understanding of the organizational environment, through their business processes [11]. An accurate requirements elicitation can be assured through the use of requirements elicitation methodologies, methods or techniques. The Work

System Method [2] presents a combined static view of the current (or proposed) system and a dynamic view of the system evolution over time. The Soft Systems Methodology (SSM) [14] is a domain-independent analysis methodology designed for tackling problematic situations where there is neither clear problem definition nor solution.

Overall, our approach suggests the derivation of a process-level logical architecture for creating context for cloud design. There are several approaches, in a product-level perspective, to support the design of software architectures, like RSEB [22], FAST [39], FORM [23], KobrA [6] and QADA [30]. The product-level perspective of the 4SRS [29] method also promotes functional decomposition of software systems.

Tropos [12] and 4SRS (in [18]) are process-level requirement modeling methods. Regarding Tropos, it uses notions of actor, goal and (actor) dependency as a foundation to model early and late requirements, architectural and detailed design. The 4SRS method is usually applied in a product-level perspective. According to [19], and in a business context, a process is executed to achieve a given business goal and where business processes, human resources, raw material, and internal procedures are combined and synchronized towards a common objective. Our processes represent the real-world activities of a software production process, like in [16].

A system logical architecture can be viewed as a constructed set of the system's design decisions. By constructed we mean that the architecture is built using a construction method that assures its correctness. Design decisions, at this level, can be analyzed by looking at the non-functional requirement that the system is intended to comply. For instance, if we intend our system to be secure, the architect should pay attention to the communication between architectural elements represented in the logical architecture diagram and also to the data flows between them or to the existence of special encryption or authentication elements. If the system is required to be redundant, the architect should care about redundant sub-systems or architectural elements.

The result of the application of the 4SRS method is a logical architecture. A logical architecture can be considered a view of a system composed of a set of problem-specific abstractions supporting functional requirements [4]. The logical architecture acts as a common abstraction of the system providing a representation of the system able to be understood by all the stakeholders regardless of their background. The process architecture represents the fundamental organization of service development, service creation, and service distribution in the relevant enterprise context [40]. A process architecture can also be defined as an arrangement of the activities and their interfaces in a process [9], takes into account some non-functional requirements, such as performance and availability [25], and can be represented with components, connectors, systems/configurations of components and connectors, ports, roles, representations and rep-maps [31], as well as by architectural elements' static and temporal features [24].

The defined and derived artifacts suggested by our approach, used alone and unaligned with each other, are of a lesser use to organizations and stakeholders. Our approach begins in a business-level perspective, by defining the organizational configurations and ends with a technological view of the system. From one perspective to the other, alignment must be assured. The alignment we refer to relates to business and IT alignment [13] and, in our case, where the business needs must be instantiated into the creation of context for proper product design.

23.3 V-Model Approach

Traditional development processes can be referenced using the Royce's waterfall model [37] that includes five typical phases in its lifetime: Analysis, Design, Implementation, Test and Deployment. Defining a simplified macro-process for supporting the requirement elicitation in a process-level approach must take into account the waterfall model lifecycle for a project. We frame our proposed V-Model approach in the Analysis phase of the lifecycle model, as depicted in Fig. 23.2. This simplified development macro-process based on the waterfall model uses the V-Model generated artifacts for eliciting requirements that, in a process-level approach, are used as input for the traditional 4SRS usage (product-level) [29]. The product-level 4SRS promotes the transition from the Analysis to the Design phase.

23.3.1 The V-Model Representation

In this section, we present our approach, based on successive and specific artifacts generation. We use Organizational Configurations (OC) [17], *A-type* and *B-type sequence diagrams* [28], use case models and a process-level logical architecture diagram. All these artifacts are properly described later in the chapter. The generated artifacts and the alignment between the business needs and the context for product design can be represented by a V-Model (Fig. 23.5).

The original V-Model is a variation of the Royce's waterfall model [37], in a V shape folded in half and having in the vertex the lowest level of decomposition.

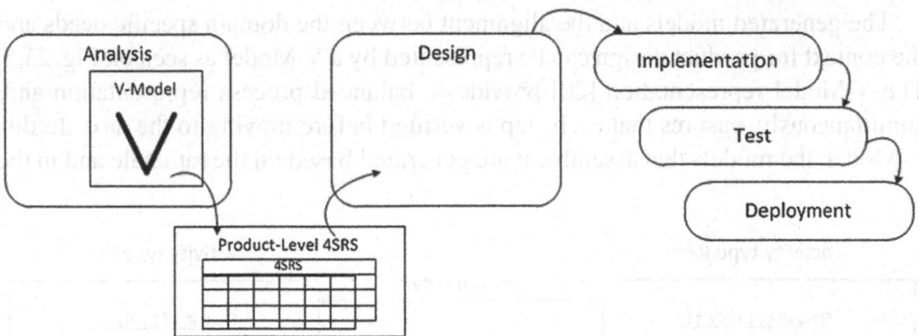

Fig. 23.2 Framing the V-Model representation in the development macro-process

The V-Model left side represents the decreasing abstraction from user requirements into components by a process of decomposition and definition. The right side of the V-Model represents the integration and verification of the previous components into greater levels of implementation and assembly, by realizing them and thus decreasing the abstraction level. The V-Model representation [20] provides a balanced process representation and, simultaneously, ensures that each step is verified before moving to the next.

In our proposed V-Model, the artifacts are generated based on the rationale and in the information existing in previously defined artifacts, i.e., *A-type sequence diagrams* are based on OCs, use case model is based on *A-type sequence diagrams*, the logical architecture is based on the use case model, and *B-type sequence diagrams* comply with the logical architecture.

The OC model is a high-level representation of the activities (interactions) that exist between the business-level entities of a given domain. Fig. 23.3 shows an example of an OC, with two activity types, each with a role and two interactions. Each OC must contain information on the performed activities, the participating professional profiles, and the exchange of information or artifacts. The set of interactions are based on business requirements and, in conjunction with the entities and the stakeholders, are represented with the intention of describing a feasible scenario that fulfills a business vision.

Our approach uses a UML stereotyped sequence diagram representation to describe interactions in early analysis phase of system development. These diagrams are presented in this chapter as *A-type* sequence diagrams. Another stereotyped sequence diagram, called *B-type* sequence diagrams, allows for deriving process sequences represented by the sequence flows between the architectural elements (AEs) depicted in the logical architecture. An AE is a representation of the pieces from which the final logical architecture can be built. This term is used to distinguish those artifacts from the components, objects or modules used in other contexts, like in the UML structure diagrams. One must assure that a process' sequences modeled in *B-type* sequence diagrams depict the same flows as the ones modeled in *A-type* sequence diagrams, as well as being in conformity with the interactions between AEs depicted in the logical architecture associations. An example of *A-type* and *B-type* sequence diagrams can be found in Fig. 23.4.

The generated models and the alignment between the domain specific needs and the context for product design can be represented by a V-Model as seen on Fig. 23.5. The V-Model representation [20] provides a balanced process representation and, simultaneously, ensures that each step is verified before moving to the next. In this V-Model, the models that assemble it are generated based on the rationale and in the

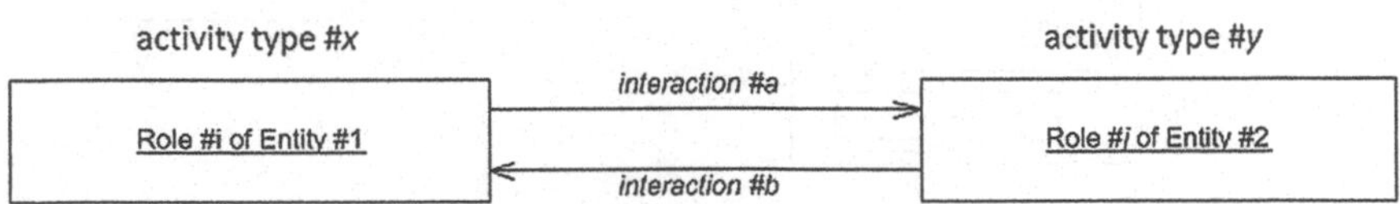

Fig. 23.3 Organizational configuration example

information existing in previously defined models, i.e., *A-type* diagrams are based on OCs, use cases are based on *A-type* diagrams, the logical architecture is based on the use case model, and *B-type* diagrams comply with the logical architecture.

A-type Sequence Diagrams can be gathered and afterwards used as an elicitation technique for modeling the use cases. It can be counterintuitive to consider that use case diagrams can be refinements of sequence diagrams. It is possible if we take into consideration that the scenarios expressed in the *A-type* sequence diagrams are built using the use-case candidates in the form of activities that will be executed and must be computationally supported by the system to be implemented. These activities in form of use cases are placed in the *A-type* sequence diagram and associated with the corresponding actors and other used cases. These use cases are later arranged in use case diagrams after redundancy is eliminated and proper naming is given. The flow expressed by the sequences creates the rationale for discovering the necessary use cases to complete the process.

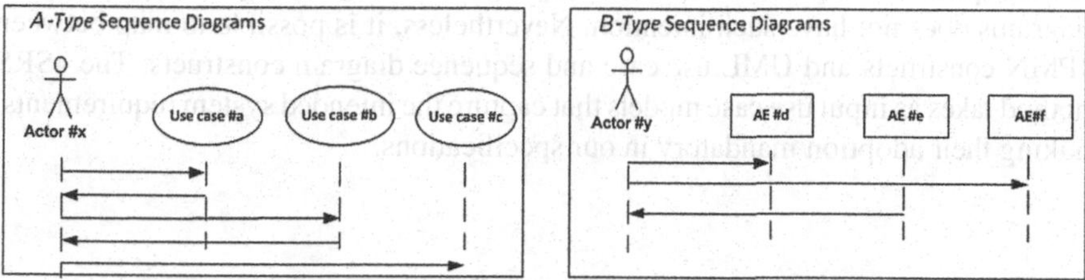

Fig. 23.4 *A*- and *B-type* sequence diagrams examples

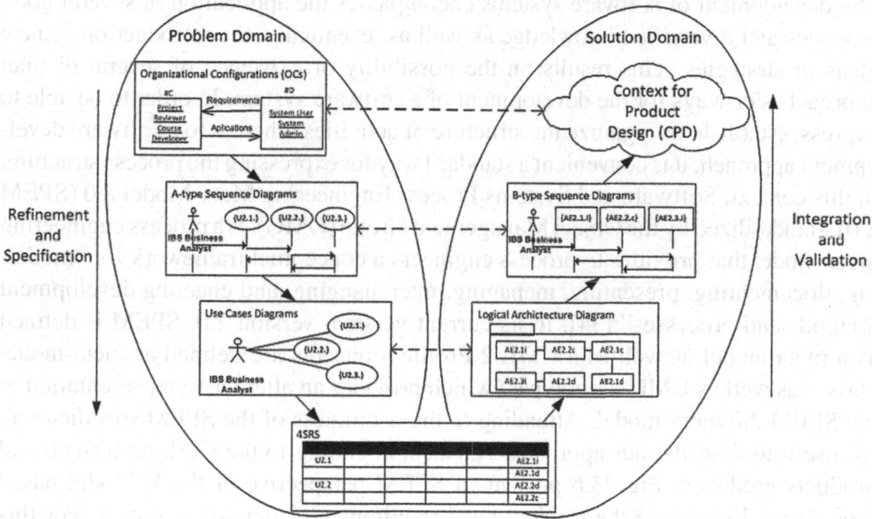

Fig. 23.5 V-Model adaption for business and IT-alignment

As suggested by the V-Model represented in Fig. 23.5, the artifacts placed on the left hand side of the path representation are properly aligned with the artifacts placed on the right side, i.e., *B-type* sequence diagrams are aligned with *A-type* sequence diagrams, and the logical architecture is aligned with the use case model. Alignment between the use case model and the logical architecture is assured by the correct application of the 4SRS method. The resulting sets of transformations along our V-Model path provide artifacts properly aligned with the organization's business needs (which are formalized through Organization Configurations).

A notation commonly associated with business process is BPMN [33]. BPMN is a graphical notation that depicts the steps in a business process by coordinating sequence of processes and the messages they exchange in a defined scenario. We have adopted UML instead of BPMN because UML takes an object-oriented approach to design of applications, focusing on software. BPMN takes that approach to modeling of systems, focusing on business process. The two are complementary views on systems. BPMN process definitions are intended to be implemented as an automated business process in a process execution language. Our usage of sequence and use case diagrams does not have such intention. Nevertheless, it is possible to map between BPMN constructs and UML use case and sequence diagram constructs. The 4SRS method takes as input use case models that capture the intended system requirements, making their adoption mandatory in our specifications.

23.3.2 A V-Model SPEM Representation

The development of software systems encompasses the application of several good practices and diversified knowledge as well as, eventually, the introduction of new ideas or strategies. This results on the possibility of existence of several distinct approaches or ways for the development of a software system. In order to be able to express, establish, or organize the structure of activities inherent to a software development approach, it is convenient a standard way for expressing the process structure. In this context, Software and Systems Process Engineering Meta-Model 2.0 (SPEM 2.0), standardized by the Object Management Group (OMG), is a process engineering meta-model that provides to process engineers a conceptual framework for "modeling, documenting, presenting, managing, interchanging, and enacting development methods and processes" [34]. In its current version, version 2.0, SPEM is defined as a meta-model as well as a UML 2 Profile (concepts are defined as meta-model classes as well as UML stereotypes) which provides an alternative representation to the SPEM 2.0 meta-model. Attending to the usefulness of the SPEM specification, we use it to describe our approach. As such, attending to the work performed and products produced, Fig. 23.6 presents a SPEM perspective of the V-Model based process used to derive the product-level requirements elicitation context. For this purpose, we use the typical SPEM representations for presenting the approach, i.e., activities (e.g., Use Case Modeling), artifacts (e.g., Use Case Model), deliverables

(Product-level Requirements Elicitation Context) and associations (input, output, predecessor and composition).

As depicted by Fig. 23.6, the V-Model representation has the purpose of providing the deliverable *Product-Level Requirement Elicitation Context*. The main activities that make up the process are *Definition of Organizational Configurations*, *Description of interactions*, *Use Case Modeling*, *4SRS Transformation*, *Architecture Traversing*, and *Collection of Artifacts* (as indicated by the composition associations). These activities are sequentially performed in a way that an activity starts only when its predecessor activity has finished (as indicated by the predecessor dependencies). The activities use and produce (as indicated by input and output associations) artifacts, namely *Organizational Configurations*, *A-Type Sequence Diagrams*, *Use Case Model*, *Process-Level Logical Architecture Diagram*, *B-type Sequence Diagrams*, and *Product-Level Requirement Elicitation Context*.

23.4 Business Requirements

The V-Model representation promotes the alignment between the artifacts on the problem domain and the artifacts on the solution domain. The presented artifacts are created in succession, by manipulating the information that results from one to make decisions on how to create the other. To assess this approach, we present a

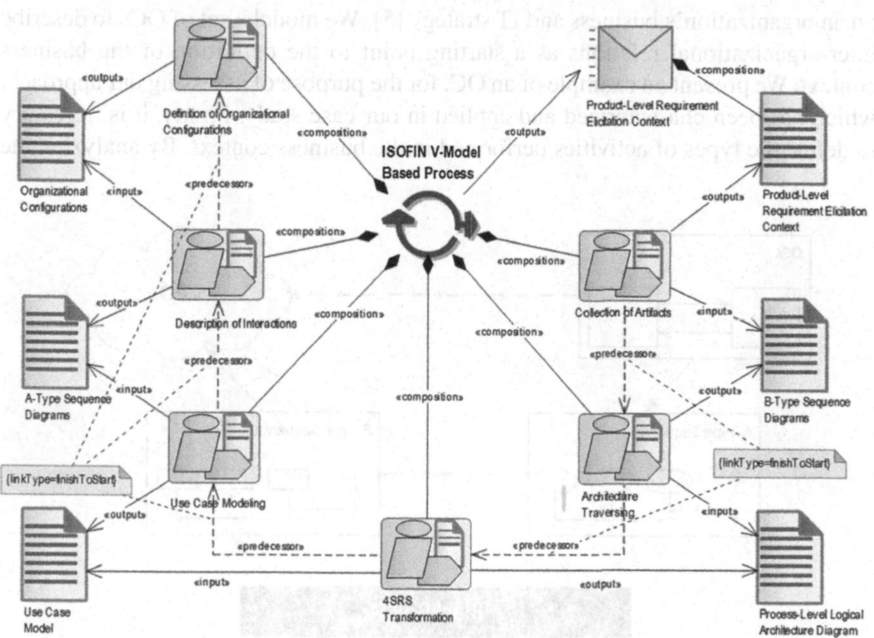

Fig. 23.6 SPEM diagram of ISOFIN V-model based process

process regarding our real case study, the ISOFIN project, as an example. The process under analysis, called "Create IBS", deals with the creation of a new Interconnected Business Service (IBS). The inter-organizational relations required to create a new IBS are described under a new OC. The definition of activities and actors required to create a new IBS are described in an *A-type* sequence diagram. A *B-type* sequence diagram allows for validation of the logical architecture required to create an IBS and also validates the requirement expressed in the corresponding *A-type* sequence diagram. After the generation of these artifacts, we assure that the "Create IBS" process is aligned with the stakeholder's needs.

In a process-level approach, in opposition to the product-level approach, the characterization of the intended system gives a different perspective on the organizational relations and interactions. When defining a business context, we consider that interactions between actors and processes constitute an important issue to be dealt. This section focuses on characterizing those interactions by using three different levels of abstraction, as depicted in Fig. 23.7: the first level is represented by OCs; the other two are represented by different types of Stereotyped UML sequence diagrams, presented as *A-type* and B-*type* sequence diagrams (later described in this section).

23.4.1 Organizational Configurations

Today's business is based on inter-organizational relations [17], having an impact on an organization's business and IT strategy [5]. We model a set of OCs to describe inter-organizational relations as a starting point to the definition of the business context. We present an example of an OC, for the purpose of assessing our approach, which has been characterized and applied in our case study. Firstly, it is necessary to define the types of activities performed in the business context. By analyzing the

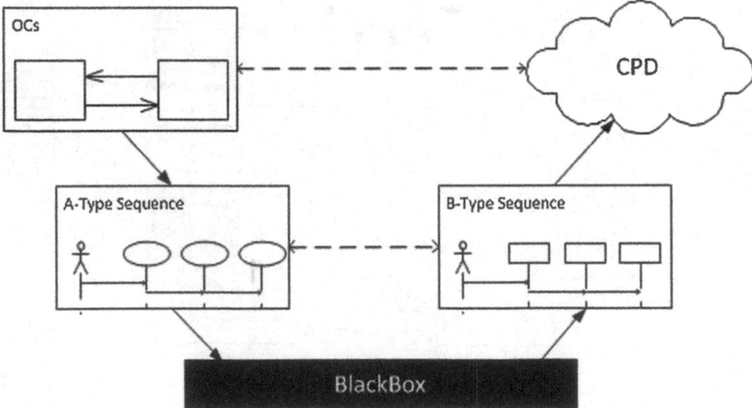

Fig. 23.7 Organizational configurations and interactions alignment

types of activities, the execution of an IBS within a business activity regards #A activities, while the creation of a new IBS regards #B activities:

(1) *#A Activities—Financial Domain Business Activities*: these are the delivered domain business activities regarding the financial institutions.

(2) *#B Activities—ISOFIN Platform Services Integration*: these are the activities that relate to the integration of supplier services.

In order to characterize an organization, it is required to relate a set of roles to the performed activity type. Finally, the interactions between organizations are specified. In Fig. 23.8, it is possible to depict the required relations between organizations in order to create an IBS and providing it to ISOFIN Customers. The description of the professional profiles and the exchange of information between organizations are not relevant in this chapter.

23.4.2 Stereotyped Sequence Diagrams

In an early analysis phase, we need to define the relations between activities and actors, defined through interactions in our approach. Interactions are used during the more detailed design phase where the precise inter-process communication must be set up according to formal protocols [35]. An interaction can be displayed in a UML sequence diagram.

Traditional sequence diagrams involve system objects in the interaction. Since modeling structural elements of the system is beyond the scope of the user requirements, Machado et al. propose the usage of a stereotyped version of UML sequence diagrams that only includes actors and use cases to validate the elicited requirements at the analysis phase of system development [28]. We also use such diagrams in our work and define them as *A-type* sequence diagrams, as shown in Fig. 23.9. In this example, we depict sequential information flows of process-level use cases that refer to the required activities for creating an IBS. These activities are executed within #B activities, after receiving business requirements from ISOFIN Customers and before delivering IBS (interactions depicted in the OC of Fig. 23.8).

The usage of *A-type* sequence diagrams is required to gather and formalize the main stakeholder's intentions, which provide an orchestration and a sequence of some proposed activities. *A-type* sequence diagrams relate the roles presented within an OC and instantiates their relations with activities. *A-type* sequence diagrams allow a pure functional representation of behavioral interaction with the environment and are

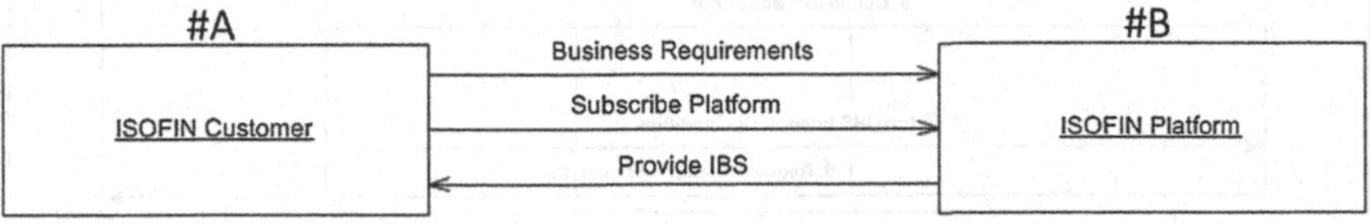

Fig. 23.8 Organizational configuration

appropriate to illustrate workflow user requirements [28]. They also provide information for defining and modeling use cases at a process-level perspective and frame the activities execution in time. Modeled diagrams must encompass all processes and actors.

One of the purposes of creating a software logical architecture is to support the system's functional requirements [25]. It must be assured that the derived logical architecture is aligned with the business needs. On the one hand, the execution of a software architecture design method (e.g., 4SRS) provides an alignment of the logical architecture with user requirements (presented in Sect. 6.1). On the other hand, it is necessary to validate if the behavior of the logical architecture is as expected. So, in a later stage, after deriving a logical architecture, to analyze the sequential process flow of architectural elements (as shown in Fig. 23.10), we adopt different stereotype of UML sequence diagrams, where architectural elements (presented in the logical architecture), actors and packages (if justifiable) interactions are modeled. Architectural elements refer to the pieces from which the final logical architecture can be built. In Fig. 23.10, we present the same activities concerning creating an IBS but in a lower level of abstraction, closer to product design. *B-type* sequence diagrams differ from the traditional ones, since they model the exchange of information between actors and logical architectural elements, thus they are still modeled at the system level.

23.4.3 An UML Metamodel Extension for A-type and B-type Sequence Diagrams

The usage of *A-type* and *B-type* sequence diagrams in our approach is perfectly harmonized with UML sequence diagram's original semantics, as described in the UML Superstructure [35]. We present in the left side of Fig. 23.11 some of the classes of

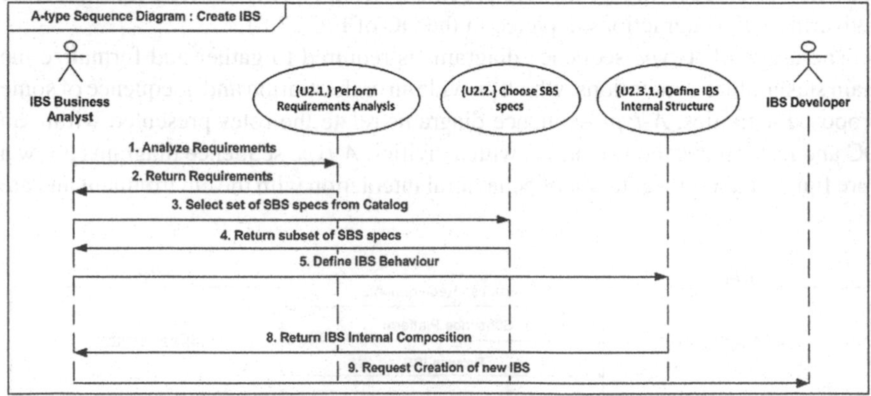

Fig. 23.9 A-type sequence diagram

the UML metamodel regarding sequence diagrams (in the *Interactions* context of the UML Superstructure). As *A-type* and *B-type* sequence diagrams differ from typical sequence diagrams in the participants of the interactions, the usage of these diagrams regards the Lifeline class. A lifeline represents an individual participant in the *Interaction*. The Lifeline notation description presented in the UML Superstructure details that the *lifeline* is described by its *<connectable-element-name>* and *<class_name>*, where *<class_name>* is the type referenced by the represented *ConnectableElement*, and its symbol consists in a "head" followed by a vertical line (straight or dashed). A *ConnectableElement* (from *InternalStructures*) is an abstract metaclass representing a set of instances that play roles of a classifier. The *Lifeline* "head" has a shape that is based on the classifier for the part that this lifeline represents.

We propose in this section, as depicted in the highlighted class in the right side of Fig. 23.11, a stereotype class to extend the UML Metamodel, so it can support AEs. The participants in the interactions in *A-type* sequence diagrams are use cases and in *B-type* sequence diagrams are AEs. Regarding *A-type* sequence diagrams, the UML Superstructure clearly defines a class for use cases. However, regarding *B-type* sequence diagrams, AEs are not considered in any class of the UML metamodel and, despite some similarities in semantics, are different from UML components. The added value of our metamodel relates to situations like these, leading to the necessity of defining a stereotype *Architectural Element* for the *NamedElement* class (depicted in the right side of Fig. 23.11). AEs refer to the pieces from which the final logical architecture can be built and currently relate to generated artifacts and not to their connections or containers. The nature of AEs varies according to the type of system under study and the context where it is applied. Like the *ConnectableElement* class, *UseCase* class is also generalized by *NamedElement* class. The information regarding abstract syntax, concrete syntax, well-formedness and semantics [3] of *UseCase* class

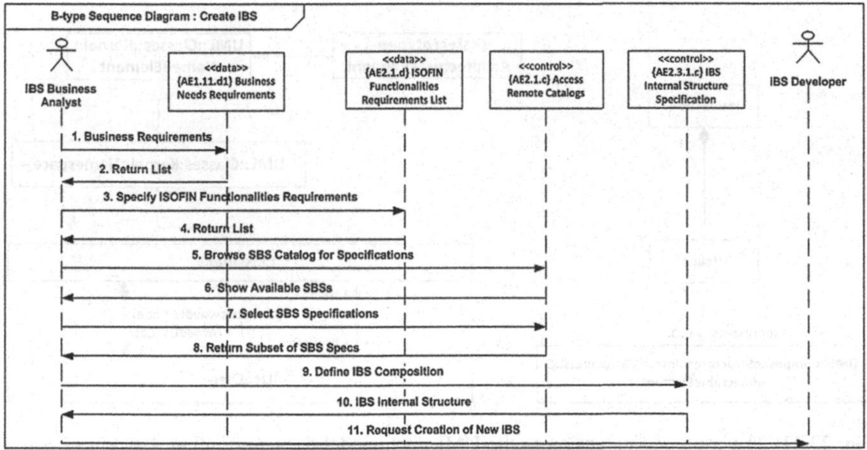

Fig. 23.10 B-type sequence diagram

and the context in which we defined the stereotype *Architecture Element* does not express any condition that restricts them of being able to act as a *ConnectableElement*.

23.5 Transition from Business to IT

The 4SRS method allows for the transformation of user requirements into an architectural model representation and is traditionally applied in a product-level perspective [29] including variability and recursive mechanisms [4, 29].

This chapter presents an extension of the traditional (product-level perspective) usage of the 4SRS method to allow its application in a process-level perspective supporting the creation of context for the product-level requirements elicitation. This application differs from the traditional by defining a set or rules that must be observed when reasoning about the execution of the method steps. Our extension of the method also defines additional micro-steps to the existing ones. Alongside the method presentation there will be presented some examples created during the method application to derive a logical architecture that acts as a basis for the requirements elicitation of a cloud SaaS solution, in this case, a subset of the ISOFIN project.

The 4SRS method takes as input a set of use cases describing the requirements for the cloud-specific processes that tackle the initial problem. These use cases are refined trough successive 4SRS iterations, representing the intended cloud concerns of the involved business and technological stakeholders. Neither KobrA, RSEB or TROPOS make use of techniques for refining use cases like the 4SRS method does. Application of the 4SRS method requires the creation of "architectural elements" (AEs). The nature of AEs varies according to the type of system under study and also with the context where it is applied. In the specific context of logical architectures, the term architectural element refers to the pieces from which the final logical architecture

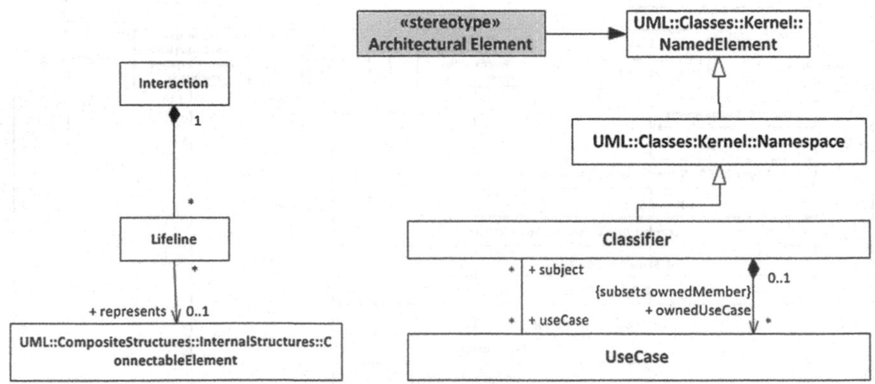

Fig. 23.11 The proposed extension to the UML metamodel for representing *A-type* and *B-type* sequence diagrams [35]

can be built. We deliberately use this term to distinguish those artifacts from the components, objects or modules used in other well established contexts, like in the UML structure diagrams. This process-level approach can be executed in several contexts. In our case for cloud design, cloud-related issues are dealt in non-automatic micro-steps in step 2 (only micro-steps 2ii and 2vi are automatic). The rest of the steps described in this section are independent of the execution context.

The execution of the 4SRS transformation steps can be supported in tabular representations as detailed in [29]. Moreover, the usage of tables permits a set of tools to be devised and built, so that the transformations can be partially automated. These tabular representations constitute the main mechanism to automate a set of decision-assisted model transformation steps. Tabular transformations are supported in a table where the cells are filled with the set of decisions that were taken and made possible the derivation of a logical architecture for the cloud design. An example of the 4SRS method execution table is represented in Fig. 23.12. Each column of the table concerns a step/micro-step of the method execution.

23.5.1 Step 1: Architectural Element Creation

This step regards the creation of AEs. The product-level 4SRS [29] rule of transforming each use case into three AEs is still valid in the process-level 4SRS. According to the MVC-like pattern applied in the product-level 4SRS, an interface, data and control AEs are created for each use case. *i-type*, *d-type*, or *c-type* stereotypes respectively are added to each AE and their names are prefixed with "AE" (the stereotypes definition will be detailed in micro-step 2i). No particular rationale or decision is required at this step since it concerns mainly the transformation of one use case into three specific AEs.

Step 1 - architectural element creation		Step 2 - architectural element elimination									Step 3 - packaging & aggregation	Step 4 - architectural element association	
		2i - use case classification	2ii - local elimination	2iii - architectural element naming	2iv - architectural element description	2v - architectural element: represented by	2v - architectural element: represent	2vi - global elimination	2vii - architectural element renaming	2viii - architectural element specification		4i - Direct Associations	4ii - UC Associations
{U2.1.}		cd											
{AE2.1.c}	Generated AE		T	IBS Analysis Pre-Start Decision	Browse the IBS and SBS Catalogs searching already existing IBS and SBS information with the intent of analyzing if the current business need isn't already fulfilled and if the ISOFIN Platform infrastructure supports the new implementation. ...	{AE2.1.c}	{AE1.11.i} {AE2.2.c} {AE2.5.c} {AE2.5.i}	T	Access Remote Catalogs	Allows browsing the available catalogs in the ISOFIN Platform (ISOFIN Application, IBS, and SBS). The user (Business User or the IBS Business Analyst) is allowed to search for information regarding the desired artifact and to select artifacts to use on his purposes. ...	{P2.2} IBS Analysis Decisions	{AE1.11.d1} {AE1.11.d2} {AE2.1.d}	{AE2.3.1.i} {AE2.3.2.i} {AE2.10.i} {AE2.11.i} {AE3.3.i} {AE3.7.1.i}
{AE2.1.d}	Generated AE		T	ISOFIN Functionalities Requirements List	Set of functional and non-functional requirements needed to fulfill identified business needs, intended system functionalities and all the constraints that may restrict design and implementation.	{AE2.1.d}		T	ISOFIN Functionalities Requirements List		{P2.1} IBS Requirements	{AE2.1.c}	
{AE2.1.i}			F										

Fig. 23.12 Tabular transformation of the 4SRS method

An addition to this step is the identification of glue elements resulting from the textual descriptions associated with the use case under analysis. If the use case depicts pre- or post-conditions in the form of validations, those can be expressed in this step as a *Glue AE*. These AEs have the *c-type* stereotypes since they require decisions to be made with computational support, that is, they must be supported by the system architecture to be represented. A sequential number is added to each Glue AE. Those elements will be used as generic process interfaces between generated AEs and act as pre- or post-condition process validations. Other AEs are expressed as *Generated AE*.

23.5.2 Step 2: Architectural Element Elimination

In this step, AEs are submitted to elimination tasks according to pre-defined rules. At this moment, the system architect decides which of the original three AEs (i, c, d) plus any glue element are maintained or eliminated taking into account the entire system.

The original step 2 of 4SRS is divided into seven micro-steps. We added a new micro-step, 2viii: Architectural Element Extended Description.

Micro-step 2i: Use Case Classification. In this step, each use case is classified ac-cording to the nature of its AEs, previously created in step 1. The nature of an AE is defined according to the suffix the AE was tagged with. In the process-level perspective more than one of each AE type can be generated according to the textual description and in the model of the use case. Each AE type must be interpreted as follows:

- *i-type*—refer to interface. These represent process' interfaces with users, software or other processes. An AE belonging to or being classified in this category is due to its ability interact with other AEs external to itself;
- *c-type*—refer to control. These represent a process focusing on decision making and such decision must have a computational support given from the overall intended system;
- *d-type*—refer to generic decision repositories (data), not computationally supported from the overall intended system. This repository stores information for a given period of time, comprising decisions based on physical repositories (like documents or databases) or verbal decisions taken and transmitted between humans.

In the process-level perspective, *c-type* and *d-type* AEs are related to decision-making processes. The difference resides on the computational support of the AE by then under design overall intended system (in hypotheses).

Micro-step 2ii: Local Elimination. This micro-step refers to determining which AEs must be eliminated in the context of a use case, guaranteeing its full representation. This is required since micro-step 2i disregards any representativeness concerns.

There are cases when there is an explicit place for a *d-type* AE and it is admittedly eliminated. Reasons for this are due to the process-level perspective: there is no need for certain types of decision repositories that only regard information for the final product and not the process.

Micro-step 2iii: Architectural Element Naming. In this micro-step, AEs that survived the previous micro-step are given a name. The name must reflect the role of the AE within the entire use case, in order to semantically give hints on what it represents and not just copy the original use case name. Usually, the AE name reflects also the use case from which the AE was originated.

Micro-step 2iv: Architectural Element Description. The resulting AEs that were named in the previous micro-step must be described and the requirements that they represent must be addressed in the process-level perspective. This micro-step is where the transition is made from the problem domain to the solution domain, so the descriptions must detail, in process terms, how, why, when by whom that AE is going to be executed. This micro-step must explicitly describe the expected behavior of the AE execution, including which decisions will be made and how will they be supported.

Micro-step 2v: Architectural Element Representation. The purpose of this micro-step is to eliminate AE redundancy in the global process. In this micro-step, all AEs are considered and compared in order to identify if one AE is represented by any other one. The identification of AE representation is the most critical task in the 4SRS method application, because the elimination of redundancy assures a semantic coherence of the logical architecture and discovers anomalies in the use case model. Since the architecture being described concerns the process-level, the identification of AE redundancy takes in consideration facts like the execution context, actors involved, used artifacts, activities and tasks, among others. If all of these factors are similar, though the AEs are originated by different use cases, the given AE can be considered to represent another. Other cases when an AE is considered to represent another:

- In similar activities, if the same actor has the same role in the both AEs, despite different execution contexts (e.g., {AE2.4.1.i} *Perform ISOFIN Supplier Request Evaluation* is considered to be represented by {AE2.4.2.i} *Perform ISOFIN Customer Request Evaluation*, the IBS Business Analyst triggers both AEs—the first AE represents the second AE, because the actor interacts with the same type of information);
- In similar activities, different actors participate in the AE, but the execution context is the same (e.g., {AE2.1.c} *Access Remote Catalogs* and {AE1.11.i} *Browse ISOFIN Catalogs*, the involved actors are different, but the execution platform is the same—both of them execute in the ISOFIN Platform, in the SaaS layer).

These cases are only applicable for *i-type* and *c-type* AEs. This set of rules cannot be applied to *d-type* AEs since they represent the decisions that need to be taken and whose computational support is not assured by the scope of the project under analysis. Also, *d-type* AEs are usually input for other decision processes (*c-type* AEs) requiring computational support.

Despite the decision making process may be similar, *d-type* AEs differ in the decision making purpose. This difference is required to assure the process variability, when the execution contexts are similar but the involved actors and activities are different.

The column "represented by" stores the reference of the AE that will represent the AE being analyzed. If the analyzed AE is going to be represented by itself, the corresponding "represented by" column must refer to itself. The column "represents" stores the references of the objects that the analyzed AE will represent.

Micro-step 2vi: Global Elimination. This micro-step refers to determining which AEs must be eliminated in the context of the global model, similar to micro-step 2ii, since its execution is automatic.

The AE that is represented by itself or represents other AEs is maintained. The rest (i.e., AEs that are represented by other AEs) are eliminated. This is a fully "automatic" micro-step, since it is based on the results of the previous one.

Micro-step 2vii: Architectural Element Renaming. In this micro-step, AEs that have not been eliminated in micro-step 2vi are renamed. In cases where the AE under analysis results of the representation of more than one AE, the new name must reflect the global execution of the AE in the project context.

Micro-step 2viii: Architectural Element Specification. This micro-step has never been considered in previous versions of the traditional 4SRS method. Though it is similar to micro-step 2iv, this micro step intends to describe AEs that, in micro-step 2v, are considered to represent other AEs. The decision of creating this micro-step arises from the need to clearly define the proper behavior of the "new" AE in a way that is clear to system architects. The specification must also include execution sequence references of the AEs. The specification information is required in the transformation from the process-level approach to the product-level approach, to infer the necessary requirements of a given product based on the processes of which the product is composed.

23.5.3 Step 3: Packaging and Aggregation

Like in the traditional 4SRS method, in this step, the remaining AEs (those that were maintained after executing step 2), for which there is an advantage in being treated in a unified process, should give the origin to aggregations or packages of semantically consistent AEs. This step supports the construction of a truly coherent process-level model.

23.5.4 Step 4: Architectural Element Association

Decisions on the identification of associations between AEs can be based in information contained in the use case model and in micro-step 2i. Thus, as an addition to the original 4SRS, step 4 was divided in micro-step 4i: Direct Associations and 4ii: Use Case Associations, with the purpose of identifying unnecessary direct associations and to help reflecting the model changes made in the previous steps. It must be also noted that any textual references to eliminated AEs in micro-step 2vi, must be included in micro-step 2viii, making it another source of information for step 4.

Micro-step 4i: Direct Associations. Direct associations are the ones that derive from AEs originated by the same use case. These associations are depicted from the classification given in the method micro-step 2i.

Micro-step 4ii: Use Case Model Associations. Use Case Model Associations are the ones that can be inferred from the textual descriptions of use cases, that is, when a use case description refers, implicitly or explicitly to another use case, the associations inferred imply that the use cases are connected.

23.6 Business Context for Cloud Design

In this section, we present the process-level logical architecture derived using the 4SRS method. The method takes use cases as input, since they reflect elicited requirements and functionalities. Use cases are derived from *A-type* sequence diagrams and from the OCs (presented in Sect. 23.4). The 4SRS method, in the examples to follow, is treated like a black box in the V-Model description (Fig. 23.13).

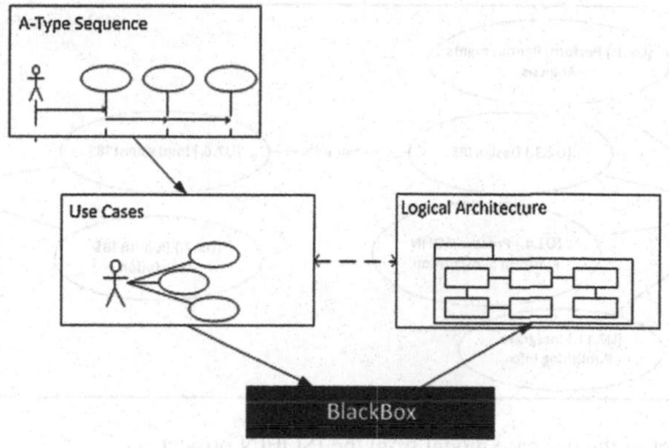

Fig. 23.13 Derivation of process-oriented logical architectures

23.6.1 Derivation of Process-Oriented Logical Architectures

Gathering *A-type* sequence diagrams (presented in 4.2) can be used as an elicitation technique for modeling the use cases. All use cases defined in the *A-type* sequence diagrams must be modeled and textually described in the Use Case artifact.

The use case model specifies the required usages of the ISOFIN Platform. In Fig. 23.14, we present a subset of such usages, regarding the development of functionalities to be accessed by ISOFIN Customers. Use cases, in the process-level perspective, portray the activities (processes) executed by persons or machines in the scope of the system, instead of the characteristics (requirements) of the intended products to be developed. It is essential for use case modeling to include textual descriptions that contain information regarding the process execution, preconditions and actions, as well as their relations and dependencies.

The turning point for eliciting requirements was the usage of the 4SRS method in the process-level perspective, which allowed for the transformation of process-level requirements into the logical diagram, presented in Fig. 23.15, which represents the logical architecture for creating IBSs. The architecture is composed by the architectural elements that derive from the use case model. The resulting subset of the logical architecture shows how activities are arranged so an IBS is generated and available to ISOFIN Customers within the intended IT solution. The architecture is composed by the AEs that survived after the execution of step 2. The packaging executed in step 3 allows the identification of major processes. The associations identified in step 4 are represented in the diagram by the connections between the AEs (for readability purposes, the "direct associations" were represented in dashed lines, and the "use case model associations" in straight lines).

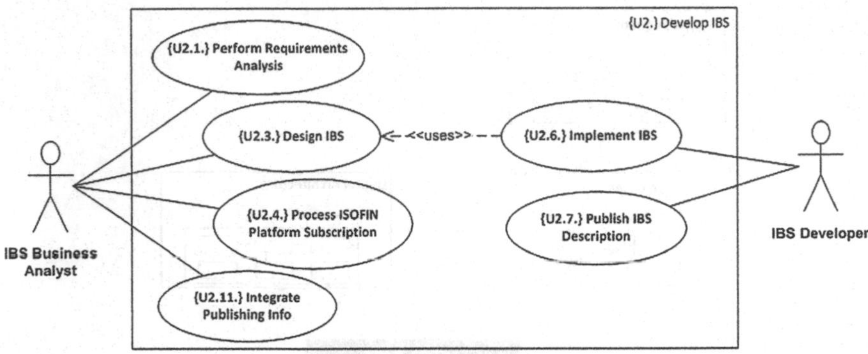

Fig. 23.14 Subset of the use case model from the ISOFIN project

23.6.2 Process Assessment Through ARID

Having a structured method makes the analysis repeatable and at the same time helps ensuring that the same set of validation questions are placed in early development stages. By this we mean that in the elicitation and elaboration phases [26] any identified problem can be mitigated at a lesser cost than if that problem was identified in the construction or transition phases.

With the purpose of assuring the attained logical architecture representation is tenable, we chose to validate it using the Active Reviews for Intermediate Designs (ARID) method [15]. Our concerns relate to discovering errors as soon as possible, inconsistencies in the logical architecture or even inadequacies with the elicited requirements. The ARID method is a combination of Architecture Tradeoff Analysis Method (ATAM) with Active Design Review (ADR). ATAM is a refined and improved version of Software Architecture Analysis Method (SAAM) that helps reviewing architectural decisions having the focus on the quality attributes requirements and their alignment and satisfaction degree of specific quality goals. The ADR method targets incomplete (under development) architectures, performing evaluations on sections of the global architecture. Those features made ARID our method of choice regarding the evaluation of the in-progress ISOFIN logical architecture.

Figure 23.16 shows the coverage of each ARID step with respect to the V-Model artifacts. There are also represented ARID specific artifacts like *Project Charter*, *Materials* and *Issues*. ARID requires that a project context is defined, containing information regarding the identification of the design reviewers. We have represented such information in our diagram using the *Project Charter* box as used in project management [36] terminology. The *Materials* box represents the supporting documentation, like presentation that needs to be made to stakeholders, seed scenarios and meeting agenda. *Issues* relates to a check-list that includes but is not limited to: notes concerning the presentation, the presented logical architecture, newly created scenarios and validation scenarios.

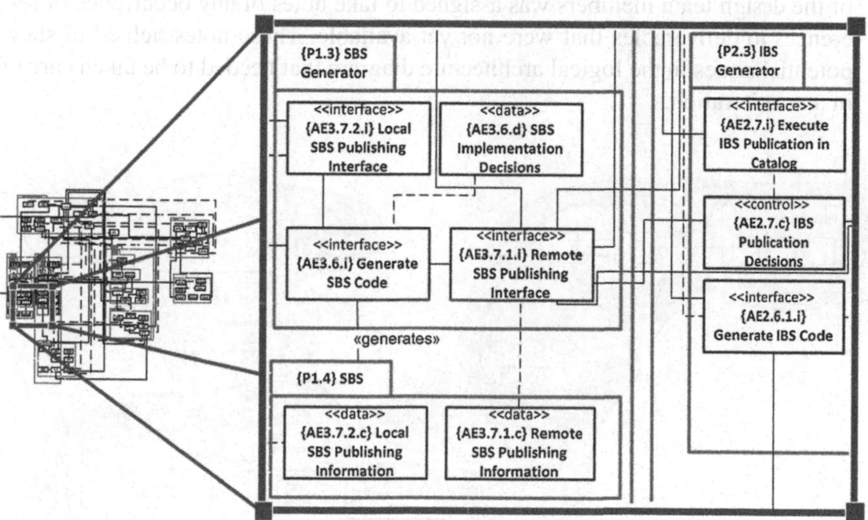

Fig. 23.15 Subset of the ISOFIN process-level logical architecture

The ARID method is divided in two phases: *Rehearsal* and *Review*. The *Rehearsal* phase was adapted to the ISOFIN project context as follows:

- ARID Step 1. *Identify the Reviewers*: We chose 10 reviewers from the ISOFIN project design team. We chose 2 stakeholders from each of the 5 entities that were involved directly or indirectly with the design decisions.
- ARID Step 2. *Prepare the design briefing*: For the purpose of demonstrating the design we prepared a presentation showing the logical architecture diagram as a background and the OCs, *A-type* sequence diagrams and use cases that were used to derive each part of the logical architecture.
- ARID Step 3. *Prepare the seed scenarios*: Associated with each OC and *A-type* sequence diagram set there was defined a feasible scenario in a total of 10 scenarios, included in the presentation with the purpose of rising questions regarding the presented logical architecture.
- ARID Step 4. *Prepare the materials*: We scheduled a meeting with all the stakeholders (reviewers), and distributed to them the presentation and the meeting agenda.

The second ARID phase, *Review*, was adapted to the ISOFIN context as follows:

- ARID Step 5. *Present ARID*: We have presented the steps of ARID to the stakeholders in order to create a context for the method execution.
- ARID Step 6. *Present the design*: Prepared materials, scenarios and logical architecture were presented. The reviewers followed the rule of not questioning the presentation contents or making any improvement comment. Only clarification questions were allowed for the sake of better understanding the materials. One of the design team members was assigned to take notes of any occurrence of references to deliverables that were not yet available. These notes helped to show potential issues in the logical architecture diagram that needed to be taken care of in a next iteration.

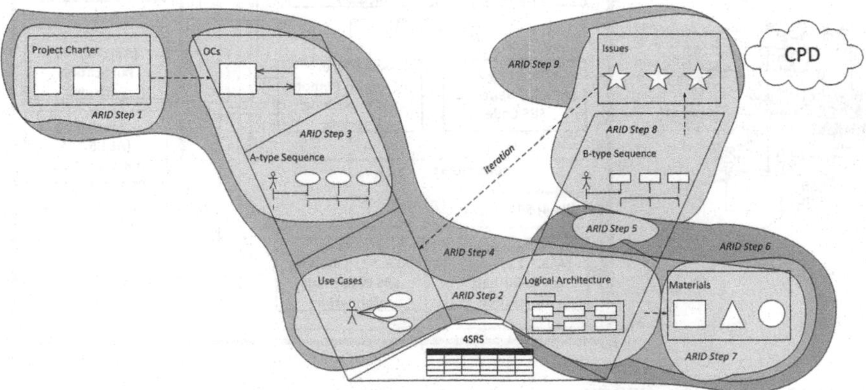

Fig. 23.16 ARID steps in the V-model

- ARID Step 7. *Brainstorm and prioritize scenarios*: Reviewers presented the new scenarios that solved problems they were dealing. Those scenarios where put in the pool with the seed scenarios. We analyzed that pool to exclude duplicates and overlaps. At this moment we had 16 feasible scenarios and formalized the *A-type* sequence diagrams as seen on Fig. 23.9. Each reviewer was allowed a vote equaling 30 % the number of scenarios. That vote could be allocated on any scenario or scenarios they wanted to be discussed.
- ARID Step 8. *Apply the scenarios*: Scenarios that won were used to test the logical architecture diagram for suitability. We began with the scenario that gathered the most votes. The reviewers, working as one and having that scenario in mind designed the *B-type* sequence diagrams (as seen in Fig. 23.10) that corresponded to the scenario under analysis. These diagrams were used to see if the logical architecture diagram solves the problem raised by the scenario. The team member allocated to taking notes recorded the *B-type* sequence diagrams. At any time the design team responsible for the logical architecture intervened to help. We have established a four-hour window to execute this step and in that time we managed to create just as many *B-type* sequence diagrams as *A-type* sequence diagrams. This is considered the necessary condition for the architecture validation.
- ARID Step 9. *Summarize*: As a last step we reviewed the notes and inquired the participants concerning the exercise. All this feedback helped improve the logical architecture diagram and define a check-list of subjects that required attention and needed to be attended before moving on to design or implementation.

In Fig. 23.16 issues discovered in *step 8* and summarized in *step 9* may promote a new iteration of the 4SRS method. This is done when there are detected severe flaws in the logical architecture diagram by not managing to create correct or the necessary *B-type* sequence diagrams to traverse all the AEs in the logical architecture diagram or to comply with all the defined *A-type* sequence diagrams. We required 4 iterations in the 4SRS method before the logical architecture passed the ARID assessment.

23.7 Conclusion

In this chapter, we have presented a process-level approach to creating context for product design based on successive derivation of artifact models in a V-Model representation. We use *A-type* sequence diagrams as a bridge from business needs to the first system requirements representation, *B-type* sequence diagrams are used as validation for *A-type* sequence diagrams and the logical architecture diagram. The used artifacts represent the system in its behavior, structure and expected functionalities. This chapter also presents the extensions to the traditional application of the 4SRS method, for creating context for requirements elicitation and later derivation of logical architectural diagrams from use cases in a process-level perspective. The approach process assessment presented in the chapter is compliant with the ARID method.

For creating a context for IT product design, the V-Model presented in this chapter encompasses a set of artifacts through successive derivation. Our approach is different from existing ones [6, 23, 39], since we use a process-level perspective. Not only do we manage to create the context for product design, but we also manage to align it with the elicited business needs.

Our stereotyped usage of sequence diagrams adds more representativeness value to the specific model than, for instance, the presented in Krutchen's $4+1$ perspective [25]. This kind of representation also enables testing sequences of system actions that are meaningful at the software architecture level [7]. Additionally, the use of this kind of stereotyped sequence diagrams at the first stage of analysis phase (user requirements modeling and validation) provides a friendlier perspective to most stakeholders, easing them to establish a direct correspondence between what they initially stated as functional requirements and what the model already describes.

The approach assures that validation tasks are performed continuously along the modeling process. It allows for validating: (1) the final IT solution according to the initial expressed requirements; (2) the *B-type* sequence diagrams according to *A-type* sequence diagrams; (3) the logical diagram by traversing it with *B-type* sequence diagrams according to ARID specifications; (4) multiple refinements of the logical architecture trough iterations of the 4SRS method, promoted by issues raised during ARID application. We also believe that our V-Model approach enables the derivation of software architectures with attributes in which [8] considers to be revealing as good software: (1) Architectures are constructed in well-defined layers of abstraction. Each layer is built upon lower levels of abstraction, is isolated and represents a coherent abstraction by itself, with an established and controlled interface; (2) Each layer isolates the interface from the implementation, allowing to make change in one without disrupting the other; (3) Architectures are simple, built using common abstractions and mechanisms. Our context for product requirements elicitation is based on such architecture.

The V-Model representation regards multiple levels of abstraction (for instance, *B-type* sequence diagrams and the logical architecture itself), AEs that constitute the logical architecture are isolated and built using as basis the MVC pattern and all the modeling is done using common notation with only simple extensions, like the presented UML metamodel extension.

References

1. Abran, A., Moore, J., Dupuis, R., Dupuis, R., Tripp, L.: Guide to the software engineering body of knowledge (swebok). 2004 ed P Bourque R Dupuis A Abran and JW Moore Eds IEEE Press (2001)
2. Alter, S.: The work system method for understanding information systems and information systems research. Communications of the Association for Information Systems **9**(1), 6 (2002)
3. Atkinson, C., Kuhne, T.: Model-driven development: A metamodeling foundation. IEEE Softw. **20**(5), 36–41 (2003)

4. Azevedo, S., Machado, R.J., Muthig, D., Ribeiro, H.: Refinement of software product line architectures through recursive modeling techniques (2009)
5. Barrett, S., Konsynski, B.: Inter-organization information sharing systems. MIS Quarterly 6(Special Issue: [1982 Research Program of the Society for Management, Information Systems]), 93–105 (Dec., 1982)
6. Bayer, J., Muthig, D., Gpfert, B.: The library system product line. a kobra case study. Fraunhofer IESE (2001)
7. Bertolino, A., Inverardi, P., Muccini, H.: An explorative journey from architectural tests definition down to code tests execution (2001)
8. Booch, G., Maksimchuk, R., Engle, M., Young, B., Conallen, J., Houston, K.: Object-oriented analysis and design with applications. Addison-Wesley Professional (2007)
9. Browning, T.R., Eppinger, S.D.: Modeling impacts of process architecture on cost and schedule risk in product development. Engineering Management, IEEE Transactions on **49**(4), 428–442 (2002)
10. Campbell, B., Kay, R., Avison, D.: Strategic alignment: a practitioner's perspective. Journal of Enterprise Information Management **18**(6), 653–664 (2005)
11. Cardoso, E.C.S., Almeida, J.P.A., Guizzardi, G.: Requirements engineering based on business process models: A case study (2009)
12. Castro, J., Kolp, M., Mylopoulos, J.: Towards requirements-driven information systems engineering: the tropos project. Information Systems (2002)
13. Chan, Y., Reich, B.: It alignment: what have we learned? Journal of Information Technology **22**(4), 297–315 (2007)
14. Checkland, P.: Soft systems methodology: a thirty year retrospective. Systems Research **17**, S11–S58 (2000)
15. Clements, P.C.: Active reviews for intermediate designs. Tech. rep., Technical Note CMU/SEI-2000-TN-009. (2000)
16. Conradi, R., Jaccheri, M.: Process modelling languages (1999)
17. Evan, W.: Toward a theory of inter-organizational relations. Management Science pp. 217–230 (1965)
18. Ferreira, N., Santos, N., Machado, R.J., Gaevic, D.: Derivation of process-oriented logical architectures: An elicitation approach for cloud design. International Conference on Product Focused Software Development and Process Improvement PROFES2012 **7343**, 45–58 (2012)
19. Hammer, M.: Beyond reengineering: How the process-centered organization is changing our work and our lives. Harper Paperbacks (1997)
20. Haskins, C., Forsberg, K.: Systems engineering handbook: A guide for system life cycle processes and activities; incose-tp-2003-002-03.2. 1 (2011)
21. ISOFIN: Isofin research project. http://isofincloud.i2s.pt/ (2010)
22. Jacobson, I., Griss, M., Jonsson, P.: Software Reuse: Architecture, Process and Organization for Business Success. Addison Wesley Longman (1997)
23. Kang, K.C., Kim, S., Lee, J., Kim, K., Shin, E., Huh, M.: Form: A feature-oriented reuse method with domain-specific reference architectures. Annals of Sw, Engineering (1998)
24. Kazman, R.: Tool support for architecture analysis and design (1996)
25. Kruchten, P.: The 4+1 view model of architecture. IEEE Softw. **12**(6), 42–50 (1995)
26. Kruchten, P.: The Rational Unified Process: An Introduction. Addison-Wesley (2003)
27. Luftman, J., Ben-Zvi, T.: Key issues for it executives 2010: judicious it investments continue post-recession. MIS Quarterly Executive **9**(4), 263–273 (2010)
28. Machado, R., Lassen, K., Oliveira, S., Couto, M., Pinto, P.: Requirements validation: Execution of uml models with cpn tools. International Journal on Software Tools for Technology Transfer (STTT) **9**(3), 353–369 (2007)
29. Machado, R.J., Fernandes, J., Monteiro, P., Rodrigues, H.: Refinement of software architectures by recursive model transformations. International Conference on Product Focused Software Development and Process Improvement PROFES2006 **4034**, 422–428 (2006)
30. Matinlassi, M., Niemel, E., Dobrica, L.: Quality-driven architecture design and quality analysis method, a revolutionary initiation approach to a product line architecture. Tech. rep., VTT Tech. Research Centre of Finland (2002)

31. Medvidovic, N., Taylor, R.N.: A classification and comparison framework for software architecture description languages. Software Engineering, IEEE Transactions on **26**(1), 70–93 (2000)
32. NIST: National institute of standards and technology - the nist definition of cloud computing (2009)
33. OMG: Business process model and notation (bpmn) v2.0
34. OMG: Software and systems process engineering meta-model (spem)
35. OMG: Unified modeling language (uml) superstructure version 2.4.1 (2011)
36. PMI: A Guide to the Project Management Body of Knowledge (PMBOK Guide), 4th edn. (2008)
37. Ruparelia, N.B.: Software development lifecycle models. SIGSOFT Softw. Eng. Notes **35**(3), 8–13 (2010)
38. Sungwon, K., Yoonseok, C.: Designing logical architectures of software systems (2005)
39. Weiss, D.M., Lai, C.T.R.: Software Product-Line Engineering: A Family-Based Software Development Process. Addison-Wesley Professional (1999)
40. Winter, R., Fischer, R.: Essential layers, artifacts, and dependencies of enterprise, architecture (2006)
41. Zou, J., Pavlovski, C.J.: Modeling architectural non functional requirements: From use case to control case (2006)
42. Zowghi, D., Coulin, C.: Requirements elicitation: A survey of techniques, approaches, and tools. Engineering and managing software requirements, Springer, Heidelberg pp. 19–46 (2005)

Chapter 24
Cloud-Based Systems Need Multi-Level Management

Luciano Baresi, Domenico Bianculli and Sam Guinea

Abstract Cloud-based systems are built and delivered using multi-level architectures, which may compose third-party services at the application level as well as at lower levels, such as the platform and the infrastructure ones. With this architectural style, the ability to automatically perform management operations, possibly in a cross-level way, is becoming more and more important as the technology matures, and its adoption increases. We argue that the multi-level management of cloud-based systems should be established at design time, and the service life cycles of the different services (and levels) should be managed accordingly. In this chapter, we present a conceptual model for manageable cloud-based systems, and a reference framework for implementing the foreseen management solutions.

24.1 Introduction

Cloud computing [2] is imposing a significant shift in the way many modern software applications are conceived. While usually computational capabilities were constant, and the design had to take them into account, cloud computing offers a wider and more flexible design space. The attention is not only at the application level anymore,

L. Baresi (✉) · S. Guinea
Deep-SE Group, Dipartimento di Elettronica e Informazione,
Politecnico di Milano, Piazza L. da Vinci, 32, I-20133 Milano, MI, Italy
e-mail: luciano.baresi@polimi.it

S. Guinea
e-mail: sam.guinea@polimi.it

D. Bianculli
University of Luxembourg, SnT Centre, 4 rue Alphonse Weicker,
L-2721 Luxembourg, Luxembourg
e-mail: domenico.bianculli@uni.lu

A. Bouguettaya et al. (eds.), *Advanced Web Services*,
DOI: 10.1007/978-1-4614-7535-4_24,

but one can (easily) control and manage all the resources down to the physical infrastructure.

The *service* abstraction is the key enabler of this change. Initially, services were used as a means to provide coarse-grained self-describing software components over a network infrastructure. Web and REST services [32, 33] indeed became consolidated technologies, and many composition solutions were devised, such as BPEL (Business Process Execution Language) [28], ESB (Enterprise Service Bus) [12], and SCA (Service Component Architecture) [29].

Nowadays, services are also used to abstract the *infrastructure* on which applications are executed, and the *platforms* that supply the key elements needed to create and deploy the applications. Execution and storage services (like the ones offered by Amazon [1]) as well as platform services (like Microsoft Azure [24], Google App Engine [19], and Heroku [21]) are becoming widely used solutions to create, deploy, and run many different applications. The same applies to OpenStack [30], which offers a complete set of open-source elements for creating a complete, private cloud infrastructure.

All these solutions provide users—and their applications—with the resources they need, but they also foster a more global approach towards the development and management of applications. There is no need to overestimate required resources at design time anymore, but they can be efficiently acquired and released on demand. From a management perspective, these resources must be properly probed, planned, and provisioned. For example, in the old days, the addition of a new server, because of a sudden increase in the number of users, would have been considered a major, significant change, taking a significant amount of time and money. Now, we can buy the computing power on the cloud as soon as we need it, for the time we need it, and put it in operation in minutes.

Besides offering new opportunities, the abstraction/virtualization of resources opens the whole development/deployment/execution stack and enables quite sophisticated management. Besides the "usual" monitoring of the behavior of the different software components and of the operation of the computing infrastructure, the cloud allows one to change the allocation of components and vary computational resources. Problems at one level, say pure performance of the application, may require multi-level solutions: e.g., the provision of a new virtual machine and the selection of faster services. More sophistication also calls for more advanced monitoring and adaptation capabilities. All the different constituents of the system, that is, the different application, platform, and infrastructure services must be probed efficiently and effectively. Retrieved data must be integrated, correlated, and analyzed. Finally, identified solutions must be communicated to all interested parties.

Achieving these goals calls for two key elements: the identification of a comprehensive conceptual model, able to accommodate all the concepts that characterize the three typical layers of cloud-based applications, and a suitable run-time framework supporting the management.

This chapter moves a significant step in this direction. It organizes the concepts and solutions that belong to today cloud initiatives. It motivates, proposes, and discusses C^2M (Comprehensive Cloud Model), which aims to accommodate all the typical concepts of a layered cloud-based application. It also draws the high-level architecture of a run-time infrastructure to support both C^2M and the multi-layered approach to the management of cloud-based applications. This architecture can also be seen as an attempt to organize and summarize the work done by the authors in the context of monitoring, managing, and adapting services and service-centered solutions at the different levels.

The rest of this chapter is organized as follows. Section 24.2 presents and discusses the nature of cloud-based systems. Section 24.3 presents C^2M, and discusses the abstractions needed to accommodate software, platform, and infrastructure services, as well as the main management concepts that need to be taken into account to build a manageable cloud-based system. Section 24.4 presents a reference framework for the holistic, multi-level management of cloud-based systems. Section 24.5 exemplifies the concepts on two different designs of a "LaTeX in the Cloud" application. Section 24.6 discusses related work in the area of run-time service management, including the authors' previous contributions in the field. Section 24.7 concludes the paper by presenting our agenda for future work.

24.2 Cloud-Based Systems

Services are coarse-grained software components that are wrapped in standard protocols and delivered through the Internet. They represent the basic building blocks of service-oriented architectures. In this architectural style, loosely-coupled services, which tackle separate concerns, are composed to build easily evolvable distributed systems. This allows them to respond to sudden changes in the execution environment or in their requirements in a smoother manner.

The service abstraction has become the cornerstone of the development of cloud computing. No longer do we solely speak of Software-as-a-Service (SaaS). Instead we now commonly apply the abstraction to software platforms (Platform-as-a-Service, PaaS), to infrastructures (Infrastructure-as-a-Service, IaaS), and to a growing number of other elements (Everything-as-a-Service, XaaS).

Cloud computing has mainly become associated with the delivery of three kinds of system components: software, platform, and infrastructure. Figure 24.1 shows the three layers commonly seen in a modern multi-layered cloud-based application.

In the *Software-as-a-Service* layer the main stakeholder is the *application developer*. Her goal is to build a software application that is delivered on demand over the Internet. Typical examples are Google Docs, which provides office utilities as a service; Dropbox, which provides file storage as a service; Blitline, which provides image processing as a service, and so on. The SaaS level is typically realized by composing software services (possibly from third parties) that expose well-defined WSDL or REST interfaces. One way to compose them is to adopt a standard service composition language, such as BPEL, but the composition may be achieved through a regular programming language.

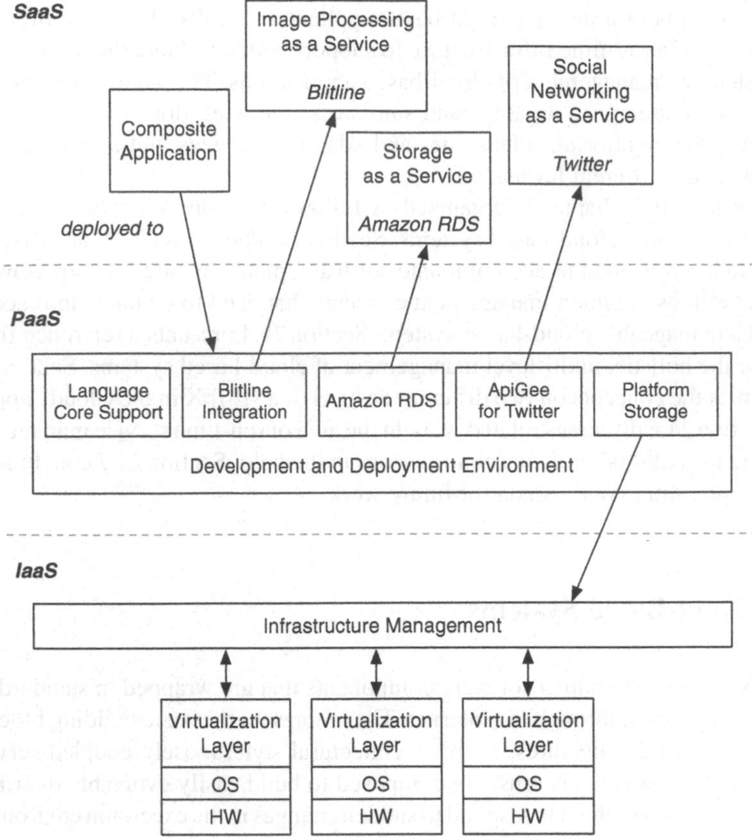

Fig. 24.1 The three classic layers of a cloud-based system

In the *Platform-as-a-Service* layer the main stakeholder is the *platform provider*. Her goal is to build a software platform within which developers can implement and deploy their applications. Typical examples are Google App Engine, Microsoft Azure, Heroku, and so on. Providing a PaaS means providing a development and deployment environment that can be easily custom-tailored for a given application. This involves provisioning a core development framework, as well as allowing the developer to extend it with additional first- or third-party libraries and tools. The extension mechanism is an important part of the platform offering, since it ensures that the library integration is achieved seamlessly. In Fig. 24.1, which depicts the three classic layers of a cloud-based system, we notice that the platform layer offers a *Platform Storage* service, which is implemented in the platform's underlying infrastructure. The platform layer also integrates various third-party libraries that allow the application to more easily interact with software services such as Blitline, Amazon RDS, and Twitter. These libraries can be either simple programmatic gateways towards these services, or they can provide additional functionality. For example, developers that access Twitter through the ApiGee service get a higher limit for the number of Twitter API requests per hour.

In the *Infrastructure-as-a-Service* layer the main stakeholder is the *infrastructure provider*. Her goal is to provide scalable on-demand provisioning of infrastructural resources, usually in terms of computing resources or virtual machines. Typical examples are Amazon EC2 (Elastic Compute Cloud), Rackspace, GoGrid, and so on. IaaS providers exploit economies of scale to provide computational resources hosted in big data centers across the globe. The computational resources can be virtual machines, block storage, firewalls, load balancers or networking I/O, and their costs are typically calculated on a usage basis.

A developer that wants to implement and deploy a cloud-based application has many options. She can decide to rely on a PaaS, on an IaaS, or on neither. This decision defines the number of technical aspects that she will have to explicitly take into account and manage. If the application is deployed within a PaaS, the developer will only need to manage the application. Other aspects such as the run-time environment, the servers, the virtualization, the hardware, and the networking will be managed for her by the provider. If the application is deployed within a IaaS, the developer will once again be responsible for the application. This time, however, she will also need to explicitly manage the run-time environment and the servers. The virtualization, the hardware, and the networking will continue to be managed for her by the provider. Finally, if the application is deployed neither on a PaaS nor on a IaaS, then the developer will need to explicitly take all these aspects into account and manage them by herself.

24.3 C^2M: A Comprehensive Conceptual Model for Multi-Level Management of Cloud-Based Systems

In this section we illustrate C^2M, the comprehensive conceptual model we developed to support the holistic management of cloud-based applications. At a bird's view, C^2M is composed of two parts:

- the concepts related to service abstraction, and to the different service composition mechanisms that are available at the software, platform, and infrastructure levels;
- the concepts related to service management.

In the following, we detail the two parts and highlight the associations that connect them to each other.

24.3.1 *Service Abstraction*

As depicted in Fig. 24.2, the cornerstone of C^2M is the concept of Service; this concept captures the different levels we have mentioned in Sect. 24.2, i.e., SaaS,

PaaS, and IaaS. Although it is possible to consider other levels underneath IaaS (e.g., Hardware-as-a-Service), in C^2M we consider IaaS to be the lowest visible (and manageable) level of our applications.

For each Service there can be different Service Instances, each of them delivering its functionality to one or more customers. Each Service Instance is an independent entity with respect to the other instances; hence, it can be managed autonomously. Anyway, some management decisions can be made in terms of a Service and then applied to all instances of that service. To enable management at these different levels, Service and Service Instances are subclasses of Manageable Entity, which is described later in Sect. 24.3.2.

C^2M defines two possible kinds of associations between services: the "uses" association and the "composes" association. The "uses" association identifies the fact that a service provided at one layer uses or depends on a service provided at a lower layer. The "composes" association identifies a stronger relationship. It means that an added-value service can be built by composing other services that exist in the same layer. The "uses" association is therefore an inter-level association, while the "composes" association is an intra-level association.

The inter-level nature of the "uses" association can lead to various combinations: a SaaS service can use a PaaS or an IaaS service, while a PaaS service can only use an IaaS service. The "uses" association defined between SaaS Service and PaaS Service characterizes the fact that an application at the SaaS level can be built on top of a platform service, relying on the functionality provided by the platform (e.g., authentication, queues). This is the case for applications developed for Google App Engine. Similarly, the "uses" association between SaaS Service and IaaS Service represents the case in which a SaaS application is built directly on the virtualized machine abstraction provided by the infrastructure level, e.g., by configuring the operating system, the middleware components, the business logic, and the storage access. For example, this is the case of applications that are deployed on Amazon EC2 by configuring a custom virtual machine image. Note that a SaaS application might use, at the same time, services provided by different vendors at the platform and infrastructure level. A platform service can be realized on top of an existing infrastructure, as modeled by the "uses" association between PaaS Service and IaaS Service. This is the case of Heroku, a well known PaaS solution supporting various language environments, such as Ruby, Java, Python, and PHP. Heroku's deployment environments are built on top of the infrastructural services provided by Amazon. On the one hand, this allows Heroku not to invest in proprietary server-farms; on the other, this means that Heroku's services depend on Amazon successfully providing the infrastructure. For example, when on June 29, 2012, Amazon's EC2 suffered a widespread and hours-long outage in its North Virginia facilities, systems built on Heroku were also made unavailable.[1]

[1] More details can be found at http://venturebeat.com/2012/06/29/amazon-outage-netflix-instagram-pinterest/.

Note that a PaaS Service can be implemented by directly accessing and configuring in-house hardware, which—as said above—is not included[2] in C^2M. This is the case of Google App Engine, which uses its own server facilities to provide its PaaS solution. Similarly, a SaaS Service can also be implemented directly on top of in-house hardware, and have no "use" associations.

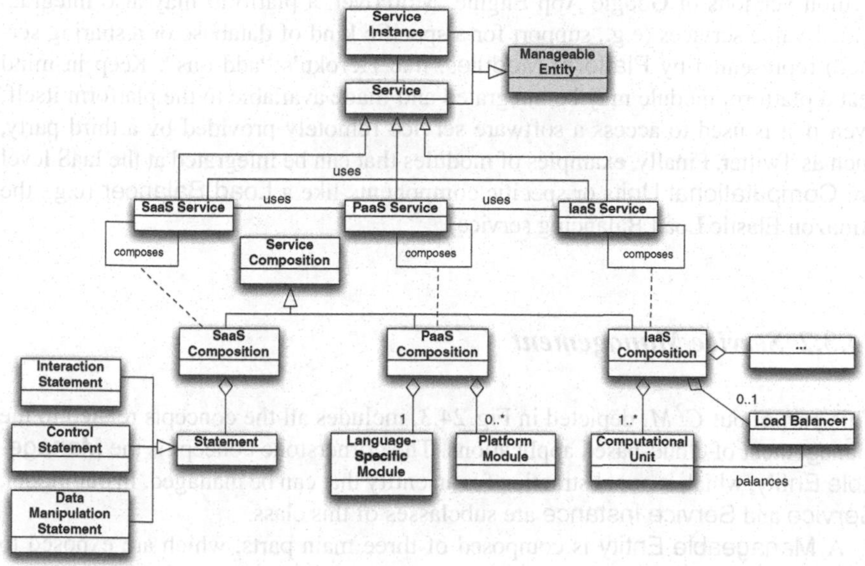

Fig. 24.2 Service abstraction concepts

The way service composition is realized is different for each level in which it is enacted. At the SaaS level, developers implement composite services using the features provided by the programming language they adopt. The concept represented by a Statement in the adopted programming language plays a fundamental role in this sense. An Interaction Statement represents an interaction with a partner service, which can happen synchronously or asynchronously. Typical examples of this class of statements are `invoke` or `receive` activities in BPEL, or a (remote) procedure call in a common programming language like Java or C. A Control Statement corresponds to the usual control structures of programming languages (selection, loops, exception handling) as well as to constructs that are specific to service interactions (e.g., the `pick` and the `wait` activities, popular in BPEL). Control Statements are used to define the control flow of a composition. Finally, a Data Manipulation Statement is used to set the fields of the messages exchanged with or the variables passed to a partner service. For example, it may correspond to an `assign` activity in BPEL. This kind of statement is very important for dealing with the heterogeneity

[2] This is also why we never define "uses" associations for IaaS Services.

of data representations used by the different partner services participating in a service composition. While a service composition is realized programmatically at the SaaS level, at the other two levels of our model, i.e., PaaS and IaaS, service composition is realized as aggregation of "modules". For example, a platform composite service could be realized by integrating Language-Specific Modules on the basis of the programming languages that the platform wants to support, like the Java and Python versions of Google App Engine. Moreover, a platform may also integrate added-value services (e.g., support for a specific kind of database or a sharing service) represented by Platform Modules, like Heroku's "add-ons". Keep in mind that a platform module may be integrated and made available to the platform itself, even if it is used to access a software service remotely provided by a third party, such as Twitter. Finally, examples of modules that can be integrated at the IaaS level are Computational Units or specific components like a Load Balancer (e.g., the Amazon Elastic Load Balancing service).

24.3.2 Service Management

This part of our C^2M, depicted in Fig. 24.3, includes all the concepts related to the management of cloud-based applications. The cornerstone concept is the Manageable Entity, which is our abstraction for an entity that can be managed. In our model, Service and Service Instance are subclasses of this class.

A Manageable Entity is composed of three main parts, which are exposed to clients:

Probes. A probe of a Manageable Entity allows its clients to profile/inspect some facets of its status. For example, a client might want to profile a service's average response time or its throughput. Other probes might be specific to the level to which the "probed" service belongs. In the case of an infrastructure service, interesting probes could be CPU, memory, network or disk usage of a virtual machine. For a platform service, users might want to check the version of a certain programming library made available on the platform, or the space occupied by the database. At SaaS level, probes are application-specific. Keep in mind that, although a probe conceptually belongs to a manageable entity, it can be installed on the client's side of an interaction to make up for the fact that the service may be hosted by a third-party.

Specifications. A service specification provides different types of information about the service itself. One kind of information is represented by Features, related to the functionality offered by the service. For example, they include the type of authentication supported by the application exposed as a SaaS, the programming languages supported by a platform, the memory configuration available at the IaaS level. The other type of Specification provided by a service is represented by the concept of Property, which groups specifications in the form of pre-

/post-conditions, invariants, behavioral protocols, quality-of-service attributes, at various level of formality.

Management Operations. This concept represents the operation that can be performed on a Manageable Entity, e.g., a service, by a management framework. There is a group of operations that can be performed at any level; they are called Lifecycle Operations and control the execution of a service, by starting, stopping, or pausing it. Other operations are specific to each level of our model. For example, at the SaaS level, management can be enacted with a Change Statement operation, such as changing the partner service of an Interaction Statement, to support dynamic binding. At the PaaS and IaaS levels, Management Operations manipulate the modules that compose the platform or the infrastructure; for examples, modules can be added, removed, or updated.

Note that the concepts related to service management included in our model are transparent to the concept of Service Composition. Since a Service Composition is an aggregation of Services, which are Manageable Entities, a service composition is itself a Manageable Entity. On the other hand, C^2M prescribes that the composition mechanisms used to realize a composition be *management-aware*. This is a crucial requirement that determines that a composition mechanism has:

- to expose Management Operations, Probes, and Specifications that are related to the composite service as a whole;
- to intercept invocations of a Management Operation, or readings of Probes and Specifications, by passing the invocation or reading requests to the proper component services, as well as correlating and aggregating the data coming from the component services.

Furthermore, since a service at the SaaS or PaaS level may "use" the services provided by the lower level(s), invoking a Management Operation or reading a Probe/Specification at the (higher) service level, should be properly translated into invocations of Management Operations and Probe/Specification readings of the services used at the lower levels. This has a strong impact in terms of multi-level manageability.

24.4 A Reference Framework for Multi-Level Management

Management of multi-level cloud-based systems needs to be holistic. We need to understand that the single parts of a system are intimately interconnected and explicable only by reference to the whole. This helps us to not confuse symptoms with causes. A functional problem (e.g., the violation of a run-time assertion) or a non-functional one (e.g., an unacceptably long response time) that is witnessed at one particular level, for example at the SaaS level, may be caused by malfunctions in one of the system lower levels, for example at the PaaS or IaaS level. For each problem we need to find the most effective, and time-and cost-efficient solution; this may require coordinated adaptations at multiple layers.

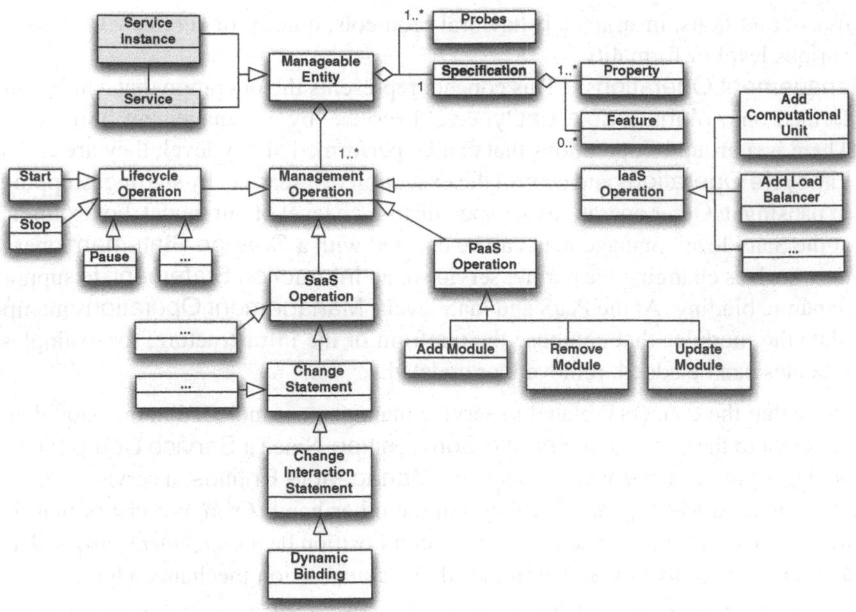

Fig. 24.3 Service management concepts

In literature there are many management approaches that concentrate on a single level, and treat it in isolation from the rest of the system [3, 7, 23]. Many of these approaches adopt some form of MAPE (Monitoring, Analysis, Planning, and Execution) control loop [22]. A MAPE control loop is built and run in parallel with respect to the system. It monitors the system behavior, analyzes it to discover functional and/or non-functional problems, plans possible solutions, and then attempts to dynamically adapt the system accordingly.

Guinea et al. have advocated that the traditional control loop could continue to be used if it were extended to support multi-level systems [20]. Figure 24.4 shows a slight variation of the reference multi-level control loop described therein. The loop is made up of four steps: *Multi-level Monitoring*, *Multi-level Analysis of Adaptation Needs*, *Multi-level Adaptation Planning*, and *Coordinated Adaptation*. The approach builds upon the fact that the levels adopt a common service abstraction, and are therefore made up of manageable entities, as defined in C^2M.

The *Multi-level Monitoring* step is responsible for capturing the run-time data needed to reason about the system functional and non-functional behavior. These data are the static and dynamic properties exposed by the manageable entities, as defined in C^2M. This is achieved by deploying appropriate software probes to the three levels. Probes are shown in Fig. 24.4 as small boxes labeled with the letter "P". The amount of data that can be produced by a cloud-based system, if we take into account all three levels, can be overwhelming. This is the reason for which this step also needs to perform an initial assessment of the data. Data from different levels are

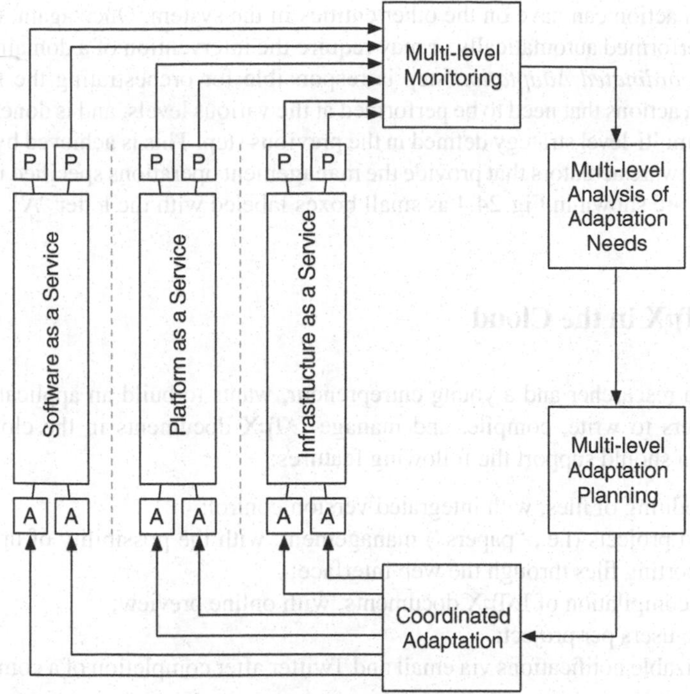

Fig. 24.4 The multi-level management reference framework

filtered, correlated, aggregated, and manipulated to produce higher-level information under the form of general or domain-specific metrics. This exercise is what makes the holistic analysis of the system's behavior possible. Run-time data can also be temporarily (or permanently) stored to optimize the correlation, and to allow for offline drill-down analyses.

The *Multi-level Analysis of Adaptation Needs* step is responsible for taking the correlated data and using them to identify anomalies within the system. This step can be performed automatically, through the evaluation of cross-level properties expressed over current and historical correlated data, or manually by a human expert. In the latter case the expert needs to be assisted by a multi-level monitoring dashboard in which the correlated data can be analyzed both as a live feed and through drill-down analysis.

The *Multi-level Adaptation Planning* step is aware of the adaptation capabilities that are available in the system, and is responsible for planning a coordinated multi-level adaptation strategy. The strategy defines what actions need to be taken, at what level and in what order, and the data that they need to exchange to accomplish their goals. The planning should take into account the dependencies that exist between the various manageable entities, and be aware of the positive or negative impact that an adaptation action can have on the other entities in the system. Once again, this step may be performed automatically or may require the intervention of a domain expert.

The *Coordinated Adaptation* step is responsible for orchestrating the multiple adaptation actions that need to be performed at the various levels, and is done according to the multi-level strategy defined in the previous step. This is achieved by engaging the software actuators that provide the management operations specified in C^2M. Actuators are shown in Fig. 24.4 as small boxes labeled with the letter "A".

24.5 LaTeX in the Cloud

Dr. Dek, a researcher and a young entrepreneur, wants to build an application that allows users to write, compile, and manage LaTeX documents in the cloud. The application should support the following features:

- online editing of files, with integrated version control;
- files and projects (i.e., "papers") management, with the possibility of uploading and exporting files through the web interface;
- remote compilation of LaTeX documents, with online preview;
- multiple users per project;
- customizable notifications via email and Twitter after completion of a compilation job.

The architecture designed by Dr. Dek for this application is sketched in Fig. 24.5. The *Frontend* module contains the web forms for editing, uploading, and exporting files, organizing projects, and browsing file revisions. The *Application Logic* module contains the business logic that authenticates users, compiles documents, manages

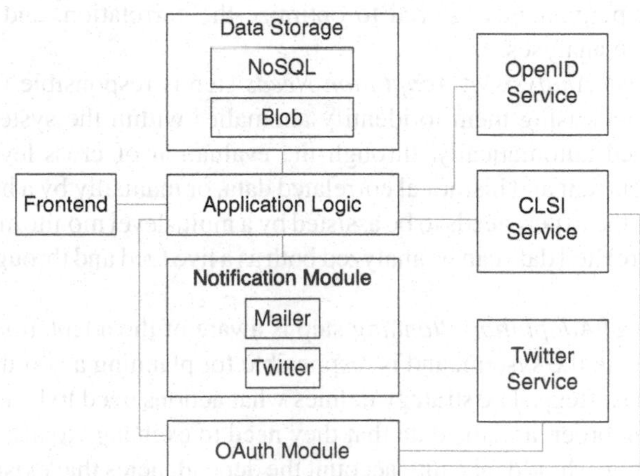

Fig. 24.5 Architectural sketch of the "LaTeX in the Cloud" application

files revisions, and controls notifications. Application users are authenticated through the OpenID standard using a third-party OpenID service. Users' settings and metadata (e.g., list of the files belonging to a project, access lists for a project, compilation flags) are stored in a NoSQL key-value store. LaTeX source files, their revisions, and the output of a compilation (log and PDF files) are stored in a datastore optimized for blob objects. Remote compilation is supported using a third-party service that implements the *CLSI-Common LaTeX Service Interface*. The *Notification* module is responsible for sending out email and Twitter notifications to all the project participants, to signal that a new version of the document has been released. An email contains the notification itself, the LaTeX compilation logs, and the resulting PDF file (or a link for its download). A tweet, on the other hand, contains only the notification and a link to get the newly compiled PDF. The Twitter and CLSI services are accessed using the OAuth authentication protocol through a dedicated module.

Dr. Dek considers two possible solutions to develop and deploy this application. The first one relies on Amazon technologies and consists of a mix of infrastructure services (e.g., computational units like Amazon EC2) that will serve to users the dynamic web pages of the application and execute the business logic of the application, and storage services[3] (e.g., Amazon SimpleDB or DynamoDB as NoSQL databases and Amazon S3 as a blob data store). Note that this solution requires that Dr. Dek personally configure all the required servers and middleware, and develop the full code base of the application, including the business logic, the interaction with the OpenID, the CLSI and the Twitter services, as well as auxiliary components, such as the Notification (including the Mailer sub-component) and the OAuth module.

In the second solution, Dr. Dek wants to leverage the services provided by a PaaS, to reduce the amount of code to write, and to simplify the management of the underlying infrastructure. He picks Google App Engine, since it provides important services used in the application, such the App Engine Datastore as a NoSQL database, Google Cloud Storage as blob datastore, the Mail API for email functionality, and the Users API with support for OpenID identifiers. It also offers additional functionality, which Dr. Dek is considering to support in the next major revision of the application, such as the possibility to convert documents file type (e.g., from PDF to HTML) through the Conversion API, and images manipulation through the Images API. Note that this solution also reduces dependencies on third-party services, since accessing the OpenID service or third-party storage services is no longer required because this functionality is provided by the platform.

24.5.1 Managing the "LaTeX in the Cloud" Application

Here we analyze how the two solutions described above can be managed with respect to the concepts defined in C^2M. We describe suitable probes and management oper-

[3] We consider storage services at the same level as SaaS; see also Fig. 24.1.

ations, and discuss three different multi-layer management scenarios. We identify the following groups of Manageable Entities:

- **Manageable Entities that are shared by both solutions.** Both solutions rely on the Twitter, CLSI, and OpenID services. These services do not expose any probe; probes have to be installed on the client's side, to monitor attributes such as the average response time, the throughput, and the invocation rate. These services also do not expose management operations to third-party users.
- **Manageable Entities used in the Amazon-based solution.** In this solution we use Amazon SimpleDB, Amazon S3, Amazon DynamoDB, and Amazon EC2. The first two services provide probes for attributes through dedicated APIs. For example, they can provide the amount of used storage using `DomainMetadata` and `get_bucket_filesize`, respectively. The other services expose probes through Amazon's own monitoring solution, called Amazon CloudWatch. For DynamoDB Amazon exposes probes such as `SuccessfulRequest Latency, UserErrors, SystemErrors, ThrottledRequests, ConsumedReadCapacityUnits, ConsumedWriteCapacityUnits,` and `ReturnedItemCount`. For Amazon EC2, Amazon exposes probes for `CPUUtilization, DiskReadOps, DiskWriteOps, DiskReadBy-tes, DiskWriteBytes, NetworkIn, NetworkOut`. When in-house software modules—such as the Frontend and the Application Logic modules—are executed on Amazon EC2, we may also want to define application-specific probes like statistics on the generation of dynamic web pages. This can be done using the standard probing capabilities that are included with the operating system, e.g., used memory or swap memory size. Moreover, these extra probes can register with CloudWatch if they want to make their data available through its standard channels. Amazon EC2 is the only service, among the ones we decided to use, to provide some form of management operations. Among others there are operations to manage virtual machines images (e.g., `CreateImage`, `RegisterImage`), to manage storage volumes (e.g., `AttachVolume`), to control a machine instance (e.g., `StartInstance, RunInstance, StopInstance, ModifyInstance Attribute`), and to enable load balancing (e.g., `CreateLoadBalancer, RegisterInstances WithLoadBalancer`).
- **Manageable Entities used in the Google App Engine based solution.** In this solution we use the App Engine DataStore, Google Cloud Storage, and the Mail API. The App Engine Datastore provides probes for capturing the response times of the RPC calls that are made to the datastore, statistics counts, usage levels by property and entity type, write operation counts, etc. The Google Cloud Storage provides probes for capturing the total storage size, entry counts, and the size of built-in and composite indexes. The Mail API provides probes for monitoring the response times of the RPC calls that are made to the mailer. When we run the Frontend and Application Logic on Google App Engine we can also receive reports on their average queries per second over the last minute, their average latency over the last minute, the number of requests they received in the last minute, how long they have been running, their current memory usage, and their availability. In

terms of manageability, Google App Engine allows service providers to choose the processing capacity of the instances running the application, as well as to configure the scheduler, by setting the number of idle instances it should take into consideration and the pending latency. The lifecycle of default ("frontend") instances is automatically managed by App Engine, while "backend" can be managed by developers. The DataStore supports data backup and restore, as well as copy and delete operations. No management operations are available for the Cloud Storage service and Mail APIs.

In addition to the probes and the managing operations described above, we assume that it is also possible to define more application-specific probes for the composite application. We also assume that other level-specific operations are available, such as code changes or datastore migration.

24.5.2 Management Scenarios

We now review three possible management scenarios that may occur while running "LaTeX in the Cloud". Each scenario begins with a description of how it plays out in the Amazon-based implementation, and then discusses the differences that arise in the Google-based implementation.

Scenario 1

In this scenario, the application-specific probe corresponding to the time perceived by the user for compiling a LaTeX project reads a value that is higher than expected. Note that this value, reported at the SaaS level, is the aggregation (e.g., the sum) of the response time of many service invocations:

- the NoSQL database queried to retrieve which files belong to the project;
- the Application Logic that determines which files have already been cached by the CLSI service and therefore do not need to be uploaded again;
- the blob datastore used to retrieve the raw artifacts to compile;
- the CLSI service that performs the actual compilation.

Although the symptom is initially seen at the SaaS level, Dr. Dek decides to look at probes at various layers, and to perform a holistic analysis. Dr. Dek notices that there are no anomalies in the execution of the CLSI, NoSQL, and S3 services; the culprit is then at the IaaS level, because the computational unit is inadequate to properly execute the application logic. Dr. Dek has two possible solutions. The first possibility is to perform the EC2 IaaS operation `ModifyInstanceAttribute` to modify the type of instance being used with one with greater resources. The second possibility is to create a new EC2 instance with the `CreateInstance` management operation, deploy the application to the new node, and then introduce load balancing with the operations

`CreateLoadBalancer` and `RegisterInstancesWithLoadBalancer`. Since the application was designed with advanced management features in mind, Dr. Dek can easily create a new virtual machine in parallel and perform a failover to the new instance.

In the Google-based implementation the scenario plays out in a similar fashion. The analysis of the data collected through the probes is mostly the same. The adaptation however is slightly different. First of all, Google does not provide fine-grained management operations for its instances; instead Dr. Dek's instances are managed for him by the platform. When the instances are no longer adequate, Google App Engine will automatically create new instances of the Application Logic and load balance them with respect to incoming requests. Dr. Dek has limited control over how this is performed. He can only use the management operations that allow him to specify the minimum and maximum number of idle instances that should remain available at all times to manage usage peaks, and the minimum and maximum latency for requests that are temporarily stored when all available instances are fully occupied. These parameters define how aggressive Google App Engine is in dynamically adding and removing instances. A second solution for Dr. Dek is to configure Google App Engine to be less aggressive and to migrate the application to an instance with more resources.

Scenario 2

In this case, the probe corresponding to the time for generating the dynamic page that displays a specific file's version history is higher than expected. In this case the components that are involved in providing the page are:

- the NoSQL database queried to retrieve the file's version history;
- the Application Logic;
- the Frontend.

Once again the symptom is seen at the SaaS level. Nevertheless Dr. Dek performs a holistic analysis that takes into account data from probes at multiple layers. This analysis determines that the virtual machines running the Frontend and the Application Logic execute as expected; moreover, the probes for the Frontend report a reasonable response time for the invocation of the Application Logic component. The problem lies in the NoSQL database. Indeed, its `DomainMetadata` probe tells him that the storage is approaching the maximum size permitted, and therefore cannot scale any further. Dr. Dek decides to change this component by upgrading to Amazon DynamoDB, a more performant and scalable NoSQL database. This decision would typically require Dr. Dek to perform a data migration from SimpleDB to DynamoDB, and to change the application code. These actions require also to stop the application, redeploy it, and (re)start it. However, Dr. Dek designed the application with a persistence layer that allows him to dynamically modify the binding to the NoSQL database. This allows him to avoid modifying the application code; however, the data migration must still be performed manually. This step can be achieved when the system is still running to avoid any down-time.

In the Google-based implementation the scenario does not occur. The reason for this is that the NoSQL datastore is provided directly within the PaaS. Amazon SimpleDB is offered as SaaS, and has finite quotas, while Google provides no maximum limit for billed data storage. The same is true for blob storage.

Scenario 3

In this scenario, the operating system of the virtual machine on which the application logic is being run reports a high-usage of the swap file as well as minimal residual amount of free memory. Here the culprit can only be the application logic, which, by the way, shows a normal invocation rate. These data drive Dr. Dek to setup profiling tools, such as DTrace, to investigate the memory leak. This is easily done since Dr. Dek has full access to the virtual machine. A bug fix is then required, and this implies that the application will need to be stopped (operation `StopInstance`), manually fixed, redeployed and restarted (operation `StartInstance`). More elaborate solutions are also possible. For example, Dr. Dek could leave the application running, produce the bug fix, create a new virtual machine instance to which to deploy it (operation `CreateImage`), and then swap the old instance with the new one (operations `StopInstance` and `StartInstance`). In both cases, the symptom is seen at the IaaS level, while the adaptation occurs at the SaaS level (e.g., bug fix), possibly involving other levels as well (e.g., swapping of virtual machine instances).

In the Google-based implementation the scenario plays out in a slightly different manner. When deploying to the PaaS, Dr. Dek no longer has direct access to the instance's operating system. This means he can no longer provide custom infrastructure probes, and must rely solely on the information that Google provides. In this particular case, Google only provides a periodic snapshot of the instance's memory usage. This is enough for Dr. Dek to understand that there is a problem, but his limited view of the system makes the application profiling and the bug hunting more difficult. His only solution is to undeploy the application, instrument the source code with statement-level probes, and redeploy it to Google App Engine. The probes collect more data than before, and these are saved in the PaaS to logs, which are then downloaded to Dr. Dek's own computer and used to profile the application through DTrace. When the bug is found and fixed, the application can finally be stopped, redeployed, and restarted.

24.6 Related Work

Here we present and briefly discuss some of the most interesting works on the runtime management of service-based systems. We start by presenting approaches that propose models for manageability, and then concentrate on isolated service monitoring and adaptation approaches that focus on multi-level systems. We conclude this section with an overview of some of the work that we have achieved in the area of run-time service management.

24.6.1 Models for Manageability

Manageability has been a hot topic for standardization by part of different consortiums. Oasis has proposed the Web Services Distributed Management (WSDM) [27], a protocol for the interoperability of management information and features. It focuses on two main aspects: how to use Web services technologies as the foundation of a resource management framework, and how these notions can be adapted to Web services themselves. An alternative standard, called WS-Management [15], has been proposed by the Distributed Management Task Force (DMTF). Its goal is similar to WSDM's one, as it provides support for generic resource management using Web service standards. It also proposes a special binding for managing resources that are defined using their Common Information Model (CIM).

Different MDE methodologies for managing extra-functional properties of service compositions have been proposed, although they focus on a single level in the system. Chowdhary et al. [13] address the specification of business-level performance indicators and their direct transformation to platform specific models, Debusmann et al. [14] define SLA (Service Level Agreement) parameters together with the specific indicators needed within the SLA itself, and Chan et al. [11] address the automatic generation of component-based instrumentations for monitoring specific quality-of-service concerns.

Momm et al. [25] provide a model-based technique for defining the monitoring and control capabilities of a manageable software service. In their work, they model how a service Key Performance Indicator is obtained through low-level processing operations (e.g., addition, subtraction, etc.). They then discuss various instrumentation alternatives that can be used to derive a service's manageability interface, and provide a manageability infrastructure capable of dealing with basic elementary data, and with their correlation and aggregation.

24.6.2 Multi-Level Monitoring and Adaptation

Multi-level control loops are still in their infancy. One of the authors participated in a preliminary study in which there was a first attempt to create an integrated multi-level control loop for service-based systems [20]. In particular, in this work the authors developed a control loop for managing BPEL processes on top of virtualized resources; there was no concrete corollary contribution for software deployed in the context of a PaaS. C^2M was designed to overcome this limitation, by providing the foundational models required to generalize the control loop for multi-level applications.

There have also been some initial research contributions that concentrate either on multi-level monitoring or on multi-level adaptation. For example, Foster et al. [18] have proposed an extensible framework for monitoring business, software, and infrastructure services. The framework allows different kinds of reasoners, tailored to different kinds of services, to be integrated and to collaborate to monitor decomposable SLA terms and expressions. The framework automatically assigns the decomposed atomic terms to specific reasoners, yet the approach does not support the correlation of terms monitored at different layers. Mos et al. [26] propose a multi-layered monitoring approach that considers service and infrastructure level events produced by services deployed to a distributed enterprise service bus. Basic computations can be performed on the events to produce aggregate information (e.g., averages) or complex event processing can be used for more complex correlations and verifications. The resulting data are analyzed by comparing them to thresholds, and the knowledge collected at the various levels are presented through appropriately differentiated user interfaces and visualization techniques. The approach does not correlate knowledge collected at the different levels.

Regarding multi-level adaptation, Efstratiou et al. [16] present an approach for adapting multiple applications that share common resources. These applications are not composed, but rather single entities affected by the same contextual attributes. Since these applications live in the same space they need to coordinate how they manage the shared resources to avoid conflicts. However, they expect the users to perceive and model the conflicts manually. Finally, Popescu et al. [31] propose a framework for multi-layer adaptation of service-based systems comprised of organization, coordination and service layers. In this approach a designer needs to prepare a taxonomy of the adaptation mismatches, and then a set of adaptation templates, known as patterns, that define generic solutions for these mismatches.

True multi-level monitoring and adaptation techniques need to be able to plan multi-layered adaptation strategies. To this end Zengin et al. [34] have developed a cross-layer adaptation manager called CLAM. The approach takes as input (a) a model of the service-based system in which the designer highlights the cross-layer relationships that exist between the services, and (b) a set of predefined domain-specific rules that can be used to establish the integration of different adaptation actuators at different levels. The authors have published preliminary results based on an initial implementation of CLAM.

24.6.3 Our Contributions to the Area

In the last few years we have provided numerous contributions to the concepts presented in C^2M, both in terms of property specification languages, and in terms of run-time management machinery. This work was mainly focused on the SaaS layer, and in particular on BPEL compositions.

24.6.3.1 WSCoL, WSReL, and Dynamo

In [7] we presented WSCoL (Web Service Constraint Language), an assertion language for specifying the functional and non-functional properties of the interactions between a BPEL process and its third-party services. A WSCoL assertion is always associated with a BPEL interaction statement. When we reach this statement in the process execution, we gather the required run-time data and attempt to verify the assertion. WSCoL allows three different kinds of probes: *internal probes*, to gather information from the process internal execution state, *external probes*, to gather context and situational information, and *historical probes*, to gather information about previous process invocations.

We also presented WSReL (Web Service Recovery Language), a language for defining complex recovery strategies that can be enacted when an anomaly is discovered. It provides both local and backward recovery. The former attempts to fix a problem in the current state of error (i.e., compensation), while the latter attempts to fix the problem by restoring the process to a previously known correct state (i.e., rollback). WSReL adopts a combination of ECA (Event–Condition–Action) rules that allows designers to mix and match atomic actions, such as ignore, notify, rebind, callback, and restore, to build a complex recovery strategy.

For WSCoL and WSReL we developed Dynamo, a process execution environment that provides WSCoL-compliant probes and analyzers, and WSReL-compliant actuators. Dynamo uses Aspect-oriented Programming to extend ActiveBPEL, an open-source BPEL execution environment. Probing, analysis, and recovery are treated as cross-cutting concerns that are activated every time the process needs to interact with a third-party service.

24.6.3.2 ALBERT

WSCoL has been the basis for the definition of a new language, ALBERT (Assertion Language for BPEL Process Interactions) [4]. ALBERT supports an assume/guarantee specification and verification pattern. In ALBERT, we specify the functional and the non-functional properties that the partner services are required to guarantee in terms of logical formulae, called *assumed assertions* (AAs). Based on these AAs the composition may offer a service whose properties can also be specified via ALBERT formulae, called *guaranteed assertions* (GAs). At design time, a formal verification tool can then be used to check that a composite service delivers on its GAs, under the assumption that the external services deliver on their AAs. Since design-time verification is not enough for evolving systems like the ones built out of dynamic services, verification must be extended to run time, where ALBERT properties become run-time assertions monitored during the execution of the composite service. Run-time monitoring of ALBERT assertions has been integrated into Dynamo; the implementation has then been optimized for efficiency [5] by defining the semantics of ALBERT through an extension of alternating automata.

ALBERT was the key element around which we developed SAVVY-WS (Service Analysis, Verification, and Validation methodologY for Web Services) [9], a methodology that provides a holistic approach to support the lifelong verification of Web service compositions. An outlook on the adoption of this methodology in the context of generic, non Web services-based, service compositions has also been proposed in [8].

WSCoL and ALBERT, WSReL, and Dynamo contribute to three out of four of the steps of the control loop presented in Sect. 24.4, that is the *(Multi-level) Monitoring*, *(Multi-level) Analysis of Adaptation Needs*, and the *Coordinated Adaptation* steps. *(Multi-level) Adaptation Planning* is achieved using a human expert that must be knowledgable of the intricacies of the process design. However, they only concentrate on the SaaS level, without taking into account any other layers.

24.6.3.3 Model-Driven Management

In [6] we furthered our studies on service management and proposed a model-driven approach to the automatic synthesis of probes, data correlators, and analyzers for BPEL processes called MDMS (Model-Driven Management of Services). This model-driven approach advocates that designers need to consider management as an integral part of a system development, from requirements elicitation to implementation. MDMS uses BPMN and natural language to define the system architecture and management needs at the CIM (Computation Independent Model) level. It uses SCA, along with a data model and a model of key performance indicators, to provide the management needs at the PIM (Platform Independent Model) level. Finally, it uses BPEL and complex event processing (CEP) techniques to provide management at the PSM (Platform Specific Model) level.

MDMS is supported by an execution environment called EcoWare (Event Correlation Middleware). Any service-based execution environment that has suitable probes can be used in conjunction with EcoWare. We implemented a tool capable of automatically generating probes for BPEL processes that are deployed to Dynamo. The probes are configured to send the data they collect to a Siena [10] publish/subscribe event notification service. Based on the models we then generate a pipe-and-filter composition of Esper-based [17] event processing components to provide the required event filtering, correlation, and aggregation.

EcoWare provided the genesis of the work presented in this chapter. While working on EcoWare we only focused on the SaaS layer, yet it was that work that pushed us to focus on the main concepts needed to build a manageable service-based system. Moreover, it also allowed us to more deeply consider the role that complex event processing techniques could play in the bigger picture of multi-level management.

24.7 Conclusions and Future Work

This chapter discussed how cloud-based applications can exploit the *service* abstraction to govern and maintain their effective operation. The complete availability of the infrastructure and platform on which applications are deployed offers unique means to tune the operation of its constituting services at run time. Besides the "usual" activities at application level, like for example monitoring the response time of a partner service or selecting a faster counterpart, probing and adaptation can also address the platform and infrastructure exploited by the application. Moreover, information that comes from the same infrastructure, but belongs to different applications, can be shared and used to improve the interdependent operation of the different applications.

As said, all these opportunities call for a unified model to accommodate all the different concepts, and to be able to exploit them in a single, integrated approach. A dedicated run-time framework must provide users with the means to properly probe deployed applications at all levels, retrieve and correlate information, decide on the corrective actions, and apply them. The chapter thoroughly discussed C^2M, which is our proposal for a conceptual model for the multi-layer management and operation of cloud-based applications. It also proposes a high-level reference framework for implementing multi-level management.

24.7.1 Outlook

This chapter moved the first steps towards the integrated and multi-level management and operation of cloud-based applications. The availability of development and deployment platforms and of run-time infrastructures is both an opportunity and a challenge. It is an opportunity since the availability of many existing solutions allows the user to design, deploy, and operate applications in more sophisticated, performant, and cheap ways. It is a challenge since some (many) issues are still waiting to be solved. This holistic approach impacts all levels of the usual cloud stack, and we think it calls for significant advances in the following directions:

- **Abstractions.** More is needed in terms of the abstractions that one can use to reason on and design these applications. We need a better agreement on the key concepts behind these applications, and cloud solutions in general, but also a neat and clear identification of the building blocks and primitives the different solutions can offer to their customers.
- **Design and specification techniques.** Since current design and specification techniques are used to reason at a single level, the interactions and interferences among levels must be properly identified and specified: this means that suitable techniques must let one think of the different layers as a single integrated solution where they exist both in isolation and as parts of a whole.

- **Standardization of run-time components.** Currently, each cloud infrastructure provides its own components, and each attempt to reason on the integrated management of cloud-based applications remains isolated. Similarly to other approaches, for example WSDM in the domain of Web service management, this new world calls for standardized APIs that one can exploit to both conceive an application and think of its integrated management.
- **Management capabilities.** The general concepts presented in this chapter must be grounded in concrete cases and needs. Real experiences are supposed to privilege some management capabilities with respect to others, and thus they should help us better tune the reasoning capabilities needed in this context.
- **Validation and verification.** This comprehensive solution opens new challenges to the verification and validation of these applications. Again, the problem is not to study one layer in isolation, but validation and verification activities must try to address applications as complete systems composed of elements (services) at different levels.
- **Thorough assessment.** The solution presented here comes more from the technologies available today and the work done by the authors in these years. Now, the model must be confronted with more concrete needs and specific requirements from the different domains that are already exploiting the cloud and will further exploit it in the future.

Advances in all these directions are key to have better means for the development of quality cloud-based applications, for their operation, and also for their effective management.

Acknowledgments This research has been funded by the European Commission, Programme IDEAS-ERC, Project 227077-SMScom (http://www.erc-smscom.org), and FP7 STREP project 257483-Indenica (http://www.indenica.eu); by the National Research Fund, Luxembourg (FNR/P10/03).

References

1. Amazon: Amazon Web Services. http://aws.amazon.com/ (2012)
2. Armbrust, M., Fox, A., Griffith, R., Joseph, A., Katz, R., Konwinski, A., Lee, G., Patterson, D., Rabkin, A., Stoica, I., et al.: A view of cloud computing. Comm. ACM **53**(4), 50–58 (2010)
3. Barbon, F., Traverso, P., Pistore, M., Trainotti, M.: Run-Time Monitoring of Instances and Classes of Web Service Compositions. In: ICWS '06: Proceedings of the 2006 IEEE International Conference on Web Services, pp. 63–71. IEEE Computer Society (2006)
4. Baresi, L., Bianculli, D., Ghezzi, C., Guinea, S., Spoletini, P.: Validation of web service compositions. IET Software **1**(6), 219–232 (2007)
5. Baresi, L., Bianculli, D., Guinea, S., Spoletini, P.: Keep it small, keep it real: Efficient run-time verification of web service compositions. In: FMOODS/FORTE 2009: Proceedings of IFIP international conference on Formal Techniques for Distributed Systems, *LNCS*, vol. 5522, pp. 26–40. Springer (2009)
6. Baresi, L., Caporuscio, M., Ghezzi, C., Guinea, S.: Model-Driven Management of Services. In: ECOWS 2010: Proceedings of the 8th European Conference on Web Services, pp. 147–154. IEEE Computer Society (2010)

7. Baresi, L., Guinea, S.: Self-supervising bpel processes. IEEE Trans. Software Eng. **37**(2), 247–263 (2011)
8. Bianculli, D., Ghezzi, C.: Towards a methodology for lifelong validation of service compositions. In: SDSOA 2008: Proceedings of the 2nd International Workshop on Systems Development in SOA Environments, pp. 7–12. ACM (2008)
9. Bianculli, D., Ghezzi, C., Spoletini, P., Baresi, L., Guinea, S.: A guided tour through SAVVY-WS: a methodology for specifying and validating web service compositions. In: E. Börger, A. Cisternino (eds.) Advances in Software Engineering, *LNCS*, vol. 5316, pp. 131–160. Springer (2008)
10. Carzaniga, A., Rosenblum, D.S., Wolf, A.L.: Design and evaluation of a wide-area event notification service. ACM Trans. Comput. Syst. **19**(3), 332–383 (2001)
11. Chan, K., Poernomo, I.: QoS-aware model driven architecture through the UML and CIM. Information Systems Frontiers **9**(2–3), 209–224 (2007)
12. Chappell, D.: Enterprise service bus. O'Reilly, Media (2004)
13. Chowdhary, P., Bhaskaran, K., Caswell, N.S., Chang, H., Chao, T., Chen, S.K., Dikun, M., Lei, H., Jeng, J.J., Kapoor, S., Lang, C.A., Mihaila, G., Stanoi, I., Zeng, L.: Model driven development for business performance management. IBM Syst. J. **45**(3), 587–605 (2006)
14. Debusmann, M., Kroger, R., Geihs, K.: Unifying service level management using an MDA-based approach. In: NOMS 2004: Proceedings of the Network Operations and Management Symposium, pp. 801–814. IEEE (2004)
15. Distributed Management Task Force: Web Services for Management. http://www.dmtf.org/standards/wsman/ (2010)
16. Efstratiou, C., Cheverst, K., Davies, N., Friday, A.: An architecture for the effective support of adaptive context-aware applications. In: MDM 2001: Proceedings of the Second International Conference on Mobile Data Management, pp. 15–26. Springer (2001)
17. EsperTech: Complex event processing. http://esper.codehaus.org (2010)
18. Foster, H., Spanoudakis, G.: SMaRT: a Workbench for Reporting the Monitorability of Services from SLAs. In: PESOS 2011: Proceedings of the 3rd International Workshop on Principles of Engineering Service-oriented Systems, pp. 36–42. ACM (2011)
19. Google: Google App Engine. https://developers.google.com/appengine/ (2012)
20. Guinea, S., Kecskemeti, G., Marconi, A., Wetzstein, B.: Multi-layered monitoring and adaptation. In: ICSOC 2011: Proceedings of the 2011 International Conference on Service Oriented, Computing, pp. 359–373 (2011)
21. Heroku: Heroku Cloud Application Platform. http://www.heroku.com/ (2012)
22. Horn, P.: Autonomic Computing: IBM's Perspective on the State of Information Technology. IBM TJ Watson Labs. (2001)
23. Mahbub, K., Spanoudakis, G.: A Framework for Requirements Monitoring of Service based Systems. In: ICSOC '04: Proceedings of the 2nd International Conference on Service Oriented Computing, pp. 84–93. ACM (2004)
24. Microsoft: Windows Azure. http://www.windowsazure.com/en-us/ (2012)
25. Momm, C., Gebhart, M., Abeck, S.: A model-driven approach for monitoring business performance in web service compositions. In: ICIW '09: Proceedings of the 2009 Fourth International Conference on Internet and Web Applications and Services, pp. 343–350 (2009)
26. Mos, A., Pedrinaci, C., Rey, G.A., Gomez, J.M., Liu, D., Vaudaux-Ruth, G., Quaireau, S.: Multi-level Monitoring and Analysis of Web-Scale Service based Applications. In: ICSOC/ServiceWave Workshops, pp. 269–282 (2009)
27. OASIS: Web Services Distributed Management (WSDM). http://www.oasis-open.org/specs/ (2006)
28. OASIS: Web Services Business Process Execution Language Version 2.0. http://www.oasis-open.org/specs/ (2007)
29. OpenSOA: Service component architecture specifications. http://www.osoa.org (2007)
30. Openstack: Openstack Cloud Software. http://openstack.org/ (2012)
31. Popescu, R., Staikopoulos, A., Liu, P., Brogi, A., Clarke, S.: Taxonomy-Driven Adaptation of Multi-layer Applications Using Templates. In: SASO 2010: Proceedings of the Fourth IEEE International Conference on Self-Adaptive and Self-Organizing Systems, pp. 213–222 (2010)

32. Richardson, L., Ruby, S.: RESTful web services. O'Reilly, Media (2007)
33. Weerawarana, S., Curbera, F., Leymann, F., Storey, T., Ferguson, D.: Web Services Platform Architecture: SOAP, WSDL, WS-Policy, WS-Addressing, WS-BPEL, WS-Reliable Messaging and More. Prentice Hall (2005)
34. Zengin, A., Marconi, A., Baresi, L., Pistore, M.: CLAM: Managing Cross-layer Adaptation in Service-based Systems. In: SOCA 2011: Proceedings of the 2011 IEEE International Conference on Service-Oriented Computing and Applications, pp. 1–8. IEEE (2011)

Chapter 25
Web Services for Things

Guangyan Huang, Jing He and Yanchun Zhang

Abstract In this chapter, we introduce an interesting type of Web services for "things". Existing Web services are applications across the Web that perform functions mainly to satisfy users' social needs "from simple requests to complicated business processes". Throughout history, humans have accumulated lots of knowledge about diverse things in the physical world. However, human knowledge about the world has not been fully used on the current Web which focuses on social communication; the prospect of interacting with things other than people on the future Web is very exciting. The purpose of Web services for "things" is to provide a tunnel for people to interact with things in the physical world from anywhere through the Internet. Extending the service targets from people to anything challenges the existing techniques of Web services from three aspects: first, an unified interface should be provided for people to describe the needs of things; then basic components should be designed in a Web service for things; finally, implementation of a Web service for things should be optimized when mashing up multiple sub Web services.

We tackle the challenges faced by a Web service for things and make the best use of human knowledge from the following aspects. We first define a context of things as an unified interface. The users' description (semantic context) and sensors (sensing context) are two channels for acquiring the context of things. Then, we define three basic modules for a Web service for things: ontology Web services to unify the context of things, machine readable domain knowledge Web services and event report Web services (such as weather report services and sensor event report services). Meanwhile, we develop a Thing-REST framework to optimally mashup structures

G. Huang (✉) · J. He · Y. Zhang
Victoria University, Melbourne, Australia
e-mail: guangyan.huang@vu.edu.au

J. He
e-mail: jing.he@vu.edu.au

Y. Zhang
e-mail: yanchun.zhang@vu.edu.au

A. Bouguettaya et al. (eds.), *Advanced Web Services*,
DOI: 10.1007/978-1-4614-7535-4_25,

to loosely couple the three basic modules. We employ a smart plant watering service application to demonstrate all the techniques we have developed.

25.1 Introduction

25.1.1 A Scenario of Web Services for Things

Things in the real world can communicate their physical situation (e.g., location, temperature etc.) to people through sensors, and people can control things by themselves or use actuators. In this chapter, we describe the development of Web services for things that allows machines to understand things: the major aim is to build a new bridge between humans and things through machines (e.g., computers, sensors, other devices). Since advanced technology has already built an interface between human and machines, defining an interface between machines and things enables human to interact with things. We design an interesting application in Fig. 25.1, expected to be understandable by average people, to demonstrate the techniques of applying human knowledge/resources through the Web and sensors to provide a Web service for things [20].

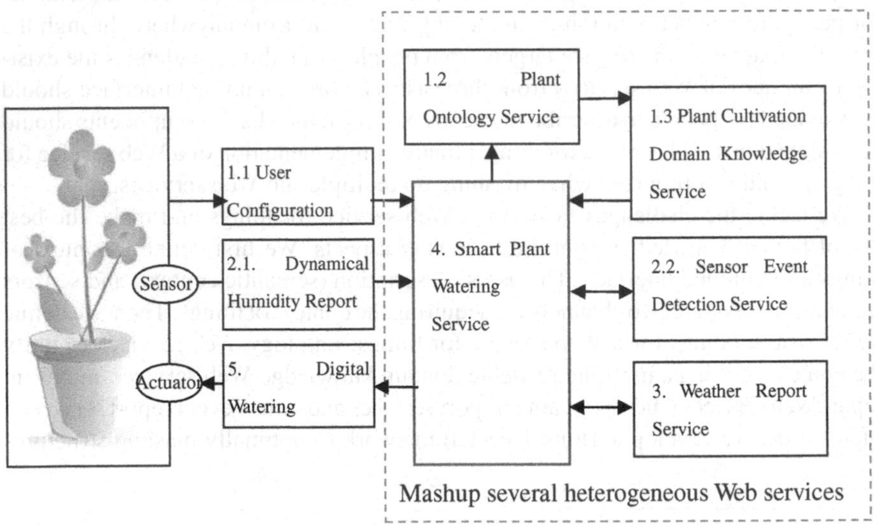

Fig. 25.1 A smart plant watering service

The object served in Fig. 25.1 is an outdoor potted plant; when it dries out, it will generate an event notifying its owner or an actuator to water it with a suitable dose. A sensor is used to monitor the humidity and temperature of the soil in the pot and an actuator is set up to execute the watering command. Different plants have different preferences (watering dose and frequency). To add human intelligence into this application, basically two inputs (e.g. context of things) are required: user configuration with the plant's name, location and life stage, and a dynamical humidity report of the soil around the plant from the sensors; then we can make the best use of human knowledge and resources (such as weather report services) on the Web to provide a service to the plant, which we call a smart plant watering service. This smart plant watering service mashups four heterogenous Web services to implement its goal. A *weather report service* combines with a dynamical humidity report that is analyzed by a *sensor event detection service* to dynamically determine whether watering is needed. A *plant cultivation domain knowledge service* allows calculation of the amount of water the plant requires by understanding the plant's context (plant name and life stage, provided in the user configuration phase). Actually, the user's configuration is unified by a *plant ontology service*, since users may call their plants in different aliases or in different languages. Then, the output of the *plant ontology service* is chained to the input of the *plant cultivation domain knowledge service*. Finally, a message specifying the dose of water will be produced to trigger the actuator when the humidity value is smaller than a threshold and no rain is forecast.

Could an equivalent service be achieved by replacing the smart plant watering service with an embedded computing unit? We can imagine a smart device including a sensor, an actuator and a computing unit, as well as some storage or memory. To provide the same smart service to the plant, the device needs to pre-store plant cultivation domain knowledge and have the capability to predict the weather. This is impractical for two reasons. First, meteorological services need supercomputers to predict weather precisely; such capacity cannot be included in a device of a size suitable for the proposed task. Second, storing knowledge of all possible plant species and individually designing embedded devices for each plant would drive costs very high.

Compared to using an embedded computing unit, the advantages of Web services for things will make them popular with the general public:

- **Low cost**. Computing services can be used in a pay-as-you-go model, thus saving the cost of buying expensive devices;
- **Quality**. The ability to make use of professional services via the Web means the best available information can be utilized;
- **Convenience**. The required service can be implemented automatically according to the contexts of things;
- **Flexibility**. The same sensor and actuator can be used for different plants.

25.1.2 Challenges and Solutions for Implementing Web Services for Things

Comparing the context of things (e.g., name, location, sensing report of things) with the people-centric context raises the following challenges for the design of context-aware Web services for things (termed smart Web services in this chapter). First, it is difficult to unify the context of things. We can analyze people's behaviors or operations on the Web to identify their preferences. But for things, we can only obtain their preferences through their classes (e.g., names). Thus, ontologies and domain knowledge are needed to unify and understand the context of things. That is, we deduce their preferences (e.g., habits or characteristics or properties) from their classes based on domain knowledge accumulated throughout human history. Also, it is difficult to implement a flexible smart Web service based on the context of things. People express their needs easily, but the time when the needs of a target thing generate can be detected only by analyzing sensor data. Also, we must explore experts' domain knowledge to provide professional services for things.

This chapter aims to make things, as physical entities in the real world, understood by machines and thus, provide smart Web services to things [20]. We first define a context of things as an unified interface. We extend the traditional context for QoS-aware Web services to the context for smart Web services (e.g., both the context of things and the user context). The users' description (semantic context) and sensors (sensing context) are two channels for acquiring the context of things. Then, we define three basic modules for a Web service for things: ontology Web services to unify the context of things, machine readable domain knowledge Web services and event report Web services (such as weather report services and sensor event report services). Meanwhile, we develop a Thing-REST framework to optimally mashup structures to loosely couple the three basic modules. We tackle the problem of mashuping heterogenous Web services based on Representational State Transfer (REST) for mashups. The Thing-REST framework is used to manage the context of things as well as user context in order to efficiently and easily implement smart Web services.

25.1.3 Extensive Applications

"Twenty-first century computers are profound technological devices that have woven themselves into the fabric of everyday life" [29]. Smart plant watering service is just one of the simple and typical applications of Web services for things; we can use general humidity and temperature sensors, or special sensors for smart plant care[1] to implement it. However, for scalable applications, we adopt general sensors

[1] http://www.koubachi.org

to describe the mechanism of smart Web services for things in Sect. 25.6. Other applications include,

- smart homes [9, 19, 32] that improve living conditions for the aged and the disabled [23],
- SmartAgriFood that addresses farming, agri-logistics and food awareness as an extreme use case for the Future Internet [35],
- smart offices for working in a convenient modern way, and
- smart hospitals [16] that can monitor and serve individual patients.

The Semantic Web provides the specialists' field knowledge and the Ubiquitous Web acts as the eyes and arms of the objects to help satisfy human goals, building a bridge between the virtual world and real world.

The rest of this chapter is organized as follows. We present State-of-the-Art Web technology for things in Sect. 25.2. We define the context of things in Sect. 25.3. We then provide a smart Web service for things in Sect. 25.4. In Sect. 25.5, we introduce a Thing-REST style for implementing the smart Web service. In Sect. 25.6, we present an implementation of the application in Fig. 25.1. Finally, Sect. 25.7 concludes this chapter.

25.2 State-of-the-Art Web Technology for Things

25.2.1 Semantic Web for Machine Readable Knowledge Reuse

Although Web 2.0 provides a set of tools to support interactive and collaborative knowledge creation, sharing and dissemination, including blogs and wikis, podcasts, webcasts, webinars, social bookmarking and social networking sites such as Facebook, Web 2.0 technologies lack support for semantics to automatically share and reuse knowledge [22]. In contrast, the future Web 3.0 will integrate the social Web and the Semantic Web, enabling people to create data stores on the Web, build vocabularies and write rules for handling knowledge, thus lowering the cost of data and knowledge creation by using volunteers and collective human intelligence [22].

Throughout history, humans have accumulated lots of knowledge about the physical world. We have studied and classified many of the things in the world, including natural things such as plants, animals, insects, mountains, seas and lakes, and man-made things such as buildings and consumer products, and we have collected information about how to create, cultivate and utilize all these things. However, human knowledge about the world has not been fully used on the current Web which focuses on social communication; the prospect of interacting with things other than people on the future Semantic Web is very exciting.

25.2.2 Ubiquitous Web for Sensing Physical World

Meanwhile, Web 3.0 merges Ubiquitous Web technology. Sensors and actuators are already interconnected through the Internet [8, 12, 18, 42], representing the beginning of the Internet of Things that helps computers monitor, react to and affect the changing status of the physical world. Sensors are the nerve cells of the system, operating as data publishers [18]; this means the Web is becoming a computing center like a brain, which is able to respond to every nerve cell in different ways, based on the contexts of things. The mechanism is the static context (e.g. name, location, preference of things) that determines how to respond and the dynamic context (sensing report of things' situation) that determines when to respond. In a Ubiquitous Web, any knowledge can be shared to serve any thing, forming a bridge between the virtual world and the real world. Thus, as Conrad Wolfram said, Web 3.0 is where the computer is generating new information, rather than humans.[2]

Thus, the two purposes of Web 3.0 are: to link data by the Semantic Web that makes online information machine-readable, and to facilitate a Ubiquitous Web that can be accessed by anything, anywhere, anytime, using a variety of devices.

25.2.3 Context of Things

By managing the context of things, the goal is to automatically reuse knowledge (e.g., domain knowledge and specialists' experiences) as a format of Web services on the Internet to create smart Web services which are easily reused. "Context of things" is a concept which enables people to understand things and translate their understanding into machine languages in order to provide services for things automatically. Context is vital in Web services. Already known contexts [1, 5, 7, 10, 11, 33, 41] are generally used for the Web of people, for instance, to improve the QoS of Web services; they do not include the context of things to enable a smart Web service for things. A widely used definition of context was proposed by Dey and Abowd [10]: "Context is any information that can be used to characterize the situation of a thing. An entity is a person, place, or object that is considered relevant to the interaction between a user and an application, including the user and applications themselves." However, it lacks an explicit definition of the context of things. In this chapter, we define the context of things as a supplement, since the already known context for Web services is not enough to be employed by smart Web services, like the application shown in Fig. 25.1.

For a Web of People [39], context is defined as any information that can be used to characterize the interaction of a user with a software system (and vice-versa), as well as the environment where such interaction occurs [5]. Here a user is generally a person, so we call this people-centric context; typical examples are people's locations, personal preferences and the characteristics of their Web access devices.

[2] http://webuser.hs-furtwangen.de/heindl/ebte-08ss-web-20-uphakorntanakit.pdf

Thus, existing context-aware Web services [1, 5, 10, 11, 33, 41], mainly focus on improving the Quality of Services (QoS) based on the contexts of users; and generally programs in Web services enumerate different implementations corresponding to different attribute values of the context. But, for a Web of things based on Web 3.0, the contexts of things in the physical world are extremely diverse, which poses new problems for implementing context-aware Web services. For example, on a Web of things, the service target is a plant and the service content is to water the plant; we cannot enumerate all the cases to implement this Web service, since a huge number of different classes of plants exist with different preferences for watering doses and frequency. A thing can be biotic (e.g., plants and animals) or abiotic (buildings and commodities). A thing may be a person; typical target examples are aged people, small children, disabled people, patients and any other special group of people.

25.2.4 Web Services for Things

25.2.4.1 Web Services

Web services are vital to transform the Web from a collection of information into a distributed computational device [14]. By using context, Web services can become smarter—that is, aware of the target things' or the applications' physical environment or situations and respond proactively and intelligently [41]. Thus, such a context-aware (smart) Web service can understand situational context and share that context with other services and produce dynamic results based on who, what, when, where, and why it was called [28]. According to IBM's Web service tutorial [14], "Web services are a new breed of Web applications. They are self-contained, self-describing, modular applications that can be published, located, and invoked across the Web. Web services perform functions, which can be anything from simple requests to complicated business processes".

25.2.4.2 REST

In REST [15, 27, 43], any resource is addressed by a unique identifier of standard format via Uniform Resource Locators (URL) using the Hypertext Transfer Protocol (HTTP) and its methods (e.g. GET[3], POST[4], PUT[5] and DELETE[6]) to access them. The state of a resource, e.g. a sensor node, can be get or set by the GET or POST HTTP methods, respectively. The REST style is suitable for loosely coupling distributed

[3] GET returns a representation of the requested resource.

[4] By using POST, it is possible to update a resource with new information.

[5] PUT is used to create a new resource with a name that is specified by the client.

[6] If a resource is no longer required, the DELETE method removes the URI from the accessible resources of a server.

networked applications that are independent and self-organized. Summarizing the work in [4, 30, 40], the main advantages of REST include:

(1) operations are defined in the message [Muehlen];
(2) there is a unique address for every process instance [Muehlen];
(3) late binding is possible [Castellani] [Muehlen];
(4) process instances are created explicitly [Muehlen];
(5) zero-knowledge network probing on client sides [Castellani] [Muehlen];
(6) no client's session state is maintained on server sides [Wilde];
(7) it allows multiple applications to interact with the same resources [Wilde].

These advantages make REST suitable for developing smart Web services. First, sensors/actuators can be assigned a global Uniform Resource Identifier (URI), for example, "http://vcrab.com/SmartWebService/Joey/Rose_Humidity_Sensor" on the Web and its states can be accessed from anywhere on the Internet. Second, a loose coupling style can support mashing heterogeneous Web services up well. For example, a TinyREST architecture [27] is used to obtain/change the state of the sensors/actuators through an addressing mechanism where all requests, e.g. POST, GET, can be forwarded by the gateway to one (or a group) of specific sensor(s)/actuator(s). The TinyREST is demonstrated to be a very efficient way to access sensor nodes or sensor networks from any Internet clients and any Internet-based applications. The loose coupling style in REST makes run-time linking practical by easily typing in the URL [37].

The Thing-REST extends the TinyREST in two aspects: first, Thing-REST not only unifies the sensing context of things provided by sensors but also unifies the semantic context of things in the natural language provided by people; second, Thing-REST also defines the user's context in an explicit way by using URIs. In summary, Thing-REST can describe all the context resources in a smart Web service for things.

25.2.4.3 REST-Based Mashup

Mashup is an approach that allows users to aggregate multiple services, each serving its own purpose, to create a service that serves a new purpose and mashup can compose heterogeneous resources [25]. Mashup tools, such as Yahoo's pipes, IBM's QEDwiki and Google's Mashup Editor often require little or no programming knowledge to create a mashup; they chain the Web resources together by piping one service's output into the next service's input while filtering content or making slight format changes [34]. Thus, the REST style is used to achieve machine-readable features. For example, an hREST (HTML for RESTful Services) [24] is provided for machine-readable descriptions of Web APIs for mashup automation in order to replace manual Web service composition (or mashup) due to plain unstructured HTML documents, or human-readable descriptions, for Web APIs. Also, in [13], a pREST (REST-based protocol for pervasive systems) aims to provide additional information about resources by supporting a loose typing system via an HTTP header. In [18], a structured XML document or a JavaScript Object Notation (JSON) object that are both machine-readable and human-readable are adopted for services of smart things (e.g., sensors, actuator networks).

In addition to the machine-readable interfaces the same as in hREST and pREST, the Thing-REST provides three mashup structures (e.g., chain, select and merge) to implement efficient smart Web services.

25.3 Context for Smart Web Services

In this section, we first provide a whole graph of context for smart Web services and then define a new concept: the context of things.

25.3.1 Context Lattice

We classify contexts into four typical classes: user's Web-access devices, user's preferences, user's physical situations and user's things, and then we plot them into a context lattice as shown in Fig. 25.2. Already known contexts for Web services describe the user's physical situation (e.g., common context, such as weather, time and location), the user preferences and the user's Web-access devices (e.g., computing context[7] and communication context).[8] But these contexts are generally used for the Web of people, for instance, to improve the QoS of Web services; they are not enough to enable a smart Web service. Thus, we will define a new concept of "context of things" (e.g. semantic context and sensing context) that is orthogonal with the context for QoS-aware Web services.

The context of things is more critical than other contexts for a smart Web service, thus, this chapter focuses more on using the context of things, as well as related common contexts to implement a smart Web service.

25.3.2 Context of a Thing

We formally define the context of a thing as follows:

Definition 25.1 (A Thing). A Thing is an entity (e.g., a pot plant, a cow, a person, a building etc.) or a group of entities that have close relations (e.g., a house filled with consumer electronics, a cornfield containing thousands of corn plants, etc.). A thing can be atomic or composite.

[7] Computing context is hardware and software for running the application of a Web service, such as computing ability and throughputs.

[8] Communication context includes physical environments and situations on communication hardware platforms, including users' devices, sensors, actuators, base station and server computers.

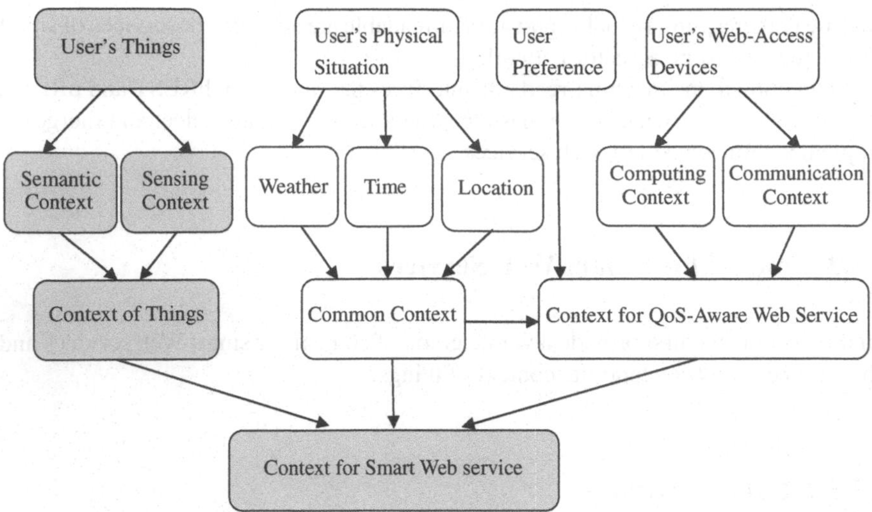

Fig. 25.2 Context lattice

Definition 25.2 (Context of a Thing). The context of a thing includes knowledge about both the situation around the thing and the thing itself.

The situation around the thing may change dynamically, which can be monitored by sensors. The knowledge representation of the thing itself can be found in the domain ontology database. We separate the thing from its situation, since its context may be static or predictable and the context related to the environment around the thing may be dynamic. For example, a person's name, life stage and preferences are static information that may not change for a long period of time, but a person's location and accessing device may change in a day. Another example is a pot plant: the plant's name (type), life stage and living habits are static information, but the soil around the plant may change from healthy to unhealthy due to lack of water or nutrients, and diseases or pests may threaten its life. We can also state that the static context of the thing can be predicted while the dynamic context of the thing may not. However, to distinguish between the situation and the thing itself, we prefer to use *sensing context* and *semantic context*, since we want to handle the whole process of managing the thing automatically. Thus, we formally define them as follows.

Definition 25.3 (The Semantic Context of a Thing). The Semantic Context of a Thing is knowledge accumulated by humans about the thing itself (e.g., name, class name etc.), and is static and predictable.

Definition 25.4 (The Sensing Context of a Thing). The Sensing Context of a Thing is dynamically changeable and unpredictable knowledge about the situations of the thing, generally sensed using sensors/actuators.

Typical semantic context includes *Basic Information of the Thing (BIT)* described by name, location and life stage, which are originally described in natural languages and are expected to be unified by *ontology services* on the Semantic Web. Typical sensing context are *Sensing Reports* that are dynamic states of the situation around things monitored by sensors/actuators and may be analyzed further by *sensor event detection services* on the future Web. *Basic Information of the Thing (BIT)* and *Sensing Reports* are two sources of information about the target thing.

25.4 A Smart Web Service for Things

25.4.1 Overview of a Smart Web Service for Things

We have illustrated a smart Web service by using a simple application: the smart watering plant Web service in Fig. 25.1. We now formally define a smart Web service based on the concept of task ontology.

Definition 25.5 (A Task Ontology). A task ontology provides a systematic vocabulary of the terms used to solve problems [26]. Information about Generic Tasks [6] includes:

(1) a task specification in the form of generic types of input and output information;
(2) specific forms in which the basic pieces of domain knowledge are needed for the task and specific organizations of this knowledge particular to the task; and
(3) a family of control regimes appropriate for the task.

Definition 25.6 (A Smart Web Service for Things). A smart Web service for things is defined as a general framework to integrate all the functions on a task ontology in which one or multiple Web services are explored automatically to satisfy specific needs of a thing (e.g., a plant, a building, a special people group).

According to the definition of the task ontology, we plot a framework of a general smart Web service in Fig. 25.3, which includes six basic components: Input (e.g., the context of things and the user context), Output (e.g., actions towards Things), Ontology Services, Domain Knowledge Services, Event Detection Services and an application logic module. For the purpose of serving things, the input is the context of things and the output is the action towards things. The component of ontology services is needed as an interface between human users and machine automation. We also take domain knowledge services as a vital component that can explore human-accumulated knowledge related to the target thing. Another important component is event detection services, since the time when the needs of the target thing generated are always recognized through analyzing the readings of sensors/actuators around the thing. If the sensing context of things is complex, sensor event detection services may need the assistance of domain knowledge services. The application logic module is actually the user interface for applications, where simple programming or application logic is designed here to loosely couple available Web services in order to satisfy the application goal while the user context may determine the QoS of executing the mashup.

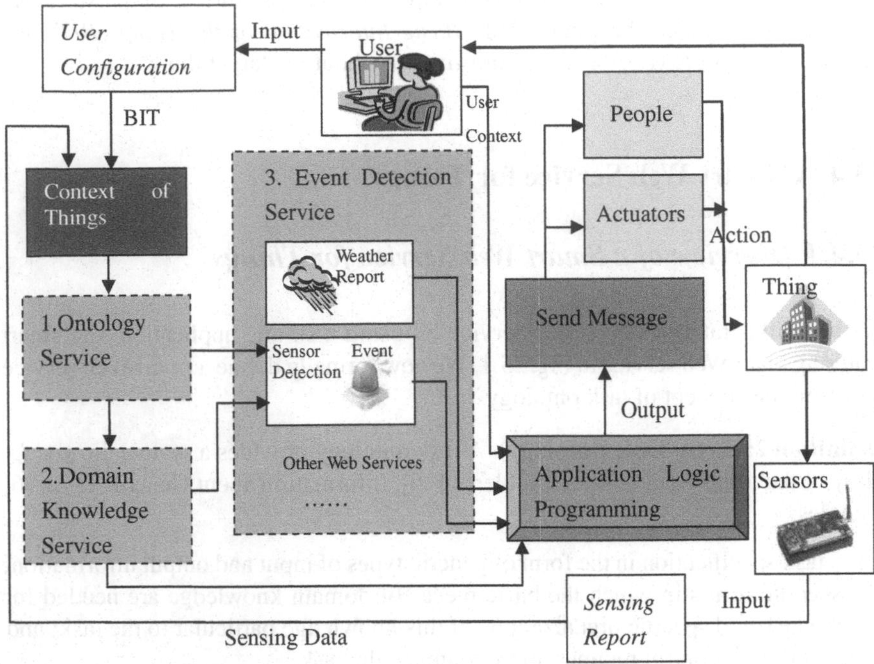

Fig. 25.3 A framework of a smart web service

We have defined a context for smart Web services (e.g., the context of things and the user context) in Sect. 25.3. We present three types of Web services and the output in the smart Web service in this section and introduce the Thing-REST-based mashup in Sect. 25.5.

25.4.2 Ontology Services and Domain Knowledge Services

The semantic context of a thing is created by people and is generally unified by ontology services on the Semantic Web. The main goal of using ontology ID to unify a semantic context of a thing is to promote machine automation, that is, interaction between different Web service applications without human intervention. On the Semantic Web, XML (eXtensible Markup Language) structures the users' documents, while RDF (Resource Description Framework) expresses the meaning of the content. XML specifies a syntactic encoding of documents allowing their exchange between applications [38]. In RDF, a triple being rather like the subject, verb and object of an elementary sentence is used to make assertions that particular things have properties with certain values. Subject and object are each identified by a Uniform Resource Identifier (URI). The triples of RDF form webs of information about related things, and the URIs ensure that concepts are not just words in a document but are tied to a unique definition that everyone can find on the Web. However, two databases may use different identifiers for what is, in fact, the same concept; thus, ontology is a solution to this problem.

Definition 25.7 (An Ontology or Domain Ontology [17]**).** An ontology is an explicit specification of a conceptualization for a systematic account of existence. In an ontology, the set of objects to represent a domain is called the universe of discourse and definitions associate the names of entities in the universe of discourse (e.g., classes, relations, functions or other objects) with human-readable text describing what the names mean, and formal axioms that constrain the interpretation and use of these terms.

Ontologies are reusable in a given domain and provide vocabularies about the concepts within a domain and their relationships [26].

Ontologies are models that represent an abstraction of a domain in a formal way, such that several parties are able to agree on the abstraction and reuse the model in their own (Web) applications [38]. According to above definition, an ontology is suitable to unify semantic context, since it provides a unified form of knowledge on the Web for reuse and automation.

To help understand the importance of ontology ID for a semantic context of a thing, we define two terms as follows:

A Human Dictionary is a dictionary containing words in natural language that is understandable by people. We use Σ to denote a human dictionary.

A Machine Dictionary is a dictionary for terms in ontologies with URIs that have explicit meaning used by machines. We use Ω to denote a machine dictionary.

The user uses words in the human dictionary to write a *BIT*, then the system will translate the type of the thing in the *BIT* into a unified ID. We assume the system of ontologies will be mature enough on the future Semantic Web such that every word in the human dictionary reflects one term in the machine dictionary and n words may reflect one term. That is

Fact 1: $\forall a \in \Sigma \Rightarrow \exists b \in \Omega \cap a = b$

Since different users may employ different vocabularies for the target thing, an ontology is needed to unify them. Taking the application in Fig. 25.1 as an example, panicle, ear and tassel are all words used to describe an inflorescence [2]. Many ontologies are now available, such as the Open Biological and Biomedical Ontologies [3] and the Ontology Lookup Service (OLS) [31]. Thus, two application descriptions by different users that may use different words to denote the same type of thing can be translated into the same unified ID.

Although answering queries in an ontology is analogous to theorem proving and thus building and maintaining a very large ontology is time-consuming and costly [21], many Web Ontology Languages (OWLs) are now available on the Web on the way to build a good ontology system. In this chapter, we build the plant ontology by refering to ontologies of plant environment conditions, plant growth and developmental stages and plant structure [2] in the plant watering application, as shown in Fig. 25.1. For example, the developmental (or life) stage is defined by characteristic morphological or physiological landmarks in a plant's life cycle, such as germination, seeding, flowering, and ripening, rather than a specific temporal framework [2].

Domain Knowledge is accumulated knowledge and experience of specialists in a domain that can be explored to understand and interact with the things. Ontology IDs are standard input for a domain knowledge service.

25.4.3 Event Detection Services

25.4.3.1 Sensor Event Detection Services

Sensing contexts are generated by sensors or sensor networks automatically and dynamically. A sensor context is generally denoted by a 2-tuple (physical parameter, value). The characteristic of a sensing context is that its data format is simple and only physical parameters need to be interpreted by an ontology. Also, for complex sensing report data, we translate the *Sensing Context* into *Sensing Event* by using a *sensor event detection service*.

Sensing reports are critical for a smart Web service as they provide information about dynamic states of the thing; however, raw sensor data may not be useful. Some patterns from continuous sensor data and the report events can be recognized as output; more often, an event detection service may need domain knowledge services to analyze the raw sensor data. Thus, the input and output interfaces of sensors/actuators are important. Although there are many types of sensors/actuators, the basic abstract of a single sensor is a 2-tuple (physical parameter, value). Also, an event may be detected through the cooperation of all the sensors in the network; we only provide one URI for a sensor network. In order to reduce communication costs between sensors and the remote server, there are two methods to report sensing events: Local Event Detection for simple events and Remote Event Detection for complex events.

Local Event Detection. For some applications in which sensor data comprise very simple information (e.g., physical parameters such as temperature and humidity), the analysis of sensing data is also very simple.

Remote Event Detection. There are some complex applications. For example, a series of images of the target thing captured by a camera sensor needs pattern recognition to detect events. Since recognizing patterns from an image is challenging, high-quality domain knowledge Web services involving intensive computing are needed. In such cases, raw sensing data must be sent to the remote server for the analysis of events. The communication cost is great since the image size is very large compared to simple physical parameter values, so it is important to reduce the frequency of sending data. For example, data can be sent periodically in over a long interval or useless raw sensing data can be roughly filtered locally and only key frames sent to the server.

25.4.3.2 Weather Report Services

Weather can be regarded as a special *event detection service*, since it is usually analyzed by online meteorological services which employ complex systems including sensors (e.g., satellite cameras). A weather report service builds a simple weather context by analyzing patterns from a huge volume of complex data sensed from the physical world.

25.4.4 Actions Towards Things

People Actions: People have many ways to receive messages instantly, such as mobile phones, MSN, emails etc., and message format can be defined by the user (for example, we can send a message in the user's native language). In this case, we may analyze user context. Not all users are experts at interacting with the target thing, thus the message generated by the smart Web service is also important to the user, as it not only notifies when to act but also reminds the user to act and communicates effective actions and methods to guide behavior towards the target thing.

Actuator Actions: When the actuator receives the messages, it will interpret the message into the control command to operate the actuator. The message can be an instant message to require actuators to act at once or a message that only gives a deadline for the action. Also, messages may provide other necessary information, for example, about quantitative control over the watering dose.

25.5 REpresentational State Transfer for Things (Thing-REST)

In this section, we present a Thing-REST style, which is a Resource-Oriented Architecture (ROA) and includes two parts: resource management and mashup structures. The aim of Thing-REST is to describe the resources of a Thing (e.g., a sensor, a person, a plant) objectively by using a set of standard interfaces and then to let Web service applications use these resources automatically.

25.5.1 Context Management in Thing-REST

According to two classes of the context of things: the semantic context and the sensing context, we define two types of URIs: concept URI (c-URI) and entity URI (e-URI) respectively in Thing-REST to manage them. In the same way, we use c-URIs and e-URIs to manage the user context. For example, c-URIs are used to manage semantic context and sensing context related e-URI addresses, and e-URIs are used to manage sensing context.

Definition 25.8 (Concept URI (c-URI)). Concept URI is a URI for an abstract thing (a concept).

Definition 25.9 (Entity URI (e-URI)). Entity URI is a URI for a concrete thing, an entity that exists in the physical world.

Both c-URI and e-URI have addresses that can be located on the Web. For every e-URI, there is a respective physical entity. Sommer et al. [36] described Internet-based access from and to services in an embedded network and built a Web service bridge between an IP-network and a sensor network. For example, 'http://193.150.15.14/light/turnon' is translated into 'Node: 193.150.15.14, Service: 5, Port: 1' through a mapping table: '$light \rightarrow 5, turnOn \rightarrow 1$'. To provide a simple and effective interface between people and things, as well as between things, we propose a communication mechanism for smart Web services. Sensors/actuators can be connected to the Web through PCs or base stations. Every thing must have a URI on the Web, then we define a uniform interface to send messages to and from a URI. We can provide the type of a URI (e.g., c-URI or e-URI) in HTTP headers just like those in [13, 43].

In the Thing-REST, we define a URI namespace for both machine-readable and human-readable purposes. An open problem in REST is that it is difficult to manage the URI namespace due to a large number of objects. In the Thing-REST, we provide an object-oriented URI namespace and organize URIs in flat structures. We actually split the definition of the resources and the citation in the applications. Examples of c-URI and e-URI as well as the flat structure to manage them are shown in Fig. 25.4.

We set two reserved words: "self" and "has" in the URI namespace. Suppose the name of the thing is a flower plant, "Rose", then we PUT a URI (e.g., "Rose/self") for the semantic context of "Rose" and PUT a URI (e.g., "Rose/has") to list the e-URIs for all sensor/actuator of "Rose"; an example is shown in Fig. 25.5. GET and POST are used frequently while PUT and DELETE are only used in the beginning configuration phase and the URI canceling phase, respectively.

We also explicitly describe the context of the owner (e.g., user context for QoS-aware Web services) by using URIs in the Thing-REST. In the example shown in Fig. 1.1, suppose the owner is "Joey", then we PUT a URI (e.g., "Joey/self") for the user context and PUT a URI (e.g., "Joey/has") to list all his contact methods; an example is shown in Fig. 25.6. We do not discuss context for QoS-aware Web services in this chapter, since much related work has already been done. We will

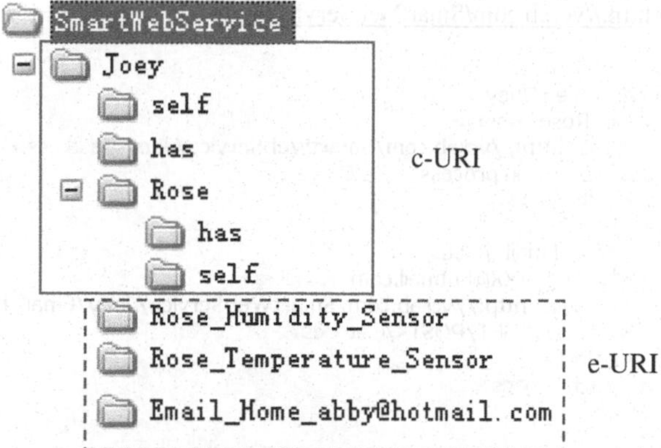

Fig. 25.4 Flat structure for management of URIs

The content in http://vcrab.com/SmartWebService/Joey/Rose:

```
<?xml version="1.0" ?>
- <thing name="Rose">
    <owner>Joey</owner>
    <address>http://vcrab.com/SmartWebService/Joey/Rose</address>
  - <SemanticContext>
      <thingclass>Rose</thingclass>
      <lifestage>3</lifestage>
      <location>Melbourne,Australia</location>
    </SemanticContext>
  - <SensingContext>
    - <sensor>
        <name>Humidity_Sensor</name>
        <address>http://vcrab.com/SmartWebService/Joey/Rose_Humidity_Sensor</address>
        <methods>GET</methods>
      </sensor>
    - <sensor>
        <name>Temperature_Sensor</name>
        <address>http://vcrab.com/SmartWebService/Joey/Rose_Temperature_Sensor</address>
        <methods>GET</methods>
      </sensor>
    </SensingContext>
  </thing>
```

Rose/self

Rose/has

Fig. 25.5 An example XML for context of a thing

show in Sect. 25.6 that it is easy to enable user contexts to be aware for QoS purposes in an explicit way in the Thing-REST.

We allocate a URL to every target thing, including things' owners. These URLs are open to the public through an authorized user name and password. Thus, every thing, including humans, has a URI on the Web for use by smart Web services. For a thing such as a plant or a house which may explore a set of sensors/actuators, we allocate URIs to all the resources; an example is shown in Fig. 25.5, where local addresses of sensors/actuators are bound to URIs and the sensor report data can be achieved through the GET operation on the URIs. We authorize different operations (e.g., POST and GET) to access URIs.

The content in http://vcrab.com/SmartWebService/Joey:

```
          <?xml version="1.0" ?>
        - <owner name="Joey">
            <thing>Rose</thing>
Joey/self   <address>http://vcrab.com/SmartWebService/Joey</address>
            <UserContext>in process</UserContext>
          - <ContactMethods>
            - <contact>
                <type>Email</type>
                <binding>XXX@hotmail.com</binding>
Joey/has        <address>http://vcrab.com/SmartWebService/Joey/Email_Home</address>
                <methods>GET/POST</methods>
              </contact>
            </ContactMethods>
          </owner>
```

Fig. 25.6 An example XML for describing owner of a thing

25.5.2 Mashup Structures in THING-REST

In this subsection, we develop a mashup style which is built on three mashup structures in Thing-REST; that is, three basic structures (chain, select and merge) for mashups are implemented by using REST techniques (e.g., HTTP and URIs).

25.5.2.1 Chain Structures in Thing-REST

In a chain structure, a sequence of Web services is chained together, where the output of a Web service is the input of another Web service. Figure 25.7 shows the mechanism of a chain implemented in the Thing-REST. We use a ChainNode to store the mid-term results between Web services. According to REST techniques, no client's session state is maintained on server sides (see Sect. 25.2.2); this reduces the burden on server sides. Thus, a client optionally chooses to store mid-term results. We provide a ChainNode.xml to store the mid-term results on the current director. In the Thing-REST, input "http://globalhost0/SWS1/WS1" will execute "GET URI of Web service 1" and store mid-term results in "http://globalhost0/SWS1/WS1/ChainNode.xml" in Fig. 25.7. So the chain of three Web services coupled for a new composite Web service can be denoted by "http://globalhost0/SWS1/WS1/WS2/WS3" and the mid-term results can be found in different directors by the same name "ChainNode.xml".

The ChainNodes are designed for efficiency purposes, just like CPU fetches instructions from a high speed cache instead of from the main memory. The advantage of ChainNodes is to ensure efficiency when break point happens in a chain; that is, if some Web service fails in a chain, the tasks that have been done are recorded in a series of ChainNodes and the chain of tasks can be restored from the broken point instead of from the beginning.

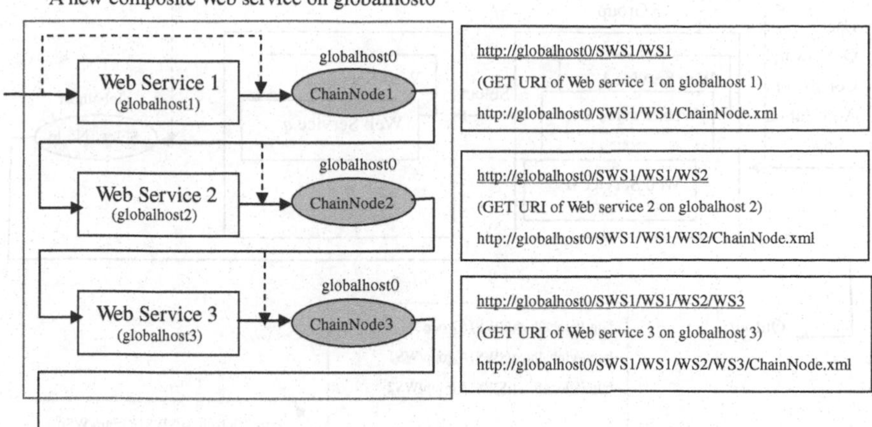

Fig. 25.7 A chain structure

25.5.2.2 Select Structures in Thing-REST

In a select structure, we select one or several URIs from a group of URIs. Figure 25.8 shows that according to the user's QoS-aware context or application aim, we generally select some URIs of Web services from a group of URIs. These URIs of Web services in a group may provide the same service with various QoS. We can see from Fig. 25.8 that there are n Web services: "WS_1, WS_2, …, WS_n" in the directory: "http://globalhost/SWS1/Group". The final results of selection: "WS_p" and "WS_q", are put in the file "http://globalhost/SWS1/Group/SelectNode.xml". Note that multiple Web services for the same function also improve the reliability of the mashup. The SelectNode is also designed for efficiency purpose. In the same way as in chain structure, if the input of the selection structure is equal to the historical input recorded in SelectNode.XML, then the output is GET directly from "SelectNode.XML" to avoid executing selection structure again.

25.5.2.3 Merge Structures in Thing-REST

In the merge structure shown in Fig. 25.9, we couple multiple Web services to create a new Web service. Different from Fig. 25.7, both WS1 and WS2 are called by WS3 directly. We use the same ChainNode mechanism as in the chain structures to store mid-term results.

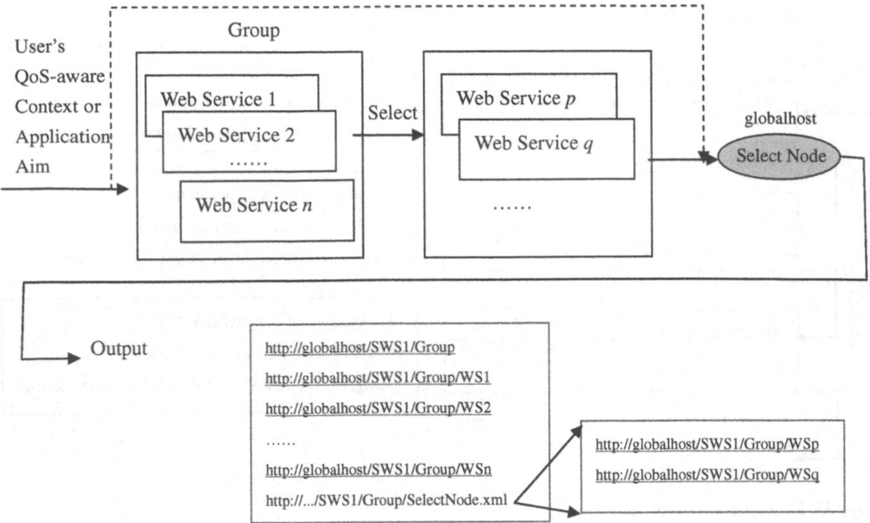

Fig. 25.8 A select structure

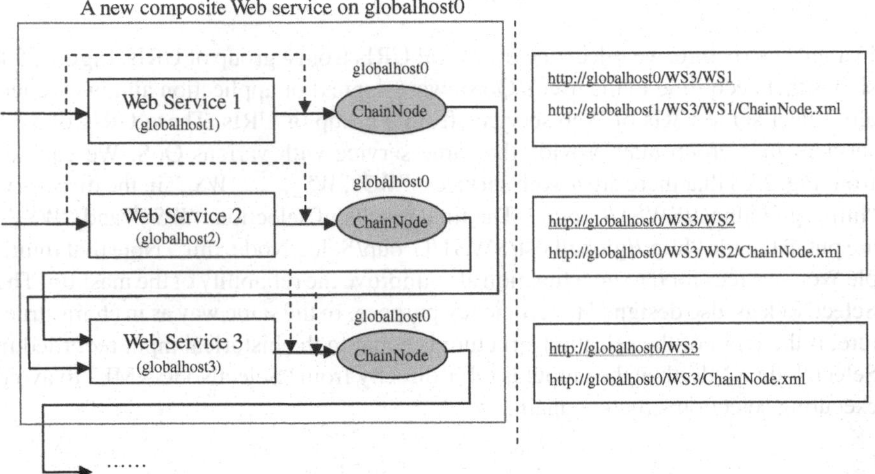

Fig. 25.9 A merge structure

25.6 A Smart Plant Watering Web Service Application

In this section, we design and implement the smart plant watering Web service in order to demonstrate the effectiveness of the Thing-REST-based smart Web service for the Web of things. We have implemented the smart plant watering Web service on the website (http://vcrab.com/SmartWebService).

25.6.1 The User Interface and Application Logic Design

We present a design of the smart plant watering Web service (shown in Fig. 25.1) by using the Thing-REST style. Figure 25.3 provides a general framework of a smart Web service, where there are four inputs of the application logic programming component: user context, sensor event, weather report and domain knowledge.

We implement this application in "http://vcrab.com/plantWatering" to mashup four Web services we introduced; and we provide the main part of its PHP code as shown in Fig. 25.10 to introduce how to use the four Web services. Suppose sensors' data have been updated online in their e-URIs. We first achieve a thing name, "Rose", from "http://vcrab.com/SmartWebService/Joey/index.XML" (shown in Fig. 25.6) and then we look for the thing's location and lifestage from "http://vcrab.com/SmartWebService/Joey/Rose/index.XML" (shown in Fig. 25.5). We use "http://vcrab.com/eventDetection?thingID=FL:0001017" (at line 2) to detect events, such as "Lack Water", where the ontology ID (e.g. "FL:0001017") of the thing will be found through "http://vcrab.com/Ontology?thing=Rose" (at line 1). We use "http://vcrab.com/weatherReport?location=Melbourne,Australia" (at line 5) to achieve the local weather conditions for the thing. Finally, if "Lack Water" event happens and weather condition is not "Rain" (at line 9), then we use "http://vcrab.com/plantCultivation?thing=FL:0001017,3" (at line 10) to compute the dose, based on the plant cultivation domain knowledge database, and action will be triggered to water the Rose plant.

```
   //Find Ontology ID
1  $myOntologyID=file_get_contents("http://vcrab.com/Ontology?thing=".$thingclass);
   //Call Event Detection Service
2  $myevent0=file_get_contents("http://vcrab.com/eventDetection?thingID=".$myOntologyID);
3  $myevent1=explode(".",$myevent0);
4  $myevent=$myevent1[0];
   //Call Weather Report Service
5  $myweather=file_get_contents("http://vcrab.com/weatherReport?location=".$location);
6  $mytemp=explode(",",$myweather);
7  $mycon=explode(":",$mytemp[1]);
8  $myconditions=$mycon[1];
   //Application Logic
9  if (strcmp($myevent,"Lack Water")==0 && strcmp($myconditions,"Rain")!=0)
   {//Call Plant Cultivation Service
10 $mydose=file_get_contents("http://vcrab.com/plantCultivation?thing=".$myOntologyID.",".$lifestage);
11 echo "Please Watering".$thing."with dose=".$mydose;}
12 else    echo "No action!";
```

Fig. 25.10 Application PHP code

From this application, we can see that the Thing-REST makes the design of a smart Web service simple. In addition, Thing-REST has all of the seven advantages presented in Sect. 25.2.2.

25.6.2 The Server and Client Control Panels

We now briefly introduce the configuration system that supports the application of Sect. 25.6.1, which includes a configuration control panel for smart Web services on the Web server and a sensor control panel that is on the client.

25.6.2.1 User Configuration on the Web Server

The user configuration interface includes three parts: context of things, user context and Web service setting.

We first input the context of things, such as the semantic context that describes the target thing itself: the name, location and the life stage of the thing and the sensing context that describes all the sensors/actuators for the target thing. Users can set the sensor data update frequency and sensor URI. For example, two sensor URI addresses in Fig. 25.5 are used to publish sensor data.

Then we input the user context, for this application, including user name and a list of contact contexts, such as E-mail addresses, mobile phone numbers and MSN etc. Particularly, every contact method is available in a special state of the user. For instance, Joey may use E-mail in his office, use MSN at home, use a mobile phone outdoors and assign his representative to receive messages when he is out of the city. We actually also generate Thing-REST URIs for all of his contact methods. We suppose Joey's state can be dynamically achieved through his location information.

Finally, the default Web services are

- a plant ontology service (http://vcrab.com/Ontology),
- a plant cultivation domain knowledge service (http://vcrab.com/plantCultivation),
- an event detection service (http://vcrab.com/eventDetection), and
- a weather report service (http://vcrab.com/weatherReport).

They also can be replaced by other similar Web services. The plant ontology service will retrieve a standard ID in the machine dictionary of the thing, based on the input thing's name described by the word in the human dictionary (see Sect. 25.4.2). The plant cultivation domain knowledge service will consider the preferences of the thing to the soil water and the thing's lifestage to compute the water dose. The weather report service can return the current temperature and conditions of a particular city, and we implemented it based on the weather forecast services provided by, for example,"www.weatherforecast.com". The event detection service will fetch sensor data from user defined URIs and look for the things' preferences to humidity and temperature in the plant cultivation domain knowledge database.

25.6.2.2 Client Sensor Control Panel

A sensor is connected to the computer as the base station shown in Fig. 25.11. The sensors and actuators that monitor the plants send a sensing report to the base station through wireless sensor networks. Then the sensing data can be POST to the URIs while a message for actuators can be GET from URIs by the sensor control panel. We can set the frequency (five hours once) for updating data on the URIs.

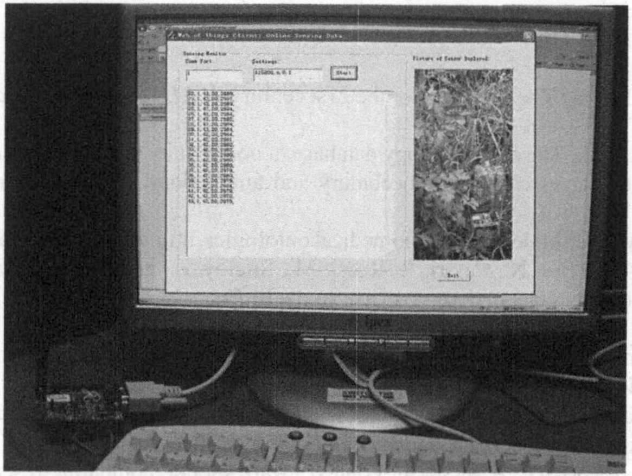

Fig. 25.11 Base station of sensors and client sensor control panel

In summary, the Thing-REST style is especially suitable for a smart Web service. The basic reason is that static semantic context and dynamical sensing context are two aspects to describe the needs of a thing. First, we can use URIs to manage these contexts and thus provide a standard interface of input and output for Web services. Then, the mashup style where chain, select, merge structures are implemented through building the relationship between URIs make automation available while providing a simple and friendly user interface. Particularly, special chain nodes in the mashup style are useful to implement an efficient smart Web service, where ontology service and domain knowledge service may only need to be executed once and their results are used repeatedly.

25.7 Conclusions

This chapter presents a RESTful smart Web service for the Web of things. A framework of a smart Web service is developed that is built on the following types of Web services: ontology service, domain knowledge service, and event detection service (e.g., weather report service and sensor event detection service) on the future Web. The first two types of Web services are reasonable on the Semantic Web, while the event detection service will become popular on the Ubiquitous Web. Particularly, a concept of the context of things is introduced explicitly for the smart Web service. Then a Thing-REST style is adopted to efficiently implement a smart Web service.

Finally, a smart plant watering service application is presented in detail for explaining the effectiveness of the Thing-REST-based smart Web service.

References

1. Abowd, G. D. et al.: The computer for the 21st century. *IEEE Pervasive Computing* **1(3)** (2002) 22–23.
2. Avraham, S. et al.: The plant ontology database: a community resource for plant structure and developmental stages controlled vocabulary and annotations. *Nucleic Acids Res.* **36** (2008) 449–454.
3. Bio-ontoloty. Open biological and biomedical ontologies. http://www.obofoundry.org/, (2011).
4. Castellani, A. P., Bui, N., Casari, P., Rossi, M., Shelby, Z., and Zorzi, M.: Architecture and protocols for the internet of things: A case study. In *Proc. 1st IEEE Int'l. Wksp. Web of Things (WoT'10) at IEEE PERCOM* (2010).
5. Ceri, S., Daniel, F., Facca, F. M., and Matera, M.: Model-driven engineering of active context-awareness. *World Wide Web* **10** (2007) 387–413.
6. Chandrasekaran, B.: Generic tasks in knowledge-based reasoning: high level building blocks for expert system design. *IEEE Expert* **1(3)** (1986) 23–30.
7. Chen, G. and Kotz, D.: A survey of context aware mobile computing research. Tech. Rep. Dartmouth Computer Science Technical, Report TR2000381 (2000).
8. de Souza, L. M. S., Spiess, P., and Guinard, D.: Socrades: A web service based shop floor integration infrastructure. In *Proceedings of the 1st international conference on The internet of things*. Springer, Switzerland, (2008) 50–67.
9. Dengler, S., Awad, A., and Dressler, F.: Sensor/actuator networks in smart homes for supporting elderly and handicapped people. In *Proceedings of the 21st International Conference on Advanced Information Networking and Applications Workshops (AINAW'07)*. Niagara Falls, (2007) 863–868.
10. Dey, A. K. and Abowd, G. D.: Towards a better understanding of context and context-awareness. Tech. Rep. Technical Report GIT-GVU-99-22, GVU Center, Georgia Institute of Technology (1999).
11. Dey, A. K. and Mankoff, J.: Designing mediation for context-aware applications. *ACM Transactionsion Computer-Human Interaction* **12(1)** (2005) 53–80.
12. Dickerson, R., Lu, J. K., and Whitehouse, K.: Stream feeds an abstraction for the world wide sensor web. In *Proceedings of the 1st international conference on The internet of things*, (2008) 360–375.
13. Drytkiewicz, W., Radusch, I., Arbanowski, S., and Popescu-Zeletin, R.: prest: A rest-based protocol for pervasive systems. In *The proc. of MASS* (2005).
14. Fensel, D. and Bussler, C.: The web service modeling framework wsmf. *Electronic Commerce Research Journal* **1(2)** (2002) 113–137.
15. Fielding, R. T.: Architectural style and the designs of network-based software architectures. Ph.D. thesis, University of California, Irvine, USA (2000).
16. Fuhrer, P., Guinard, D.: Building a Smart Hospital using RFID Technologies. In *ECEH (2006)*, pp. 131–142.
17. Gruber, T.: Toward principles for the design of ontologies used for knowledge sharing. *International Journal Human-Computer Studies* **43(5-6)**, (1995) 907–928.
18. Guinard, D., Trifa, V., Pham, T., and Liechti, O.: Towards physical mashups in the web of things. In *The proceedings of Sixth International Conference on Networked Sensing Systems (INSS)*. Pittsburgh, USA, (2009) 1–4.
19. Haryanto, R.: Context-awareness in smart homes to support independent living. M.S. thesis, University of Technology, Sydney (2005).

20. He, J., Zhang, Y., Huang, G., and Cao, J.: A Smart Web Service based on the Context of Things. *ACM Transactions on Internet Technology*, 11(3), (2012).
21. Horrocks, I.: Ontologies and the semantic web. *Communications of the ACM* **51(12)** (2008) 58–67.
22. Ivanova, M. and Ivanova, T.: Web 2.0 and web 3.0 environments: Possibilities for authoring and knowledge representation. *Revista de Informatica Sociala* **12** (2009) 7–21.
23. Kim, Y. B., and Kim, D.: Healthcare service with ubiquitous sensor networks for the disabled and elderly people. In *ICCHP 2006*, LNCS 4061, (2006) 716–723.
24. Kopecky, J., Gomadam, K., and T., V.: hrest: an html microformat for describing restful web services. In *2008 IEEE/WIC/ACM International Conference on Web Intelligence and Intelligent Agent Technology* (2008).
25. Lorenzo, G. D., Hacid, H., and Paik, H.: Data integration in mashups. *SIGMOD Record* **38(1)** (2009).
26. Lu, R. and Jin, Z.: Formal ontology: Foundation of domain knowledge sharing and reusing. *Journal of Computer Science and Technology* **17(5)** (2002) 535–548.
27. Luckenbach, T., Gober, P., Arbanowski, S., Kotsopoulos, A., and Kim, K.: Tinyrest- a protocol for integrating sensor networks into the internet. In *REALWSN* (2005).
28. Manes: Enabling open, interoperable, and smart web services. http://www.w3.org/2001/03/WSWS-popa/paper29. (2001).
29. Mark, W.: The computer for the 21st century. *Scientific American* **265** (1991) 94–104.
30. Muehlen, M. Z., Nickerson, J. V., and Swenson, K. D.: Developing web services choreography standards - the case of rest vs. soap. *Decision Support Systems* **40** (2005) 9–29.
31. Ontology lookup service. http://www.ebi.ac.uk/ontology-lookup/, (2011).
32. Rasch, K., Li, F., Sehic, S., Ayani, R., and Dustdar, S.: Context-driven personalized service discovery in pervasive environments. *World Wide Web* **14** (2011) 295–319.
33. Sheng, Q. Z., Pohlenz, S., Yu, J., Wong, H. S., Ngu, A. H. H., and Maamar, Z.: Contextserv: A platform for rapid and flexible development of context-aware web services. In *The proceedings of the 31st International Conference on Software Engineering (ICSE'09)*. Canada (2009).
34. Sheth, A. P., Gomadam, K., and Lathem, J.: Sa-rest: Semantically interoperable and easier-to-use services and mashups. *IEEE Internet Computing* **11**(6) (2007) 91–94.
35. Inventory of Future Capabilities of Internet to Meet Future Long and Short Term Needs of the Food Sector. http://www.smartagrifood.eu/sites/default/files/content-files/downloads/SAF_D700-2_V011_Final_0.pdf. (2012).
36. Sommer, S., Scholz, A., Buckl, C., Kemper, A., Knoll, A., Heuer, J., and Schmitt, A.: Towards the internet of things: Integration of web services and field level devices. In *International Workshop on the Future Internet of Things and Services - Embedded Web Services for Pervasive Devices (at FITS 2009)* (2009).
37. Swenson, K. D.: Workflow and web service standards. *Business Process Management Journal* **11(3)** (2005) 218–223.
38. Volz, R.: Web ontology reasoning with logic databases. Ph.D. thesis, Institute AIFB, University of Karlsruhe (2004).
39. Wayne: Tim berners-lee's web of people, the online journalism review, 4th december 2007. http://www.ojr.org/ojr/stories/071204wayne/ (2007).
40. Wilde, E.: Putting things to rest. Tech. Rep. UCB iSchool Report 2007-015, UC Berkeley, USA (2007).
41. Yu, J., Sheng, Q. Z., Liao, K., and Wong, H. S.: Model-driven development of context-aware web services. In *Enabling Context-Aware Web Services: Methods, Architectures, and Technologies* (2009).
42. Zeeb, E., Bobek, A., Bohn, H., Priiter, S., Pohl, A., Krumm, H., Luck, I., Golatowski, F., and Timmermann, D.: Ws4d: Soa-toolkits making embedded systems ready for web services. *The proc. of Open Source Software and Productlines (OSSPL07)*. Ireland (2007).
43. Zhao, H. and Doshi, P.: Towards automated restful web service composition. In *2009 IEEE International Conference on Web Services* (2009).

Index

A. Bouguettaya et al. (eds.), *Advanced Web Services*,
DOI: 10.1007/978-1-4614-7535-4,

Printed in the United States
By Bookmasters